Also in the Variorum Collected Studies Series:

STEPHAN KUTTNER, edited by PETER LANDAU
Gratian and the Schools of Law, 1140–1234
Second Edition

JACQUES van der VLIET
The Christian Epigraphy of Egypt and Nubia

PETER MEREDITH, edited by JOHN MARSHALL
The Practicalities of Early English Performance: Manuscripts, Records, and Staging
Shifting Paradigms in Early English Drama Studies

MEG TWYCROSS, edited by SARAH CARPENTER and PAMELA KING
The Materials of Early Theatre: Sources, Images, and Performance
Shifting Paradigms in Early English Drama Studies

SEYMOUR DRESCHER
Pathways from Slavery
British and Colonial Mobilizations in Global Perspective

DAVID JACOBY
Medieval Trade in the Eastern Mediterranean and Beyond

GILES CONSTABLE
Medieval Thought and Historiography

GILES CONSTABLE
Medieval Monasticism

MICHAEL J.B. ALLEN
Studies in the Platonism of Marsilio Ficino and Giovanni Pico

ALEXANDRA F. JOHNSTON, edited by DAVID N. KLAUSNER
The City and the Parish: Drama in York and Beyond

BENJAMIN Z. KEDAR
Crusaders and Franks
Studies in the History of the Crusaders and the Frankish Levant

DAVID MILLS, edited by PHILIP BUTTERWORTH
To Chester and Beyond: Meaning, Text and Context in Early English Drama
Shifting Paradigms in Early English Drama Studies

https://www.routledge.com/history/series/VARIORUMCS
VARIORUM COLLECTED STUDIES SERIES

Gratian and the Schools of Law
1140–1234

Stephan Kuttner, edited by Peter Landau

Gratian and the Schools of Law
1140–1234

Second Edition

LONDON AND NEW YORK

First published 2018
by Routledge
2 Park Square, Milton Park, Abingdon, Oxon OX14 4RN

and by Routledge
52 Vanderbilt Avenue, New York, NY 10017, USA

First issued in paperback 2020

Routledge is an imprint of the Taylor & Francis Group, an informa business

© 2018 selection and editorial matter, Peter Landau; individual chapters, Stephan Kuttner

The right of Peter Landau to be identified as the author of the editorial material, and of Stephan Kuttner for the individual chapters, has been asserted in accordance with sections 77 and 78 of the Copyright, Designs and Patents Act 1988.

All rights reserved. No part of this book may be reprinted or reproduced or utilised in any form or by any electronic, mechanical, or other means, now known or hereafter invented, including photocopying and recording, or in any information storage or retrieval system, without permission in writing from the publishers.

Trademark notice: Product or corporate names may be trademarks or registered trademarks, and are used only for identification and explanation without intent to infringe.

British Library Cataloguing in Publication Data
A catalogue record for this book is available from the British Library

Library of Congress Cataloging in Publication Data
A catalog record for this book has been requested

ISBN 13: 978-0-367-58391-0 (pbk)
ISBN 13: 978-0-86078-408-1 (hbk)

Typeset in Times New Roman by
Servis Filmsetting Ltd, Stockport, Cheshire

VARIORUM COLLECTED STUDIES SERIES CS1071

TABLE OF CONTENTS

Preface ix
Preface to the Second Edition xi

1. The Scientific Investigation of Medieval Canon Law:
   The Need and the Opportunity
   in: Speculum 24 (Cambridge, Mass. 1949) 1

2. Graziano: L'uomo e l'opera
   in: Studia Gratiana 1 (Rome 1953) 13

3. Zur Frage der theologischen Vorlagen Gratians
   *in: Zeitschrift der Savigny-Stiftung für Rechtsgeschichte,
   Kan. Abt. 23 (Weimar 1934)* 25

4. New Studies on the Roman Law in Gratian's Decretum
   *in: Seminar: An annual extraordinary number of The Jurist 11
   (Washington, D.C. 1953)* 45

5. Additional Notes on the Roman Law in Gratian's Decretum
   *in: Seminar: An annual extraordinary number of The Jurist 12
   (Washington, D.C. 1954)* 73

6. Les débuts de l'école canoniste française
   in: Studia et documenta historiae et iuris 4 (Rome 1938) 79

7. Bernardus Compostellanus Antiquus
   in: Traditio 1 (New York 1943) 93

8. Anglo-Norman Canonists of the twelfth century
   *in collaboration with Eleanor Rathbone in: Traditio 7
   (New York 1949–51)* 163

9. Réflexions sur les brocards des glossateurs
   in: Mélanges Joseph de Ghellinck, S.J., II (Gembloux 1951)   251

10. Papst Honorius III. und das Studium des Zivilrechts
    *in: Festschrift für Martin Wolff, ed. E. von Caemmerer et al.
    (Tübingen 1952)*   273

Retractationes   291

Indices
    1. General Index   333
    2. Papal Letters   347
    3. Initia Operum   349
    4. Manuscripts   353

PREFACE

For this volume ten essays were selected in which I have dealt with the growth of canon law as a learned discipline during the nearly one hundred years that preceded the official publication by Pope Gregory IX in 1234 of the Book of Decretals – the period one may well call the Century of Gratian. Admittedly, we possess little verifiable information on his period, and there remain many problems to solve on the genesis of his work. But it is a matter of record that the 'Concordia discordantium canonum' of the elusive Magister marked a turning point in the history of canon law: it became the text on which formal teaching of the *decreta* began at Bologna in the 1140s, soon to spread to other centers of learning in the European West.

The papers here presented do not deal with the substance of Gratian's doctrines or with those of the masters in the schools, but rather with literary and academic history; they discuss such matters as the methods and the transmission of canonistic writing and lecturing. I have excluded some early papers of which the main contents were later absorbed in others here republished; I have also excluded short notes on individual texts or manuscripts which over the years have regularly appeared in the *Bulletin* of the Institute of Medieval Canon Law, first published as an annual appendix to *Traditio* (1955–70), and since 1971 as an independent 'New Series' in Berkeley.

It is a measure of the great strides taken by research in the glossators of canon law since the end of the Second World War that some of the major essays in this volume stand in need of considerable revision, of new manuscript information, and other *addenda*. Therefore the *Retractationes*, which, as on previous occasions, I have appended to the papers here republished, occupy many more pages than in earlier volumes.

I wish to express my sincere thanks for permission to reprint these essays to the editors and publishers of the periodicals where most of these essays (Nos. I–VIII) first appeared, as well as to the publishing houses of J. Duculot, S.A. (Gembloux, for No. IX) and J.C.B. Mohr/Paul Siebeck (Tübingen, for No. X). I wish to thank my granddaughter Ann Kuttner, M.A., and Fred Paxton, M.A., for their assistance in making the indices of the volume. I owe particular gratitude to my friend, Professor Stanley Chodorow (University of California, San Diego) who again, as twice before in this series, generously shouldered the burden of programming the computer for typesetting the front matter, the *Retractationes*, and the indices, with all the attendant labor of repeated proofreading and incorporating a tiresome author's alterations.

There is one word of thanks which, alas, must remain unsaid. Eleanor Rathbone, co-author of the eighty-page essay on Anglo-Norman canonists, would always gladly have given her permission to reprint it here (No. VIII) with additions and corrections. The gentle, immensely learned, and unpretentious lady died in London on 15 November 1979 at the age of seventy-five. She will always be fondly remembered by all students of the intellectual history of the Middle Ages who crossed her path in England, the United States, and the reading rooms of the world's great libraries.

I dedicate this volume
 To the memory of Eleanor Rathbone (1904–1979)

University of California   STEPHAN KUTTNER
Berkeley
April 1983

In an earlier volume of collected studies, *The History of Ideas and Doctrines of Canon Law in the Middle Ages* (1980), the inscription of the article No. VI, 'La réserve papale du droit de canonisation' (1938), was omitted from the reprinting by editorial oversight. I repeat it here:

> Piae memoriae
> UDALRICI STUTZ
> domini mei ac magistri
> sacrum

PREFACE TO THE SECOND EDITION

The second edition of Stephan Kuttner's volume of articles with the title 'Gratian and the Schools of Law' can now be republished more than 20 years after Kuttner's death in 1996. The author had asked me to take care for a second revised edition of this volume.

In his preface to the volume Kuttner points out that the collected essays do not deal with the substance of Gratian's doctrine or those of the following masters in the schools but rather with literary and academic history, especially with matters as the methods and transmission of canonistic writing and lecturing between 1140 and 1234.

The century after Gratian's Decretum could be called the Century of Gratian according to Kuttner.

The ten essays selected for this volume had been published first by Kuttner between 1934 and 1954. For the volume of 1983 he added 47 pages of *Retractationes*. In his personal copy of the Gratian volume Kuttner wrote many further additions as '*New Retractationes*' (abbreviation: NR). I used these notes for the second edition and supplemented them by addenda of my own about research in the history of medieval canon law during the last 30 years since 1983. For Kuttner's additions I used the logogram (*S.K.*), for my own supplements I used (*P.L.*).

A last word should be added about the value of Kuttner's volume for future research. His articles on Gratian and his sources (no. I–V) are still fundamental for questions of Gratian's sources in his Decretum, especially in Roman law and in the field of scholarly discussions about Gratian as jurist and as theologian. The essay 'Bernardus Compostellanus Antiquus' (no. VII, 1943) is a major study on canon law in Bologna at the beginning of the thirteenth century. The essay 'Les débuts de l'école canoniste française' (no., VI, 1938) gave the first description of the specific features of the French school of Canon Law during the twelfth century.

The famous essay on 'Anglo-Norman Canonists', published together with *Eleanor Rathbone* in 1951 – the volume 'Gratian and the Schools of Law' was also dedicated to her – certainly discovered this previously forgotten school in England during the Anglo-Norman period of English history (no. VIII, 1951); it is one of Kuttner's most remarkable accomplishments in intellectual history. The

PREFACE TO THE SECOND EDITION

two last articles 'Réflexions sur les brocards des glossateurs' (no. IX, 1951) and 'Papst Honorius III. und das Studium des Zivilrechts' (no. X, 1952) describe an important literary genus (Brocarda) and give a convincing explanation of Pope Honorius III much discussed prohibition of Roman law lectures at the University of Paris in 1219.

Altogether it can be summarized that 'Gratian and the Schools of Law' is an indispensible supplementary volume to Kuttner's famous 'Repertorium der Kanonistik' (1937).

Prof. Dr. Dr. h.c. mult. Peter Landau, University of Munich

THE SCIENTIFIC INVESTIGATION OF MEDIAEVAL CANON LAW: THE NEED AND THE OPPORTUNITY

This study by Kuttner, published in 1949, was deliberately not brought up to date by the author in his volume of 1983. He only mentioned his study 'The Revival of Jurisprudence' (1982). (P.L.)

I

It is hardly possible to overlook the fundamental importance of canon law in the texture of mediaeval civilization. The student of the Middle Ages finds himself confronted with a world in which canonical institutions were an integral part of the social and political structure; with an intellectual framework for which canonical doctrines were living realities in the realm of thought and learning. The conspicuous place held by the *magistri decretorum* in mediaeval universities is as significant as is the appalling number of canon law books in mediaeval libraries. In the ever-recurrent conflicts between the spiritual and the temporal powers, canon law and its interpretation played a crucial role. From the Carolingian times to the Gregorian Reform canonical collections were frequently instruments as well as mirrors of reform movements and related ideologies. The economic history of the Middle Ages is largely determined by the financial system of tithes, of ecclesiastical benefices, and by the consequences of the canonical doctrine of usury. In the legal history of nearly all Western nations, the impact of canon law on contracts, wills, marriages, corporations (to name only a few institutions), on the judicial system and procedure is easily traced. Gaines Post has shown how this impact extends to the nascent constitutional law;[1] borrowings in Bracton

---

* Paper read at the annual meeting of the Mediaeval Academy of America in Toronto, Canada, 8 April 1949. In view of the general nature and purpose of the paper, bibliographical references and details of erudition have been kept to a minimum. A forceful plea for restoring canon law to its proper place in the *universitas litterarum* has recently been made by G. Le Bras, 'Études latines et droit canon,' *Mémorial d' études latines ... offert ... à J. Marouzeau* (Paris, 1943), pp. 416–435. See also the same author's chapter 'Canon Law,' in C. G. Crump and E. F. Jacob, *The Legacy of the Middle Ages* (Oxford, 1926), pp. 321–361.
1 Cf. in particular his 'Plena Potestas and Consent in Medieval Assemblies,' *Traditio,* I (1943), 355–408; 'A Romano-Canonical Maxim, "quod omnes tangit," in Bracton,' *ibid.,* IV (1946), 197–251.

from canonical treatises have been discovered by Schulz and Richardson.[2] The canonists' practical needs and devices became of great importance for the arts of dictamen and the notariate; Latin and vernacular literatures, liturgical texts and sermons, offer numerous instances of a penetration of canonical terms and concepts.

Again, a web of interrelations connects the growth of scholastic theology, the mediaeval development of rhetoric, the revival of Roman law, and the canonists' methods of scientific inquiry. It is now nearly forty years since the late lamented Monsignor Grabmann demonstrated in his *Geschichte der scholastischen Methode*[3] the decisive role which the hermeneutics of Ivo of Chartres, of Bernold of Constance played in the beginnings of scholasticism. Since then, a number of interesting details concerning the share of the jurists in the early elaboration of dialectical methods has come to light. The extent to which the *sententiae* of the theologians were indebted to the canonists for their systematic approach as well as for the transmission of patristic material, and the extent to which theology and canon law stimulated each other in the teaching on the sacraments, is most impressively presented in the work of another venerable mediaevalist, Père de Ghellinck's *Mouvement théologique du XIIe siècle* — which, after having served many of us for more than thirty years as a companion of studies, has just been reissued in a revised and enlarged edition.[4] No corresponding study, unfortunately, exists for the thirteenth century, although it would be most rewarding to trace, for instance, the absorption of canonistic material in certain parts of the *Summa* of St Thomas Aquinas.[5]

Kuttner mentions Grabmann's 'Geschichte der scholastischen Methode' for the beginnings of scholasticism and de Ghellinck's 'Mouvement Théologique du XIIe siècle' for the extent in which theologians and canonists stimulated each other in the twelfth century. He explains that no corresponding study exists for the thirteenth century, especially for St. Thomas Aquinas. A short summary of Thomas Aquinas' doctrine of natural law is given by *Ch. Lefebvre* in: *Le Bras/Lefebvre/ Rambaud*, L'Age Classique 1140–1378. Sources et Théorie du Droit (Histoire du Droit et des Institutions de l'Eglise en Occident VII, Paris 1965), 382–384 (p. 3: Les conclusions Thomistes). See also *P. Mikat* 'Gesetz und Staat nach Thomas von Aquin unter besonderer Berücksichtigung der Lehre vom Gesetz

---

2 F. Schulz, 'Critical Studies in Bracton's Treatise,' *Law Quarterly Review*, LIX (1943), 172–180; 'A New Approach to Bracton,' *Seminar*, II (1944), 41–50; 'Bracton on Kingship,' *English Historical Review*, LX (1945), 136–176; H. G. Richardson, 'Tancred, Raymond and Bracton,' *ibid.*, LIX (1944), 376–384; 'Studies in Bracton,' *Traditio*, VI (1948), 61–75.
3 II (Freiburg, Germany, 1911), 86, 213 ff., 302 f.
4 (Louvain: Museum Lessianum, 1948) *passim*, esp. ch. v, pp. 416–547. The first edition appeared in Paris, 1914.
5 The book by B. C. Kuhlmann, *Der Gesetzesbegriff beim Hl. Thomas von Aquin im Lichte des Rechtsstudiums seiner Zeit* (Bonn: Hanstein, 1912), is not satisfactory. Dom O. Lottin's fine study, *Le droit naturel chez St. Thomas d' Aquin et ses prédécesseurs* (2nd ed., Bruges, 1931) stands in need of a revision. Some interesting observations in I. Th. Eschmann, 'The Notion of Society in St. Thomas Aquinas, I,' *Mediaeval Studies*, VIII (1946), 1–42.

in der Summa Theologiae, in: Beiträge zur Rechtsgeschichte, Gedächtnisschrift für Hermann Conrad (Rechts- und Staatswissenschaftliche Veröff. der Görres-Gesellschaft, N.F., H. 34, Paderborn etc. 1979), 439–465. (P.L.)

Let us add that the very strictures of Roger Bacon or Dante on the legalistic spirit that led the clergy to run to the law schools in search of the canonist's promising career; the very railings of the satirists against the ambitious, greedy, artful canon lawyers, reflect in a way the actual truth that in the mediaeval world canon law was an all-prevading social and cultural power.

And yet, compared with the organized efforts and achievements of modern scholarship in other fields of mediaeval research, active interest in its scientific investigation has remained the concern of a handful of specialists. From the days of Antonio Agustín, the learned archbishop of Tarragona in the sixteenth century, to our own time, it has always been a few scholars only who carried in succeeding generations the burden of patiently advancing the frontiers of our knowledge: a fact which makes the progress achieved in the last eighty-odd years all the more respectable.[6] The fascinating historical process which stretches over the early centuries of the Middle Ages and in which a huge mass of accumulated, heterogeneous sources grew into the consistent body of common law of the church universal, has become known in its major phases, thanks in particular to the labors which filled the lifetime of the late Paul Fournier and are being carried on by Professor Le Bras. The researches of Maassen and Schulte, continued and corrected in numerous details by the studies of Singer, Gillmann, and others, have made it possible to discern the outlines of the rational perfection of this law in the ever more elaborate doctrines of the schools from the twelfth to the fourteenth century. The counterpart of this scholastic development, viz., the crystallization of new doctrines into legislative authority by the decretal letters and conciliar enactments of the popes, has been particularly explored by Friedberg, Seckel, and Professor Holtzmann. The greater part of a body of manuscript material that runs into thousands of codices has been recorded, identified and classified, at least for the period down to the mid-thirteenth century.

The yield of all these researches is as unexpected as promising, but the more the material has increased at the hands of pioneer scholars, the more it becomes evident that its full utilization is beyond the forces of individuals: only a fraction of the mediaeval works which have become known are at present completely analyzed and evaluated; still smaller is the number of those that have been edited, competently or otherwise. Except for the parallel case of Roman law — of which the mediaeval revival, scholastic interpretation, and gradual transformation into a system of common law has likewise remained the domain of an almost esoteric

---

6 For what follows, general bibliographical information will be found in J. F. von Schulte, *Geschichte der Quellen und Literatur des Canonischen Rechts*, I and II (Stuttgart, 1875–77); P. Fournier and G. Le Bras, *Histoire des collections canoniques en Occident* (Paris, 1931–32); S. Kuttner, *Repertorium der Kanonistik* (Studi e Testi, LXXI; Città del Vaticano, 1937); A. van Hove, *Prolegomena* (Commentarium Lovaniense in Codicem Iuris Canonici, I, 1; 2nd ed. Malines-Rome, 1945).

scholarship[7] — this situation is not found in other fields of so universal a significance for the intellectual context of the Middle Ages.

II

To substantiate the preceding general observations, I wish to state some specific and urgent needs. Let me begin at a central point. It is commonly known that the *Concordia discordantium canonum* composed by Gratian at Bologna about 1140 — later on simply called the *Decreta* or *Decretum* — constitutes the great divide in the history of mediaeval canon law. As a collection of canons, it marks the end of a plurisecular development of assembling, in ever new selection and combination, the authorities of the past in all their bewildering variety. As a methodical treatise, which submits the thousands of *auctoritates* to the analysis of reason, it became the starting point and fundamental text of a new science in the schools, as well as the foundation for the juristic reasoning by which the popes since the mid-twelfth century — in particular, since Alexander III — created in their responses and judicial decisions the new law of the decretals. With Gratian, briefly, canon law enters into its specifically juristic stage as a highly technical subject of specialized learning. This fact explains perhaps why historians on the whole have been less attracted by his work than by the canonical collections of the early Middle Ages,[8] which lend themselves more easily to a description of their trends and tendencies in general matters of ecclesiastical policy. But to the canonist proper the *Decretum* remains fundamental.

Kuttner points out that Gratian's Decretum constitutes 'the great divide in the history of mediaeval canon law and that with Gratian canon law enters into its specifically juristic stage'. He also demands to trace anew the transmission of Gratian's original sources in the preceding collections he did put to use. For this question I can refer to my contribution: P. Landau, Gratian and the Decretum Gratiani, in: W. Hartmann/K. Pennington (ed.), The History of Medieval Canon Law in the Classical Period, 1140–1234. From Gratian to the Decretals of Pope Gregory IX (Washington D.C. 2008), 22–54, mainly pp. 30–32. Kuttner counted ca. 50 manuscripts from the twelfth century — I estimated for this time a total number of about 160 manuscripts (p. 48). Five codes contain the first recension of the Decretum, discovered by *Anders Winroth* — cf. A. Winroth, The Making of Gratian's Decretum

---

7 For orientation on the state of scholarship with regard to the glossators, cf. in particular E. Genzmer, 'Die justinianische Kodifikation und die Glossatoren,' *Atti del Congresso Internazionale di diritto romano, Bologna,* I (Pavia, 1934), 345–430; H. Kantorowicz, *Studies in the Glossators of the Roman Law* (Cambridge, England, 1938); for the period of the post-glossators the studies of E. M. Meijers, W. Engelmann, and W. Ullmann are of especial importance. The modern Italian school of legal historians has added much to our knowledge of the growth of the *diritto comune* (bibliographical references in Van Hove, *op. cit.*, p. 463, n. 3).

8 A glance at the amount of bibliographical reference offered for the early collections in Van Hove's *Prolegomena* (pp. 265–337) will bear out this contention.

(Cambridge Studies in Medieval Life and Thought. Fourth Series, Cambridge 2000). A separate edition of this first recension is planned by Winroth. (P.L.)

There is no lack of studies on Gratian. His book, preserved in hundreds of manuscripts, and part of the *Corpus iuris canonici* in force till 1918, has been printed time and again since the fifteenth century. A critical edition, however, does not exist.[9] What passes for one, the edition of Friedberg (1879), is based on eight manuscripts only, all chosen from German libraries, and at that not even all chosen with good judgment. As arbitrary as the national restriction is the *recensio mixta* of the text; the recording of variants is unreliable, the historical apparatus composed without method, outmoded, and full of misleading statements. A new edition, however, is a task of immense proportions. In the codices, the *Decretum* usually fills between two hundred and three hundred large folios, and about fifty of the extant manuscripts date from the twelfth century; all these will have to be examined before a stemma can be established and the best manuscripts selected for the recension of the text. The transmission of the original sources in the collections preceding Gratian has to be traced anew in the light of all the discoveries made by Fournier and others — a problem of fundamental significance for determining the genesis of Gratian's text. It cannot be answered by a mere listing of the earlier *testimonia*, for we have to ascertain which of the intermediary collections that Gratian may have used he did put to use. But here it is necessary to remember that only a few among the earlier collections are available themselves in critical editions: of the indispensable works of Burchard of Worms and Ivo of Chartres we have only the worthless texts printed in Migne; the so-called Polycarpus and other collections of the early twelfth century which may have served Gratian are not printed at all.[10] Still another problem is presented by certain groups of Roman law texts in Gratian which Professor Vetulani has recently indicated must have been inserted by way of afterthought: an observation which reopens the question as to whether it was Gratian alone who composed the whole of the *Decretum*.[11]

Kuttner thought that Vetulani's research on the use of Roman law by Gratian reopened the question whether it was Gratian alone who composed the whole of the Decretum. (P.L.).

These are only a few of the difficulties to be surmounted, and it is but fair to state that it would be foolhardy to attempt their solution by other means than the co-ordinated effort of a great Institute.

---

9 For a detailed justification of the statements which follow see Kuttner, 'De Gratiani opere noviter edendo,' *Apollinaris*, XXI (1948), 118–128.

10 A critical edition of Burchard's *Decretum* is now being prepared for the *Monumenta Germaniae Historica* by O. Meyer. An edition of the *Polycarpus* was planned by the late Carl Erdmann.

11 A. Vetulani, 'Gratien et le droit romain,' *Revue historique de droit français et étranger*, 4th ser., XXIV (1946–47), 11–48; cf. Kuttner, *Apollinaris*, XXI, 127; de Ghellinck, *Mouvement théologique* (2nd ed. cited n. 4 *supra*), p. 205, also p. 512 f. (on the authorship of the *tract. de poenitentia*).

III

To take another example. After Gratian, it was left for nearly eighty years to the initiative of the canonists to incorporate the rapidly accumulating papal cases, responses, and conciliar legislation into the body of canon law. Over sixty private collections of the contemporary new material, differing in selection and arrangement, originated during this period. The first pope ever to make himself a choice among the decretals of his pontificate in an official collection was Innocent III, in 1209; the pope who united all of the recognized new decretal and conciliar texts in a definitive compilation was Gregory IX, in 1234. Additional decisions and enactments of his successors — likewise in a first stage the object of minor, official or private collections — received their final shape in Boniface VIII's *Liber Sextus* (1298); and in 1317, John XXII published the *Constitutiones Clementinae* of his predecessor, Clement V.

As mediaeval authors already knew, the official 'codifications' had achieved clearness of systematic presentation and conciseness of text at the cost of sacrificing the integrity of the original documents. The trend to cut apart the individual papal letter, to omit what was juridically irrelevant, and to distribute the remaining fragments under the appropriate rubrics of a topical arrangement, appears first among the private collectors toward the end of the twelfth century. One topical system, devised by Bernard of Pavia *ca* 1190, was adopted as a standard pattern by the schools as well as by the redactors of all official papal law books to come. The more often an individual decretal passed through successive collections, the more complex grows the problem of reconstructing the original text. To unite its divided fragments, to recover its narrative part and with it, the names and facts of the case, to restore its often badly mauled inscription, are tasks which require a comprehensive study of the entire tradition. Since the registers of the chancery are lost for the twelfth, and are neither complete nor always reliable for the thirteenth century, the decretal collections become the most important tool of investigation in this field. Moreover, a great number of pieces were never included in the officially promulgated books; of the decretal letters of the twelfth century, e. g., over 1050 are preserved in early collections; the Gregorian compilation comprises only 540 of them.

But only a few of the early collections have been printed or completely analyzed. It is most welcome news, therefore, that under the sponsorship of the Academy of Göttingen. Professor Holtzmann has undertaken to edit a *Corpus* of the twelfth-century decretals.[12] One of the saddest gaps in our knowledge of papal diplomatics will thus be filled.

There still remains much work to be done for the thirteenth century, although for this period the preservation of the papal registers eases the situation. But decretal letters were often not registered in the chancery, and only with the aid of

---

12 W. Holtzmann, 'Über eine Ausgabe der päpstlichen Dekretalen des 12. Jahrhunderts,' *Nachrichten der Akademie der Wissenschaften in Göttingen*, Phil.-hist. Kl., 1945, pp. 15–36; cf. Kuttner, 'Notes on a Projected Corpus of Twelfth-Century Decretal Letters,' *Traditio*, vi (1948), 345–351.

the canonistic tradition can we hope to solve a number of historical problems. This applies to the general councils of the Middle Ages no less than to the decretal letters. To cite two examples only:[13] it has been demonstrated that for the legislation of Innocent IV in the First Council of Lyons the papal register presents only a preliminary, incomplete draft; vice versa, for the legislation of the Second Council of Lyons the register of Gregory X contains the final redaction, while recently an interesting, preliminary text has come to light in a canonical manuscript now at Washington. Also, the manifold interrelations between the enactments of the general councils and legislation on the local level that preceded them or followed in their wake — diocesan statutes, provincial and legatine synods — constitute a field of urgent historical interest, both as to the genesis and the actualization of the common conciliar law.[14]

IV

The preceding observations were all connected with collections of law. But by far the greatest problems lie ahead in the field of mediaeval canonistic science: the work of the schools in which *ratio* welded the *auctoritates* — canons and decretals into a coherent, universal system of jurisprudence. The unredeemed treasures of the canonists' literary production would make a library of colossal proportions. Their value lies in the intellectual as well as in the practical order. Stimulated by, and influencing in their turn the teachings of the contemporary masters of the civil law; equal in the mastery of all the methods of analysis and discovery to their confreres of the schools of theology and the arts, the *magistri decretorum* exerted at the same time a profound action on forensic life. The all but binding authority of the leading commentaries and of the formal opinions rendered on individual cases by the ranking professors illustrate the guiding function of the schoolmen in the practice of the courts; and it is significant that throughout the thirteenth and fourteenth centuries the popes as a rule addressed their official collections of decretal law, not to the episcopate, but to the schools.

The whole vast territory of research in this field has barely been staked out, yet from the discoveries made during the last three generations it has become increasingly clear that one of the most urgent needs is that of studying the growth of canonical science in the century between Gratian and Gregory IX. For it is during this period that all the methods and most of the fundamental doctrines were created on which all later developments are based. To appraise the achievements of the

---

13 Cf. Kuttner, 'Die Konstitutionen des ersten allgemeinen Konzils von Lyon,' *Studia et documenta historiae et iuris,* VI (1940), 71–131; 'Conciliar Law in the Making: the Lyonese Constitutions (1274) of Gregory X in a Manuscript at Washington,' *Miscellanea Pio Paschini* (Rome, 1949), II, 39–81.

14 Cf. e.g., C. R. Cheney, 'Legislation of the Medieval English Church,' *English Historical Review*, L (1935), 193–224, 385–417; *id.*, *English Synodalia of the Thirteenth Century* (Oxford, 1941); Sten Gagnér, 'Zur Entstehung der europäischen und der schwedischen Diözesansynode,' *Kyrkohistorisk Årsskrift*, XLVIII (1948), 1–31.

great commentators of the post-Gregorian period we have to recover the material of canonistic thought which they found ready at their disposal for further perfection, adaptation to changing circumstances, and refinement. The more manuscripts of the twelfth and early thirteenth centuries come to light, the more we realize — and again, the parallel with contemporary Roman legal science is striking — that this was not just a period of 'first beginnings' but a full-fledged scientific system in its own right. But it so happened that the Gregorian decretals made the output of the preceding generations largely obsolete for practical purposes. Points disputed in the earlier authors had in the meantime been settled by legislation; old interpretations and references did no longer fit the official text. While the glosses, commentaries, and treatises on the new *liber decretalium* could make ample use of the material contained in the corresponding works of the early thirteenth century, these works themselves were needs discarded. As for Gratian's *Concordia*, the book of authorities for the ancient law, it remained the subject of *lectio ordinaria* in the schools, but its interpretation had become static. Thus gradually the canonical literature of an entire century fell into oblivion, while its results were absorbed in the progress of new thought. By the time of the invention of printing, the *Glossa ordinaria* on Gratian, composed *ca* 1216 by Johannes Teutonicus, but revised after Gregory IX by Bartholomew of Brescia, was the only work which had not been forgotten and which appeared in incunabula and sixteenth-century editions.

Today we have a fairly complete knowledge of the volume of production during this fundamental, first century of canonistic science. We know of glosses transmitted, by a constant process of accretion, in ever changing combinations; or formally published in coherent *apparatus glossarum*. We know of a large output of *summae*, collected *distinctiones, solutiones contrariorum, quaestiones disputatae, generalia*, and other literary forms; and of a complex pattern of interrelations between the various species of canonical writing. Earlier belief in a monopoly of Bologna for twelfth-century studies in canon law has been shattered by the discovery of numerous works which show that the schools of France and Norman England were holding their own; for a short time, Cologne also may have been a center of teaching. We know that from 1190 on, collections of decretals became the subject of formal lecturing, and an equally varied literature on the decretal law grew side by side with the works of the *Decretum*.

Dealing with the earlier belief in a monopoly of Bologna for twelfth-century studies in 'canon law', Kuttner mentions 'numerous works on the schools of France and Norman England holding their own'. Fundamental research dealing with these schools by himself is included in this volume no. VI (France) and no. VIII (Anglo-Norman school). Cologne 'may have been a center of learning for a short time'. The Cologne school and its numerous products are described by P. Landau, Die Kölner Kanonistik des 12. Jahrhunderts (Kölner Rechtsgeschichtliche Vorträge H. 1), Badenweiler 2008. This school existed at least from 1165–1190. (P.L.)

The historical value of this immense production has been vindicated wherever monographic studies have been undertaken on the development of individual problems or doctrines. Often anonymous *summae*, existing only in one or few copies, prove of no smaller interest than the great works of the leading masters that were copied time and again at the schools. Specific trends with regard to the use of arguments from Roman law; or to the borrowing of terminologies and figures of thought from the arts and theology; or to a differentiation of schools in the style of reference and argumentation, have come to light as the critical analysis of the material proceeds. As in other mediaeval literatures, the minutiae of style and form require as much attention in properly determining the historical place of a given text as do the more obvious criteria offered by the conflict or identity of opinion. But methods of textual criticism and historical interpretation have hardly begun to be evolved and tested in our field.

Above all, the size and number of writings to be studied has made scholars shy away from the task of editing at least the representative works of this period. What has been edited so far makes less than half a row of books on a library shelf, covers only the initial stage of canonistic production, and has only in part been done with competence.[15] The student of canon law thus finds himself in a position which could not be worse: while, e.g., the historian of mediaeval theology, quite apart from the numerous editions due to the intensified modern research in twelfth-century scholasticism, has always a Migne at his disposal, the canonist lacks even that. It has been suggested merely to reproduce in print the leading canonistic *summae* from one or the other 'good' manuscript on hand.[16] Such a procedure would obviously result in texts that are unreliable, since more often than not even the best manuscripts of mediaeval work are faulty, let alone the frequent occurrence of variant redactions of a given text. But once an uncritical text is printed, the stimulus for doing better will be gone for a long time.

Nothing short of the standards of rigid scholarship will do. A collection of monographic studies and critical editions is, however, a task which will need the efforts of many, at times even for one individual work, as in the case of Huguccio, the teacher of Innocent III, where it means the establishing of a text which would run approximately into four printed volumes of folio size and for which over thirty manuscripts would have to be examined. The quantitative difficulties are considerably less in many other cases, but equally frightening for some of the great *apparatus* of glosses of the early thirteenth century on Gratian or the decretal collections. Moreover, since all of these commentaries discuss, incorporate, and adapt the teachings of their predecessors, they present the hugest problems for assembling and sifting the *testimonia*. The *Glossa ordinaria* of Johannes Teutonicus, e.g., requires a previous tabulation of the entire earlier tradition of mixed gloss compositions, which can be traced in more than 150 manuscripts of Gratian; it also requires a complete study of three other great *apparatus glossarum* produced at Bologna shortly before the work of John. Again, for editing the great collections of *quaestiones disputatae* of the glossators, a catalogue of the traditional lemmata, fictitious cases or antinomies, would impose itself as a prerequisite.

---

15 Editions listed in the present writer's *Repertorium* (n. 6 *supra*), pp. 125, 127, 131, 133, 220, 387.
16 Le Bras, in *Mémorial Marouzeau* (note* *supra*), p. 420.

V

The few examples chosen at random in this paper, from a relatively short but significant period of canonistic activity, may convey an idea of the magnitude of problems we face in the scientific investigation of mediaeval canon law. The later centuries of the Middle Ages present similar problems of their own. Manuscript research has been only sporadic for the second half of the thirteenth and the early fourteenth century; it has not been carried beyond this time at all.[17] From about 1350, the most signal contribution of the jurists, in both laws, is to be found in the collections of *consilia, repetitiones*, and monographic treatises rather than in their commentaries. A *catalogue raisonné* of such collections, even of the printed ones alone, as Professor Le Bras recently pointed out,[18] would be highly desirable lest this wealth of material remain buried.

To sum up. It may sound disappointing to hear the needs of research in canon law defined primarily in terms of what one may call juristic philology. Still, each historical science has to go through a stage in which the critical study and editing of texts must take the first place — not as an end in itself, but as a necessary prerequisite for a valid interpretation of history. The historian of mediaeval canon law is interested in texts first of all because they convey canonical doctrine; he will want to go beyond textual criticism and arrive at a classification of doctrinal positions, of mediaeval methods of inquiry, of literary influences and trends — in brief, at a true history of the science of canon law in the Middle Ages.[19] He will want to proceed further and test the vital force of doctrine against the realities of ecclesiastical life in all their colorful variety, as they may be gleaned from archival and narrative sources — which means to co-ordinate the history of canonical jurisprudence and the history of canonical institutions. Yet, all such aims of the historian will remain futile, given the present state of our source material. This situation is now the concern of a small, scattered group of scholars alone: it ought

---

17 The printed editions of late mediaeval commentaries are full of dangerous pitfalls. A good illustration in F. Gillmann, 'Dominus Deus noster papa?' *Archiv für katholisches Kirchenrecht*, xcv (1915), 266–282. The shocking expression which is quoted in the title of this article and has played a certain role in controversialist literature is commonly held to have been used by the canonist Jesselin de Cassagnes (Zenzelinus, d. 1334) in his gloss on John XXII's decretal *Cum inter (Extrav. Joan. XXII*, 14, 4, v. *declaramus* i. f.). Gillmann shows that the words, as found in 29 out of 40 printed editions, are based on a faulty reading of the manuscript used in the *editio princeps* (Paris: Rembolt, 1500); the correct manuscript tradition of the incriminated passage is: '... credere autem dominum nostrum papam conditorem dicte decretalis et istius sic non potuisse statuere ...' (*loc. cit.*, pp. 276–280).

18 *Mémorial Marouzeau*, p. 421 f.

19 The methodological problems of such a history are somewhat akin to those which have been frequently discussed in the field of patristic studies; cf. (most recent) B. Altaner, 'Der Stand der patrologischen Wissenschaft und das Problem einer neuen altchristlichen Literaturgeschichte,' *Miscellanea Giovanni Mercati*, I (Studi e Testi, CXXI; Città del Vaticano, 1946), 483–520; J. de Ghellinck, 'Les recherches patristiques, progrès et problèmes,' *Mélanges offerts au R. P. Ferdinand Cavallera* (Toulouse: Bibliothèque de l'Institut Catholique, 1948), pp. 65–85.

to be the concern of all who behind the many departments of knowledge perceive the inner coherence of the intellectual order of the mediaeval world. If this be generally realized in the great centers of learning, the opportunity for an organized investigation of mediaeval canon law will come.

THE CATHOLIC UNIVERSITY OF AMERICA.

GRAZIANO: L'UOMO E L'OPERA

This essay contains the 'Discorso commemorativo' during the Congress on Gratian in Bologna on April 17th, 1952. A supplement to this paper for a new edition of Gratian's Decretum is S. Kuttner, De Gratiani opere noviter edendo, Apollinaris 21 (1948), 118–128. (P.L.)

Ci siamo adunati in questa città[1], venuti dalle Università, statali e pontificie, d'Italia, d'oltralpe e di oltremare, per celebrare con voi, docenti e scolari dello Studio di Bologna, la festa giubilare di un Maestro che, umile di persona, portò, con la sua opera insigne, gloria alle vostre aule; il Maestro al cui ingegno si deve il fatto memorabile che per la prima volta, nella storia della civiltà cristiana e qui, sorse una vera scienza del diritto della Chiesa, trasformando la mole complessa di regole e tradizioni ecclesiastiche in un sistema ragionato, universale, per sè stante. Con Graziano e la sua *Concordia discordantium canonum* una nuova scuola s'innestò accanto alla sorella maggiore, che era la scuola, giovine essa stessa, dei glossatori del diritto giustinianeo.

Da allora Bologna parve destinata a divenire la città madre e maestra del *ius utrumque,* di ambedue i diritti. Da essa generazioni di scolari, formati sia nelle leggi di Cesare, sia nei decreti della Chiesa, uscirono per portare con sè le nuove fonti e la nuova giurisprudenza nei vari paesi d'origine; e ovunque vediamo sorgere, dal secolo XII in poi, una produzione giuridica letteraria e centri d'insegnamento di diritto nell'Europa occidentale, che possono dirsi rampolli, diretti o indiretti, dello Studio bolognese. Quale che sia l'elemento caratteristico locale o particolare che concorreva qua e là, all'origine di tali scuole, le fondamenta furono gettate dalla opera d'Irnerio per i legisti, e da Graziano per i canonisti.

Si è detto giustamente che noi giuristi moderni siamo tutti figli spirituali di Bologna; ma se questa osservazione si deve alquanto restringere per il diritto secolare — cioè a quei paesi la cui cultura giuridica nel corso della storia è stata impregnata a fondo del pensiero romanistico —, essa è certamente verissima per il diritto canonico, del cui sistema universale l'opera del monaco bolognese è rimasta parte integrante attraverso i secoli. Il suo libro, in quanto collezione di

---

[1] Discorso commemorativo tenuto nell'Aula Magna dell'Università di Bologna nella mattina del 17 aprile 1952.

canoni (di *sacri canones* e *decreta sanctorurn patrum,* come si diceva allora), riuscì subito e si mantenne come compilazione definitiva dello *ius antiquum,* cioè della tradizione canonica del passato; in quanto primo manuale ragionato didattico, esso segnò la via per l'esposizione e l'interpretazione giuridica delle istituzioni e delle dottrine canoniche; esso, finalmente, con la nuova scienza così inaugurata, creò le basi e il clima intellettuale per l'opera legislativa dei grandi papi giuristi del medio evo, cioè per lo *ius novum* delle decretali e costituzioni pontificie dei secoli XII, XIII e XIV.

* * *

Per ben capire il significato storico della *Concordia discordantium canonum* (che nella scuola fu chiamato in breve il *Liber decretorum,* o *Decreta* o *Decretum*), bisogna insistere sul punto che il nostro omaggio solenne a Graziano non è soltanto intendimento dei canonisti di professione. E non è nemmeno, vogliamo aggiungere, pensiero ristretto ai soli giuristi, ai quali la storia del diritto insegna che in quasi tutti i Paesi europei numerose istituzioni e dottrine civilistiche, processualistiche, pubblicistiche, penalistiche (che non potremmo discutere in questa sede) ricevettero nel corso del loro sviluppo storico profondi influssi dalla giurisprudenza canonistica.

La vera portata della nostra commemorazione sta in questo che il diritto della Chiesa è parte integrante della coltura medioevale; e senza renderci conto di ciò non potremmo mai arrivare a conoscere il medio evo, vale a dire non saremmo in grado di valutare una delle componenti essenziali della civiltà occidentale. Nè la storia politica o ecclesiastica dai tempi di Carlomagno all'epoca del conciliarismo; nè i conflitti ricorrenti tra potere spirituale e potere temporale; nè le origini delle teorie politiche dello Stato, possono giustamente interpretarsi senza una conoscenza dei problemi inerenti al diritto canonico, ampiamente discussi dai decretisti e dai decretalisti del medio evo. I movimenti di riforma spiritual richeggianti nella storia del cristianesimo medioevale sono in larga misura accompagnati da sviluppi canonistici. La storia economica del medio evo non potrebbe capirsi senza il diritto delle decime, dei benefici ecclesiastici, dei divieti canonici contro l'usura; nè la storia delle istituzioni senza la teoria canonica delle persone morali. L'arte del dettame letterario, brani importanti delle letterature latine e volgari riflettono concetti, termini e istituzioni canoniche, senza dire della teologia sacramentale e morale, di tutta la storia del pensiero scolastico, intimamente connesse col crescere della scienza canonistica. Il diritto canonico è davvero come un filo sottile che si può scoprire ovunque si esamini da vicino la tessitura della civiltà cristiana nei secoli di mezzo.

Questa compenetrazione era possibile solo in una società per la quale l'unità e l'universalità dell'ordine ecclesiastico erano un dato reale e vivo, e per la quale, quindi, il significato universale degli aspetti giuridici di quell'ordine era un fatto che si spiegava da sé. Quantunque fossero violenti e appassionati i conflitti e le controversie tra Chiesa e Stato; quantunque fossero esorbitanti, alle volte, le pretese di superiorità lanciate da una parte o dall'altra, non si perdeva mai di vista il fatto che società ecclesiastica e società politica, ossia ordine spirituale e ordine temporale, rappresentavano due lati distinti di una unità piú sublime: l'unità della città di Cristo rè (*Christianitas, civitas Christi* ovvero *respublica Christiana,* come si soleva dire piú tardi). Compenetrandosi l'uno e l'altro, indirizzati l'uno verso l'altro, sotto lo stesso sovrano celeste, i due ordini sono però due «Stati» o popoli distinti: ognuno con la propria funzione e vita sociale, ognuno con il proprio principio di governo (sacerdozio e regno), ognuno con la propria giurisdizione.

Kuttner refers to the medieval dualism of two laws as two sides of a sublime unit. This medieval dualism was abandoned in modern times. (P.L.)

L'ordine giuridico dovendo rispecchiare l'ordine divino delle cose, ne seguiva logicamente che altro dev'essere il diritto del corpo ecclesiastico, altro quello del corpo politico; ognuno è un'ordine perfetto in sè, in funzione dell'organismo sociale da cui emana, autonomo per definizione sotto il diritto divino, naturale e positivo, che è fonte e norma di ambedue le giurisdizioni.

La cultura giuridica dell'età moderna ha abbandonato le concezioni medioevali. Dalle dottrine regalistiche, sorgenti già nel basso medio evo, fino al positivismo del secolo XIX e oltre, si può tracciare uno sviluppo, certamente non rettilineo, ma nondimeno progressivo, che finí in una nozione monistica del diritto. Le norme dell'ordinamento giuridico non vengono piú concepite se non nei termini di una funzione dello Stato sovrano. Quel monismo giuridico non ha soltanto, frequentemente, fatto perdere di vista la verità elementare che anche l'autorità suprema politica — qualunque sia il suo nome — soggiace ad un diritto piú alto di essa (e forse ci voleva il cataclisma della guerra mondiale per far rinascere tale verità, almeno nella coscienza dell'Occidente); ma l'equazione monistica tra diritto e volontà statale doveva pure condurre — il che anzitutto entra nelle nostre considerazioni — a rimuovere il diritto canonico dalla sua prístina posizione imponente nell'ordine universale giuridico della società. I sistemi moderni giuridici in genere riconoscono l'ordinamento canonico come un diritto speciale, al quale, per il rispetto dovuto alla religione, si concede forse una certa autonomia, comunque condizionata e limitata; ma non riescono piú a concepire il diritto canonico come ordinamento universale, essenzialmente e congenitamente autonomo, al di là di ogni potere civile. Questo mutamento d'idee ha pure rimosso, dobbiamo aggiungere, il diritto canonico dal suo prístino posto d'onore nelle Università pubbliche.

Tuttavia si può notare ai tempi nostri un rifiorire degli studi canonistici. Da una parte l'opera di codificazione, da quando fu cominciata sotto il Beato Pio X, ha dato, e continua a dare, sempre nuovi impulsi alla dogmatica del diritto della Chiesa; e d'altra parte hanno fatto scuola i grandi maestri della storia del diritto canonico, i quali in queste ultime generazioni ci hanno insegnato a trovare nello sviluppo di tante istituzioni ecclesiastiche, nella complessità della storia delle fonti canoniche, qualche cosa di piú che oggetti di mera curiosità antiquaria. È testimonianza di questo rifiorire d'una consapevolezza piú profonda se oggi una schiera folta di studiosi viene a commemorare il centenario di Graziano.

* * *

Torniamo al secolo XII. Se mai ci fu un grande iniziatore la cui personalità — come quella degli architetti delle cattedrali maestose del medioevo — è nascosta nell'ombra della propria opera, tale fu il nostro monaco camaldolese. Possiamo dire con qualche probabilità che egli nacque in un piccolo paese tra Orvieto e Chiusi verso la fine del secolo XI. Sappiamo che fu maestro di teologia nel monastero bolognese dei SS. Felice e Naborre, ove la *Concordia discordantium canonum* dev'essere stata compiuta non molto dopo il 1140; che aveva discepoli ai quali spiegò i canoni sulla base del suo libro; che diede un parere in una causa giudiziaria nel 1143; e che era già morto quando il decretista Rufino, tra il 1157 e il 1159, scrisse la sua *Summa decretorum*.

Rufinus finished his Summa in 1164—cf. *A. Gouron*, Sur les Sources civilistes et la datation des Sommes de Rufin et d'Etienne de Tournai, BMCL 16 (1986), 55–70; also in: *A. Gouron*, Droit et coutume en France aux XIIe et XIIIe siècles (Aldershot 1993), no. X. Cf. also *R. Deutinger*, The decrtist Rufinus—a well-known person?, BMCL 23 (1999), 10–15. (P.L.)

L'immaginazione fertile dei cronisti medioevali non voleva contentarsi di questi dati così magri.

Some details on Gratian's biography have been corrected by recent research. He was no Camaldolite monk in the Bolognese monastery of S. Felix and Nabor. We have no reliable information about his place of birth. But there are no doubts that he taught canon law in Bologna at the time of the first glossators of Roman law and that he probably was a monk. (P.L.)

Notiamo la leggenda dei tre fratelli: Graziano, il maestro dei *decreta*, Pietro Lombardo il maestro delle sentenze, e Pietro Comestore, il maestro della *Historia scholastica*. Al senso medioevale di simmetria simboleggiante doveva dare soddisfazione il pensiero che gli autori dei tre libri di testo più diffusi nell'insegnamento teologico, canonistico, e di storia biblica volgarizzata fossero nati dalla stessa madre.

Un'altra tradizione, ugualmente fittizia, si compiacque immaginare che Graziano diventasse vescovo, perfino cardinale, anticipando così, per il fondatore della scuola, le alte dignità alle quali non pochi tra i suoi discepoli e successori dovettero di fatto ascendere. Ma il figlio spirituale di S. Romualdo, benché non destinato agli onori della prelatura, doveva col suo libro determinare il pensiero e il perfezionamento giuridico della Chiesa in una misura molto più larga che non avessero mai fatto gli autori più illustri delle grandi collezioni canoniche nel secolo che lo precedette; fra cui tanti — come i vescovi Burcardo di Worms, S. Anselmo di Lucca, Ivone di Chartres, i cardinali Deusdedit e Gregorio di S. Crisogono — erano stati uomini d'azione non meno che di studio; consiglieri di papi e di principi, figure ben in vista negli affari ecclesiastici e politici.

* * *

Qual'è dunque il merito intrinseco per il quale la *Concordia discordantium canonum* doveva dare forma definitiva alla tradizione millenaria canonica antica?

Il problema si risolve soltanto se l'opera di Graziano viene inquadrata in quel movimento di idee che è il periodo degli albori della Scolastica. Dopo secoli di un tradizionalismo lineare che in genere s'era contentato di accumulare, compilare e ricompilare le autorità del passato, le nuove generazioni, anzitutto dall'ultima parte del secolo XI, scoprivano la forza costruttiva della ragione. In tutte le province del pensiero umano, una volta eliminata la diffidenza verso la dialettica, una volta adottato il programma del grande Sant'Anselmo di Canterbury, mirante all'armonia di *auctoritas* e *ratio* nel processo della *fides quaerens intellectum,* si procedeva dalla riproduzione conservatrice alla analisi ragionata, all'espansione costruttiva, alla sistemazione sintetica degli elementi presentati dalla tradizione. Sarebbe futile voler determinare a quale disciplina appartiene la priorità — o precedenza — in quel germogliare del rinascimento medioevale: teologia e filosofia, giurisprudenza canonica e giurisprudenza civile diedero e ricevettero a vicenda impulsi ed influssi; contribuendo ugualmente al perfezionamento del nuovo mondo intellettuale.

Nel libro di Graziano varie correnti di quel movimento di idee confluiscono; e la sua sintesi a sua volta dà spunto a nuove correnti e a sviluppi nuovi.

Quanto alle origini dell'opera possiamo distinguere anzitutto quattro fattori storici: 1) i nuovi atteggiamenti teorici e pratici risultanti dalla riforma gregoriana; 2) la consolidazione dei principî dell'ermeneutica verso la fine del secolo XI; 3) i progressi scientifici della teologia nelle scuole della Francia; 4) la formazione di una nuova scienza legale nella scuola di Irnerio a Bologna.

Kuttner enumerated four major influences on Gratian: 1.) the Gregorian Reform movement, 2.) the consolidation of hermeneutics in Canon Law, 3.) French Theology, 4.) Teaching of Roman Law in Bologna. (P.L.)

1) L'epoca della riforma gregoriana e della lotta detta delle investiture, saturata di conflitti di idee e di forze opposte tanto nell'ordine politico-ecclesiastico quanto nell'ordine teorico-dogmatico, accompagnata da sismi violenti, aveva svegliato nella mente degli uomini un nuovo senso dei contrasti, delle antitesi esistenti sotto la superficie della tradizione canonica. La battaglia per la libertà e la purità della Chiesa — cioè la reazione contro il processo di feudalizzazione dell'ordine gerarchico — doveva condurre i riformatori a domandarsi quali fossero nella massa enorme di testi antichi e recenti gli elementi del diritto vero, comune, della Chiesa. Accumulata dai collettori attraverso i secoli in una maniera arbitraria su documenti svariatissimi — concili generali e particolari, lettere di papi, statuti di vescovi, frammenti patristici, libri penitenziali e liturgici, brani di cronache, formulari, testi del diritto romano volgare e capitolari dei re franchi — come poteva una tale tradizione servire a chiarificare e a reggere la disciplina universale ecclesiastica? In un processo paziente di ricerca per le fonti dell'antichità cristiana, e di eliminazione di tutto quanto non poteva concordarsi con la suprema autorità giurisdizionale e magistrale del Romano Pontefice, i riformatori cercarono di stabilire una nuova tradizione più rigorosa dei testi canonici.

Ma, come nelle soluzioni politiche, da Urbano II in poi, il periodo dei compromessi prudenti succedeva a quello del rigore inflessibile gregoriano, cosí nella storia delle collezioni canoniche con l'opera di Ivone di Chartres si manifestava una nuova tendenza, mirante all'armonizzazione delle idee contraddittorie, piuttosto che alla eliminazione delle consuetudini cresciute nell'alto medio evo. A questo punto si accentua la portata dell'arte ermeneutica come strumento del pensiero canonico.

2) L'ermeneutica, tecnica dell'interpretare i testi al fine di appianare i contrasti, faceva parte necessaria del corredo della disciplina retorica antica. L'alto medio evo, tanto per il tramite dell'ermeneutica biblica dei Padri, quanto (piú direttamente) per il tramite dell'insegnamento tradizionale nel trivio, ne aveva sempre avuto qualche conoscenza. Ma, per accorgersi della necessità urgente dei processi ermeneutici, erano necessarie le crisi e le tensioni dell'era gregoriana, e poi il desiderio di vedere ristabilito l'equilibrio della disciplina sacramentale ed ecclesiastica in genere, senza sacrificare le conquiste della Riforma.

Bernaldo di Costanza nel suo trattato *De excommunicatis vitandis* e il gran vescovo di Chartres nel prologo alla sua compilazione canonica diedero alle regole ermeneutiche un nuovo orientamento, dirigendo i luoghi comuni dei retori verso la soluzione dei problemi specifici presentati dalla tradizione multiforme e dalla stratificazione storica dei sacri canoni; problemi per i quali il badare alle autorità relative dei legislatori, ai loro motivi, alle condizioni di tempo, luogo, persona, all'elucidazione del testo per il contesto, alle categorie di precetto e consiglio, di norma assoluta e norma dispensabile, si imponeva. In ispecie per Ivone, l'equilibrio tra giustizia e carità diventa il criterio supremo della *consonantia canonum*.

About the new orientation in hermeneutics of canon law he mentions *Bernold of Constance* and *Ivo of Chartres* with his Prologue. The famous Prologue was edited with a French translation, an Introduction and an Index by *Jean Werckmeister* (ed.), Yves de Chartres. The Prologue (Sources canoniques 1), Paris 1997; and by *Bruce C. Brasington* (ed.), Ways of Mercy. The Prologue of Yves of Chartres, in: *Gert Melville* (ed.), Vita regularis. Editionen 1 (Münster 2004), with an extensive commentary on Ivo's sources and an analysis of his concepts. (P.L.)

For Bernold of Constance cf. also *M. Therialt*, L'interprétation des normes canoniques chez Bernold de Constance, REDC 47 (1990), 411–421. (P.L.)

The influence of Ivo's Prologue on Gratian is according to Kuttner the equilibrium between iustitia and caritas. (P.L.)

3) Ma dalla formulazione di certi principi ermeneutici non si arriva d'un passo a un sistema ragionato di diritto. Nel mezzo secolo che correva tra l'opera di Ivone e quella di Graziano, troviamo soltanto applicazioni isolate di quei principî; applicazione ad alcune questioni speciali ch'erano diventate acutissime durante le lotte dell'era gregoriana. D'altra parte (e questo ci porta al terzo elemento storico che contribuì all'opera del nostro) le idee

metodiche enunciate da Bernaldo e Ivone ebbero nei decenni successivi un influsso profondo sui progressi raggiunti nelle scuole teologiche della Francia.

Con Abelardo, non solo il catalogo delle regole d'interpretazione si allarga e si perfeziona in una dissertazione critica, ma nel *Sic et Non* egli procedette anche ad organizzare tutta la massa enorme di autorità patristiche sistematicamente in diverse serie di proposizioni antinomiche, disposte sotto capi distinti: libro che doveva servire da arsenale classificato della disputazione dialettica — non (come s'è creduto) in uno spirito di scetticismo, ma per dimostrare che la scienza teologica si deve concepire come un insieme di problemi da risolvere; problemi che richiedono l'uso della piena facoltà di discernimento razionale non meno che una padronanza perfetta dei testi autoritativi, se dall'applicazione meccanica, esteriore, dei luoghi retorici si vuol arrivare ad una sintesi di dottrina. E quel metodo (quantunque le conclusioni dommatiche abelardine siano state spesso inaccettabili e perfino eterodosse) dava direzione e forma alla teologia scolastica del secolo XII: qui, la *solutio contrariorum* non è piú un rimedio per spiegare certe difficoltà (come fu per i canonisti della generazione d'Ivone), ma principio centrale euristico di tutto un edificio dottrinale.

Kuttner's evaluation of Gratian as a theologian must be partially revised by research since the discovery of two recensions of the Decretum. The latest description of the present knowledge is given by *John C. Wei*, Gratian the Theologian (Studies in Medieval and Modern Canon Law 13), Washington D.C. 2016. Wei has doubts that Gratian (the author of the first recension) was familiar with Abelard and his 'Sic et non', but had links to anonymous works associated with the study of law. Gratian was interested in penitential theology, but was no sacramental or liturgical theologian. He created a new science of canon law on a theological but non-sacramental basis. Kuttner's formulation that Gratian created 'un ordinamento essenzialmente giuridico' and that he developed 'una teoria universale delle fonti del diritto' is also confirmed by Wei who ends with 'Gratian the jurist'. (P.L.)

4) Si deve sempre insistere sull'influsso esercitato dai movimenti teologici di Francia su Graziano, sotto piú d'un punto di vista: perché ciò entra pure nella sostanza dell'opera grazianea. Basta ricordare che tutto il campo della disciplina dei sacramenti, l'imputabilità dei delitti, per non dire dei concetti fondamentali del diritto divino e della costituzione della Chiesa, fa parte della teologia nonché dei *sacri canones*. Anzi, fino a Graziano i *sacri canones et decreta sanctorum patrum* si consideravano sempre soltanto come un lato particolare della *sacra pagina,* cioè della teologia. Ma con tutta l'importanza dell'aspetto teologico della *Concordia discordantium canonum* (e nuove ricerche hanno tracciato, per es., certi influssi dottrinali della scuola Porretana), non bisogna dimenticare che uno dei meriti principali di Graziano sta nell'aver dato alla tradizione canonica la forma d'un sistema di diritto, di un'ordinamento essenzialmente giuridico.

Con questa osservazione torniamo al *genius loci*: il quarto fattore storico decisivo nella formazione dell'opera di Graziano è ch'essa fu scritta appunto a Bologna.

Non spetta a noi di discorrere qui a lungo della parte d'Irnerio e della scuola dei glossatori nella sinfonia intellettuale del secolo XII. Il sincronismo e parallelismo tra la nascita della teologia scolastica e la rinascita della giurisprudenza romana rimane uno dei fenomeni piú stupendi per lo storico del medioevo: stupendo perché l'attività d'Irnerio, partendo da presupposti del tutto diversi, si diresse verso gli stessi principî metodici quali eran quelli testé descritti nella teologia. La scoperta del Digesto, rilevando agli iniziatori della scuola bolognese il pensiero maturo di una coltura giuridica altissima, la cui tradizione era stata interrotta da secoli, doveva condurli ad acquistare una piena conoscenza e comprensione dello *ius civile* e ad investigare la coerenza intrinseca dell' intera codificazione giustinianea. Nelle loro glosse, esplorando il *mare magnum* di migliaia di testi, procedevano dalla registrazione dei luoghi paralleli e delle antinomie alla soluzione dei *contraria,* ad emulare e sorpassare i giuristi classici nelle loro distinzioni e questioni, ad organizzare e sintetizzare le materie complesse dei vari titoli del *Corpus iuris civilis* nelle loro *summae*. Con tutto questo nacque una nuova dialettica giuridica che si inquadrava senz'altro nelle correnti tipiche del periodo.

È assai difficile valutare con precisione l'influsso di Irnerio e dei quattro Dottori su Graziano, perchè il problema non è identico con quello dell'uso diretto dei testi giustinianei nel libro dei *decreta*. Ricerche recentissime sembrano confermare certe osservazioni già fatte nel secolo XVII, e cioè che Graziano nel suo piano originale forse non contemplò di racchiudere nella propria opera i frammenti tolti dal Digesto e dal Codice che oggi vi troviamo. Ma prescindendo da questo problema delicatissimo di critica del testo, risulta da altri passi non sospetti che il nostro era al corrente delle dottrine e dei metodi dei glossatori civilisti; e la loro opera ricostruttrice, analitica e sintetica nel campo delle *leges,* lo ispirava a dare la stessa coerenza dottrinale ai *canones*. Coerenza, diciamo, giuridica in quanto da stabilirsi non nel regno dell'astratta speculazione, ma nel mondo reale dei problemi concreti giudicabili, che comporta di giorno in giorno la molteplicità di funzioni e relazioni nel corpo sociale della Chiesa.

Difatti, il concetto stesso di *ius canonicum*, nel senso d'un complesso universale di norme giuridiche ecclesiastiche, non si trova prima di lui (si parlava nell'alto medio evo di *iura canonica* solo nel senso di diritto subiettivo della Chiesa), e un tale concetto poteva prendere forma soltanto in un periodo e in un ambiente ove il concetto di *ius*, nel senso d'un complesso normativo coerente, aveva acquistato un significato razionale. In quel senso è lecito di asserire che la nuova scienza dei glossatori fu un presupposto necessario per il lavoro di cristallizzazione della disciplina ecclesiastica quale complemento concettuale dello *ius civile*: il *ius canonicum*.

* * *

La cristallizzazione, dovendo compiersi coi mezzi d'un processo razionale, prendeva la forma storica della «concordia» dei discordanti canoni. Poichè, a differenza del diritto civile, una codificazione autorevole (un «digesto») dei canoni non esisteva, Graziano dovette lui stesso provvedervi. Le collezioni esistenti non potevano servire come tali, non essendo esse organizzate in una maniera che permetteva di mettere in rilievo, passo per passo, le antinomie, le discrepanze, e quindi, i problemi. D'altra parte, egli non poteva piú contentarsi di un catalogo secco di antitesi, di un *Sic et Non* canonico, in un tempo nel quale le conquiste dottrinali dei teologi e dei glossatori civilisti avevano già rivendicato il valore creativo dei principi scolastici. Cosí la *Concordia discordantium canonum* diventò collezione canonica a guisa d'un manuale di ragionamenti e soluzioni — o, se vogliamo, manuale composto di argomenti di ragione e di autorità giustificative; composto in una maniera che dovette ispirare, un po piú tardi, il maestro delle Sentenze, Pietro Lombardo, — ma che troviamo assai sproporzionata secondo il gusto letterario moderno, giacché la mole dei testi probativi piú d'una volta ci fa perdere il cammino del pensiero grazianeo.

Questo pensiero era tutt'altro che una semplice applicazione delle regole ermeneutiche svolte dalla generazione dei Bernaldo e Ivone; era un pensiero non soddisfatto di ridurre le antinomie nei canoni alle distinzioni facili tra norme di precetto e di consiglio, norme di rigore e di dispensa; ma pensiero che arriva a distinzioni piú sottili analitiche dei concetti stessi e delle situazioni stesse che fanno l'oggetto delle norme. Pensiero che s'istrada coraggiosamente fin dall'inizio verso una teoria universale delle fonti del diritto, e che pure indovina la differenza fondamentale tra la giudicabilità delle cause nel foro esterno, umano della Chiesa e il giudizio perfetto di Dio. Pensiero, ancora, ricco di esempi e d'analogie storiche e bibliche, ma alle volte (dobbiamo aggiungere anche questo) pensiero oscuro, mal coordinato, perdentesi in questioni incidentali o secondarie, e perfino dimentico del proprio programma sistematico.

Il sistema stesso del libro si mostra soltanto in parte concepito su un piano generale logicamente disposto, mentre per la maggior parte si tratta di una concatenazione delle varie istituzioni canoniche fatte secondo le lievi associazioni suggerite da certi punti di contatto fra di loro.

Quei difetti furono già notati dai primi decretisti, eppure essi non sognavano (salvo poche eccezioni) di abbandonare il sistema di Graziano. Perché grandi ne erano i meriti: il metodo di indagine che consiste nel costante rintracciamento di problemi da assoggettarsi all'operazione dialettica di concordare le antinomie allo scopo di derivarne una dottrina conclusiva, praticabile. E tal metodo era piú accentuato ancora per l'uso frequentissimo della forma classica di muovere problemi e dubbi: la *quaestio*. Graziano vi ricorse spesso nel lungo trattato delle fonti e dell'ordinazione sacra che costituisce la prima parte dell'opera; inoltre, la fece elemento formale della struttura di tutta la parte seconda — le trentasei cause fittizie giudiziarie, di cui ciascuna è trattata in una serie di questioni: *Hic primum queritur... secundum queritur...* ecc... Quale fosse la validità, nella specie, delle risposte e dottrine grazianee, il principio scientifico — nient'altro che la *solutio contrariorum* applicata su grandissima scala — implicava per i decretisti la possibilità di un'ulteriore revisione e di una sempre maggiore perfezione, di un progresso continuo verso definizioni piú esatte, verso distinzioni piú fini, sistemazioni piú equilibrate, sunti piú comprensivi.

Nel fare il proprio libro base del suo insegnamento, Graziano diede alla scienza decretistica una direzione che la scuola doveva conservare durante tutto il medioevo. Il *liber decretorum* diventava il *liber auctoritatum* ad esclusione di ogni altra collezione canonica; il Digesto dei canonisti, che presentò in forma definitiva un *corpus* integrale (eccezion fatta per un certo numero di canoni supplementari) della tradizione disciplinare antica della Chiesa. In quanto *concordia* o manuale, diventava il modello dell'insegnamento e dell'attività letteraria, per la forma e il metodo, piuttosto che per la sostanza delle sue dottrine. La scuola rimaneva piú fedele allo spirito indagatore e costruttivo del Maestro nel sentirsi non legata alle sue opinioni, ma nel cercare invece sempre nuovi problemi e possibilità dottrinali per mezzo dell'analisi minuta dei canoni stessi.

Il progresso scientifico si svolse di pari passo con quello della scuola dei legisti. I margini dei manoscritti si riempivano di glosse: serie di rimandi a luoghi paralleli o contrari, che diedero occasione a nuove *solutiones contrariorum* non previste da Graziano; distinzioni, notabili, brocardi, *summulae* e tanti altri tipi didattici. Staccandosi dalla connessione esterna col testo dei *Decreta*, i commentari, le somme, le distinzioni redatte per sé si moltiplicarono. Ancora nelle *quaestiones disputatae* dei canonisti possiamo notare l'incrociarsi di due elementi d'origine: le esercitazioni di scuola sul modello di quelle condotte nella scuola di Bulgaro legista, e la veste didattico-letteraria delle *causae* nel libro di Graziano. Il contatto con il lavoro dei legisti andava intensificandosi di generazione in generazione: poiché Graziano aveva insegnato la validità degli argomenti tolti dalle leggi, ove queste non contraddicono i canoni, la scienza canonistica (e tra poco l'attività giudiziaria e legislativa dei papi) non esitò di servirsi ampiamente delle fonti e dei concetti del diritto romano per perfezionare le proprie dottrine giuridiche, nonché la propria procedura forense.

L'opera scientifica della scuola dei decretisti bolognesi rapidamente acquistò un carattere europeo. Fu di qui che Stefano di Tournai, ritornando in Francia, importò la nuova scienza nella patria; e dalla scuola di Parigi ulteriori ramificazioni dovettero dare origine ai centri di studi decretistici nella Renania e nei paesi anglo-normanni.

* * *

Anzitutto la scuola, producendo un sistema sempre piú compatto di un diritto ragionato, gettava le basi per il diritto nuovo delle decretali pontificie. Graziano non ha introdotto nessuna innovazione riguardo al potere legislativo dei papi, ma semplicemente riasserito la formula gregoriana che il papa è il supremo guardiano e maestro del diritto della Chiesa. Però, se dalla metà del secolo XII in poi il vecchio strumento della *epistola decretalis* si usava a Roma con sempre maggior frequenza, se da tutte le parti del mondo le consultazioni, gli appelli e richieste dirette al Pontefice di commettere le cause a giudici delegati, si moltiplicarono di giorno in giorno, questo sviluppo presuppone (tra altre ragioni storiche) uno slancio del ragionamento tecnico giuridico in seno alla curia che sta in relazione diretta con la nuova scienza canonistica; relazione, che si fa subito evidente, se ricordiamo che con Alessandro III nel 1159 il primo canonista, il maestro bolognese Rolando Bandinelli, che era stato tra i primissimi espositori della opera di Graziano, salí sulla cattedra di Pietro.

Il *ius novum* delle decretali e delle costituzioni conciliari dei grandi papi giuristi, da Alessandro a Innocenzo III e a Gregorio IX, da Innocenzo IV a Bonifacio VIII, andava dalla seconda metà del secolo XII a sviluppare e trasformare profondamente il sistema canonico, facendolo rispondere con sempre maggior precisione alle esigenze emergenti dalla complessa vita giuridica della Chiesa. Sviluppo di massima portata, che spesso rendeva inefficaci certi canoni del diritto antico da leggersi sul libro di Graziano; sviluppo che spesso o confermava o rigettava le interpretazioni e le teorie dei decretisti; ma — a differenza dei processi legislativi moderni — il *liber decretorum* non fu mai svalutato né formalmente abolito. Le successive collezioni ufficiali del nuovo diritto pontificio, promulgate nei secoli XIII e XIV, non erano intese come codificazioni totali del diritto canonico vigente, ma anzi come integrazione del diritto antico con quello nuovo, in un solo «diritto comune» della Chiesa universale. Da parte dei pontefici legislatori, l'opera di Graziano come tale fu sempre presupposta, lasciata intatta, quale parte necessaria e fondamentale del *Corpus iuris canonici*. d'ora innanzi l'ordinamento vigente per qualsiasi istituzione canonica poteva determinarsi soltanto con un esame complessivo dei testi contenuti tanto nei *Decreta* quanto nelle *Decretali* (le quali, caratteristicamente, durante il medio evo, ritenevano il nome di *extravagantes*, cioè non racchiuse nel corpo dei *Decreta*).

L'esposizione del *liber decretorum* rimaneva nelle scuole, attraverso i secoli di mezzo, la prima *lectio ordinaria*, nella quale si formava la mente giuridica dei canonisti in erba. Certamente nel basso medio evo la trattazione dei *Decreta* era diventata stazionaria, poiché tutti i progressi e nuovi sviluppi oramai risultavano dal diritto pontificio delle *Decretales;* ma nondimeno perfino i gradi accademici, che i canonisti attinsero alla fine dei loro studi, continuavano a designarsi col nome di *magister* e *doctor decretorum*, e con buona ragione: essi servivano a rammentare ai laureati che la loro scienza in fin dei conti si fondava sull'opera di Graziano; nome, che per sempre sarà legato alla storia della giuriprudenza della civiltà cristiana del medio evo, la cui eredità è patrimonio imprescrittibile nostro.

ZUR FRAGE DER THEOLOGISCHEN VORLAGEN GRATIANS[1]

Kuttner starts with the thesis that Gratian's work was the beginning of canon law as a specifically juristic science, contradicting Rudolf Sohm's theory of Gratian's Decretum as a work of sacramental theology (so-called 'altkatholisches Kirchenrecht'). (P.L.)

I

Für die Geschichte der Beziehungen zwischen Theologie und Kanonistik im 12. Jahrhundert[2] hat das Werk Gratians schon darum eine besondere Bedeutung, weil mit ihm die Kanonistik in ein völlig neues Stadium tritt, in das Stadium der spezifisch wissenschaftlichen Entfaltung. Indem Gratian nicht nur — wie seine Vorgänger — die altkirchlichen Quellen sammelt und ordnet, sondern darüber hinausgehend in wissenschaftlicher Reflexion deutet, erläutert, distinguiert und harmonisiert, gestaltet er aus der Fülle der Canones ein Lehrgebäude. Diese Arbeit bedeutet, von der Seite des kirchlichen Rechts gesehen, den Beginn einer juristischen Theorie, den Anfang der Kanonistik als juristischer Wissenschaft, — sofern man eben unter „Jurisprudenz" systematisch-wissenschaftliche Bearbeitung von Rechtsstoff versteht.[3] Die großen vorgratianischen Sammlungen sind und bleiben

---

1 Vgl. dazu diese Zeitschrift LIII 1933 Kan. Abt. XXII S. 403 Anm. 2. Zu ebenda S. 401 Anm. 1 sei bei dieser Gelegenheit nachgetragen, daß die dort erwähnte Hüffersche Abschrift des Polycarp sich wiedergefunden hat und jetzt auf der Bonner Universitätsbibliothek Handschr. S. 1451 sich befindet. U. St.

2 J. de Ghellinck, Le Mouvement théologique du XIIme Siècle, Paris 1914 p. 277 ss.: Théologie et Droit canon au XIme et au XIIme siècle; Derselbe, Artikel „Gratien, la théologie dans ses sources et chez les Glossateurs" im Dict. de théol. cath. VI 1920 col. 1731 ss.; M. Grabmann, Die Geschichte der scholastischen Methode II 1911 S. 131, 213ff.; P. Fournier et G. Le Bras, Histoire des collections canoniques en occident II, 1932 Chap. V: Théologie et droit canon.

3 Das spezifisch juristische Moment bei Gratian leugnet R. Sohm, Das altkatholische Kirchenrecht und das Decretum Gratiani, 1918 S. 8ff., Kirchenrecht II, 1923 S. 79ff. Er faßt eigenwillig das Dekret als ein der Sakramentaltheologie gewidmetes Werk auf, wobei der an Umfang größte Teil des Dekrets (die Causae 2 bis 26) nur ein Exkurs zur Ordinationslehre sein soll. Sohms These ist von F. Gillmann, Einteilung und System des Gratianischen Dekrets usw., Arch. f. kath. KR. CVI 1926 S. 472ff. aus den Quellen widerlegt worden. Auch begrifflich ist sie abzuweisen.

Materialsammlungen, auch wo ihre Autoren von Konkordanzbestrebungen geleitet waren (wie z. B. Ivo von Chartres)[4]; denn es fehlt ihnen das Wesentliche der gratianischen Leistung: der Versuch zur Gewinnung einer Doktrin, die aus den Quellen erwächst.[5]

Dieser Unterschied Gratians von seinen Vorgängern ist auch für die theologische Seite seines Werkes bedeutsam. Nicht so sehr die Tatsache, daß in den kirchlichen Rechtsstoff, d. h. den Stoff der äußeren Kirchenordnung so mannigfaches theologisches Material (über die Sakramente des ordo, der Buße, der Ehe, der Taufe, der Eucharistie usw.) eingeflochten ist, charakterisiert die Concordia discordantium canonum; — denn die Gemeinsamkeit des patristischen Materials mit den eigentlich theologischen Sentenzensammlungen[6] kommt auch dem Dekret Burchards, dem Dekret Ivos und anderen Kanonessammlungen vor Gratian zu[7]; ganze Bücher sind ja bei Burchard (lib. 19 „corrector", lib. 20 de contemplatione) oder bei Ivo (Decr. Lib. 1, 2) theologisch-dogmatischen Problemen gewidmet. Die Frage nach dem Verhältnis Gratians zur theologisch-scholastischen Wissenschaft läßt sich auch nicht rein methodengeschichtlich allein durch eine Untersuchung des Anteils der beiden Disziplinen, Kanonistik und Theologie, an der Konkordanzmethode beurteilen.[8]

Vielmehr liegt die Bedeutung Gratians auch für die theologischen Partien seines Werkes in dem Übergang vom bloßen Sammeln und Disponieren patristischen Stoffes zur materiellen Behandlung dogmatischer Probleme an Hand der Quellen. Gratian ist ebenso produktiver Theologe wie produktiver Jurist und als solcher in seiner Beziehung zu den theologischen Dogmatikern, nicht nur zu den theologischen Stoffsammlern des 12. Jahrhunderts zu beurteilen. Den

---

Sohms Deutung des Dekrets ruht auf einer Unklarheit über den Begriff des „Juristischen"; für ihn ist nämlich Jurisprudenz offenbar nur in den Kategorien römischen Rechtsdenkens möglich und mit Legistik identisch; eine Aequivokation, die wiederum auf die These von der nichtrechtlichen Natur des „altkatholischen" Kirchenrechts, Kirchenrecht II S. 58 ff. zurückgeht und den exakten Begriff des Juristischen als des methodischen Rechtsdenkens einseitig verengt. Zur rechtsphilosophischen Kritik an der ganzen vorgefaßten Einstellung Sohms gegenüber „Recht" und „Jurisprudenz" vgl. auch W. Schönfeld, Die juristische Methode im K.R., Arch. f. Rechts- u. Wirtsch.-Philos. XVIII 1925 S. 58ff.

4 Grabmann a. a. O. I 1909 S. 240ff.
5 Zur Würdigung des Dekrets als eines Lehrsystems, in dem die gesammelten Quellen nur Belege sind, vgl. U. Stutz, Gratian und die Eigenkirchen, in dieser Zeitschrift XXXII 1911 Kan. Abt. I S, 3. Der erste Kanonist, der vor Gratian die gesammelten Texte bereits kommentiert, ist Alger von Lüttich im Liber de iustitia et misericordia M[igne] P[atrologia] L[atina] CLXXX, vgl. jetzt Fournier-Le Bras II p. 340; Le Bras, Alger de Liège et Gratien, Rev. des Sciences philos. et théol. XX 1931 p. 5 ss.
6 de Ghellinck p. 44 ss.; Fournier-Le Bras II p. 326 ss.
7 de Ghellinck p. 44, 297 ss. (über Ivo), 280 ss. (über Burchard), 286 ss. (nachburchardische Sammlungen). Fournier-Le Bras II p. 326 s.
8 Fr. Thaners Versuch, die methodische Beziehung einzig mit dem Einfluß von Abaelards Sic et Non auf Gratian zu erklären (Abaelard und das kanonische Recht, Graz 1900), ist durch neuere Forschungen überholt, welche gezeigt haben, wie an der Entstehung der Konkordanzmethode Theologie und Kanonistik vor Gratian gleichermaßen Anteil haben, ja wie Abaelard die Methode von kanonistischen Sammlern im wesentlichen vorgebildet gefunden hat (Bernold von Konstanz,

dankbarsten Gegenstand für eine solche Untersuchung wird stets der „Tractatus de poenitentia" bilden[9], der als umfangreiche Abhandlung über die Dogmatik des Bußsakraments die ausgeprägteste theologische Färbung besitzt, wofür es charakteristisch ist, daß in nachgratianischer Zeit, als die kanonistische Jurisprudenz mehr und mehr zur Sonderdisziplin wurde, eine Behandlung der Bußlehre durch die Dekretisten zumeist unterblieb.[10]

Seeing in Gratian as well a productive theologian and a productive jurist he stresses the importance of the 'Tractatus de penitentia' in the Decretum. This treatise has now be dealt with in the fundamental and first full-scale study by *Atria A. Larson*, Master of Penance. Gratian and the Development of Penitential Thought and Law in the Twelfth Century (Studies in Medieval and Early Modern Canon Law 11), Washington D.C. 2014. (P.L.)

II

Einen starken Einfluß haben die im Anfang des 12. Jahrhunderts entstandenen theologischen „Sententiae Magistri A." (die man früher Alger von Lüttich zugeschrieben

---

Ivo, Alger). Vgl. Fournier, Les collections canoniques attribuées à Ives de Chartres, Bibl. de l'école des chartes LVIII 1897 p. 661; Grabmann II S. 199, 213 ff., dessen allzu absprechendes Urteil über die wissenschaftsgeschichtliche Bedeutung des „Sic et Non" aber von de Ghellinck p. 49, 331 ss. und neuerdings von J. Cottiaux, La conception de la théologie chez Abélard, Rev. d'hist. ecclés. XXVIII 1932 p. 791 ss. korrigiert wird. Vgl. auch Fournier-Le Bras II p. 339 n. 3, p. 348.

9 Einen Ansatz zu solcher Untersuchung geben E. Hugueny, Gratien et la confession, Rev. sciences phil. théol. VI 1912 p. 81, und vor allem A. Debil, La première dist. du „de paenitentia" de Gratien, Rev. d'hist. eccl. XV 1914 p. 251 ss., 442 ss., der jedoch nur die Lehre Gratians und die der Theologen vergleicht, ohne die quellengeschichtlichen Zusammenhänge zu untersuchen. Über andere theologische Materien des Dekrets handeln zahlreiche Aufsätze F. Gillmanns im Katholik und im Arch. f. kath. KR.

10 Nur Huguccio kommentiert den tract. de poen. ausführlich. Schon Rolandus (Alexander III.) hatte in seinem kanonistischen Stroma (ed. Thaner 1874) ad C. 33 q. 3 die Erörterung der Bußlehre ausdrücklich seinem theologischen Sentenzenwerk reserviert. In den glossierten Hss. des Dekrets vor Johannes Teutonicus wie in der johanneischen Glosse ist die spärliche Glossierung des tract. de poen. schon für den Blick auffallend. Dagegen hat die Glossenhs. des Cod. Vat. Pal. 624 eine reichere, offenbar dem Laurentius zuzuweisende Schicht ad C. 33 q. 3 (Teetaert, La confession aux laiques usw., Bruges 1926 p. 227); ähnlich der erste Apparat des Joh. Teutonicus im Cod. Pal. 658 (Kuttner, diese Zeitschrift LII 1932 Kan. Abt. XXI S. 168; die Laurentiusschicht in dieser Urform der Glos. ord. ist überhaupt größer, als ich angenommen habe: Fr. Gillmann, Arch. f. kath. KR. CXII 1932 S. 514 Anm. 1). — Teetaerts Vermutung, daß Cod. Pal. 624 im übrigen die reine johanneische Glosse enthalte, ist zutreffend. Dagegen ist die Summierung des tract. de poen. in der von Teetaert (1. c. p. 228) bekanntgemachten Hs. der Summa des Stephanus Tornacensis Cod. Vat. Borghes. 287 unecht: Die Summa endet hier fol. 109 v. mit pars II des Dekrets, daran schließen sich anderthalb Spalten kurzer Summierung der 7 Distinktionen des tract. de poen. und eine kurze Sammlung (bis fol. 110) zivilistischer Prozeßformeln. Außerdem enthält jedoch die Handschrift ad C. 33 q. 3 (fol. 102) die Erörterungen des Stephanus über das Problem der D. 1 de poen., wie sie sonst überall überliefert sind (ed. v. Schulte 1891 S. 246) und von denen die Behandlung der D. 1 im genannten Anhang sachlich abweicht. Dies, wie überhaupt die anhangsweise Behandlung zusammen mit den Klagformeln, spricht gegen die Echtheit der Stücke auf fol. 109 v.

hat[11], jetzt aber als Werk eines unbekannten Sammlers ansieht)[12] bekanntermaßen auf die Behandlung der Sakramente der Ehe, der Priesterweihe, der Eucharistie und der Taufe bei Gratian gehabt.[13] Nun enthalten zwei Handschriften dieser Sentenzen (Troyes 1317, Florenz Laurent. S. Crucis plut. V sin. Cod. 7) einen Titel de poenitentia, die Florentiner Hs. außerdem noch Titel de caritate, de falsis testibus, de periurio[14]; vier Titel, die in der von Friedberg für die Quellengeschichte zum Dekret herangezogenen Hs. (Paris Bibl. nat. lat. 3881, mit der Vatic. lat. 4361 im Aufbau übereinstimmt) fehlen. Fournier und Le Bras regen an, den Titel de poenitentia im Vergleich mit Gratians tract. de poen. zu untersuchen[15]; diese Untersuchung ist auch auf den Titel de caritate auszudehnen, da ja Gratian Probleme der Caritaslehre in de poen. D. 2 (z. T. auch noch in D. 3) behandelt.

An edition of the 'Sententiae Magistri A' was published by *Paule Maas*, The Liber Sententiarum Magistri A. Its place amidst the sentences collections of the first half of the 12th century (Middeleeuwse Studies XI), Nijmegen 1995 — Edition pp. 221–293. (P.L.)

Ich habe nun den Cod. S. Crucis in Florenz geprüft und in beiden Titeln eine Fülle patristischen Materials, das auch bei Gratian de poen. vorkommt, gefunden. Auffallend ist vor allem das übereinstimmende Vorkommen ganzer zusammenhängender Partien mit nicht nur in der Art der Exzerpierung und Inskription völlig gleichem patristischem Material, sondern auch gleichen verbindenden Dicta. Hier einige Beispiele aus dem Tit. de caritate:

Sent. Mag. A. fol. 73	Gratian de poen. D.2
Augustinus super genesim ad litteram:[16] Quomodo ... lapsus est primus homo.[17] *Et paulo post:* Expoliantes ... per peccatum. *Et post pauca:* Stola ... Adam.	c. 31

Sent. Mag. A. fol. 73.	Gratian de poen, D. 2
Idem in homelia XI: Princeps ... subiugavit. *et paulo post:* Amissa ... factus est.	c. 32
Illud idem ad Iulianum comitem, licet per alia verba. His auctoritatibus habemus Adam ante peccatum habuisse caritatem et post perdidisse.	(fehlt.)[18]

---

11 So der Entdecker H. Hüffer, Beiträge zur Geschichte der Quellen des Kirchenrechts, Münster 1862 S. 1ff., auch noch Fournier in dem oben S. 27 Anm. 8 zit. Aufsatz in Bibl. éc. chart. p 651.
12 Fournier-Le Bras II p. 332; Le Bras, Alger de Liège (oben S. 26 Anm. 5) p. 23.
13 Vgl. das Stellenregister in Friedbergs Ausgabe, Prolegom. Sp. LXXIIIf.
14 Fournier, Bibl. éc. chart. 1. c. p. 652.
15 Fournier-Le Bras II p. 330, wo versehentlich der Hinweis auf das Vorkommen von de poenitentia in der Hs. von Troyes und von de caritate in der Florentiner Hs. fehlt.
16 *Unde Aug. in genesi ad litt.:* Gratian.
17 primus homo: fehlt bei Gratian.
18 Vgl. aber den Schluß des Dict. p. c. 30: *Colligitur ergo quod Adam* usw.

Ambrosius[19] *ad Sabinum:* Quando Adam... Deo.	c. 33
— —.[20]	c. 34
Idem <in> Exameron: Illa anima ... deposuit.	c. 35
Idem de fuga seculi: Similem ... perfectum.	c. 36
Idem de vita beata: Sapiens ... inventus est.	c. 37
Idem in libro de Ysaac et anima: Sed nec Adam ... vestiebat.	c. 38
Idem in libro de paradiso: Et[21] cognoverunt ... tegumento virtutum.[22]	c. 39
Postremo opponitur illud[23] *... intrat.*[24]	Dict. p. c. 39 (Anfang)
Sent. Mag. A. fol. 73 ᵛ.	Grat. de poen. D. 2
Augustinus[25] *de correctione et gratia:* Quicumque ... redeunt *et cet.*	Dict. p. c. 24 (Mitte)
In eodem: Firmum fundamentum ... deputantur.	c. 25
Idem in eodem[26]*:* Nullus ... hanc vitam.	c. 26
In eodem: Talibus deus ... in bonum *et cet.*[27]	c. 27
Ad Galathas[28]*:* Circumcisio ... dilectione.	c. 28
Item ad Hebreos: Non est tam ... vestri et cet.	c. 29
Sent. Mag. A. fol. 73ᵛ.	Gratian de poen. D. 2
Operis ... vobis deus.	Dict. p. c. 29 (Anfang)
Opponitur etiam de Benedicto ...	(fehlt)
fol. 73 ᵛ/74	Gratian 1. c.
De reprobis etiam qui caritatem habuisse videntur, (fol. 74) *Augustinus de correctione et gratia*[29]*:* Apostolus ... sunt sancti *et cet. In eodem:* An adhuc ... non accepi. *In eodem de eisdem*[30]*:* In bono ... permanserunt. *In eodem:* Propter huius ... cadere *et cet.*	Dict. p. c. 40 c. 41

19 *Item Ambrosius ad Sab.:* Gratian.
20 Die Stelle (Primus homo) steht aber im Tit. de poenitentia, fol. 78, wo auch die vorhergehende und die folgende noch einmal wiederholt werden.
21 Ut: Gratian. (Et: orig.)
22 virtutum tegumento: Gratian.
23 *Opponitur etiam illud:* Gratian.
24 Von hier an bis z. Schluß des Dictum im Text verschieden, aber materiell übereinstimmend. Sent. A. schließen den Paragraphen mit dem Zitat aus Ambrosius de Isaac et anima, das bei Grat. im Dict. § 3 a. E. steht.
25 *Unde Augustinus in libro de ...:* Gratian.
26 *In eodem:* Gratian (Friedb.); *Idem in eodem libro:* Corr. Rom.
27 *et cet.:* fehlt bei Gratian.
28 *Item Apostolus ad Galathas:* Gratian.
29 *... de reprobis etiam videndum est, an ipsi karitatem habeant, qua amissa postea dampnentur. De his ita scribit Augustinus in libro de ...:* Gratian.
30 *de eisdem* fehlt bei Grat.

In eodem[31]: Multa similia ... in finem *et cet. Et* *iterum*[32]: Homo iste incepit *et cet.*	Dict. p. c. 41
fol. 75/75 ᵛ	Gratian 1. c.
Augustinus[33] *de gratia et libero arbitrio:* Qui vult ... nemo habet *et cet. Et paulo post:* Ipsam caritatem ... pro te ponam. *Quod autem caritas sit perfecta et imperfecta, Augustinus*[34] *super epistolam Johannis:* (fol. verso) Si quis tantam ... mori lucrum.	c. 16
In eadem: Forte nata ... suffocetur.	c. 18[35]
In eadem: Crescit caritas ... converso.	c. 17 Satz 2
Idem ad Ieronimum: Karitas in quibusdam ... non potest.	c. 19
Gregorius[36]): Si sermo ... studete. *Et paulo post:* Flate ... consumat.	c. 20
Set opponitur postremo ...	(fehlt)

Der hier an mehreren Beispielen angedeutete Befund würde nun für eine starke Abhängigkeit Gratians von den Sent. Mag. Λ. im tract. de poen. sprechen, für eine Abhängigkeit, die über die sonst bekannte Benutzung des Mag. A. als einer Quelle patristischer Texte durch Gratian weit hinausginge. Denn hier käme eben zur Übernahme der Einzelstücke[37] im Zusammenhang und in gleicher Textgestaltung — vor allem auch dort, wo Canones aus einer patristischen Quelle durch Zusammenziehungen und Auslassungen geformt sind[38] — noch die Übernahme einzelner Dicta in auffallender Weise. Aber gerade dieses Auffallende gibt zu Bedenken Anlaß:

---

31 *In eodem* fehlt bei Gratian, der folgende Satz dort als eignes dictum. Die Zuschreibung in den Sent. ist jedenfalls unrichtig.
32 *In eodem:* Iterum homo iste ...: Gratian. Nach Friedberg (Note 645 a. a. O) ist der Satz nicht als Zitat zu verifizieren. Die Lesart der Sent., wonach „iterum" nicht zu homo gehört, scheint mir besser als die gratianische.
33 *Hinc etiam Aug. ait in libro de* ...: Gratian.
34 *Quod autem — Augustinus:* fehlt bei Gratian. Es heißt dort: *Idem super* ...
35 In allen der Friedbergschen Ausgabe zugrunde liegenden Hss. steht c. 18 vor c. 17 (Fr. Note 235).
36 *Item Gregorius:* Gratian.
37 Von weiteren Einzelstücken seien notiert: Cod. S. Cruc. fol. 71 c. Si quis autem (c. 49 de poen. D. 3), fol. 72 c. Karitas que (c. 2 d. p. D. 2), fol. 79 c. Qui recedit (c. 14 d. p. D. 4), fol. 80 ᵛ c. Qui admissa (c. 13 d. p. D. 3), fol. 81 cc. Irrisor, Inanis, Perfecta (cc. 11, 12, 8 1. c.) fol. 81ᵛ c. Ille penitentia<m>, Nichil profuit (cc. 9, 38 1. c.). Diese Liste wäre noch zu verlängern.
38 Wie die cc. Quomodo (c. 31 de poen. D. 2), Princeps (c. 32) Quicumque (Dict. p. c. 24), Apostolus (c. 41), Qui vult (c. 16), Si sermo (c. 20). — Die vorkommenden Varianten sind geringfügig, wie ein Beispiel zeigen mag: fol. 73: Quomodo renovati (renovari *Grat.*) dicimur, si non recipimus quod primus homo perdidit (perd. pr. ho.: *Gratian*), in quo omnes moriuntur? (in ... moriuntur: *om. Grat.*) Hoc plane recipimus, quia iustitiam, ex qua per peccatum lapsus est primus homo (pr. ho.: *om. Grat.*) *Et paulo post:* Expoliantes (vos: *add. Grat.? cf. Friedberg n.* 321 *ad c. cit.*) veterem

Die anderen Hss. der Sententiae Mag. A. enthalten überhaupt nur auctoritates, keine eignen dialektischen Verbindungstexte; die Florentiner weicht hierin von allen ab.[39] Der Abschnitt de caritate ist ferner in den anderen Hss. nicht vorhanden, ein Abschnitt de poenitentia nur noch in der von Troyes, offenbar jedoch in einer Fassung, die von der Florentiner abweicht; denn der Titel reicht im Cod. S. Crucis von fol. 76 ^{v} bis 87^v, im Cod. Trecens. dagegen nur von fol. 157 bis 158^v.[40] Dazu kommt, daß gerade von den mit Gratian so auffallend übereinstimmenden Stücken viele in den Titeln de carit. und de poen. noch ein zweites Mal und zwar oft in abweichender Textüberlieferung stehen; ein Verfahren, das, wo solche Doppelüberlieferungen sich häufen, auf eine recht unaufmerksame Kompilationsarbeit schließen läßt. Ich notiere:

fol. 73 Quando Adam ...   fol. 78 Quando Adam ...
(= c. 33 de poen. D. 2)   (um einen Satz des Originals Ambros. ep. 49 n. 2
                                   erweitert)
fol. 73 Illa anima ...   fol. 78 Illa anima ...
(=c. 35 1. c.)   (gleiche Fassung)
fol. 73 Similem ...   fol. 78^v Similem ...
(= c.36 1.c.)   (gleiche Fassung)
fol. 73 Sapiens ...   fol. 78^v Sapiens ...
(= c. 37 1. c.)   (um einen Zwischensatz des Originals Ambros. de
                                   Jacob II c. 5 n. 22 erweitert)
fol. 73 Set nec Adam ...   fol. 78 ^{v} Set nec Adam ...
(= c. 38 1. c.)   (gleiche Fassung)
fol. 73 Et cognoverunt ...   fol. 78^v Et cognoverunt ...
(= c. 39 1. c.)   (um mehrere Sätze des Originals Ambros, de
                                   Parad. c. 13 n. 63 erweitert)
fol. 75 Qui vult ...   fol. 71^v Qui vult ...
(= c. 16 1. c.)   (ein größerer Abschnitt des Originals Augustin. de
                                   grat. et lib. arb. n. 33 ohne Zusammenziehungen)
fol. 75 ^{v} Si sermo ...   fol. 71^v Si ergo sermo ...
(= c. 20 1. c.)   (ein größerer Abschnitt des Originals Augustin.
                                   Serm. 178 n. 11 ohne Zusammenziehung)

So kann die Frage auftauchen, ob die weitgehende Verwandtschaft zwischen den besonderen Teilen des Cod. S. Crucis, dessen Schrift auf die Mitte des 12.

---

hominem induite novum, qui renovatur in agnitionem Dei (agnitione fidei: *Grat.*) secundum imaginem eius qui creavit eum. Hanc imaginem in spiritu mentis impressam perdidit Adam per peccatum. *Et post pauca:* Stola illa prima ipsa iustitia est, unde lapsus est Adam.

39 Hüffer a. a. O. S. 4; Fournier Bibl. éc. chart. 1. c. p. 653 n. 2.
40 Ich entnehme diese Angabe über den Umfang dem Bericht von F. Patetta, Il msc. 1317 della Bibl. di Troyes, Atti della R. Accad. delle scienze di Torino XXXII 1897 p. 456. Die dort beigegebenen Photographien einzelner Seiten des Cod. Trecens. — leider nicht der foll. 157f. — zeigen, daß die Differenz nicht etwa auf größerem Blattformat oder engerer Schrift beruhen kann.

Jahrhunderts weist[41], und dem tract. de poen. Gratians nicht umgekehrt erklärt werden muß: daß hier eine plagiatorische, nachgratianische Umarbeitung der Sent. Mag. A. vorliegt, die aus Gratian und aus anderen theologischen Sentenzenwerken schöpft. Zum mindesten lassen alle genannten Auffälligkeiten des Cod. S. Crucis — Verbindungstexte, die sonst nicht überliefert sind und streckenweise mit Gratian übereinstimmen, vier Titel mehr als die anderen Hss., häufige Doppelüberlieferung patristischer Texte in verschiedenen Formen — es als sehr bedenklich erscheinen, die Abschnitte de caritate und de poenitentia als echte Bestandteile der ursprünglichen Sent. Mag. A. anzusehen. Erst eine vergleichende Analyse der übrigen Titel in allen Hss. der Sentenzen wird aber ergeben können, welche Überlieferung die echte sei. Vorher können die Einschübe des Cod. S. Crucis jedenfalls nicht mit Sicherheit als Quelle für den tractatus de poenitentia in Anspruch genommen werden.

Kuttner compared MS Florenz Laurent. S. Crucis plut. V sin. Cod. 7 of the Sententiae Magistri A with the Decretum Gratiani and found many identical texts. He was reluctant to see in Cod. S. Crucis the source of Gratian and discussed also a possibility that the Florentine manuscript had inversely taken Gratian as its source. (P.L.)

III

Neuerdings ist nun die Frage, von welchen Theologen die dogmatischen Ausführungen Gratians beeinflußt seien, von Fr. Bliemetzrieder aufgegriffen und dahin beantwortet worden, daß Gratian zur Schule Anselms von Laon gehöre.[42] Die Nachprüfung der Beweise, die der verdienstvolle Herausgeber der dem Laoner Kreis entstammenden „Sententiae Anselmi" und „Sententiae divinae paginae"[43] für seine These vorträgt, wird jedoch zeigen, daß eine solche Einordnung Gratians sich nicht halten läßt.

Discussing the thesis of *Franz Bliemetzrieder* on Gratian having been influenced by the theological school of Laon, Kuttner refers to the 'Sententiae Anselmi' and the 'Sententiae divinae paginæ'. (P.L.)

---

41 Die Ähnlichkeit des Schriftbildes mit dem zahlreicher mir bekannter italienischer juristischer Handschriften aus der zweiten Hälfte des 12. Jahrhunderts spricht hierfür mehr als paläographische Einzelmerkmale (rundes d, Anfänge der Schaftbrechung, Ähnlichkeit von c und t; dagegen aber: keine Striche über ii, s auch am Ende nur selten gegenüber ſ).

42 Fr. Bliemetzrieder, Gratian und die Schule Anselms von Laon, Arch. f. kath. KR. CXII 1932 S. 37 ff. (im folgenden stets nur mit Namen und Seitenzahl zitiert.) — Über Anselm und seine Bedeutung für die Wissenschaft des 12. Jahrhunderts vgl. de Ghellinck, The sentences of A. of L. usw., Irish Quarterly Review 1911 p. 427; Bliemetzrieder, Autour de l'oeuvre théologique d'Anselm de L., Recherches de théol. anc. et médiév. I 1929 p. 435; Derselbe, L'oeuvre d'A. de L. et la littérature théol. contemp., ebenda V 1933 p. 275; H. Weisweiler, L'école d'A. de L. et Guillaume de Champeaux, ebenda IV 1932 p. 237 ss., 371 ss.

43 Anselms von Laon systematische Sentenzen, ed. Bliemetzrieder, Münster 1919. Seine ursprüngliche Annahme, Anselm selber sei der Autor der Sent. Ans., hat Bliemetzrieder jetzt fallen lassen. Arch. a. a. O. S. 59.

Bliemetzrieders Untersuchungen sind von dem Wunsch getragen, die Annahme irgendeines Einflusses Abaelards auf Gratian für hinfällig erklären zu können. Mag nun auch Thaner[44] die Beziehungen zwischen Abaelard und Gratian überschätzt haben, so ist doch eine völlige Leugnung dieser Beziehungen bei unvoreingenommenem Studium und Vergleich der Quellen nicht möglich; die Rigorosität aber, mit der Bliemetzrieder den möglichen Einfluß Abaelards zurückweist, ohne ihn aus den Quellen, d. h. aus einem Vergleich von Stellen in Abaelards Werken mit den entsprechenden Partien bei Gratian zu widerlegen, wirkt wie Abneigung gegen den Gedanken, den Haeretiker Abaelard mit dem Vater der Kirchenrechtswissenschaft in Zusammenhang zu bringen. Freilich wäre ein solches Vorurteil nicht zu verstehen: die neuere — auch die katholische — Forschung hat gezeigt, daß der Kampf des hl. Bernhard gegen Abaelards Haeresien von Leidenschaft getrübt war, daß das Urteil des Konzils von Sens (1140) in manchen Punkten nicht gerechtfertigt ist und auf Mißverständnissen beruht[45], und schließlich braucht Abhängigkeit von Abaelard kein Makel zu sein, wenn ein Alexander III. zu seiner Schule gehört.[46]

Bliemetzrieder geht von folgender Prämisse aus: Wenn Abaelard Einfluß auf Gratian hatte, dann ist eine Beziehung Gratians zur Schule Anselms ausgeschlossen, da Abaelards Schüler dessen Gegensatz gegen Anselm geerbt hätte (S. 37). Gratian steht aber ganz im allgemeinen in engem Abhängigkeitsverhältnis zu Ivo von Chartres, der zur Schule Anselms gehört (S. 38). Also gehört auch Gratian zur Schule von Laon, mithin ist Thaners These von der Beziehung zu Abaelard hinfällig (S. 62). Diese Argumentation übersieht, daß ein solches „entweder — oder" in der Frage der Quellen gar nicht existiert. Der prinzipielle Gegensatz Anselms zur abaelardischen Lehre schloß es z. B. nicht aus, daß in vielen Fragen der Bußdisziplin Abaelard und Anselm übereinstimmten (s. u. S. 40 ff.); ferner hat nachgewiesenermaßen Abaelard selber Ivo — also die gegnerische Schule — methodisch und quellenmäßig (als „dossier patristique") benutzt[47], so daß kein Grund besteht, Abaelard mit Ivo und Ivo mit Abaelard für Gratian auszuschließen, zumal das Verfahren, für einen patristischen Text mehrere Quellen zu benutzen, wie dem 12. Jahrhundert überhaupt, so auch Gratian durchaus geläufig ist.[48] Daß endlich ein formaler und quellenmäßiger Einfluß Abaelards auch dort möglich

---

44 Vgl. oben S. 26 Anm. 8.
45 Cottiaux a. a. 0. p. 822 ss. mit zahlreichen Literaturnachweisen. — Von neuerer Abaelardliteratur im allgemeinen sei hier genannt: A. Landgraf, Beiträge zur Erkenntnis der Schule A.s, Zschr. f. kath. Theol. LIV 1930 S. 360ff.; G. de Giuli, Abelardo e la morale, Giornale critico della filos. ital. 1931 p. 33 ss.; W. v. d. Steinen, Vom heiligen Geist des Mittelalters, Breslau 1926 (dazu P. E. Schramm, Hist. Zschr. CXLVII 1933 S. 544f.); J. G. Sikes, Peter Abailard, Cambridge 1932; C. Ottaviano, Pietro Abelardo, la vita, le opere, il pensiero, Roma 1932; P. Lasserre, Un conflit réligieux au XIIme siècle, Abélard contra S. Bernard, Paris 1930. G. Delagneau, Le concile de Sens, Rev. apolog. LII 1931 p. 385ss.; J. Rivière, Les capitula d'Abélard condamnés, Rech. de théol. anc. et médiév. V 1933 p. 5ss. H. Waddell, Peter Abelard, London 1933.
46 Über Roland als Schüler Abaelards: Denifle, Die Sentenzen Abaelards usw., Arch. f. Lit. Kirch. Gesch. des MA. I 1885 S. 402ff.; de Ghellinck, Mouvement p. 100.
47 Grabmann II S. 216; de Ghellinck p. 44, 104; Fournier in Bibl. éc. chart. 1. c. p. 663.
48 Fournier-Le Bras II p. 349 n. 2.

war, wo seine Dogmatik materiell abgelehnt wurde — nämlich in der Schule Hugos von St. Viktor —, zeigt die pseudohugonische „Summa Sententiarum"[49], in der abaelardische und Viktoriner Strömungen zusammenfließen.[50]

Kann so die allgemeine Argumentation, daß sich aus den Beziehungen Gratians zu Ivo[51] seine ausschließliche Zugehörigkeit zum Laoner Kreis ergebe, nicht überzeugen, so ist nun zu prüfen, wieweit mit den Vergleichungen und Gegenüberstellungen von Stücken aus den Sententiae Anselmi und Gratians Tractatus de poen. Bliemetzrieder ein Beweis für seine These gelungen ist. Wenn man bedenkt, welche Zeitspanne zwischen der Abfassung der Sent. Ans. (Anfang des 12. Jahrhunderts) und der des Dekrets liegt, so hätte Bliemetzrieder sich mit dieser Gegenüberstellung nicht begnügen dürfen; denn um in diesem Fall einen positiven Zusammenhang behaupten zu können, müßte zuvor die Möglichkeit, daß Gratian von zeitlich ihm näher stehenden Werken beeinflußt wurde, widerlegt werden; vor allem, wenn sich darunter Werke von solcher historischen Tragweite wie die Abaelards oder Hugos von St. Viktor befinden. Abaelards Hauptwerke erschienen zwischen 1123 und 1140[52], Hugos Hauptwerk „de sacramentis Christianae fidei" war wenige Jahre vor seinem Tode († 1141) beendet[53]; die Möglichkeit einer Einflußnahme dieser Werke auf Gratian ist also zum mindesten zu prüfen und — wie im folgenden gezeigt werden soll — nicht von der Hand zu weisen.

Gratians dist. 1 de poen. behandelt die scholastische Streitfrage, ob zur Sündenvergebung in der Buße die Reue genüge, oder ob Beichte und priesterliche Absolution ebenfalls ein konstitutiver Bestandteil des Sakraments seien. Es war dies eins der umstrittensten Probleme des 12. Jahrhunderts.[54] Die umfangreiche

---

49 Die Bibliographie zur (jetzt überwiegend verneinten) Frage der Echtheit der Sum. Sent. bei Überweg-Geyer, Grundriß der Gesch. d. Philos. II[11] 1928 S. 709; de Ghellinck in Mélanges Mandonnet, 1930 II p. 82 n. 1. — Zu der Streitfrage, ob Hugo von Mortagne (um 1156) oder Odo von Lucca (vor 1150) als Autor anzusprechen sei, kann hier nicht Stellung genommen werden. Die erste Meinung ist von M. Chossat, La Somme des Sentences, oeuvre de Hugues de Mortagne vers 1156 (Spicil. Sacr. Lovan. V 1923 p. 1 ss.); die andere von B. Geyer, Verfasser und Abfassungszeit der sog. Sum. Sent. (Theol. Quart.-Schr. CVII 1926 S. 89ff.) aufgestellt worden. Neuerdings tritt M. Grabmann, Gesch. der kath. Theol. 1933 S. 37 und 288 für die Autorschaft eines sonst unbekannten Magister Hugo Parisiensis und für Abfassung nicht nach 1147 ein.

50 Vgl. darüber de Ghellinck, Mouvement p. 118 ss.; Betzendörfer, Art. „Sentenzenwerke" in Religion in Gesch. u. Gegenwart[2] 1931.

51 Für diese Beziehungen ergibt sich aber nichts aus der von Bliemetzrieder S. 39 nachgewiesenen Tatsache, daß die Palea c. 51 C. 27 q. 2 (cap. incertum) aus dem Kreise Anselms von Laon stammt und wahrscheinlich auf Ivo zurückgeht. Mit einer Palea exakte Beweise für Gratian zu führen, weil Paucapalea sich eng an die Methode des Meisters gehalten habe (Bliemetzrieder S. 38), geht nicht an.

52 Chronologie der Abaelardschen Werke jetzt bei Cottiaux l. c. p. 268. — Benutzte Ausgabe: MPL CLXXVIII.

53 Vgl. Fournier-Le Bras II p. 350. — Benutzte Ausgabe: MPL CLXXVI.

54 Lit.: K. Müller, Der Umschwung in der Lehre von der Buße während des 12. Jahrhunderts, Theol. Abhdlgen. f. K. v. Weizsäcker, 1892; Schmoll, Die Bußlehre d. Frühscholastik, 1909; R. Sohm, Altkath. KR. und Decr. Grat. S. 318ff.; O. D. Watkin, A history of penance, 1920; A. Landgraf,

Darstellung dieses Problems bei Gratian (dist. 1 umfaßt außer den dicta 90 canones) soll nun nach Bliemetzrieder von der Darstellung bei Anselm (16 Druckzeilen in der Ausg. der Sent. Ans.) abhängig sein. Zunächst enthalte dict. pr., cc. 1 et 2 de poen. D. 1 die Fragestellung und die gleiche Aufeinanderfolge ähnlicher Sätze wie Sent. Ans. p. 124. (Bliemetzrieder S. 45/46.) Hierzu ist zu bemerken:

Sent. Ans.	Grat. dict. pr.
Sciendum est penitentiam non sufficere sine *confessione*,	(... ad ... questionem, ... qua) queritur, utrum sola *cordis contritione* et *secreta satisfactione* absque *oris confessione* quisque possit Deo *satisfacere* (redeamus).

Anselm bejaht die Auffassung, nach der Beichte gefordert und ein Genügen der Reue abgelehnt wird, während Gratian untersuchen will, ob die Reue genügt. Gratian gelangt auch im Verlaufe der Erörterungen nicht zum Ergebnis Anselms, wie dict. p. c. 89 zeigt, wo er die Frage offenläßt:

Quibus auctoritatibus vel quibus rationum firmamentis utraque sententia satisfactionis et confessionis nitatur, in medium breviter proposuimus. Cui autem harum potius adherendum sit, lectoris iudicio reservatur. Utraque enim fautores habet sapientes et religiosos viros.

Das spricht nicht für Abhängigkeit von Anselm. — Ferner trägt Gratian das Problem in ganz anderer Terminologie als Anselm vor. Zwar ist bei Anselm im nächsten Satze (s. u.) von „cordis compugitio" die Rede (bei Gratian heißt es „cordis contritio"); aber daß Gratian die Nennung der Bußelemente nicht aus Anselm hat, ist klar: bei diesem fehlt die charakteristische Gegenüberstellung von „secreta satisfactio" und „oris confessio"; während z. B. die „secreta confessio", das „Deo confiteri" als Gegensatz zur „oris confessio" bei Ivo Decr. XV c. 155, Abaelard Eth[ica] c. 24 steht. Anselm kennt nur „confessio". Auch der Ausdruck „Deo satisfacere" (als Endziel der Buße) kann nicht aus Anselm stammen. — Die sachliche Problemstellung aber konnte sich für Gratian ebensogut (und klarer als Problem gefaßt denn bei Anselm) aus Hugo [de] Sacr[amentis] II p[ars] 14 c. 1 oder Abaelard Sic et Non c. 151 ergeben.[55]

Es heißt weiter:

Sent. Ans.	Grat. dict. pr.
quamvis quidam dicant conpugitionem cordis solam esse necessariam, *non confessionem,*	*Sunt enim qui dicunt* quemlibet criminis veniam *sine confessione* ecclesie et sacerdotali iudicio posse promereri,

Grundlagen f. e. Verständnis d. Bußlehre usw., Zschr. f. kath. Theol. LI 1927 S. 161 ff.; Teetaert l. c. p. 85 ss.; Debil l. c.; Amann, Art. „Pénitence" im Dict. de théol. cath. XII 1 1933 col. 935 ss.
55 Zur Darstellung des Problems bei Abaelard und Hugo s. Debil l. c. p. 444 ss.; Teetaert l. c. p. 87 ss. Weitere Autoren des 12. Jahrhunderts bei Schmoll S. 54ff.

Auf die (hier von ihm) kursiv hervorgehobenen Stellen legt Bliemetzrieder offenbar großen Wert. Wie sollte aber Gratian, der sich noch nicht festgelegt hat, anders vorgehen, als indem er mit „sunt qui dicunt" oder einer ähnlichen Wendung die eine Meinung einführt? (und nur einführt; bei Anselm ist es schon Ablehnung). Das ist doch nichts anderes als die gebräuchliche scholastische Methode, die verschiedenen Theorien mit „quidam dicunt","alii dicunt" aufzuzählen.[56] (In dict. p. c. 37 heißt es dann auch „alii e contrario testantur".) Und daß das Wort „confessio" bei Ans. und Grat. vorkommt, ist auch nicht weiter merkwürdig, wo die Frage der Confessio das Thema der Abhandlung bildet. Dagegen ist gerade das Charakteristische der Gratianischen Ausdrucksweise, die Wendung „confessio ecclesiae et sacerdotale iudicium" aus Anselm nicht zu erklären. Bliemetzrieder hebt zwei farblose Worte hervor, übergeht aber das Wesentliche (hier Stellungnahme, dort Frage; verschiedene Terminologie).

Es heißt weiter:

Sent. Ans.

quia scriptum est: Recte Petrus flevit ... et quod voce negaverat, lacrimis confitetur. Sic verbis beati Maximi commendatur interior affectus ex quo lacrimae procedunt.

Wie der eigentliche Text bei Anselm hier lautet, wird aus Bliemetzrieders Apparat in seiner Ausgabe (S. 124) nicht ersichtlich; er sagt dort nur, in der Handschrift stände „Unsinn" und Angabe von Varianten usw. sei an dieser Stelle „Papierverschwendung". — Jedenfalls findet sich dieser Teil des Textes nicht bei Gratian. Dieser fährt nach „promereri" (s. o.) vielmehr fort:

Sent. Ans.	Gratian
	(c. 1) iuxta illud Ambrosii super Lucam: [a] Petrus doluit et flevit, quia erravit ut homo. Non invenio quid dixerit, scio[b] quod fleverit. Lacrimas eius lego, satisfactionem non lego.
Penitentiam Petri legi, confessionem non inveni.	(c. 2) [c] Item Joannes Crisostomus[c]: [d] Lacrime lavant[d] delictum, quod voce pudor est confiteri.

---

56 Auch bei Abaelard Sic et Non c. 151 heißt es im Titel: Quod sine confessione non dimittantur peccata et contra.

Varianten bei *Abaelard* Sic et Non c 151:
a) Abael. hat hier zuvor noch einige andere Sätze und beginnt dann mit: Doluit et flevit... b) invenio *Abael., Corr. Rom.* c—c) *om. Abael.* d—d) Lavant lacrymae *Abael.*

Eine Verwandtschaft zwischen Gratian und Anselm ist hier nicht zu finden und jedenfalls nicht durch den einen dem Sinn nach gemeinsamen Satz (der aber textlich bei beiden verschieden ist) zu beweisen. Der gratianische Text, nebst der Angabe des „Ambrosius super Lucam" ist vielmehr offensichtlich ein Auszug aus Abael. Sic et Non c. 151. (Die geringen Abweichungen sind oben in der Anm. zum gratianischen Text notiert. Vgl. auch Abael. Eth. c. 25.) Es ist jedenfalls unhaltbar, wenn Bliemetzrieder die Verschiedenheit in der Zuschreibung zwischen Gratian und Anselm (dort wird Ambrosius, hier Maximus zitiert) erklärt: „Die Sent. Ans. sind unklar ausgedrückt, zuerst anonym eingeführt, so daß es den Anschein hat, als ob auch Gratian sich nicht ausgekannt und den Eigentümer der Stelle suchend, den Ambrosius gefunden hätte." (Bliemetzrieder S. 46). Die nächstliegende Erklärung dagegen, daß Gratian nicht den in Text und Zuschreibung abweichenden Anselm, sondern den fast wörtlich übereinstimmenden Abaelard benutzt haben könnte, wird nicht einmal erwogen. Näher mit dem gratianischen Text als Anselms Formulierung ist übrigens auch die Hugos (Sacr. II p. 14 c. 1 Sp. 554) verwandt:

... Opponis adhuc lacrymas illas Petri, quas legis, confessionem non legis. Lacrymae lavant delictum quod ore pudor est confiteri. Has igitur lacrymas opponis... Dicis ergo, quia lacrymas Petri legis, satisfactionem non legis. Audisti quia fleverit, sed quid dixerit non audisti. Ideo lacrymae lavant delictum quod ore pudor est confiteri.

Ungewiß bleibt, woher Gratian die Johannes-Chrysostomus-Zuschreibung des letzten Satzes (c. 2) hat, der in Wahrheit die Fortsetzung der Ambrosiusstelle ist, sich im übrigen fast wörtlich bei Abaelard und Hugo, nicht aber bei Anselm findet.

Bliemetzrieder stellt übrigens die Behauptung auf, daß auch Petrus Lombardus die vorliegende Stelle bei Anselm benutzt habe. (Bliemetzrieder S. 52). Lomb. Sent. IV dist. 17 c. 2 bringt nämlich zunächst die Ambrosiusstelle wie Gratian, fügt dann aber hinzu: „hoc idem etiam Maximus dixit episcopus". Für dieses Maximuszitat findet Bliemetzrieder nur die Alternative, daß der Lombarde dies „selbst entdeckt" oder sich an die Sent. Ans. gehalten habe, übersieht aber, daß bei Abaelard c. 151 sowohl die Stelle aus Ambrosius, wie eine sehr ähnlich lautende aus Maximus steht; daß ferner bei Pseudo-Hugo Sum. Sent. tract. 6 c. 10 nur Maximus zitiert ist, und daß der Lombarde notorisch neben Gratians Dekret Abaelards Sic et Non und die Summa Sententiarum benutzt hat.[57] Dabei machen die Befunde bei Abaelard und Pseudo-Hugo jede weitere Erklärung des lombardischen „hoc idem etiam Maximus dixit eps." überflüssig: der Lombarde mußte doch bei Pseudo-Hugo auf das Maximuszitat, bei Abaelard gar auf die Parallelstellen Ambrosius-Maximus stoßen. Eine Textanalyse zeigt, daß auch beim Lombarden, ganz wie bei Gratian, Wortlaut und Textschichtung nichts mit Anselm zu tun haben:

Lomb. Sent. IV d. 17 c. 2:
Item Ambrosius: „[a]Ideo flevit Petrus quia culpa obrepsit ei[a]. [b]Non invenio quid dixerit, invenio quod fleverit[b]. [c]Lacrimas eius lego, satisfactionem non lego[c]. [d]Set quod defendi non potest, ablui potest[d]. [e]Lavant lacrimae delictum, quod voce pudor est confiteri[e]. [f]Veniae fletus consulit et verecundiae[f]." Hoc idem etiam Maximus[g] dixit episcopus.

a—a): *Abael. Grat. Ambrosiuszitat:* ... quia erravit ut homo. *(orig. Ambr. super Luc. X 88 n. 1523. Zur Lesart des Lomb. vgl. ebenda n. 1522 a. E.)* b—b): *Abael., Gratian Ambrosiuszitat.* — *Abael. und Ps. Hugo Maximuszitat:* Invenio quod (Petrus *add. Ps. Hugo)* fleverit, non invenio quid dixcrit. c—c) *Abael. Gratian Ambrosiuszitat.* — *Abael., Ps. Hugo Maximuszitat.* d—d) *Ambros. orig.* — *Abael. Maximuszitat:* Quod defleri solet, non solet excusari, et quod defendi– – –potest. e—e) *Abael. Grat. Ambrosiuszitat.* — *Abael. Maximuszitat:* Lavant enim lacrimae ... *Ps. Hugo Maximuszitat:* Lavat enim lacrima ... f—f): *Abael. Ambrosiuszitat:* Et veniae fletus consulunt ... (*om. Gratianus*). g) *Homil. 53 n. 166.*

Weiter führt Bliemetzrieder für seine These Dict. Grat. p. c. 34 de poen. D. 1 an. Hier rede Gratian in gleichem Zusammenhang wie die Sent. Ans. von den gereinigten Leprosi und dem zum Leben erweckten Lazarus, „allerdings in entgegengesetzter Anwendung" (Bliemetzrieder S. 46).

Nun besteht textlich hier überhaupt keine Verwandtschaft zwischen Gratian und Anselm; und für die inhaltliche Verwandtschaft ist die entgegengesetzte Deutung der beiden Allegorien kein sehr starkes Argument. Vor allem wird die Vermutung Bliemetzrieders hinfällig, wenn man bedenkt, daß der allegorische Vergleich der Leprosenreinigung (Lev. 14) und der Auferweckung des Lazarus (Joann. 11) mit dem Bußsakrament das geläufigste Argument für das Problem des Anteils des Priesters an der Buße (Problem der Schlüsselgewalt) in der mittelalterlichen Diskussion bildet. Es geht auf Hieronymus, Comm in Mt. 16 v. 19[58], Augustin, Serm. 67 2 3; 98 6; 295 3[59]; in Jo. tract. 49 24[60], und Gregor d. Gr., Hom. in Ev. II

---

57 Das lehrt ein Blick in den Apparat der Ausgabe der Väter von Quaracchi (Petr. Lomb. Sententiarum libri IV, 2da ed., Ad Claras Aquas 1916).
58 MPL XXVI col. 122.
59 MPL XXXVIII col. 434, 594, 1349.
60 MPL XXXV col. 1756.

26[61], zurück, findet sich bei zahlreichen Vor- und Frühscholastikern[62], ist also patristisches Gedankengut und keine Besonderheit der Sent. Ans. Abaelard bringt es in Eth. c. 26 (col. 674, 676), Hugo in Sacr. II p. 14 c. 8. Und als einer von vielen benutzt auch Gratian dieses geradezu klassische Gleichnis: so wie Gott die Leprosen reinigte, die Priester sie aber nur für „rein" erklärten, oder wie Christus Lazarus vom Tode erweckte, die Jünger aber nur draußen seine Binden lösten, so vergibt auch Gott in der Reue die Schuld, während der absolvierende Spruch des Priesters nur deklaratorisch ist. Dies war die Deutung Abaelards; daß freilich auch eine entgegengesetzte Deutung (auch der Anteil des Priesters ist konstitutiv) möglich war, zeigen die Sent. Ans., Hugo Sacr. 1. c. und Gratian dict. § 2 p. c. 87 1. c.

Im dict. p. c. 37 de poen. D. 1 führt Gratian aus, daß nach der Sündenvergebung die Liebe im Menschen lebt, er also nicht mehr böse sein kann:

> Si ergo vivit, et diligit; si diligit, dilectio in corde est; dilectio autem in malo non est.

Der nächste Satz soll nun Gratians Verwandtschaft mit Anselm beweisen (Bliemetzrieder S. 46):

Sent. Ans. p. 83	Grat. dict. p. c. 37 1. c.
Haec caritas *fons* est, de quo alienus non communicat, nisi boni et beati et ad vitam praedestinati.	Est enim *fons bonorum proprius,* in quo non communicat alienus.

Quelle dieses Satzes ist Augustin, Enarr. in Ps. 102. Er steht bei Abaelard und bei Hugo, in Gratian viel verwandterer Form:

Abael. Sic et Non c. 138 (Sp. 1578)	Hugo Sacr. II p. 13 c. 11 (Sp. 542)
Ipse enim est *fons proprius bonorum,* proprius sanctorum, de quo dicitur: nemo alienus communicet tibi.	Quomodo charitas *fons proprius* nominatur, de quo non communicat alienus?

Der Satzanfang bei Gratian: „Est enim fons bonorum proprius" stammt offenbar aus der abaelardischen Überlieferung, kann aus Anselm textlich nicht hergeleitet werden; und auch das "fons proprius" bei Hugo steht der gratianischen Formulierung noch näher als das bloße "fons est" bei Anselm. Die Ähnlichkeit des zweiten Satzteils dagegen bei Anselm und bei Gratian ("in quo non communicat alienus") soll nicht bestritten werden, beweist aber nichts, da auch Abaelard eine sehr ähnliche und Hugo sogar eine mit Gratian bis auf die Anknüpfungspraeposition (hier „in", dort "de") gleichlautende Wendung hat. Gegen Anselm spricht wiederum, daß bei ihm der Satz durch einen neuen

---

61 MPL LXXVI col. 1200.
62 Nachweisungen bei Debil 1. c. p. 442 s.

Gedanken (nisi boni et — praedestinati) erweitert ist, der sich weder bei Gratian, noch bei Abaelard, noch bei Hugo findet. Jedenfalls ist die Behauptung unhaltbar, Gratian führe "wie aus dem Gedächtnis (!) denselben Beweissatz" wie Anselm, „nur etwas voller" vor (Bliemetzrieder S. 46).

Das im selben dict. von Gratian gegebene Analogon zur bloß deklaratorischen Bedeutung der confessio — die Beschneidung sei Abraham „in signum iustitiae, non in causam iustificationis" gegeben — lese man auch bei Ans. Sent. p. 89 (Bliemetzrieder S. 46). Hierzu wäre aber zu sagen, daß Anselm a. a. O. diesen Gedanken über das alttestamentarische Sakrament an einer gar nicht zur Bußlehre gehörigen Stelle bringt, wie auch schon der Satz über die caritas bei ihm nicht in der Bußlehre stand. Was in den Sent. Ans. p. 89 in der Lehre von der Circumcisio steht, soll dort in keiner Weise eine Parallele zur Bußlehre sein; die Parallelisierung beider Sakramente unter dem Gesichtspunkt: signum oder causa? ist aber gerade für Gratian charakteristisch. Und wiederum übersieht Bliemetzrieder, daß der Gedanke, Abraham selbst habe der Beschneidung zur Rechtfertigung nicht bedurft, bei Abaelard Sermo III (In circumcisione Domini) col. 398, ferner in der Expositio in epistolam Pauli ad Romanos col. 840 und 842, und bei Hugo Sacr. I p. 12 c. 2 steht, bei Abaelard ausdrücklich unter Bezugnahme auf die Bußlehre. Auch sprachlich ist Gratian mit Abaelard wieder verwandter als mit Anselm: während es bei diesem heißt: „Abraham ... circumcisionem accepit, ... ut iustificatus ostenderetur", lautet es bei Abaelard Sermo III: „... pro *signo* autem *iustitiae* iam habitae", bei Gratian „in *signum iustitiae*". Im übrigen geht die ganze Deutung der Beschneidung Abrahams auf Rom. 4 v. 1, 2 zurück und ist keine Erfindung Anselms.

Bis zu dict. p. c. 37 de poen. D. 1 hatte Gratian die erste These (von dem Genügen der Reue zur Sündenvergebung) behandelt; von dict. pars II eod. ab behandelt er nun die Gegenthese von der Notwendigkeit der confessio und satisfactio. Bliemetzrieder nennt das: „der § 1 pars II enthält dann die These der Sent. Ans. (p. 125), daß zur Sündenvergebung ..." usw. Das klingt, als ob nur Anselm diese These vertreten habe, während doch kein Theologe der Zeit an dem Problem vorüberging. Und vor allem Hugo von St. Viktor war der gewichtigste und für das Mittelalter einflußreichste Vertreter der gegen Abaelards Bußlehre gewandten These.[63] Gratian will damit, daß er hier auf sie zu sprechen kommt, doch nur ganz allgemein den Streitstand darstellen; aus dem Aufwerfen eines Problems als umstritten, in welchem Streit Anselm auf der einen Seite stand, folgt noch nichts über den Einfluß Anselms.

Ferner zieht Bliemetzrieder Argumente daraus, daß von den nun bei Gratian folgenden canones (es sind 53 canones von c. 38 bis c. 90) zwei auch in dem kurzen Absatz bei Anselm über die Beichtfrage stehen. Es handelt sich um c. 63 und c. 84 de poen. D. 1. Nun finden sich aber ausweislich der Friedbergschen Ausgabe des Dekrets: c. 63 auch im Polycarpus VI 20, Anselmus Lucens. XI 6; c. 84 in Ivo Decr. XV 23, Coll. trium part. III 28 (29) 3, Polyc. VI 20 (19) 22. Über

---

63 Vgl. Schmoll a. a. O. S. 47; Sohm, Altkath. KR. und Decr. Grat. S. 320; Debil l. c. p. 444; Teetaert l. c. p. 124.

die notorische Benutzung dieser Quellen durch Gratian ist hier nicht zu reden; das bloße Vorkommen in den Sent. Ans. liefert angesichts dieser Tatsache dann aber noch keinen Beweis für die Benutzung durch Gratian.

Zu dict. Grat. p. c. 87 de poen. D. 1 findet Bliemetzrieder weitere Übereinstimmungen mit Anselm von Laon in den Begriffen „poenitentia interior — exterior" und „crimina occulta — manifesta" (Bliemetzrieder S. 46). Aber die Einteilung der crimina in occulta und manifesta durchzieht das ganze gratianische Kirchenrecht; so sind D. 50 und C. 2 q. 6 auf ihr aufgebaut; wenn diese Distinktion in der Bußlehre wieder auftaucht, so braucht sie daher noch nicht auf Anselm zurückzugehen; ebenso könnte man eine Verwandtschaft zweier beliebiger Autoren konstruieren, die über die Einteilung der Exkommunikation in namentliches Anathem und gewöhnliche Exkommunikation handeln. Im übrigen findet sich die Einteilung der crimina in „occulta" und „manifesta" gerade mit Bezug auf die Buße auch bei Hugo Sacr. II p. 14 c. 7, die Einteilung der poenitentia in „interior" und „exterior" bei Hugo Sacr. II p. 14 c. 2.

Zur dist. 2 de poen. bemerkt Bliemetzrieder, es sei merkwürdig, daß diese über die Frage: unica poenitentia oder Möglichkeit einer reiteratio poenitentiae handle, eine Frage, die auch in den Sent. Ans. ihren Platz habe. Dabei ergab sich das Problem ohne weiteres für jede Bußabhandlung des 12. Jahrhunderts, die — wie Gratian — den pseudo-augustinischen „Liber de vera et falsa poenitentia" (11. Jahrhundert) benutzte. So beschäftigt sich zum Beispiel Hugo mit dem Problem: Sacr. II p. 14 c. 4. — Und bei Gratian umfaßt die Frage 45 canones, bei Anselm wird sie in 13 Zeilen besprochen.

Die dist. 2 (und zum Teil auch noch dist. 3) handelt von der „caritas"; auch das führt Bliemetzrieder auf Anselm zurück, aber ohne andere Belege als die „dialektische Bewegtheit und inhaltliche Wendung", die an Anselm p. 82–85 erinnere. Die Caritasprobleme finden sich aber ebensogut bei Abaelard, Sic et Non c. 137, c. 138; Hugo Sacr. II p. 13 cc. 7 ss. — Für eine Stelle stützt sich Bliemetzrieder auf die zum anselmischen Kreis gehörigen Sententiae divinae paginae:

Sent. div. pag.p. 16	Grat. pr. de poen. D. 3
… sententiam quam quidam tenent, quod qui semel habuerit caritatem, nunquam eam amittat …	… asserentes, quod sicut caritas semel habita nunquam amittitur …

Auch hier kann man wieder auf Abaelard und Hugo verweisen:

Abael. Sic et Non c. 138	Hugo Sacr. II p. 13 c. 11
Quod charitas semel habita nunquam amittatur, et contra.	Utrum charitas semel habita amittatur. … si autem charitatem aliquando habuerunt, … quia secundum sententiam ipsorum semel habitam amittere non potuerunt. (col. 540)

In der passivischen Formulierung „quod (utrum) caritas semel habita nunquam amittatur" sind Abaelard und Hugo wiederum Gratian verwandter als die aktivisch sich ausdrückenden Sent. div. pag.

Im dict. § 2 p. c. 22 de poen. D. 3 trägt Gratian die Ansicht von der Wiederholbarkeit der Buße vor; auch hier kann man nicht Anselm als Quelle suchen (wie Bliemetzrieder S. 47), da es sich lediglich um die dialektische Gegenmeinung zu pr. D. 2 handelt, die sich aus der Fragestellung Gratians zwangsläufig ergibt und z. B. auch bei Hugo Sacr. II p. 14 c. 4 behandelt wird. Vor allem aber wird die Lösung der Frage, die Gratian im dict. p. c. 49 de poen. D. 3 gibt — daß nämlich die Verweigerung eines „secundus locus poenitentiae" nur für die poenitentia sollemnis gelte — von Anselm gerade nicht akzeptiert. Es trifft auch nicht zu, daß Gratian in diesem dict. p. c. 49 die „auctoritates" in gleichem Zusammenhang und in gleicher Fassung wie Sent. Ans. zitiere (so Bliemetzrieder S. 47); denn Gratian interpretiert hier zwei Stellen, die Ambrosianische: „Poenitentia semel usurpata — usum sequentis amittit" und die (bereits im dict. p. c. 61 D. 50 angeführte): „Non est secundus locus poenitentiae". Sent. Ans. aber bringt von diesen nur die zweite, die sich indessen ebensogut bei Hugo Sacr. II p. 14 c. 4 (col. 559) nachweisen läßt: Auch Hugo geht von dem Zitat aus „Quod autem dictum est, quod non est secundus locus poenitentiae", und erwähnt die von Gratian befolgte Deutung: „ ... Alii hoc dictum intelligunt de publica poenitentia ...", akzeptiert sie freilich so wenig wie Anselm. Angesichts dieses Tatbestandes spricht für die Sent. Ans. als Quelle der Gratianstelle keine größere Wahrscheinlichkeit als für Hugo von St. Viktor.

c. 45 de poen. D. 2 behandelt Fragen der Angelologie. Nach Bliemetzrieder S. 47 ist diese Stelle mit Sent. Ans. p. 51 zu vergleichen. Doch übertrifft — ganz abgesehen davon, daß die Sent. Ans. die Engellehre in ganz anderem Zusammenhange als Gratian bringen — z. B. Abaelard Sic et Non c. 46 (col. 1413) Anselm hier an Zahl patristischer Zitate, die in Gratians c. 45 eingehen.

Auch das Thema der dist. 4 („an peccata dimissa redeant") soll den Zusammenhang mit Sent. Ans. beweisen (Bliemetzrieder S. 47). Aber bei Gratian sind es 24 canones, bei Sent. Ans. 4½ Zeilen. Daß das Problem ausführlich bei Hugo II p. 14 c. 9 (col. 570–578!) und bei Abaelard Expos. in Ep. ad Rom. (col. 864) behandelt wird, übergeht Bliemetzrieder.

In dict. p. c. 24 de poen. D. 4 streift Gratian die Frage nach dem Einfluß der Sünden der Eltern auf die Kinder, eine Frage, „welche in der Schule von Laon ihren ständigen Platz hatte". (Sent. Ans. p. 74–76; Bliemetzrieder S. 47). Sie wird indessen ebenso erörtert bei Abaelard Expos. in Ep. ad Rom. col. 872, Sic et Non c. 116, Hugo Sacr. I p. 7 c. 38.

De poen. D. 7 über das tempus poenitentiae (usque ad ultimum articulum vitae) soll nach Bliemetzrieder S. 47 auf Sent. Ans. p. 122 zurückgehen, woselbst sich eine kurze Bemerkung über die Buße in praesenti vita — in futura vita findet. Man vergleiche indessen auch Hugo Sacr. II p. 14 c. 3 (De iis qui in hac vita poenitentiam non complent), c. 5 (De iis, qui in extremis poenitent).

Hiermit sind die Argumente Bliemetzrieders aus dem Tractatus de poenitentia erschöpft. Für jeden Einzelpunkt seiner Beweisführung ließ sich die

Unhaltbarkeit der These nachweisen, daß die Sent. Ans. die theologische Quelle Gratians seien, und daß man die theologischen Partien bei Gratian „fast als deren (d. h. der Sent. Ans.) Erweiterung und Nachahmung" (Bliemetzrieder S. 47) ansprechen könne. Von allen Einwänden gegen die Möglichkeit eines solchen Abhängigkeitsverhältnisses erwähnt Bliemetzrieder nur die auffallenden Unterschiede im Umfang der beiderseitigen Erörterungen, schiebt aber auch diesen Einwand als unbeachtlich beiseite (Bliemetzrieder S. 47). Die Hauptfrage aber, ob nämlich außer Anselm nicht andere gewichtige Autoren Einfluß auf Gratian gehabt haben könnten, übergeht er schweigend. Die vorstehenden kritischen Ausführungen dienen demgegenüber einzig dem Zweck, an zwei der einflußreichsten Theologen vor 1140 nachzuweisen, daß sie mindestens mit dem gleichen Recht wie die Sent. Ans. für Gratian als Quelle in Anspruch genommen werden können, ja daß in vielen Punkten ihr Einfluß auf Gratian aus textkritischen Gründen wahrscheinlicher ist als der Anselms. Jede der von Bliemetzrieder untersuchten Stellen ließe sich auf Abaelard oder Hugo zurückführen:

Gratian de poen.	Abaelard	Hugo de Sacr.
dict. pr. D. 1	Sic et Non c. 151	II p. 14 c. 1
cc. 1, 2	eod.; Ethica c. 25	eod. (Sp. 554)
dict. p. c. 34	Ethica c. 26	II p. 14 c. 8
dict. p. c. 37	Sic et Non c. 138	II p. 13 c. 11
	Serm. III (Sp. 398)	I p. 12 c. 2
	In ep. ad Rom. Sp. 840	
dict. p. c. 87		II p. 14 cc. 2, 7
D. 2		II p. 14 c. 4
c. 45	Sic et Non c. 46	
dict. pr. D. 3	Sic et Non c. 138	II p. 13 c. 11
dict. p. c. 22		II p. 14 c. 4
dict. p. c. 49		eod.
D. 4	In ep. ad. Rom. Sp. 864	II p. 14 c. 9
dict. p. c. 24	eod. Sp. 872	I p. 7 c. 38
	Sic et Non c. 116	
D. 7		II p. 14 cc. 3, 5

(cc. 63, 84 D. 1 sind zwar nicht bei diesen, aber in anderen Quellen nachweisbar: oben S. 40.)

Mehr als die Möglichkeit einer solchen Zurückführung auf Abaelard und Hugo läßt sich freilich ohne breiteres Studium der vorgratianischen Theologie positiv nicht behaupten. Und auch wenn Gratian — was ich für wahrscheinlich halte — die Werke Abaelards und Hugos ausgeschöpft haben sollte, so sind wir darum noch nicht der Nachforschung nach weiteren Quellen seiner theologischen Ausführungen enthoben. Nur ein Negatives ergibt sich mit Gewißheit: die

Unwahrscheinlichkeit der Benutzung des zeitlich und meist auch textlich viel ferner stehenden Anselm. Angesichts dieses Ergebnisses beim tract. de poen. bedarf es keines Eingehens mehr auf die Argumente Bliemetzrieders aus dem Vergleich der gratianischen und der anselmischen Ehelehre; auch hier wird bei Bliemetzrieder (S. 48ff.) die Frage nach möglichen anderen Einflüssen nicht gestellt, obwohl wir bereits Untersuchungen über die Zusammenhänge zwischen Hugos von St. Victor „de sacramentis" sowie „de B. Mariae virginitate" und Gratians Eherecht besitzen.[64]

Refuting Bliemetzrieder's thesis Kuttner sees the possibility of Abelard and Hugh of Victor having influenced Gratian and the 'Tractatus de penitentia.' This main thesis cannot be maintained after Winroth's discovery of two recensions of Gratian's Decretum. Abelard and Hugh of St. Victor were only used for the second recension which probably was not composed by Gratian himself. Gratian's theological sources for 'De penitentia' were anonymous theological treatises preserved in Italian manuscripts. Cf. mainly *John C. Wei*, Gratian the Theologian (Studies in Medieval and Early Canon Law 13), Washington D.C. 2016, passim. (P.L.)

So sei festgehalten: Die Bedeutung Hugos für das kanonische Recht muß mehr als bisher beachtet, die Abaelards sollte nicht aus irgendwelchen Vorurteilen verkleinert werden.

---

[64] Le Bras Art. „Mariage" im Dict. de théol. cath. IX 2 1927 col. 2149. — Fournier-Le Bras II p. 321. — Über Hugos Lehre von der Zahl der Sakramente im Zusammenhang mit dem Kanonisten vgl. de Ghellinck, Mouvement p. 359 ss.

NEW STUDIES ON THE ROMAN LAW IN GRATIAN'S DECRETUM

This article by Kuttner, published first 1953 in 'Seminar', was his most important contribution to the problems of Roman Law in Gratian's Decretum. He started with a commentary to *Adam Vetulani's* essay 'Gratien et le droit romain', RHD[4] 24/25 (1946/47), 11–48, which he called 'to have opened up entirely new roads to an understanding of the composition of the Decreta.' (p. 49) Vetulani's thesis, that an extensive use of the sources of Roman Law was not part of Gratian's original plan, and that numerous texts were inserted only at a late stage of redaction, found Kuttner's general approval. Since 1953 the discovery of two recensions of Gratian's Decretum by Anders Winroth confirmed Vetulani's thesis again. According to Winroth's results the following texts of Roman Law are already included in the first recension: 1.) Dict. p. D. 25, c. 3 (Kuttner p. 47); 2.) Dict. p. D. 34, c. 17 (Kuttner p. 48); 3.) C. 2, q. 6, c. 28 (Kuttner, p. 50) — unique text from the Authenticum in Gratian; 4.) C. 15, q. 3, c. 1–3 (Kuttner p. 50); 5.) C. 15, q. 3, c. 4 (Kuttner p. 60: late insertion), 6.) C. 1, q. 4, Dict. p. c. 12 (Kuttner p. 67), Item ignorantia iuris alia naturalis, alia civilis (§ 2, first sentence), probably influenced by *Bulgarus*, Summula de iuris et facti ignorantia; 7.) C. 15, q. 3 pr. (Kuttner p. 67s: probably from Codex Theodosianus 9.1.3); 8.) C. 16, q. 1, c. 40 (Kuttner p. 70s: from the Polycarpus), but actually from 3 L 2. 27. 12 (ed. *Motta*, Collectio trium librorum, MIC, Ser. B, vol. 8, p. 367)—3 L 2. 27. 13 = C. 16, q. 1, Dict. p. c. 40, sentence 1. Most of the texts from Roman Law in Gratian's Decretum are only in the second recension ; the first recension has Roman Law in some Dicta. (P.L.)

I

The recent celebrations of the eighth centenary of the *Decretum Gratiani* at Bologna and Rome, 17–22 April 1952, have focused once more the interest of legal historians on the all-important work of the "Father of the Science of Canon Law." The fact that after nearly four hundred years of canonistic erudition since the days of the *Correctores Romani* we still do not have a satisfactory critical edition of the *Concordia discordantium canonum* has been often lamented;[1] and

---

1 Cf. the present writer's "De Gratiani opere noviter edendo," *Apollinaris* 21 (1948) 118–28.

the resolutions taken at the commemorative convention[2] give promise for the first time of an organized, international cooperation of scholars toward this formidable task. Encouragement for such an enterprise came from the lips of Pope Pius XII in his allocution of 22 April 1952:[3]

> ... It is evident that the edition of the *Correctores Romani* should remain in the large collection which constitutes the *Corpus Juris Canonici*. But there is nothing to prevent the preparation for printing of a new critical edition, as certain scholars have laudably proposed; in fact, it is altogether desirable... Such a critical edition should be prepared in keeping with the demands of present-day scholarship, since the edition of Friedberg, notwithstanding its undeniable merits, no longer measures up to the wants of ranking experts in the history of canon law...

Prout nunc temporis ars et ratio exigit: textual criticism in many fields of medieval research has come to recognize that the really intricate problems are presented not so much by the corruptions of a finished text at the hand of later copyists as by the "internal" history of a given text. We may be faced, e.g., with successive editions published by the author; with works that show traces of rewriting, or of substitution or interpolation of fresh matter by the author in the course of revising again and again his first draft (here Peter Lombard[4] or Bracton[5] come easily to mind); with publication by pupils from lectures which the master never cast into definite literary form, etc. Phenomena of this kind are by no means unknown to students of ancient literature—Aristotle's *Metaphysics* are a case in point[6]—but occur far more often in medieval writing, particularly with works of the schoolmen, in the wider meaning of the term, destined for the classroom or practical consultation.[7] In their case, matters are further complicated by the fact that we have to do with *textes vivants,* upon which the author himself and subsequent generations

---

2 Cf. *The Jurist* 12 (1952) 396 f.
3 *Acta Apost. Sedis* 44 (1952) 375; English text from *The Jurist* 12.270 f. The translation in *The Jurist* is based on the Latin text which appeared in *L'Osservatore Romano* on 23 April 1952, and consequently repeats some of the minor verbal mistakes of this printing, which later were corrected in the official text of the *Acta* (where, however, the allocution is erroneously dated of 29 April). It should therefore be mentioned that the Holy Father, in treating of the decretists of the twelfth and thirteenth centuries, spoke of "the Bolognese, French, Anglo-Norman (not: Anglo-Saxon, as in trans. p. 267), and Spanish schools"; and again, of "the golden age ... of classical canon law, especially in Bologna, Paris (not: Pavia, as in trans. p. 269), and other Universities."
4 A. Landgraf, *Einführung in die Geschichte der theologischen Literatur der Frühscholastik* (Regensburg 1948) 94 f.; cf. D. Van den Eynde, "Nouvelles précisions chronologiques sur quelques oeuvres théologiques du XIIe siècle," *Franciscan Studies* 13 (1953) 114 f.
5 H. G. Richardson, "Studies in Bracton," *Traditio* 6 (1948), 61–104, esp. 87 ff., 93 ff., 100 ff.
6 W. Jaeger, as cited by F. Schulz, *History of Roman Legal Science* (Oxford 1946) 157 n. 1; I do not feel competent to pass judgment on Schulz's brilliant thesis (p. 160 ff.) which regards the *Institutes* of Gaius as lecture notes published after Gaius' death.
7 Cf. e.g. E. Gilson, "Doctrinal History and Its Interpretation," *Speculum* 24 (1949) 486 f.

of scholars and scribes felt free to "improve" by addition or subtraction. The history of the *paleae,* for instance, in Gratian's *Concordia* reflects to a large extent the critical attitudes of the several schools of decretists of the twelfth and thirteenth centuries towards the work of the Master; attitudes expressed both by the addition of new authorities (at first in marginal notes, comparable to the *Authenticae* of Irnerius and his school, entered in the manuscripts of the Code) and by marking off or omitting duplications and other "chaff" among Gratian's texts.[8]

The more we realize that Gratian's work is not likely to have been composed and published in one magnificent thrust, the less can we share the optimism of earlier generations of scholars who believed that one may easily arrive at the "original" shape of the book by merely counting and tabulating the *paleae* in the manuscripts. Such reasoning must fail in particular since we have to reckon with an early beginning of the process of eliminating original duplicates, and no criteria for distinguishing these from intruded-and-dropped ones have as yet been evolved.[9] While the heuristic value of manuscripts with a low number of *paleae* remains unquestionable,[10] the critical problems that arise in the twilight zone between original revisions and early accretions cannot be solved by them alone. To find here the golden mean between a mechanical tabulation of variants and the flight of fancy—which elsewhere has so often discredited higher criticism—is not always easy. At times, nothing but internal criteria will remain to establish the traces of an early reworking undergone by the extant text. Thus, e.g., the dictum of Gratian after c.3 D.25 shows an original plan of proceeding as follows:

> Nunc autem per singulos gradus ordine recurrentes, qui, ex quibus ordinibus, in quem gradum conscendere possint; qui post lapsum ualeant reparari, uel non; quibus culpis a proprio gradu mereantur deici; quo accusante, quibus testificantibus possint conuinci; cuius sententia sint soluendi uel dampnandi, breuiter consideremus,

—a plan which must have been abandoned at an early stage of the work. The inconsistency of the dictum with the actual shape of part I was of course noticed by the glossators;[11] but there exists no shred of evidence that Gratian ever got to

---

8 F. Gillmann, "Paucapalea und Paleae bei Huguccio," *Archiv für katholisches Kirchenrecht* (AKKR) 88 (1908) 466–79; A. Vetulani, "Ueber die Distinktioneneinteilung und die Paleae im Dekret Gratians," *Zeitschrift der Savigny-Stiftung* (ZRG), Kanon. Abt. 22 (1933) 346–70; "Les manuscrits du décret de Gratien conservés dans les bibliothèques polonaises," *Revue historique de droit français et étranger*[4] (RHD[4]) 15 (1936) 344–58, esp. 353 ff.; A. Van Hove, *Prolegomena* (Comm. Lovaniense in Cod. iur. can. I 1; 2nd ed. Malines-Rome 1945) 342; and W. Ullmann's paper, "The Paleae in the Cambridge Manuscripts of the Decretum," presented at the Congress of 1952 and just published in *Studia Gratiana* I (Bologna 1953) 161–216. (By the author's courtesy I was able to use a set of proof sheets before publication.)
9 Vetulani, in RHD[4] 15.355 f.
10 *Ibid.* 345 f.; Kuttner, *loc. cit.* (n. 1 *supra*) 120.
11 *Summa Parisiensis ad loc.:* "... quae diligentius in causis quam in distinctionibus exsequetur" (ed. T. P. McLaughlin, Toronto 1952, p. 26); cf. F. Gillmann, "Einteilung und System des

the point of drafting a treatise corresponding to the program he announced.[12] Any attempt at reconstruction would be foolhardy.

Or again, at the end of D. 31 Gratian interprets a number of canons, as is his wont, quoted in the preceding discussion; the last of these, however ("Illud quoque Martini papae: *Si subdiaconus secundam duxerit uxorem,* non dissimiliter intelligendum est"), has up to this point not been seen by the reader and is found only as D.34 c.17: an incongruity which prompted the author of the *Summa Parisiensis* to consider this sentence as added by Gratian after the completion of his book.[13] Then, there is the epilogue of pt. I, D. 81–101, with its ample reconsideration of matter already treated, thus indicating a rather fitful working method.[14] But who will say that there ever existed one finished copy not containing it?

The prudent critic will do well to limit conjectural reconstruction to the instances in which internal evidence is borne out by some external signs of textual or transcriptional disturbance in the manuscripts.[15] Without such restraint, he might find himself easily presenting hypotheses as facts.

Such disturbances have been found of late, e.g., by Mme. Rambaud and by the Abbé Guizard in a number of Paris manuscripts with regard to the transmission of both the *tractatus de poenitentia* and the *tractatus de consecratione*.[16]

Gratianischen Dekrets ...," AKKR 106 (1926) 525, where many other relevant texts are cited *passim;* see esp. Huguccio *ad loc.* (pp. 562–3; also on D.60 pr.: p. 565), on whom the *Glossa ord.* here is based (p. 572). For the text of *Summa Antiquitate et tempore* see AKKR 112 (1932) 519 n. 2. On Gratian's word *breviter,* Huguccio and *Glos. ord.* note ironically: "i. e. usque ad xii. causam."

12 While the first items of the proposed disposition may be recognized in portions of pt. I *(qui:* D. 25–49, D. 51–59; *ex quibus ordinibus:* D.60–61; *reparatio post lapsum:* D. 50), the rest has been submerged in the superimposed order of *negotia* in pt. II. Of the *culpae* deserving deposition only simony has remained (C. 1); accusers and witnesses are dealt with in the course of C.2–6 (on procedure), and the competent judge, in C. 7–11 (on bishops). An untenable interpretation of our dictum is found in R. Sohm, *Das altkatholische Kirchenrecht und das Dekret Gratians* (Leipzig 1918) 28 ff.

13 "...datur intelligi quod post ordinationem huius operis quasdam apposuit determinationes" (p. 31 McLaughlin, cf. introd. p. xi). Elsewhere the *Summa* considers part of a dictum (C.35 q.2 & 3 p.c.21) as added by the masters of Bologna (cf. pp. 262, xi); probably a conjecture based on a misunderstanding of the commentaries *ad loc.* of Rolandus Bandinelli (*Stroma* ed. F. Thaner, Innsbruck 1874, p. 214), Rufinus (*Summa* ed. H. Singer, Paderborn 1902, p. 519), Stephen of Tournai (ed. Schulte, Giessen 1891, p. 253).

14 See Rufinus' criticism of Gratian, ad D.81 pr. (p. 170 f. Singer), and the rejoinder by the *Summa Antiquitate et tempore* (quoted by Gillmann, in AKKR 112.525 n.1).

15 A case in point: C.13 q.2 p.c.7, in discussing funeral rights and bequests, Gratian refers to a specific rule *secundum Leonem* as if known to the reader, i. e., to Leo IX's decretal *Relatum* (JL 4269), which must have been somewhere near this point in his original draft and is indeed found here (in varying positions) in several manuscripts, but not in the best ones nor in the vulgate tradition. Other manuscripts, however, insert here, or after c. 12, the decretal of Urban II, *Mortuorum* (JL 5775); cf. *Notae Corr. Rom.* and Friedberg (n.90) *ad locc.* The matter puzzled the early glossators (cf. testimonies collected by McLaughlin, *Sum. Par.* p. xiv, to which add Rufinus, C.13 q.1, p. 334 Singer) as well as the *Correctores.* We have to do with obvious traces of multiple recension.

16 J. Rambaud-Buhot, "Plan et méthode de travail pour la rédaction d'un catalogue des manuscrits du Décret de Gratien," *Revue d'histoire ecclésiastique* 48 (1953) 213; "L'étude des manuscrits

They bear out the misgivings scholars have felt, almost since the earliest times, about the disproportionate length and digressive nature of the *De poenitentia,* which throws C.33 q.3 out of all balance; similarly, the serious discrepancies in the manuscript tradition of the *De consecratione*[17] should be viewed in conjunction with the well-known fact that this treatise (pt.III) differs from the rest of Gratian's work by the absence of all *paragraphi,* i.e., by altogether abandoning the dialectical procedure of *concordia discordantium canonum.* The French scholars' new researches, then, allow us a glimpse into early stages of recension in which, to say the least, neither C.33 q.3 nor the matter following upon C. 36 had as yet been given their present form.

The most remarkable methodical advance, however, and the most startling discovery which modern decretist scholarship has made to date came from the enforced leisure of a distinguished Polish scholar in a Swiss internment camp during World War II: this is Adam Vetulani's article on "Gratien et le droit romain," which appeared in 1947[18] and has opened up entirely new roads to an understanding of the composition of the Decreta. With little else but a copy of Friedberg's edition at his disposal, Vetulani was able to demonstrate that, contrary to the traditional view, an extensive direct use of the sources of Roman law was not part of Gratian's original plan, and that the numerous excerpts from Justinian's codification were inserted only at a late stage of redaction. Further, since the composition of these texts shows the skill of a trained civilian, the question arises whether in its final shape Gratian's book must not be considered the work of a team rather than an individual—a hypothesis not to be rejected *a limine,* as Pius XII has said,[19] but for which no direct proof can be expected to be forthcoming from our sources, whereas sufficient internal and external evidence is on hand to warrant Vetulani's conclusions regarding the late introduction of the Roman law matter. It is worth while to recapitulate the main lines of his argument.[20]

II

If we eliminate the surprisingly few Roman texts Gratian took over from intermediary sources, i.e., from previous canonical collections (Vetulani counts 22 fragments altogether), there remain some 200 fragments of Justinian law, distributed

---

du Décret de Gratien conservés en France," *Studia Gratiana* 1 121–146; and L. Guizard, "Les manuscrits du Décret de Gratien de l'Université de Paris," to appear in Vol. II of *L'Année canonique.*

17 Even Friedberg's best MS, Cologne 127 (=A) has some peculiarities, cf. proleg. col. xcv.

18 RHD^4 24–25 (1946–47) 11–48; the date-line reads *Camp d'internement militaire en Suisse, 1944–45.*

19 Allocution of 22 April (n. 3 *supra*), *Acta AS* 44.373; *Jurist* 12.268.

20 In the following, Vetulani's basic article (n. 18 *supra*) will be referred to by initial and page; the supplementary article, "Encore un mot sur le droit romain dans le Décret de Gratien," *Apollinaris* 21 (1948) 129–34, by the siglum *Ap.* and page.

in 46 original units of composition, i.e., 46 *capitula* or *dicta* (*paragraphi*)[21] as they appear in the early manuscripts, not in the arbitrary division and numbering of the printed editions. (E.g., cc.126–130 of C.1 q.1 are actually one with c.125; or C.3 q.7 dict, p.c.1—c.2—dict.p.c.2 are one, etc.) Some of these original chapters follow each other immediately (Nos.1–2, 10–13, 36–37, 42–43 of the chart): this means that the Roman texts are actually concentrated in only 40 places. The fragments all come from the Digest, the Code, and the *Authenticae* of the Bolognese vulgate of the Code; none from the *Epitome Iuliani* and the Institutes; one exceptional chapter from the *Authenticum* (2 q.6 c.28: *Nov.23* = *Auth.* 4.2).[22] The texts are often put together, mosaic-fashion, from various fragments widely scattered in the sources, which the compiler feels at liberty to paraphrase, abridge, reshuffle, and combine, much more so than he ever does with the canon law texts. This technical skill in composing what one may call *summulae,* and the use of the *Authenticae* point to the Irnerian school; however, for the inscriptions of the several fragments, a style of citation prevails which differs from that current among the Bolognese glossators.[23]

No.	V. No.	Gratian	No.	V. No.	Gratian
1	(1)	D.50 c.45	24	(22)	3 q.11 p.c.3(§1)-p.c.4
2	(2)	— c.46	25	(23)	4 q.2 & 3 p.c.2-c.3
3	(3)	D.54 c.20	26	(24)	— q.4 p.c.2
4	(4)	1 q.1. cc.126–130	27	(25)	5 q.1 p.c.3
5	(5)	— q.4 p.c.9 (*al.* c.6)	28	(26)	— q.3 p.c.1
6	(6)	— — p.c.12 (§3 *fin.*)	29	(27)	— q.6 p.c.3
7	(7)	— q.7 c.26	30	(28)	6 q.1 cc.22–23
8	(8)	2 q.1 c.14	31	(29)	— q.4 c.7 (*al.* q.5 c.2; *al.* q.4 c.4)
9	(9)	— q.3 p.c.8	32	(30)	10 q.2 cc.1–3
10	(10)	— q.6 c.28	33	(31)	11 q.1 p.c.9
11	(11)	— — c.29	34	(32)	12 q.2 p.c.58–c.60
12	(12)	— — c.30	35	(33)	15 q.1 c.2
13	(13)	— — c.31	36	(34)	— q.3 cc.1–3
14	(14)	— — p.c.39	37	(35)	— — c.4
15	(15)	— — c.41-p.c.41	38	(36)	16 q.1 p.c.40 (*al.* c.40 §§3–4)
16	(*Ap.*p.132)	— q.8 c.2	39	(37)	— q.3 p.c.15–p.c.16
17	(16)	— — p.c.5	40	(—)	17 q.4 p.c.29
18	(17)	3 q.3 p.c.4	41	(38)	19 q.3 c.9
19	(18)	— q.7 p.c.1–c.2	42	(39)	25 q.2 cc.14–15
20	(*Ap.*p.132)	— q.8 c.1 §2	43	(39)	— — p.c.16
21	(19)	— q.9 p.c.15	44	(40)	32 q.1 p.c.10
22	(20)	— — p.c.18	45	(42)	De poen. D.1 cc.6–21
23	(21)	— q.11 c.2	46	(41)	36 q.2 c.3

---

21 See the chart; the difference in numbers from Vetulani's original 42 (V. pp. 16–28) is explained below, IV A. The 22 texts from pre-Gratian collections are listed in V. p. 14 (correct there Ivo, *Panormia* VI, 127–131 to IV, 127–131).
22 Cf. on this below, IV C.
23 V. pp. 57–58.

In pt.I the small number of Roman law texts is striking: 3 from earlier canonical collections, and 3 directly taken from the Roman sources; and of the latter, one is even suspect as an intruded gloss and a second, as coming perhaps from an intermediary collection.[24] At any event, there is no direct quotation where one should expect it most: in his treatise on the sources of law (D.l–15) Gratian relies for his information on *leges* and *constitutiones* entirely on Isidore's Etymologies and canonical collections, without attempting to use the pertinent opening titles of the Digest.[25]

In pt. II one notices a heavy concentration of Roman law texts in the sections dealing with procedure: they account for two thirds (29 out of 43) of all passages. Moreover, of the 14 passages concerned with other branches of the law, 5 may in Vetulani's opinion come from intermediary collections, 3 may be later intrusions or glosses, and 1 cluster of texts belongs to the *tract. de poen.*, the original composition of which, as we know, presents problems of its own.[26] If one accepts these conjectural eliminations,[27] the ratio of procedural to nonprocedural texts becomes even more impressive (although it seems somewhat exaggerated to dismiss the latter as "infinitesimal in number," "insignificant" and "of little importance,"[28] especially since some of them deal with basic topics such as alienation of ecclesiastical goods [No.32], or *praescriptio* [No.39]).

If Gratian refrains from more abundant quotation of Roman texts on all except procedural topics, this reserve cannot stem from lack of knowledge: witness the workmanlike composition of the passages that do quote Roman sources. But if not lack of competence, there must be another, intentional reason for this attitude: the compiler appears to have conceived of a plan to supplement the ecclesiastical rules on judicial procedure by the pertinent, and technically more advanced, texts and doctrines of Roman law, but to forego, on the whole, major Romanistic borrowings in regard to other topics. The resulting lack of balance in the use of Justinian's texts leads to the obvious question: was this the original scheme of Gratian's work?[29] Vetulani points to the following signs that it was not, and that a revision must have taken place at a late stage of composition:

(*a*) Terminal position: in 14 instances the Roman law fragments are placed together in one cluster at the end of the *quaestio,* often without regard to the line of argument, whereas normally Gratian does not practice—different in this from, e.g., Ivo of Chartres—arrangement by "masses"; [30]

---

24 V. pp. 31–32; but see below, IV B (No. 1), F (No. 2).
25 V. p. 33; cf. J. Gaudemet, "La doctrine des sources du droit dans le Décret de Gratien," *Revue de droit canonique* 1 (1951) 5–31, for the material used by Gratian.
26 V. pp. 33–38 (counting 12 non-procedural passages); the 14 are Nos. 5–7, 32, 35, 38–46, and the suspected ones are Nos. 38, 42, 43, 44, 46, Nos. 5, 6, 35, and No. 45, respectively.
27 But see below, IV B (No. 35), E (Nos. 42, 43), F (Nos. 44, 46).
28 V. pp. 34, 38.
29 V. pp. 38–39.
30 V. p. 40: Nos. 4, 6, 7, 9, 15, 17, 18, 24, 25, 26, 27, 30, 31, 41 of our list.

(b) Mechanical attachment: in 11 cases the Roman law fragments are tacked onto the preceding canon without interruption, and without fitting always the rubric of that canon;[31]

(c) Lack of rubrics: in contrast to Gratian's usual method of introducing a canon, the Roman law fragments are nearly always—there are but 5 exceptions—presented without a rubric of their own;[32]

(d) Transcriptional disturbance: in numerous instances the Roman Law passages are found to be of uncertain position in the manuscripts, or absent from some manuscripts;[33]

(e) Material and formal inconsistency: there are several instances—and these are perhaps the most interesting cases—of Roman law texts quoted in a wrong context, or adduced by way of afterthought, or leaving even jarring inconsistencies with a preceding or following dictum, inscription, or rubric;[34]

(f) Glossators' critique: a Bolognese tradition, which can be traced back to Johannes Faventinus, asserted that the lengthy *summula de praescriptione* in C.16 p.3 p.c.15–p.c.16 (No.39) was not Gratian's own work but had been supplied "ab alio"—perhaps, as the *Glossa Palatina* and the *Glossa ordinaria* have it, but without proof, by the civilian glossator Jacobus.[35]

The cumulative force of the evidence assembled is, I believe, overwhelming in favor of Vetulani's thesis up to this point. We may leave aside his further speculation as to the identity of the "redactor"—here, as in other cases of work that grew by accretion in the original shop, caution seems indicated, and Vetulani himself is not eager, for instance, to give too much credit to Johannes Faventinus' story on the *De praescriptione,* even though it was told by a near-contemporary. As to the main issue, however, while some points of detail may be questioned, the soundness of Vetulani's conclusions appears clearly established by his material and may be corroborated by further observations. But before we turn to such critical and supplemental notes (below, IV), a more exciting question has to be discussed: the traces that exist of at least one manuscript which represents a stage of Gratian's work before the final redaction.

III

The slender pamphlet with the title page reading, "Diomedis Brava/ Patricii Tranensis/ Disquisitio Critica/ de Interpolatione / Gratiani/ Bononiae Apud

---

31 V. p. 41 (counting 9): Nos. 22, 27, 28, 29, 31, 32, 33, 35, 42; add 4, 16.
32 V. p. 41 f., counting four exceptions, but see below, IV C.
33 Discussed in V. *passim*; also *Ap.* 131–3; more below, IV E.
34 V. pp. 42–47, discussing Nos. 22, 25, 28, 33, 34; cf. also pp. 16, 31 (No. 1), 18 (No. 7); more below, IV H.
35 *Ap.* 131, quoting from J. Juncker, "Summen und Glossen," ZRG *Kan. Abt.* 14 (1925) 390 n. 1 (but for *Summa Parisiensis,* read *Summa Lipsiensis* in *Ap. cit.),* Johannes Teutonicus' *Glos. ord.* C.16 q.3 p.c.15, v. *non potest* (cited by Juncker, *loc. cit.)* comes verbatim from *Glos. Pal.* (MS Vat. Pal. 658, fol. 59ra).

Haeredes Benatii/ 1694./ Super. permissu," (pp.xxiv), was already in Sarti's day a great bibliographical rarity.[36] I have seen a microfilm of the copy owned by the University Library of Pisa.[37] Two eighteenth-century reprints, however, are of easier access: one, in Justus Henning Boehmer's edition of the *Corpus iuris canonici*, with the editor's notes;[38] the other, in Paul Riegger's *Dissertatio de Decreto Gratiani*, with Boehmer's and Riegger's notes.[39]

Behind the pseudonym, Diomede Brava, and the false imprint one of the representative figures of that great age of polyhistors is hiding: Gratian's confrere, the Camaldulese Guido Grandi (1671–1742), who died as professor of Mathematics in Pisa and whose work in the mathematical sciences appears to be better remembered than his numerous writings on topics of history, philosophy, theology, hagiography, etc.,[40] though his share in the discussion of the *littera Pisana* will be recalled by the student of the textual transmission of the Digest.[41] The *Disquisitio* was actually printed in Pisa, in 1730, and Don Guido always stoutly denied having written it;[42] but he adopted a number of "Brava's" arguments on interpolation when—under another pen-name again—he wrote his *Nuova Disamina della Storia delle Pandette Pisane*.[43] There were not many to follow him.[44] The veil of mystification thrown around himself and his printer unduly discredited Brava in the eyes of Sarti; and Sarti remained, it seems, the only scholar after Boehmer and Riegger seriously to discuss Grandi's interesting observations: the great modern authorities on Gratian do not even mention the *Disquisitio*.

The striking discovery on which "Brava" reported in detail was a manuscript of Gratian's book, identified as "in bibliotheca monasterii S. Blasii apud Vesontionem diu seruatum, nunc in suburbano amici praesulis musaeo positum." He describes it as consisting of 340 folios, and containing neither *paleae* (but see below) nor glosses; above all, he records the absence of many texts never before—and, we

---

36 M. Sarti et M. Fattorini, *De claris Archigymnasii bononiensis professoribus* (Bologna 1769–72) I 274 = 2nd ed. (Bologna 1888–96) I 346 f.
37 Shelf-mark A-Y9–58, bound after Guido Grandi's *Epistola de Pandectis* (Florence 1727) and his *Vindiciae pro sua Epistola de Pand.* (Pisa 1728). I wish to thank Dom Anselm Strittmatter, O.S.B., for his kind help in locating this rare copy and having it microfilmed for me.
38 Halae Magdeburgicae 1747: I pp. xlii–xlviii.
39 Vindob. 1760 (not seen); reprinted in *Thesaurus iuris ecclesiastici*, ed. Ant. Schmidt, S.J. (Heidelberg 1772) I 129–238: pp. 186–204.
40 See the brief notice by A. Agostini in *Enciclopedia Italiana* 17.718 and the bibliography listed in L. Ferrari, *Onomasticon* (Milan 1947) 373.
41 Cf. for instance C. F. von Savigny, *Geschichte des Römischen Rechts im Mittelalter* (2nd ed. Heidelberg 1834–51) III 462 etc. (see Index s.v.); B. Kübler, *Geschichte des Römischen Rechts* (Leipzig 1925) 408 n.4. See n.37 *supra*, 43 *infra* for titles.
42 J. B. Mittarelli et A. Costadoni, *Annales Camaldulenses* VIII (Venice 1764) 622; cf. G. M. Mazzucchelli, *Gli scrittori d'Italia* II. iv (Brescia 1763) 2038.
43 Bartolo Luccaberti, *Nuova Disamina* ... (Faenza 1730); cf. Mittarelli *loc. cit.*; Sarti I 274 and note *d* (2nd ed. 347 and n. 2, where the pseudonym is wrongly given as Lucchetti).
44 See however J. B. Bartholus (Bartoli), *Institutiones iur. can.* (Ausugii [Borgo di Val Sugana] 1749) 501 f.; cf. Sarti *loc cit.* n. *e* (n.3).

may add, except for Vetulani never since—suspected. A comparison shows that of the 46 items of our list only 14 appear to be present in Brava's manuscript (=*Br*): Nos. 2, 3, 11–14, 16, 20, 21, 23, 33, 39, 40, 44. Br omits 30 pieces altogether, while in 2 instances constitutions from the *Codex Theodosianus*, i.e. from the tradition of the Visigothic Breviary, take the place of the usual quotations from Justinian's Code: Nos. 36, 42.[45] In a good many cases Brava supports the external evidence by arguments of internal criticism, scrutinizing the accepted text of Gratian for signs of "interpolation"; the point is nearly always well taken.[46]

Sarti (and, to a lesser extent, Boehmer) discounted the evidence of *Br*—since no further corroborating manuscript turned up—by arguing that the scribe of this unique codex must have been an overscrupulous canonist, who on principle eliminated, wherever possible, Gratian's genuine quotations from civil law. But this hypothesis is easily rebutted if we remember, (1) that in the two cases mentioned there is little to commend to an overzealous canonist the Theodosian Code instead of that of Justinian; (2) that by all standards of philological method at least in the cases of formal inconsistency[47] the original absence of the suspect text is more plausible than its later elimination; (3) that *Br* includes nearly all those Roman law texts which Gratian took from intermediary canonical sources: of these 22 texts all but 2 are found in the manuscript, and the two significantly occur in contexts the omission of which in *Br* is borne out by other critical considerations.[48]

The presence in *Br* of most of the second-hand Roman texts disposes not only of the theory of the anti-civilian "editor" of the manuscript, but also of the suspicion—not voiced in so many words by Sarti but still to be considered—that the whole "codex" of Brava might be a hoax, cleverly conceived on the basis of a merely conjectural elimination of certain Roman law texts. While misgivings are understandable, the intrinsic trustworthiness of *Br* cannot be impugned. In this connection, a second look at the texts from Justinian that are present (or at least not reported absent by Brava) is in order.

Of the 14 passages, the following 5 only are beyond suspicion: Nos. 2 (D.50 c.46: CJ. 9.16.5), 3 (D.54 c.20: 5 *Authenticae* of CJ. 1.3.36, 37), 14 (C.2 q.6 p.c.39: CJ. 7.70.1), 21 (3 q.9 p.c.15: *Auth. Si debitum*[49] CJ. 4.20.18), 44 (32 q.1

---

45 Cf. below, IV E, IV G (*d*). Brava claims to have seen also in other manuscripts Justinian law replaced by Theodosian law: (No. 4) C. 1 q.1 c.126; CTh. 9.27.6 for CJ. 9.27.4; (29) 5.q.6 p.c.3: CTh. 11.39.10 (Brev. 11.14.5) for CJ. 1.3.8; (30) 6 q.1 cc.22–23: CTh. 9.14.3, 9.35.1 for CJ. 9.8.5, 4; (43) 25 q.2 p.c.16 § 4: CTh. 1.2.6 (Brev. 1.2.4) for CJ. 1.22.4; (45) (46) De poen. D.1 c.6 = 36 q.2 c.3: CTh. 9.25.2 (Brev. 9.20.2) for CJ. 1.3.5. See Brava §§ 31, 52, 53, 75, 81, 84; all these are texts absent from *Br*.
46 Nos. 1 (see below, IV B), 7 (IV D), 8 (IV C), 19, 25, 28 (IV H), 31 (IV D), 34, 38 (IV H), 46 (IV F).
47 Below, IV H; above at n.34.
48 C.16 q.1 c.40 (bound up with No. 38, see below, IV H) and 19 q.3 c.10 (Epit. Jul. 115 cc.62–63, bound up with No. 41 [cf. V. p. 26 f. No. 38], which is absent from *Br*, see Brava § 69).
49 *Si enim scriptum sit debitum* (Nov. 90.2–3), cf. Vacarius 4.17 n.5 (ed. F. de Zulueta, Publ. Selden Soc. 44; London 1927, p.126; p.lix No. B 16); Vetulani, "Les Novelles de Justinien dans le Décret de Gratien," RHD⁴ 16 (1937) 472 f.

p.c.10: CJ. 9.9.2, 1). The other 9 can be attacked on various grounds and are, in part at least, on Vetulani's list of suspects.[50] Had Brava-Grandi been out to invent a manuscript characterized by the absence of what he considered interpolations, he would at least have eliminated C.3 q.8 c.1 §2; 11 q.1 p.c.9; 16 q.3 p.c.15–p.c. 16 (Nos.20, 33, 39); for they would have been about the most convincing specimens to be had.[51] That he remains silent about these, is perhaps the best indication of his sincerity: as elsewhere, so in the world of manuscripts reality is never as beautifully symmetrical as fiction.

This impression is confirmed if we test *Br* for *paleae*. By no means does the manuscript represent a particularly "pure" text. Instead of an expected low number of *paleae*, over 60 seem to be present; and even if we take into account possible oversight in the case of *paleae* not easily spotted (e.g. those appearing as a portion of text within a given canon),[52] or a slackening of Grandi's interest as the survey went on, there remains a goodly number of cases in which it would have been tempting for him to assert absence of a given piece from his manuscript so as to enhance its age. Yet he himself points to the fact that many texts which *in vulgatis* are marked as *paleae* do appear in *Br.*[53] The manuscript thus represents indeed a textual tradition of curiously mixed ancestry: on the one hand, a stage earlier than the last original revision; on the other, a text already enlarged by numerous additions to the completed book.

Under these circumstances it is exasperating that Grandi remained so vague about the provenance and location of his source. A *monasterium S. Blasii* does not seem to have existed near Besançon; could one assume that the manuscript came from Sankt Blasien in the Black Forest—where so many celebrated codices now scattered in various libraries originated—and had traveled via Besançon to Italy? And where should one place the *musaeum suburbanum amici praesulis?* Not at Trani in Apulia, to be sure, the home of "the Patrician Brava"; but could it be Florence, or Pisa, where the true author of the *Disquisitio critica* spent his academic years? A scrutiny of the largely unedited correspondence and other papers

---

50 V. pp. 21, 46 (Nos. 23, 33 [21, 31]); *Ap.* 130, 132 (Nos. 39, 16, 20); and see below IV A (No. 40), IV B (Nos. 11–13), etc.

51 No.20 is a gloss slipped into the text of 3 q.8 c.1 (below, IV D: but Grandi might have merely overlooked this case), No.33, a glaring case of inconsistency of inscription caused by incomplete revision (V. p. 46), and No. 39 was suspected even by the early glossators (above, at n. 35; cf. below, IV E).

52 They are (numbers refer to Friedberg's list of *paleae*, col. xiii ff.) Nos. 2, 6, 7, 11, 53, 77, 106, 121, 148, and C.22 q.4 c.19 § 1 (on this *palea* see Vetulani, ZRG *Kan. Abt.* 22 [n.8 *supra*] 363; Ullmann, *Stud. Grat.* I 198).

53 Brava § 16: "... nam quandoque capita quaedam quae in vulgatis *paleae* nomine recensentur, hic inserta vidi, suppresso tamen *paleae* vocabulo." In the case, e.g., of several *paleae* following each other immediately in the vulgate text, one would expect total absence or total presence in a given manuscript. Not so in *Br,* where of such pairs or triplets we sometimes find one single *palea* present (here indicated by italics): Friedberg's Nos. 4–*5* (Dist. 9 cc.1–*2*), 22–*24* (Dist. 35 cc.5, 6, *7*), *26*–28 (Dist. 38, cc. *13*, 14, 15), 60–*62* (Dist. 88 cc.11, 12, *13*), *142, 143,* 144 (C. 23 q.8 cc.*1, 2,* 3).

of Grandi in the University Library of Pisa[54] may or may not lead us onto the trace of the manuscript. If it still exists, it will eventually be reached by the group of researchers now engaged[55] in the project of a *catalogue raisonné* of all the manuscripts of Gratian. But *Br* may be lost, just as another, famous *codex Vesontinus*—the one from which Cujas was able to supply certain portions of the *Sententiae* of Paulus—is lost,[56] and in that case no one will ever answer the riddle of its origin.

IV

The observations that follow here are offered by way of a supplement to Vetulani.

A. *Number of passages from Roman law.* In the article of 1946/7 this was given as 42 units; two more were discussed in *Apollinaris* in 1948 (Nos. 16, 20 of our list); and Vetulani's No. 39 should have been counted as two according to his own principle, since in the manuscripts cc.14–15 and dict. p. c. 16 of C.25 q.2 are two distinct units (Nos. 42, 43 of our list). To be added is the following:

(40) C.17 q.4 p.c.29, on punishment in secular law of various species of sacrilege. Sources: (pr.:) CJ. 1.3.10, paraphrased ("... sicut in primo libro Codicis legitur titulo de episcopis et clericis et lege Si quis in hoc genus sacrilegii proruperit") and with the addition of a garbled reference, "et in Digestis tit. ad legem Juliam pecuniarum repetundarum, 1. ultima"; (§1:) CJ. 9.29.1–3, paraphrased ("... lib. ix. Codicis tit. de crimine sacrilegii").—The first part of the dictum duplicates a quotation found as early as Gregory the Great's famous *commonitorium* to the *defensor* Johannes (JE 1912: *ep.* 13.50 in MGH *Epp.* 2.415 lin.10–18), cf. C.2 q.1 c.7 §7; but, as the form of reference shows, neither this text nor Anselm of Lucca 4.23 (ed. Thaner, Innsbruck 1906–15, p. 201)[57] were Gratian's source. The form of reference in both paraphrases from the Code is in keeping with a style found elsewhere in Gratian (see below, B) but the reference to the Digest is given in the "Irnerian" style, i.e. by citing only rubric and *lex*.

The glossators had no difficulty observing that the reference was wrong.[58] Dig.48.11.9 *(de lege Julia repetundarum l. ult.)* makes no sense whatever in the

---

54 Agostini, *Enciclop. Ital.* 17.718.
55 Cf. Mme. Rambaud, "Plan et méthode" (n. 16 *supra*) 211.
56 Jac. Cuiacius, *Observationes* 21.13 ff.; cf. G. Haenel, *Lex Romana Visigothorum* (Berlin 1849), praef. pp. xvii, lxxxix; P. Krüger, *Collectio librorum iuris anteiust.* II (Berlin 1878) 44; A. Berger, in Pauly-Wissowa, RE 10.732; *id.,* "In tema di derelizione" (1914), *Bullettino dell'Istituto di diritto romano* 32 (1922) 151, with further bibliography in n.1.
57 Gregory the Great cites "Cod. lib. primo tit. tertio const. undecima, Imperatores Archadius et Honorius Augusti Theodoro p. p."; Anselm of Lucca omits all reference to the Code, giving only the inscription *(Imperatores* etc.). The text occurs also in *Coll. Caesaraugustana* (cf. Savigny, *Geschichte* II 491) but no details are known.
58 *Glossa Palatina ad loc.*: "Hic falsum dicit, quia hoc non dicitur in illo tit. ff. ad leg. iul. repe. set in illo tit. ff. ad leg. iul. peculatus, sacrilegii (7, *al.* 6) et l. sacrilegii capite (11, *al.* 9). Errauit ergo in titulo, et utinam in hoc solo errasset" (MS Pal. 658, fol. 61rb); *Glos. ord. ad loc.*: "Magister errauit in nomine huius tituli…"

context, but the nearby Dig. 48.13.7(6) does; this is *ad legem Juliam peculatus l. Sacrilegii* (not the last of the title), which treats of punishments for various forms of sacrilege. A rubric as cited by Gratian does not even exist;[59] the wording *"ad* 1. Jul. *pecu*niarum repetundarum" points to original contamination, and a misreading or dittography of some abbreviation for "pec*ulatu*s" (such as *pecul't'*) might account for the otherwise incomprehensible "1. ult." (which in turn would have led to the dropping of the initial word, *Sacrilegii,* of the *lex* actually meant). Such heavy textual disturbance indicates intrusion of a marginal note in the final stage of redaction. If such a note began with "et repetas" or the like, this could be one way of explaining the strange aberration to the Julian law on *repetundae:*

et repetas in Dig. tit. ad 1. Jul. pecul't'. Sacrilegii
et in Dig. tit. ad 1. Jul. pec. repet. 1. ult.

Another explanation could be offered by the fact that the first mistake ("ad 1. Jul. pecul't'. 1. ult.") led to a text (fr.16, *al.* 14) in which "publica iudicia peculatus et de residuis et repetundarum" are jointly named.

B. *Critical value of inscriptions.* The foregoing may be added to the cases, discussed by Vetulani, in which Irnerian style of reference can be taken as a sign of late intrusion. This much, however, should be clear: (*a*) If Gratian, as a rule, does use a different style for the inscriptions he gives the texts from Justinian's law, this does not mean that he "n'a pas subi—au moins dans cette direction—l'influence de l'Ecole de Bologne" (V. p.31), but is to be explained by the fact that the brief Irnerian style (rubric of title and initium of *lex),* while sufficient in glosses and references for identifying a passage, is not *per se* a satisfactory way of introducing a passage quoted in a collection of *auctoritates;* (*b*) In the early generations of Irnerius' school, so uniform a style of reference as postulated by Savigny did not exist;[60] (*c*) Variety of style is found also in Gratian's inscriptions to a larger extent than Vetulani admits; e.g., in inscriptions of constitutions from CJ. the name of the issuing emperor is often but not always given.[61]

Suspicion against texts introduced in the Irnerian style is borne out by other signs of disturbance in the following cases:

(1) D.50 c.45: material inconsistency, variations of inscription, cf. V. pp. 16, 31 n.3; Brava §19.

---

59 Hence the Roman edition omits the word "pecuniarum," but cf. Friedberg n. 293 *ad loc.* for the MSS.
60 M. Conrat, *Die Epitome exactis regibus* (Berlin 1884) lxviii ff., ccxxxvi ff.; H. Kantorowicz, *Studies in the Glossators of the Roman Law* (Cambridge 1938) 165 f., 196 f.
61 Cf. Nos. 17, 18, 22–24, 29 of Vetulani's (Nos. 18, 19, 24–26, 31 of our) list, and No. 40 (above, A).

(5) 1 q.4 p.c.9 (*al.* c.6): missing in some MSS, designated as *palea* in others, variations of position, cf. V. pp. 17, 36.

(6) 1 q.4 p.c.12 §3 *fin.*: reference to CJ. 8.4.7, which in the vulgate MSS follows as *palea,* cf. V. pp.18, 34, 36; the entire sentence, "Nam si putat" *rell.* is lacking in many MSS, cf. Friedberg n. 133 *ad loc.*[62]

(19) 3 q.7 p.c.1–c.2: formal inconsistency of dict. p.c.2, see below, H.

(22) 3 q.9 p.c.18: modifying but inconsequential afterthought, missing in one of Friedberg's MSS, cf. V. pp. 41, 45; reported as marginal gloss in another MS by Brava §46.

(35) 15 q.1 c.2: variations of position, cf. V. pp.25, 37.

(40) 17 q.4 p.c.29: contamination, see above, A.

(45) De poen. D.1 cc.6–21: variations of position, insufficient coordination of c.22 and dict p.c.22, cf. Brava §81; Rambaud, "Plan et méthode" (n. 16 *supra*) p. 222.

Except for No. 40, they all are absent from Brava's manuscript; Nos.5 and 6 should probably be classed as *paleae.* In the other cases, however, one would hesitate to say with Vetulani that "il s'agit ici, à coup sûr, d'intercalations postérieures dues aux décrétistes" (V. p.30). While it is very likely for these texts to have originated in marginal notes—hence the Irnerian form of reference instead of inscriptions proper—there is no reason why the transference from margin to text could not have taken place during some stage of original revision. The disturbances are no greater in these than in many other texts from Roman law that have the "right" kind of inscription. Also the fact that many of these passages were glossed unsuspectingly by the earliest decretists would seem to corroborate our explanation.

(11, 12, 13) Of the series C.2 q.6 cc.29–31, not criticized in this context by Vetulani, the first (c.29) is inscribed in Friedberg's best manuscripts: "Digest, tit. Quando appellandum sit, lege I." (Dig.49.4.1); the subsequent chapters have no inscriptions but instead the rubrics, c.30: "De appellationibus recipiendis uel non," c.31 pr.: "De libellis dimissoriis," c.31 §1 (separate chapter in the oldest MSS): "Titulo Nichil nouari," which are actually verbatim the rubrics of the respective titles of the Digest (Dig. 49.5, 6, 7)[63] from which Gratian's texts were taken—that is, they are not rubrics proper, i.e., summarizing statements of Gratian's own making, but "Irnerian" references turned into "rubrics." If we notice further that cc.29–31 are a consecutive series of excerpts from Digest 49.4–7, their origin from a marginal notation seems obvious. Other traces of this may be found: in c.30 some MSS offer readings closer to the Digest than to Gratian's text;[64] some

---

[62] Cf. M. Boulet-Sautel, "Les 'Paleae' empruntées au Droit romain ...," *Studia Gratiana* I 153 for MSS in France.

[63] The title of 49.7 *Nihil innovari* (al. *novari) appellatione interposita* is shortened by haplography, since c.31 §1 (Dig.49.7.1) begins, "Appellatione interposita ..."

[64] Gratian's text (pr.), "...sed et si mater ex pietate prouocauerit, dicendum est," cuts short the emendations attempted by the vulgate MSS of the Digest in the corrupt passage Dig. 49.5.1.1 (for which

glosses have crept into the text of c.29;[65] positional uncertainty is evinced by the Cracow MS, where the entire series cc.29–31 is repeated after c.41.[66] Finally, some MSS have a rubric (preceding the inscription) for c.29: "Forma uero appellationis hec est,"[67] which makes no sense in this place, as c.29 treats of *tempus,* not of *forma appellationis.* It can be only explained by contamination with the first sentence of dict. p.c.31 ("Forma apostolorum[68] hec est..."), and this must have occurred in the archetype when cc.29–31 were still in the marginal stage and the words in question followed immediately upon c. 28.

Yet in *Br* the three chapters are not only present but even provided with inscriptions in the "correct" Gratian style instead of the title rubrics,[69] and the same is found in some of Friedberg's MSS.[70] The verdict, then, again must be: original revision, not interpolation.

C. *Critical value of rubrics.* Vetulani notes the extremely rare occurrence of rubrics for the texts quoted directly from Justinian; of the four cases he cites (Nos. 8, 10, 12, 13), two have just been discussed and should be eliminated as being merely miscarried inscriptions. Instead, No. 37 should be added. Vetulani considers at least one of the texts in question (No.10) as taken from an intermediary canonical collection, not from the Roman source directly, and hence, he believes, it is possible that the others too may turn out to belong to that category (V. pp.19, 42). The argument, not compelling in itself, fails with regard to the two texts that came from a series of marginal references (Nos. 12, 13, discussed above); it can be disproved for the others as well.

(10) C.2 q.6 c.28 is Gratian's only quotation of a Novel from the *Authenticum* (Nov.23: Auth.4.2), a unique departure from his regular practice to quote from the *Authenticae* of the Code. Therefore Vetulani in an earlier article had postulated a hypothetical, intermediary collection as source;[71] in the article of 1946/7 the hypothesis is treated more or less as an established fact.[72] But the absence from *Br* of the chapter and of the preceding dictum indicates on the contrary the introduction

---

see Mommsen's apparatus *ad loc.*); the readings of Friedberg's MSS *EGH* (n.353), *CEG* (n.356) follow in a garbled fashion the Digest vulgate. Also, some MSS supply Dig. 49.5.3 (Gratian's c.30 has: 49.5.1, 2, 4), before or after c.30 §2 (fr.4), see Friedb. n.363 (*EH, C*).

65 Cf. *Notae Correctorum* c.29; *Summa Parisiensis, ad loc.* v. *cum quis:* "hoc est glossa" (p.110 ed. McLaughlin).

66 *Ap.* 132f.

67 Friedberg, n. 283 *ad loc.* (The rubric given in the Roman edition is of later making).

68 appellationum *AD,* appellationis *B*: Friedb. n.385 *ad loc.*

69 Brava §40: "Rursus in rubrica praecedente c. *Biduum* 29 eiusdem quaestionis, citatur immediate *Vlpianus lib.1 de appellationibus*: quemadmodum et in alia rubrica ante cap. *Non solent.*30. idem *Vlpianus lib.29. ad edictum* laudatur, vti et *Scaevolae, Martiani* [=c.31], et *Macri* [Boehmer, Riegger: *Marci,* but Macer is meant] testimonia ex eorum libris infra citantur, necnon *Vlpiani lib.4. de appell.* absque mentione tituli digestorum."

70 Cf. his nn. 349, 359, 361 (c.30), 365, 376 (c.31).

71 "Les Novelles ..." (n.49 *supra)* 476 f.

72 V. pp. 19, 42.

of this text in a late stage of revision (later, perhaps, than the series cc.29–31 from the Digest?), and it cannot be overlooked that the chapters now stand in a substantially wrong order: for the dictum and Nov.23, in which (to use Gratian's words) "Justinianus in constitutionibus suis corrigens, infra decem dies appellationis remedium cuique dandum decreuit," should logically have followed rather than preceded the text from the Digest, which supposes a *biduum vel triduum*. The whole juxtaposition remains clumsy; in Gratian's workshop two sets of marginal notes may have been made, one from the Digest and one from the *Authenticum*, to modify the abstracts from the *Theodosianae leges* (i.e. from the *Sententiae* of Paulus with the Visigothic *interpretatio*) which Gratian here in cc.22, 24–27 had taken over from Ivo, *Panormia* 4.127–131.[73]

(8) C.2 q.1 c.14 (Dig.48.2.8–11, 13) with the rubric "Qui ab accusatione prohibeantur et qui recipiantur" is placed at the end of the affirmative part of q.1 (V.p.18); in the Cracow MS it has been supplied in the margin without rubric (*Ap.* p.131), and it is absent from *Br.* The chapter does not properly fit its place, as was justly observed by Grandi (Brava §35), for C.2 q.1 deals with the observance of *ordo iudiciarius* (cf. dict. pr. and p.c.14), not with the question of capacity of accusation, which is considered *ex professo* under various aspects in C.2 q.7; 3 qq.4, 5; 4 qq.1–5; 6 q.1; 15 q.3. All this suggests late insertion.[74]

(37) C.15 q.3 c.4 (CJ. 1.3.30.5) with the rubric "Lese maiestatis et publicorum iudiciorum et symonie accusatio equaliter proponatur" (not discussed by Vetulani) is absent from *Br.* The text from the Code serves Gratian's argument (equal right of accusation in cases of simony and lèse majesté) only by a *tour de force*, since it treats chiefly of the equality of punishment. Gratian's unusual interpretation would explain why he found it necessary to underscore his point by a special rubric. Significantly the same text with the same interpretation is referred to in the dictum p.c.22 of C.6 q.1 (No.30), where the traces of late insertion are quite obvious (see below, E).

D. *Revision or interpolation?* In addition to some texts already discussed (above, B), the following have been suspected as being inserted by the schools after Gratian, i.e., equal to *paleae*:

(16) C.2 q.8 c.2 (CJ.4.19.25) is found as only a marginal entry in some of the oldest and best MSS (*Ap.*p.132), yet seems to be present in *Br.*[75]

(20) C.3 q.8 c.1 §2: the brief quotation from CJ. 7.45.14 interrupts the canonical text of Ps.-Zephyrinus and is obviously intruded from the margin; it has a very irregular tradition in the MSS and was criticized early by the glossators.[76] But

---

73 On Ivo as Gratian's source for these texts see *Summa Parisiensis,* C. 2 q.6 c.25 (p.109 McLaughlin), a passage of great interest for the history of the transmission of the Theodosian Code; cf. *inter al.* Mommsen, *Proleg. Theod.* (Berlin 1905) pp. lxxviii, cv.
74 Boehmer's note 41 on Brava *ad loc.* erroneously asserts that the text came from the *Panormia.*
75 Also Ullmann, *art. cit.* (n.8 *supra*) 177 remains in doubt.
76 *Ap.* p.132; cf. *Not. Corr. ad loc.* (v. *ut codice*); Friedberg n.7; Ullmann p. 180 f. (where a critical gloss by Simon of Southwell is quoted); *Summa Paris. ad loc.* (p. 122 ed. McLaughlin, cf. p.xiii).

Friedberg's best MSS have the text and Brava remains silent (or did he overlook the matter because it concerns a passage in the middle of a canon?).

(31) C.6 q.4 c.7 *fin.* (*al.* c.4 *fin., al.* q.5 c.2) shows uncertainty of position even in the best MSS (V.p.23, *Ap.*p.132); it is absent from *Br* and others. Suspicions voiced by earlier writers are borne out by the designation as *palea* in several MSS studied by Mme. Boulet-Sautel.[77]

Two of these three cases show the difficulty of finding a sharply defined demarcation line between interpolation and original revision. But there are also some instances in which we find the two stages side by side. Nos.4, 7, 18, 25, 32 of our list are present in all manuscripts but not in *Br.* and must be considered late original insertions. They attracted further additions in the schools as follows:

(4) 1 q.1 cc.126–130: in some MSS c.127 is enlarged by CJ. 9.27.2, 3 (to be added to Friedberg's list of *paleae*).[78]

(7) 1 q.7 c.26: *palea* c.27 follows, and according to *Summa Parisiensis* a further *palea,* CJ. 1.3.30, was read here by some.[79]

(18) 3 q.3 p.c.4: *palea* c.4 precedes and *palea* p.c.4 §7 follows.

(25) 4 q.2 & 3 p.c.2–c.3 (see below, H): *palea* c.2 precedes.

(32) 10 q.2 cc.1–3 (see below, E): first portion of c.3 is *palea.*

To these may be added Gratian's Romanizing dictum in C.1 q.4 p.c.12 §§2–3, to which the reference No.6 (§3 *fin.*: probably *palea,* see above, B) and *palea* c.13 are attached; §§2–3 are not found in *Br.* (see below, G).

E. *Transcriptional disturbances.* Uncertainty in the position of the Roman texts, or omission in some manuscripts, with or without later correction, was reported by Vetulani in various cases, some of which have been examined above.[80] The following observations may be added to illustrate two symptoms of revision, not discussed by Vetulani, which we may characterize as "internal duplication" and "split-and-shift."

(26) C.4 q.4 dict. p.c.2, originally attached without interruption to c.2 (Ps.-Damasus, JK †243 c.15 *fin.*-c.16 *med.*: ed. Hinschius p.504), is absent from *Br.* In the vulgate MSS, c.2 § 1 "Inscriptio semper fiat—dampnari,[81] cum et seculi leges hec eadem retineant," is followed by:

(*a*) three vague references to the Code, "Codice libro ix. titulo de accusationibus, Codice libro ix. de adulteriis, titulo de abigeis et inscriptionibus" (Friedberg n.27 relegates the last two words in the apparatus) = CJ. 9.2, 9.9, 9.37;

---

[77] *Art. cit.* (n.62 *supra*) 151 f. For the Cambridge MSS, see Ullmann 176 f.; for MSS used by different glossators, e.g., Singer, *Rufinus* p.249 note *b*; McLaughlin, *Sum. Paris.* p.xiv.
[78] Cf. Boulet-Sautel p.152; Friedberg *ad* c.128, n.1793.
[79] Ed. McLaughlin p.100; cf. p.xii. (The passage stands in need of emendation.)
[80] E.g., Nos. 5, 11–13 (above, B), 8 (C), 16, 20, 31 (D).
[81] Source: CTh. 9.1.11 *Interpr.*

(b) Gratian's own words, "Aliquando etiam sine inscriptione accusatio fieri potest" (dict.§1);

(c) abstracts and paraphrases from the titles referred to in *a*, without any inscriptions and separated only by "item": CJ.9.2.7, first sentence[82] (dict.§1 *fin.*); 9.9.6 paraphr. (§2); 9.37 un. (§3); 9.2.8 (§4); 9.2.16, first sent. (without "item": §5).

A number of MSS repeat here c.2 §1 "Inscriptio—retineant," but some of the best MSS have it *only* here,[83] thus clearly indicating that the cluster of Roman law texts was in a first stage of composition inserted—most probably by expanding a marginal note—between the two sections of the Pseudo-Damasus and gradually shifted to the end of the canon. (After the last quotation from the Code, the vulgate text concludes with another sentence of Gratian's, "De domo etiam—incidat iudex," and c.3, from Nicholas I, JE 2796—both, however, are missing here and transferred to the end of q.6 in some of the oldest MSS.)[84] Even apart from these positional variations the awkward make-up of the passage is telling. The series of references at the beginning—obviously the original nucleus of the dictum—should have been distributed and prefixed by way of inscriptions to the several texts in dict. §§1–5. As it stands now, it leaves the impression of unfinished, untidy work, and the nonsensical reading "de accusationibus ... de abigeis et inscriptionibus" at the beginning, which is even in the best MSS, suggests that possibly a first, correct reference *"Cod. lib.ix tit. de accusationibus et inscriptionibus"* was subsequently split by the additional references to the titles *de adult.* and *de abigeis.*

Early copyists made things worse by prefixing the particle *ut* to the initial references, thus making the words "ut Codice..." appear as though they were meant to corroborate the preceding c.2 §1 ("... quia ante inscriptionem nemo debet iudicari uel dampnari" etc.) while on the contrary they introduce the exceptions (*accusatio sine inscriptione*) to this rule. Yet this became the common Bolognese reading;[85] hence the lame explanation in the *Glossa ordinaria*: "istud *ut* respicit uerba sequentia."

(30) C.6 q.1 cc.22–23. For the sources of this *summula* on accusation for lèse majesté, originally part of the dictum p.c.21, see V.p.23. In *Br.* the whole series, with Gratian's introductory observation, "Hec licet ratione..." (dict.p.c.21 §1), is missing. Within this *summula* one passage (p.c.22) shows marks of having been split by an interpolated reference; it reads in Friedberg's edition (italics mine):

---

82 More in one of Boehmer's MSS (cf. his n. 46 *ad loc.*).

83 Cf. *Nota Corr.*; Friedberg n.18 *ad* c.2. Also in the text used by the *Summa Parisiensis*, cf. *ad loc.*: "Leges vero hic appositas [oppositas MS] sic lege ut *ultimam* ponas tamquam pro rubrica, hoc modo: 'Inscriptio vero semper fiat,' etc...." (p. 127 ed. McLaughlin, italics mine).

84 Friedberg n. 40 *ad* dict.p.c.2; cf. also Rambaud, "Plan et méthode ..." (n. 16 *supra*) 220 for MS Paris 3888.

85 *Ed. Rom.*; Friedberg's MS *D* (n.22); cf. also the *casus* of Bartholomaeus Brixiensis v. *Inscriptio*, where the difficulties felt by Huguccio and Benencasa ("Beneuen." *ed.Rom.*) are reported.

> Porro symonie accusatio ad instar lese maiestatis *procedere debet*, sicut Leo inperator in I. libro Codicis decreuisse legitur, tit. de episcopis et clericis, 1. Si quenquam *procedere debet.* Quod de accusatione, non de pena intellegi oportet.

The *lex* referred to is CJ. 1.3.30, the pertinent part of which (§5 ... *Sane quisquis hanc sanctam*) Gratian quotes in 15 q.3 c.4, proposing the same interpretation (No.37, see above, C).[86] The constitution does of course not begin "Si quenquam procedere debet," but nearly all of Friedberg's MSS have this dittographic nonsense (so does one early 13th-cent. MS in the Library of Congress),[87] whereas the vulgate text (=*ed.Rom.*) tacitly corrects the passage by suppressing the second "procedere debet." At least one other MS of the 13th cent. replaces the reference by quoting the fragment itself ("Quisquis igitur sanctam—retrahatur").[88] The key to the correct reading is found in the Cologne MSS, which Friedberg should have followed instead of merely reporting on them (nn.281, 282 *ad loc*):

> Porro symonie accusatio ad instar lese maiestatis—sicut Leo imp. in I. lib. Cod. decreuisse legitur, tit. de epis. et cler. 1. Si quenquam uel in hac urbe[89]—procedere debet. Quod...

(32) C.10 q.2 p.c.1–c.3, originally part of c.1: an important *summula* on alienation of ecclesiastical goods, made up from fragments of CJ.1.2.21 and 1.2.14, with a number of traditional *Authenticae*.[90] Here we have again positional uncertainty, causing a split of the original canon to which these Roman texts were attached: in the vulgate tradition the canon (c.7 of the Council of Agde) begins as c.1 "Casellas—presumant" and continues in c.3, after the Roman texts (CJ. 1.2.14.9–10,[91] *Auth.Hec usus, Auth. Quibuscumque*: c.3pr.-§2), with the words "Quodsi necessitas—permittimus" (§2 *fin.*- §3). But already the *Correctores* noted that "in aliquot melioribus codd." the two sections of the canon are given together as c.1 and that it was thus read by the author of the *casus* on c.1. So also two of Boehmer's, and several of the MSS employed by Friedberg, who consequently prints it that way (though his account of the MSS in the apparatus remains

---

86 The full text was read by some as *palea* at the end of 1 q.7, see at n.79 *supra*.
87 Law Library of Congress MS G.71 (from Weissenau) fol.98 va.
88 *Ibid.* MSG.7, fol.144va–b; formerly Phillipps MS 14953, the whereabouts and contents of which were given as uncertain in my *Repertorium der Kanonistik* (Città del Vaticano 1937) 320. The MS was acquired in 1948 from Christensen, Bloomfield, N. J.
89 This is the correct initium of CJ. 1.3.30.
90 For the sources in detail see V.p. 24; but add *Auth. Perpetua quoque* and *Qui rem huiusmodi* (c.2 §§6–7). The sentence "Sed melius dicitur ..." (§10), which V. attributes to Gratian, is part of the *Auth. Qui res iam dictas* (§9) as formulated by Irnerius; cf. *Glos. ord. ad loc.* v. *Sed melius*.
91 The preceding portion of §9 is a *palea*.

somewhat confused).⁹² Yet the splitting of the *canon Agathensis* is the only arrangement that yields a point of contact for the series of Roman texts: they begin after c.1 with a brief clause, "excepta uidelicet causa captiuitatis," quoted from CJ. 1.2.21;⁹³ and the exception here stated to the prohibition of alienation—viz. redeeming of prisoners, later on amply documented in 12 q.2 cc.13–16, 70, etc.— becomes incomprehensible if it is read after the permissive (c.1 *fin.* Friedberg "... in usum prestare permittimus" = c.3 vulg.) instead of the prohibitive part of the canon ("... neque ... alienare presumant" c.1 vulg.). In *Br.* cc.2–3 are omitted, but Brava remains silent as regards the short dictum p.c.1, although its origin in a marginal note seems obvious.

(39) C.16 q.3 p.c.15–p.c.16: the celebrated *summula de praescriptione,* which an early Bolognese tradition—or gossip?—declared to be interpolated by someone else,⁹⁴ but which is found in all manuscripts, including *Br.* Commenting on p.c.15, dict.pr.,

> Huius ergo longi temporis prescriptio auctoritate Gelasii et secularium legum ecclesiis obici non potest,

i.e. before the beginning of the Romanistic distinction (dict. §1) "Prescriptionum alie," the glossators advised to continue reading farther down, after the end of the long *summula* (p.c.16 §4 *Auth. Quas actiones*), at the words,

> sed sola prescriptio xxx. annorum et deinceps, a qua tamen prescriptione priuilegia Romane ecclesie sunt exclusa *rell.,*

with the subsequent c. *Nemo* (17), thus implying that here Gratian's original text had been split. The *Correctores Romani* observed that one of their MSS repeats after *Auth. Quas actiones* the passage, "Huius ergo—non potest," thus reconnecting by duplication the end of the dictum with its beginning; Friedberg lists three such MSS.⁹⁵ The uncertainty of the reading, "sed sola prescriptio" (which fits the end of dict.pr.) or "sed sola prescriptione"⁹⁶ (which fits the end of *Quas actiones*), points in the same direction. Multiple recension is further suggested by two internal duplications:⁹⁷ p.c.15 §6 briefly cites *Quas actiones* and the initial words of *Epit. Jul.* 119.6; the first of these reappears in a longer excerpt at the

---

92 Friedberg n.9 *ad loc.* seems to imply that *ABC*—his oldest MSS—offer the vulgate position. So does MS Paris 3888, cf. Rambaud, *art. cit.* 220.

93 According to V.p.24 this fragment is found before Gratian, in Anselm of Lucca 4.22 and in *Polyc.* But the excerpt from CJ. 1.2.21 in Anselm (pr.-§1 v. "... in factum actionem") stops short before the passage employed by Gratian. The *Polycarpus* is not accessible to me.

94 Cf. at n.35 *supra.*

95 *Not. Corr. ad loc.* §4, v. *habentibus,* with Friedberg's notes in brackets.

96 *Ibid.* and Friedb. n. 251.

97 Cf. *Glos. Pal.* (n. 35 *supra*) and *Glos. ord.* p.c.15 v. *non potest*: "... quod etiam conicitur [conuincitur *ed. Rom.*] ex eo quod ille concordantie bis ponuntur."

end of the *summula*, p.c.16 §4, and the other—which comes from an intermediary collection, *Polycarpus* 3.12.34—reappears paraphrased in full as q.4 c.3 of the same *Causa*.

(42, 43) C.25 q.2 cc.14–15, p.c.16: a *summula* on rescripts, divided by c.16 (Pelagius I: JK 1033) and made up of fragments from CJ. 1.19, 1.22, and 1.23, some of which are found also in collections prior to Gratian (V. pp.35, 37; however, no material for collations is available). The whole cluster of texts, including the decretal of Pelagius, is not in its usual place in several of the oldest MSS,[98] and in Friedberg's best MSS the rubric of c.16 is missing.[99] All this points to origin in a marginal notation on c.13, a fragment from Gregory the Great's *ep.* 9.197 (JE 1724), which expressly refers to *imperialis constitutio* for the maxim, "ut ea que contra leges fiunt non solum inutilia sed etiam pro infectis habenda sint" (actually quoted from CJ. 1.14.5.1). Among the parallel texts, cc.14–16, suggested to Gratian by this maxim, Pelagius' decretal JK 1033 is itself a summary of what "clementissimus princeps generalibus legibus constituit," and thus in turn prompted the compilation of the Roman fragments p.c.16.[100] In *Br.* this latter *summula* is lacking, and instead of c.14 (CJ. 1.19.3) Constantine's *Contra ius rescripta* (CTh. 1.2.2 [Brev. 1.2.1]) is read.

F. *Intermediary sources?* For a number of texts Vetulani contemplates the possibility of Gratian's having taken them, at least in part, from earlier canonical collections rather than directly from the Roman sources. Some of these have been disposed of above;[101] one will be considered in connection with formal signs of double recension (below, H: No.38); there remain Nos. 2, 44, 46.

(2) D.50 c.46: the mere fact that this piece from CJ. 9.16.5 occurs also in the *Collatio legum Mosaicarum et Romanarum* (V. p.32) does not suffice to support the suggestion of a possible canonical intermediary, especially since Gratian's readings are those of Justinian's Code.

(44) C.32 q.1 p.c. 10: CJ.9.9.2, 1;

(46) C.36 q.2 c.3: CJ. 1.3.5; absent from *Br.* Even if part of these texts can also be found before Gratian (V. pp. 27–28, 35, 37), no conclusion is justified unless we have a connection positively established by textual comparison. Friedberg's apparatus offers no material, and the collation of the first part of No.44 (CJ.9.9.2)

---

98 *Ap.* 132 (MSS of Cracow and Plock); Rambaud, *art.cit.* 221 (Paris 3888); Friedberg n.85 *ad* c.12 (MSS *EG*).

99 Friedberg n.98 *ad* c.16.

100 CJ. 1.22.2–6 and 1.23.3, 4, 7. It is worth noting that modern authorities who discuss the imperial constitutions Pope Pelagius had in mind cite no other texts than those quoted here by Gratian: see M. Conrat, *Geschichte der Quellen und Literatur des Römischen Rechts im früheren Mittelalter* (Leipzig 1891) 6 n.5, Nos.4–5 (also the fragment left by Conrat of a second edition, which H. Kantorowicz published in ZRG Rom. Abt. 34 [1913] 29 n.1, No. 5); V. Wolf von Glanvell, *Die Kanonessammlung des Kardinals Deusdedit* (Paderborn 1905) 444 n. 7 on Deusd. 4.99 (JK 1033).

101 Nos. 8, 10, 12, 13: above, IV C; Nos. 42, 43: IV E.

with the printed text of Ivo, *Decr.* 8.266 remains inconclusive.[102] In any event, an *argumentum e continuo* for the rest of the dictum is hardly admissible.

G. *Implied proficiency in Roman law.* For this aspect of Gratian's work, which was not discussed by Vetulani, only a few examples will be given in the present paper.

(a) D.5 pr., on Natural law: "... cepit enim ab exordio rationalis creature, nec uariatur tempore sed immutabile permanet"; D.6 p.c.3 §1: "Naturale ergo ius ab exordio rationalis creature incipiens, ut supra dictum est, manet immobile." Gaudemet, in his excellent analysis of the opening sections of the Decretum, finds here a Ciceronian influence,[103] but the glossators were nearer the truth when they noted[104] such parallels as Inst.Just. 2.1.11 ("... a vetustiore iure incipere: ... vetustius esse naturale ius, quod cum ipso genere humano rerum natura prodiit..."); Dig. 41.1.1. pr. ("... et quia antiquius ius gentium cum ipso genere humano proditum est..."); Inst. 1.2.11 ("Sed naturalia iura... semper firma atque immutabilia permanent..."). Gratian's definition may of course be based on an intermediary source, especially since no direct use by him of the Institutes is otherwise known. Still, it is skilfully composed and in its marked Roman character cuts sharply across Gratian's original definition, D.1, pr., which equates *ius naturale* with the divine law "quod in lege et euangelio continetur" (also D.5 pr. after "immutabile permanet": "Sed cum naturale ius lege et euangelio supra dicatur esse comprehensum..."). This juxtaposition of concepts was to create certain difficulties of interpretation for the early decretists.[105]

(*b*) D.34 p.c.3: Gratian's definition of concubine,

> Concubina autem hic ea intelligitur que cessantibus legalibus instrumentis unita est et coniugali affectu asciscitur; hanc coniugem facit affectus, concubinam uero lex nominat,

contains civilian terms not derived from the canons he quotes (cc.4, 5) but from the *Auth. Licet* of CJ. 5.27.8 ("... concubina... quae sola fuerat ei indubitato affectu coniuncta," *ex* Nov. 89.12.4) and CJ. 5.27.10 ("... minime dotalibus instrumentis compositis, postea autem ex eadem adfectione etiam ad nuptialia pervenerit instrumenta..."),[106] quite possibly by way of one of the collections of

---

102 The wrong assumption (V. p.27) that this fragment occurs also in the *Coll. Caesaraugustana* is based on the poorly aligned tables in A. Theiner's *Disquisitiones criticae* (Rome 1836) 265; cf. instead, Savigny, *Geschichte* II, 491 and 514.
103 Gaudemet, *art. cit.* (n. 25 *supra*) 25 n.2, referring to *De republ.* 3.22.33 ("lex diffusa in omnes").
104 Cf. *Glos. ord.* D.1 pr. v. *Humanum genus*, D.5 pr. v. Haec quae, etc.
105 Some tentative remarks in the present writer's paper, "Natural Law and Canon Law," *University of Notre Dame Natural Law Institute Proceedings* 3 (1949) 99 f.; cf. O. Lottin, *Le droit naturel chez St. Thomas d'Aquin et ses prédécesseurs* (2nd ed. Bruges 1931) 12; G. Le Bras, "Les écritures dans le Décret de Gratien," ZRG Kan. Abt. 27 (1938) 56 f.
106 Nov. 18.5 (Epit. Jul. 118) adduced in the *Nota Corr.* is much less likely and has no verbal parallels.

THE ROMAN LAW IN GRATIAN'S DECRETUM

legal definitions current at the time.[107] Gratian's speaking of *legalia instrumenta* instead of *dotalia* or *nuptialia instrumenta* indicates, however, that he had not fully grasped the precise technical meaning. The dictum shows further marks of incomplete revision in that the beginning, "... *hic* ea intelligitur" has no point of reference in the immediately preceding canon D.34 c.1 (cc.2–3 are *paleae*); hence the glossators referred *hic* back to D. 33.[108] This saves the meaning but certainly does violence to the words, for Gratian always uses "illud Gregorii" or similar expressions when he wants to point back to an earlier text. The solution seems to be given in *Br.,* where between D.34 c.1 and dict.p.c.3 Brava read a canon, "Ex concilio Bituricensi: Presbyteri et diacones et subdiaconi, sicut lex canonum praecipit, neque uxores neque concubinas habeant,"[109] which must have disappeared during the process of revision.

(c) C.1 q.4 p.c.12: In Gratian's important distinction of *ignorantia facti* and *iuris*, the subdivisions of *ignorantia facti* are based on theological criteria and illustrated by biblical examples;[110] the discussion of *ignorantia iuris,* however, subdivided into *ign. iuris naturalis* and *iuris civilis,* is entirely built upon civilian conceptions, but without direct quotation (leaving aside the dubious last sentence, probably a *palea*).[111] The distinction was quite possibly modelled upon Bulgarus' *Summula de iuris et facti ignorantia,* as Kantorowicz has shown.[112] In respect of *ignorantia facti*, the Romanistic criteria of *ign. crassa et supina, ign. quae caderet in virum discretum, ign. probabilis,* were introduced in the teaching of the canonists only after Gratian.[113] It is therefore interesting to learn (Brava §33) that in *Br.* the entire subdistinction of *ign. iuris* is absent, i.e. that the earliest recension seems to have had no Roman law whatever in this context.

(*d*) C.15 q.3 pr.: In discussing the question, "an mulier sacerdotem accusare ualeat," Gratian argues for the negative by saying, *inter al.*:

> Legibus quoque cautum est ut ob uerecundiam sui sexus mulier apud pretorem pro alio non intercedat, nisi forte suas uel suorum iniurias persequi maluerit...

---

107 "That floating mass of legal glossaries"—Kantorowicz, *Studies* (n. 60 *supra*) 18, with bibliography in nn.7, 8.
108 Cf. Rufinus *ad loc.* ("... in superioribus capitulis," p.80 ed. Singer); *Summa Paris. ad loc.* (p.33 ed. McLaughlin; emend as follows: "quod autem dicit 'concubina hic intelligitur,' i.e. precedenti decreto secundo [= c.7 D.33]; *hic,* i. e. supra"); *Glos. ord. ad loc.* ("*hic* respicit id quod dixi supra proxima dist. cap. i").
109 Brava §12; Council of Bourges 1031 c.5, first sentence: Mansi 19.503.
110 Kuttner, *Kanonistische Schuldlehre von Gratian bis auf die Dekretalen Gregors IX.* (Città del Vaticano 1935) 153.
111 Above, IV B, No.6.
112 *Studies* 79 f.—The problem of identifying other civilian glossators who may have influenced Gratian in one or another of his Romanizing dicta cannot be examined in the present paper. For No. 39 cf. above, II (*f*) at n.35; for No.15 (C.2 q.6 dict. *fin.*) see *art.cit.* (n.1 *supra*) in *Apollinaris* 21.127 at n.41 (Bulgarus? Irnerius? Henricus de Bayla?).
113 *Kanon. Schuldlehre* 145 f., 154 ff.

The first part of the passage is apparently based on Dig. 50.17.2 ("... Feminae ... nec postulare nec pro alio intervenire nec procuratores existere..."); Dig. 3.1.1.5[114] ("...dum feminas [praetor] prohibet pro aliis postulare... ne contra pudicitiam sexui congruentem alienis causis se immisceant; ... improbissima femina quae inverecunde postulans..."); the *nisi*-clause is borne out by the texts subsequently quoted in cc.1, 2 §1, 3 §2 (CJ. 9.1,12; Dig. 48.2.1; CJ. 9.1.4). But again, we notice confusion as to technical language: *intercedere pro alio* is an undertaking of surety or, generally, of an obligation for others; should Gratian have misunderstood the famous opening sentence of Dig. 16.1, "Senatusconsulto Velleiano plenissime comprehensum est ne pro ullo feminae intercederent," so as to mean prohibition of acting and pleading in court, i.e., as equal to the passages quoted above which speak of *postulare* and *intervenire pro alio?* The confusion of terms is understandable inasmuch as *intervenire* in the Roman sources covers either meaning,[115] and Dig. 50.17.2 "nec pro alio intervenire" was indeed construed by some glossators as referring to the *sc. Velleianum*[116]—which, however, in the context could be of no interest to Gratian.

But there might be another explanation. *Br.* omits the series of texts from Cod. Just. and Digest in cc.1–3 (No. 36); instead of c.1 (CJ. 9.1.12) Brava read the constitution CTh. 9.1.3 (Brev. 9.1.2), followed immediately by Dig. 48.4.8 (= c.3 §§3–4). Now, in CTh. 9.1.3 the incapacity of women for criminal actions is formulated thus: "... ut intendendi criminis publici facultatem non nisi ex certis causis mulieres habeant, hoc est si suam suorumque iniuriam *rell.*" A scribal mistake of *intercedere* for *intendere* would palaeographically be easy to explain, and this is how a first draft of Gratian's dictum might have developed into what we read now. His argument demands that criminal accusation be mentioned, and he may have written something like this: "... apud pretorem pro alio non inter*ueniat nec publicum crimen intendat, nisi forte...*" Once the second verb had been miscopied as *intercedat*, "emendation" and homoeography (*inter-inter*) would have done the rest.

(*e*) *Ibid.* dict. p.c.4: In the course of his tortuous and often criticized[117] argument on parallels and differences between *leges* and *canones* in regard to the right of accusation, Gratian appeals to an analogy from the law of celibacy and states: "... legibus enim soli cantores et lectores, canonibus autem etiam acoliti uxores ducere possunt." The *Correctores Romani* wrote a long criticism of this passage—Gratian's line of reasoning is indeed specious, since acolythes were not an order in the East—and pointed to Nov.22.42 as a source. Gratian, we may

---

114 Quoted in 3 q.7 c.2 (No. 19: below, H).
115 Cf. *Vocab. iurispr. rom.* s.v.
116 Bulgarus, *Ordo iudiciorum,* app. § *Feminae* (ed. Wahrmund, *Quellen* 4.1 [Innsbruck 1925] 13f.) "... *nec postulare,* nisi pro se tantum; neque *intercedere,* nisi cum suum negotium gerunt, ut cum intercedunt pro [nisi pro *Wahrm.*] creditore suo; nec *procuratores* [pro curatore *Wahrm.*; existere *add.?*] litigando, nisi causa cognita pro parente ..." (italics and emendations mine). See also the Accursian gloss *ad loc.* and Heumann-Seckel, *Handlexikon* s.v. *intervenire.*
117 Cf., e.g., Stephanus Tornacensis, *Summa ad loc.* ("... unde Gratianum hic aut errare puto aut vagari ...," ed. Schulte [Giessen 1891] p. 221); *Summa Paris,* q.3 pr. (p. 175 McLaughlin), etc.

add, probably read this Novel as *Auth. Multo magis* of CJ. 1.3.19. And it is even more astonishing that this *Authentica* is adduced here, where it fits exceedingly ill, but is bypassed in the long tractate on celibacy, Dist. 26–34, where the differences between oriental and Roman discipline are repeatedly touched upon.[118]

In any event, the weakness of Gratian's logic in dict. pr. and p.c.4, as well as the considerable differences for cc.1–4 in *Br.*,[119] point to a particularly inept ultimate recension of the entire *quaestio* 3.

H. *Formal inconsistencies.* In addition to the interesting cases discussed by Vetulani (Nos. 22, 25, 28, 33, 34)[120] and the incidental observations made in the preceding pages, some further, striking instances of incongruities left untouched in the final revision should be noted.

(19) C.3 q.7 p.c.1–c.2. After this long *summula* composed from Digest and Code (for details see V.p.20f.) on disqualifications of judges, Gratian's words, "Idem testatur Felix papa et eisdem uerbis," make no sense. They were commonly referred by glossators and commentators to 3 q.5 c.11 (Ps.-Felix II, JK †230 c.12 §15 on the exclusion of *servi, infames,* etc. from testimony and accusation), but this text admittedly did not use "the same words" as any portion, and in particular the end, of q.7 c.2. In *Br.* however, the whole *summula* is lacking and "Idem testatur..." follows immediately upon c.1, quoted from *Romana sinodus,* "Infamis persona nec procurator potest esse, nec cognitor," which is based on Angilr. c.4 (ed. Hinschius p. 759 at n.32; inscr. "Sancta synodus Romana dixit," p. 758). And this text indeed is found *eisdem verbis* in Ps.-Felix I, *ep.*2.13 (JK †143, ed. Hinschius p.202). The *Correctores Romani* in their note on c.1 came close to recognizing this truth, yet failed to draw the obvious conclusion and repeated (on dict.p.c.2) the wrong reference to q.5 c.11, as does also Friedberg (n.89 *ad loc.*). Brava §45 pointed to the incongruity of the vulgate text, but without adverting how neatly c.1 and p.c.2 agree.

(25) C.4 q.2 & 3 p.c.2-c.3 has been competently discussed by Vetulani, who points out (p.43) that this Romanistic *summula* on witnesses belies Gratian's dict.pr., "secunda autem et tertia questio *eodem concilio* [i.e., Carth. VII] *uno eodemque capitulo* terminatur." One might add, as did Brava §48, that the final dictum (p.c.3), "sed obicitur illud beati Bricii, qui uoce pueri triginta dies ab ortu habentis innocens probatus est," with its solution,[121] makes sense only if read as an objection to the last sentence of c.1, "... ad testimonium autem intra annos quatuordecim etatis sue constituti non admittantur," which it follows directly (c.2 is a *palea*) in *Br.*

---

118 D.28 p.c.13 §4; D.31 p.c.13; D.32 *passim,* etc.
119 See above, *d* for cc.1–3 (No. 36); IV C, for c.4 (No. 37).
120 V.pp.42–47; all but No.33 (11 q.1 p.c.9; V.p.46) are absent from *Br.* On Nos. 28 (5 q.3 p.c.1) and 34 (12 q.2 p.c.58–c.60) Brava's critical comments (§§ 51,61) are identical with those by Vetulani (pp. 44, 46f.); for No. 25 see below.
121 Not properly understood in V. p.22.

(38) C.16 q.1 c.40-p.c.40, a series of texts on clerical and monastic immunity, is perhaps the only instance of double recension in which Roman materials were demonstrably added from intermediary canonical sources.

c.40: C.J. 1.3.51, from the *Polycarpus*
p.c.40 (c.40 §3 *ed. Rom.*): CTh. 16.2.8 (not CJ. 1.3.1), from Ans. Luc. 4.13
— *(ibid.* §4): CJ. 1.2.5 (not CTh. 16.2.40), from Ans. Luc. 4.21

The proof for the derivative nature of the text[122] is the unquestionably Theodosian reading "meruisse perhibemini" (CTh. Ans. Grat.) for "meruistis" (CJ.) in the first fragment of dict p.c.40. That Gratian's text belonged to the tradition of Anselm of Lucca is further shown by the variant "fundos et máncipia" (Ans. Grat.) for the authentic "et uos et mancipia" (CThJ.; not noted in Friedberg).[123] But Gratian did not follow Anselm's tacking onto the Theodosian text of the interpretation by Hincmar of Reims, "cum enim dicit—concluditur."[124] Thus an intermediary source between Anselm and Gratian is likely; and this assumption is confirmed by some variants in the second fragment, especially by Gratian's reading with the original (CJ 1.2.5), "post debite ultionis," against Anselm "predicte ultionis" (not recorded by Friedberg).

What the presumable intermediary collection was we cannot say at present. But the entire series of Roman texts is of uncertain position in some manuscripts;[125] it is not found at all in Br. Now, Gratian's own words which follow immediately (dict. p.c.40 *ed. Rom.;* dict. ps.II Friedb.), read thus:

> Hoc idem datur intelligi ex uerbis b. Siluestri, qui obedientiam minorum erga maiores assignans ait: "Abbas hostiario, monachus abbati sit subditus," ...

and, as Brava §66 rightly observed, *hoc idem* can only refer to the end of the dictum preceding c.40, where the non-clerical status of monks in antiquity is discussed, but does not fit with the intercalated texts on immunity. The presence of the latter in this place is probably to be explained by the passage, "et praecipue monachos, licet non sint clerici" in CJ. 1.3.51: it provided Gratian with a civilian parallel for his remark p.c.39 §3, "monachos autem ... monachos simpliciter et non clericos fuisse ecclesiastica testatur ystoria," and then by its context attracted the other material on immunities. After inserting the three pieces, Gratian forgot to change the wording of the first draft where he had interrupted himself; thus, the "seams" of double recension remain visible to the critical reader.

---

122 For other considerations see V.pp. 26, 34, 37. The *Polycarpus* is not available to me for collations.
123 The *Correctores Romani* noted both variants (v. *meruisse),* but not their derivation from Anselm.
124 Hinemar's *ep. ad Carolum imp.* (Mansi 16.757), quoting CTh. 16.2.8 was Anselm's model, not the Theodosian Code (Brev.) itself, cf. the inscription of the chapter in the *Coll.* 74 *tit.,* his immediate source; ed. Thaner, note *b* on Ans. 4.13 (p.197).
125 *Ap.* p.133.

Texts discussed in this paper

[This index replaces the *Summary list of texts* originally printed on this page, where references were given only by numbers of the tabulation p.50 above and sections A, B, C, etc. of part IV (pp.56ff.) as 1 (B), 2 (F), etc. An asterisk after, or instead of, page references indicates discussion in 'Additional Notes …' (No. V of this volume), at pp.77–78 unless otherwise noted. The siglum R after a page number refers to the 'Retractationes'.]

(–) D.5 pr.: 66
( ) D.34 p.c.3: 66–67
(1) D.50 c.45: 57
(2) — c.46: 54, 65
(3) D.54 c.20: 54
(4) C.1 q.1 cc.126–130: 61*
(5) — q.4 d.p.9 (*al.* c.6): 58*
(6) — — p.c.12 (§3 *fin.*): 58, 61, 67
(7) — q.7 c.26: 61*
(8) C.2 q.1 c.14: 60*
(–) — q.3 p.c.7: *[71R]
(9) — — p.c.8: *
(10) — q.6 c.28: 59–60
(11) — — c.29: 58–59*
(12) — — c.30: 58–59*
(13) — — c.31: 58–59*
(14) — — p.c.39: 54
(–) — — p.c.40: *
(15) — — c.41–d.p.41: 67 n.112*
(16) — q.8 c.2: 60*
(18) C.3 q.3 p.c.4: 61, *[71n]
(–) — q.6 p.c.2: *[71f.]
(19) — q.7 p.c.1–c.2: 58, 69, *[71R]
(20) — q.8 c.1 §2: 60–61*[73n]
(21) — q.9 p.c.15: 54*
(22) — — p.c.18: 58
(23) — q.11 c.2: *

(24) C.3 q.11 p.c.3–p.c.4: *[73n]
(25) C.4 q.2 & 3 p.c.2–c.3: 61, 69*
(26) — q.4 p.c.2: 61
(28) C.5 q.3 p.c.1: 69 n.120*
(29) — q.6 p.c.3: 54 n.45
(30) C.6 q.1 cc.22–23: 54 n.45, 60, 62–63*
(31) — q.4 c.7 (*al.* q.5 c.2; *al.* q.4 c.4): 61*
(32) C.10 q.2 cc.1–3: 61, 63–64*
(–) C.11 q.1 cc.1,5,36: *[70n]
(33) C.11 q.1 p.c.9: 55 n.51, 69 n.120*
(34) C.12 q.2 p.c.58–c.60: 69 n.120
(35) C.15 q.1 c.2: 58
(–) — q.3 pr.: 67–68
(36) — — q.3 cc.1–3: 68
(37) — — c.4: 60, 63
(–) — — p.c.4: 68–69
(38) C.16 q.1 p.c.40 (*al.* c.40 §§3–4): 70
(39) — q.3 p.c.15–p.c.16: 64–65
(40) C.17 q.4 p.c.29: 56, 58
(41) C.19 q.3 c.9: 54 n.48
(42) C.25 q.2 cc.14–15: 65
(43) — — p.c.16: 54 n.45, 65
(44) C.32 q.1 p.c.10: 54–55, 65
(45) De poen. D.1 cc.6–21: 58
(46) C.36 q.2 c.3: 54 n.46, 65

ADDITIONAL NOTES ON THE ROMAN LAW IN GRATIAN

This essay by Kuttner is a supplement to n. IV, published in 'Seminar' one year later. It was inspired by a study of *J. Rambaud-Buhot* on an early Abbreviatio decreti in a Parisian manuscript and also deals with the Abbreviatio of *Omnebene* (ca. 1156). Here Kuttner explicitly argues for distinguishing stages of revision in the Decretum (p. 70). But he does not resolve the question whether we have to do 'with an original multiple recension' or 'with later accretions due to the activities of the earliest glossators'. He hopes that 'a secure answer will be possible in times to come' (p. 34). Winroth's discovery of the two recensions has given that 'secure answer'. (P.L.)

In last year's volume of this magazine, the critical problems connected with the texts of Roman law in the *Decretum Gratiani* were discussed by the present writer.[1] The article was designed to correlate and supplement with new observations the evidence which Guido Grandi ("Diomede Brava") in the eighteenth century and, recently, Professor Vetulani have assembled to show that the numerous excerpts from the legislation of Justinian found in Gratian's work were inserted only at a late stage of redaction. Meanwhile, Vetulani's conclusions have been corroborated by new findings made in the course of an inquiry into the manuscripts of Gratian preserved in France, an inquiry which is at present being conducted by a group of French scholars under the inspiring direction of Madame Jacqueline Rambaud-Buhot, of the manuscripts division of the Bibliothèque Nationale.[2] The new findings, first presented by Mme. Rambaud at the *Journées d'histoire du droit* in Paris, 6 June 1953, are now discussed in her paper, "Le 'Corpus Juris Civilis' dans le Décret de Gratien."[3] Since the two articles, hers and mine, were published without either writer's being aware of the other's parallel endeavors, the following notes are offered by way of a supplement.

---

1 S. Kuttner, "New Studies on the Roman Law in Gratian's Decretum," *Seminar* 11 (1953) 12–50, hereafter cited as K.
2 Cf. the articles cited in K. p.16 n.16.
3 J. Rambaud-Buhot, "Le 'Corpus Juris Civilis' dans le Décret de Gratien d'après le manuscrit lat. nouv. acq. 1761 de la Bibliothèque Nationale," *Bibliothèque de l'École des chartes* 111 (1953 [1954]) 54–64, hereafter cited as R.

1. In the thirty Gratian manuscripts of the Bibliothèque Nationale and in nine manuscripts of other Parisian and provincial libraries which were examined by Mme. Rambaud and her associates, omissions, interpolations, uncertainties of position, and other transcriptional disturbances of one or another Roman law text have come to light.[4] Even more revealing, however, are two of the earliest *Abbreviationes decretorum,* one being the anonymous MS *nouv. acq. lat.* 1761 of the Bibliothèque Nationale, which heretofore was generally considered a mere uncompleted copy of Gratian's work (it breaks off with C.12 q.2 c.39[5]), but which Mme. Rambaud has established as a peculiar abridgment written in northern Italy *c.* 1160–1170;[6] the second is known as the work of Master Omnebene (Omnibonus), *c.* 1156, and in many respects amounts to more than a straight *abbreviatio,* in that its author frequently replaces Gratian's *dicta (paragraphi)* by summaries and expositions of his own.[7] Omnebene's epitome had a respectable manuscript tradition;[8] its literary relations to other works of the early decretists deserve a fresh examination.[9]

2. As for the *Abbreviatio* of MS *nouv. acq. lat.* 1761 (= *Pa*), Mme. Rambaud, after describing its characteristic traits in general, states that the manuscript does not contain any of the canons and dicta which in the standard text of Gratian quote or cite passages directly from the Digest, the Code, and the *Authenticae.*[10] However, with regard to the dicta the evidence offered is not quite conclusive. R. p.58 n.5 lists the following as absent from *Pa*: C.1 q.4 p.c.9, p.c.12 (=Nos. 5–6 of our list,

---

4 R. pp.60–64.
5 Kuttner, *Repertorium der Kanonistik* (Città del Vaticano 1937) 108.
6 R. pp.54–9.
7 R. pp.54–5, 60. In another, forthcoming paper, Mme. Rambaud will present the evidence for the proposed reassessment of Omnebene's work as a combination of *summa* and *abbreviatio.*
8 Seven MSS listed in *Repertorium* 259 (of which only Bibl. Nat. MS lat. 3886 was accessible to Mme. Rambaud); add the Vatican MS Reg. lat. 1039, which Maassen (*Geschichte der Quellen* [Graz 1870] 807) believed to be a copy of Cresconius' *Concordia canonum,* while Patetta considered it a MS of Gratian (*R. Accademia nazionale dei Lincei, Rendiconti*[6] 13 [1937] 432–3).— The statement that the Bodleian MS Tanner 8 of Omnebene presents in part I a different *Abbreviatio* (so *Repert.* 259, following Le Bras, who first recorded the MS) has upon re-examination proved to be mistaken. (But the initium, "Humanum genus" *rell.,* which is the only argument adduced for Omnebene by A. Teetaert, "Commentationes historiae iuris canonici," *Collectanea Franciscana* 14 (1944) 243, remains inconclusive, since it merely reproduces Gratian's opening sentence.)
9 Such relations can be established, e.g., with the *Abbreviatio Lex alia* (cf. *Traditio* 7 [1949/51] 294 n.13) and the *Summa Sicut uetus testamentum* of Florence, Bibl. Naz. MS *Conv. soppr.* G.IV.1736 (*Trad.* 1 [1943] 279 n.1; a fragment also in Madrid, Bibl. Nac. MS 87, cf. G. Fransen, in *Revue d'histoire ecclésiastique* 48 [1953] 230). One of the common characteristics of these is the application of St. Jerome's trichotomic division of the Old Testament (*lex—prophetae—hagiographi*) to the concept of *lex divina* (Omnebene, D.1 p.c.1; for *Abbr. Lex alia* cf. *Repert.* 262) and its extension by analogy to the New Law (*euangelium—epistule—expositiones et canonice sanctiones* in Omnebene; *iiii^{or} euangelia—dicta apostolorum—expositiones ... et institutiones sanctorum patrum* in *Summa Sicut uetus test.*), which in turn is based on Hugh of St. Victor, *De scripturis et scriptoribus sacris,* cf. Migne, PL 175.15.
10 The mention of Justinian's Institutes (R. p.58) is a slip of the pen, as the Decretum does not use this part of the *Corpus iuris.*

K. p.19); C.2 q.3 p.c.8 (No. 9), q.6 p.c.39 (No. 14), p.c.40 (introduction to No. 15), p.c.41 (No. 15), q.8 p.c.5 (No. 17); C.3 q.3 p.c.4 (No. 18), q.6 p.c.2 (on this Romanizing dictum see below, section 4), q.9 p.c.15 (No. 21), q.11 p.c.3 (No. 24); C.4 q.2 & 3 p.c.2 (No. 25), q.4 p.c.2 (No. 26); C.6 q.1 p.c.21, p.c.22, p.c.23 (No. 30 with the introductory and concluding statements); and C.11 q.1 p.c.9 (No. 33: R. p.59, not in p.58 n.5). But the dicta C.3 q.7 p.c.1, q.9 p.c.18; C.5 q.1 p.c.3, q.3 p.c.1, q.6 p.c.3 (Nos. 19, 22, 27–29) are not accounted for; this would seem to imply that *Pa* does, after all, reproduce 5 of the 33 Roman law passages usually contained in that portion of Gratian's text (pr.- C.12 q.2 c.39) which is covered in this manuscript.

However this may be, *Pa* strengthens the case for distinguishing stages of revision in the Decretum. An argument to the contrary, viz. that nothing can be proved by an *abbreviatio* because the epitomator might merely have suppressed the Roman texts he found in his complete model, is not valid. For, *Pa* preserves nearly all the fragments of Roman law which Gratian took over from intermediary canonical collections, especially from Ivo of Chartres.[11] Hence, no intentional elimination of Romanistic material as such, no anticivilian bias can be assumed as an explanation for the shape of the manuscript: the case parallels exactly that of the lost codex of Brava.[12]

3. The evidence from Omnebene (=*O*) points in the same direction, although the fact that a greater number of texts from the *Corpus iuris* is included in his work presupposes a more advanced stage of redaction in the model he abbreviated. Mme. Rambaud, who has published the data from *O* only for the part which corresponds to *Pa,* found that about one half of the texts absent from the latter do appear in *O.* Her tabulation,[13] when expressed in terms of our list, shows the presence of Nos. 5–7, 12–14, 15 (with the preceding dictum C.2 q.6 p.c.40, but dict. p.c.41 is considerably shortened), 17–18, C.3 q.6 p.c.2, Nos. 21, 23–24, 25 (shortened), 31. If we add the 5 passages not recorded as missing in *Pa* (Nos. 19, 22, 27–29), this amounts to 19 out of the 33 texts in question up to this point (C.12 q.2 c.39), plus C.3 q.6 p.c.2. The list differs from the one that can be established for Brava's lost manuscript (K. p.54: Nos. 2, 3, 11–14, 16, 20–21, 23, 33 ...), which includes only 11 numbers for this part of Gratian, the only common passages being Nos. 12–14, 21, 23, and the dictum just mentioned.

4. This dictum, C.3 q.6 p.c.2, belongs to the noteworthy class of statements in Gratian's work which show some proficiency in Roman law without expressly quoting from the sources. A few typical specimens were analyzed in last year's article;[14]

---

11 R. pp.57–8: only C.11 q.1 cc.5 and 36 are omitted. From Mme. Rambaud's list of the second-hand Roman law texts, the reference to C.11 q.1 c.1 "Gaius" (R. p.57 n.6) should, however, be stricken: Gratian here quotes not the Roman jurist but Pope Gaius of the Pseudo-Isidorian letter JK †157 (ed. Hinschius p.214). The reference to cc.21–28 of C.2 q.6 (R. p.57 n.5) should read cc.22–27.
12 K. p.54.
13 R. p.60 nn.1–3.
14 K. pp.66–69.

like some of these,[15] the present dictum leaves the impression of an amateur's insecure grasp of the technicalities involved in his source materials:

> Exceptio fori dilatoria est atque ideo in initio litis debet opponi et probari. Peremptorias autem exceptiones (ut sunt prescriptiones longi temporis) sufficit in initio litis contestari.

The little distinction is based, as the glossators were quick to notice, on CJ. 8.35.8 ("Praescriptionem peremptoriam, quam ante contestari sufficit ..."), *ibid.* 13 ("Praescriptionem fori in principio a litigatoribus opponendas esse legum decrevit auctoritas"), and 4.19.19 ("Exceptionem dilatoriam opponi quidem initio, probari vero postquam actor monstraverit quod adseverat oportet").[16] But the assertion that the *exceptio fori* has to be pleaded *and proved* at the outset of the suit *because* it is a dilatory exception is founded on a premise which the sources won't bear out; it was left, however, to later canonists to rectify Gratian's notions concerning dilatory exceptions by more precise subdistinctions.[17]

In some manuscripts, the texts from Justinian's Code are themselves found interpolated at this place;[18] moreover, Gratian's dictum appears for a second time in many manuscripts, at a not very distant place within the same *Causa,* i.e. at the end of C.3 q.3 p.c.4 (§7), where it follows upon a series of Roman law texts on judicial adjournments.[19] This duplicate is generally considered a *palea,*[20] but its presence in some of the oldest manuscripts may argue for an original duplication, which was eliminated as "chaff" by the schools at an early date.[21] To all these signs of instability of the textual tradition we have now to add the evidence of *Pa,* where the dictum is also absent from its "authentic" place, q.6 p.c.2.

---

15 Cf. K. p.66 for D.34 p.c.3; pp.67–69 for C.15 q.3 pr. and p.c.4.
16 Cf. *Glossa ord.* v. *exceptio;* also (on the parallel passage, C.3 q.3 p.c.4 § 7) the marginal note of the *Correctores Romani,* Boehmer's note *o,* and Vetulani, "Gratien et le droit romain," *Revue historique de droit français et étranger*[4] 24–25 (1946–47) 20.
17 *Exceptio declinatoria iudicii—dilatoria solutionis:* e.g., Ricardus Anglicus, *Ordo iudiciarius* 28 (ed. Wahrmund, *Quellen* II 3 [Innsbruck 1915] 89); *Glossa Palatina* C.3 q.3 *fin.* (Vatican MS Pal. lat. 658, fol. 35rb); *Glossa ord. loc. cit.* Cf. also the Accursian gloss on CJ. 4.19.19 v. *exceptionem.*
18 Boehmer nn.22, 23 on C.3 q.6 p.c.2.
19 The last of the excerpts preceding C.3 q.3 p.c.4 § 7 is the *Auth. Quod fieri* of CJ. 3.11.2 (*ex* Nov. 53.1): evidently the cause of the mistaken identification by Mme. Rambaud of C.3 q.6 p.c.2 with Nov. 53.1 (R. p.62).
20 *Summa Parisiensis ad loc.* (ed. McLaughlin p.119); *Corr. Romani* note β; Boehmer n.52; Friedberg n.70 (= *palea* No. 86); M. Boulet-Sautel, "Les 'Paleae' empruntées au Droit romain ...," *Studia Gratiana* I (Bologna 1953) 154, 157.
21 Cf. K. p.14; W. Ullmann, "The Paleae in the Cambridge Manuscripts of the Decretum," *Studia Gratiana* I 168ff., esp. 172–4 (who overlooks, however, the pun implied in the double meaning of the sobriquets *palea* and *granum*—the allusion to Paucapalea and Gratianus being twisted into "chaff" and "grain"—when he tries to revive the humanists' pseudo-etymology, *palea* < πάλιν).—Huguccio had nothing to say about C.3 q.3 p.c.4 §7, cf. F. Gillmann, in *Archiv für katholisches Kirchenrecht* 88 (1908) 475, but the *Glossa Palatina* commented on exceptions in this place (cf. n.17 *supra*) and not in q.6 p.c.2.

5. A number of observations made in last year's article with regard to the textual tradition of the Roman law passages Nos. 1–33 can now be supplemented by Mme. Rambaud's findings in other manuscripts of Gratian.[22] The following survey is given, in general, without further reference to the omission of such passages in *Pa* and *O*.[23]

(4) C.1 q.1 cc.126–130, enlarged in some MSS by CJ. 9.27.2, 3 (K. p.61): several such MSS listed, R. p.62–3.

(5) C.1 q.4 p.c.9, missing in some MSS, designated as *palea* in others, variations of position (K. p.58): several MSS listed, R. pp. 60 n.4 (omissions), 61 (transposed, also in *O*), 64 (*palea* in one MS).

(7) C.1 q.7 c. 26, followed sometimes by CJ. 1.3.30 according to *Summa Parisiensis* (K. p.61): cf. R. p.62–3 (several MSS) and L. Guizard, in *L'Année canonique* 2 (1953) 87 (Ste.-Geneviève MS 342).

*(9) C.2 q.3 p.c.8, a *summula* on the delicts of accusers (*calumnia, tergiversatio, praevaricatio*), absent from Haenel's codex[24] (Friedberg's F; cf. his n.87 *ad loc.*) and *Br* (Brava § 36): also from *Pa* and *O*, R. pp.58 n.5, 60.

(11, 12, 13) C.2 q.6 cc. 29–31, provided in some MSS with inscriptions citing the Roman jurists by name and book (K. p.59): several MSS listed, for cc. 30–31 only, R. p.62–3.—Paul Dig. 49.5.3 inserted in c.30 (K. p.59 n.64): other MSS listed, R. p.62–3, for c.31 (? this would seem to be out of place, since c.31 is made up from Dig. 49.6 and 7, but c.30 from Dig. 49.5).—*In c.29 §3 from Ulp. Dig. 49.4.1.7, the passage here bracketed, "[Dies autem istos ... erit. Quare] si forte ...," which appears in the older editions, is a later insertion (cf. Boehmer, nn.65, 67 *ad loc.*; Friedberg n.298 *ad loc.*): addition found in Bibl. Nat. MS 3893, listed as *palea* in Douai MS 585, R. pp.63, 64.

*(15) C.2 q.6 c.41-dict. p.c.41, omitted in *Br* together with Gratian's preceding dictum (p.c.40, cf. Brava § 41): the same in *Pa*, R. p.58 n.5.

---

22 Nothing new is added, however, by her observations on C.3 q.8 c.1 §2 (R. p.63: intrusion of a fragment from CJ. 7.45.14—this is merely No. 20 of the usual Roman texts, K. p.60) and C.3 q.1 c.4 (R. *ibid.*: inscription "Codicis libro VIII tit. 1" added—merely a verbal variant of the usual inscription of No. 24).

23 To repeat the evidence of these two and that of Brava's codex (=*Br*, cf. K. pp.53–56): *Pa* omits Nos. 1–18, 20–21, 23–26, 30–33; *O* om. Nos. 1–4, 8–11, 16, 20, 26, 30, 32–33; *Br* om. Nos. l, 4–10, 15, 17–19, 22, 24–32. Thus, 8 omissions are common to *BrPaO*, 9 to *BrPa*, 6 to *PaO*, while 5 each are peculiar to *Br* and to *Pa*—In the following survey, passages not expressly discussed in K. are marked by an asterisk.

24 This is now Leipzig, University MS Haen. 17. Haenel's own description, "Ueber eine ihm gehörige Handschrift des Decretum Gratiani," *Berichte über die Verhandlungen der kgl. sächsischen Gesellschaft der Wissenschaften* 29 (1877) 104–10, is still valuable, since Friedberg collated the MS only in part and had an unjustly low opinion of it (cf. his *prolegomena*, col. xii and xcvi–vii). In the light of recent discoveries concerning the instability of Gratian's *tractatus de poenitentia* in certain MSS (cf. K. p.48 n.16), it is of especial interest that the original scribe of cod.

(16) C.2 q.8 c.2, only as marginal addition in some of the oldest MSS (K. p.60): absent from other MSS, marked as *palea* in St.-Omer MS 433, R. pp.60 n.4, 64.

(21) C.3 q.9 p.c.15, present in *Br* (K. p.54), but not in *Pa* and in Mazarine MS 1287, R. pp.58 n.5, 60 n.4.

*(23) C.3. q.11 c.2, only as marginal addition in Haenel's codex (Friedberg n.9 *ad. loc.;* Vetulani p.21): absent from *Pa* and Mazarine MS 1287, R. *ibid.*

(25) C.4 q.2 & 3 p.c.2-c.3, shows formal inconsistency with dict. pr. and dict. p.c.3 (K. p.69): considerably shortened in *0*, R. p.60.

(28) C.5 q.3 p.c.1 (*al.* c.1 *fin.*), shows formal inconsistency (K. p.69 n.120), position varies in Vetulani's Cracow MS (*Apoll.* 1948 p.133): also in Bibl. Nat. MS 16899, R. p.61.

(30) C.6 q.1 cc.22–23, omitted in *Br* together with the preceding dictum (p.c.21 § 1, K. p.62–63): the same in *Pa*, where also the concluding dictum is absent, R. p.58 n.5.—In dict. p.c.22, one MS replaces Gratian's reference to CJ. 1.3.30 by quoting the fragment itself ("Quisquis igitur sanctam ...," K. p.63): the same in *O*, R. p. 61 ("Quisquam [?] hanc sanctam ...").

(31) C.6 q.4 c.7 *fin.*, absent from some MSS, of uncertain position in others, sometimes marked as *palea* (K. p.61): several MSS listed, R. pp.60 n.4 (om.), 61 (transp., also in *O*), 64 *(palea* in one MS).

(32) C.10 q.2 cc.1–3, of uncertain position (K. pp.63–64): shortened in several MSS, inscription from Nov. 120 (the source of many of the *Authenticae* here assembled) added in Bibl. Nat. MS 16898, R. pp.60 n.4, 63.

(33) C.11 q.1 p.c.9, inconsistency of inscription (K. p.55 n.51): text absent from *Pa, O,* and Bibl. Nat. MS 3884, R. p.59.

Among the capitula Gratiani marked with an asterisk C. 2, q. 3, Dict. p. c. 8 (no. 9) is already found in the first recension, whereas C. 2, q. 6, c. 41—Dictum p. c. 41 (no. 15) and C. 3, q. 11, c. 2 (no. 23) are only in the second recension. (P.L.)

Today one cannot doubt any more that the Roman law texts in Gratian were the outcome of a complex process of revising and adding. It is another question whether we have to do with stages of original, multiple recension or, as Mme. Rambaud is inclined to believe,[25] with later accretions due to the activities of the earliest glossators. Our materials at present do not suffice to resolve this question; it remains to be seen whether a secure answer will be possible in times to come.

THE CATHOLIC UNIVERSITY OF AMERICA

Haen. refrained from copying it, with the remark at the end of C.33 q.2: "Hic quidam interponunt penitentie tractatum, quem tamen iudicio rationis nos preterimus" (Haenel p.107, cf. Friedberg *loc. cit.*), whereas the canons *De poen.* D.1 cc.22–30, D.5 cc.2–7 and c.8 form part of an appendix he put at the end of C.11 q.3 (cf. Haenel p.106).

25 R. p.64.

LES DÉBUTS DE L'ÉCOLE CANONISTE FRANÇAISE*

This essay was first given as a lecture during the 'Journées d'Histoire du Droit' in Paris 1937. The lecture gave the first summary of the French school in medieval canon law. (P.L.)

SUMMARIUM. — Tractatur de variis operibus, pro maxima parte anonymis, saec. XII et XIII ineuntis, quae scholas scientiae canonicae post Gratianum etiam extra Bononiam, in Gallia necnon in provinciis anglo-normannis ortas esse demonstrant. De scriptorum habitudine ad Bononienses, ad facultates Theologiae et artium parisienses, ad ius civile, ad RR. pontificum decretales, et de exitu huius scholae aliqua adnotantur.

Il a existé des canonistes en France déjà à l'époque qui précédait le décret de Gratien; c'est-là un fait généralement connu: il suffit de citer à cet égard les noms d'Yves de Chartres ou d'Alger de Liége. Mais on ne peut considérer ces auteurs comme représentants d'une *école* canoniste: il n'y a école que du moment que se trouve professé un enseignement destiné à transmettre la tradition d'une doctrine. Et cette étape n'a été franchie qu'après l'apparition du décret de Gratien environ en 1140. C'est à partir de ce moment que l'on voit se former de véritables écoles décrétistes et qu'on peut parler d'une science canoniste proprement dite. Or, pendant des siècles, on n'a prêté attention qu'à l'histoire des anciens décrétistes bolonais, et bien que des personnalités comme Giraud le Cambrien[1] ou Jean de Salisbury[2] nous aient laissé des descriptions de l'enseignement canoniste à Paris

---

* Communication faite aux Journées d'Histoire du Droit Paris 1937. Nous avons conservé à ce travail le caractère de conférence et d'un premier essai de synthèse historique de données et de dates peu connues et peu explorées. Quant à la documentation de nos thèses, nous devons nous borner à renvoyer le lecteur aux recherches et à la bibliographie encadrées dans notre *Repertorium der Kanonistik* (1140–1234). *Prodromus Corporis Glossarum* I, Città del Vaticano 1937 (Studi e Testi, vol. 71) et à notre article *Sur les origines du terme Droit positif*, dans la *Revue historique de droit français et étranger*, IVme série, 15 (1936) p. 728 et ss.
1 cf. infra p. 88 et suiv.
2 cf. OTT, *Rhetorica ecclesiastica*, dans *Wiener SB* 125 (1891) VIII p. 49.

pendant la deuxième moitié du douzième siècle, on ne savait presque rien de l'histoire de cet enseignement et absolument rien des ouvrages qui en sont sortis. Et même après qu'au cours du dix-neuvième siècle on eut découvert quelques écrits des premiers décrétistes français — comme le Spéculum de Pierre de Blois trouvé par Lappenberg en 1831 ou la Summa Parisiensis trouvée par Maassen en 1857[3], l'historien classique de la littérature canoniste, von Schulte, qui avait lui-même trouvé et décrit encore d'autres ouvrages français (parfois à la vérité sans en reconnaître la véritable origine), pouvait émettre l'opinion que la science du droit canon en France au douzième siècle n'avait été que peu développée et n'avait guère d'importance[4]. Après Schulte d'autres savants (comme Singer, Thaner, Ott, Caillemer, Tanon et Gillmann) augmentèrent la liste des écrits décrétistes français[5], mais aucun d'eux ne fit l'effort de reconstituer dans cette liste le profil historique d'une école. Il est vrai que la découverte de tous les écrits qu'on connaissait, avait été plutôt une aubaine due au hasard que le fruit de recherches systématiques. Et c'est ainsi que les fouilles minutieuses auxquelles je me suis livré dans un grand nombre de bibliothèques de l'Europe occidentale et dont j'ai réuni les résultats dans mon Répertoire canonistique, nous ont révélé l'existence de presque autant d'ouvrages inconnus d'origine française que ceux qu'on connaissait jusquc-là. C'est ce qui m'encourage à entreprendre de donner ici une première esquisse d'histoire littéraire de cette école.

Le premier témoignage de la réception du Decret de Gratien nous est fourni par une *abbreviatio*, écrite en Provence vers 1150. C'est l'abbrevatio «Quoniam egestas», conservée dans sept mss. dont quatre sont munis de gloses, qui selon toute apparence ont utilisé les «Exceptiones Petri legum Romanorum»[6].

Kuttner starts with the Abbreviatio 'Quoniam egestas' of Gratian's Decretum as the earliest work, written ca. 1150 in the Provence. A major essay on this work was published by *R. Weigand*, Die Dekretabbreviatio "Quoniam egestas" und ihre Glossen, in: Fides et Ius. Festschrift für Georg May (Regensburg 1991), 249–265; also cf. *A. Gouron*, Le manuscript de Prague, Metr. Knih. J. 74; à la recherche du plus ançien décrétiste à l'Ouest des Alpes, ZRG Kan. Abt. 83 (1997), 223–248; also in: *A Gouron*, Pionniers du droit occidental au Moyen Âge (Ashgate 2006), no. I. Gouron discovered Elzéar d'Avignon as author of 'Quoniam egestas'. For „Quoniam egestas" cf. now also *E. de Leon*, La abreviación "quoniam egestas" del decreto de Graziano, in: P.Erdö/A. Szuromi (ed.), Proceedings of the Thirteenth International Congress of Medieval Canon Law Esztergom 2008 (MIC, Ser. C, Vol. 14, Città del Vaticano 2010), 303–310, comparing this abbreviation with other abbreviationes Decreti. (P.L.)

---

3 LAPPENBERG, dans *Zeitschrift für geschichtliche Rechtswissenschaft*, 7 (1831) p. 207. MAASSEN, dans *Wiener SB* 24 (1857) p. 11 n. 6.
4 SCHULTE, *Geschichte der Quellen und Literatur des Canonischen Reehts* ... I, Stuttgart 1875 p. 238.
5 Voir les indications bibliographiques des pages suivantes.
6 cf. *Repertorium der Kanonistik* p. 263 et s. — Découverte par SCHULTE, cf. *Wiener SB* 57 (1867) p. 221 et ss.

Mais la véritable pénétration scientifique du Décret ne commence qu'après le retour en France d'Etienne, le futur évêque de Tournai. Ayant étudié le droit canon à Bologne, il publia à Orléans après l'année 1160 sa fameuse Somme sur le Décret[7]. Cette somme était encore entièrement tributaire de l'école bolonaise; mais depuis et probablement sous l'influence d'Etienne le genre littéraire des sommes commence à fleurir en France même.

The date of the Summa decreti by Stephen of Tournai was now determined as being 1165 by *A. Gouron*, Sur les sources civilistes et la datation des Sommes de Rufin et d'Etienne de Tournai, BMCL 16 (1986), 55–70; or 1166 by *H. Kalb*, Studien zur Summa Stephans von Tournai (Forschungen zur Rechts- und Kulturgeschichte, ed. *N. Grass*, XII, Innsbruck 1983), 108–112. (P.L.)

Une *summa* proprement dite est un résumé systématique d'une matière destinée à l'enseignement[8] et qui ne s'arrête pas à donner une exégèse du texte. Le premier ouvrage de ce genre en France est la somme «Elegantius in iure divino» (dite Summa Coloniensis), publiée à Cologne vers 1169 par un clerc français[9]. Ce clerc avait fait ses études à Bologne et à Paris; aussi voit-on s'unir dans son ouvrage l'influence des Bolonais à celle des théologiens et des rhétoriciens de Paris. Quant à la méthode, l'auteur ne se borne pas, pour justifier ses déductions, à alléguer les canons, mais il en communique le texte, avec la tendance donc d'épargner au lecteur le travail de consulter lui-même le texte du Décret. Cette méthode, qui ne se trouve pas chez les Bolonais, est adoptée aussi par l'auteur de la deuxième somme parue en France, maître Odon de Dour, qui écrit son ouvrage, intitulé «Decreta minora», vers la même époque, en utilisant largement les dicta Gratiani et des passages d'Etienne de Tournai[10].

The author of the Summa 'Elegantius in iure divino' (Summa Coloniensis) was not a 'clerc français', but could be identified as Berthold (Bertram) of St. Gereon in Cologne, later bishop of Metz—cf. *P. Gerbenzon*, Bertram of Metz, the Author of 'Elegantius in iure divino' (Summa Coloniensis)?, Traditio 21 (1965), 510–511; and *P. Landau*, Die Kölner Kanonistik des 12. Jahrhunderts (Kölner rechtsgeschichtliche Vorträge, H. 1, ed. *D. Strauch*, Badenweiler 2008), 16–18. (P.L.)

Une troisième somme a été écrite entre les années 1175 et 1178 par un auteur anonyme originaire de la Carinthie. C'est la somme «Inperatorie maiestati» (dite Monacensis)[11], fortement empreinte d'influences théologiques et réthoriques parisiennes. D'une diction limpide et non interrompue par l'insertion de pièces justificatives, le grand succès de cette somme se manifeste par le grand nombre d'écrits qui en ont subi l'influence: notamment quatre sommes fragmentaires anonymes

---

7 *Repertorium* cité p. 133 et ss.
8 Définition de E. M. Meijers, *Sommes, Lectures et Commentaires*, dans *Atti del Congresso Internazionale di Diritto Romano Bologna-Roma 1933* I pag. 433. *Repertorium* cité p. 123.
9 Découverte par Maassen, cf. *Wiener SB* 31 (1859) p. 461; décrite par Schulte, dans *Wiener SB* 64 (1870) p. 93 et ss. — *Repertorium* cité p. 170 et ss. (avec bibliogr.).
10 *Repertorium* cité p. 172 et ss. (première description).
11 Découverte par Maassen, cf. *Wiener SB* 24 (1857) p. 13 n. 2, décrite par Singer, dans *Archiv für katholisches Kirchenrecht* 69 (1893) p. 369 et ss. — *Repertorium* cité p. 179 et s. (avec bibliogr.).

et le prologue de maître Pierre de Louveciennes[12]; et non moins certains écrits qui sortent du genre des résumés systématiques et dont nous aurons encore à nous occuper. Enfin même le grand Bolonais Huguccio a emprunté des arguments à la somme «Inperatorie maiestati».

The Summa 'Inperatorie maiestati' (Summa Monacensis) was not written in Carinthia, but in Paris already ca. 1173. Its author was *Peter of Louveciennes*. Cf. *P. Landau*, Master Peter of Louveciennes and the Origins of the Parisian School of Canon Law around 1170, in: Proceedings of the Fourteenth International Congress of Medieval Canon Law, Toronto 2012 (MIC, Ser. C, Vol. 15, Città del Vaticano 2016), 379–394. (P.L.)

Un esprit plus modeste que ce grand summiste carinthien, un moine de Clairvaux du nom d'Evrard, né à Ypres, étudiant des arts libéraux «et aliarum facultatum» à Paris, confesse dans son épilogue sa connaissance des ouvrages de quelques maîtres Bolonais: «Johannis, Rufini et aliorum». Il cache prudemment sous cet «aliorum» Sicard de Crémone auquel il a emprunté presque tout son opuscule et dont il imite la méthode, notamment en ce qu'il donne son précis systématique sous forme de questions et de réponses, d'où le titre «Summula decretalium questionum». On peut en fixer la date à l'année 1181 environ[13].

On n'ignore pas qu'à côté des sommes proprement dites les décrétistes du douzième siècle cultivaient encore un autre genre de traités systématiques, nommés eux aussi «summae», mais qui à l'élément synthétique du résumé ajoutaient l'élément analytique de l'exégèse du texte légal. Ce type littéraire, précurseur des «commenta» du treizième siècle, fleurissait chez les Bolonais[14]; et Etienne de Tournai l'introduisit aussi en France avec sa somme. Comme première de ces *sommes exégétiques* nous nommerons l'ouvrage anonyme «Magister Gratianus in hoc opere», écrit vers 1170. Bien que souvent influencé par Rufin et Etienne, il se plait à citer surtout des théologiens français et parfois même à se mettre en opposition avec les «magistri Bolonienses»[15]. Maassen, qui a découvert cette somme, lui a donné le nom de «Summa Parisiensis»[16]. Elle a influencé la somme «Antiquitate et tempore» que Savigny, Maassen et Schulte considèrent comme l'ouvrage de Rufin, mais dont l'origine française a été revendiquée avec succès par Tanon et Singer[17]. Nous trouverons des traces de la somme «Magister Gratianus» encore dans une collection de «distinctiones».

The Summa 'Antiquitate et tempore' had no French origin, but was written in Cologne by *Gottfried of St. Andreas*—cf. *P. Landau*, Die Kölner Kanonistik des 12. Jahrhunderts (see above), 18–21; and *P. Landau*, Die Dekretsumme 'Fecit

---

12 cf. *Repertorium* cité p. 181 et ss.
13 *ibid.* p. 187 et ss. (première description).
14 *ibid.* p. 123 et ss.
15 *ibid.* p. 177.
16 *Wiener SB* 24 (1857) p. 11 n. 6; 31 (1859) p. 465 et ss.
17 cf. *Repertorium* cité, p. 178 (avec bibliogr.).

Moyses Tabernaculum', ein weiteres Werk der Kölner Kanonistik, ZRG Kan. Abt. 96 (2010), 602–608. (P.L.)

L'influence de la Summa Monacensis, citée plus haut parmi les sommes proprement dites, s'étend d'ailleurs aussi aux sommes exégétiques: entre autres à la somme «Tractaturus magister»[18] et à la somme «Permissio quedam»[19], écrites l'une et l'autre dans les années 1179 à 1187. Cette époque est particulièrement riche en ouvrages de ce genre. Nous pouvons y placer encore deux sommes exégétiques de l'école parisienne: la somme «Reverentia» qui témoigne d'une remarquable connaissance de la philosophie contemporaine[20], et la somme «Et est sciendum» qui allait influencer la jeune école anglo-normande[21].

For the Summa 'Tractaturus magister' cf. now *P. Landau*, Die Dekretsumme 'Tractaturus magister' und die Kanonistik in Reims in der zweiten Hälfte des 12. Jahrhunderts, ZRG Kan. Abt. 100 (2014), 132–152. The Summa was composed in *Reims*; its author was probably *Jean de Breteuil*. For the Summa 'Permissio quedam' cf. *A. Gouron* 'Sur les gloses siglées d et p dans les manuscrits du XIIe siècle, Rivista internazionale di diritto comune 8 (1997), 21–34; also in: *A. Gouron*, Pionniers du droit occidental au Moyen Âge (Aldershot 2006), no. IV. Cf. also *T. Genka*, Die Hallenser Handschrift ULB Ye 2° 52 im Licht der Überlieferung der Summa Permissio quedam zum Dekret Gratians, in: *P. Carmassi/G. Drossbach* (ed.), Rechtshandschriften des deutschen Mittelalters. Produktionsorte und Importwege (Wolfenbütteler Mittelalter—Studien 29, Wiesbaden 2015), 147–165. The authors of 'Permissio quedam' were the jurists *Donnedieu* (Donadeus) and *Ponce de Saint-Césaire* in Southern France (Provence) around 1185/86. (P.L.)

The Summa 'Reverentia sacrorum canonum', composed around 1187, is only preserved by a manuscript in Erfurt. It is also a product of the Cologne school of canon law; its author was probably a pupil of Gérard Pucelle. Cf. *P. Landau*, Die Kölner Kanonistik des 12. Jahrhunderts (above at p. 81), 21–24; and *P. Landau*, Gérard Pucelle und die Dekretsumme Reverentia sacrorum canonum. Zur Kölner Kanonistik im 12. Jahrhundert, in: *B. d'Alteroche* et al. (ed.), Mélanges en l'honneur d'Anne Lefebvre-Teillard (Paris 2009), 623–638. An edition of 'Reverentia sacrorum canonum' will soon be published by John Wei. (P.L.)

En effet pendant ces années, une nouvelle branche se détache de l'école française. Vers 1186 un Normand, après avoir étudié à Paris, rédige une grande somme exégétique où se mêlent les influences des décrétistes bolonais, du théologien parisien Gérard Pucelle et de la somme parisienne «Et est sciendum» que nous mentionnions tout à l'heure. Il s'agit du riche commentaire «Omnis qui iuste» (dit

---

18 *ibid.* p. 184 et ss. (première description).
19 *ibid.* p. 192 et ss. Découverte et décrite par SCHULTE, dans *Wiener SB* 64 (1870) p. 184; 65 (1870) p. 63 et ss., qui pourtant n'a pas reconnu l'origine' française.
20 *Repertorium* cité p. 194 (première description).
21 GILLMANN, dans *Archiv für katholisches Kirchenrecht* 106 (1926) p. 523 n. 2; 107 (1927) p. 192 et ss. — cf. *Repertorium* cité p. 195 et s.

Summa Lipsiensis)[22] qui a été connu même du Bolonais Huguccio, mais auquel on est redevable avant tout de l'initiation aux études canonistes des deux côtés de La Manche: deux autres sommes-commentaires parues dans ces pays[23] se trouvent en étroite relation avec «Omnis qui iuste», et la même école anglonormande devait produire encore vers la fin du siècle une quatrième somme, celle-là non-exégétique, la somme «Prima primi uxor» où ont été introduites en outre des doctrines de Huguccio[24].

For 'Et est sciendum' cf. now P. *Landau*, Der Dekretglossenapparat «Et est sciendum»—ein Werk des Kanonisten Rodoicus Modicipassus, Rivista Internazionale di Diritto comune 24 (2013), 19–26. It has close relations to the Summa Lipsiensis; its author was the English canonist Rodoicus Modicipassus, who wrote it in Sens 1181–1185. The Summa Lipsienis ('Omnis qui iuste iudicat') can also be assigned to Rodoicus Modicipassus—cf. P. *Landau*, Rodoicus Modicipassus—Verfasser der Summa Lipsiensis?, ZRG Kan. Abt. 92 (2006), 340–354. (P.L.)

En France, pendant cette dernière période du douzième siècle, nous ne possédons que le fragment «Quamvis leges seculares»[25]. Et c'est seulement au treizième siècle, entre les années 1206 et 1210, que va paraître un dernier ouvrage de la catégorie des sommes exégétiques. C'est la somme «Animal est substantia» (dite Bambergensis), la plus étendue des sommes françaises et qui est caractérisée par le large emploi qu'elle fait du droit romain, dont elle allègue les sources avec une abondance jusqu'alors inconnue chez les canonistes[26].

For the fragmentary Summa 'Quamvis leges seculares' cf. also B. *Tierney*, Two Anglo-Norman Summae', Traditio 15 (1959), 483–491. (P.L.)

The Dutch legal historian Chris Coppens recently developed a very probable hypothesis about the author of 'Animal est substantia': it was *Reginald of Orléans* (1183–1220), a Parisian canonist, who taught canon law in Paris 1206–1210 and later entered the Dominican order in 1217. Cf. C. *Coppens*, L´auteur d'Animal est substantia: une hypothèse, in: B. d' Alteroche et al. (ed.), Mélanges en l'honneur d'Anne Lefebvre-Teillard (Paris 2009), 289–298. Cf. also C. *Coppens*, "Roma communis nostra patria", in: V. Colli/E. Conte (ed.), Iuris Historia. Liber Amicorum Gero Dolezalek (Berkeley / Cal. 2008), 177–191. (P.L.)

Cet ouvrage termine la liste des sommes françaises au Décret. Pendant l'époque relativement courte de 1169 à 1210 environ on a donc vu se développer une activité prodigieuse dans ce genre littéraire. Mais ce n'est pas seulement dans les résumés systématiques et dans les commentaires exégétiques que l'école excellait. Par exemple quelques écrits importants nous ont été conservés en outre sous la forme de Distinctiones.

---

22 Découvert et décrit par Schulte, dans *Wiener SB* 66 (1870) p. 51 et ss. — cf. *Repertorium* cité p. 196 et ss.
23 Décrites pour la première fois dans notre *Repertorium* p. 198 et ss.
24 *ibid.* p. 205 et s. (première description).
25 *ibid.* p. 204 et s.
26 Découverte par Schulte, cf. *Wiener SB* 65 (1870) p. 59 et s. — *Repertorium* cité p. 206 et s.

La *distinctio*, comme méthode dialectique, est un des éléments fondamentaux de la science médiévale dans toutes ses branches: théologie, philosophie, science du droit etc. Elle consiste à établir des divisions et des subdivisions progressives d'une notion, d'un terme, d'un fait, d'une règle, d'une relation juridique[27]. Il ne faut pas confondre la méthode de distinguer, qui s'applique au besoin dans les gloses, les sommes, les questions etc., avec les Distinctiones comme genre littéraire, c.-à-d. les écrits composés exclusivement d'une série de Distinctiones qui se succèdent parfois librement et sans ordre, parfois selon l'ordre des diverses notions dans le système légal. Comme les sommes, les Distinctiones des canonistes doivent leur origine à l'école bolonaise[28]. Le premier en France à se servir de cette forme est l'auteur inconnu des Distinctiones Monacenses, un clerc de Westphalie qui écrit après 1170 sous l'influence de la somme «Magister Gratianus in hoc opere» (dite Summa Parisiensis) et non sans polémiser çà et là contre les «Bolonienses»[29]. Un autre ouvrage anonyme, les Distinctiones «Consuetudo»[30], dépend de la somme «Inperatorie maiestati» dont nous avons déjà mentionné l'influence sur toute la production canoniste française[31]. Cette influence s'étend aussi aux distinctions de Pierre de Blois le jeune, neveu du fameux épistolographe, qui écrit son opuscule vers 1180 à Chartres où il était chanoine. Ses distinctions, d'une originalité et d'une fraîcheur remarquables, ont été éditées en 1837 par Reimarus sous le titre de Speculum iuris canonici[32].

For the Distinctiones Monacenses we have now two modern editions: 1.) *A.J. De Groot* (ed.), Distinctiones 'si mulier eadem hora' seu monacenses (Rechtshistorische Reeks Gerard Noodt Instituut 36), Nijmegen 1996; 2.) *R. Sorice* (ed.), Distinctiones 'Si mulier eadem hora' seu Monacenses, MIC, Ser. A. Vol. 4 (Città de Vaticano 2002). The second edition is preferable—cf. *A. Gouron*, Sur les "Distinctiones Monacenses", RHDFE 81 (2003), 345–352, here p.346. (P.L.)

Cf. also *C. H. F. Meyer*, Gratian in Westfalen. Landesgeschichtliche Befunde zur Verbreitung kirchenrechtlicher Literatur um 1200, in: *V. Colli* (ed.), Juristische Buchproduktion im Mittelalter (Studien zur europäischen Rechtsgeschichte 155, Frankfurt/M. 2002). (P.L.)

Outre les sommes et les distinctiones, d'autres documents de l'approfondissement de la doctrine, cette fois au moyen de disputes casuistiques,

---

27 Voir E. SECKEL, *Distinctiones Glossatorum*, dans *Festschrift der Berliner Juristischen Fakultät für Ferd. von Martitz*, Berlin 1911 p. 281.
28 cf. *Repertorium* cité p. 208 et ss.
29 ibid. p. 215 et s. (avec bibliogr.). Ouvrage découvert par SINGER, cf. *Archiv für kath. Kirchenr.* 69 (1893) p. 378.
30 Découvert par SCHULTE, cf. *Wiener SB* 64 (1870) p. 137; décrit par SINGER *loc. cit.* p. 416, 420 et ss., 434 et ss.; classifié dans *Repertorium* cité p. 219.
31 supra p. 195.
32 *Petri Blesensis opusculum de distinctionibus in canonum interpretatione adhibendis, sive ut auctor voluit Speculum Iuris Canonici*.... ed. Th. A. REIMARUS, Berolini 1837. — Découvert par LAPPENBERG, cf. supra n. 3. — *Repertorium* cité p. 220 et ss.

nous ont été transmis sous la forme des *Quaestiones*. Je citerai pour la France du douzième siècle les Quaestiones Bambergenses où les cas faisant l'objet des disputes sont empruntés pour la plupart, vraiment ou fictivement, à la vie ecclésiastique de Paris et de Meaux[33]; puis les Quaestiones Andegavenses, riches en allusions à des événements dans la France d'alors[34]; les Quaestiones Laudunenses[35], et enfin les Quaestiones Londinenses de l'école anglo-normande[36], discutées et écrites après l'année 1192.

The Questiones Bambergenses were edited partially by G. *Fransen*, Les "Questiones" des canonistes I, Traditio 12 (1956), 566–592, and Les "Questiones" des canonistes II, Traditio 13 (1957), 481–501. (P.L.)

The Questiones Londinenses (ca. 1196/98) were partially edited by *J. Brundage*, Mediaeval Studies 24 (1962), 158–160, and Speculum 38 (1963), 448–452. (P.L.)

Une activité notable s'est déployée en France dans le domaine des monographies de *procédure canonique*, où il semble qu'au douzième siècle les Français aient même eu la préséance sur les Bolonais. Cette activité nous est attestée par le Ordo iudiciarius, écrit en 1171 environ à Amiens ou à Reims[37], édité par Kunstmann[38], par la Rhetorica ecclesiastica éditée par Wahrmund[39], ouvrage très intéressant par sa méthode et par son style purement rhétoriciens, écrit lui aussi probablement dans l'archidiocèse de Reims avant le troisième concile du Latran[40]; par le petit Ordo de Pierre de Blois[41], par le Ordo Bambergensis édité par Schulte[42], écrit entre les années 1182 et 1185 et dont on peut constater les relations avec les premières sommes de l'école anglo-normande[43]; enfin par la «Practica legum et decretorum» du normand Guillaume de Longchamps[44] qui devait être plus tard chancelier du roi Richard Cœur-de-lion et évêque d'Ely; publiée entre les années 1183 et 1189, editée par Caillemer[45]. Dans un autre Ordo, édité par Gross, il s'agit moins de droit canonique que d'un abrégé de

---

33 SCHULTE, dans *Wiener SB* 64 (1870) p. 137 et s.
34 *Repertorium* cité p. 251.
35 Note préliminaire dans notre *Repertorium* p. 255. Une révision du ms. (*Laon* 371-bis) en juin 1937 nous a révélé l'origine française ou bien normande, et la date de la composition: 1186 à 1192. On y reviendra dans un autre travail.
36 *Repertorium* cité p. 251 et s.
37 GILLMANN, *Zur Lehre der Scholastik vom Spender der Firmung und des Weihesakraments*, Paderborn 1920 p. 23 n. 1.
38 Dans *Kritische Ueberschau der deutschen Gesetzgebung und Rechtswissenschaft* 2 (1855) p. 17 et ss.
39 *Quellen zur Geschichte des römisch- kanonischen Prozesses im Mittelalter* I fasc. 4, Innsbruck 1906.
40 Cf. OTT *loc. cit.* (supra n. 2), *passim*, p. 67 et ss.
41 cf. THANER, dans *Wiener SB* 79 (1875) p. 228; SECKEL, *Distinctiones Glossatorum* p. 343.
42 Dans *Wiener SB* 70 (1872) p. 285 et ss.
43 FITTING, dans *Zeitschrift der Savigny-Stiftung, Romanist. Abt.* 6 (1885) p. 183; SCHULTE *loc cit.*
44 HAURÉAU, dans *Histoire littéraire de la France* XXVIII 1881 p. 498.
45 *Le droit civil dans les provinces anglo-normandes au XIIme siècle*, Caen 1883 p. 50–72 (Extrait des *Mém. de l'Acad. nationale de Sciences, Arts et Belles-Lettres de Caen*). cf. FITTING *loc. cit.*, p. 184 et s.

droit procédurier romain, destiné à l'usage du clergé[46]. Il a été écrit en France vers 1170.

Kuttner refers to six Ordines on procedure during the 12th century from France stating that the French authors had in this literature priority to the Bolognese authors. This priority has been confirmed by new studies—cf. *P. Landau*, Die Anfänge der Prozessrechtswissenschaft in der Kanonistik des 12. Jahrhunderts, in: *O. Condorelli* et al. (ed.), Der Einfluss der Kanonistik auf die europäische Rechtskultur I: Zivil- und Zivilprozessrecht (Norm und Kultur 37/1, Köln 2009), 7–23. For the Rhetorica ecclesiastica cf. *L. Fowler-Magerl*, Ordo Iudiciorum vel ordo iudiciarius (Ius commune, Sonderhefte 19, Frankfurt/M. 1984), 45–56, and *P. Landau*, Die 'Rhetorica ecclesiastica'—Deutschlands erstes juristisches Lehrbuch im Mittelalter, in: *F. Theisen/W.E. Voß* (ed.), Summe-Glosse-Kommentar (Osnabrücker Schriften zur Rechtsgeschichte 2.1, Osnabrück 2000), 122–139. This ordo was composed in the diocese of Hildesheim around 1160/61 and might have been the first work of classical canon law written in Germany. (P.L.)

The Ordo Bambergensis and the 'Practica legum et decretorum' by *William of Longchamp* are now edited in English translation by *B.C. Brasington*, Order in the Court. Medieval Procedural Treatises in Translation (Medieval Law and Its Practice 21, Leiden/Boston 2016), 182–196 and 203–275. (P.L.)

For the ordo 'Tractaturi de iudiciis', edited by *Gross* 1870, cf. *A. Gouron*, Une école de canonistes anglais à Paris: maître Walter et ses disciples (vers 1170), Journal des Savants 2000, 47–72; also in: *A Gouron*, Pionniers du droit occidental au Moyen Âge (Aldershot 2006), no. VI. I could identify this canonist Walter as *Walter of Coutances*—cf. *P. Landau*, Walter von Coutances und die Anfänge der anglo-normannischen Rechtswissenschaft, in: *O. Condorelli* (ed.), «Panta rei», Studi dedicati a Manlio Bellomo III (Roma 2004), 183–204. My identification was accepted by Gouron in his Addenda et Corrigenda to 'Pionniers', p. 3. (P.L.)

Jusqu'à présent nous n'avons pas encore examiné le genre littéraire qui est pourtant le plus caractéristique de la science médiévale des deux droits: à savoir les *gloses*. Or, pour les gloses au Décret il ne saurait être douteux que pendant le douzième siècle, l'école bolonaise ne l'importe sur l'école française. Parmi les quelque cent mss. du Décret munis de ces constellations multiformes de gloses qui caractérisent l'époque précédant la première Glose ordinaire, trois seulement décèlent l'origine française et quatre ou cinq seulement l'origine anglo-normande des gloses marginales[47]; tout le reste des mss. est aux Bolonais. Mais par compensation, c'est la France qui au début du treizième siècle nous donne le premier «apparatus glossarum» au Décret, c'est-à-dire le premier commentaire marginal cohérent et publié tel quel, contrastant donc avec les combinaisons variables de

---

[46] *Incerti auctoris Ordo iudiciarus, pars Summae Legum et Tractatus de praescriptione*, ed. C. Gross, Innsbruck 1870. Voir la préface de l'éditeur.
[47] Cf. la liste dans notre *Repertorium* p. 9 et la description des mss. y cités aux pp. 13, 22, 25 et s., 36, 37, 40.

gloses hétérogènes du douzième siècle. Nous avons eu la bonne chance de pouvoir signaler ce premier Apparatus «Ecce vicit leo», écrit par un maître français peu après l'année 1202, en sept mss.[48] Ses affinités avec la somme «Animal est substantia», d'à peu près la même époque, sont évidentes; et sa valeur incontestable lui aurait certainement valu un succès encore plus grand, si la réception en France de la Glose ordinaire bolonaise de Jean le Teutoniqne n'avait pas marqué la fin d'une école décrétiste indépendante au nord des Alpes.

Kuttner mentions the Apparatus "Ecce vicit leo" on the Decretum Gratiani, preserved in two recensions (1202/1210). The author of this Apparatus was the Parisian canonist *Petrus Brito*—cf. *A. Lefebvre-Teillard*, Petrus Brito, Auteur de l'Apparat Ecce vicit leo?, Proceedings of the Thirteenth International Congress of Medieval Canon Law, Esztergom 2008, (MIC, Ser. C, Vol. 14, Città del Vaticano 2010), 117–135. Kuttner's thesis about the French school to have composed the first 'Apparatus glossarum' on the Decretum could be disproved by the discovery of the Bolognese Apparatus 'Ordinaturus magister' (ca. 1180–1190) with two recensions, cf. among others *R. Weigand*, Der erste Glossenapparat zum Dekret: 'Ordinaturus magister', BMCL 1 (1971), 31–41. (P.L.)

Permettez-moi, messieurs, d'ajouter à ce catalogue des écrits de l'ancienne école décrétiste française quelques observations d'ordre général. Ce qui nous frappe de plus dans cette école française, c'est l'anonymité de la plupart de ses ouvrages. Parmi les trente-neuf écrits que nous connaissons à présent[49], il n'y en a que six pour lesquels le nom de leurs auteurs nous a été transmis. Ce sont le prologue de Pierre de Louveciennes, les sommes d'Odon de Dour et d'Evrard d'Ypres, la Practica de Guillaume de Longchamp, enfin les distinctions et le Ordo iudiciarius de Pierre de Blois. Réussira-t-on à découvrir les auteurs de tous les autres ouvrages? Je l'ignore. Nous possédons certaines indications qui peuvent peut-être nous mettre sur leurs traces. Quelques lettres initiales nous sont offertes par les signatures des gloses ajoutées à la somme d'Etienne de Tournai dans un ms. de Berlin et dont Thaner a prouvé l'origine française[50]. A part les noms de Pierre de Louveciennes et de Pierre de Blois on y trouve les sigles M., G., O. et W.R. Au maître G. est encore attribué un prologue au Décret dans le même ms.[51] L'initiale O. nous cache-t-elle Odon de Dour? L'initiale M. Mathieu d'Angers, dont Giraud le Cambrien nous atteste l'enseignement[52]? L'initiale G. Gérard Pucelle, dont l'enseignement canoniste nous est confirmé par une citation dans la somme «Omnis qui iuste»[53]? Mais G. peut signifier aussi Giraud le Cambrien lui-même qui parle des cours qu'il a tenus à Paris[54]. Et comment conclure de l'attribution, déjà douteuse, de quelques gloses, à l'identification de

---

48 *Repertorium* cité p. 59–66.
49 (Y compris les trois mss. glosés du Décret).
50 *Wiener SB* 79 (1875) p. 211 ss., 225 ss.
51 *ibid.* p. 229.
52 GIRALDUS CAMBRENSIS, *opp.* ed. BREWER (*Rer. Brit. Scriptores* vol. XXI) I, London 1861 p. 48.
53 Cf. *Repertorium* p. 197 n. 3.
54 *Opp.* I p. 48.

l'un ou de l'autre des auteurs de ces gloses avec l'auteur anonyme de l'une ou de l'autre somme ou collection de distinctions etc? Et ne paraîtra-t-il pas également trop osé d'identifier le chancelier Guillaume de Longchamp ou le magister Rogerus Normannus, dont nous parle Giraud[55] et qui avait étudié à Bologne et tenu des cours à Paris, avec l'auteur d'une des sommes de l'école anglo-normande? On pourrait multiplier les hypothèses de ce genre en tenant compte de tous les noms de prétendus professeurs canonistes, cités au neuvième vol. de l'Histoire littéraire de la France[56]. Mais je crains quant à moi que, tant que nous ne posséderons pas de données plus précises[57], ce ne soit-là une entreprise par trop aventureuse, quelque légitime que soit notre désir de connaître le nom de tant de modestes savants.

Ce qui me semble plus important, c'est de fixer les traits caractéristiques de l'école française et de montrer quelles en sont les relations avec l'école bolonaise. Ce serait-là un beau champ d'études futures de critique littéraire. Je me bornerai ici nécessairement à quelques considérations générales. Les maîtres français ont utilisé et souvent cité les auteurs bolonais, et certainement ils les ont connus non-seulement par l'entremise d'"Etienne de Tournai, mais aussi directement. D'autre part on peut noter, en confrontant les écrits des deux écoles, des notions et des distinctions propres aux maîtres français, et non moins leur indépendance stylistique et terminologique. Cette indépendance est due surtout au lien étroit qui unissait au douzième siècle les canonistes français et la théologie, la philosophie, la rhétorique parisiennes. Presque tous les écrits de la première époque nous fournissent une preuve de cette liaison, tantôt par leur érudition philosophique et théologique, tantôt par le style qu'ils empruntent aux rhétoriciens[58]. Ces traits se retrouvent même chez le cardinal Laborans qui, si c'est à Rome qu'il composa sa Compilatio decretorum, avait dans sa jeunesse étudié à Paris[59].

Kuttner's thesis about the close connection of the French school of Canon Law with theology, philosophy and rhetorics was generally confirmed by recent research—cf. R Weigand, The Transmontane Decretists, in: *W. Hartmann/K. Pennington (ed.)*, The History of Medieval Canon Law in the Classical Period (Washington D.C. 2008), 174–210, here p. 208. (P.L.)

Mais au commencement du treizième siècle cette influence des facultés de théologie et des arts libéraux sur les canonistes français s'efface devant une orientation décisive vers le droit civil romain. Un exemple éclatant de ce changement, documenté surtout par le grand Apparatus «Ecce vicit leo» et la somme «Animal est substantia»[60], nous est fourni par Giraud le Cambrien, qui dans son autobiographie

---

55 *ibid.* p. 46.
56 p. 216.
57 cf. OTT *loc. cit.* (supra n. 2) p. 94 n. 5.
58 cf. par exemple notre *Repertorium* pp. 60, 171, 175, 179, 184, 191, 194, 207 et la bibliographie y citée, surtout SINGER dans *Archiv für kath. Kirchenr.* 69 (1893) p. 400; 73 (1895) pp. 42 et ss., 57 et s.
59 cf. *Repertorium* cité p. 268.
60 *ibid.* pp. 66, 207.

nous a non seulement transmis le «principium» de ses Disputationes parisiennes de l'année 1177, mais aussi un plaidoyer prononcé dans son procès devant le pape en 1202. Tandis que le Principium parisien, bourré de lieux communs rhétoriques, se plait à citer Pline et Sénèque[61], le plaidoyer de 1202 abonde en allégations du Code et de Digestes; les rares allégations du Décret et des Décrétales en sont, pourrait-on presque dire, étouffées[62].

Pourquoi l'école décrétiste française n'a-t-elle pas survécu aux premières années du treizième siècle et a-t-elle entièrement cèdé la place aux Bolonais? Je crois qu'on peut en trouver une forte raison dans les hésitations qu'inspirait aux Français le nouveau droit des décrétales des papes. On connait la lettre d'Etienne de Tournai où il se plaint de l'influence croissante des nouvelles collections de décrétales[63]; on connaît de même les lamentations de Pierre le Chantre à cet égard[64]. Et bien que les decrétistes français depuis la fin du douzième siècle commencent à alléguer par-ci par-là quelques décrétales, il semble qu'ils n'aient tout de même pas compris toute la portée du nouveau droit pontifical. Autrement on ne saurait s'expliquer le fait étrange qu'à côté d'une production abondante d'ouvrages relatifs au Décret il n'ait pas paru chez eux de commentaire aux décrétales[65] depuis la Compilatio prima jusqu'à Grégoire IX, ainsi donc pendant plus de quarante ans. Pendant cette période l'école bolonaise glosait, commentait, résumait les Compilationes Antiquae sans relâche et adaptait l'interprétation du Décret aux Décrétales.

Kuttner's thesis about the hesitation of French canonists to the ius novum in the papal decretals was already revoked by himself 1983 in the Retractationes to this essay (p. 290). For English commentaries to the new decretal law around 1185/90 cf. *P. Landau*, Studien zur Appendix und den Glossen in frühen systematischen Dekretalensammlungen, BMCL 11 (1981), 1–21, here pp. 8–21; also in: *P. Landau*, Kanones und Dekretalen (Bibliotheca Eruditorum 2, Goldbach 1997), 257–277. (P.L.)

Or, il est à considérer que déja pour les ouvrages du douzième siècle, le succès effectif des Bolonais était plus grand que celui des Français; le nombre de mss. des écrits publiée de part et d'autre nous en fournit la preuve. Par exemple, nous connaissons trentetrois mss. de la somme de Huguccio, vingt-quatre de la somme de Sicard de Crémone et même quarante mss. de celle de Jean de Faenza[66], alors que la plupart des sommes françaises ne nous sont conservées que dans un seul exemplaire, que quelques-uns seulement de ces ouvrages existent en deux ou trois

---

61 GIRALDUS, *opp.* I p. 46.
62 *ibid.* p. 146 et ss.
63 cf. DENIFLE, *Die Universitäten des Mittelalters bis 1400* I, Berlin 1885 p. 745 n. 1.
64 cf. *opp.* in MIGNE, *Patrol. lat.* 205 col. 164. Pour l'influence de Pierre le Chantre sur les canonistes français voir notre *Repertorium* pp. 60, 180[4], 207. Des traces du prologue de Pierre à son «Verbum abbreviatum» se délignent dans maintes écrits canonistes.
65 Il n'y a que sur l'origine de l'apparatus «Militant siquidem patroni» à la Compilatio I (*Repertorium* p. 326) que je n'ose pas encore me prononcer définitivement.
66 Voir les listes de mss. dans notre *Repertorium* pp. 143 et ss., 150 et s., 155 et ss.

mss.[67] et que le nombre de sept, atteint par l'Apparatus «Ecce vivit leo» et celui de dix, atteint par les distinctions de Pierre de Blois[68], sont tout-à-fait exceptionnels. Si l'on ajoute à ces données statistiques l'empressement des Bolonais à s'occuper du nouveau droit des décrétales, contrastant avec la réserve observée par les Français, on comprend que le sort des deux écoles ait été si différent. La gloire bolonaise continuait à briller d'un éclat égal, tandis que l'ancienne école décrétiste française fut bientôt oubliée. Le souvenir en était déjà effacé quand, après les Décrétales de Grégoire IX, une nouvelle école canoniste française apparut, illustrée par les grands noms de Henri de Suse, de Pierre de Sampson, de Guillaume Durand et de tant d'autres. Mais c'est-là un nouveau chapitre qui va s'ouvrir et qui est beaucoup mieux connu que celui dont nous avons essayé de vous donner un bref aperçu.

---

67 *Repertorium* cité pp. 170, 178, 181, 183, 192, 195, 196, 215, 219.
68 *ibid.* p. 59 et p. 220.

BERNARDUS COMPOSTELLANUS ANTIQUUS
A Study in the Glossators of the Canon Law[1]

1. Master Bernard, archdeacon of Compostella, and a member of the Canon Law School of Bologna in the early thirteenth century, is generally known as the author of a collection of decretals which he compiled in 1208 at the Roman Curia, with the aid of Pope Innocent III's registers, covering the first ten years (February 22,

---

[1] Abridged references will be made in this article to the following publications:
(i) Periodicals: *Archiv für katholisches Kirchenrecht* = *AKKR*; *Revue (.Nouvelle Revue) historique de droit français et étranger* = *RHD (Nouv. RHD)*; *Sitzungsberichte der kaiserlichen Akademie der Wissenschaften in Wien, philosophisch-historische Klasse* = *SBWien*; *Zeitschrift der Savigny-Stiftung für Rechtsgeschichte, Kanonistische (Romanistische) Abteilung* = *ZRGKan (ZRGRom)*.
(ii) Reference works: K. Eubel, *Hierarchia catholica medii aevi*, I (2d ed., Monasterii, 1913) = Eubel; A. Gloria, "Monumenti della Università di Padova, 1222–1318", *Memorie del Reale Istituto Veneto di scienze, lettere ed arti*, XXII (1882–1886), 232–670 = Gloria; Ph. Jaffé, *Regesta Pontificum Romanorum ab condita Ecclesia ad annum post Christum natum MCXCVIII*, 2 vols (2d ed., S. Loewenfeld, F. Kaltenbrunner, P. Ewald; Berolini, 1885–1888) = *JL (JK, JE)*; S. Kuttner, *Repertorium der Kanonistik (1140–1284); Prodromus Corporis Glossarum*, I (Studi e testi, LXXI, Città del Vaticano, 1937) = Repertorium; A. Potthast, Regesta Pontificum Romanorum inde ab anno 1198 ad annum 1304, 2 vols. (Berolini 1874–1875) = *Po.*; M. Sarti et M. Fattorini, *De claris archigymnasii Bononiensis professoribus*, 2 vols. (2d ed. Bononiae, 1888–1896) = Sarti; F. C. von Savigny, *Geschichte des Römischen Rechts im Mittelalter*, 7 vols. (2d ed., Heidelberg, 1834–1851) = Savigny; J. F. von Schulte, *Die Geschichte der Quellen und Literatur des Canonischen Rechts von Gratian bis auf die Gegenwart*, 3 vols. (Stuttgart, 1875–1880) = Schulte, *QL*.
(iii) Monographs and Articles: F. Gillmann, *Des Johannes Galensis Apparat zur Compilatio III, ... mit einem Anhang: Zur Inventarisierung der kanonistischen Handschriften aus der Zeit von Gratian bis Gregor IX* (Mainz, 1938; the first part but not the "Anhang", pp. 54–94, appeared also in *AKKR*, CXVIII [1938], 174–222) = Gillmann, *Zur Inventaris.*; id., *Des Laurentius Hispanus Apparat zur Compilatio III ...* (Mainz, 1935) = Gillmann, *Laur. Hisp.*; R. von Heckei, "Die Dekretalensammlungen des Gilbertus und Alanus nach den Weingartner Handschriften", *ZRGKan*, XXIX (1940), 116–357 = Heckel, *Gilb. Alan.*; Kuttner, "Eine Dekretsumme des Johannes Teutonicus", *ZRGKan*, XXI (1932), 141–189 = Kuttner, *Dekretsumme*', E. Th. A. Laspeyres, *Bernardi Papiensis Faventini Episcopi Summa decretalium ...* (Ratisbonae, 1860) = Laspeyres, *Bern. Pap.*; G. Post, "The So-called Laurentius-Apparatus to the Decretals of Innocent III in Compilatio III", *The Jurist*, II (1942), 5–31 = Post, *So-called Laur*; J. F. von Schulte, "Die Glosse zum Decret Gratians von ihren Anfängen bis auf die jüngsten Ausgaben", *Denkschriften der kais. Akademie der Wissenschaften in Wien, phil.-hist. Kl.*, XXI, ii (1872), 1–99 = Schulte, *Glosse*; H. Singer, "Die Dekretalensammlung des Bernardus Compostellanus Antiquus", *SBWien*, CLXXI, ii (1914), 1–119 = Singer, *Bern. Comp.*; A. Vetulani, "Projet d'un catalogue des manuscrits

1198–February 21, 1208) of that pontificate. Bernard's contemporary, the celebrated master Tancred, further tells us that the Spaniard's compilation was used by the school for some time as *Collectio Romana*, until in 1210 Pope Innocent promulgated an official collection of his decretals, arranged by his subdeacon and notary, Petrus Collivaccinus of Benevento. One of the Pope's reasons for issuing the authentic law book—the first of its kind in Church history—had been the fact that some of the decretals in Bernard's work, though genuine papal letters, were not considered by the Curia as universally binding.[2] The new official collection, commonly known as *Compilatio tertia*, at once superseded Bernard's private collection, and for centuries the latter was known only from hearsay until rediscovered in modern times.[3]

No wonder the figure of the old Spanish canonist soon became effaced; already Johannes Andreae (d. 1348) complained that writers confused our Bernard with his namesake, the younger Bernard of Compostella, who was a chaplain of Innocent IV and a renowned canonist about the middle of the thirteenth century.[4] But even Johannes Andreae had not much to say about *Bernardus antiquus*, save that his compilation had not long been in force, and that he had lectured and written glosses (*apostillae*) on the two first of the five *Compilationes antiquae*.[5] However, the *apostillae* seemed to be lost, and only a few references made to the Compostellan by his younger contemporaries have been traced so far.[6]

2. It is attempted in this study to reconstruct, from new discoveries in canonical manuscripts, the *oeuvre* of the half-forgotten Spanish master, i.e. his glosses on the *Decreta* of Gratian (ch. II), on the *Compilatio prima* (ch. III), and his

---

juridiques du moyen-âge conservés dans les bibliothèques polonaises", *Collectanea Theologica*, XVIII (1937), 436–451 = Vetulani, *Projet*.

Gillmann's articles 'Des Johannes Galensis Apparat zur Compilatio III' and 'Des Laurentius Hispanus Apparat zur Compilatio III' were republished in: *R. Weigand* (ed.), Gesammelte Schriften zur klassischen Kanonistik von Franz Gillmann. Schriften zu den Dekretalisten I (Forschungen zur Kirchenrechtswissenschaft 5/2, Würzburg 1993), no. 25 (Johannes Galensis) and Schriften zu den Dekretalisten II (Forschungen zur Kirchenrechtswissenschaft 5/3, Würzburg 1993), no. 29 (Laurentius Hispanus). (P.L.).

2 Tancred, preface to his *Apparatus* on *Comp. III*; cf. Singer, *Bern. Comp.*, pp. 3 (n. 2). 29; Kuttner, *Repertorium*, p. 319.

3 Cf. Singer, *Bern. Comp.*, p. 5 ff.; *Repertorium*, p. 317 f.

4 Joh. Andreae, *Additiones in Speculum Durantis*, lib. III, tit. *de inquis.*, §1, gl. *Puto quod non bene* (ed. Venet., 1577, III, 28vb, gl. *k*). On the younger Bernard, see G. Barraclough's biographical notes in *English Historical Review*, XLIX (1934), 487–494, and in *Dictionnaire de Droit Canonique*, II (Paris, 1937), 777–779; also Kuttner, *ZRGKan*, XXVI (1937), 455 f., *Studia et documenta historiae et iuris*, VI (1940), 73, n. 7. Two typical cases of confusion between the two Bernards are recorded in *Repertorium*, p. 318, n. 1.

5 Joh. Andreae, *Add. in Spec.*, preface, § *Porro*; cf. also the preface of his *Novella*. Both texts are reprinted in Schulte, *QL*, I, 240 f.; Singer, *Bern. Comp.*, p. 4, n. 4.—In *Repertorium*, p. 408, n. 2, I wrongly interpreted the passage "... et apostillas dederat super illas" as referring to some lost *Notabilia*, instead of glosses.

6 Joh. Hispanus de Petesella, *Summa decretalium* (c. 1236, cf. Schulte, *QL*, II, 81; Kuttner, *Repertorium*, p. 33, n. 1) cites several times a master *b.*, meaning probably the Compostellan; cf.

Quaestiones disputatae (ch. IV); also, some new observations concerning the *Compilatio Romana* will be offered (ch. V). The lengthy introduction (ch. I) is necessitated by the lack of a comprehensive history of the Canon Law Glossators in general, and in particular of Bernard's fellow canonists in Bologna with whose productions his own works were intimately connected. The general development, the trends, types and stages of gloss writing in the twelfth and the thirteenth centuries are even less well known than the figures of the individual glossators. A common prejudice conceives the history of medieval learning too often as but a mosaic of antiquarian curiosities; the history of glosses in particular is mostly considered as an arcanum, of no interest but to a few punctilious experts.[7]

This study contains also numerous and lengthy footnotes. Since I published, in 1937, a reference work which was intended as a first step towards a comprehensive handbook, new researches by others and by myself have brought out much additional information about medieval canonists: biographical data, newly discovered writings, bibliography and unclassified manuscripts. All information of this kind is recorded here in the temporary form of footnotes, as, owing to war conditions,[8] the continuation of the above mentioned reference book is not yet possible.[9]

I. Bolognese Glosses on Gratian, before and during Bernard's Time

3. About the year 1190, what might be called the first period of the Canon Law School of Bologna had come to its end. For nearly fifty years, the early generations of *Magistri decretorum* had put forth a series of remarkable *Summae*— sometimes systematic text books, sometimes detailed commentaries[10]—and written numerous glosses on the *Decreta*, as the School used to call Gratian's *Concordia discordantium canonum*.[11] The history of these glosses is one of the most intricate

---

Schulte, "Beiträge zur Literatur über die Decretalen Gregors IX ... ", *SBWien*, LXVIII (1871), 79. Quite recently, the late lamented Msgr. Gillmann disclosed in one of his last articles two quotations from *b. Conpostell'.*, the one made by an anonymous glossator of *Comp. I*, the other by Laurentius, on the same compilation, both in Erlangen, University Library, MS 349. Cf. Gillmann, "Petrus Brito und Martinus Zamorensis ... ", *AKKR*, CXX (1940), 64, n. 2.

Gillmann's article 'Petrus Brito und Martinus Zamorensis' was republished in *R. Weigand* (ed.), Schriften Gillmann 2 (see above), no. 22. (P.L.)

7 A similar complaint regarding the general neglect of medieval scriptural glosses was recently made by Miss Beryl Smalley in the introduction to her brilliant book, *The Study of the Bible in the Middle Ages* (Oxford, 1941).

8 Not even the fate and present whereabouts of all MSS in occupied countries can be ascertained. In this study, MSS are cited according to their pre-war location.

9 As to important publications, since 1937, by Gillmann, Post, Heckel and Vetulani, see above, n. 1.

10 Cf. *Repertorium* pp. 123–167. Two newly discovered works can be added: the *Summa "Sicut uetus testamentum"*, Florence, Natl. Libr., MS *Conv. soppr.* G. IV. 1736, on parts i and ii of Gratian, and the *Summa "Ius aliud diuinum"*, Milan, Ambrosian Libr., MS H. 94 *sup.* (fols. 73r, 74r-80v), covering D. 1–54 of pt. i only. Both writings belong to the early period of the school, c. 1148–1159.

11 The use of the singular number, *Decretum*, is of relatively recent origin. Cf. Kuttner, "The Father of the Science of Canon Law," *The Jurist*, I (1941), 15, n. 29.

problems of medieval research, for we have to remember that the time of the *Apparatus glossarum*, i.e. of the coherent marginal commentaries which were formally published by individual authors or compilers as definite literary works, was to come only in the beginning of the thirteenth century.[12] Until that time, the enormous bulk of gloss production was handed down, in Bologna as well as in the French and the Anglo-norman schools, in an embarrassing variety of mixed gloss compositions, i.e. in agglomerations of marginal and, sometimes, interlineary notes that grew gradually and irregularly, by a fluctuating process of selection and accretion of the materials in the respective schools. Among the numerous MSS of Gratian with glosses previous to the period of the apparatuses, hardly two will look exactly alike, and yet the mixed compositions are witnesses to a certain tradition in the schools.[13]

For the early glosses and gloss compositions of the Decretum Gratiani we have now the fundamental work by *R. Weigand*, Die Glossen zum Dekret Gratians, Studien zu den frühen Glossen und Glossenkompositionen, Stud. Grat. XXV and XXVI (Roma 1991). (P.L.)

At least 150 such MSS are still preserved,[14] and if we eliminate those representing the tradition of the Western schools,[15] we shall find that by far the

12 Cf. *Repertorium*, p. 59 ff.
13 *Op. cit.*, p. 1 ff.
14 Some 120 MSS are recorded in *Repertorium*, pp. 13–58; I can add now thirty more: Admont, Benedictine Monastery, MS 48; Cologne, Cathedral Libr. MS 129 (information furnished by Mr. R. Most); Florence, Laurentian Libr., MSS *S. Croce* I *sin.* 1 (sets i-iii of the various gloss strata), *Aedil. Flor. Eccl.* 96 (set i), *Acquisiti* 93 (set i); Natl. Libr., MSS *Conv. soppr.* A. II. 376 and A. II. 403; Graz, Univ. Libr., MSS 52 (set i), 69 (set i), 71 (sets i-iv), and 80 (set i) (formerly MSS 40/18, 40/4, 40/26, and 40/5 respectively); Heiligenkreuz, Cistercian Monast., MSS 43 and 44; Krakow, Bibl. Jagiellonska, MS 357 (set i; information furnished by Dr. Vetulani); Lilienfeld, Cistercian Monast., MSS 222 (sets i-iii) and 223 (set i); Milan, Canons Regular of St. Ambrogio, unnumbered MS; New York, Pierpont Morgan Libr., MS M. 446 (sets i-iv); Olmütz, Metropolitan Chapter, MS 266 (sets i-iv); Plock, Diocesan Seminary, MS 64 (sets i and iii; cf. Vetulani, *Projet*, p. 446); St. Paul in Lavant, Bened. Monast., MS XXV. 2.6 (formerly XXV. a/25); Treves, Municipal Libr., MS 907 (set i; information furnished by the Rev. P. J. Kessler); Venice, Marcian Libr., MS *lat.* IV. 117 (Valentinelli's catalogue, VIII. 16; set i); Vercelli, Cathedral Chapter, MS XXV (sets i-ii); Verona, Cath. Chapt., MS CLXXXIV (formerly 164; sets i-ii); Vicenza, Bibl. Bertoliana, MS 17 (formerly 15.2.2; catal. no. 627; sets i-ii); Vienna, Natl. Libr., MSS 2061 and 2102 (sets i-iii); Washington, D. C., Library of Congress, Law Division, unnumbered MS (set i); Zwettl, Cistercian Monast., MS 31.

On the other hand, the MSS of Einsiedeln, Bened. Monast., 193 and of Florence, Laurentian Libr., *Gadd. reliq.* 2 (formerly MS *Magliabecch.* XXXI. 46), listed in *Repertorium*, pp. 48.51 on a conjectural basis, are to be discarded: the first contains the *Glossa Ordinaria* of Bartholomaeus Brixiensis, the other fragments of the *Apparatus "Ecce vicit leo"* (cf. below §6, n. 50). In some other cases, again, our conjectural suppositions of early glosses have been confirmed: Lucca, Archbishop's Libr., MS 20 (formerly MS 6); St. Florian, Canons Regular, MS III.5; and (information by the Rev. Kessler) Cues, Hospital, MS 223; Treves, Diocesan Seminary, MS 8. Six further MSS (cf. *Repertorium*, pp. 18.19. 44. 48. 50) remain still unexplored.
15 Their number is more conspicuous than is commonly believed, and includes also some items not properly recognized in the *Repertorium*. Full evidence for the MSS (at least 25) of the French and the English Schools will be given on another occasion.

majority give account of some stage of Bolognese glossing between the forties and the eighties of the twelfth century. This was the period running from Paucapalea, Gratian's first disciple, to Huguccio, the teacher of Innocent III, and only a relatively small number of MSS[16] tells of the twenty odd years from that time to the first apparatuses.

The names[17] of Paucapalea[18] (in the forties), of Rufinus[19] (in the fifties), of John of Faenza,[20] Peter of Spain, Cardinalis and the theologian Gandulph (in the sixties and early seventies), of Simon of Bisignano[21] (in the later seventies), are the milestones on the way of the glossators before the time of Huguccio. Selections from

---

16 Some examples are cited in *Repertorium*, p. 9.
17 On the following glossators and their works, see *Repertorium*, s. hh. vv., and the bibliography given by A. Van Hove, *Prolegomena* (Commentarium Lovaniense in Codicem Iuris Canonici, I, i, Mechliniae-Romae, 1928) p. 223 f.
18 Add to the bibliography (n. 8): A. Mocci, "Documenti inediti sul canonista Paucapalea", *Atti della R. Accademia delle scienze di Torino*, XL (1905), 316 ff., who identifies the canonist with the homonymous bishop (since 1146) of S. Giusta, Sardinia (?).—Among the MSS of Paucapalea's *Summa* (*Repertorium*, p. 125 f.) the presumed fragment of Oslo has to be cancelled; according to recent information, it contains pieces of Stephen of Tournai's *Summa*.

For Johannes Faventinus cf. N. Höhl, Wer war Johannes Faventinus? Neue Erkenntnisse zu Leben und Werk eines der bedeutendsten Dekretisten des 12. Jahrhunderts, Proceedings of the Eighth International Congress of Medieval Canon Law, San Diego 1988, (MIC, Ser. C, Vol. 9, Città del Vaticano 1992), 189–203, and *Id.*, Die Glossen des Johannes Faventinus zur Pars I des Decretum Gratiani (Diss. Würzburg 1987), 17–38. (P.L.)
19 Add to the bibliography, for Rufinus' career and pastoral writings: Dom G. Morin, "Le discours d'ouverture du concile général de Latran (1179) et l'oeuvre littéraire de Maître Rufin, évêque d'Assise', *Atti della Pont. Accademia Romana di Archeologia*, Memorie, II (1928), 113–133.—Of Rufinus' *Summa* (cf. *Repertorium*, p. 131 f.), two new MSS were discovered by the Rev. P. J. Kessler in Monza, Cathedral Chapter: MS i. 18/156 (formerly T. VII, invent, no. ccxvii), and fragments in MS i. 19/161 (formerly T. XII, invent, no. ccxxiv; fols. 31–110), bound together with fragments of Stephen's *Summa*.

The Summa in Decretum written by *Simon of Bisignano* was recently edited by P. V. Aimone Braida, Summa in Decretum Simonis Bisianensis, (MIC, Ser. A, Vol. 8, Città del Vaticano 2014). (P.L.)
20 Add to the bibliography: J. Argnani, "Joannes Faventinus glossator", *Apollinaris*, IX (1936), 418–443; 640–658, who refutes conclusively (p. 418 ff.) Schulte's unwarranted identification of master John with an homonymous bishop of Faenza (*QL*, I, 137), and shows his true identity to be that of a canon of the cathedral chapter, 1174–1187. But Argnani errs in making (p. 424 f.) one person of this canon *magister Johannes* and a *Johannes presbyter* who subscribes chapter documents between 1203 and 1220. The further discussion on the writings of the glossator (pp. 425 ff. 640 ff.) is an absurd compilation from second hand sources, full of misunderstandings, inconsistencies and unacknowledged quotations.— For John's *Summa* (cf. *Repertorium*, p. 143 f.), add two new MSS: Krakow, Cath. Chapter, MS 88 (information by Prof. Vetulani), and Nürnberg, Municipal Libr. MS *Cent. IV. 94* (information by Mr. Most).
21 Add to the bibliography: A. Lambert, "Bisignano, Simon de", *Dictionn. de Droit Canonique*, II (1937), 900. For the *Summa* (cf. *Repertorium*, p. 147), add a copy of the prologue alone, Vienna, Natl. Libr., MS 2121, on the margin of fol. 84r. Among the MSS of Gratian listed above, n. 14, the copies of the Pierpont Morgan Library (set iv) and of Zwettl are particularly rich in Simon's glosses.

their glosses, as transmitted by the various consecutive mixed compositions,[22] and occasional glosses of minor decretists like *b.* (Bernard of Pavia?[23]), *d.* (David of London?[24]), *f.* (Fidentius? Philip?[25]) and *Ro.* (?—not the French master Rodoicus Modicipassus[26]), were the warp with which, in the eighties, Huguccio's generation interwove their own abundant productions, mainly that of the leading master

22 A critical account of the various types of these gloss compositions, with full MS evidence, is much needed, but beyond the scope of this study. Suffice it to say that the preliminary groupment of the MSS into three main types (*Repertorium*, pp. 3 ff. 13 ff.) can now be abandoned in favor of a more exact classification of at least five types from Paucapalea to Huguccio.
23 See below, §9.
24 For the siglum *d.* see *Repertorium*, pp. 19.51, also the new MSS (above n. 14) Cues 223, Treves Sem. 8, Vercelli XXV. Schulte proposed the authorship of a magister *D. canonicus Londiniensis* (*QL*, I, 151). If he were right, this would be the same master David of whose correspondence much was published from the MS *Vatic, lat.* 6024 by F. Liverani, *Spicilegium Liberianum* (Florence, 1863), pp. 554 ff. 603–628.735.740 f. (some letters are already in Sarti, II, 161 ff.). Recently, Z. N. Brooke, "The Register of Master David ... ", *Essays in History presented to R. L. Poole* (Oxford, 1927), pp. 227–245, analyzed in full the Vatican MS and sketched the career of David as a student of Clermont, Paris, Bologna, and as agent and procurator of bishop Gilbert Foliot.
   The canonist D. may be *Daifer*, discovered by Weigand—cf. *R. Weigand,* Die Glossen zum Dekret Gratians Teil III und IV, Stud. Grat. XXVI (Romae 1991), 630, referring to a gloss in the Summa Lipsiensis ad D. 54, c. 15. (P.L.)
25 The siglum *f.* occurs in Cues, MS 223 and in Munich, State Libr., MS lat. 10244 (cf. *Repertorium*, p. 19). Also the *Glossa Palatina* (see on this apparatus below, §6 C) quotes on C. 15, q. 6, c. *Auctoritatem* (2): "... quicquid dicat h (ugguccio), b. et f. dicunt ... " (Vatican Libr., MS *Pal. lat.* 658, fol. 56ra). Who was this *f.*?
   (i) A master Fidentius or Fidantius, *canonicus Civitatensis*—which might be Ciudad Rodrigo in Spain, or Città-Tempio in Sardinia, or Civitate in Calabria—was once entrusted by Alexander III with the decision of a case (*JL* n. 13854; the address is corrupted in almost all the decretal collections, cf. Singer, "Neue Beiträge ... ", *SBWien*, CLXXI, i [1913], 34, n. 1). But was this master ever a member of the Bolognese school?
   (ii) As to *f.* = Philip, chronological reasons rule out the only Italian master of that name who is found, in 1229, in the school of Padua (cf. Gloria, p. 547: Filippo d'Aquileja), and who wrote, after 1216, gloss additions with the sigla *ph., phi., phy., fi., f.*, on Gratian (cf. *Repertorium*, pp. 95.100), on the *Comp. I* (Admont, Bened. Monast., MS 22 [fols. 1–85v, in set ii]; Graz, Univ. Libr., MS 106 [formerly 41/9, fols. 1–90v, in set ii]), the *Comp. II* (Admont, MS *cit.*, fols. 86–128v, in set ii), and the *Comp. IV* (*ibid.*, fols. 246v–270, in set ii). Schulte also claimed to have seen his glosses on the *Comp. III* in Chartres, Municipal Libr., MS 296 (formerly 354; cf. *Repertorium*, p. 362) but according to my own inspection of the MS, he must have been mistaken.
   (iii) Finally, the siglum φ in glosses on the *Collectio Cassellana* (c. 1185–1187, cf. *Repertorium*, p. 293) points to a master of the French school, perhaps the *Philippus iureconsultus*, or the *Philippus Sarracenus, ... decreta et sacras claudens in pectore leges*, both of whom Gilles de Paris names in his poem, *Carolina* (1198), ed. Bulaeus, *Historia Universitatis Parisiensis*, II (Paris, 1665), 526.—Thus, the signature *f.* in the early Bolognese glosses remains a riddle—or is it simply a corrector's mark, for *falsum*, as Juncker, *ZRGKan*, XV (1926), 356, suggested?
   The master Phi. in the Collectio Cassellana was probably a German canonist—cf. *P. Landau,* Die Phi.-Glossen der Collectio Cassellana, in: *W. P. Müller/M. E. Sommar* (ed.), Medieval Church Law and the Origins of the Western Legal Tradition 'A Tribute to Kenneth Pennington' (Washington D. C. 2006), 159–169. (P.L.)
26 For the siglum *Ro.*, see *Repertorium*, pp. 20.49, also Salzburg, St. Peter's Abbey, MS a. XII. 9. Schulte counted Rodoicus among the Bolognese, as a member of the Picciolpassi family

himself, and that of Bazianus and Melendus.[27] Also included in the standard gloss compositions of this epoch were references to, or quotations from, scholars who only for a short time had belonged to the school and left no original glosses; as, e.g., Albert of Benevento who had become a Roman Cardinal in 1157 and was Pope Gregory VIII in 1187;[28] or Master Stephen who returned from Bologna to his native France before 1160 and whose long career ended on the episcopal see of Tournai.[29]

4. And now, about 1190, the intense activity of interpreting the *Decreta* came to a standstill. It was the time when Huguccio[30] had just published, after long years of writing, the great commentary, *Summa super decretis*, unfinished as

(*QL*, I, 186, cf. *Repertorium*, p. 20, n. 1). But master Robert Courçon, in his theological *Summa* (c. 1204–1208) had named Rodoicus Modicipassus among masters of the French school; cf. B. Hauréau, *Notices et extraits des MSS de la Bibl. Nationale*, XXXI, ii (1886), 269.271; Juncker, *ZRGKan*, XV (1926), 493, note. From a gloss of Johannes Galensis on *Comp. III* we know that Rodoicus was precentor of Sens, and appeared for the chapter in an election suit at the Curia, 1200 A.D. (*Po.* n. 1043); cf. Gillmann, "Des Johannes Galensis Apparat ...," *AKKR*, CXVIII (1938), 219. Thus, the *Ro.*-glosses in Bologna cannot be his.

The Bolognese *Ro.*-Glosses may be products from Rodoicus Modicipassus, who taught for some time in Bologna before he became precentor of Sens—cf. P. Landau, Rodoicus Modicipassus— Verfasser der Summa Lipsiensis ?, ZRG Kan. Abt. 92 (2006), 340–354, here p. 349. (P.L.)

27 On these two, see below, §§8.9.12.

28 For such quotations from Albert, see Schulte, *QL*, I, 130, n. 4. Albert is commonly believed to have written also original glosses, cf. Schulte, *Glosse*, pp. 37.51; *QL*, I, 130 f.; Kuttner, *Repertorium*, pp. 7.10. But Schulte's main piece of evidence was a blunder: The glosses with the siglum *Al.*, quoted by him (*Glosse*, p. 51) from MS XVII.A.12 (formerly I. B. 1) of the National Museum in Prague, are not found among the *pre-ordinaria* materials of this MS, but in its very last stratum (set vi) which contains additions of late Bohemian origin (14th cent.) to the *Glossa Ordinaria*. The sigla *Al.* and *steph.*, occurring frequently in this stratum, evidently refer to Albertus Ranconis, scholastic of the Prague cathedral (1369–1372) and to Stephen of Prague, archdiocesan chancellor and lector (c. 1350). Both Schulte, *QL*, II, 431 f. and E. Ott, "Das Eindringen des kanonischen Rechts ... in Böhmen und Mähren", *ZRGKan*, III (1913), 59.81.87, overlooked the testimony of the Prague MS for the two Bohemian masters.—We can prove also for the few glosses in other MSS which are said to be by Albert of Benevento (cf. *Repertorium*, pp. 18.47.49) that the attribution is false.

29 For Stephen's biography, see now J. Warichez, *Etienne de Tournai et son temps* (Tournai-Paris, 1937). It can be proved that all the early glosses with the siglum *ste.*, or otherwise attributed to him by recent authors (cf. *Repertorium*, pp. 12.18; also Juncker, *ZRGKan*, XV [1926], 391, n. 1) are abstracted from his *Summa* which was written in France after 1160 but, as is well known, much read in Bologna. A great number of such excerpts are found as glosses, e.g. in St. Florian, Canons Regular, MS III.5.—For the *Summa* (cf. *Repertorium*, p. 133 f.), four MSS can be added: Milan, Ambrosian Libr., MS R.73 *sup.* (misbound); Monza, Cath. Chapter, MS i. 19/161 (fols. 3–30, fragment, see above, n. 19); Oslo, National Archives, coll. of fragments, no. 159 (4 leaves); Turin, Natl. Libr., MS D. IV. 40 (Pasini's no. 909; catal. no. 514). On the other hand, the MS 119 of Boulogne-sur-mer, Municipal Libr. (cf. *Repertorium*, p. 134) does not contain Stephen's work but two writings of the French school: (i) an anonymous *Summa* (fols. 2–62), influenced by Stephen and by Sicard of Cremona, beg. "In eadem ciuitate"; (ii) an interesting composition of *Distinctiones* and *Generalia* (fols. 73–81v), beg. "Breuiter quid contrarietatis".

30 For the famous canonist's activity as a lexicographer and grammarian, see M. Manitius, *Geschichte der lateinischen Literatur des Mittelalters*, III (Munich, 1931), 191 f. A *modicus libellus* on the

it was, between 1188 and his elevation to the see of Ferrara (1190).[31] An unknown pupil of his had already taken care of the parts not treated by the master, even before the latter had abandoned the idea of finishing his work.[32] For the moment, apparently not much was left to be said about Gratian's work in the way of commenting and glossing. No other *Summa* appeared after Huguccio in Bologna,[33] and the only writings published on Gratian during the nineties, the *Distinctiones decretorum* of Richardus Anglicus,[34] and Benencasa of Arezzo's

    calendar which Huguccio himself cites in his *Summa* under the title of *Agiographia*, beginning "Laboris assiduitas" (cf. Gillmann, *AKKR*, XCI [1911], 61, n. 2; *Zur Inventaris.*, p. 63), seemed to be lost. But we can identify it with the anonymous fragment of an etymological glossary, described by B. Hauréau, *Notices et extraits*, XXXIV, i (1891), 34 f., from Paris, Bibl. Nat., MS *lat.* 14877, fol. 124: this fragment begins "Laboris assiduitas" and explains the names of the months, the days, and the saints of the Roman calendar.—The attribution to Huguccio of an *Expositio de symbolo apostolorum*, by G. C. Trombelli, *Bedae et Claudii Taurinensis ... opuscula* (Bononiae, 1755), p.205ff., seems very doubtful to me.
31 Cf. *Repertorium*, pp. 155–159, with 33 MSS. Add now: Klosterneuburg, Canons Regular, MS 89 (without C. 23–26 and *tract. de poen.*, cf. Gillmann, *Zur Inventaris.*, p. 62) and MS 295 (fols. 110–238; fragment as described in the catalogue); Milan, Ambrosian Libr., MS A. 238 *inf.* (fols. 89rb–162rb: only *tract. de cons.*, as continuation of a commentary on C. 33, q. 3—C. 36 [fols. 37ra–89rb] which is based on Bartholomaeus Brixiensis' *Glossa Ordinaria*, and begins "Johannis quinto in principio dicitur" [misread and misjudged by Teetaert, cf. *Repertorium*, p. 80, n. 2]); Vienna, Natl. Libr., MS 2061 (only C. 2–C. 11, q. 1, c. 39; written as intercapitular gloss in a fragmentary copy of Gratian). Gillmann, *loc. cit.*, noted also Cambrai, Munic. Libr., MS 567 as an addition to my list; but this is simply an old class-mark of the already known MS Cambrai 612. Further bibliography on the peculiarities of the one or the other MS may be found in Gillmann, *loc. cit.*; Le Bras, *RHD*, 4, XVI (1937), 728; N. del Re, *I codici Vaticani della "Summa decretorum" di Uguccione da Pisa* (Roma, 1938).
32 Cf. *Repertorium*, p. 158: Huguccio's commentary on the *causae haereticorum* (C. 23–26) breaks off with C. 23, q. 4, c. 33. This fragment is preserved in several of the MSS, along with the continuation (C. 23, q. 4, c. 34–C. 26, q. 6, c. 3) written by the pupil c, 1185–1187. Four such MSS are listed *loc. cit.*, add Admont, Bened. Monast., MS 7; Florence, Laurentian Libr., MSS *S. Croce* I *sin.* 4 and *Medic.-Fesul.* 126. But in other MSS, the same continuator begins already with C. 23, *pr.* (six MSS listed *loc. cit.*); and in Montecassino, MS 396, we have as a separate writing this pupil's commentary not only on C. 23–26 (pp. 136–175) but also on C. 1 and *tract. de cons.* (pp. 113–135,175–190; listed as an uncertain *Summa Casinensis* in *Repertorium*, p. 166).—For three other continuations on C. 23–26 see *Repertorium*, p. 158 f.; still another is contained in Verona, Cath. Chapter, MS CXCIV (formerly 169, misbound). It begins, after Huguccio's original C. 23, q. 4, c. 33, again with c. 33: "*Est iniusta*] "Casus: ostenditur hie duabus."
    For the text of C. 23–26 in Huguccio's Summa, so-called 'Continuatio prima' cf. now W. P. Müller, Huguccio (Studies in medieval and early modern Canon Law 3, Washington D.C. 1994), 87–108. It was composed in 1185/86, and reflected the teaching of *Bazianus* rather than Huguccio. (P.L.)
33 The anonymous *Summa Reginensis* was written during Huguccio's professorship (*Repertorium*, p. 160 ff.), and refers to him as *magister meus* (*op. cit.*, p. 165, n. 2; Gillmann, *Zur Inventaris.*, p. 63 f.), or also as *ut in summa dicitur*, and as *hug.* (Vatican Libr., MS *Reg. lat.* 1061, fol. 41 va).—An anonymous collection of *Summulae* and *Distinctiones* in Montecassino, MS 396 (pp. 20–31.82–84; not *Quaestiones*, as presumed in the catalogue and in *Repertorium*, p. 250), belongs to the same period.
34 Cf. *Repertorium*, p. 222 ff. Additional MSS: Douai, Munic. Libr., MS 649 (fols. 7–25v; formerly MS 582, given wrongly as no. 581 by Schulte and Tailliar, cf. *Repertorium*, p. 222, n. 5); Lucca,

Casus decretorum,[35] were both intended for other purposes than that of adding to the exegetic discussion: Richard aimed at systematizing in clear-cut diagrams the canonical concepts found in the *Decreta*, and Benencasa chiefly at abstracting the cases and contents of Gratian's canons for the better aid of memory.

The slackening of decretist production was due to a fundamental innovation in the study of canon law. Hitherto, the new decretals of the recent popes, circulating in more or less arbitrary, unsystematic collections,[36] had been used occasionally as *extravagantes* (i.e. *decretales extra decreta vagantes*) by the Bolognese school, in interpreting Gratian's texts.[37] But now, for the first time, a collection of decretals was formally made the subject of lecturing, apart from the *Decreta*: the *Breviarium extravagantium* by Bernard Balbi of Pavia, composed between 1188 and 1192, and which later on was called the *Compilatio prima*.[38] With its system of five books subdivided into titles, it established the permanent pattern for all other decretal collections and decretalist science to come. It was only natural that with this change in teaching methods, the whole attention of the Bolognese canonists was diverted for a while to the new compilation, while in the schools of France and England the *Compilatio prima* was accepted only somewhat later. The Western schools stuck first to their own systematic collections of decretals,[39] but without making them a

---

Governmental Libr., MS 2698 (fols. 163v–191v); Paris, Bibl. Nat. MS *lat*. 3922 B; Zwettl, Cist. Monast., MS 162 (fols. 105–122v).—The identity of the English master Richard in Bologna is still an unsolved riddle. The main solutions proposed are: Bishop Richard Poore (cf. the older bibliographers and Schulte, *QL*, I, 183 f.; rejected now by all historians); Richard de Lacy (cf. *Repertorium*, p. 223, n. 1); Richard de Mores (Morins, Mora), the later prior of Dunstable (cf. J. C. Russell, *Dictionary of Writers of Thirteenth Century England* [London-New York-Toronto, 1936], p. 111 ff.). The case for the latter seems strongly supported by the subscription "Explicit summa breuis magistri Ricardi de Mores super decreta Graciani" in Dublin, Trinity Coll., MS 275, fol. 183 (Russell, p, 112). But this *Summa brevis* (MS *cit*., p. 169–183) is different from all the ascertained writings of the Bolognese canonist. The whole problem and Richard's numerous works will be discussed in a forthcoming study on the early English canonists. See also below, §§10 (n. 128). 18 (nn. 224, 226).23 (n. 279).24 (nn. 292, 293).

35 Cf. *Repertorium*, p. 229 f. Additional MSS: Plock, Diocesan Seminary, MS 80 (fols. 1–101v; Vetulani, *Projet*, p. 449); Vienna, Natl. Libr., MS 2142 (fols. 49–118v); Zwettl, Cist. Monast., MS 297 (fols. 1–85v). An additional proof against Siena, and for Arezzo, as the canonist's home town (cf. *Repertorium*, p. 230, n. 1) is found in the obituary of S. Maria di Reno, Bologna, edited by G. C. Trombelli, *Memorie istoriche concernenti le due canoniche di S. Maria di Reno e di S. Salvatore* (Bologna, 1752), p. 329 ff., under the date of October 4, 1206: *obiit magister Benincasa aretinus* ... (cf. the reprint in Sarti, II, 287).—Many incorrect statements are in R. Naz, "Benencasa", *Dictionnaire de Droit Can.*, II, 747.

36 Cf. *Repertorium*, pp. 272–288.

37 On the primitive style of Bolognese decretal references before the *Comp. I*, cf. Kuttner, "Zur neuesten Glossatorenforschung", *Studia et documenta historiae et iuris*, VI (1940), 313 f.

38 On the date, cf. *Repertorium*, p. 322, n. 1.

39 For the systematic collections of France and England—among which some were openly intended to substitute the *Comp. I*—see *Repertorium*, pp. 290–299; some rectifications are given by W. Holtzmann, *ZRGKan*, XXVII (1938), 300–302; Kuttner, *RHD*, 4, XVII(1938), 197.—We can add now (i) to the family of the *Appendix Concilii Lateranensis*: Vienna, Natl. Libr., MS 2172 (fols. 2–52v); (ii) to the family of the *Coll. Bambergensis*: a fragment in Paris, Bibl. Nat., MS *Baluze* 77

special subject of teaching,[40] and consequently continued for a longer time to concentrate their lecturing and commenting upon Gratian's work.[41]

For Bologna, then, the prevailing interest in the interpretation of the new decretals—reflected soon in a number of glosses and apparatuses on the *Compilatio prima*—explains in our opinion the stagnation of decretist production after the time of Huguccio. It explains why the process of consistently adding new gloss materials to the previous compositions on the *Decreta* was interrupted; in fact, the tradition of Huguccio's time was now maintained without substantial changes.[42] And where attempts to enlarge this standard tradition are found in a few MSS, they are rather private interpolations and arbitrary experiments: they do not mark further progress in the school. For instance, the scribes of the traditional gloss strata in MS 222 of the Cistercian Monastery of Lilienfeld, and in the Vatican MS *Ross. lat.* 595, have occasionally incorporated younger glosses which contain references to the *Compilatio prima*, and which certainly stood apart, as private notes, in the respective exemplars.[43] In Munich, State Libr., MS *lat.* 10244, the original glosses have been frequently retouched[44] with afterthoughts, additional

(fols. 324–328; discovered by Dr. Holtzmann, copy of a lost MS of Tours); a fragment in Florence, Laurent. Libr., MS *S. Croce* III *sin.* 6 (fols. 2 and 1); an index of rubrics in Verona, Cath. Chapter, MS CLXXXIV (formerly 164; fol. 254v); (iii) to the family of the *Coll. Francofortana*: Troyes, Munic. Libr., MS 961.
For the Collectio Francofurtana cf. now the analysis by P. *Landau/G. Drossbach*, Die Collectio Francofurtana: eine französische Decretalensammlung (MIC, Ser. B, Vol. 9, Città del Vaticano 2007). The manuscript Troyes 961 from Clairvaux is the oldest manuscript of this collection and comes from the region of the origin of the collection (p. 15s.). (P.L.)

40 This is shown by the fact that only few of the MSS are furnished with some scanty glosses: cf. *Repertorium* pp. 290 (*Appendix*). 291 (*Coll. Bamb.*). 292 (*Coll. Cass.*). 296 (*Coll. Franc.*), and the MSS of Vienna and Troyes, cited above. As to the use of the various collections for réference in writings of the Western schools, cf. *Repertorium*, pp. 17.23.24.199. 200.252.

41 Some *Summae* in *Repertorium*, p. 204 ff., *Apparatus, ibid.*, p. 59 ff. and below, §6, n. 59.

42 This tradition is represented by at least thirty-six of the MSS listed in *Repertorium*, pp. 13 ff. and above, §3, n. 14: Bamberg *Can.* 13 (set i), Cambrai 646 (set ii), Cividale 96 (i), Cues 223 (i), Douai 590 (i), Durham C. I. 7 (i), Florence, S. *Croce* IV *sin.* 1 (ii, iii) and *Aedil.* 96 (i), Graz 71 (iii, iv) and 80 (i), Hereford P. VII. 3 (ii), Jena *El. fol.* 56, Leipzig *Haen.* 18 (i), Lilienfeld 222 (i), London, B.M. *Add.* 24658 (ii), Montecassino 66 (i, ii), Munich *lat.* 10244, Naples XII. a. 5 (ii) and XII. a. 9 (i), New York, Morgan M. 446 (iii), Oxford, New College 210 (i), Paris, Arsenal 677 (ii[iii]) and Ste.-Geneviève 342, Prague, Metropolitan Chapter J. XIX (i), Reims 676 (iii), Rome, Angelica 1270 (iii), Salzburg a. XII. 9 (i), Treves, Munic. Libr. 906 (ii) and Semin. 8, Vatican, *Vat. lat.* 2494 (ii), *Pal. lat.* 625 (ii), *Ross. lat.* 595 (i) and St. Peter's Chapter A. 27 (i), Vercelli XXV (i?), Verona CLXXXIV (i, ii), Wolfenbüttel *Helmst.* 33.—In this large group, conformities are found especially among the MSS of Bamberg, Graz, Jena, Leipzig, Lilienfeld, Munich, Paris (Ste.-Genev.), Prague, Vatican (*Ross.*), Wolfenbüttel; also between Salzburg and Treves 906.

43 In Lilienfeld, the citations commonly run: *alex. iii. Licet preter solitum* (fol.57v), or *extra. Cum in cunctis* (fol. 76r), but sometimes with citation of titles: *ex. de eo qui dux. in matrim. quam poll. adult., Significauit* (fol. 139v: *1 Comp.* IV, 7, 2). In MS Ross., commonly: ex. *Relatum est* (fol. 53r), or *alex. iii. Litteras, et cap. Concessit, et decr. eug(enii), Iuuenis* (fol. 223v), but in pt. iii we frequently find references like arg. *ex. de uerbor. signif. Quesiuit* (fol. 285r: *1 Comp.* V, 36, 9).

44 Abundant evidence is found for this statement if one compares the texts printed from *Cod. Mon.* by Gillmann, "Die Abfassungszeit der Dekretglosse des Clm. 10244",*AKKR*, XCII (1912),

102

references to Huguccio,[45] and the like, probably by the unknown *m(agister) .g.* whose siglum appears in one of these interpolations.[46]—In one of the Western schools, the scribe of MS 342 of the Ste.-Geneviève Library in Paris, combined into one stratum the gloss composition of the Huguccio-period with a group of younger decretal references, *continuationes, summulae,* and with a selection from Richard's *Distinctiones decretorum.*[47]

5. All these interpolations do not affect our statement regarding the virtual standstill of gloss production after 1190. However, we have to fortify this statement over against a thesis that was put forward thirty years ago by the late Msgr. Gillmann, and that has remained unchallenged ever since. In studying some of the very gloss compositions which we consider as representing the standard tradition of Huguccio's time,[48] the learned prelate claimed that they include materials borrowed from the *Apparatus* of Laurentius Hispanus, written after 1210.[49] This would mean that there was no such gap between the earlier mixed glosses and the time of the apparatuses as we have asserted above, but that the stream of decretist gloss production flowed continuously, right down to the *Glossa Ordinaria* (c. 1216–1217).[50]

But Gillmann's thesis is untenable for the simple fact that in his MSS the glosses refer to decretals only of the twelfth century, and this without making

---

204–210. 368 (note)–369; XCIII (1913), 450–458; XCIV (1914), 436–439, with the readings of the same glosses in Bamberg, MS *Can.* 13 which Gillmann has carefully recorded in his footnotes. Strangely enough, he failed to draw the obvious conclusion from the eloquent facts. The MSS of Paris and the Vatican Library which I checked agree with the readings of Bamberg. See also Juncker, "Summen und Glossen", *ZRGKan,* XIV (1925), 465, n. 4.

45 In these interpolated references, we read *N. dicit ...,* or *secundum N ...,* or simply the siglum *N.* This corruption of the initial *H* (uguccio) is easily understood with the help of some paleographic experience; it occurs also in other MSS, cf. Juncker, *ZRGKan,* XV (1926), 344.347, n. 3; Gillmann, *AKKR,*CXVI (1936), 457, note.—R. Trifone, "Gli scritti di Guglielmo Nasone ...", *Rivista di storia del diritto italiano,* II (1929), 245, is badly mistaken in interpreting this *N.* as siglum of the 13th century decretalist William Naso.—Such extra references to Huguccio as in Munich, and even more lengthy excerpts from his work, are not uncommon in private marginal notes outside the proper gloss compositions, e.g. in Douai, MS 586 (set iii); Edinburgh, Natl. Libr., MS 3.1.12; Lilienfeld, MS 222 (set ii); Naples, MS XII.a.9 (set ii); Paris, Bibl. Nat., MSS *lat.* 3885 and 3886 A (set ii, copious abstracts); Reims, MS 676 (set iv); MS *Vatic, lat.* 2494 (set iii). They are based generally on Huguccio's *Summa,* not on his glosses. His name, when not suppressed, is abridged on such occasions by the decretists, and also later by the decretalists, in all possible manners: *N., h., hu., hugu.* (cf. *Repertorium,* pp. 19.20.40.41.43.49.53.54.78.205, n. 1), *ȳ., yḡ., vḡ.* (cf. Juncker, *ZRGKan,* XIV [1925], 415, n. 1; *Repertorium,* p. 71), or even *wiz.* (cf. Gillmann. *AKKR,* CXVIII [1938], 214, note; CXX [1940], 62; *Zur Inventaris.,* p. 78). The latter form is evidently a corruption derived from *vgvitio—vvitio.* His genuine siglum, however, is found only as *vḡ.*

46 Gloss on D. 74, c. 6, printed in *AKKR,* XCII, 204.

47 Similar selections from Richard appear also, as a separate stratum, in Prague, Metrop. Chapter, MS J.XIX (set ii).

48 MSS Munich *lat.* 10244, Bamberg *Can.* 13.

49 "Die Abfassungszeit der Dekretglosse ... ", *AKKR,* XCII (1912), 201–224, particularly p. 217 ff.—On the *Apparatus* of Laurentius, see below, §6 B.

50 On the *Ordinaria,* see below, §6 D.

any use of the *Compilatio prima*.⁵¹ Laurentius could not, and did not write such outmoded references after 1210, i.e. after the twelfth year of Innocent III, and that in an apparatus which frequently cites not only the first, but also the second and the third of the *Compilationes antiquae*. Who could think, at that time, of converting the correct decretal references of a glossator, when borrowing from him, into an antiquated style, unintelligible for the contemporary reader? By all the rules of textual criticism, the glosses in the MSS of mixed composition which return also in Laurentius' work (or under his name in later apparatuses) must therefore be older than Bernard of Pavia's decretal compilation, and they cannot be an offspring, but must be a source of the Laurentian apparatus.⁵²

Now, one could perhaps assume that these glosses were originally written by that master as individual notes, long before his formal apparatus.⁵³ Yet this hypothesis is ruled out not only by the fact that in the mixed compositions the said glosses never bear a genuine siglum of Laurentius,⁵⁴ but also and chiefly by chronological reasons: if Laurentius had already glossed before the time of the *Compilatio prima*, the long interval from about 1190 to his *Apparatus* and his other works⁵⁵ (all about and after 1210) would remain unexplained; and since his later, long and eventful activity in Spain and Portugal, as bishop of Orense from 1218 to 1248,⁵⁶ does not give the impression of a very old prelate, the presumed

---

51 Gillmann concedes this, *art. cit.*, p. 214, but discards the fact as insignificant. Cf. also his remark in *AKKR*, XCIV (1914), 242.
52 I select only two examples: (i) the gloss on D. 87, c. 3, v. *remedia* (Gillmann, p. 218) returns in Laurentius, in the *Glossa Palatina*, and in the *Ordinaria*, but with its primitive decretal reference changed, to fit in the *Comp. I*; (ii) on D. 73, c. 3, v. *Et hic sciendum est*, the mixed compositions have a gloss, "Nota uigiliam pentecosten. quod abhinc ... mutantur"; the three said apparatuses drop the first sentence, and add, as an afterthought, "scil. statuimus ... sacras" (cf. Gillmann, p. 219).
53 This solution was proposed in *Repertorium*, pp. 19.77 f.; I argued then that individual glosses by Laurentius were found also in other MSS. But the argument is not conclusive: the glosses in the MSS Cambrai 646 (set iv), Reims 676 (set v), Tours 559 (set iii), and *Vatic, lat*. 1367 (set ii) are strata of younger origin than the Laurentian apparatus and, as far as his glosses are concerned, derived from it.
54 Additions of the siglum by later hands occur, rarely, in the Vatican MS Ross. 595, and have, of course, no critical value. Cf. also *Repertorium*, p. 84, n. 2; 85, n. 1.
55 Mainly glosses on the various *Compilationes antiquae* of decretals, cf. *Repertorium*, pp. 326.346.356.383. His part in the composition of the *Apparatus "Servus appellatur"* on *Comp. III* has been overrated as formal authorship by Gillmann, *Laur. Hisp.* (above, §1, n. 1), *passim*, and by myself in *Repertorium*, p. 356. Cf. now Post, *So-called Laur.*, who proves that this work is an anonymous compilation from various authors' glosses (including also many by Laurentius). The same could be shown, I believe, for the gloss composition on *Comp. I* in Erlangen, Univ. Libr., MS 349 (set ii) which Gillmann, *Zur Inventaris.*, pp. 72–80, considers as a formal apparatus by Laurentius.—Additional MSS of the *Apparatus "Servus appellatur"* have been discovered in a fragment of Kassel, Landesbibl., MS *jur*. 11 (Gillmann, *AKKR*, CVXII [1937], 436–452), and in Plock, Diocesan Seminary, MS 67 (fols. 121–239v; Vetulani, *Projet*, pp. 441.450).
56 Gillmann, *Laur. Hisp.*, p. 125 f. On the bishop's various activities in Church and politics, see H. Florez, *España Sagrada*, XVII (Madrid, 1763), 102 ff. As late as 1244, Pope Innocent IV employed him as judge delegate in various cases; cf. E. Berger, *Les registres d'Innocent IV*, I (Paris, 1884), nn. 109.112.412. Cf. also A. E. Reuter, *Königtum und Episkopat in Portugal im*

glosses would have been written by a mere youth.—The only unobjectionable and intrinsically most probable explanation of the so-called Laurentius-glosses in the mixed composition is the reversal of Gillmann's thesis: they are all anonymous productions of the school before 1190, and they were used, some twenty years later, by Laurentius in the compilation of his apparatus.

For the whole history of glosses to the Decretum Gratiani in the 12th century one has to refer now to *Rudolf Weigand, Die Glossen zum Dekret Gratians*, Stud. Grat. XXV and XXVI (1991). (P.L.)

6. Commenting on Gratian's *Decreta* had again become an important feature of the activities of Bologna, when Laurentius wrote this work. The temporary stagnation after Huguccio could not last for ever, and with the steady increase of decretal legislation, especially after the accession of Pope Innocent III (1198), there arose the necessity not only of studying intensely the new papal law, but also of avoiding a possible gulf between decretist and decretalist teaching. After all, Gratian's book was still the fundamental text of the schools, and consequently, a new generation of canonists saw one of their main tasks in accommodating its interpretation to the decretal law. For this reason, the outstanding canonists of the early thirteenth century were productive in both decretist and decretalist glosses. Among these men, we shall find Bernard of Compostella.

The revived gloss production on the *Decreta* was now laid down, except for a few mixed gloss compositions after the old fashion, in coherent marginal commentaries, and formally published as *Apparatus glossarum* by individual authors who generally selected for this purpose materials from other glossators and combined them with their own notes. This literary form had already been in use for some time among Bolognese civilians,[57] glossators of the *Compilatio prima*,[58] and French decretists.[59] Within a period of less than ten years, four great apparatuses on Gratian appeared now in Bologna:

---

13. Jahrhundert (Abhandlungen zur mittleren und neueren Geschichte, hrsg. von Below, Finke, Meinecke, LXIX, Berlin, 1928), pp. 18.31.

57 A concise review of the early apparatuses on the various parts of the *Corpus Iuris Civilis* is found in E. Genzmer, "Die justinianische Kodifikation und die Glossatoren", *Atti del congresso internazionale di diritto romano ...*, *MCMXXXIII*, pt. i: *Bologna*, 1 (Pavia, 1934), 390–396; see also H. Kantorowicz's note, included in B. Smalley, *The Study of the Bible in the Middle Ages* (Oxford, 1941), p. 36 ff.

58 Cf. *Repertorium*, p. 322 ff.

59 On the outstanding *Apparatus "Ecce vicit leo"*, written in the French school after 1202, cf. *Repertorium*, pp. 59–66; the glosses of Douai, Munic. Libr., MS 592, and of Evreux, Munic. Libr., MS 106, set ii (*Repertorium*, p. 36). are also to be considered as formal apparatuses.— For *Ecce vicit leo*, seven MSS are listed *op. cit.*, p. 59; add now: Plock, Diocesan Seminary, MS 64 (set ii; cf. Vetulani, *Projet*, p. 446), and Florence, Laurentian Libr., MS *Gadd. reliq.* 2 (formerly MS *Magliabecch.* XXXI. 46) where the apparatus is however destroyed in great part by the scribe who entered later the *Glossa Ord.* of Bartholomaeus Brixiensis. (The identity of the Magliabecchian with the Gaddian MS was overlooked in *Repertorium*, pp. 48.110. See for the history of the so-called *Codices Gaddiani reliqui*: A. M. Bandini, *Catalogus codicum bibliothecae*

(A) The *Apparatus* "*Ius naturale*",[60] which we may safely attribute to the outstanding Englishman Alanus.[61] He must have composed it somewhat before 1210, and revised it shortly after that date, since the MSS present different redactions,[62] and the *Compilatio tertia* (1210) is not used in all of them consistently for citing Pope Innocent III' decretals.[63]

(B) The *Apparatus* of Laurentius Hispanus, written between 1210 and 1215.[64] The tradition of this important text is very unsatisfactory. Three MSS are extant,[65] but only one of them (*Lp*) presents the commentary in a nearly complete and relatively pure shape.[66] The second (*Lm*) contains a mere

---

Mediceae-Laurentianae, IV [Florentiae, 1777] xxxiv, and *Bibliotheca Leopoldina-Laurentiana*, I [1791], dedication page and p. xv).

60 Cf. *Repertorium*, pp. 67–75 where five MSS are listed. Add now: Klosterneuburg, Canons Regular, MS 101 (set i); Vatican Library, MS Ross.lat. 595 (set ii, not identified in *Repertorium*, p. 58).

61 Full proof for this statement will be given on another occasion. The pieces of evidence are (i) the frequent sigla, *a.,al.*, in the Vatican MS; (ii) a comparison with Alan's decretalist glosses; (iii) the inscription of a lost MS of the Grande-Chartreuse, *Jus.can*. XXXVII: *Summa Alani super decretum*, *3° folio "Jus naturale"*; cf. the old catalogue (15th cent.), edited by P. Fournier, "Notice sur la bibliothèque de la Grande-Chartreuse", *Bulletin de l'Académie Delphinale*, IV, i(1886), 383.— Alanus' other works are: an *Apparatus* on *Comp. I*, written after 1207, some glosses on *Comp. II*, and his *Collectio decretalium*, published c.1206. Cf. *Repertorium*, pp. 316.325.346; some rectifications in *RHD* 4, XVII (1938), 198, n. 5 and in Gillmann, *Zur Inventaris.*, p. 71 f. The collection of decretals has now been analyzed in detail by R. von Heckel in his scholarly study on Gilbert and Alan (above, §1, n. 1); a newly discovered second redaction of this collection, Salzburg, St. Peter's Abbey, MS a. IX. 18 (fols. 169–243), and Vercelli, Cath. Chapter, MS LXXXIX (fols. 51–136, with glosses by Alan himself), will be discussed on another occasion.

62 Cf. *Repertorium*, p. 70 f.

63 E.g. in the Vatican and the Klosterneuburg MSS.

64 Cf. *Repertorium*, pp. 76–80.

65 Paris, Bibl. Nat., MS lat. 15393, set ii (= *Lp*); Bibl. Mazarine, MS 1287, set ii (= *Lm*); Charleville, Munic. Libr., MS 269, set ii. (= *Lc*). An alleged fourth MS has to be discarded: Schulte, *Glosse*, p. 23, claimed to have discovered the *Apparatus* in Prague, Natl. Museum, MS XVII. A. 12 (formerly I.B.I); cf. *Repertorium*, pp. 52.77. Actually, the Prague MS contains: two early gloss compositions (sets i, ii); the *Ordinaria* of Joh. Teutonicus (set iii); a selection from the *Casus* of Benencasa (set iv); various additions, from Bartholomaeus Brixiensis' second redaction of the *Ordinaria*, and from the *Rosarium* of Guido de Baysio (set v); Bohemian additions, mainly by Albert Ranconis and Stephen of Prague (set vi; cf. above, n. 28). The siglum of Laurentius appears frequently in set v, and has been interpolated often in set iii, as a result of the copious, though not always trustworthy quotations from Laurentius in Guido's *Rosarium* (written in 1300; on Guido's *testimonia* and their value, see *Repertorium*, p. 87 f., below n. 84). Schulte's mistake, and his assertions regarding the Prague text of the *Ordinaria* (cf. Kuttner, *Dekretsumme*, pp. 164, n. 1; 168) are thus explained.— 'Another MS, now lost, is mentioned in a Bolognese deed of 1286: sale of *unum decretum cum apparatu Laurentii; cf. Chartularium Studii Bononiensis*, IX (Bologna, 1931), no. lxiv (3316).

66 Sometimes the texts are abridged because a similar gloss stands already in set i (Alanus); on the other hand, glosses sometimes begin with *lau. dicit ...*, yet are signed by *l.*; this denotes rather a *reportatio* than an original gloss. A conspicuous example is found on C. 1, q. 3, c. *Si quis obiecerit* (7), v. *nec pastum*] "Lau. dicit quod ... pro consuetudinibus. *la.*" The siglum is cancelled, and the gloss continues, as only a member of the Parisian school could write: "et ita uidi parisius, quod episcopus Odo (d. 1208) dedit palafredum arcidiacono, postquam fuit deportatus a sancta genouefa ad maiorem ecclesiam, quia erat ecclesie consuetudo. *La.*"

fragment;[67] and the third (*Lc*) gives, in the form of supplements to Johannes Teutonicus' *Glossa Ordinaria*, only selections which are often abridged,[68] and sometimes altered by the incorporation of other glosses, by Jacobus de Albenga, Petrus Brito, Willielmus Vasco, Martin of Zamora, and a master *b*.[69] Also, the critical value of *Lc* is lessened by the fact that it is a "conflated" MS as far as the work of Laurentius is concerned; i.e. the scribe tried to improve his text by comparison with other *testimonia* of the master's activity, particularly with the *Glossa Palatina* where many of Laurentius' glosses are incorporated in a wording different from the more reliable *Lp*.[70] Therefore, we find the readings of *Lc* sometimes in agreement with *Lp*, sometimes with the MSS of the *Palatina*.[71] All this makes the restoration of Laurentius' texts extremely difficult. For his glosses on C. 33, q. 3, the *tractatus de poenitentia*, the confusion is almost discouraging.[72]

(C) The so-called *Glossa Palatina*, composed by an unknown author between 1210 and 1215.[73] The complex genesis of this able and influential compilation is as yet unravelled, for gloss materials of Laurentius,[74] Johannes Teutonicus,[75] Vincentius,[76] Alanus,[77] Jacobus de Albenga,[78] Melendus,[79]

---

67 *Repertorium*, p. 77.
68 The reason for the abbreviations was the same as in *Lp*; but here, set i (the *Glos. Ord.*) gave more opportunities for this procedure. Cf. *Repertorium*, p. 76.
69 The sigla *Ja*. and *ber*. are mentioned already loc.cit.; in the meantime I also found *M*., *W*., and *brito*. On Martin and William, see below, *Appendix*; on Petrus Brito, below, §20, n. 258.
70 For these discrepancies between Laurentius and *Glos. Pal.*, see *Repertorium*, p. 83 f.
71 One example is mentioned below, §7, n. 92.
72 In *Repertorium*, p. 78 f., I thought it possible that Laurentius had published a separate apparatus on this tract, transmitted by MSS of the *Glossa Ordinaria*, the *Palatina*, and others. Among the MSS listed *loc. cit.*, Bamberg *Can*. 14 and *Vatic. lat*. 1367 are copies of the *Ordinaria*, and a separate tradition is given in Paris, MS *lat*. 14317, and St. Omer, MS 192. (The fragment on the fly-leaves of Paris, MS *lat*. 3903, has to be discarded: it consists of pieces from Barth. Brixiensis and Guido de Baysio). But almost every other MS of the *Ordinaria* or the *Palatina* could be added, and each time, the glosses by Laurentius appear in another arbitrary selection and with the most discrepant readings. This would be hardly consistent with a formal apparatus.
73 Cf. *Repertorium*, pp. 81–92, where 10 MSS are listed. Add now: Salzburg, St. Peter's Abbey, MS a. XII. 9 (set ii), and Vienna, Natl. Libr., MS 2102 (set iv). In Vienna, most of *Glos. Pal.* has been later erased for the *Glossa Ordinaria* (Barth. Brix.).
74 *Repertorium*, p. 82 ff.
75 " *Op.cit.*, p. 91 f.; other examples in Kuttner, *Dekretsumme*, pp. 177. 183; below, §9, n. 121.
76 E.g., the introductory gloss of the *Palatina* on C. 4, q. 6: "Hic depingitur. vi. questio, an scil. accusator ... uel crimine excepto", returns in the gloss composition of MS *Vatic. lat*. 1367, set ii (on this composition see below, *Appendix*), fol. 106rb, with the siglum *v*.
77 Cf. the interesting gloss "Omnis uirtus ... on *De poen.*, D. 2, p. c. 14, which was taken over by Johannes Teutonicus in the *Ordinaria*, with the siglum *a*. (but see below, n. 83). It contains quotations from *aristotiles* (= *Eth. Nicom.*, 1107a) and *oratius* (= *Epp.* I, 18, 9). Also the gloss "Hec clausula ..." on *De poen.*, D. 5, c. 4, likewise incorporated later by Johannes, belongs to Alan.
78 A gloss of the *Palatina*, on C. 6, q. 1, c. *Quicumque* (18), v. *periurauerit*] "Set utrum periurium ... magis canonica opinio", returns in the Vatican compilation (above, n. 76), somewhat altered, with the sigla *Ja. la.*, indicating both its author and its redactor.
79 Beyond frequent references to this master (cf. Kuttner, *Dekretsumme*, pp. 148 f., 158. 167), there are also original glosses with his siglum (*ibid*. pp. 161.171). See also below, §12.

master *b.*,⁸⁰ and others⁸¹ flowed together in the apparatus. The main contribution came undoubtedly from Laurentius, and it would be tempting to see in him also the compiler of the work, did not the all too frequent discrepancies between the texts of the *Palatina* and *Lp* or *Lc*, the absence of his siglum, and various other critical reasons forbid this assumption.⁸² But even contemporaries sometimes quoted by mistake glosses of others from the *Palatina* as being by Laurentius,⁸³ and with the dim transmission of the latter's original apparatus it is not astonishing that Guido de Baysio in his *Rosarium*, some eighty years later (1300 A.D.), took Laurentius' authorship in almost every gloss of the *Palatina* for granted.⁸⁴

(D) The *Apparatus* of Johannes Teutonicus,⁸⁵ completed shortly after the Fourth Lateran Council (1215), and retouched by the author with some references to the *Compilatio quarta* (c., 1216–1217).⁸⁶ It was soon accepted by the schools as *Glossa Ordinaria*, i.e. as the standard commentary the opinions of which could possibly be contradicted, but had always to be considered first in the class-room

---

80 Cf. below, ch. II.
81 The compiler incorporated also materials from the gloss compositions of the twelfth century, and even whole groups of glosses. For instance, all the glosses that are found on Gratian's important little treatise on prescription (C. 16, q. 3, p. c. 15) in the standard compositions of Huguccio's time (I checked MS *Vatic. Ross.* 595, fol. 167rb), return unchanged in *Glos. Pal.*, even including the outmoded citation (in gl. "Non enim uiolento ...") of *ex. alex. iii. In literis*, for *I Comp.* II, 9, 5.—A similar example is found on C. 6, q. 3, c. *Placuit* (3).
82 Cf. *Repertorium*, p. 89 ff. Note the striking similarity of critical problems in the *Palatina* and the so-called Laurentius-apparatus on Comp. III (above, §5, n. 55).
83 E.g., the Vatican composition (above, n. 76) has on C. 2, q. 6, c. *Si quis* (21), v. *senserit*, the gloss: "In quocumque ... quedam mulier. *la.*"; but in the *Palatina*, on c.cit., v. *iudicem*, it stands with the siglum *b.*—The first gloss of Alanus mentioned above, n. 77, is given with the correct siglum *a.* in the Vatican MSS *Pal. lat.* 625 and *Vat. lat.* 1367 (set i) of Johannes' *Ordinaria*, but with the sigla *a. l.* in MS *Pal. lat.* 658 of the *Palatina*, and with *l.* in MS *Pal. lat.* 624 of the *Ordinaria*. In the second Alanus-gloss, only *Vat. lat.* 1367 has the correct siglum, all the others give *l.*
84 Cf. *Repertorium*, p. 87 f.; an example for unwarranted attribution *ibid.*, p. 91, n. 1. Another, amusing, case: on C. 13, q. 2, c. *Illud* (5), v. *obstrictum*, the gloss of the *Palatina* (see the full text below, §11) concludes thus: "... dicit 1. quod sic, cum ad officium eius spectat quicquid ex prima amministratione deberet ad secundam rationem transire: ff. mandati, Qui mutuam, §Non omnis". Guido (ed. Venet., 1577, fol. 240rb) reproduces this as: "... dic quod sic, cum ... §Non omnis. *la.*" But in the original text, *dicit l.* means *dicit lex*, i.e. the Roman law in the cited passage (*Dig.* 17, 1, 56, 2), and Guido mistook the abbreviation *l (ex)* for the glossator's siglum!
85 For Johannes' other works—*Apparatus* on *Compp. III* and *IV*, on the Constitutions of the Fourth Lateran Council, glosses on *Comp.* V, and Quaestiones *disputatae*—see *Repertor.*, pp. 254.357.370.374.383. We shall deal on another occasion with his previously unknown *Apparatus* on the *Arbores consanguinitatis et affinitatis*, with the problem of his being the redactor of *Comp. IV* (cf. *Repertorium*, p. 372), and with Gillmann's objections, *AKKR*, CXVII (1937), 453–466, concerning the *Apparatus* on the Lateran Constitutions.
86 Cf. *Repertorium*, pp. 93–99, where 35 MSS are listed. Add now seven more: Avranches, Munic. Libr., MS 148; Graz, Univ. Libr., MSS 71 (set v) and 80 (set ii); Klosterneuburg, Canons Reg., MS 87; Krakow, Bibl. Jagiellonska, MS 357 (set ii; information by Dr. Vetulani); Olmütz, Metrop.

interpretations of the *Decreta* as well as in court. A second redaction of Johannes' work was published, after 1240, by Bartholomaeus of Brescia, mainly in order to adapt it to the further development of the decretal legislation.[87] This second redaction only is found in the printed editions.[88]

II. Bernard's Glosses on Gratian

7. Bernard of Compostella did not publish a full *Apparatus* on the *Decreta*. But it can be proved that he is the Master *b*. to whom a great many passages in the contemporary apparatuses refer, and who appears in some mixed gloss-compositions of the early thirteenth century. Quotations from *b*., or glosses incorporated with his siglum, are mainly preserved by Laurentius and in the *Glossa Palatina*; in the additions to Laurentius of the MS Charleville 269 (*Lc*);[89] and in the mixed compositions of Arras, Municipal Library, MS 500 (set iv; siglum *b*. = *ber*.), St.-Omer, Municipal Library, MS 476 (set ii; siglum *b*.), Vatican Library, MS *Vat. lat.* 1367 (set ii; sigla *B., b., b., B'*.).[90] Of these manifold witnesses I have examined in detail only the Vatican gloss-composition[91] and the *Glossa Palatina*. The few passages concerning master *b*. which I had the opportunity to collate also in Laurentius show a substantial agreement between him and the *Palatina*, even where the reports are differently phrased, as e.g. in a lengthy gloss on imputation of homicide,[92] or as in the following gloss:

Chapter, MS 401 (without Gratian's text); Venice, Marcian Libr., MS *lat*. IV. 117 (set ii). For the earlier strata of the MSS of Graz, Krakow, and Venice, see above, §3, n. 14.—On the other hand, Montecassino, MS 68, listed in *Repertorium*, p. 98, on a conjectural basis, contains only the later redaction by Bartholomaeus Brixiensis. In some other cases, our conjectures have been confirmed: Klosterneuburg. MS 101 (set iii); Treves, Municipal Libr., MS 907 (set ii); Vienna, Natl. Libr., MS 2082 (set i). The two MSS of Frankfurt and Madrid (*Repertorium*, pp. 95.98) remain still unexplored.

87 Cf. *Repertorium*, pp. 103–115, with hundreds of MSS; pp. 116–122 for a peculiar redaction of the fourteenth century.
88 On the editions, see Schulte, *Glosse*, pp. 26 ff. 91 ff.
89 Cf. above, §6 B.
90 Cf. *Repertorium* pp. 31 (siglum tentatively attributed to Bernard of Pavia). 45.53.
91 Cf. below, §14.
92 On D. 50, §*Casu quoque* (p. c. 36). This complex gloss will be edited and discussed with all its historical implications on another occasion, since at present I have not at my disposal the indispensable variant readings of Laurentius in the Parisian MS *lat*. 15393 (*Lp*). The version of the *Palatina* was published in Kuttner, *Dekretsumme*, p. 150, but not quite correctly: cf. some emendations in *Repertorium*, p. 89, n. 2; it might be added that the first words are *Fit homicidium ...*, not *Est homicidium*, and that the passage towards the end, concerning the distinction *a corpore in corpus* (cf. *Dekretsumme*, p. 150, lines 23–24; *Repertorium, l. c.*) is corrupted by a homoeography in *Glos. Pal.*, to be healed with the aid of *Lc*: "... et hoc uidetur dicendum, cum est datum dampnum de non corpore in corpus; ⟨si uero de corpore in corpus,⟩ non sunt promouendi ...". The differences between *Lc, Glos. Pal.*, on one side, and *Lp* on the other side, begin at the passage: "Set dico quod ipso iure ..." (*Lc, Glos. Pal.*) which in *Lp* reads: "Set b'. dicit quod ipso iure ..." (cf. *Repertorium*, p. 90).

Laurentius (*Lc*)

C.15,q.6,c.*Nos predecessorum* (4)[93]. *prohibemus*] respectu ergo communionis cum eo habende, dicit *b*. Alias enim secundum eum papa non potest soluere uinculum fidelitatis quo tenentur milites secundum consuetudinem regionis dominis suis uel regibus; unde dicit quod si non iuuarent talem excommunicatum, si inimici terram eius intrarent, infamiam incurrerent secundum leges suas, licet non debeant iure poli. Non tamen ueniat ille ad exercitum, uel si uenerit, recedant. *b.l.*

Glos.Pal.

prohibemus] Dicit *b*. quod hoc[a] papa prohibere non potest, nisi tantummodo[b] eo respectu, quod non debent[c] omnimodo[d] communicare et ex toto[e], non quo possit soluere illud uinculum fidelitatis quo milites tenentur secundum consuetudinem regionis[f] dominis suis uel regibus; unde dicit quod si[g] non iuuarent excommunicatum talem, si inimici intrarent terram eius, incurrerent[h] infamiam secundum leges suas, licet non debeant[i] iure poli. Non tamen ueniat ille ad exercitum, uel si ueniret,[j] recedant[k].

a) hic *P*.   b) solummodo *P*, soluendo *R*.   c) debet *PR*.   d) excommunicato *PR*.
e) et ex toto *om*. *PR*.   f) regionum *PR*.   g) set *Ov*.   h)   *om*.   *R*.
i) *om*. *Ov*.   j) uenerint *R*.   k) recedent *P*.

However, we must refrain from going into further details regarding the transmission of the texts, and shall concentrate in the first place on the identification of Master *b*. in the *Glossa Palatina*.

8. The siglum *b*. in itself is ambiguous, and therefore could easily be misjudged as denoting Bazianus,[94] the well known decretist of the late twelfth century.[95] But Bazianus wrote his glosses[96] and *Quaestiones*[97] in the time of Huguccio,[98] never cited the *Compilatio prima*,[99] and died in 1197.[100] On the contrary, Master *b*. is

---

93 *Lc* (folios not numbered) .—*Glos. Pal.*: Vatican Libr., MSS *Pal. lat.* 658 (= *P*), fol. 56ra; *Reg. lat.* 977 (= *R*), fol. 157r. The text appears also in.the mixed composition of MS *Vat. lat.* 1367 (= *Ov*), fol. 154va.

94 Wrong attributions of *b*.-glosses to Bazianus are found e.g. in Gillmann, *Laur. Hisp.*, p. 109, n. 1 ff.; in Kuttner, *Dekretsumme*, p. 149 f., and "La réserve papale ... ", *RHD*, 4, XVII (1938), 202.221. Paleographical reasons should be sufficient as a warning against attribution to Bazianus in all those cases where the siglum is written *b'*. or *b*., because these are standard abbreviations for *ber.* ·

95 Schulte, *QL*, I, 154 ff.

96 Glosses on Gratian: Schulte, *loc.cit.*, and Kuttner, *Repertorium*, pp. 7.10. Glosses on the *Summa* of Joh. Faventinus: *Repertorium*, p. 143 f. (MSS Angers 370 and Reims 684).

97 Disputations by Bazianus are reported in two collections of *Quaestiones*: Montecassino Abbey, MS 396 (pp. 32–80; 84b–112) and Vienna, Natl. Libr., MS 1064 (fols. 81–91), both still to be analyzed.

98 Schulte, *QL*, I, 153, n. 3.

99 Schulte, *Glosse*, pp. 57.58.62; *QL*, I, 155. The same is true for the *Quaestiones*.

100 Schulte, *QL*, I, 154. The latest known writing of Bazianus, a *consilium*, is dated of April 20, 1192; cf. *Repertorium*, p. 7, n. 2.

quoted in the *Palatina* frequently as citing and interpreting decretals of the said compilation:

C. 10, q. 2, c. *Ea* (2), §*Hoc ius*, v. *conflata*[101] Quia res desinit esse sacra per conflationem, arg. de cons. di. i. Ecclesias (c. 20). Amittit enim formam, et forma rei est esse rei: ff. ad exhib. Iulian. §Si quis (*Dig.* 10, 4, 9, 3); sicut et ager, si sit alueus: ff. de acquir. rer. dom. Adeo, §ii (*Dig.* 41, 1, 7, 2). Arg. contra ⟨ff.⟩ de contrahen. empt. Ede (*Dig.* 18, 1, 73). Vestimenta etiam sacra in necessitate in eadem forma ad tabernam^a obligari possunt: *ex. i^b. de pigno. c. i.* (*1 Comp.* III, 17, 1 = X. III, 21, 1). Honestum tamen est, si fieri potest et creditor sustinet, ut apud aliquam ecclesiam collocetur: de cons. di. i. *In sancta* (c. 41).—*b. dicit* quod, cum res sacra extimari non possit—ff. de rer. diu. Sciendum, §ult. (*Dig.* 1, 8, 9, 5)—, nec locus sacer uendi possit: C. de relig. *Locum* (*Cod.* 3, 44, 9); nec obligari, ut C. que res pig. *Si monumento* (*Cod.* 8, 16, 3). *Dixit super illo ex(trauaganti)*, nexum pignoris non constare in huiusmodi sacris rebus mobilibus,[102] nec creditorem habere ypothecariam utilem uel directam. Set habet doli exceptionem et detinere potest pro pecunia, et est simile; nam pignus etiam retineri potest, etc.: C. etiam ob cirographum pec. (*Cod.* 8, 26, un.). Set tu dic cum *h* (uguccione), quod tam calix quam palle quam alia uendi possunt, licet *b*. in omnibus contradicat.
    a) taberna *P*.   b) i. *om. P*.

C. 13, q. 2, §*Nunc queritur* (p. c. 1)][103] Hic^a explicatur unus articulus ...; et dicit *h*. de isto iure funerandi, quod de iure communi quilibet debet sepeliri in ecclesia sua, nisi in tribus casibus ...; *b*. uero dicit quod ubicumque uoluerit, potest, dumtamen hoc non faciat ex odio uel temeritate: j(nfra) e(adem), *Placuit* (13, q. 2, c. 7); ex.i.^{b} de sepultur. c. ii (*1 Comp.* III, 24, 2).
    a) Et hic *R*. b) i. *om.P*.

Still less do references of Master *b*. to later decretals[104] fit into the chronology of Bazianus'publications.

9. Also, the usual siglum of, and designation for Bazianus was *baç.* or *baz.* It is true that copyists disfigured this often into *bar*.,[105] but all the velleities of

---

101 *P* 36ra, *R* 127vb.
102 For the corresponding gloss of *b*. on *Comp. I*, see below, §13, at n. 158.
103 *P* 52vb, *R* 149va.
104 See the glosses on D. 50, p. c. 36 (*Dekretsumme*, p. 150), and on C. 22, q. 4, c. 22 (below, at n. 122).
105 This disfiguration is discussed at length by Schulte, *Glosse*, pp. 56 ff. 63. Also in the *Quaestiones*, the siglum is often bar.—I cannot agree with Kantorowicz's proposal to explain this spelling by

medieval scribes being granted, there existed a well observed tradition of distinguishing different authors by different sigla.[106] In Bazianus' case, this was all the more imperative, as confusion with another canonist of his own time had to be avoided, namely with one *b*., or *b*'. (= *ber*.) whose siglum appears in Bolognese gloss compositions from c. 1175 onwards,[107] and particularly in the standard compositions of the Huguccio epoch.[108] I think this earlier *ber*. (the Compostellan is out of the question) can be identified as Bernard Balbi of Pavia. It is true that this outstanding author is generally classified only as the first decretalist and as writer of monographs,[109] not as a glossator of Gratian.[110] But we can consider it certain that, as a pupil of the decretists Johannes Faventinus and Gandulph,[111] he would have begun his literary activities, as every one else in the school, by writing notes on the *Decreta*. The assumption that he did so in the seventies[112]

---

assuming the glossator's true name to have been *Barzianus*; H. Kantorowicz, "De pugna", *Studi di storia e diritto in onore di Enrico Besta*, II (Pavia, 1938), 11.

106 Cf. the observations regarding sigla for Simon, Stephanus and Silvester, by Juncker, "Die Summe des Simon von Bisignano und seine Glossen", *ZRGKan*, XV (1926), 390 ff.

107 E.g., Lilienfeld, Cistercian Monast., MS 223; London, B.M., MS *Stowe* 378 (*Repertorium*, p. 28); Paris, Bibl. Nat., MS *lat*. 3888 (*ibid.*, p. 38); all three of them represent the stage of glossing in the period of Johannes Faventinus.

108 Among the MSS of this epoch (cf. above, §4, n. 42) the siglum *b*. or *ber*. is relatively frequent in the MSS Cues 223, Hereford P. VII.3, Oxford, New College 210, Treves, Sem. 8, *Vat. lat.* 2494, Vercelli XXV, Verona CLXXXIV; one quotation *secundum ber*. also in Treves 906 (cf. Juncker, *ZRGKan*, XV, 394, note). The siglum is also found in one MS of Simon de Bisignano's epoch: Berlin, State Libr. MS *Phill*. 1742 (cf. *Repertorium*, p. 16).

109 Schulte, *QL*, I, 175–182; Kuttner, *Repertorium*, pp. 290.292 (n. 1).322 f. 387 ff. 398 f., G. Le Bras, "Bernard de Pavie", *Dictionnaire de Droit Canonique*, II (1937) 782–789. Bernard's main writings were edited with an excellent introduction, in 1860, by E. Th. A. Laspeyres (see above, §1, n. 1).

110 Some unsubstantiated and partly incorrect hints in *Repertorium*, pp. 29 (n. 1). 31.518.

111 Schulte, *QL*, I, 176 f., named as Bernard's teachers correctly Gandulph, but wrongly Huguccio and one Johannes Hispanus. This is repeated, although with some reserve, by Le Bras, *art. cit.*, col. 782.—(i) As to Huguccio, chronological reasons alone should suffice to exclude him; and in fact, the one passage where *magister meus Vg*. is quoted in Bernard's *Summa de matrimonio*, has been definitely exposed as an interpolation by Kunstmann, "Das Eherecht des Bischofs Bernhard von Pavia", *AKKR*, VI (1861), 219.229, n. 16, and by Gillmann, *Der Katholik*, 1904, i, 205; *AKKR*, CXVI (1936), 115.—(ii) Johannes Hispanus is a personality invented by Schulte as the presumptive author of the Anglo-Norman *Summa "Omnis qui iuste"* written c. 1186 (*Summa Lipsiensis*, cf. *Repertorium*, p. 197). Schulte, *QL*, I, 176, n. 6, asserted that the citations of *meus doctor magister Jo*. in Bernard's writings must be referred to that *Summa*; he brushed aside the obvious chronological and geographical objections, and suppressed the fact that already Kunstmann (*art. cit.* p. 221) had proved the citations of *magister Jo*. to fit perfectly in the *Summa* of Johannes Faventinus (written before 1171).

112 Since Bernard cannot have glossed earlier than his teachers—John's and Gandulph's glosses belong to the sixties and early seventies, cf. above, §3—, we must distinguish him from still another master *b*. whose glosses appear, together with those of Rufinus, in two MSS prior to this period: Cambridge, Sidney Sussex College, MS 101, and London, Chester Beatty Collection, MS 46 (*Repertorium*, pp. 24.29). In both these MSS the glosses are written by French or English hands (for the first MS see M. R. James, *A Descriptive Catalogue of MSS in the Library of Sidney Sussex College* [Cambridge, 1895], p. 123 f.); this *b*., therefore, was probably a master of

and early eighties agrees also perfectly with the data of his career: we know that Bernardus Papiensis published his *Summa de matrimonio* between 1173 and 1179,[113] the so-called *Collectio Parisiensis secunda* of decretals between 1177 and 1179,[114] and the *Summa de electione* during the same years.[115] In the eighties, he was appointed provost of Pavia where he published his final decretal collection, the *Breviarium extravagantium* (*Compilatio prima*), between 1188 and 1192.[116]

Thus, authors and copyists of glosses on the *Decreta* had good reasons for not simply writing *b.*, when they intended to quote Bazianus, and we can conclude therefore from both the chronological and the transcriptional argument that *b.* in the *Glossa Palatina* and similar texts is generally a master different from Bazianus. Sometimes, the distinction made by the *Palatina* between the two becomes evident:

---

one of the Western schools. Note that an unidentified, and certainly not Bolognese, master *b.* is frequently cited in the Anglo-Norman *Summa "Omnis qui iuste"*: Schulte, "Die Summa Decreti Lipsiensis. *SBWien*, LXVIII (1870), 45 f. In *Repertorium*, p. 29, n. 1, I failed to consider this possibility.

Master *b.*, whose glosses appear in the manuscripts of Cambridge, Sidney Sussex College 101, and London, Chester Beatty Collection 46, might be the same author as in glosses in MS Pommersfelden 142; cf. R. Weigand, Stud. Grat. XXVI (1991), 612s.

But see *Kuttner*, Retractationes p. 122 on p. 304. (P.L.)

113 Editions by Laspeyres, pp. 287–306, and by Kunstmann (above, n. 111), pp. 223–262. Additional MSS are mentioned by Gillmann (n. 111) and in *Repertorium*, p. 292, n. 1. Add further: Montecassino, MS 396 (pp. 1–20); Turin, Natl. Libr., MS D. V. 2 (Pasini's no. 880; catal. 516; fols. 99—109); Zwettl, Cistercian Mon., MS 162 (fols. 66–70r).—The question of the date has never been seriously examined, but can be settled as follows: (i) The *terminus ad quem* (1179) is given by Bernard's own *Collectio Parisiensis II* (c. 1177–1179), for in the treatise on marriage Bernard cites decretals and other *extravagantes* still without referring to the titles of that compilation, while later, in his *Summa de electione*, he used to refer to it. The statement by Friedberg, *Die Canonessammlungen zwischen Gratian und Bernhard von Pavia* (Leipzig, 1897), p. 31, *viz.* that Bernard, when writing *Sum. de matr.*, "had the individual decretals before him generally in the same (textual) shape as they appeared afterwards in *Coll. Par. II*", has been misunderstood by Le Bras, *art. cit.*, col. 787, who asserted apodictically that the collection was used in the treatise.—(ii) For the *terminus a quo* (1173) we have but to examine the dates of Alexander III's six decretals cited in the course of the treatise (ed. Laspeyres nn. 8.11.64.69.79.92). We find:

JL n. 12254, of Nov. 26, 1163–1164 (cf. *Repertorium*, p. 283).
JL n. 12180, of Jan. 31, 1171–1172 (cf. *ibid.*)
JL n. 12293, of June 2, 1173–1174
JL n. 13162, of Sept. 4 (or 1), 1167–1169 (*ibid.*, p. 287)
JL nn. 14055.13970, both of uncertain date.
The treatise, then, was not written before June 2, 1173.

114 Cf. *Repertorium*, p. 290; Le Bras, *art. cit.*, col. 787. The date of Alexander III's arrival in Venice, *terminus a quo* for the most recent decretal in this collection (*JL* n. 14157), was March 24, 1177 (cf. *JL* before n. 12794), not May 11th, as given in *Repertorium*, *loc. cit.*—Bernard wrote also some glosses on this collection; his siglum occurs twice in the MS of Paris, *lat.* 1566.

115 Edition by Laspeyres, pp. 307–323. For the date, cf. *Repertorium*, p. 290.
116 *Op. cit.*, p. 322, n. 1.

C. 13, q. 2, c. *Illud* (5), v. *obstrictum*][117] Hoc dicas conniuentibus ecclesiis ...; *b.* intelligit hoc secundum consuetudinem ..., *bazianus* intellexit de seruo dediticio....

C. 1, q. 5, c. *Presentium* (3), v. *fratrumque*][118] Et ita episcopus in tali casu dispensare non potest sine consilio fratrum et auctoritate, arg. xv. q. vii. Episcopus nullius (c. 6). *M.* et *b.* Nam in omni dispensatione consensus capituli requirendus. Preterea nota per cap. istud dispensari[a] circa symoniam in ordine; nam si ipse ordinatus[b] dedit pecuniam uel alius etiam, dum tamen det episcopo, non poterit episcopus hoc casu dispensare. Et hoc notauit, cum dixit 'non episcopo', quasi dicat: secus si episcopo esset data. Unde strictior erit potestas episcopi dispensandi in symonia commissa in ordine, quam commissa in beneficio: s(upra). e.q., c.i.—*b.* concedit quod nec in beneficio possit dispensare ubi ipsi data fuit pecunia. Huiusmodi autem dispensatio peti non potest, ut episcopus compellatur ad dispensandum: de pen. di. vi Quicumque (c. 1), in fine; 1. di. De hiis (D. 50, c. 34). *baç. contra.*

a) *om. P.* b) *est add. P.*

C.29, q.2, pr.[119]

Glos.Pal.

Secunda questio] Hic intitulatur ii. q., an scil. conditione seruili reperta liceat libere seruum dimittere. Et quidem sic, si, cum contraxit[a] cum eo, ignorauit seruum esse: j(nfra) e(ad.) Si quis ingenuus(c.4). Si autem sciuit, non, immo tenet matrimonium: j.e.c.i.iii.et ii.Et quia hic tractatur de errore conditionis, nota quod *h.* dicit quod tantum deterior conditio impedit. *baç.* uero dixit quod et melior et deterior impedit; nam si seruus meus credit contrahere cum serva et contrahit cum libera, non est matrimonium. *h.* dicit illam rationem, quia dicit hoc introductum fuisse causa

Johannes Teutonicus, *Glos.Ord.*

Secunda questio] Hic intitulatur ...

Et nota quod secundum *h.* non omnis error conditionis impedit matrimonium, set tantum error seruilis conditionis ...; *alii* autem dicunt quod siue erret in meliori, siue in deteriori, semper dirimitur matrimonium.

---

117 *P* 53ra, *R* 149vb. The full text of this gloss is printed below, §11.
118 *P* 28va (not collated with *R*).
119 *P* 79va, *R* 228va.—*Glos.Ord.*: MS *Vat.lat.* 1367 (set i), fol. 237va.

libertatis, et quia uerisimile est quod libentius uellet liberum quam seruum quem non diligit[b], et ut occurratur malicie seruorum. *b*. uero dicit quod ubicumque interuenit error conditionis in inpari, nunquam contrahitur matrimonium, siue in meliori, siue in[c] deteriori interueniat error: C.de incest.nupt.l.iii. (*Cod*.5,5,3). Ubi uero interuenit error, tamen conditio par[d] est, puta seruus uoluit contrahere cum libera, set tamen ipsa erat scrua, uel liber[e] cum serua, tamen erat libera, tenet matrimonium; licet *h*. dicat quod tantum deterior impediat.

De ascriptitia conditione uel originaria[f] non reperitur in canone quod impediat, unde dicit *h*. quod non impedit. *Jo*. tamen dicit contra, quod scil.impediat: in aut. de nupt. §Asscriptitio, coll.iiii. (*Auth*.4,1,17 = *Nov*.22,17). Nec error conditionis impedit ex natura, set ex constitutione.

Tertii dicunt quod si interueniat error in dispari conditione, dirimitur matrimonium;

set si in pari, non dirimitur ...

... Dubitari autem consueuit, si libera contrahit per errorem cum homine ascriptitie conditionis, an teneat matrimonium. *h*. dicit quod teneat, lex tamen contradicit, in aut. de nupt. §Ascriptitio, et C. de senatuscons. Claudia. 1. una (*Cod*. 7,24,1).

a) Contraxerit *P*. b) quam ... diligit] quem diligit seruum *PR*, *R. corr. ut supra*.
c) *om. P*.   d) pars *P*.   e) *om. P*.   f) originalia *R*.

This last gloss reports three different opinions regarding the invalidating force of *error conditionis* in marriage consent (error concerning the freedom or servitude of the spouse): Huguccio holds that only the mistake of the free spouse who is ignorant of the servile status (*conditio deterior*) of the other, renders the marriage void; Bazianus holds that the corresponding mistake of a slave who is ignorant of the free status (*conditio melior*) of his, or her, spouse, has the same effect. Master *b*. finally sides with Bazianus, if the contracting parties are really of unequal condition, one free and one slave; but if two persons of equal condition contract marriage under the erroneous assumption of inequality, *b*. declares the marriage to be valid.[120] The rest of the gloss regards another controversy,

---

120 A somewhat confused report on this controversy is also found in a gloss of the *Apparatus "Servus appellatur"* on *Comp. III* (Laurentius? cf. above §5, n. 55), printed by Gillmann, *Laur. Hisp.* p. 110, note; *De coniugio serv.*, c. *Ad nostram* (*3 Comp*. IV, 7, un. = X. IV, 9, 4), v. *separavit*]" ... De isto errore dicunt quidam ba(zianus) bi.(?) quod utriusque conditionis error, et melioris et deterioris, impedit. Hug̃. uero dicit quod tantum deterioris conditionis ...; pro opinione ba. et(!) est argumentum ..." (The parentheses are Gillmann's who rightly suspects the text to be

on *conditio ascriptitia* vel *originaria* (i.e. praedial serfage), where Huguccio's opinion is contradicted by *Jo.*, i.e. by Johannes Teutonicus, as the parallel text in the *Ordinaria* shows.[121]—In the following gloss, Huguccio, Bazianus and *b*. hold again three different opinions:

> C. 22, q. 4, c. *Inter cetera* (22), v. *impendere*][122] ... dicit *baz*. hoc consilium esse, cum enim coactus iurauit, habet exceptionem: ff. quod metus ca. Nec timorem (*Dig.* 4, 2, 7). Nam et matrimonia debent esse libera: ex. i.ª de sponsal. Requisiuit (*1 Comp.* IV, 1, 12. = X. IV, 1, 17).[123] Set *h*. dicit hunc compellendum eam ducere, arg. s. ead. Si aliquid (c. 16); non[b] tamen dicit quod finaliter sit compellendus, ut ex. Requisiuit. *b*. dicit quod ubi quis iurat absolute, compellendus est etiam finaliter, ut consentiat, arg. ex. iii. de spon. Sicut ex litteris[c] ... (*3 Comp.* IV, 1, 1 = X. IV, 1, 22).[124]
>
> a) *om. P*. b) nec *R*. c) ex. ii. de spon. Sicut ex litt. *P*, ex. ii. de iureiur. Item si quis *R, super rasura*.

10. Who, then, was this Master *b*.? One could think perhaps again of Bernard of Pavia, since the author of the *Compilatio prima* still continued his literary activities after having been raised, between April 1191 and June 1192, to the bishopric of Faenza: he illustrated his own compilation by short glosses,[125] by a *Summa titulorum*,[126] by a series of *Argumenta*

---

corrupted. Perhaps it can be bettered by the following emendations:"... dicunt quide*m* ba. *et* ber.; ... pro opinione ba. et *ber*. est arg.").

121 The invalidating effect of this error had been previously asserted by Johannes Faventinus; cf. Kunstmann, *art. cit.* (above, n. 111), p. 221, and the quotation in Bernard of Pavia's *De matrim.* (ed. Laspeyres, p. 294; ed. Kunstmann, p. 234). But in *Glos. Pal.* "Johannes" is said to have contradicted Huguccio; therefore, he cannot be the Faventinus who wrote before Huguccio. The attribution to Johannes Teutonicus is also inferred by the corresponding references to *Nov.* 22,17, in both *Pal.* and *Ord.*

122 *P* 65rb, *R* 187ra.—A lengthy gloss in which *b*. cites *baç*. is also found on C. 16, q. 1, c. *Monachi* (33), v. *vagantes*.

123 It is evident that the citation, *ex. i. de sponsal. Requisiuit*, presents a modernized form of Bazianus' and Huguccio's original references. For Huguccio, cf. *Repertorium*, p. 161, n. 1: "... Lucius etiam tertius in illa decretali *Requisiuit* dicit ...". A similar wording must be found in Bazianus' original text, for which, at present, I have no MSS on hand.

124 The substitution of Celestine III's *Item si quis* (*2 Comp.* II, 16, 7) in *R* is evidently spurious; also, this decretal would not make the glossator's point, for it permits exceptions in the fulfilment of the oath.

125 *Repertorium*, p. 323; see also below, §18.

126 Edition by Laspeyres, pp. 1–283. Cf. *Repertorium*, pp. 387 ff. 462, with 23 MSS. Add Montecassino, MS 46 (pp. 1–278: *Comp. I* with excerpts from the *Summa*, on the lower margins). The MS of Mr. Vollbehr, formerly in Washington (*Repertorium*, p. 388) cannot be located at present.—Schulte, *QL*, I, 181 and Le Bras, *art. cit.* (above, n. 109), col. 785, find fault with Bernard's book: they contend that it is not properly a *Summa decretalium*, but a *Summa* of Canon Law, with but occasional references to the decretals (among other references: to Gratian,

(or *Notabilia*)[127]—which were to become the canvas for the *Generalia* (*Brocarda*) of Richardus Anglicus[128]—; and finally he wrote *Casus decretalium*, after his translation (1198) to the see of his home town Pavia.[129]
Indeed, in one case, the *Glossa Palatina* might have referred by the initial *b*. to Bernardus Papiensis. In the controversy on *error conditionis*, an opinion was held by the latter, in both his *Summa de matrimonio* and his *Summa titulorum decretalium*, which resembles very much—although it does not correspond exactly—to the report of the *Palatina* on Master *b*.[130] But even if we admit this one possible instance, no generalizing conclusion is allowed; for elsewhere the *Palatina* treats *b*. and Bernard of Pavia distinctly as two persons:

C. 17, q. 1, §*Si ergo* (p. c. 4), v. *confitebor*][131] j. de pen. di. i. Dixi (c. 4). *in corde*] Et ita potest quis obligari, quod concedit *b*., licet gratianus sentiat aliter, ut infra sequitur. *pro opere*] uocis et confessionis. *computandus est*] et sine dubio computandus esset, si non esset mente alienatus. Quod postea dicit de ore uel de corde, nichil est, quia nichil obligatur, sicut et alio. Nec contradicit ex. qui clerici uel uouent. c. ult^a. (*1 Comp*. IV, 6, 8 = X. IV, 6, 5); nam illud intelligo de comparatiua permissione. *b. uero pap̄*. dicit ibi alexandrum dormitasse.
a) l(ibro). i. *add. R*.

---

to Roman Law, etc.). This reproach is void, for a *Summa decretalium* has as its subject the *tituli decretalium*, i.e. the canonical institutes and concepts expressed by the rubrics of the titles, and not the individual decretals, the explanation of which would make a *Lectura*, not a *Summa*.— Also unfounded is Schulte's and Le Bras' further thesis that the book had been originally written before, and only revised after the *Compilatio prima*.

127 Already in Bernard's glosses, *Argumenta* are frequent: cf. e.g. Laspeyres, p. 323 f., nos. 1.2.6–9.11.17.19.20.23.24.26 (and, developed into *Generalia* with solutions, nos. 3.22). As a separate collection I found the *Argumenta* in Melk, Benedictine Monast., MS 333 (formerly F. 33, catal. 190; fols. 252v–254v), beg. "Argumentum quod nullus iure suo priuatur sine culpa".

128 On Richard's *Generalia*, see *Repertorium*, p. 417 f., with two MSS. Add: Avranches, Munic. Libr., MS 149 (fols. 139–147v); Bamberg, State Libr., MS *Can*. 45 (formerly P. II. 4; fols. 45.1–7 [fragment])—both not identified in *Repertorium*, pp. 421, n. 2; 422—, and Zwettl, Cist. Mon., MS 162 (fols. 73–82).—For genetic relations between the literary species of *Argumenta* and *Generalia*, cf. *Repertorium*, pp. 3.239; the relation between Bernard's and Richard's respective works in particular will be discussed on another occasion.

129 *Repertorium*, p. 398 f.; specimens edited by Laspeyres, pp. 327–352. To the MSS, add Zwettl, MS 297 (fols. 86–106); but Novara, Cath. Chapter, MS XCVI (formerly 76; listed as dubious in *Repertorium*, p. 399) has to be cancelled: it contains, like the MS 225 of Vendôme (wrongly named by Le Bras, *art. cit.*, col. 787), the *Casus* by Bernard Bottone of Parma on the decretals of Gregory IX.

130 *Summa de matr*., ed. Laspeyres, p. 294; ed. Kunstmann, p. 234. *Summa titul*., IV, 9, §5, ed. Laspeyres p. 154. Bernard discusses the error of the slave who intends to marry a free woman, and *vice versa*, like master *b*. in the gloss on C. 29, q. 2, pr. But he does not use the characteristic distinction, *in inpari—in pari*, nor does he mention the *error in meliori*, when speaking of unequal spouses. Thus it is not quite certain whether the *Palatina* refers to him.

131 *P* 60vb, *R* 169vb–170ra. Also on C. 16, q. 1 §*De his vero* (p. c. 41; *P* 57va), Bishop Bernard is quoted expressly as "... *b*. tamen papi(ensis) ...".

Also, for all the other numerous b.-glosses of this *Apparatus*, no corresponding texts are found in Bishop Bernard's writings; often he holds quite different opinions.[132] In particular, there exists no relation whatsoever between Master *b*. of the *Palatina* and Bernard of Pavia's glosses on Gratian which appear in the earlier mixed compositions. Finally, we may anticipate here that our Master *b*. in one of his other works, the glosses on the *Compilatio prima*,[133] quotes Bernardus Papiensis expressly and objects several times to his opinions, e.g.:

De decimis, c. *Ex parte* (*1 Comp*. III, 26, 10 — X. III, 30, 10), v. *propriis manibus*][134]s. ead. Fraternitatem (c. 8) contra. *bernaldus papi*. refert in summa sua super hoc uolumine[135] se super his decretalibus domino alexandro questionem mouisse et ab eo accepisse huic[a] decretali, sc. Ex parte, standum fore. *Set uerius credo* hanc decretalem fuisse priorem et per superiorem correctam, fauore illius episcopi ad quem scribitur sibi specialiter indultam. Fouere enim religiossimos monachos debemus per quos ecclesia dei redunita fulcitur. Unde credo standum epistolis antiquis in contraria parte. *b'*.
a) hac *MS*.

11. By way of elimination, then, Bernard of Compostella remains the only Bolognese master of the early thirteenth century to whom the numerous passages in the *Glossa Palatina* with the siglum *b*. (or quoting from *b*.) can refer in general. The same is true for the corresponding quotations by Laurentius, for the glosses by *b*. or *ber*. in the mixed composition of MS *Vat. lat.* 1367, and for the additions by *b*. to Laurentius in the Charleville MS.[136] An examination of the other pertinent gloss compositions of the same period[137] will probably not affect this conclusion. What we still need is a positive evidence for the Compostellan's gloss writing, and this too is offered by the *Palatina*:

C. 13, q. 2, c. *Illud* (5), v. *obstrictum*][138] Hoc[a] dicas conniuentibus ecclesiis[b], ut ff. de reg.iur. Neque (*Dig*. 50, 17, 45) et[c] de usuc. Non solum,

---

132 For instance, master *b*.'s important distinctions on homicide (Kuttner, *Dekretsumme*, p. 150; above, §7, n. 92) are entirely different from those given by Bernardus Pap., *Summa titul.*, V, 10 (ed. Laspeyres, p. 220 ff.); or, master *b*.'s admission of the defendant's *purgatio canonica*, even after his crime has been attested by witnesses (below, §12, at n. 152) is contrary to Bern. Pap., *Summa titul.*, V, 29, §3 (ed. Laspeyres p. 259): "... Praeterea si accusator offert probationem et reus offert purgationem, probatio et non purgatio est audienda, quia tunc demum recipitur, cum deficit accusator."
133 Cf. below, ch. III.
134 Modena, Bibl. Estense, MS a. R. 4.16, fol. 40ra. Further examples see below, §19.
135 Cf. *Summa titul.*, III, 30, §3 (ed Laspeyres, p. 105).
136 In *Lc*, such additions are found e.g. on D. 5, c. *Ad eius* (4), v. *prohibentur*; C. 16, q. 7, c. *Sicut Domini* (19). For the Vatican glosses, see below, §14.
137 MSS Arras 500, St.-Omer 476; see above, §7.
138 *P* 53ra, *R* 149vb.

§Si rem (*Dig.* 41,3,33,6). Nam domino res sua uendi uel^d obligari non potest, *b. intelligit hoc secundum consuetudinem compostell'. ecclesie*, secundum quam^e seruus habet proprium. bazianus^f intellexit de seruo dediticio: C. de latina libert. 1. i. (*Cod.* 7, 6, 1). Set pone quod aliquis gessit procurationem ecclesie usque ad certum tempus, postea dictum est ei, ut iterum gerat per aliud tantumdem tempus^g. Numquid^h compelletur^i reddere rationem primi temporis? Dicit l(ex) quod sic,^{139} cum ad officium eius spectat quicquid ex prima amministratione deberet ad secundam rationem transire^j: ff. mandati, Qui mutuam §Non omnis^k (*Dig.* 17, 1, 56, 2).

a) Hec *P* b) oculis (!) *R*. c) et C. *P*. d) nec *P*. e) quamuis *P*. f) baçanus *P*. g) per ... tempus *om. R*: h) *om. R*, posseat (!) *add. P.* i) compellentur *P*. j) redire *R*. k) Non ideo minus *Dig*.

Certainly, nobody would have interpreted the legal capacity of serfs "according to the custom of the church of Compostella," were this bishopric not his home. With this gloss, the key to master *b*.'s identity is found: not Bazianus, nor Bernard of Pavia, but Bernard of Compostella was meant by the siglum *b*. in the *Glossa Palatina* and other contemporary apparatuses.

12. It has become evident from the texts quoted in the preceding paragraphs that Bernard's teaching had its own personal note, for he held his own views on many canonical problems. The examples of his independent reasoning could be easily multiplied; but from these polemical glosses one must not deduce that Bernard was an habitual dissenter. We learn from the *Palatina* that on the contrary he frequently followed the doctrines of his fellow countryman Melendus. This Spanish canonist[140] was Bernard's senior, for he belonged to the Bolognese school as early as in Huguccio's days.[141] At the beginning of the thirteenth century, he must have been very renowned. When Thomas Marlborough came to Bologna, in 1205, and searched for lawyers who would plead the case of Evesham Abbey against the Bishop of Worcester in the papal court, he hired among others one *magister Merandus Hispanus*, who is nobody else than Melendus.[142] At the same time, the

---

139 On the misinterpretation of this passage by Guido de Baysio, see above, §6, n. 84.
140 Schulte, *QL*, I, 151; Kuttner, *Repertorium*, p. 7, n. 3. The glosses of *Magister M.* on Stephen of Tournai, which I mentioned *loc. cit.*, were, however, more probably written by a master of the French school, perhaps by Matthew of Angers; cf. Kuttner, "Les débuts de l'école canoniste française", *Studia et docum. hist. et iuris*, IV (1938), 201, n. 52.
141 Cf. above, §3, at n. 27.
142 *Chronicon Abbatiae de Evesham*, ed. W. Dunn Macray (London, 1863, Rolls Series), p. 153. The passage has been noted, but without identification of the glossator, by Pollock and Maitland, *The History of English Law before the Time of Edward I*, I (2d ed., Cambridge, 1898), 122, n. 1.— Thomas engaged, besides Melendus, "quendam ... militem Papiensem, Bertrandum nomine, dominum legum, qui nulli totius Lumbardiae post dominum Assonem (i.e. Azonem) habebatur secundus" (this civilian lawyer and knight of Pavia is otherwise not known); "magistrum Petrum

Bishop of Winchester secured Melendus' services, and had him appear in Rome as attorney for King John, in that fateful Canterbury election case which preceded the papal appointment of Stephen Langton to the primatial see of England.[143] Thomas Marlborough also states that he met Melendus again as a bishop on the Lateran Council (1215); thus we can identify the glossator with Bishop Melendus of Osma (c. 1210–1225).[144] Before his election, Melendus had taught for a short time, c. 1209, in Vicenza.[145]

It is striking how often the *Glossa Palatina* names *m. et b.* as holding the same opinions in controversial matters. E.g.:

D. 95, c. *Pervenit* (1), v. *concedimus*][146] ... de collatione autem huiusmodi sacramentorum dicunt *b.* et *m.* ...

C. 1, q. 5, c. *Presentium* (3), v. *fratrumque*][147] ... arg. xv. q. vii. Episcopus nullius. *M.* et *b.*... .

C. 11, q. 1, c. *Sacerdotibus* (41), v. *specialiter*][148] Ita hec intelligunt *M.* et *b.*, idest non tam pro istis. ...

C. 23, q. 3, pr., v. *fugiens*][149] ... unde dic cum *b.* et *m.* baldaciter... .

C. 33, q. 2, In *adolescentia* (14), v. *regulam*][150] ... *B.* uero et *M.* qui dicunt... .

De cons., D. 2, c. *Sicut* (2), v. *calix*][151] ... nam dicunt *b.* et *m.*... ., item dicunt *b.* et *m.*...

Beneventanum, capellanum domini Papae, postea cardinalem et episcopum Portuensem", i.e. Petrus Collivaccinus, the future redactor of the *Compilatio tertia* (cf. *Repertorium*, p. 355; for his biography, see F. Heyer, *ZRGKan*, VI [1916], 395–405); "magistrum Willielmum Provincialem, clericum domini cancellarii", who was a notary of the Chancery under Innocent III (cf. H. Bresslau, *Handbuch der Urkundenlehre*, I [2d ed., Leipzig 1912], 248), and Vice-Chancellor of the Roman Church, 1220–1222 (cf. P. M. Baumgarten, *Von der apostolischen Kanzlei* [Köln, 1908], p. 73).—For the variant spellings of Melendus' name (Merandus, Monendus, Melandus, Merendus, etc.) cf. Gillmann, *Zur Inventaris.*, p. 57.

143 *Chron. Evesh., loc. cit.*: "Hunc, cum regeret scholas Bononiae, dominus Wintoniensis Romam adduxerat, et stetit ibi pro domino rege Angliae contra monachos Cantuarienses super iure eligendi Cantuariensem episcopum."

144 *Loc. cit.*: "... quem postea tempore concilii vidi episcopum." At that time, the only Spanish bishop by the name of Melendus is found at Osma; cf. Eubel, I, 383.

145 See the document of 1209 in Sarti, I, 381, n. 9. For the short-lived school of Vicenza (1204–1209) in general, cf. Savigny, III, 307 ff. Melendus cannot have been one of the founders of that school, as Sarti, *loc. cit.*, and Schulte, *QL*, I,. 151, presumed, since Thomas Marlborough found him in 1205 still teaching at Bologna.

146 Kuttner, *Dekretsumme*, p. 158.

147 Above, §9, at n. 118.

148 *P* 46va, *R* 131 vb.

149 Cf. below, §15, at n. 189.

150 *Dekretsumme*, p. 167.

151 *Ibid.*, p. 149.

Sometimes, also, the two friends opposed each other:

C. 2, q. 1, c. *Multi* (18) v. *convictum*]¹⁵² Nec adhuc uult satisfacere ...; dicit tamen *h.* quod clericus non potest reconueniri a laico super crimine uel actione famosa. *M.* contra, quia pro socio, depositi, bene: Instit. de pena temere litig. §Ex quibusdam (*Inst.* 4, 16, 2). Non tamen infamabitur clericus lata contra eum sententia. Set *b.* contra, arg. ff. de hiis qui notantur inf. 1. i. (*Dig.* 3, 2, 1); de pena temere litig. §Ex quibusdam; vi. q. i. Infames . (c. 17). Item pone actum esse cum clerico de seruo occiso^a, et probatur ei crimen: numquid priuabitur officio? Distingue an infamia sequatur ex eo^b facto, et tunc^c priuabitur; an non, et tunc secus. Item numquid recipies eius purgationem post crimen sibi^d probatum? Videtur quod non, quia testes iurauerunt de scientia, compurgatores^e de credulitate.^f Set *b.* dicit eam recipiendam, maxime quia compurgatores debent esse plures, quod uerum est.

a) ocioso *P*.   b) om. *P*   c) ita *R*.   d) sic *P*.
e) et purgatores *R*.   f) crelitate *P*, crudelitate *R*.

And in a collection of *Quaestiones disputatae* we shall find them delivering contrary opinions on a practical case.¹⁵³

13. Another problem to be considered is that of the approximate date of Bernard's glosses. The usual method of examining for that purpose his citations of decretals fails in our case, for most of his glosses we do not know in their original shape,¹⁵⁴ but through the reports of Laurentius and the *Glossa Palatina*. The two apparatuses, composed c. 1210–1215, gave of course all references to decretals according to the then acknowledged compilations (*Compp.* I—III); yet from this method of citation we can by no means conclude that the Compostellan wrote after 1210. What we know is that he used the *Compilatio prima*;¹⁵⁵ we know further that his academic activities fall in the early thirteenth century, as his own decretal collection (*Compilatio Romana*) dates from 1208.¹⁵⁶ But within the space of c. 1200–1215, an exact chronological determination of his glosses is not possible. We can infer only that Bernard began writing on the *Decreta* before 1206, as this is the *terminus ad quem* for his glosses on the *Compilatio prima*,¹⁵⁷ and in these glosses he sometimes refers to his decretist production:

De decimis, c. *Fraternitatem* (*1 Comp.* III, 26, 8), v. *ab exactione*]¹⁵⁸ De iure communi, i.e. de iure ueteris testamenti, credo quemlibet predium

---
152 *P* 30rb, *R* 91vb.
153 See below, §25.
154 Except a few examples from the Vatican MS: below, §14.
155 Above, §8.
156 Above, §1.
157 Below, §21.
158 MS of Modena (above, n. 134), fol. 39vb.

habentem ad functionem decimalem teneri ...; uel melius solue, *ut notaui xvi. q.i. in nota 'In iure uet. test.'*; et illud omnino approbo. Sunt enim quidam qui contrarium predicant, quod ibidem ad plenum intellectum clericalis decimationis—ut eod., c. Parrochianos (*1 Comp.* III, 26, 26 = X. III, 30, 14)—inuenies. *b'*.

Bernard testifies here, before 1206, to have written a gloss on Gratian, C. 16, q. 1, that begins: "In iure ueteris testamenti"; unfortunately, it is not preserved, although the *Glossa Palatina* on C. 16, q. 1, cites frequently Bernard's opinions.[159] But in another case,

> De pignor. c. Nullus (*1 Comp.* III, 17, 1 = X. III, 21, 1), v. *vel vestimentum*][160] In quo casu non credo quod nexus pignoris teneat. Unde, si a pignoris detentatione (!) caderet creditor, non darem sibi ypothecariam. Dum tamen tenet, habet doli exceptionem, *ut dixi x.q.ii. Hoc ius.b'*. Set secus in libro, cum non sit res sacra, *b'*.

the gloss on C. 10, q. 2, c. 2, which Bernard cites, is reported indeed by the *Palatina*, and moreover, the *Palatina* refers back to the gloss on the decretal compilation: "b. dicit ...; dixit super illo extrauaganti... ."[161]—These cross-references account for an early beginning of Bernard's glossing on Gratian. However, he may very well have continued to write glosses after 1206; and since he never gathered them, as far as we know, in a formal apparatus, he may even have carried on after the *Glossa Palatina* was published. This is all the more likely, as we have evidence that Bernard took up his pen again, after 1216–1217, in order to write additional notes on the *Glossa Ordinaria*.

14. This evidence is found in MS *Vat. lat.* 1367 (= *Ov*), in a very interesting stratum of glosses (set ii) compiled after 1217, probably by a pupil of the scarcely known Bolognese master William Vasco.[162] This text consists of selected glosses from earlier authors, and of supplementary annotations on the *Ordinaria*. In both groups Bernard of Compostella is well represented. His glosses—if we abstract from those which have been incorporated into the composition through the medium of the *Palatina*[163]—are signed by the siglum *B*. (on over 30 pages), or *b*. (fol. 125va), *dicit ber...* . (fol. 131va), *B'*. (fol. 303va). In one case, the full signature is found under a moralising verse:

---

159 E.g. *Glos. Pal.* on C. 16, q. 1, c. *In sacris* (56), v. *vel beneficiis*] "... *h*. dicit .. *b*. uero dicit ..., et nos, secundum *b*." (*P* 57vb, *R* 162vb). On cc. 57.58, *eod.*, see below, §15, at nn. 187. 188.
160 MS of Modena, fol. 36ra.
161 Cf. above, §8, at n. 101.
162 See below, Appendix.
163 E.g. the gloss on C. 15, q. 6, c. 4: above §7, n. 93.

De cons., D. 4, c. *Mulier* (20)][164]   Mulier semel docuit
                                            Et totum mundum subuertit.b'nād'.

But in this case I think the compiler quoted an adage circulating, as its spirit would suggest, under the flag of St. Bernard of Clairvaux.[165]

Among the Compostellan's glosses in *Ov*, many can be determined as originally written in his early period, because the *Palatina* already knew them:

D.10, c.*Lege* (1).[166]   *Glos.Pal.*
Glos.Vat.

duorum] Set nonne isti testes sunt domestici, ergo non sunt admittendi? R.bene possunt recipi, cum in causa ecclesie inducantur, ut xiii.q.ii.Super prudencia (c.1). *B.*	*dicantur*] Isti testes domestici sunt, et tamen eis creditur, quia causa ecclesiastica est: xiii.q.ii.c.ii.; et quia sunt tales persone de quibus dubitari non potest, sicut et X[c] (Christus) dixit: 'Quare testimonium meum et patris mei non recipitis?' (cf.*Jo.* iii,11;v,36–38; viii,18).

C. 18, q. 2, c. *Dudum* (27).[167]

Glos. Ord., v. fraternitati] Set nonne, cum aliquid precipitur, sufficit quod preceptum sit predecessori ad hoc, ut successor teneatur? ut in auth. Ut nulli iudicum, Et hoc iubemus, coll. ix (*Auth.* 9, 9, 6 = *Nov.* 134, 6). Licet aliud sit in mandato, quia illud extinguitur morte, ut ex. i. de off. deleg. Gratum (*1 Comp.* I, 21,23 = X. I, 29, 20). Dicunt quidam quod siue sit preceptum siue mandatum, dummodo expressis nominibus scribatur, semper expirat morte, ut ex. de off. deleg. Quoniam (*eod.*, c. 19 = X, c. 14). Alii dicunt aliud esse in precepto quam mandato.

Glos.Vat.   *Glos.Pal.*

Nam preceptum est tale quod contineat factum, nec exspirat morte mandantis uel etiam mandatarii[a], et ita intelligit *az.* illam aut(henticam) 'Et hoc uero iubemus'. Si uero iurisdictio, distinguitur utrum re integra, etc. *B.*	... Set *b.* in precepto non admittit distinctionem illius c.extra. Quoniam, quia quocumque modo non finitur morte alterutrius persone: §Et hoc uero ...

a) mandatoris *Ov.*

---

164 *Ov* 306vb.
165 I failed, however, to find the dictum among his writings.
166 *Ov* 4va, *P* 2vb.
167 *Ov* 171vb, *P* 62rb. In *Glos. Pal.*, the problem is treated at length, and the author, before quoting master *b.*'s opinion, writes, among other remarks: "... alias morte mandatoris uel mandatarii non extinguitur huiusmodi preceptum, *ut dixi* in aut. ut nulli iudicum, §Et hoc uero, coll. ix..."; attributing thus to himself the explanation of *Nov.* 134, 6, which, according to Bernard, had been offered by the civilian Azo.

In the gloss on D. 10, the Vatican compiler probably gives Bernard's original wording; in the second gloss, he evidently reshaped Bernard's text at the beginning, in order that it might match, with the conjunction *nam*, the last sentence of the *Ordinaria*.

Other glosses were obviously written by the Spanish master as additions to the *Ordinaria*, e.g.:

C. 6, q. 1, c. *Illi qui* (3).[168]
Glos. Ord.: Secundum quosdam prima pars de criminosis non excommunicatis, secunda de *excommunicatis; secundum alios loquitur prima pars de occultis, secunda de criminosis** manifestis.
Glos. Vat.: *hoc tenet *W*. **pocior est prior intellectus, nam de occultis non cogitur quis ad penitentiam. *B*.

C. 18, q. 2, c. *Abbates* (16).[169]
Glos. Ord., v. *acquisierit*] Ergo fugitiuus. ... Set ponamus quod aliquis sepius deliquid, propter quod monasterium ipsum nolit recipere: quero si id quod postea acquirit, priori monasterio acquirit uel sequenti? Videtur quod sequenti ... . Set hanc questionem plene notaui inter dominicales questiones.[170]
Glos. Vat.: Dic quod, si intrauit aliud monasterium, illi acquirit; alias si uagatur, quicquid acquirit primo acquirit, ut in aut. de sanctiss. episc. Si monachus (*Auth.* 9, 15, 42 = *Nov.* 123, 42). *B*.

Still in other cases, no clue is offered as to the chronological relations between Bernard and the *Ordinaria*, e.g.:

Glos. Vat. on C. 3, q. 7, c. *In gravibus* (5)][171] Set numquid iudex potest recusari obiectu criminis, ut uidelicet si dicatur uel adulter uel aliter criminosus? Videtur quod sic, per omnia ista c(apitula), et ex. i. de testib. Super eo (*1 Comp.* II, 14, 4 = X. II, 21, 3). In contrarium uidetur xv. q. ult. c. ult. (q. 8, c. 5), et viii. q. iiii. Nonne (c. 1), et j. ead. §ult. (3, q. 7, p. c. 7). Dic quod non potest, per iura preallegata. *B*.

C. 3, q. 9, pr.][172] Omnia ista capitula a principio usque ad c. Decreuimus (c. 10) intellige, quando reus est absens ex iusta causa et probabili, uel tantum probabili. *B*.

C. 16, q. 3, §*Sic etiam* (p. c. 16), v. *Romane ecclesie*][173] Set quas ecclesias intelligis romane ecclesie? *h*. dicit quod omnes ecclesie exempte, que nullo medio spectant ad dominum papam, intelliguntur, unde non prescribitur contra eas, nisi spatio c. annorum; et uidetur ipsius opinio canonizari ex. iii. de prescript. Cum uobis (*3 Comp.* II, 17, 4 = X. II, 26, 14), et ex. iii. de confirm. utili c. i. (*3 Comp.* II, 20, 1 — X. II, 30, 4) ultra medium. *B*.

---

168 *Ov* 108va. Regarding the addition by *W*. (William Vasco), see below, Appendix, at n. 411.
169 *Ov* 170vb.
170 Bartholomaeus Brixiensis, by placing in the second redaction of the *Ordinaria* the siglum *Jo*. before, and his own siglum *B*. behind the last sentence, stole this passage and made it appear as a reference to his own *Quaestiones*. The *Quaestiones disputatae* of Johannes Teutonicus to which the original gloss referred are preserved in a collection of Klosterneuburg, cf. *Repertorium*, p. 254; below, §24, n. 291. As to the Bolognese custom of naming *Quaestiones* after the day on which they were disputed in class (here: *dominicales*), cf. Savigny, III, 570, n. *a*.
171 *Ov* 102va.
172 *Ov* 103ra.
173 *Ov* 163va.

The last gloss seems to be written after 1210 (*Comp. III*)—unless the compiler of the Vatican glosses changed the style of the references which Bernard may well have originally given according to his own decretal collection or *extra titulos*.[174] In any event, there are enough glosses in *Ov* to show that the Compostellan was stirred to new activity by the appearance of Johannes' *Glossa Ordinaria*.[175]

15. Johannes Teutonicus himself does not seem to have esteemed Bernard very highly. When we compare the abundant testimony given by Laurentius and by the author of the *Palatina* for the Compostellan's earlier gloss production, and on the other hand the parsimony of Johannes in acknowledging his achievements, the contrast is astounding: only in a few cases Bernard's initial accompanies the report on his opinions in the *Ordinaria*;[176] usually, Johannes refers to those opinions by an impersonal *alii* or *quidam*:

Glos. Pal.	*Glos. Ord.*[177]
C.10,q.2, c.*Ea* (2), §*Hoc ius. conflata*][178] Quia res desinit ... *b*.dicit quod, cum res sacra extimari non possit, ... nec locus sacer uendi possit... . Dixit super illo extra. nexum pignoris non constare in huiusmodi sacris rebus.... Set ... detinere potest pro pecunia	*conflata*] Quia ad profanos ... dicunt tamen quidam quod nec uendi nec obligari possunt, cum sint res sacre ...; et dicunt ibi non esse nexum pignoris, set solum detentionem habet, quousque reddatur ei sua pecunia ...
C.22, q.4, c.*Inter cetera* (22). impendere*][179 ... *b*.dicit quod ubi quis iurat absolute, compellendus est etiam finaliter ...	*matrimonium*] ... alii dicunt quod omnibus modis est cogendus ...
C.29, q.2, pr.[180] ... *b*.uero dicit ...	... tertii dicunt ...

---

174 The two decretals appear, under the same rubrics as in *Comp. III*, in Bernard's *Coll. Rom.*, II, 15, 4 and II, 19, 1. They regard the same case and were issued on the same day: June 17, 1206 (*Po.* nn. 2812.2813).'
175 Further examples are found in *Ov*, fols. 89rb. 90rb. 108va. 110va. 121r. 125va ("hanc solutionem approbat *b*."). 147rb. 160va. 236ra. 244va. 289vb.
176 Cf. *Glos. Ord.* on D. 95, c. 1, v. *concedimus*; on *De cons.*, D. 2, c. *Sicut* (2), v. *calix* (both texts printed in *Dekretsumme*, pp. 158.149); also on *De cons.*, D. 3, c. 1, v.*festivitates* (printed in Kuttner, "La réserve papale ... ", *RHD*, 4, XVII [1938], 220 f.). In all these cases, I previously supposed the siglum *b*. to denote Bazianus.
177 The following texts have been collated in the Vatican MSS *Pal. lat.* 624 (= Op^1), 625 (= Op^2) and *Ov*, for the original *Ordinaria*. Most of them are also found in the printed editions of the second (Barth. Brix.) redaction.
178 The full text is given above, §8, at n. 101.
179 Cf. above, §9, at n. 122.
180 See both texts above, §9, at n. 119.

Glos. Pal.

C.30, q.l, c.*Pervenit* (l).[181]
ex lavacro] Dicit B....

De cons., D.2, c.*Etsi non* (16).
natali][182] *b*.dicit tantum in pascha preceptum esse.

Glos. Ord.

ex lavacro] Dicunt quidam ...

natali] Alii dicunt tantum in pascha preceptum esse.

Or he presents Bernard's glosses as his own, tacitly or expressly:

D.95, c.*Pervenit* (l).[183]
crismate] j.de cons.... nunc uero minime, *b*.

C.l,q.5, *Presentium* (3).
fratrumque][184] Et ita ... nullius, M. et *b*. Nam in omni ... s.e.q.c.i.—*b*.concedit quod nec in beneficio ...

C.13, q.2, §*Nunc queritur* (p.c.l).
Hic[185] explicatur unus articulus ... et dicit *h*. de isto ... *b*. uero dicit quod ubicumque uoluerit, potest, dumtamen hoc non faciat ex odio uel temeritate... . ex.i. de sepult.c.ii. (*1 Comp.* III, 24,2).

Ibid., c.*Unaquaque* (3).
in morte][186] Hoc consilium est, similiter ex.de sepult.De uxore (*1* Comp. III,24,7 = X.III,28,7). Set pone[a] quod plures uiros habuerit: quem sequeretur?

Ibid., c.*Unaquaque* (3).
Secundum b. planum est, quia quem voluerit[b] ...

a) ipse *PR*. b) uolunt *P*.

crismate] j.de cons.... nunc uero minime. *Jo*.

fratrumque] Et ita ... nullius. Nam in omni ... s.e.q., c.i.—Set hoc non admitto ...

Hic explicatur alter articulus ... *h*. dicit ...; *ego* credo quod libere potest quis eligere sepulturam ubicumque uoluerit, ut ex.eod.tit. Volumus (c.2); et omnia contraria intelligo, quando uel est illectus, uel quando ex contemptu uel temeritate ...

in morte] Hoc est consilium, ut ex.i. eod. c.penult.(7).
Querit *h*.: pone quod mulier plures uiros habuit: quem illorum debet sequi? Secundum *me* non est questio,

quia potest eligere sepulturam ubi voluerit ...

---

181 Cf. *Dekretsumme*, p. 148.
182 *P* 97vb, *R* 280ra. See also the report of the *Apparatus "Servus appellatur"* on Comp. *III* (cf. above, §5, n. 55), *De penitent.*, c. *Deus qui* (V, 20, 1 = X.V, 38, 8), v. *consuetis festivitatibus*] "Pasca, pentecosten ... communicare. Set ber. (*scr.* b'.) de festo pascali hoc concedebat ..." (printed by Gillmann, *Laur. Hisp.*, p. 111, note, who relates the citation to Bazianus).
183 The full text is in *Dekretsumme*, p. 150.
184 The full text is given above, §9, at n. 118.
185 Cf. above, §8, at n. 103.
186 *P* 53ra, *R* 149va.

Glos. Pal.	Glos. Ord.
C.16, q.l, c.*In canonibus* (57). *cartarum*][187] i.e.lectionis, quia non tantum lectioni debet insistere, lxxxvi. Fratrem (D.86, c.6). *b*.	*cartarum*] i.e. librorum, quia episcopus non debet semper libris insistere, ut lxxxvi. di. Fratrem.
Ibid., c.*Similiter* (58). *ecclesie ... facultatibus*][188] *b*. dicit quod sunt ecclesie ...	*ecclesie*] Quia episcopus ... uel dic quod res sunt ecclesie ...
C.23, q.3, pr. *fugiens*][189] Hoc dicit allegando ...; unde dic cum *b.et m.*[a] baldaciter quod clericus etiam uerberare potest et etiam interficere, ne interficiatur ...	*fugiens*] Quidquid hic dicitur allegatio est; nam bene licitum est cuilibet se defendere, etiam clerico, ut *notaui* s. q. i. in principio ...

a) dic cum b. m. *P*, dicunt b. et m. *R*.

Finally, in a good many cases, Johannes passes over the opinions held by Bernard without any mention.[190]

This attitude of Johannes Teutonicus towards a fellow master of the same school was not an isolated phenomenon in Bologna. In general, Johannes ignored the *Apparatus* on the *Decreta* by Alanus also; and in Tancred's *Glossae Ordinariae* on the first three of the *Compilationes antiquae*,[191] we can notice that this leading decretalist, too, acknowledged one group only of colleagues with consistent fairness, citing and incorporating their glosses with the pertinent sigla on almost every page of his commentaries, while passing over the not less important production of others with but a few occasional references.[192] Reticent attitudes of this kind reveal something unpleasant that has existed at all times among professors: academic factions, jealousies, and clique domination. When the teaching

---

187 *P* 57vb, *R* 163ra.
188 *PR eod.*
189 *P*66rb, *R* 187va. A further example is found on C. 32, q. 5, c. *Proposito* (4), v. *adultera*, where the gloss " Videtur augustinus male ... secundum canones" is given with the siglum *b*. in the *Palatina*, unsigned in *Op*[1] *Op*[2], and given with *h*. in *Ov*. (The continuation of the same gloss in the printed editions of the *Ordinaria* belongs to the second redaction). Cf. also the incorrect attribution of a gloss "*B*. tamen dicit ..." to *G*. (Gandulph?), in *Glos. Ord.* on C. 32, q. 2, c. 13; and of a gloss "*B*. uero et *M*. ..." to "*h*. uero et *laur*. et *M*.", in *Glos. Ord.* on C. 33, q. 2, c. 14 (*Dekretsumme*, pp. 148, n. 1; 167).
190 Nothing is found in *Glos. Ord.* that corresponds to the *Palatina* on D. 50, p. c. 36 (*Dekretsumme*, p. 150); C. 2, q. 1, c. 18 (above, §12, at n. 152); C. 11, q. 1, c. 41 (above, at n. 148); C. 13, q. 2, c. 5 (above, §11); C. 16, q. 1, c. 56 (above, §13, n. 159); C. 17, q. 1, p. c. 4 (above, §15, q. 10, at n. 131).
191 Cf. on these apparatuses, *Repertorium*, pp. 327 f. 346. 358 f.; below, §17, n. 219.
192 This is, e.g. in the *Glos. Ord.* on *Comp.* III, his policy towards Johannes Galensis. I cannot subscribe to the harmless explanation proposed by Gillmann, "Des Johannes Galensis Apparat ... ", *AKKR*, CXVIII (1938), 200: "One could suppose that Tancred had the apparatus by Johannes Galensis not on hand". Other examples of Tancred's unfairness could be easily supplied.

of "orthodox" authors only was honored by the leaders of the school, Johannes and Tancred, and when the "outsiders" were intentionally neglected, we are at once reminded of the well known situation in the contemporary Civil Law school where for generations the *nostri doctores*—Bulgarus, Johannes Bassianus, Azo, Accursius—treated in a similar way the outsiders Martinus Gosia, Placentinus, Pillius, and the *Gosiani* in general.[193]

16. The result was, in the case of Bernard of Compostella, that his achievements as a decretist glossator were soon forgotten. In fact, throughout the later Middle Ages, one man only took care to recall his glosses: Guido de Baysio, archdeacon of Bologna (*d.* 1313)[194] who in his voluminous *Rosarium* (1300 A.D.) assembled, with the zeal of an antiquarian, from writers past and present a unique supplement to Bartholomaeus Brixiensis' edition of the *Glossa Ordinaria*, recording all that he deemed noteworthy in Huguccio and the *Palatina* (which he regarded as Laurentius' work[195]), in decretists and decretalists since Johannes Teutonicus' days down to his own time. In this inestimable—even if not always reliable—mine of literary antiquities, quotations from B*er(nardus) Hisp(anus)* constitute a considerable part: in fact, we find under that name many of our master's opinions recorded, e.g.:[196]

C. 2, q. 1, c. *Multi* (18)] ... et post crimen sic probatum dicebat *Ber. Hisp.* purgationem recipiendam...,[197]

C. 10, q. 2, c. *Ea* (2)] ... sed *H. et Lau.* dicunt quod tam calix quam palle quam alia uendi possunt, licet *B. hisp.* in omnibus contradicat...[198]

C. 11, q. 1, c. *Sacerdotibus* (41)] ... sed quod sequitur fuit sententia *M.* et *B. Hispa.*, secundum *Lauren.*[199]

C. 16, q. 1, c. *Monachi* (33)] ... secundum *Bar.* (!) *Hisp.*....[200]

Ibid., c. *Similiter* (58)] ... tenet etiam *B. His.*, cuius fuit sententia que proxime sequitur in glosa....[201]

---

193 Cf. Savigny, IV, 127 ff.; Genzmer's article (cited above, §6, n. 57), p. 395; H. Kantorowicz and W. W. Buckland, *Studies in the Glossators of the Roman Law* (Cambridge, 1938), p. 87 f., and *passim, s.v. Gosiani*.—Whether Rogerius belonged to the orthodox wing or to the *Gosiani*, is disputed between Kantorowicz-Buckland, pp. 124.155.180, and E. M. Meijers, "Le conflit entre l'équite et la loi chez les premiers glossateurs", *Tijdschrift voor Rechtsgeschiedenis*, XVII (1939/1940), 119, n. 1; 120 f.
194 For his life and works, cf. Schulte, *QL*, II, 186 ff.
195 Cf. *Repertorium*, p. 87 f., above, §6 C.
196 In the following notes, Guido is cited from the Venice edition, 1577. Texts which refer to Bernard simply by the initial are omitted.
197 *Ed. Ven.*, fol. 136vb; cf. above, §12, at n. 152.
198 *Ven.* 203ra; cf. above, §8, at n. 101.
199 *Ven.* 211rb; cf. above, §12, at n. 148.
200 *Ven.* 256vb; cf. above, §9, n. 122.
201 *Ven.* 261 vb; cf. above, at n. 188.

C. 29, q. 2, pr.] ... in ea glosa, ibi 'alii', adde: ut *Baz.*; in ea glosa, ibi 'tertii', adde: ut *Ber. His.*[202]

De cons., D. 2, c. *Etsi non* (16)] In glosa 'alii', adde: ut *Ber.*[203]

But already Guido's outstanding disciple, Johannes Andreae (d. 1348), had forgotten the Compostellan's glosses on the *Decreta*.[204] And since that time, the memory of his activities in this field has become entirely obliterated.

III. Bernard's Glosses on the Compilatio Prima

17. For the decretalist production of Bernard of Compostella, we have Johannes Andreae's word: "... he lectured on the first two compilations, and published glosses (*apostillas*) on the same."[205] The glosses on the *Compilatio secunda* seem to be lost, but with regard to the *Compilatio prima*, Johannes' report is confirmed by some quotations from Bernard in contemporary authors;[206] and as already stated in the course of this study,[207] we have recently come across his original glosses also, in a MS of Modena. This MS, Bibl. Estense *a*. R. 4. 16 (*lat*. 968, formerly XII. L. 8) was insufficiently described by Blume in 1834.[208] Actually, the volume (= *M*) contains:

(i) fols. 1–76v: the *Compilatio prima*, with several strata of glosses.
(ii) fol. 77r–v: Pope Innocent III's decretal *Pastoralis* (*Po.* n. 2350), with hitherto unknown glosses by the Portuguese Silvester,[209] who was one of Tancred's professors[210] and a glossator of the *Compilationes antiquae* and the *Decreta*.[211] Incidentally, we can identify this canonist of Bologna with Master Silvestre Godinho whom Gregory IX appointed archbishop of Braga on July 5, 1229,[212] and who died on July 8, 1244.

---

202 *Ven.* 344va; cf. above, §9, at n. 119. In this case, however, we can not be certain whether *in ea glosa* (i.e. of the *Ordinaria*) the opinion of the *tertii* was that of Bernard of Compostella, or that of Bernard of Pavia—or of both. Cf. above, §10, n. 130.
203 *Ven.* 392 va; cf. above, §15, at n. 182.
204 Cf. above, §1.
205 Above, §1, n. 5.
206 *Ibid.*, n. 6.
207 §§10.13.
208 F. Blume, *Bibliotheca librorum manuscriptorum Italica* (Gottingae, 1834), pp. 36.37.40; cf. *Repertorium*, pp. 317.340.352.
209 The siglum is *sil.*, or *m(agister) sil.*
210 Gillmann, "Magister Silvester als Glossator", *AKKR*, CVI (1926), 154; G. Post, "Additional glosses of Johannes Galensis and Silvester ... ", *AKKR*, CXIX (1939), 373.
211 *Repertorium*, pp. 18. 355. 359. For Glosses on Gratian, see also Gillmann, *art. cit.*, p. 149; on *Comp. I: ibid.*, p. 154; on *Comp. III*: Gillmann, *Laur. Hisp.*, p. 117, and Post, "Some unpublished glosses ... ", *AKKR*, CXVII (1937), 405.414.422 f.; *AKKR*, CXIX, 369–373; *So-called Laur.*, pp. 25 f. 29.—One short gloss on the decretal collection of Gilbert (cf. n. 9) was published by Juncker, *ZRGKan*, XV (1926), 486, n. 1.
212 The unprinted rescript, addressed to the Chapter *of* Braga, is calendared in Auvray, *Les registres de Grégoire IX* (Paris, 1890 ff.), n. 318, from the Vatican Archives, *Registr. Vat.* 14,

(iii) fols. 78–117v: a previously unknown decretal collection, composed in or after 1210 from the collections of Gilbertus (c. 1202–1203)[213] and Alanus (c. 1206),[214] by way of combining their pre-Innocentian materials into one new compilation. With regard to Pope Innocent III's decretals both Gilbert's and Alan's collections had been superseded, in 1210, by the official *Compilatio tertia*;[215] thus, rearrangements of the earlier decretals recorded by the two Englishmen were much in demand: at the same time as the text of Modena, a similar recompilation was made by the Bolognese master John of Wales; and still another version, by an anonymous compiler, is found in MS *lat.* 15398 (fols. 281–288) of the Bibliothèque Nationale of Paris.[216] But of the competitors, only John of Wales was successful: his arrangement was acknowledged by the school as *Compitatio secunda*,[217] while the *Collectio Estensis*[218] and the *Collectio Sorbonica*—as we propose to call the other two—were soon forgotten. The *Coll. Estensis* was annotated, however, with a few scanty glosses,

---

fols. 125v–126, which I have checked. Silvester, at the time dean of the chapter, had been invalidly elected; the Pope quashed the election, but conferred the archbishopric to him by sovereign provision, praising him as *uirum fame celebris et note scientie*. The document gives Silvester's name only as *Magistrum S. Decanum uestrum*; but the full name of Archbishop Silvestre Godinho of Braga, 1229–1244, (Eubel, I, 144 has it wrongly; Simon) is recorded in other sources. Cf. on his pontificate, Fortunato de Almeida, *História da Igreja em Portugal*, I (Coimbra, 1910), 405.411.609; João Pedro Ribeiro, *Dissertações cronológicas e críticas* ..., V (2d ed., Lisboa, 1896), 143; E. A. Reuter, *Königtum und Episkopat in Portugal* (above, §5, n. 56), pp. 31 ff. 37. The decretal X.V, 31, 18, and other papal letters were addressed to him, cf. Reuter, p. 31, n. 171.

213 On Gilbert's collection, see *Repertorium*, pp. 310–313, and the full analysis of the first redaction by R. von Heckel, *Gilb. Alan.* (above, §1, n. 1). Of the second redaction (*Repertorium*, p. 312), two new copies have been discovered: Salzburg, St. Peter's Abbey, MS IX. 18 (fols. 118–168), and Vercelli, Cathedral Chapter, MS LXXXIX (fols. 1–50r), both annotated with Gilbert's own glosses.
214 Cf. above, §6 n. 61.
215 *Repertorium*, p. 355; for the (mostly indirect) dependence of *Comp. III* upon the two collections, see the list in Schulte, "Die Compilationen Gilberts und Alanus", *SBWien*, LXV (1870), 695 ff.; Friedberg, *Quinque Compilationes Antiquae* (Lipsiae, 1882), p. xxiv f; Heckel, *Gilb... Alan.*, p. 172.
216 The compilations of Modena and of Paris were believed hitherto (also in *Repertorium*, pp. 351.352) to be copies of the *Comp. II*. A full analysis of both of them will be given on another occasion. For the further contents of MS Paris *lat.* 15398 (among them also *Comp. II*: fols. 74–105v), see *Repertorium*, pp. 302.338.351.363.391; below, nn. 219.258; for its provenience and further bibliography, see Post) *So-called Laur.*, p. 8, n. 14. A collection of Tortosa, Cathedral Chapter, MS 160 (Coll. *Dertusensis III*; cf. *Repertorium*, p. 319), may belong to the same type of recompilations.
217 *Repertorium*, p. 345. For the relation of John's collection to Gilbert and Alan, cf. Heckel, *Gilb. Alan.*, p. 173 f.
218 I choose this name in order to avoid confusion with the so-called *Collectio Mutinensis*, in the miscellaneous volume of the Bibl. Estense,. MS a.0.6.9 (*lat.* 164, formerly V.C. 11), item no. 9. Kantorowicz, *ZRGKan*, XII (1922), 427, n. 4, citing the MS with a wrong number (49), believed this text to be a collection of decretals made after 1179 (cf. *Repertorium*, p. 285); actually, it contains nine older canons from Gratian (MS cit., item no. 9, pp. i–ii), and the statutes of the third Lateran Council (ibid. pp. ii–xiiii).

and one scribe copied in the margin of *M* the first redaction of Tancred's *Apparatus* on the *Compilatio secunda*.[219]
The *Collectio Estensis* (MS Modena, Bibl. Estense a. R. 4. 16, fol. 78r–117v) and the *Collectio Sorbonica* (Paris Bibl. nat. 15398, fol. 281–288) were discovered by Kuttner as independent compilations; they had before been believed to be copies of the Compilatio II. For the Collectio Estensis see now my analysis in *P. Landau*, Magister Silvester, die Collectio Estensis und die Compilatio secunda, ZRG Kan. Abt. 93 (2007), 154–181. I could identify the Portuguese Magister *Silvester Godinho*, who taught in Bologna ca. 1200–1217, as the compiler of the Collectio Estensis (pp. 179–181). Johannes Galensis used the Collectio Estensis when he compiled the Compilatio II. For the Collectio Sorbonica cf. now *P. D. Clarke*, The Collection of Gilbertus and the French Glosses in Brussels, Bibliothèque royale, MS 1407–09, and an early Recension of Compilatio Secunda, ZRG Kan. Abt. 86 (2000), 132–184, here pp. 180–184 (Appendix 5).For Clarke the Collectio Sorbonica represents an early draft of Compilatio secunda (p. 143). (P.L.)
This could be easily done, for that collection differed from the *Estensis* more in arrangement than in substance.
(iv) fols. 119 (118 is blank)—235 v: Bernardus Compostellanus, *Compilatio Romana*, with some particularities and glosses.[220]
(v) fols. 237 (236 blank)—255ra: a supplement to the *Compilatio Romana*, drawn from the *Compilatio tertia*, and containing only those decretals of the latter collection which are not covered already by Bernard;[221] the pertinent glosses from Tancred's *Apparatus* are added.

---

219 Tancred published both his *Apparatus* on *Comp. I* and *Comp. II* for the first time c. 1210–1215, and revised and re-edited them c. 1220: cf. *Repertorium*, 327 f. 346; *RHD*, 4, XVII (1938), 203, n. 3; Gillmann, *Zur Inventaris.*, pp. 82–85.—MSS of the respective first redactions are more numerous than generally believed: besides those mentioned already by Gillmann and by myself (*RHD*, loc. cit.), I found copies in Florence, Laurentian Libr., MSS *S. Croce* III sin. 6 (*Comp. I*: fols. 3–96v) and *S. Croce* IV sin. 2 (*Comp. II*: fols. 79–129); Lisbon, National Libr., MS *Alcob.* 381 (formerly 305; *Comp. II*: fols. 76v–116v); Padua, Antonian Libr., MS II. 35 (*Compp. I* and *II*); Paris, Bibl. Nat., MSS *lat.* 15398 (*Comp. I*, fragm.: fols. 3–52v), *lat.* 15996 (*Comp. I*), and *nouv. acq. lat.* 2127 (*Compp. I* and *II*: fols. 1-57v.58-89); Treves, Munic. Libr., MSS 864 (*Comp. I*: fols. 1–66) and 876 (*Comp. I*: fols. 1-21.32-82 [misbound]; both MSS according to information by the Rev. P. J. Kessler); Vercelli, Cath. Chapter, MS XXIII (*Compp. I* and *II*: fols. 1-54v.55-86v); and here in *M*.—On *Comp. III*, Tancred published only one *Apparatus* (c. 1220), but earlier, his private notes on that compilation had been circulated without his knowledge by certain students; cf. *Repertorium*, p. 358, and Post, *So-called Laur.*, p. 30, nn. 66.67.
220 See below, §27.
221 Such supplementary excerpts from later collections, made in order to integrate an earlier one, were not infrequent in the schools. To this category belongs, e.g., the *Collectio Abrincensis*, abstracted from *Coll. Sangermanensis* as a supplement to *Comp. I* (*Repertorium*, p. 299); or the excerpt from *Comp. III* in Fulda, Landesbibl., MS D.5 (fols. 215v-246) which has the function of integrating Gilbert's and Alan's collections (Heckel, *Gilb. Alan.*, p. 126); and other similar texts.

(vi) fols. 255rb–257rb: an analogous supplement to the *Collectio Estensis*, drawn from the *Compilatio secunda*,[222] also with the pertinent glosses from Tancred.

18. In the glosses of *M* on the *Compilatio prima* (fols. 1-76v), we have to distinguish four strata. Set i contains the glosses by Bernard of Pavia, the compiler himself: as usual, concordances to the individual titles, cross-references, *notabilia* and *argumenta*, occasionally also *solutiones contrariorum and solutiones generalium*,[223] Along with these glosses, the same stratum includes portions of the *Apparatus* written between 1193 and 1198 by Richardus Anglicus, the outstanding commentary in the first decade of the new decretalist teaching.[224] The scribe of *M*, set i, however soon tires of copying Richard's work; from the end of book II he inserts his glosses but at random among those of the Papiensis.

Set ii appears irregularly at intervals throughout the MS, more coherently in book IV, and includes other portions of Richard's *Apparatus*. The bulky rest of the English canonist's glosses (particularly those of books III and V) are incorporated, sometimes unchanged, sometimes in an enlarged and revised shape, into the mixed composition of set iii. In this extensive and most interesting stratum of our MS,[225] Richard's production is used, even as in many other gloss compositions of the early thirteenth century on the *Compilatio prima*, as the groundwork for a miscellaneous commentary.[226] In *M*, the unknown redactor filled it with a

---

222 The excerpt ends with 2 *Comp.* V, 22, 2. On Blume's mistake, caused by this item, see below, §27.
223 For Bernard of Pavia as a glossator of *Comp. I*, see *Repertorium*, p. 323. *Solutiones contrariorum* and *Generalia* are already found among the specimens edited by Laspeyres, *Bern. Pap.*, pp. 323–326 (nos. 3.14.15.16.22) and by Gillmann, "Des Cod. Halen. Ye 52 Glossenbruchstück ... ", *AKKR*, CVIII (1928), 486 ff.; also below, §19, at n. 30.—To the earliest mixed compositions, usually including Bernard's glosses, we can add: Admont, Bened. Monast., MS 55 (fols. 1–85v: set i); Avranches, Munic. Libr., MS 149 (fols. 7–77v: set i); Lisbon, Natl. Libr., MS *Alcob*. 173 (formerly 304; fols. 10v–115r); Montecassino, MS 46 (pp. 1–178: set i; abstracts from the *Summa* in set ii: above §10, n. 38).
224 For this *Apparatus* cf. *Repertorium*, p. 324 f. Besides the MS of Modena, we can add: Avranches, MS 149 (set ii); Salzburg, St. Peter's Abbey, MS a. IX. 18 (fols. 2–117: set i); Zwettl, Cistercian Monast., MS 34 (fols. 2–81v, with but fragments of the glosses, on fols. 2–6v. 33–42).
225 Begins fol. 1ra, on *De constit.*, c. *Canonum* (*1 Comp.* I, 1, 1 = X. I, 2, 1), v. *custodiantur*] "Con(stituti)o ergo sciatur. Ut enim Boetius ait: malum nun (!) fugitur nisi cognitum ... "; c. *Cognoscentes* (2 = X. I, 2, 2)] "Pone casum: constitutum est ut nulli detur dignitas infra xxv. annum ... *b*." The last glosses, fol. 76r, are on *De reg. iur.*, c. *Indignum* (*1 Comp.* V, 37,13 = X. V, 41, 11)] "Collige casum extra ..." (= Richard, cf. *Repertorium*, p. 325); c. *Quamvis* (14 = X. V, 41, 10)] "jnfra di. lxxxi. Dictum ... c. ult. in fine" (= Richard, *ibid.*); v. excusatio] "Nonne pro spiritualibus episcopi ... adquirendis uel concedendis. *b*."
226 For mixed compositions, based on Richard's work, see *Repertorium*, p. 325. Also the MSS of Lambeth Palace, 105, and Worcester Cathedral Chapter, F. 122 (*Repertorium*, p. 335) should be listed in this group, and not as copies of Richard's *Apparatus*. Add further: Admont, MS 55 (fols. 1–85v: set ii, together with glosses by Petrus Hispanus), and two anonymous commentaries, written without the decretal text, in Klosterneuburg, Canons Regular, MS 1045 (fols. 1-7v. 9), beg. "Ad iuste iudicandum"; and in Zwettl, MS 162 (fols. 1-48v, shortly mentioned in *Repertorium*, p. 392), beg. "Materia auctoris in hoc opere".

conspicuous layer of other glosses: many anonymous, one by Bernard of Pavia (*b. pa.*),[227] some by Melendus (*Mel.*),[228] some by Pelagius (*p., pe., pel'., pell., pl'., pl'a.*), that Spanish master whom Vincentius used to quote as a decretalist, and who later on became a Cardinal and Bishop of Albano (d. 1232).[229] Above all, however, the redactor of the Modenese composition availed himself of numerous glosses by master *ber.* (*b'.* or *ƀ.*) in whom we shall recognize Bernard of Compostella.

The fourth stratum, finally, contains anonymous and irregular additions, and can be conveniently dated, because it cites contemporary decretals expressly from the *conp(ilatio) G(ilberti)*, the *conp(ilatio) ala(ni)*, and the *conp(ilatio) b'(ernardi)*[230] This accounts for the years from 1208 to 1210.

19. The identification of the Compostellan as author of the *ber.*-glosses in set iii is not too difficult. Any confusion with Bernard of Pavia is easily avoided, as the gloss production of the two namesakes is distributed in sets i and iii respectively, with one exception only.[231] Also, the younger Bernard often refers to, or criticizes the opinions of the elder, as in the gloss cited above on *1 Comp.* III, 26, 10: " ... bernaldus papi. refert in summa sua ... ",[232] or as in the following examples:

De elect., c. *Nullus* (*1 Comp.* I, 4, 1 = X. I, 6, 1), v. *convocatis*][233] Vocari ergo debent absentes, arg. huius cap., et arg. lxv. di. Non debet (c. 2). Esse enim potest, quod presentium sententia per absentes in melius conuertatur; arg. ff. de arbitr. Si tres (*Dig.* 4, 8, 18 'Sicuti tribus'). Preterea consensus omnium quos electio tangit debet interuenire, ut lxiii. di. c. ult.; ff. de adobtionibus, l. ii (*Dig.* 1, 7, 2); C. de autor, prestanda, l. ult.

---

227 *M*, fol. 70ra.
228 *M* 3ra, and repeatedly.
229 Cf. *Repertorium*, p. 53; below, Appendix, at n. 385. He was created a Cardinal in 1206, Bishop of Albano in 1213; cf. Eubel I, 4.—Glosses in *M*: lv. 4ra. 20rb. 28ra. 59vb, *etc.*
230 In the following examples, the references to Gilbert and Alan are given with the numbers as used in the analysis by R. von Heckel; for Alan, the corresponding numbers of the unpublished second redaction (see above, §6, n. 61) are added in parentheses from my notes, taken in Vercelli, MS LXXXIX. References to Bernard are given as in Singer's analysis.
 M 53ra: ". . ex. Cle(mentis). iii. Martinus bertam. con. g.... ": *Gilb.* IV, 6, 1 = *2 Comp.* IV, 6, 1 (X. IV, 11, 4).
 M 53rb: "...ex. in(nocentii). de conuers. coniug. Ex parte, conp. b'; ex. jn. c. Fraternitatis, conp. *b.*":
 Bern. Compost. III, 26, 1; IV, 11, un. = *3 Comp.* III, 25, 1; IV, 11, un. (X. III, 32, 14; IV, 15, 6).
 M 53vb: "... ex. jn. de usuris, conp. ala. Illo uos ... ": *Alan.* V, 11, 3 (V, 12, 6) = *3 Comp. III*, 17,1 (X. III, 21, 4).
 M 54rb: "... ex. alex. t(it). de penit. et remiss. c. Quod quidam, conp. ala... . Alan. V, 20, 4 (2d ed. *vacat*) — *2 Comp.* V, 17, 3 (X. V, 38, 5).
 M 54v: "...ex. cele(stini). c. Quod dei timorem, conp. ala.; ex. de religiosis et transeunt. ad relig. c. Consulti sumus, conp. b' ... ": *Alan.* III, 16, 4 (III, 16, 4) and *Bern. Compost.* III, 25, 7 = *3 Comp.* III, 27, 1 and III, 24, 7 (X. III, 35, 5 and III, 31, 20).
231 Above, at n. 227.
232 Above, §10, at n. 134.
233 *M* 2rb.

(*Cod.* 5, 59, 5, 2). Set expresse contradicit C. de legation, lib. x. 1. ii (*Cod.* 10, 65, 2). Nam ibi dicitur quod hii qui in urbe sunt tantum uocari debent, et vii. q. i. Factus (c. 5); x. q. ii. Hoc ius (c. 2). Nam, ut dicit imperator, accidere potest ex eorum mora aliquod ciuitati detrimentum, ut C. de decurion. Nominationum (*Cod.* 10, 32, 45). *b'. dicit* quod si due partes sunt presentes, eligere possunt, alioquin non; arg. ff. de decretis ab ordine fac. 1. iii. (*Dig.* 50, 9, 3). Absentes uero dicit esse uocandos, si sunt in eadem diocesi, ad instar episcoporum qui de eadem prouincia uocantur. *Mel.* dat eis tantum spatium quantum est a Mediolano usque Ianuam, arg. lxiii. di. Quanto (c. 10). Si uero plus distarent, non, et uenientes eis consentire tenentur: ff. de pact. Rescriptum, resp. primo (*Dig.* 2, 14, 10, pr.). *b'*.

De appell., c. *Nos in eminenti* (*1 Comp.* II, 20, 36).[234]

(Set i)

delegare] s(upra) de off. et pot. iud. deleg. c. i. (I, 21, 1) Quamuis (c. 7 = X. I, 29, 6); ff. quis a quo appell. 1. i. in fine (*Dig.* 49,3,1).

Solutio: hic ante sententiam appellatur, ibi post; uel hic in causis ecclesiasticis, ibi in secularibus; uel illud intelligitur, quando iuris(dictio) demandatur, hic quando aliqua specialis causa delegatur.[a]
a) delegatis *M*.

(Set iii)

arbitrium] ff. quis a quo appell. 1. i. in fine contra.

Solutio:hic ante sententiam appellaverat, ibi post; uel hic in causis ecclesiasticis, *illud* in secularibus; uel *illud* intelligitur, quando iurisdictio demandatur, hoc quando aliqua specialis causa delegatur. *b'*. Ultimam credo meliorem; uel hoc in delegato a principe, illud in delegato priuati. Et intelligetur quod delegauerat lite contestata, arg. C. de procurat. Nulla[a] (*Cod.* 2, 12, 23). Alias enim delegatus a priuato non potest delegare. Ultimam approbo. *b'*.
a) 'Nullam a hanc etiam' (?) M.

Here Bernardus Compostellanus antiquus following Bernardus Papiensis distinguishes appellatio ante sententiam and appellatio post sententiam in canon law. Cf. now for this distinction in canon law my essay: P. Landau, Die Anfänge der Appellation in Mitteleuropa im hohen Mittelalter, in: Y. Mausen et al. (ed.), Der Einfluss der Kanonistik auf die europäische Rechtskultur 4: Prozessrecht (Norm und Struktur 37/4, Köln etc. 2014), 307–324. (P.L.)

For Petrus Brito as author of the Apparatus 'Ecce vicit leo' cf. A. Lefebvre-Teillard at p. 88. (P.L.)

De decimis, c. *Ad audientiam* (*1 Comp.* III, 26,13 = X. III, 30, 12), v. *novalibus*][235] Quod tamen in ceteris non obtinet. Nam licet de laboribus ponat, tamen de noualibus intelligitur

---

234 *M* 28rb. Because of the repetition in set iii, the gloss of set i has been subsequently cancelled, from the words *ff. quis* a *quo* to the end, by the corrector's remark *va-cat*.
235 *M* 40rb.

in ceteris, quam in istis de quibus fit mentio; secundum *Ricar.* et *b'*. et alios multos. Ego contra sentio, et *ūgo. b.*

Ibid., c. *Nobis in eminenti* (c. 15)]²³⁶ j. eod. Certam (c. 21) contra; xvi. q. i. Decimas (c. 47) contra; s. eod. c. prox. (14) contra.—Solutio: secundum *Ri.* et *b'* et eorum sequaces hec omnino obtinet, et contraria secundum hoc sunt intelligenda, quia labores[a] interpretandi sunt tantum pro noualibus. Quod autem dicitur in c. Fraternitatem (8), correctum est per c. Ex parte (10 = X. III, 30, 10). *Vgo* uero contra sentit, cui et ego assentio propter fauorem religionis. Quod ergo dicit hic Adrianus, dico potius pro uoluntate sua hic dixisse[b], quam de ratione, ut Alexander testatur in c. Fraternitatem. Quod autem dicitur in c. Ex parte, quod uidetur nostre solutioni obuiare, intellige ut ibi.²³⁷ *b'*.

a) lobores *M*.   b) dississe *M*.

Another argument for the Compostellan's authorship is furnished by the cross-references to his glosses on Gratian, and corroborated in one case by the *Glossa Palatina's* referring back to the present glosses on the decretals.²³⁸ Finally, as in his decretist interpretations, Bernard betrays here also his origin and identity by discussing a particular problem of the Church of Compostella:

Ne prelati vices suas, etc., c. Quoniam enormis (1 Comp. V, 3, 3 = X. V, 4, 3), v. *sub annuo*]²³⁹ Quid de cardinalibus compostellanis qui ecclesias habent?²⁴⁰ Dicimus ... *b'*.

20. From the numerous glosses with the siglum of Bernard²⁴¹ in set iii, we obtain valuable materials for studying the Compostellan's scientific personality. We perceive, e.g., that he had an outspoken preference for illustrating the text with casuistry;²⁴² we learn that he heard Civil Law in Azo's classes,²⁴³ and that like most of the contemporary canonists he had a fairly good knowledge of the civilian glossators in general.²⁴⁴ In one case, where Bernard speaks of the line of demarcation

---

236 *M* 40va.
237 The reference, *ut ibi*, is to the gloss printed above, §10, at n. 134. Another example below, §20, at n. 249.
238 See above, §13.
239 *M* 63r.
240 On Cardinals of metropolitan and cathedral churches outside of Rome, see P. Hinschius, *Das Kirchenrecht der Katholiken und Protestanten*, I (Berlin, 1869), 318 f.; for the Cardinals of Compostella in particular, *ibid.*, p. 319, n. 4. The title *cardinalis* became reserved to the Roman Cardinals as late as 1567, by Pius V.
241 But caution is indicated for the unsigned glosses. I observed, e.g., that the unsigned explanations of the title *De homicidio* (*1 Comp.* V, 10) are mostly elaborated on the basis of Richard's glosses, and often opposed to Bernard's theory of imputation, as developped in his gloss on D. 50, p. c. 36 (Kuttner, *Dekretsumme*, p. 150; cf. above, §7, n. 92).
242 See the glosses: "Pone casum ..." (above, n. 225), "Set pone quod ad eos ..." (below, at n. 248), "Quidam in mortis articulo ..." (below, at n. 259); other glosses opening with "Pone sic ... ", "Pone quod ... ", *etc.*, are very frequent.
243 *De testibus*, c. *Cum A. de Plano* (*1 Comp.* II, 13, 6), v. *publicate*] "Nota quod publicatis attestionibus ..., et in ea opinione est *aço*, ut audiui. Set numquid ... The gloss is signed by *p(elagius)* and *b'*. (*M* 20rb).
244 Besides Azo, the Roman Law glossators Albericus, Bulgarus, Cacciavillanus, Johannes Bassianus, are quoted.

between the Pope's and the Emperor's legislative powers, Azo seems to have made an additional note to his canonist pupil's gloss:

Qui filii sint legit., c. *Conquestus* (*1 Comp.* IV, 18, 1 = X. IV, 17, 1)][245] Set quid ad dominum papam statuere de talibus, cum huiusmodi potius ad dominum imperatorem spectare uideantur, ut di. xcvi. Cum ad uerum (c. 6)?. R., multum ad dominum papam: cum ad eum de principali causa, sc. de matrimonio statuere pertineat, non est mirum, si de eius sequela uel quasi accessorio statuat. *b.*—j. eod. Causam, secundo (c. 7 = X IV, 17, 7) contra. Solutio: ibi non erat questio hereditatis, set interdicti 'unde ui' *az*.[246]

If the siglum is correct, and if it does not refer simply to an oral utterance, we would have here a unique instance for decretalist glossing by the great civilian.

As for Bernard's relations to other canonists, the MS of Modena does not bring his name together with that of Melendus as frequently as the *Palatina* did,[247] but we find him here in a peculiar connection with another fellow countryman, Pelagius. Sometimes their glosses are chained together in a way which looks as if the two of them had discussed certain problems in common:

De rescript., c. *Ceterum* (*1 Comp.* I, 2, 3 = X, I, 2, 3), v. *mentio*][248] Si ergo de priori rescripto non faciat mentionem, ei non derogat, ut hic. Set numquid idem dices in priuilegiis? arg. infra ... priori derogatur. *b'*. §Infra de off. iud. deleg. Sane (I, 21, 3 = X. I, 29, 2) contra. Solutio: uel ibi dubitatur, utrum litere prius posteriusue fuerint inpetrate ... fuerat destinata. *p.*

§Set pone quod ad eos litere peruenerunt, set ante earum inspectionem sententiam protulerunt: tenet? arg. ff... . et hoc concedit *b'*.[249] si dolo caruerunt, i.e. si ii caruerunt dolo in non aspiciendo. In contrarium mouet, quia ipsa receptione literarum iudices esse desierunt ... Set dic quod non tenuit; queritur an illi ideo possint retractare. Et uidetur ... , in contrarium facit ... *b'*.

De divortiis, c. *Significasti* (*1 Comp.* IV, 20, 4 = X. IV, 19, 4), v. *adulterium*][250] §Hoc uidetur esse contra id quo legitur ... *b*.

§Non uidetur michi absonum quod quidam dicunt ... quod *b'*. concedit. Quod tamen non assero, immo contradicunt.

§Idem est secundum *bal*[251], si per sententiam separati essent ..., set *ūgō* huic sentẹntie non concordat, nec ego. *p.* Nam sententiam ... nisi sola morte. *b.*

---

245 *M* 58ra.
246 On the political background and implications of the decretal *Causam*, see Mary Cheney, "The Compromise of Avranches of 1272 and the Spread of Canon Law in England", *English Historical Review*, LVI (1941), 190.
247 See however the gloss on I, 4, 1, above, at n. 233.—For Bernard and Melendus in the *Palatina*, see above, §12.
248 *M* Iva.
249 i.e. Bernard of Pavia.
250 *M* 59vb.
251 By putting a dot under the *b*, the scribe changed the doubtful *bal.* into *al.* But this "emendation" which suggests the name of Alanus has neither transcriptional nor historical probability. Alan's *Apparatus* on *Comp. I* appeared after 1207 (above §6, n. 61), i.e. after Bernard's glosses (c. 1205–1206; below, §21); also the English master is nowhere else quoted by the Compostellan. The mysterious *bal.* returns on fol. 12ra ("... quod *ugo* concedit, *bal.* uero contra ... *b'*.") and fol.

Although in these glosses the initial *p.* is not as unequivocal as the siglum *pel'.* or *pl'a.* (= *pela.*), adopted in other glosses of the stratum, it should be interpreted as meaning Pelagius, not Petrus: for the elder Peter of Spain who had been active as a decretist in the seventies of the twelfth century,[252] published his glosses on the *Compilatio prima* about ten years before Bernard of Compostella;[253] and the younger Peter of Spain (Petrus Hispanus Portugalensis), author of *Notabilia* on the *Compilatio quarta*,[254] was a member of the school long after Bernard. He taught in Bologna, later in Padua, during the twenties of the thirteenth century,[255] and might be identical with that master Pedro Salvadores whom Gregory IX in 1235 consecrated bishop of Porto.[256] Finally, less famous Peters than these two were hardly ever referred to without a distinctive surname, such as Petrus Apulus (thus quoted by Vincentius),[257] or Petrus Brito,[258] or an otherwise unknown Petrus de Cardo whom Bernard mentions himself in a delightful problem of the construction of a will:

De testam., c. *Quorundam* (*1 Comp.* III, 22, 2=X. III, 26, 1), v. *conditio*][259] Quidam in mortis articulo constitutus condidit testamentum, quod si uxor eius pregnans susciperet filium, ipse habeat duas partes bonorum suorum et uxor tertiam; si filiam haberet, filia

---

32vb. Probably the decretist Bazianus is meant: the spelling *bas* (*ianus*) occurs sometimes in MSS (cf. Gillmann, *AKKR*, CVII [1927], 640, n. 4), and a semi-uncial *s* could easily be misread as *l.*
252 Above, §3.
253 *Repertorium*, p. 324: c. 1193–1198. Add to the mixed compositions containing his glosses: Admont, MS 55 and Lambeth, MS 105 (above, §18, n. 226).
254 *Repertorium*, p. 414. He probably was also the author of two small treatises on procedure, beg. (i) "Ad summariam notitiam consueti cursus causarum", and (ii) "Quoniam utilissimum fore putaui", both of which will be discussed on another occasion.
255 *Petrus Hispanus magister decretorum* signs a document in Bologna, March 31, 1223: cf. Sarti, I, 363, n. 6 (and p. 626 where the date is misprinted); *Chartularium Studii Bonon.* III (Bologna 1916), 197. He signs as *magister Petrus Spagnolus* in Padua, March 27, 1229: cf. Gloria, p. 544.
256 On Pedro Salvadores, Bishop of Porto (d. 1247), cf. Auvray (above, §17, n. 212), nos. 2792.2812; Almeida (*ibid.*), pp. 293.405.411.570.632; Reuter (above, §5, n. 56), pp. 30.33 f. 37.39 f.— Eubel, I, 406 dates the beginning of Pedro's pontificate as of 1231.
257 Cf. *Repertorium*, p. 54.
258 In *Repertorium*, p. 16, Petrus Brito was wrongly classed among the authors of the twelfth century. Actually, he was active as a glossator of *Comp. I* until after 1216; cf. Gillmann, *Zur Inventaris.*, p. 58 f.; "Petrus Brito und Martinus Zamorensis ... ", *AKKR*, CXX (1940), 60–64. Also in a newly discovered French *Apparatus* on *Comp. I*, written c. 1205–1210 (beg. "In quibusdam libris": Paris, Bibl. Nat., MS *lat.* 15398, fols. 204–279), references to the teaching of *P. B.* are frequently found. For additions by *brito* to Laurentius, see above, §6 B.—Probably he was a member of the Bolognese, but of a Western school, as the quotations by the Parisian *Apparatus* and by Geoffroy of Poitiers (cf. *Repertorium*, p. 16) would suggest; he may be the *magister Petrus Prepositi, rector ecclesie S. Germani in Cerulo*, of the diocese of Le Mans (Brittany), who obtained from Pope Honorius III, on April 28, 1218, certain privileges while he stayed *in scholis* or in the service of the English Ex-Queen Berengaria: *Regesta Honorii Papae III*, ed. P. Pressutti, I (Romae, 1888), n. 1270.
  For Petrus Brito as author of the Apparatus 'Ecce vicit leo' cf. *A. Lefebvre-Teillard* at no. VI, p. 88. (P.L.)
259 *M* 37ra.

unam partem et uxor duas. Tamdem utroque nato dubitatur de successione bonorum; et petrus de cardo iudicauit quod de vii. partibus bonorum filius haberet iiii. partes et uxor duas et filia unam, secundum le(gem) ff. de liberis et postum. Si ita scriptum est (*Dig.* 28, 2, 13),[260] *b*.

If this Peter were meant in the foregoing chains of glosses, he probably would not have been denoted by a simple *p*. And with the two Spaniards of the name of Peter excluded by chronological reasons, Pelagius remains the most likely solution.

21. We are so positive about the chronological argument, because the date of Bernard's decretal glosses can be determined, in contrast to his decretist glosses, rather closely, at about 1205–1206. For it will be noted that, when the Compostellan is citing decretals not contained in the first compilation, he introduces them sometimes as *extra titulos*, but adding a rubric, and sometimes as *extra omnes titulos*, or under the name of the Pope in question, without any rubric. Now, the following table shows the distribution of all those decretals in the collections of Gilbert (c. 1202–1203) and Alan (c. 1206) respectively:[261]

M 1rb.: "Ex In(n)o(centii). Pastoralis, §Quoniam autem ...": *Alan., de rescr.*, app. 94 b (*de off. et pot. iud. del.* I, 17, 4, §2), in the middle[262] = *3 Comp.* I, 2, 3 (X. I, 3, 14), in the middle.

M 2va: (i) "... ex. t(itulos). de iure patro. Per nostras ...": *Gilb.* III, 24, 3 = *3 Comp.* III, 20, 2 (X. III, 38, 27).

(ii) "... Innocen. ex. ti. de heret. Vergentis in ...": *Gilb.* V, 4, un. = *3 Comp.* V, 4, 1 (X. V, 7, 10).

M 12ra: "...ex. ti. Ino. Pastoralis, circa prin(cipium)...": *Alan., de off. iud. deleg.*, app. 94 a (I, 17, 4, pr.-§1) = *3 Comp.* I, 18, 7 (X. I, 29, 28), pr.-§1 and I, 20, 5 (X. I, 31, 11), pr.

M 18ra: "... ex. Inn. Cum super consultatione ...": *Alan., de iureiur.* II, 13, 8 (II, 15, 10).[263]

M 20rb: "... ex. ti. Inno. De testibus[264] ...": *Gilb., de except.* II, 12, 1 = *3 Comp.* II, 12, 2 (X. II, 20, 29) and V, 17, 4 (X. V, 34, 13).

M 20vb: (i) "... ex. ti. de except. Denique ...": *Gilb.* II, 12, 2 = *2 Comp.* II, 11, un. (X. II, 25, 1).

---

260 Already the Roman jurisconsult Julianus gave this ingenious solution in the cited *lex* of the Digest; Petrus de Cardo only paraphrases it.

261 References to Gilbert and Alan (second redaction in parentheses) as above, n. 230. The rubrics of titles in these two collections are added only where they do not result from Bernard's citations.

262 From the context of Bernard's gloss, it results that the passage "Quoniam autem sub huiusmodi forma ..." is meant, and not the section "Quoniam autem per dilatoriam ... " (*Alan., de except.* II, 10,2 [II, 11, 3] = *3 Comp.* II, 16,3 [X. II, 25,4]).

263 This is the decretal *Super consultatione* which Bernard later, in the epilogue of his own collection, rejected as spurious, cf. Singer, *Bern. Comp.*, p. 115, ed. p. 116.

264 As the chapter *De testibus* stands in Gilbert under the rubric *De exceptionibus*, the text of *M* might be due to a homoeographic slip of the scribe.

(ii) "... ex. ti. de restit. spol. Dilectus ...": *Gilb.* app. 7 (II, 7, 3)[265] = *3 Comp.* II, 4, un (X. II, 10, 2).

(iii) "... ex. o(mnes). tit. Inno. Super his ...": *Alan., de accus.* V, 1, 5 = *3 Comp.* V, 1, 3 (X. V, 1, 16; V, 37, 8; II, 21, 8).

M 28rb: (i) "... ex. ti. Inno. Super questionum ...": *Alan., de off. et pot. iud. deleg.* I, 13, 3 (I, 17, 3) = *3 Comp.* I, 18, 6 (X. I, 29, 27).

(ii) "... ex. Inno. iii. Ad hec deus ...": *Gilb., de dolo et contum.* II, 8, 1 = *3 Comp.* II, 3, 1 (X. II, 6, 1).

M 31ra: "... ex. tit. o(mnes). Inno. Licet Ely ...": *Alan., de accus.*, app. 29 (*de except.* II, 11, 1) = *3 Comp.* V, 2, 3 (X. V, 3, 31).

M 33vb: (i) "... ex. ti. de suppl. negl. Quoniam ...": *Gilb.* I, 7, 1 = *3 Comp.* III, 8, 2 (X. III, 8, 5).

(ii) "... ex. de filiis presb.[266] Inotuit ...": *Gilb.* I, 10, 4 = *3 Comp.* I, 6, 5 (X. I, 6, 20).

(iii) "et ex. o(mne)s. ti. Inno. Licet dilecti": *Alan., de suppl. negl.*, app. 55 (I, 9, 3)[267] = *4 Comp.* I, 6, 1 (X. I, 10, 3).

M 38vb: "Ex. ti. de testam. Certificari[268] .. *Gilb.* III, 15, un. = *2 Comp.* III, 15, 3 (X. 111,28,9).

M 50v: (i) "... ex. t. de spons. Tertio .. *Gilb.* IV, 1, 6 = *2 Comp.* IV, 1, 8 (X. II, 23, 13).
(ii) "... ex. t. de presumpt. Litteris ...": *Gilb.* II, 16, 2 = *2 Comp.* II, 15, 2 (X. II, 23, 12).

M 67rb: (i) "... ex. Cel(estini). Inspectis .. *Gilb., de homic.* V, 5, 5 (Clement III) = *2 Comp.* V, 6, 5.

(ii) "... ex. de etate et qual. or(dinandorum et) pre(ficiendorum). Ad aures .. *Gilb.* I, 9, 1 = *2 Comp.* I, 8, 2 (X. I, 14, 7).

M 75ra: (i) "... ex. I(nnoc). iii. Cum illorum ... *Gilb., de sent. excomm.* V, 14, 14 = *3 Comp.* V, 21, 5 (X. V, 39, 32).

(ii) "... ex. ti. In. Recte agis .. *Alan., de sent, excomm.*, app. 48 (V, 23, 5).[269]

This decretal with the Incipit 'Recte agis' (WH 849a) is from Celestine III, not from Innocent III—cf. *W. Holtzmann*, Kanonistische Ergänzungen zur Italia Pontificia (Tübingen 1959), 148 s. (no. 226), = QF 38 (1958), 166s. (P.L.)

---

265 Cf. Heckel, *Gilb. Alan.*, p. 219 for the considerable differences of this text in Gilbert from the official collections where the chapter begins with the words *Cum dilectus*, and is much shorter.
266 "ex. de fi. eps." *M.*
267 Cf. Heckel, p. 319, for the particularities of Alan's text.
268 In this gloss, on *De sepult.*, c. *Cum super quosdam* (*1 Comp.* III, 24, 8 = X. III, 28, 8), Bernard indulges in a pun: "Ex. ti. de testam. Certificari certificabit te super hac diuersitate".
269 Alanus attributes the decretal to Celestine III (ed. Heckel, *Gilb. Alan.*, p. 317); the same inscription is given in the spurious appendix of two MSS of Gilbert (*H* and *L*: V, 16, 5); cf. *Repertorium*, p. 313. On the other hand, the *Collectio Palatina II*, an offspring of Gilbert, written c. 1204 (cf. *op. cit.*, p. 314 ff.), has this decretal calendared in V, 14, 26 with the inscription *Idem*, meaning Innocent III.

From these passages we obtain the following results: (1) All the ten references with rubrics[270] fit into the titles of Gilbert's collection. (2) In four cases however, Bernard fails for some unknown reason to indicate the rubrics of that collection.[271] (3) No reference whatsoever is made to the collection of Alan, and all the decretals that could be found there are constantly cited as *extra omnes titulos*, or *extra Innocentii*.[272](4) The youngest of the eight decretals in this latter group is the rescript *Pastoralis*, of December 19, 1204 (*Po.* n. 2350).—We can conclude therefore that Bernard used Gilbert's, but not Alan's collection, and that he wrote, or at least completed, his glosses during the years 1205 and 1206.[273]

22. Bernard's success was none too brilliant. He was cited by some of his younger contemporaries;[274] but the one who really mattered, Tancred, paid little attention to the Compostellan's glosses,[275]—although he was always eager to include in his standard apparatuses the productions of Richard, Alan, Vincentius, Laurentius, and others. The chief of the decretalists evidently considered Bernard, even as Johannes Teutonicus did, as a lesser outsider. Perhaps it was on account of the failure of Bernard's *Compilatio Romana* that the two leading professors all but ignored him.

IV. Bernard's Quaestiones

23. In the medieval Law schools, *Quaestiones disputatae*[276] had the important function of supplementing with practical exercises the lectures of the glossators.

---

270 *M* 2va (i, ii). 20vb (i, ii). 33vb (i, ii). 38 vb. 50v (i, ii).67rb (ii).
271 *M* 20rb. 28rb (ii). 67rb (i). 75ra (i). But for the first case, see above, n. 264.
272 *M* 1rb. 12ra. 18ra. 20vb (iii). 28rb (i). 31ra. 33vb (iii). 75ra (ii).
273 The result would be the same, if we substituted for Gilbert the *Coll. Palat. II*, derived c. 1204 from his collection (n. 269). But a consultation of *Palat. II* by Bernard is unlikely, as its titles included many of the materials that later were to be recompiled by Alanus; and there would be no reason why Bernard should have missed them all in the pertinent rubrics.
274 Above, §1, n. 6(?).
275 Tancred mentions Bernard occasionally, e.g. on *Comp. I, De eo qui cognov. consang.*, c. *De illo* (IV, 13, 4), v. *occultum*] "Ita quod probari ...; arg. est pro opinione *melendi hyspani*... ex. ii. de diuort. Comes W.; ex. ii. eod. tit. Super eo (*2 Comp.* IV, 13, 2; IV, 7, 1). *b'. et lau.* dicunt ... et respondent illis decretalibus ... c. ult. *Vinc.*—Ego approbo opinionem *laur.* et *b'.* cum illa distinctione quam fecit innoc. iii. jnfra de sent. excomm. Inquisitioni, lib. iii. (*3 Comp.* V, 21, 17 = X. V, 39, 44). *t.*" For the full text of this gloss, cf. Gillmann, *AKKR*, CV (1925), 155, n. 1. The *b'.* who is cited here among other Spaniards (Melendus, Laurentius, Vincentius), and as discussing decretals younger than *Comp. I*, must be the Compostellan, although I have at present no opportunity to check whether such a gloss is found in *M.*—Also, in the *Apparatus "Servus appellatur"*, a gloss on *Comp. III, De rescript.*, c. *Sedes apostolica* (I, 2, 4 = X. I, 3, 15), v. *minores*, is signed by *b*. Tancred, however, gives the same gloss with the siglum of Laurentius; cf. Gillmann, *Laur. Hisp.*, p. 8, n. 1; Post, *So-called Laur.*, p. 10, n. 22.
276 For general information, see H. Kantorowicz, "The *Quaestiones disputatae* of the Glossators", *Tijdschrift voor Rechtsgeschiedenis*, XVI (1937/1938), 1–67, which is the best study on civilian

They originated from formal discussions[277] of the pro's and con's of cases or casuistic problems which were held by the students under the direction of their *magister* who gave the final *solutio*. As experiments of induction, they were distinct from a merely catechetical questioning for didactic purposes, and also from the dialectical considerations on theoretic problems of interpretation,— even if such consideration was likewise clad, sometimes, in the form of question, argument, and solution, as were the so-called *Quaestiones legitimae* of the civilians, and *Quaestiones decretales* of the canonists.[278] The *Quaestiones disputatae* are further distinct from the *Summae quaestionum*, i.e. from the systematic textbooks that annexed to each abstract explanation (*in summa*) of a legal institute a series of illustrative cases (*quaestiones*),—an amphibious literary form much in fashion during the late twelfth century in the French and Anglo-norman schools whence it was introduced, probably by Richardus Anglicus, in Bologna.[279]

Quaestiones. See also: U. Nicolini, *Pillii Medicinensis Quaestiones sabbatinae* (Modena, 1933); E. Genzmer, "Die justinianische Kodifikation und die Glossatoren" (above, §6, n. 57), p. 415 f.; "Seckel und Ugo Nicolini über die Quaestionen des Pillius", *ZRG Rom*, LV (1935), 315 ff.—For canonical *Quaestiones*, see *Repertorium*, pp. 243 ff., 423 ff. Comparative notes also in Kuttner, "Zur neuesten Glossatorenforschung", *Studia et documenta historiae et iuris*, VI (1940), 286 ff., 303 ff.—The best summaries on theological *Quaestiones* are found in R. M. Martin, *Les oeuvres de Robert de Melun*, I (Louvain, 1932), xxxii–xlvi; Paré-Brunet-Tremblay, *La Renaissance du XII*ᵉ *siècle: Les écoles et l'enseignement* (Paris-Ottawa, 1933), p. 128 ff.; G.Lacombe and A. Landgraf, "The *Quaestiones* of Cardinal Stephen Langton", *The New Scholasticism*, III (1929), 154 ff.; IV (1930), 162 ff.; and particularly in A. Landgraf, "Quelques collections de 'Quaestiones' de la seconde moitié du XIIᵉ siècle", *Recherches de théologie ancienne et médiévale*, VI (1934), 368–393; VII (1935), 113–128.

277 We are not dealing here with *quaestiones* incidentally raised and solved by the glossators in their lectures, as are frequently found in the apparatuses of glosses; e.g. above, §20, n. 242. On the parallel problem of theological *quaestiones* originating from the *lectio*, and *quaestiones* outside the *lectio*, see Martin, *op. cit.*, p. xliii; Lacombe-Landgraf., *art. cit.*, IV, 162f.; Landgraf, *art. cit.*, VII, 124.

278 The distinction between *Quaestiones disputatae*, catechetical questions, and *Quaestiones legitimae*, has been worked out by Kantorowicz and Buckland, *Studies in the Glossators* (above, §15, n. 193), p. 129 ff.; additions and canonical parallels in Kuttner, *art. cit.* (n. 1), p. 304 ff. A theological analogy to the *Quaestiones legitimae* (*decretales*) is offered by the *Quaestiones on contraria*, mentioned by Landgraf, *art. cit.*, VII, 122 f. On primitive (didactic) questions without dialectical disputation, see also M. Grabmann, *Geschichte der scholastischen Methode*, II (Freiburg, 1911), 16 ff., 25 ff.; H. Weisweiler, *Das Schrifttum der Schule Anselms von Laon* ... (Münster, 1936), p. 165 ff.

279 This literary species—a forerunner of the form adopted by St. Thomas in the *Summa theologiae*—is almost unknown to modern authorities. Some hints in Landgraf, *art. cit.*, VII, 122; cf. also Kuttner, *art. cit.*, p. 305, n. 43, where the canonical *Summa quaestionum* by the English master Honorius (written c. 1185–1190) is mentioned. This work, previously known imperfectly as *Quaestiones decretales Bambergenses I* (cf. *Repertorium*, p. 424), exists in at least six MSS: to the three listed *loc. cit.*, add: Laon, Munic. Libr., MS 371 *bis* (fols. 171–176v; a fragment not identified in *Repertorium*, p. 255); Douai, Munic. Libr., MS 640 (formerly 584; fols. 1–42va); Zwettl, Cistercian Monast., MS 162 (fols. 179–213). On the authorship of master Honorius— the same whose struggle for the archdeaconry of Richmond has been told at length by Roger Hoveden, *Chronicon*, ed. Stubbs, IV (London, 1871, Rolls Series), 52.89.158 f. 177 ff.—, and on other *Summae quaestionum* of his school, including the newly discovered work by Richardus

Different from all these types of literature, where the *quaestio* is but an accidental element of form, the real *Quaestiones disputatae* were primarily class exercises. As a rule, they were written down and collected without any established order by student *reportatores*, more or less under the supervision of the professor.[280] We therefore find frequently a common stock of *Quaestiones* reported in various collections which are closely related to each other, and yet different in selection, groupment, and textual shape of the materials.[281] *Quaestiones* collected, arranged, and put into definite literary form by the master himself at his desk (*Quaestiones in scriptis redactae*), were the exception at the beginning, but became more frequent during the thirteenth century.[282]

The function of the *Quaestio disputata* as a practical training in casuistry explains also why frequently identical themes (*casus*) were handed down from one

Anglicus (Montecassino, MS 396 [pp. 191–247] and Zwettl, MS 162 [fols. 145–173]), we shall have to report in a forthcoming essay on early English canonists. See also below, n. 17, no. vii (*Summa Quaest. Vindobonensis*).

Gérard Fransen's numerous studies on canonistic questions are now collected in: *G. Fransen, Canones et Questiones I, 2. La Littérature des "Questiones" des Canonistes et Civilistes*, Bibliotheca Eruditorum 25 (Goldbach 2002).

A survey on research concerning the collections of quaestiones by canonists was given by me in a colloquy of the Historisches Kolleg in Munich 1995—cf. *P. Landau, Kanonistische Quaestionenforschung*, in: *M. Bellomo* (ed.), Die Kunst der Disputation (Schriften des Historischen Kollegs. Kolloquien 3, München 1997, 73–84. In my article I also mention desiderata in this field of research (p. 84).

For the Summa questionum, written by the English master Honorius circa 1188–1190, cf. now *W. Kozur*, Die Dekret- und die Quaestionensumme des Magister Honorius im Lehrbetrieb des 12. Jahrhunderts, in: Proceedings of the Thirteenth International Congress of Medieval Canon Law, Esztergom 2008 (MIC, Ser. C, Vol. 14, Città del Vaticano 2010), 419–429, and *W. Kozur/K. Miethaner-Vent*, Titel in der Quaestionen- und Dekretsumme des Magister Honorius. Neues zu Aufbau und Abfassung der beiden Summen, in: Proceedings of the Eleventh International Congress of Medieval Canon Law Catania 2000, (MIC, Ser. C, Vol. 12), Città del Vaticano 2006), 153–168. Portions of the Summa quaestionum, bearing on marriage doctrine, have been edited by *B. Grimm*, Die Ehelehre des Magister Honorius. Ein Beitrag zur Ehelehre der anglonormannischen Schule, Stud. Grat. xxiv (Romae 1989), 231–387. A complete critical edition is planned with support by the Deutsche Forschungsgemeinschaft (DFG). (P.L.)

280 Cf. Kantorowicz, *Quaest. disp.*, p. 32 f.; Landgraf, *art. cit.*, VII, 113 ff.
281 The outstanding examples of such families in Civil Law are the Bulgarus-group, the Johannes Bassianus-group, the Pillius-Roffredus-Hugolinus-group; cf. Kantorowicz, *art. cit.*, pp. 1–17. Theological examples in Lacombe-Landgraf, *passim*; Landgraf, *art. cit.*, VII, 114.116.121.—A canonical example for such varying *reportationes* of the same stock are the *Quaestiones Palatinae I, Bambergenses I*, and *Lipsienses I*, of the twelfth century (*Repertorium*, p. 246); a previously unknown collection in Prague, University Library, MS XIV. E. 31 (catal. 2565; fols. 35–43) can be added to this group, and the origin of this whole family can be proved to be French. Another family is formed by the *Quaestiones Palatinae II, III*, and *VI* (*Repertorium*, p. 247 f.), together with the Prague MS, fols. 43–45. Examples of the early thirteenth century are furnished by a family comprising the *Quaestiones Borghesianae* (*op. cit.*, p. 429) and the *Quaestiones Patavinae* (*op. cit.*, p. 255), and by the group described below, §24.
282 Kantorowicz, *art. cit. p.* 32 ff.—*Quaestiones redactae* in Canon Law are, e.g., the *Stuttgardienses* (*Repertorium*, p. 245), the collection of Damasus (*ibid.*, p. 426), and most of the collections of the later thirteenth century.

class to another, discussed repeatedly and with different solutions.[283] Such themes came to be called *Quaestiones quaternales*.[284]—As to the intrinsic structure, the *Quaestio disputata* can present the elements of dialectic reasoning in all possible variations: from a mere case with its arguments, or a short question with its answer, to the most elaborate patterns consisting of *casus, quaestio, divisio, argumenta, solutio,* and *refutatio contrariorum*;[285] patterns which may have been determined, to some extent, by the study of Cassiodorus and the ancient Rhetoricians.[286]

Unfortunately, the history of the canonical *Quaestiones disputatae* has been much neglected. The overabundant manuscript materials are as yet recorded only in part, and even the fundamental notions on concept, function, transmission, and structure, are far from generally known.[287] Also, similarities and differences between the canonical disputations, and the generally better known *Quaestiones* of the sister disciplines, Theology and Civil Law,[288] still await a thorough examination. But only when the *Quaestiones disputatae* of the Canon Law glossators have been sufficiently explored, can the much needed comparative study of the *Quaestio*, as of the outstanding dialectical instrument of medieval scholasticism in all its fields, be undertaken.

24. A large group of anonymous canonical *Quaestiones*, dating from the first decade of the thirteenth century,[289] is reported four times, with due variations of selection and arrangement, (i) in Bamberg, State Library, MS *Can.* 45 (formerly P. II. 4, fols. 41–56);[290] (ii) in Klosterneuburg, Canons Regular, MS 656 (fols. 19–33v);[291] (iii) in Vienna, National Library, MS 2163 (fols.

---

283 For Theology, cf. Landgraf, *art. cit.*, VII, 115.127; for Canon Law, the *Quaestiones Palatinae II* and *VI* (n. 281); see also below, nn. 296, 297.
284 The term is used by Johannes de Deo in the epilogue of his *Liber Quaestionum* (c. 1246), a book which he proudly recommends as containing not a single *quaestio quaternalis*: "... hoc est, a nullo fuerunt ante disputatae." See the text in Schulte, *QL*, II, 102, n. 26.
285 Cf. Kantorowicz, *art. cit.*, p. 17ff.; Kuttner, *Repertorium*, p. 243 f.; *Studia et documenta hist. et iur.*, VI (1940), 429 f.
286 Cf. Cassiodorus, *Institutiones*, II, 2, 9 (ed. Mynors [Oxford, 1937], p. 103), or Cicero, *De inventione*, I, 14, 19 (ed. Friedrich, *M. T. Ciceronis Opp. rhetorica*, I [Lipsiae, 1893], 130), for the rhetorical pattern consisting of *exordium, narratio, partitio, confirmatio, reprobatio, conclusio*.
287 Schulte's standard handbook yields hardly any information about this branch of medieval canonical literature. A first attempt of reviewing the *Quaestiones* of the early glossators was made in my *Repertorium*, pp. 243 ff., 423 ff., but is open to many corrections and additions.
288 Some parallelisms are hinted at in the preceding notes.
289 The *Compilatio tertia* (1210) is not used.
290 For the other contents of this miscellaneous MS, see H. Fischer, *Canonistische Handschriften* (Katalog der Handschriften der königlichen Bibliothek zu Bamberg, I, i, 5 [Bamberg, 1906]), p. 913 ff.; Kuttner, *Repertorium*, pp. 387.424 f. 426, and above, §10, n. 128. The *Quaestiones* begin: "Veniens quidam ad regimen ciuitatis".
291 The MS of Klosterneuburg is described by H. Pfeiffer and B. Černik, *Catalogus codicum mss. qui in bibliotheca ... Claustroneoburgensi asservantur*, I (Wien, 1922), no. 656, and by G. Hugelmann, "In den ban mit rechte kommen", *ZRGKan*, VII (1917), 83, n. 1. The contents are: (i) fols. 1–18r: a fragment of Damasus, *Quaestiones*; cf. *Repertorium*, p. 426; (ii) fols. 19–33v: the

75–100);[292] (iv) in Zwettl, Cistercian Monastery, MS 162 (fols. 123–144v, 173–178v).[293] Only the Bamberg collection of this family has been known

presently discussed collection of *Quaestiones*, beg. "Vocatus quidam ad regimen ciuitatis", with the rubric, *Incipiunt Bone Quaestiones*, to which a later hand wrongly has added *Bartholomei brixiensis dominicales et ueneriales*; (iii) fol. 34r: an *Arbor affinitatis* with glosses, beg. " Affinitas est propinquitas proueniens in nobis", by Johannes Teutonicus, as will be shown on another occasion; (iv) fol. 34v: an anonymous treatise on consanguinity, mostly faded and illegible; (v) fols. 35–42v: Johannes Teutonicus, *Quaestiones disputatae (dominicales)*, cf. *Repertorium*, p. 254 and above, §14, n. 170. Contrary to Hugelmann's assertion, *loc. cit.*, they clearly contain references to the *Compilationes I–III*; (vi) fols. 43–47v: Tancred, *Ordo iudiciarius* (Schulte, *QL*, I, 202), incomplete.

292 The MS of Vienna, insufficiently described in the catalogue, is rich in interesting and partly unknown writings. It contains (i) fols. 1–24r: an *Abbreviatio Decretorum*, beg. "Humanum genus", identical with the fragmentary abbreviation in Avranches, Munic. Libr., MS 149 (fols. 136–138v); (ii) fol. 24r–24v: the decretal *Pastoralis* (*Po.* n. 2350) by Innocent III; (iii) fols. 25r–42v: Richardus Anglicus, *Ordo iudiciarius*; cf. *Repertorium*, p. 225; (iv) fol. 42r–42v: five minor items, (a) a *Summula de dispensatione*, beg. "Canones dispensabiles propositi sunt"; (b–e) four *Quaestiones*, beg. "Queritur utrum clericus possit compromittere", of French origin, after 1210; (v) fols. 43r–51r: an incomplete commentary of glosses on Richard's *Ordo* (no. iii), beg. "Quoniam sententia contra solitum ordinem iudiciorum prolata uim rei iudicate non habet", and on Richard's first words: *Edi*[*c*]*tio, etc.*]"Hec sunt uerba magistri qui dicit edictionem posse fieri"; the same commentary accompanies Richard's work in Douai, MS 644: cf. Witte, *Magistri Ricardi Anglici Ordo iudiciarius* (2d ed., Halle, 1853), p. 67; (vi) fol. 51v: a lecture (*quaestio decretalis*?) on *3 Comp.* IV, 13, 2; beg. "De accusationibus quesitum est; primo queritur de illa decretali extra, iii. qui matrim. accus. possunt, Per tuas, in hunc modum"; (vii) fols. 52–74v: a *Summa quaestionum*, beg. "De constitutionibus. Videndum est quid sit constitutio et quot sint species", written c. 1205–1210; (viii) fols. 75–100: the presently discussed collection of *Quaestiones*, beg. "Agitata est causa coram episcopo, appellatum est ab eo"; (ix) fol. 101: a fictitious story on King David, beg. "Hec est materia processus regis dauid".

293 The MS of Zwettl, practically unknown, is of an extraordinary value for the history of early canonical literature, particularly for Richardus Anglicus (cf. nos. vii. viii. x. xii). It contains (i) fols. 1–48v: a commentary on *Comp. I*, beg. "Materia auctoris in hoc opere", based in part upon Richard's *Apparatus*; cf. above, §18, n. 226; (ii) fols. 48v–49v: *Notabilia* on the decretal collection of Gilbert, beg. "Non ualet rescriptum contra aliquos religiosos impetratum"; (iii) fols. 50–65v: a commentary on Gratian's *Tractatus de poenitentia*, beg. "Ego dico tibi, tu es Petrus"; (iv) fols. 66–70r: Bernard of Pavia, *Summa de matrimonio*; cf. above, §9, n. 25(?); (v) fols. 70–72v: *Notabilia* on Gratian, beg. "Gregorius: Qui multum emungit, sanguinem elicit", not identical with a similar collection of *Notabilia* (cf. *Repertorium*, p. 235) in London, B. M., MS *Addit*. 18325; (vi) fol. 72v: short notes on Civil Law; (vii) fols. 73–82r: Richardus Anglicus, *Generalia*; cf. above §10, n. 128; (viii) fols. 83–94r: the same author's *Ordo iudiciarius* (cf. above, n. 292), with a paragraph on *iuramentum calumniae* and a few *quaestiones* on procedure appended; (ix) fols. 95–104|r: Jacobus Columbi, *Summa feudorum*; cf. on this feudist treatise (which Palmieri, *Bibliotheca iuridica medii aevi*, II [Bononiae, 1892], 181 ff., edited wrongly under the name of Hugolinus): E. Seckel, "Ueber neuere Editionen juristischer Schriften aus dem Mittelalter", *ZRG Rom*, XXI (1900), 250 ff., and Genzmer, *art. cit.* (above, §6, n. 57), p. 412; (x) fols; 105–122v: Richardus Anglicus, *Distinctiones*; cf. above, §4, n. 34; (xi and xiii): fols. 123–144v. 173–178v: the presently discussed *Quaestiones*, beg. "Agitata est causa coram episcopo" and "Quedam rogauit quendam"; (xii) fols. 145–173: Richardus Anglicus, *Summa quaestionum* (cf. above, n. 279), beg. "Circa ius naturale uarie questiones solent fieri", with the colophon, *Explentur questiones ueneriales magistri Ricardi super tota decreta*; (xiv) fols. 179–213: Honorius, *Summa quaestionum* (cf. above, n. 279), beg. "De questionibus decretalibus tractaturi", with the rubric, *Incipiunt questiones ueneriales secundum magistrum Honorium*.

thus far,[294] and the interrelations of the very interesting group[295] have still to be studied in detail. Some of its questions have a surprising flavor of anecdotes or *exempla;*[295a] some were evidently *quaternales*, since their themes returned later in the disputations of Johannes Teutonicus[296] and of Tancred,[297] or even in disputations of the French school, and in theological literature.[297a]

The Vienna and the Zwettl collections, however, are not homogeneous. In Vienna (*W*), amidst the *quaestiones* of the common stock, the *reportator* suddenly changes his impersonal manner,[298] and presents, from fol. 87 onwards, a

---

The MS Zwettl 162 was discussed in my essay: *P. Landau*, Feudistik und Kanonistik. Ein neuer Quellenfund zum lombardischen Lehnrecht, in: *T. J. Chiusi* et al. (ed.), Das Recht und seine historischen Grundlagen. Festschrift für Elmar Wadle zum 70. Geburtstag (Schriften zur Rechtsgeschichte 139, Berlin 2008), 525–535—also in: *P. Landau*, Deutsche Rechtsgeschichte im Kontext Europas (Badenweiler 2016), 289–300. The text on fol. 95–104r does not contain the Summa feudorum written by Jacobus Columbi, as Kuttner thought (no. IX), but the Obertine recension of the Libri Feudorum. (P.L.)

294 Cf. *Repertorium*, p. 425.

295 The collections of Bamberg (*B*) and Klosterneuburg (*K*) on one side, and of Vienna (*W*) and Zwettl (*Z*) on the other, seem to be more closely related. At least we find: *B*, qq. 1–4 = *K*, qq. 1–4, and *Z*, qq. 1–3 = *W*, qq. 1–3; while *BK*, qq. 1–4 return in *W* towards the end (fol. 94), and *W*, qq. 3–5 stand among the last ones in *K*. On the other hand, we have also *K*, q. 9 = *W*, q. 9, and *B*, q. 12 = *W*, q. 12.

295a E.g., the case of a prince who goes on pilgrimage and for whom an impostor returns; the case of a woman who makes love, at the request of her husband, to the physician who otherwise would not cure him (can the husband divorce her?); the case of a youth who, disguised as a girl, makes profession as a nun and seduces the abbess (can the bishop compel him to be a monk?); the case of a prisoner who swears that he will return to the jail, if he were allowed to go to Mass on a certain feast day and who, once in the church, refuses to go back, claiming the right of asylum; and so on.

296 The themes of *K*, qq. 9.24.35, and many others are found again in the same MS (above n. 291, no. v) among Johannes' *Quaestiones*.

297 *Quaestiones* by Tancred, hitherto unknown, are reported among many anonymous ones in a large collection of Klosterneuburg, MS 1048, fols. 75–116v. The collection cites decretals from the fourth compilation (1216–1217); the case of wife, man, and doctor, and other themes are repeated.—For another collection, in Fulda, containing *Quaestiones* by Tancred, see *Repertorium*, p. 430.

297a The case of the prisoner (*K*, q. 24 = *W*, q. 39) is also discussed in Douai, Munic. Libr., MS 649 (formerly 582), fol. 145v, in a hitherto unknown collection of *Quaestiones* of French origin, early thirteenth century (fols. 143–148v, beg. "Papa scribit episcopo parisiensi"). As late as 1264, a Dominican theologian, the Blessed Peter of Tarentaise (Pope Innocent V), took up the problem, "utrum qui iurauit redire in carcerem teneatur redire", in his *Quodlibet* q. 1 (ed. P. Glorieux, *Recherches de théologie ancienne et médiévale*, IX [1937], 242). Compare also *B*, q. 10 of our group, "an sacerdos compelli possit ad purgationem qui uouit se numquam iuraturum" (Schulte, *SBWien*, LXVI [1870], 65), with Peter's q. 2: "utrum ille qui uouit nunquam iurare, debeat iurare uel possit de mandato superioris". It should be noted that among the thirty-seven questions of this *Quodlibet*, fourteen (qq. 1–4.6.11. 15.24–26.28.30.34.35) are concerned with canonical problems.

298 In the common stock, if I am not mistaken, only two questions are reported with signatures: *W* 86v: "... Solutio: dicit Ro. ..." (Robertus? Rodulphus? See below, n. 307); *W* 96b: "... Solutio secundum Bar. ..."

set of cases with nearly all the solutions[299] attributed to a master Bernard (*dicit ber. ...*, or *b'. dicit ...*). This ends on fol. 90v; the rest of that page is blank, and on fol. 91 the anonymous *quaestiones* are taken up again by another hand. In the peculiar middle series, sometimes the themes of questions discussed on previous pages are repeated, with new arguments and answers, confirming thus the impression that we have on fols. 87–90v a *reportatio* of disputations not belonging to the main group, e.g.:

W 86r	W 90r
Episcopus Vicentinus[a] impetebat monasterium sancti felicis de quadam subiectione; monasterium profert priuilegium exceptionis. Defertur causa ad papam... a) Innocentius *W*.	Episcopus Vicentinus mouens questionem[a] super subiectione monasterio sancti felicis, in presentia[b] summi pontificis pro monasterio fuit productum[c] quoddam priuilegium ...; *b* stat ... a) questioni *W*. b) presis *W*. c) prodicet *W*.

The series of questions solved by *ber.* is also found, in its greater part and with the same attribution, in the collection of Zwettl where it clearly stands apart (fols. 173–178v) from the common stock of the four MSS (fols. 123–144v).

25. No other Bernard than the Compostellan could be the master who held these disputations inserted in the two collections. Bernard of Pavia was a bishop at that time, and no longer an active member of the school; yet *Quaestiones disputatae* differ from any other written production precisely in this that they presuppose a master *actu regens in scholis*. A positive clue to Bernard of Compostella is given in one of the disputed cases (*W* 87v)[300] where *ber.* is named again, as in his glosses, in connection with Melendus.[301] This time, however, they deliver contrary opinions on a boundary conflict between the sees of Lisbon and Evora, and on a benefice conferred upon the Portuguese master Vincentius:[302]

Episcopus ulixbonensis bona fide possidebat partem diocesis elborensis; assignauit eam in beneficium magistro *V*. Mouit postea ei elborensis

---

299 A few only are anonymous, with *dico* in the solutions; one is given (*W* 89v) as *lu. dicit*, perhaps denoting *L*(*a*)*u*(*rentius*)?
300 I give this and the following examples from *W* alone, as I have not collated the texts of *Z* in detail.
301 Cf. above, §12.
302 If the case be based on real facts, this benefice would be the earliest available datum of Vincentius' ecclesiastical career in Portugal. The able canonist became dean of the chapter of Lisbon in 1212, administrator of that diocese in 1217, royal chancellor in 1224, bishop-elect of Idanha-Guarda in 1228, was unsuccessfully postulated by the chapter of Lisbon as bishop in 1234, confirmed c. 1235 for Idanha-Guarda, and died in 1248. Cf. F. de Almeida, *História da Igreja em Portugal*, I (Coimbra, 1910), 368.381.393.622 f.; Gillmann, "Wo war Vincentius Hispanus Bischof?", *AKKR*, CXIII (1933), 99 ff; Reuter, *Königtum und Episkopat in Portugal* (above, §5, n. 56), pp. 14.20.24.28.32. A list of his canonical writings is given in *Repertorium*, p. 374, n. 2, with a correction in *RHD*, 4, XVI (1938), 209, n. 2.

super parte illa questionem et obtinuit; uult auferre dicto *V.* illas ecclesias: queritur an possit. ... Solutio: *M* aufert ei, *b*' asserit.

The case looks rather like a real issue than a fictitious problem, but I have not been able to find any record of such a law suit between Lisbon and Evora.[303] Most probably it was settled without the intervention of the Holy See; at any rate it was likely to be known, and chosen for a class discussion, only by Iberian canonists, as the issue was of but limited national interest.—On the other hand, when Bernard shortly afterwards (*W* 88v) discusses a case of English provenance:

Cantuariensis archiepiscopus uult constituere quandam ecclesiam ...
Solutio: *b*'. sententiat pro monachis, nisi ...,

we need not be astonished: the long-lasting struggle (1186–1200) between the monks of Christ Church and Archbishops Baldwin and Hubert Walter of Canterbury, over the collegiate churches founded by Baldwin at Hackington (1186) and Lambeth (1193), was watched anxiously through the entire world;[304] Pillius, the famous civilian, had acted as attorney for the monks in the Papal court,[305] and the issue involved must have been familiar to every Bolognese professor.

Several times, we find among Bernard's *quaestiones* cases dealing with the city or the church of Vicenza:

Habens quidam ius ducatie siue ius patronatus, quod idem est in ecclesia uicentina ... (*W* 89r)
Episcopus Vicentinus mouens questionem ... (*W* 90r, see §24)
Quidam in potestatem uicentinam electus[a] iurauit per annum regere ... (*W* 90r) a) clericus *W.*

---

303 I have in vain examined the Register of Innocent III, and C. Erdmann, *Papsturkunden in Portugal* (Abhandlungen der Gesellschaft der Wissenschaften zu Göttingen, phil.-hist. Klasse, Neue Folge, XX, 3, Berlin, 1927).

304 The materials of the *cause célèbre* are preserved in the *Epistolae Cantuarienses*, ed. Stubbs (London, 1865, Rolls Series), and in the chronicle by Gervase of Canterbury, ed. Stubbs, *Gervasii monachi Cantuar. Opera* ..., I (London, 1879, Rolls Series). Stubbs' introduction to the *Epp. Cant.* is still worth reading; among the more recent bibliography, I mention particularly Dom D. Knowles, *The Monastic Order in England* (Cambridge, 1940), pp. 319 ff., 325 ff. But the complex case awaits as yet a thorough analysis by a Canon Law historian.

305 Cf. *Epp. Cant.*, pp. xlix, liv, 68. The text of his pleading is given by Gervase, *Opp.* I, 366 ff. See also Savigny, IV, 325, notes *e-g*; Pollock and Maitland (§12, n. 142), I, 121. The remark on Pillius in the *Glossa Ordinaria*, C. 23, q. 2, c. 2, v. *civitas*] "... et per hoc decretum Pileus obtinuit contra nuntios regis anglie ... ", does not refer, however, to this case (as Savigny, note *f*, assumed) but to the Canterbury election case of 1205 in which Pillius appeared for the monks, and Melendus (cf. above, §12, n. 143) for King John.

and also in the surrounding *quaestiones* of the common stock, references to that city are strikingly frequent.[306] The whole group of disputations, then, may have originated in the short-lived school of Vicenza, between 1204 and 1209,[307] and Bernard, like his friend Melendus,[308] may have taught there for some time. Yet we must concede that examples chosen from Vicenza, Padua, Modena, Ravenna, and other cities of Northern and Eastern Italy, are often found in Bolognese literature; and even though speaking about the oath of the *podestà*, or about the identity of patronage and *ius ducatiae* in Vicenza, seems to presuppose at least a certain knowledge of local conditions, the assumption of the Compostellan's temporary stay at that university remains but an attractive conjecture.

V. Notes on the Compilatio Romana

26. The collection of decretals by the master of Compostella needs no elaborate introduction. It has been carefully studied, described, and analyzed by Singer in 1914.[309] The circumstances of its origin at the Roman Curia in 1208,[310] Bernard's scrutiny of the papal registers, his interviews with Pope Innocent about the authenticity of certain decretals, the initial success of the new collection in the schools, until it was superseded by the official *Compilatio tertia*,—all these facts are well known.[311] Recently, R. von Heckel supplied additional information concerning the method used by Bernard in composing his work:[312] Bernard selected from the collections of Gilbert and Alan 277 Innocentian decretals, compared them critically with the official copies in the papal registers, and added to this stock 154

---

306 Particularly in *W* 97 ff., *Z* 143 f.
307 On these dates, see Savigny, III, 307 ff.—If our supposition be true, Master *Ro.* who solves in *W* 86v (cf. above, n. 300; also in *Z* 173r) a case: "Rex anglie concessit quandam uillam cum iure suo cuidam monasterio ... ", might be identified with *magister Robertus de Anglia*, who was one of the founders of the school of Vicenza (cf. Savigny, III, 307, note *a*). But if the disputations were held in Bologna, he might rather be *magister Rodulphus Anglicus*, whose death is recorded on September 12, 1235 in the obituary of S. Maria di Reno, ed. Trombelli (above, §4 n. 35), p. 347; Sarti, II, 287.
308 Cf. above, §12, n. 145.
309 "Die Dekretalensammlung des Bernardus Compostellanus Antiquus", *SBWien*, CLXXI, ii (1914).
310 The tenth year of Innocent III, i.e. the last one exploited by Bernard (cf. his Epilogue: Singer, *Bern. Comp.*, p. 115), ended on February 21, 1208. P. Ourliac, "Bernard de Compostelle l'ancien", *Dictionnaire de Droit Canonique*, II (1937), 775, asserts that the compilation was made shortly after 1208, and that one decretal of the eleventh year (*Po.* n. 3664 = *Bern.* I, 21, 10) was used. But he overlooks the fact that Singer, p. 24, proved *Po.* n. 3664 to belong to an earlier, uncertain year; see also Kuttner in *RHD*, 4, XVII (1938), 198, n. 5; Heckel, *Gilb. Alan.*, p. 160.—Also Ourliac's contention that Bernard included (II, 18, 1) a decretal of Celestine III (*JL* n. 17648) had been disproved beforehand by Singer, p. 23 f.
311 Cf. Singer, *Bern. Comp.*, pp. 3 ff. 29 ff.; Kuttner, *Repertorium*, p. 319.
312 Heckel, *Gilb. Alan.*, pp. 170–172, correcting Singer who denied, *Bern. Comp.*, p. 17, any influence of earlier collectors upon Bernard's choice of decretals.

other decretals which he chose from the registers by himself;[313]—or almost by himself: for in a few instances we can presume that his choice was influenced by a still earlier collection, that of Rainer of Pomposa (1201)[314]. Compare, e.g.:

Bern. Compost.	Rain. Pomp.
De summa trinitate et fide catholica, c. Apostolicae servitutis (I, 1, 1)	Si personae divinae proprium nomen possint habere, c. Apostolicae servitutis (1, 1)
De primatu apostolicae sedis, c. Apostolicae sedis (I, 2, un.)	De primatu apostolicae sedis, c. Apostolicae sedis (3, un.)[315]

But these coincidences with Rainer are exceptional;[316] on the whole, we can say that one third of the 431 decretals, distributed over the 497 chapters of the *Compilatio Romana*, consists of new materials, whereas two thirds are taken from previous collections and critically revised.

The decretal collection of Rainer of Pomposa (1201) was a source of the Compilatio Romana by Bernardus Compostellanus (1208). For Rainer's collection cf. now also F. Theisen, Die Dekretalensammlung des Rainerius von Pomposa und ihre Hintergründe, in: R. H. Helmholz et al., Grundlagen des Rechts.

---

313 Heckel, *loc. cit.*, counts 267 in the first, and 164 in the second group. But he overlooks the identity of six decretals in Alan (first redaction) and Bernard respectively; and four more decretals can be added from Alan's second redaction (cf. above, §6, n. 61; this redaction will be cited here in parentheses):
Bern. I, 26, un. = *Alan.*—(I, 24, 5).
Bern. II, 2, 6 = *Alan.* II, 1, 6 (II, 2, 6).
Bern. III, 20, 2 = *Alan.* III, 16, 5 (III, 16, 5).
Bern. III, 24, 3 = *Alan.* V, 3, 4 (V, 3, 4).
Bern. III, 37, 2 = *Alan.*—(VI, 3, 4).
Bern. IV, 12, 5 = *Alan.* IV, 12, 6 (IV, 12, 7).
Bern. V, 16,1 = *Alan.* VI, 13 (VI, 6, 2).
Bern. V, 18,1 = *Alan.*—(V, 18, 3).
Bern. V, 18, 2 = *Alan.* V, 17, 3 (V, 18, 4).
Bern. V, 22,15 = *Alan.*—(V, 23,11).
Incidentally, the parallelism of *Bern.* V, 18, 1.2 and *Alan.*, 2d. ed. V, 18, 3.4, shows that the second redaction was really Bernard's source.
314 Cf. on this collection, *Repertorium*, p. 310. We can add a new MS, Paris, Bibl. Nat., lat. 3922 A (fols. 235–242).
315 Cf. Singer, *Bern. Comp.*, pp. 19.37.38, who however admits no influence.
316 If we single out, in the group not derived from Gilbert and Alan, the decretals issued during the period from 1198 to June, 1201 (i.e. the period covered in Rainer's collection), we find but a very small number of texts common to Rainer and Bernard. In Bernard's first book, e.g., they are five only:
Bern. I, 1, 1 = *Rain.* 1, un.
Bern. I, 2, 1 = *Rain.* 3, un.
Bern. I, 8, 2 = *Rain.* 4, 5.
Bern. I, 8, 4 = *Rain.* 4, 1.
Bern. I, 25, 3 = *Rain.* 2, 2;

Festschrift für Peter Landau zum 65. Geburtstag (Paderborn etc. 2000), 549–577, here p. 556s. (P.L.)

In the following observations, we shall offer a few minor corrections of, and additions to Singer's learned monograph, without any intention of impairing its unquestionable value. We shall deal in brief with the MSS (§27), some identifications of texts (§28), and the influence of the collection (§29).

27. Singer knew and used two copies of the British Museum, MS *Royal* 9. B. XI = *R*; MS *Harleian* 3834 (fols. 202–356v) = *H*; and the MS *lat.* 18223 = *B*, of the Bibliothèque Nationale of Paris. The fourth copy, in Modena, Biblioteca Estense, MS a. R. 4.16 (*lat.* 968, formerly XII. L. 8) = *M*, had escaped his attention.[317] In this MS, the contents of which are listed above (§17), Bernard's compilation occupies fols. 119–235v; beginning without title, it ends with the subscription: *Explicit conposicio Bernardi spam.* (= *hyspani?*) *Innocencii. iii.* When Blume, in 1834, described its last chapter as identical with *2 Comp.* V, 22, 2,[318] he overlooked the fact that the *Compilatio Romana* is followed in *M* by two supplementary collections,[319] and that it is the second supplement which ends (fol. 257r) by the said decretal. On the margins of Bernard's text we find in *M* two sets of additions, by two different hands. One consists of glosses selected from Tancred's Apparatus on the *Compilatio tertia*[320] and transferred by a scribe to the corresponding chapters of the *Compilatio Romana*. The second set is the result of a comparison between the texts themselves of these two compilations: since Bernard abridged the original letters of Pope Innocent more recklessly than Peter of Benevento did later in the official collection,[321] the annotator supplied the portions omitted by Bernard in the individual chapters (*partes decisae*), from a copy of the *Compilatio tertia* which he had on hand. In doing so, he evidently intended to make the Compostellan's collection useful, together with the supplement[322] on fols. 237–255r, as a combined substitute for the authentic law book of 1210.

The MS *B* is said to have been discovered by Maassen, in 1860;[323] but actually, H. d'Arbois de Jubainville had identified the MS, two years earlier, in his study on the medieval library of Clairvaux to which it belonged before the French revolution.[324]

---

while thirteen other decretals of this period are not in Rainer: *Bern.* I, 4, 8.11; I, 7, 3.4; I, 10, 3.5; I, 13, un. and I, 22, 1; I, 16, 1; I, 21, 2; I, 23, 1; I, 25, 2; I, 29, 1.5 (*Po.* nn. 1027. 230.352.942.241. 1173.1112.11.665.57.1002.1110.1013). The proportions are similar in the other books.

317 Cf. *Repertorium*, p. 317.
318 Cf. *ibid.*, p. 318.
319 Cf. above, §17 (v) (vi).
320 On this *Apparatus*, see *Repertorium*, p. 358.
321 Cf. Singer, *Bern. Comp.*, p. 27 f.
322 Above, §17 (v).
323 Singer, *Bern. Comp.*, p. 12.
324 H. d'Arbois de Jubainville, *Etudes sur l'état intérieur des abbayes cisterciennes* (Paris, 1858), p. 437 f., established the identity of MS R. 88, correctly described in the old catalogue of Clairvaux, with the MS of the Bibliothèque Impériale, *fonds Bouhier*, 137 (now MS *lat.* 18223).

The shape of *R* has puzzled scholars ever since that MS was discovered, over one hundred years ago, by Augustine Theiner.[325] *R* contains for a large number of decretals only the addresses, and refers the reader for the texts themselves to a certain *secunda compilatio* which must have preceded Bernard's collection in the scribe's exemplar. It is evident that the so-called *Compilatio secunda* by John of Wales cannot have been meant, as that collection consists chiefly of pre-innocentian decretals. Theiner supposed the references in question to denote the collection of Gilbert;[326] Schulte agreed, although not all the examples given by Theiner fitted into Gilbert's text as Schulte knew it;[327] Singer dropped the problem because of his aversion against contemplating any possible influence of earlier collections upon Bernard.[328]

The question can now be solved, since we know at present Gilbert's second redaction and its peculiar form (.= *HL*) in two English MSS, the *Harleian* 3834 (fols. 140–201v) and Lambeth Palace, MS 105 (fols. 220v–267v).[329] When we examine Theiner's examples[330] for Bernard's first book in *R*, and correct his notoriously wrong numbering of titles and chapters,[331] we obtain the following result:

Theiner's number	is *Bern. Compost.*	refers in *R* to *secunda compilatio*	which corresponds to Gilbert, lst. ed.	Gilbert, *HL*
I, 6, 9	I, 8, 5	*De fil. presb., Innotuit*	I, 10, 4	I, 10, 4
I, 7, 2	I, 9, 2	*De renunt., Quod in dubiis*	I, 5, 4	I, 5, 4
I, 7, 11	I, 10, 6	*De fil. presb., Litteras;* but should be: *De tempor. ordin., Litteras* [332]	I, 10, 3 I, 8, 3	I, 10, 3 I, 8, 3
I, 7(17), 3	I, 23, 3	*De off. et pot. iud. ord., Duo simul*	I, 14,2	I, 14, 2
I, 7(17), 4	I, 23, 4	*De eo qui agit vicem alt., Quod sedem*	I, 19, un.	I, 19, un.

---

325 Theiner, *Disquisitiones criticae in antiquas iuris canonici collectiones* (Romae, 1836), p. 129 ff.
326 *Op. cit.*, p. 131.
327 Schulte, "Die Compilationen Gilberts und Alanus", *SBWien*, LXV (1870), 610 f.
328 Cf. Singer, *Bern. Comp.*, p. 8 f.—Ourliac, *art. cit.* (above, n. 310), suggests, without sufficient reason, that the references were made to a mixed collection containing elements from both Gilbert and Alan.
329 Cf. *Repertorium*, p. 312 f.
330 Theiner, *op. cit.*, p. 131, n. 5.
331 On Theiner's mistakes and carelessness in general, see Singer, *Bern. Comp.*, p. 9, n. 31.
332 *Gilb*. I, 10, 3 is the decretal *Litteras*, *JL* n. 16633, by Clement III (*2 Comp*. I, 9, 5 = X. I, 17, 14), which of course does not correspond to any text in Bernard. The scribe of *R* wrote the correct address and *initium* of Bern. I, 10, 6: *Idem* (Innocentius III) *Mutinensi. Litteras uestre*, but then confused the reference which should have been to Innocent III's decretal *Litteras, Po.* n. 1327, *Gilb*. I, 8, 3. Evidently his eye was caught by the identical *initium* of a decretal two titles below.

Theiner's number	is *Bern. Compost.*	refers in *R* to *secunda compilatio*	which corresponds to *Gilbert*, lst. ed.	*Gilbert, HL*
I, 17, 10	I, 23, 10	*De depos. episcop., Expectans expectauit*	—	V, 17, un.[333]
I, 24, un.	I, 30, un.	*De arbitr., Dilecti filii*	—	I, 21, 2[334]

The *secunda compilatio* referred to by *R* was therefore the collection of Gilbert in the *recensio HL*,[335] and it is significant that in *H* this text precedes indeed the *Compilatio Romana*.

28. Singer failed to identify, as far as I can see, one chapter only of Bernard's collection, viz. the decretal *Licet quod legalis* (II, 2, 6) which, actually, is the letter *Po.* n. 1858, and which is also found in Alanus (II, 1, 6 [II, 2, 6]: *Licet quidem legalis*), and in the *Compilatio quarta* (II, 2, 4: *Licet quedam legalis*). Another identification which he missed does not concern Bernard's collection itself, but a calendar of its rubrics. Theiner had discovered this item in a MS of Halle,[336] and as usual had described it in a very confused manner. He believed it to be a list of Alanus' titles;[337] Schulte contested, and Singer dismissed his claim without further examination.[338] Yet if we redress Theiner's mistakes in numbering the rubrics of Bernard,[339] we find:

Theiner's calendar:	*Bern. Compost.*
De summa trinitate	= I, 1
De primatu apost. sedis	= I, 2
B. Th. I, 2	= I, 3
B. Th. I, 3	= I, 4
B. Th. I, 4	= I, 5
3 Comp. I, 4	= I, 6
De irregular. preficiendorum	= I, 7[340]
3 Comp. I, 6	= I, 8

---

333 Cf. *Repertorium*, p. 313.
334 *Gilb. HL*, I, 21, 1 = *Gilb.* app. 5; *Gilb. HL*, I, 21, 2 = *Alan.* app. 17 (I, 24, 4).
335 Also Alanus, in the glosses on his own compilation (MS of Vercelli, cf. above, §6, n. 61), calls Gilbert's collection *liber secundus*.
336 Theiner, *Disquis. crit.*, p. 126, n. 14. According to him, this calendar stands "tabulae rubricarum epitomes Bernardi Papiensis calci adiecta"; this may be either in MS Ye. 80 or in MS Ye. 52 of the University Library, both of which contain the *Comp. I*, cf. *Repertorium*, p. 331 f.
337 Theiner, *op. cit.*, p. 126.
338 Schulte (above, n. 327), p. 596 f.; Singer, *Bern. Comp.*, p. 20, n. 56.
339 This can be done by collating his careless description of the Compostellan's rubrics, p. 134, n. 13 (his numbers are given in our table as *B. Th.*), with Singer's analysis.
340 The original title in Bernard differs: *De irregulari translatione electi confirmati et episcoporum*. The wording in Theiner's list may be due to his own or to the scribe's inadvertence.

Theiner's calendar: Bern. Compost.
3 Comp. I, 8   = I, 9
Gilb. I, 8   = I, 10
etc.   *etc.*

29. Bernard's collection exercised an influence mainly upon Petrus Collivaccinus of Benevento, the redactor of the *Compilatio tertia*. A glance at Singer's analysis imparts a sufficient impression of Peter's obvious dependence upon Bernard in selection and arrangement of the materials.[341] It is known that, apart from minor changes, he differed from Bernard only by treating the common texts with greater conservatism,[342] by adding more decretals, particularly from Pope Innocent's eleventh and twelfth years,[343] and by omitting certain decretals, because the Curia did not want them to be considered as generally binding law.[344] A small number of Bernard's texts reappeared, after 1216, in the *Compilatio quarta*, but no direct influence upon this collection can be proved.[345]

Tancred stated that, before the official *Compilatio tertia* came out, Bernard's *Compilatio Romana* had been accepted for some time at Bologna.[346] We still can trace some ways in which the school made use of it. An anonymous glossator of the *Compilatio prima* in the MS of Modena frequently referred to the *conpilatio bernardi*;[347] another writer condensed it in a summary;[348] and, in a MS of Salzburg, we find a collection of decretals[349] which was evidently abstracted from Bernard:

Coll. Salisb.	*Bern. Compost.*	*3 Comp.*
1	I, 3, 4	I, 1, 4 (different)
2	I, 4, 1	I, 2, 1
3	I, 4, 5	—
4	I, 4, 8	I, 2, 6
5	I, 4, 11	V, 23, 6
6	I, 5, 5	—
.	.	.
.	.	.
.	.	.
ult.	V, 24, 5 (*ult.*)	—

341 See also Heckel, *Gilb. Alan.*, p. 172 f.
342 Singer, *Bern. Comp.*, p. 27.
343 In regard to a few pieces from earlier years, see Heckel, *Gilb. Alan.*, p. 173.
344 Tancred, in the preface of his *Apparatus* on *Comp. III*, says: " ... quas Romana curia refutabat". Cf. on the meaning of this passage, Singer, *Bern. Comp.*, p. 29 ff. For editions of Tancred's preface, see *Repertorium*, p. 309, n. 1.
345 Singer, *Bern. Comp.*, p. 25. Add to his list, n. 73, of sixteen pieces in *Comp. IV*: Bern. II, 2, 6 = *4 Comp.* II, 2, 4 (above, §28).
346 Tancred, *loc. cit.*
347 Glosses of *Comp. I* in *M*, set iv: see above, §18, n. 230.
348 Paris, Arsenal, MS 769 (fols. 74v–84v); cf. *Repertorium*, p. 435.
349 Salzburg, St. Peter's Abbey, MS a. IX. 18 (fols. 244–275v). The MS, hitherto unknown, contains (i) fols. 2–117: *Compilatio prima*, with the *Apparatus* of Richard (cf. above, §18,

It is characteristic for the Salzburg MS that it omits with preference those decretals of the *Compilatio Romana* which can be found in Gilbert and Alan.[350] Probably the compiler's intention was to furnish a supplement to these two collections, both of which were copied in the same MS. We cannot say, however, why he was not more consistent in his task and did not give all the 154 decretals which are peculiar to Bernard.[351]

Even after the *Compilatio tertia*, some authors continued to cite occasionally from the Compostellan's collection. So did Ambrosius in his *Summa*,[352] Damasus in his *Quaestiones*,[353] Vincentius,[354] Albertus, and Tancred[355] in their respective decretalist glosses, and so did the *Glossa Palatina*.[356] Even St. Raymond of Peñafort paid some attention to the *Compilatio Romana*. When he undertook to prepare, about 1230, from the five acknowledged Compilationes antiquae, the materials for the comprehensive collection of Pope Gregory IX (1234), he collated in a few instances the Compostellan's texts for critical purposes.[357] He did

---

n. 224), the *Apparatus* of Alan (on this work, cf. *Repertorium*, p. 325 and above, §6, n. 61), and several additions; (ii) fols. 118–168: Gilbert's collection of decretals, second redaction, with Gilbert's glosses; cf. above, §17, n. 209; (iii) fols. 169–243: Alan's collection, second redaction, without glosses; cf. above, §6, n. 61; (iv) fols. 244–275v: the collection presently discussed.

350 When we examine *Bern.* I, tit. 1–5 (whence *Coll. Salisb.*, c. 1–6 are excerpted), we find that I, 3, 1–3; I, 4, 3-4.6.9.10.12-14; I, 5, 1–4 are covered by the collection of Alan. But beyond these 15 decretals, *Coll. Salisb.* omits five more, viz. *Bern.* I, 1, 1–2; I, 2, un.; I, 4, 2.7.

351 In our examples, the omission of *Bern.* I, 1, 1–2 and I, 2, un. may be due to the theological nature of these pieces, but for I, 4, 2.7 that reason does not hold good.

352 Cf. Kuttner, "La réserve papale du droit de canonisation", *RHD*, 4, XVII (1938), p. 207, n. 1; p. 227.—On Ambrosius and his *Summa* see *Repertorium*, p. 392 f.; add the MS of Venice, Marcian Libr., *lat.* IV. 25 (Valentinelli VIII. 22; fols. 23–71v) concerning which several wrong guesses were made formerly by others and by myself (cf. *Repertorium*, pp. 341.389, n. 6).

353 In Damasus, *Quaest.*, tit. *de officio iudicis ordin.*, there is a passage: "... et erat bonum argumentum in bernardo, Licet." This reference was misunderstood by Schulte, "Literaturgeschichte der Compilationes Antiquae", *SBWien*, LXVI (1870), 152; actually, it means *Bern.* II, 2, 6 (= *4 Comp.* II, 2, 4).—On the *Quaestiones* by Damasus, see *Repertorium*, p. 426 ff.; add the MS of Plock, Diocesan Seminary, 78 (fols. 77–103), according to Vetulani, *Projet*, p. 451.

354 Gillmann, "Der Kommentar des Vincentius Hispanus zu den Kanones des vierten Laterankonzils", *AKKR*, CIX (1929), 263, n. 1.

355 Albertus, in a gloss on *Comp. II*, incorporated by Tancred, *De iudeis*, c. *Significavit* (*2 Comp.* V, 4, 5 = X. V, 6, 11), v. *per alios*] "... ex. b'. de emunit. eccles. Expectauimus, lib. iii. ... quotiens. a." This refers to *Bern.* III, 38, 2.—On Albert's *Apparatus*, cf. *Repertorium*, p. 345; Gillmann, *Zur Inventaris.*, p. 87; additional copies are in Melk, Bened. Monast., MS 518 (formerly I. 37; fols. 1v–34v, set i) and Zwettl, Cisterc. Monast., MS 30 (fols. 65–101). For Tancred on *Comp. II*, see *Repertorium*, p. 346, and above, §17, n. 219.

356 The *Glossa Palatina* refers twice (on D. 89, c. *Volumus* [2], v. *eligant*, and on C. 9, q. 3, c. *Cum simus* [3] v. *licentia*) to ... ex. in (nocentii). de concess. preb. Licet." (*P*, fols. 21va. 44ra). This decretal appears in *Alan.* app. 55 (2d ed. I, 9, 3), and later in *4 Comp.* I, 6, 1 (X. I, 10, 3), always under the rubric *De supplenda negligentia prelatorum*; only *Bern.* III, 10, 2 contains it under the quoted title, *De concessione prebende (uel dignitatis non uacantis)*.

357 Singer, *Bern. Comp.*, p. 28, with some examples in n. 79.

not use them, however, as a direct source, nor did he always accept the results of Bernard's textual criticism.[358] After this modest service rendered to the cause of unification of the decretal law, the *Compilatio Romana* was soon forgotten; and here ends the story of Bernard of Compostella, an eager and gifted, but unsuccessful canonist.[359]

Appendix (cf. above, §14)

Willielmus Vasco and the Glosses on Gratian of MS Vatic. lat. 1367

MS *Vatic. lat.* 1367 contains Gratian's *Decreta* with five different strata of glosses:[360] (set i): Johannes Teutonicus, *Glossa Ordinaria*;[361] (set ii) a mixed gloss composition, written at a short interval from the *Ordinaria*; (set iii) sporadic glosses by St. Raymond of Peñafort, c. 1218–1221;[362] (set iv) the additions of Bartholomaeus Brixiensis to the *Ordinaria*, incomplete;[363] (set v) an irregular stratum of later additions, c. 1294–1300,[364] including many glosses by the Provençal master Étienne Bonnier (Stephanus Provincialis) who taught in Bologna between 1290 and 1297,[365] and glosses by Richard of Siena,[366] who is generally known as one of the redactors of Pope Boniface VIII's collection of decretals, *Liber Sextus*,[367]

---

358 For instance, Bernard rejected as spurious in his epilogue, among other decretals, the letter *Miramur non modicum* (*Alan.* 1, 10, un; 2d ed. 1, 14, un.; cf. Singer, p. 114 f.). St. Raymond nevertheless included it in X. 1, 18, 7. Cf. Singer, p. 35; Heckel, *Gilb. Alan.*, p. 175.
The decretal 'Miramur non modicum' was usually ascribed to Innocent III in decretal collections from the beginning of the 13th century, but was probably written by Celestine III; cf. P. Landau, Innocenz III. und die Dekretalen seiner Vorgänger, in: *A. Sommerlechner* (ed.), Innocenzo III. Urbs et Orbis. Atti del Congresso Roma 1998 (Miscellanea della Società Romana di Storia Patria XLIV, Roma 2003, Vol. I), 175–199, here p. 196s. Celestine III is mentioned as author in Collectio A. Rot. 1.10.6 (MS Paris lat. 3922A) (P.L.)

359 Further research may bring out other writings by the Compostellan. An addition, e.g., with the siglum *B'.*, to the *Apparatus* by Vincentius on the Statutes of the Fourth Lateran Council (Bamberg, MS Can. 20; cf. *Repertorium*, p. 369) might be his—but it might as well belong to his younger contemporary, master Bertrandus (*Repertorium, l.c.* and p. 100).

360 A first but insufficient account of the MS (= *Ov*) was given in *Repertorium*, p. 53 f.

361 Cf. *op. cit.*, p. 99.

362 Cf. *op. cit.*, p. 102.

363 Cf. *op. cit.*, p. 54.

364 The *terminus a quo* results from a gloss of set v, on C. 2, q. 1, c. *In primis* (7), v. *accusatores*] "Nota istam caudam ... et hoc fuit de facto tempore potestatis bon(oniensis), scil. d(omini) Jo. de lu." (*Ov*, fol. 84ra). Giovanni da Lucino was *podestà* in 1294; cf. *Corpus Chronicorum Bononiensium*, ed. Muratori, *Rerum Italicarum Scriptores*, XVIII (Mediolani, 1731), 298; and ed. Sorbelli, *Rer. Ital. Script.*, Nuova edizione, XVIII, i, 2 (Bologna, 1938), 238.

365 On Stephanus Provincialis, see Schulte, *QL*, II, 164; P. Fournier, "Notes complémentaires pour l'histoire des canonistes du XIVe siècle", *Nouv. RHD*, XLIII (1919), 637. His siglum in *Ov* is a semi-uncial *s.*, or *ste.* The same siglum appears in a stratum of additions on the *Glossa Ordinaria* (2d redaction) in Padua, Cathedral Chapter, MS A. 23.

366 *Ov* 17va. 18rb. 89rb. The siglum is *R. de Senis*.

367 Cf. the Pope's decree of promulgation, *Sacrosanctae*, in the editions of the *Corpus iuris canonici.*—Schulte, *QL*, II, 35.

but who also taught for some time Roman Law at Naples,[368] and wrote, when he was a Cardinal (after 1298), a series of *Casus* on the *Liber Sextus*.[369] We are concerned here with set ii only. This very instructive gloss composition presents two kinds of supplements to the standard *Apparatus* of Johannes: (A) glosses supplied from authors preceding the *Ordinaria*, and (B) new, explanatory or critical annotations.[370] Both groups are carefully marked by the pertinent sigla.

In group A we find many familiar names: (i) abundant excerpts from Laurentius and from the *Glossa Palatina*;[371] (ii) numerous glosses by Johannes Teutonicus himself, partly mere fillings of accidental gaps in set i, but partly also true *glossae extravagantes* which never belonged to his formal *Apparatus*;[372] (iii) numerous glosses by Bernardus Compostellanus;[373] (iv) less frequently, glosses of Huguccio (*h.*),[374] and (v) of Alanus (*ala.*);[375] (vi) occasional excerpts from the *Distinctiones decretorum* of Richardus Anglicus.[376]—Still of greater historical interest are the glosses, contained in this group, of those Bolognese authors of whom elsewhere no, or not much, decretist production is preserved: (vii) the prolific Hungarian decretalist Damasus (*da.*);[377] (viii) Jacobus of Albenga (*Ja.*),[378] the chief glossator of the *Compilatio quinta*[379] who later contrived to be elected bishop of his home town,[380] but who is wrongly believed to have become

---

368 E. M. Meijers, *Iuris interpretes saec. XIII* (Neapoli, 1924), p. 217 ff. Concerning Richard's alleged professorate in Siena, cf. H. Denifle, *Die Universitäten des Mittelalters*, I (Berlin, 1885), 436.
369 H. Finke, *Aus den Tagen Bonifaz' VIII.* (Vorreformationsgeschichtliche Forschungen, II, Münster, 1902), p. 106, n. 1, reproduces the inscription of the copy he discovered in Munich, State Libr., MS *lat.* 329 (fol. 165v): *Incipiunt casus sexti decretalium per dominum Ricardum de Cenis cardinalem.*—Richard was Cardinal from 1298 to his death, 1314; cf. Eubel, I, 13. A copy of his will, dated January 27, 1314, was discovered by Mme J. Bignami-Odier in the Vatican Library, MS *Reg. lat.* 377 (fols. 47–51).
370 These were overlooked in *Repertorium*, p. 53.
371 Cf. *op. cit.*, p. 84.
372 Cf. *op. cit.*, p. 92; more *glossae extravagantes* are on fols. 123va. 219rb. 300rb. 301ra. 303rb. 306ra.
373 Cf. above, §14.
374 *Ov* 2vb. 3ra. 4ra. 172ra. 229ra. 258va. 261v. 264r. 278rb. 282ra. On Huguccio's original siglum, *vg.*, and the various abbreviations used for his name by others, see above, §4, n. 36(?).
375 *Ov* 112ra. 123ra. 162vb. 169ra. For his *Apparatus* on Gratian, see above, §6A.
376 *Ov* 56r. 270va, unsigned. On the *Distinctiones*, see above, §4, at n. 25(?).
377 *Ov* 84ra. 85ra. 106ra. 173ra. On Damasus' decretalist writings, see *Repertorium*, pp. 328. 346. 370. 378. 393 ff. 419 ff. 426 ff. 428, n. 3; *RHD*, 4, XVII (1938), 209, n. 2; for the *Quaestiones*, also above, §23, n. 282; §29, n. 353.
378 *Ov* 109 va. 254 rb. The first of these glosses is signed: *Ja. la.*, indicating the appropriation of a Jacobean gloss by Laurentius; cf. above, §6, n. 78. There exist also, *vice versa*, additions of Jacobus to Laurentius; cf. above §6 B.
379 *Repertorium*, p. 383. He wrote also additions to Tancred's *Apparatus* on *Comp. I*: Admont, Bened. Monast., MS 22 (fols. 1-85v, in set ii).
380 Bernard of Montmirat (*Abbas Antiquus*) says in his *Lectura* on the Decretals, *De electionibus*, c. *Dudurn* (X. I, 6, 54): "… sicut fecit magister Jacobus de Alben. qui dimisit quendam archidiaconatum quem habebat cum ecclesiis, tempore quo uacauit Alban. ecclesia, licet postea electus non fuerit". (ed. Venet., 1588, fol. 24, num. 8). On Bernard of Montmirat (d. 1296), see E. M. Meijers, *Responsa Doctorum Tholosanorum* (Haarlem, 1938), p. viii f.; Kuttner, "Wer war der

finally bishop of Faenza;[381] (ix) the Spaniard Martin of Zamora (*Mar.*),[382] otherwise known as glossator of the *Compilatio prima*,[383] and who may perhaps be identified with Martin Roderici, archdeacon of León, bishop of Zamora (1217) and later (1238–1247) of León;[384] (x) Pelagius (*Pe.*),[385] the later Cardinal-bishop of Albano (d. 1232), likewise a glossator of the first compilation;[386] (xi) finally, the famous Portuguese Vincentius (*v.*),[387] one of the most fertile decretalists, who was to become royal chancellor and bishop of Idanha-Guarda (d. 1248).[388]

Among the glosses of this group, we also find the sigla of three Bolognese civilians, Azo (*az.*), Hugolinus (*Hugol.*, *hug̃.*, *h.*), and Lanfrancus (*lāfñ.*).[389] This does not indicate, however, a decretist activity of these authors,[390] as one might believe on first sight. In fact, such glosses appear only in places where Gratian had included in his work certain pieces of Justinian's legislation, and they are simply

Dekretalist Abbas Antiquus?", *ZRGKan*, XXVI (1937), 471–489; *Studia et documenta historiae et iuris*, VI (1940), 426, n. 1.
381 Thus by Willielmus Durantis (d. 1296), *Speculum iudiciorum*, prologue: "... Jac. de Albenga episcopus Faventinus". Sarti I, 407, and F. Lanzoni, *Cronotassi dei Vescovi di Faenza* (Faenza, 1913), p. 133, therefore insert the name in the list of bishops of that see, between Bishop Albert (d. 1239 or 1241) and the Bishop-elect Julian (1242). But this insertion is not warranted by any document. Schulte, *QL*, I, 206, identifies the glossator with Bishop Jacobus Petrella (1258–1273), regardless of the difference of names and of the chronological discrepancy. A mistake by Durantis seems more likely.
382 *Ov* 213vb. 254v. 259r. 261va. 267ra; and *M.* on fol. 82va. Notes by *M.* (not Melendus) are found also in the additions to Laurentius of the MS *Lc* (cf. above, §6, n. 69). In *Ov* 247va, two distichs are marked *MaR.*, but this refers to Martialis, *Epigrammata*, XI, 104, 21–22; XI, 16, 9–10 (ed. Lindsay [Oxford, 1902], pp. 281.259).—The surname *Zamorensis* was found by Gillmann, *Laur. Hisp.*, p. 20; *Zur Inventaris.*, p. 80 if. This glossator is not to be confused with Master Martin of Florence (cf. Sarti, I, 397).
383 Cf. Gillmann, *AKKR*, CVIII (1928), 527; *Zur Inventaris.*, pp. 75 (note). 80ff.; "Petrus Brito und Martinus Zamorensis ... ", *AKKR*, CXX (1940), 63 f.—Martin also wrote glosses on *Comp. IV*, beg. "Nam dubius in fide hereticus est": Olmütz, Metrop. Chapter, MS 589 (set iii; leaves unnumbered, behind *Compp. I-III*); in the same MS, set ii, the *Notabilia* "Nota argumentum quod aliter possumus confiteri" on *Comp. IV* (cf. *Repertorium*, p. 414) are likewise signed by *M.*, *mar.*
384 On Martinus Roderici, see Eubel, I, 538.299; II (1914), xxxxiv.
385 *Ov* 108rb.
386 Cf. above, §18, at n. 229; §20.
387 *Ov* 87vb. 91rb. 101vb. 105ra. 105vb. 106rb (above, §6, n. 76). 123va. 154ra (interlinear). 156va. 164va. 168va.
388 Cf. above, §25, n. 302.
389 Azo: *Ov* 100vb. 123vb. Hugolinus: *Ov* 92rb. 158r. Lanfrancus: *Ov* 123 va.
390 To Lanfrancus, scholars have frequently attributed decretalist glosses (e.g., Schulte, *QL*, I, 198; Van Hove, *Prolegomena*, p. 232), which actually are by Laurentius Hispanus. The confusion, caused by the similitude of the sigla, *lan.* and *lau.*, was definitely clarified by Gillmann, "Lanfrankus oder Laurentius?", *AKKR*, CIX (1929), 598–641; CX (1930), 157 ff.—Azo is positively credited in the MS of Modena (above, §20, at n. 246) with having commented on a decretal of the *Compilatio prima*; but this does not prove that the celebrated civilian lectured *ex professo* on the decretals, to say nothing of teaching on Gratian.

borrowed from the Roman Law writings of the three glossators, in order to illustrate these *leges canonizatae*,[391]

(B) All the materials here enumerated were combined in the Vatican composition with glosses written after the *Ordinaria*, and which are partly real notes on Gratian's text, partly critical or supplementary remarks on the opinions of Johannes Teutonicus.[392] Here we find Bernard's siglum again,[393] but by far more numerous are the glosses bearing the siglum of a Master *W.* or quoting his sayings. This *W.* was not the decretalist William Naso[394] who flourished at a much later period,[395] but the less well known Master William of Gascony, Willielmus Vasco or Guascus, whom we find in Bolognese documents of 1219 and 1222,[396] and later, from 1226 onwards, as professor in Padua.[397] Wahrmund's

---

391 (i) The first gloss with Azo's siglum is given on C. 3, q. 6, pr. (*Ov* 100vb), i.e. on a text corresponding to *Cod.* 3, 15. The gloss begins: "Reus autem illius prouincie ... " and continues with an exposition "Item nota quod de criminibus agitur tribus locis ... transmittatur ad locum ubi deliquit: in aut. ut nulli iudic. §Si uero cog. (*Auth.* 9, 9, 5 = *Nov.* 134, 5) *az.*" This is taken verbatim from Azo's *Summa Codicis*, 3, 15 (ed. Venet., 1581, fol. 183).—(ii) Two other glosses with the siglum az. are found (*Ov* 123vb) on C. 10, q. 2, c. *Hoc ius*, §*Perpetua quoque* and *§Si quas uero ruinas* (c. 2, §§6.8) where Gratian had incorporated a group of *authenticae* from *Cod.* 1, 2, 14 (cf. A. Vetulani, "Les Novelles de Justinien dans le Décret de Gratien", *RHD*, 4, XVI [1937], 675.679). The glosses correspond exactly to Azo's *Lectura Codicis*, 1, 2, 14 (ed. Paris., 1577, p. 14, num. 55; p. 13, num. 53).—(iii) The gloss by Lanfrancus is found on the same *lex canonizata*, C. 10, q. 2, c. 1, §1 (*Ov* 123va), and runs: "Ex argumento huius legis ... unde huic littere sto tanquam iudeus. lāfñ." Here, too, origin from a Roman Law Lecture is evident.— (iv) The first gloss by Hugolinus is reported (*Ov* 92rb) on C. 2, q. 6, §*Si quis in quacumque* (p.c. 39 = *Cod.* 7, 70, un.); cf. below, at n. 418.—(v) A distinction, "Munerum alia sordida ... ", with the signature *Hugol.*, and four short glosses (signed *hug̃.*, *h.*, *hu.*) are given in *Ov* 158r, on C. 16, q. 1, §*Placet* (p. c. 40, §4) where Gratian repeats the text of *Cod.* 1, 2, 5.—"Munerum alia sordida" is the opening piece of Hugolinus' famous *Collectio distinctionum*, and was written to illustrate this very *lex*; cf. Savigny, V, 63 ff. 629; E. Seckel, "Distinctiones glossatorum", *Festschrift der Berliner Juristischen Fakultät für F. von Martitz* (Berlin, 1911), p. 420f.
392 Sometimes they consist only of additional references to the *Compilatio quarta*. An example in *RHD*, 4, XVII (1938), 221.
393 Cf. above, §14, at n. 168 ff.
394 Contrary to the supposition expressed in *Repertorium*, p. 54.
395 All the works of William Naso are concerned with the Decretals of Gregory IX, of 1234. Cf. the writings listed in Schulte, *QL*, II, 78 f., and in R. Trifone, "Gli scritti di Guglielmo Nasone ... ", *Rivista di storia del diritto italiano*, II (1929), 242 ff.—Sarti, I, 421, n. 4, and Schulte, *loc. cit.*, following an unsupported assertion by Thomas Diplovatatius (d. 1541), date Naso's activity from about 1227 onwards, and Trifone, *art. cit.*, p. 243 even asserts that this master was mentioned by a Bolognese judicial document as early as 1222. But the *Guillielmus doctor decretorum* of that document (July 24, 1222: Sarti, II, 169 = *Chartularium Studii Bonon.*, III [1916], 193) was another William, surnamed Normannus, as can be seen from a second document in the same case (March 31, 1223: Sarti, I, 626 = *Chartul.*, III, 197). Naso's writings will be discussed on another occasion; for Trifone's misinterpretation of the siglum *N.*, see above, §4, n. 45.
396 March 14, 1219: Sarti, I, 402; *Repertorium*, p. 453.—July 24, 1222: in the same document as master William of Normandy.
397 Gloria, p. 541 f.

supposition that this master might have been the author of a procedural treatise, the Ordo "*Scientiam omnes naturaliter*",[398] is wrong, since two MSS of this *Ordo* give the author's name in full as *G(u)alterus*,[399] and since the work comes from the French school.[400] But William Vasco wrote glosses on the *Compilationes antiquae*[401] on the constitution *Super speculam* of Honorius III (1219),[402] and on the *Arbor consanguinitatis*.[403] He sometimes signed with his

---

398 L. Wahrmund, *Quellen zur Geschichte des römisch-kanonischen Prozesses im Mittelalter*, II, i (Innsbruck, 1913), xii. His argument was founded on the premises that (1) the author of this treatise, *magister G.*, resolves in the prologue to follow the vestiges of a *magister Petrus Penerclii* (or *Penercho, Penerell, Peneressi, Prevelli*—the name is corrupted in all the MSS); and that (2) a formulary in the *Summa dictaminis* of Guido Faba (1229) reproduces a letter of invitation, sent from Padua by *G. Guascus* to his friend *Petrus Hispanus* (cf. also Sarti, I, 364. 401; Schulte, *QL*, I, 152; Gloria, *loc. cit.*). According to Wahrmund, the couples, G.—Petrus Penerclii, G. Guascus—Petrus Hispanus, might be identical. The syllogism, weak in itself, is voided in its first member by the disclosure of the true author and origin of the treatise *Scientiam* (cf. the text, above). But also the second premise is invalid, since other MSS of the *Summa dictaminis* give the invitation as written by one E., or R., *Castellanus*; cf. Denifle, *Universitäten des Mittelalters* (above, n. 368), p. 278, n. 227. There exists no critical edition of Guido Faba's *Summa* (the text printed by A. Gaudenzi in *Il Propugnatore*, Nuova Serie, V, ii [1892], is of no value); at any rate, this form letter in a text book of *dictamen* should not be used as a historical document, either for William Vasco, or for the younger Petrus Hispanus, even though both of them taught at Padua in 1229. For Petrus Hispanus (Portugalensis), see above, §20, n. 255.
399 On the MS of London, see *Repertorium*, p. 33, n. 1; for Montecassino, MS 136 (p. 241), cf. Dom M. Inguanez, *Codicum Casinensium Manuscriptorum Catalogus*, I (1915), 219.
400 J. Bry, review of Wahrmund's edition, *Nouv. RHD*, XXXVII (1913), 700 ff.
401 Glosses on *Comp. I*: Admont, Bened. Monast., MS 22 (fols. 1-85v, in set ii); Graz, Univ. Libr., MS 106 (formerly 41/9; fols. 1-80v, in set ii); Paris, Bibl. Nat., MS *lat.* 3932 (fols. 1-69v, in set ii; cf. *Repertorium*, p. 337).—Glosses on *Comp.* IV: Admont, MS *cit.* (fols. 246v-270, in set ii).—Reference to Vasco's decretalist glosses is probably made when the anonymous glossator of *Comp.* I in the MS of Modena, set iv (cf. above, §18, at n. 230) cites: "Dicebat W. quoniam non solum ... " (*M* 54v), and when Gilbert in the glosses on his own collection (cf. *Repertorium*, p. 313; above, §17, n. 213) speaks several times of *magister Wil.* or *Gwil.* (cf. *Repertorium*, p. 327, n. 2).
402 The famous statute—which decreed, among other provisions, the much discussed prohibition of Civil Law studies for the clergy, and the dissolution of the Civil Law school of Paris—was frequently copied separately in canonical MSS. In Florence, Laurentian Libr., MS *S. Croce* V *sin.* 4 (fly-leaf), and in Lisbon, National Libr., MS *Alcob.* 381 (formerly 305; fol. 224), it is divided into three chapters (corresponding to *5 Comp.* V, 12, 3; III, 27, un.; V, 2, un. = X. V, 38, 28; III, 50, 10; V, 5, 5) and furnished with an apparatus, beg. "Nota in causis ecclesiasticis debere principaliter canones allegari". The glosses are unsigned in Lisbon, but in Florence many of them bear the sigla *G., Guill'.*; or *Jo.* (Teutonicus). In Lisbon, two other decretals of Honorius III (*5 Comp.* II, 12, 1; I, 5, 6 = X. II, 20, 48; I, 6, 48) are appended, without glosses.
403 In Florence, MS *cit.*, on the *verso* of the fly-leaf, there is an *Arbor consanguinitatis* with glosses by one Master *R.* to which another hand adds towards the end: "*Magister Guill'. Wasco dicit, et credo bene dicat. ...*"

full name,[404] and he proves to be the author of our decretist glosses, for the compiler refers to him sometimes as *W.*,[405] and sometimes as *Vasco.*[406] There can be no objection against attributing to him also the glosses with the siglum *W.* in other mixed compositions of the early thirteenth century, as in Arras, Municipal Libr., MS 500 (set iv, together with Bernard of Compostella),[407] Beaune, Munic. Libr., MS 5 (set ii),[408] and as in the additions to Laurentius of the MS *Lc.*[409]

In the Vatican composition, William's glosses frequently consist of annotations on the doctrines of the *Ordinaria*, e.g.:

C. 2, q. 4, c. *Nullam* (3), gloss *Hec quinque capitula*][410] Hoc non approbo, quia ibi dicitur totum contrarium. *W.*

C. 6, q. 1, c. *Illi qui* (3), gloss *Secundum quosdam*, v. de *excommunicatis*][411] Hoc tenet *W.*

C. 6, q. 3, c. *Placuit* (4), gloss *Set numquid episcopus*, v. *ex. iii. de priuil. Tuarum*][412] Immo ea ratione, quia facilius perditur priuilegium quam ius commune: ex. iii. de const. Cum accessissent (*3 Comp.* I, 1, 4 = X. I, 2, 8); et talibus aufertur ius commune, ut ex. i. de appell. Consuluit (*1 Comp.* II, 20, 16 = X. II, 28, 14), ergo et priuilegium, et hoc credo. Et per illam decretalem, Tuarum (*3 Comp.* V, 16, 1 = X. V, 33, 11) non probatur hoc, quia illi non erant priuilegiati, set ribaldi falsa cruce signati. *W.*[413]

But not less frequently, he comments directly on Gratian's text. In many places, finally, we find him cited as introducing, and enlarging by his own remarks, gloss materials from Laurentius and the *Glossa Palatina*:

---

404 In the MS of Graz (above, n. 401), the opening gloss, v. *Iuste iudicate. etc.*] "Sic pone casum: diuiditur in quinque partes ... ", is signed in full, *Wil'. Wasco.* See also the preceding note. Elsewhere, *W.*, or *G.*, or *Guill.* is the usual siglum.

405 This siglum is found on 37 pages in *Ov*, and often repeatedly on the same page.

406 See the glosses below, at nn. 415.416; also on C. 16, q. 1, §*Hoc idem* (p.c. 40) v. *imperfecti sumus*] "Vasco dicit aliam litteram esse in apostolo ..." (*Ov* 158 va).

407 Cf. *Repertorium*, p. 31; above, §7.

408 Cf. *op. cit.*, p. 32 f.—I am doubtful about the siglum *W.* in New York, Morgan Libr., MS M. 446 (set iii). The MS represents in this stratum the standard tradition of Huguccio's time, c. 1180–1190 (cf. above, §4, n. 42), and strong chronological reasons prevail against William's having contributed to it. In fact, the siglum *W.* has here in general been substituted for other erased sigla (e.g., on fols. 39. 89 ff.).

409 Cf. above, §6 B.

410 *Ov* 89rb.

411 *Ov* 108va; for an addition of Bernard to the same gloss of the *Ordinaria*, see above, §14, at n. 168.

412 *Ov* 110vb.

413 Other examples of this kind are found in *Ov* 88ra. 91va. 154vb. 155ra. 158rb. 159va. 160rb. 167vb. 172va. 174vb.

| *Glos. Pal.* | *Glos. Vat.* |

C. 2, q. 6, cc. 18–21.[414]

Non ita (18), v. *in foro*] Si clericus conueniatur ... ex imperiali, coll. ix.

Non ita, v. *non licet*] Arg. quod si clericus reconueniatur ... ex imperiali, coll. vi. *la*.

ante peractam] nisi questionem ... ante sententiam.
dicta causa] i.e. lite contestata ... c. unico.
Quisquis (19)] Casus xi. q. i. ... compellendus est.

§*Quia vero*] Sic continua ... priuabitur. *Quisquis*] Casus xi. q. i.... compellendus est; uel pone casum sic: episcopus ... hoc posset.

prime sedis] i.e. episcopalis ... augustino, §i. Episcopus, ceterum sacerdos ... sacerdotem.

prime sedis] i.e. episcopalis ... augustino. *la*.

probatum] Nota contumaciam ... in fine. Preterea nonne ... notificatum.
Licet etiam (20)] Istud 'etiam' ... appellare.
sententia] Set numquid ... supplicium.

probatum]
Preterea nonne ... notificatum. *la*.
Licet etiam] Istud 'etiam' ... appellare, uel dic ... set etiam appellare.
sententia] Set numquid. ... supplicium. *la*.

Si quis iudicem (21)] In quocumque ... quedam mulier. *b*.[a]
a) h. *R*.

Si quis iud., v. *senserit*] In quocumque ... quedam mulier. *la* (!).

C. 13, q. 2, c. *Ubicumque* (7).[415]
Quidam intelligunt hoc capitulum de peregrinis et alienigenis, et quod dicitur[a] in fine de decimis intelligunt de personalibus.

Quidam hoc capitulum intelligunt de peregrinis et aduenis et alienigenis, et quod dicitur in fine de decimis intelligunt de personalibus; *et hoc approbat uasco.*

Alii intelligunt de indigenis ... non licet eligere. Episcopus autem ... xii. q. ii. Bone (74).
a) dicit *P*.

Alii intelligunt de indigenis ... non licet eligere. *lau*.

---

414 *P* 32ra, *R* 95v, *Ov* 90r.
415 *P* 53ra, *R* 150ra, *Ov* 146va.

Glos. Pal.	Glos. Vat.
C. 15, q. 6, c. *Si a sacerdotibus* (1).[416]	*a suis*]
a suis] Nisi soluant per occasionem gratis; tunc non repetent[a]: C. quod metus ca. 1. ii. (*Cod.* 2, 20, 2). Et ita uidetur quod non transtulit dominium; set secus est. Nam si dominium non transferreretur, non daretur hec actio: ff. quod metus ca. Metum. § Ex hoc edicto (*Dig.* 4, 2, 9, 7). Dic ergo 'suis': olim, sicut exponitur xxvii. q. i. Si quis rapuerit (c. 30), uel 'suis': quoad effectum.	Et ita uidetur quod non transtulerunt dominium; set secus est. Nam si dominium non transferreretur, non daretur hec actio: ff. quod metus ca. Metum, § Ex hoc edicto. Dic ergo 'suis': olim, sicut exponitur xxvii. q. i. Si quis rapuerit, uel 'suis': quoad effectum, quia repetere potest; *uel intelligo de rebus ecclesie, sicut uasco.*
a) reputent *P*.	

These examples could be increased. On C. 17, q. 1, c. 4, e.g., we find a chain of glosses in which William reproduces from the *Palatina* a controversy between Huguccio, Bernard of Compostella, and Laurentius, intersperses it with his own observations ("Ego intelligo ... "secundum me et alios ..."), eventually sums up the discussion, and adds his siglum.[417] Or, on another occasion, he introduces, and approves of, the opinion of the civilian Hugolinus concerning a *lex canonizata*:

C. 2, q. 6, *Si quis in quacumque* (p. c. 39 = *Cod.* 7, 70, un.), v. *excellentissimorum*][418] Istud uult dicere: sicut non licet tertio appellare, ita nec a sententia prefecti pretorio de secunda appellatione ad ipsum facta cognoscentis suplicare. Et probatur iste intellectus ex rubrica ipsa, ibi 'post duas sententias'. *Hugol'*. et *W*.

In all the cases reported here, we perceive from the additions and from the inserted notes of assent or dissent that older gloss materials were read and discussed in the school of William Vasco. Now, if we consider (1) this manner of enlarging part of the older texts by Master William's observations, (2) the striking frequency of his siglum, (3) the fact that these glosses belong to the most recent elements of the stratum, we have a perfect clue to the origin of the entire gloss composition in set ii of the Vatican MS: it was most probably compiled, shortly after the Ordinaria, by a pupil of William Vasco, from the latter's own glosses, and from numerous interpretations by previous authors which the master used to quote and to discuss in his classes.

The Catholic University of America.

---

416 *P* 56va, *R* 157rb, *Ov* 154rb. An interlinear gloss on the same text (*Ov* 154ra) runs thus: *suis*] "i.e. sibi commissis; hoc enim intelligo de rebus ecclesie. *v*"

417 *P* 60vb, *R* 169vb, *Ov* 166vb. The texts are too extensive to be reproduced here.

418 *Ov* 92rb. The gloss is followed by another: "Si suplicabis a sententia prefecti pretorio ... la *(urentius)*."

ANGLO-NORMAN CANONISTS OF THE TWELFTH CENTURY
An Introductory Study

BY STEPHAN KUTTNER AND ELEANOR RATHBONE

This essay written by Kuttner in collaboration with *Eleanor Rathbone* was the first monograph on the anglo-norman school, published in Traditio 7 (1951). It is still the corner-stone for all research in this field of medieval jurisprudence. (P.L.)

Among the various aspects of the operation of canon law in medieval England, the history of the Anglo-Norman school of canonists which flourished in the late twelfth and the early thirteenth centuries remains largely unexplored. Modern historians have frequently emphasized, to be sure, the eager interest which English churchmen of the twelfth century took in problems and issues of canon law; and it can now be considered an established fact that the English Church throughout this period was well abreast of the developments which everywhere resulted from the growing centralization of ecclesiastical procedure, from the work of Gratian and his school, and from the ever-increasing number of authoritative responses and appellate decisions rendered by the popes in their decretal letters.[1] The importance of the system of delegate jurisdiction in the cases referred back by Rome to the country of origin has been noted,[2] and so has the conspicuous number of twelfth-century English collections of decretals, which testifies to a particular zeal

---

1 As G. Barraclough, *English Historical Review* 53 (1938) 492–5 (book review), and Mrs. M. Cheney, 'The Compromise of Avranches of 1172 and the Spread of Canon Law in England,' *ibid.* 56 (1941) 177–97, have shown, it can no longer be maintained that the flow of decretals to England began after 1172 only and that the English Church, up till then, lagged behind in the full knowledge and practice of canon law, as was held by Z. N. Brooke, 'The Effect of Becket's Murder on Papal Authority in England,' *Cambridge Historical Journal* 2 (1926–8) 213–28; *The English Church and the Papacy* (Cambridge 1931) 213f. But aside from this point, the late Dr. Brooke's work remains fundamental in many respects; it definitely laid to rest the old controversy on the authority of the common law of the Church in England. — Cf. further C. R. Cheney, 'Legislation of the Medieval English Church,' *Engl Hist. Rev.* 50 (1935) 193–224, 385–417; Raymonde Foreville, *L'église et la royauté en Angleterre sous Henri II Plantagenet* (Paris 1943) 19f., 389ff.
2 F. W. Maitland, *Roman Canon Law in the Church of England* (London 1898) 122–31; Pollock and Maitland, *The History of English Law before the Time of Edward I* (2nd ed. Cambridge 1898) I, 115; S. E. Thorne, 'Le droit canonique en Angleterre,' *Revue historique de droit français et étranger*[4] 13 (1934) 499–513; Dom A. Morey, *Bartholomew of Exeter, Bishop and Canonist*

and tradition, among Anglo-Norman canonists, in supplementing Gratian's work by records of the new papal law.[3] The problem, also, of the influence exercised by Roman and canon law on the early development of the Common Law is being discussed with growing interest among students of English legal and constitutional history.[4]

The whole question, however, of the place of canon law in England cannot be properly determined without a full inquiry into the range and nature of canonist teaching and writing in the dominions of the English king. In general, the contribution of Anglo-Norman masters to the development of legal and canonical science has been altogether underrated, although the data available are not as meager as customary presentation would have it — are, in fact, sufficient to demonstrate the existence in its own right of an Anglo-Norman school of canonists toward the turn of the twelfth century. This contention is borne out by the abundant if scattered evidence which modern research in the manuscripts of the period between Gratian and Gregory IX has yielded of literary work produced in canon law on either side of the Channel. The writers of this joint paper believe that by summarizing the evidence, by integrating it with additional findings, and by correlating it with information gleaned from narrative and documentary sources, they can throw new light on the history of this half-forgotten school.[5]

I. English Canonists and the Early Collections of Decretals

Enthusiasm for the study of canon and civil law was prevalent throughout the ecclesiastical hierarchy of the country. The new science could not but fascinate the minds of alert young students in a period hardly equalled for its intellectual pioneering. The recurring clashes between ecclesiastical and royal jurisdiction were bound to stimulate the sense of sharp juridical argument. The need for specialized

---

(Cambridge 1937) 44ff.; and the authors cited above. The enormous growth of delegate jurisdiction was a general, not a specifically English development of the twelfth century, cf. Barraclough, *loc. cit.* 494 n.3.

3 References below, ch. I.

4 F. M. Powicke, *Henry III and the Lord Edward* (Oxford 1947) I, 30–50; *Ways of Medieval Life and Thought* (London 1950) 114–212, esp. 119, 128f., 146.; T. F. T. Plucknett, 'The Relation between Roman Law and English Common Law ...,' *University of Toronto Law Journal* 3 (1939–40) 24ff., esp. 30–6; H. G. Richardson and G. O. Sayles, *Select Cases of Procedure without Writ under Henry III* (Selden Soc. 60; London 1941) lix ff., cix ff.; G. Post, 'Plena Potestas and Consent in Medieval Assemblies,' *Traditio* 1 (1943) 355–408. Renewed interest in civilian and canonistic influences on Bracton, stimulated by the late Dr. Kantorowicz's controversial book, *Bractonian Problems* (Glasgow 1941), is witnessed by a number of important studies, especially of Dr. Schulz, Mr. Richardson, and Professor Post; cf. articles listed in the latter's study on 'quod omnes tangit,' *Traditio* 4 (1946) 197 n.2 and 216 n.96; Richardson, 'Studies in Bracton,' *ibid.* 6 (1948) 61–104.

5 The plan of the present paper was outlined when the co-authors first met early in 1947 and decided to pool the results of their research, some of which had been stated by both authors independently in unpublished lectures since 1938. For various reasons this article, originally designed to appear in 1948, could only recently be made ready for publication.

knowledge in handling the growing complexities of diocesan administration and of procedure, ordinary or delegate, was recognized by prelates and clerks alike. For the ambitious, legal training possessed the added value of serving as a stepping stone to the higher careers in the service of the Church or the king: administration, both secular and spiritual, as it expanded and became centralized in the course of the century, demanded an increasing number of expert personnel. This came to be recruited chiefly from the prominent bishops' *familiae*, that is to say, from a working class of clerics among whom the title of *magister* was almost a matter of course. The bishops, themselves often well instructed in law, shared and fostered the enthusiasm of their clerks. They made a practice of sending young archdeacons and promising members of their households to study at Bologna or at other schools, and of filling the canonries of their cathedrals with lawyers.[6]

The monasteries, too, which we should expect to regard with disfavor the worldly pursuits of the secular clergy, found themselves in need of advocates for the defense against the encroachments of royal and episcopal authorities. The monks of Battle, for instance, in the course of their suit against Godfrey de Lucy, reproached their abbot for not having allowed some of the brethren to go to Bologna,[7] while the monks of Canterbury, many of whom had brought to the priory on their profession one or more law books,[8] were able to carry their suits to Rome in person and knew well which lawyers to choose as advocates in Bologna and the Curia.[9] A country parson, Master Peter of Paxton — the agent, it is true, of a great landed family — was the possessor of a complete set of civil and canon law treatises.[10] The many surviving manuscripts and the medieval library catalogues reveal the range and variety of legal works available in all parts of the country.[11]

---

6 Cf. C. R. Cheney, *English Bishops' Chanceries 1100–1250* (Manchester 1950) for the careers of some of these clerks. The question will be discussed in detail by E. Rathbone in her forthcoming book, *English Cathedrals and the Schools in the Twelfth Century*, shortly to be published by the Warburg Institute.
7 *Chronicon monasterii de Bello* (ed. J. S. Brewer, Anglia Christiana Soc.; London 1846) 173.
8 Cf. the lists of books of individual monks, e.g., in M. R. James, *The Ancient Libraries of Canterbury and Dover* (Cambridge 1903) 67ff.
9 On Pillius and Lotharius as attorneys for the monks in the first, and Hugolinus of Segni (the future Gregory IX) in the final stage of their suit against the archbishop, see *Epistolae Cantuarienses* (ed. W. Stubbs, Rolls Series; London 1865) 68, 471, 476, 506; Gervase of Canterbury, *Opera* I (ed. Stubbs, R. S.; London 1879) 366ff.; cf. Stubbs' Introduction, *Epp. Cant.* xliv, liv, ciii; C. F. von Savigny, *Geschichte des römischen Rechts im Mittelalter* (2nd ed. Heidelberg 1834–51) IV, 325; Pollock and Maitland I, 121; Kuttner, 'Bernardus Compostellanus Antiquus,' *Traditio* 1 (1943) 326 n.30. It is uncertain who drew up the formal brief for the monks, *Epp. Cant.* 520–30; Pollock and Maitland presume that it was written by one of the Italian lawyers.
10 *The Registrum Antiquissimum of the Cathedral Church of Lincoln* (ed. C. W. Foster and K. Major, Lincoln Record Soc. 27–29, 32, 34; 1931–40) III, 164. Another country parson, Galfridus de Croppere, shortly after the Fourth Lateran Council obtained a dispensation from the law of residence, for three years, to study 'in s. scriptura et canonibus': *Rotuli Hugonis de Welles* (ed. W. P. W. Phillimore, Canterbury and York Soc.; London 1905–9) I, 39.
11 For MSS of canon law cf. S. Kuttner, *Repertorium der Kanonistik (1140–1234)* (Studi e Testi 71; Città del Vaticano 1937) *passim*: for MSS of civil law cf. e.g. W. Senior, 'Roman Law MSS.

For the law suit of the monks of Battle Abbey against Godfrey de Lucy cf. now Ch. Donahue, Gérard Pucelle as a Canon Lawyer: Life and the Battle Abbey Case, in: R. H. Helmholz et al., Grundlagen des Rechts. Festschrift für Peter Landau zum 65. Geburtstag (Paderborn etc. 2000) 333–348, here p. 340–348. (P.L.) Among the items frequently recurring in such records are early collections of decretals. Benedict, prior of Canterbury and later abbot of Peterborough, left three copies to the abbey at his death, together with two complete texts of the *Corpus iuris civilis*, two copies of Gratian, and several treatises on Roman and canon law.[12] Nowhere, it seems, was the need of making the new papal rulings available for reference—either as supplementary entries in manuscripts of the *Decreta*[13] or as separate books — felt more strongly than in England. The specific English contribution appears most strikingly in the 'primitive' class of decretal collections before Bernard of Pavia, i.e. those which string their material together without dissecting the individual rescripts for systematic distribution into titles. At the present state of research, based chiefly on the findings of Dr. Holtzmann, the foremost expert in the field, fifteen among the twenty-seven collections known of the primitive type can be assigned an English origin,[14] and this ratio will probably not be greatly changed by further discoveries.

We may point to a number of interesting details. It cannot be mere chance, for example, that so many manuscripts containing early collections of decretals come from the cathedral libraries of Canterbury and Worcester;[15] that one of the

---

in England,' *Law Quarterly Review* 47 (1931) 337–44; other MSS and references from library catalogues will be given by E. Rathbone in her forthcoming book. — Copies of Gratian were, however, rare in Wales, according to Gerald of Wales, *Gemma ecclesiastica* 1.1 'Set quoniam in partibus illis canonum copia non habetur, ipsa capitula ... vobis quoque scripta transmisimus' (*Giraldi Cambrensis Opera* ed. Brewer [Rolls Series; London 1861–91] II, 12).

12 M. R. James, *Lists of Manuscripts formerly in Peterborough Abbey Library* (Supplement to the Bibliographical Society's Transactions 5; Oxford 1926) 21.

13 Cf. Kuttner, *Repertorium* 273f., 276; M. Cheney, *Engl. Hist. Rev.* 56 (1941) 181. Such supplements are not always concerned with new texts alone; for example, an appendix made up of older canons abstracted from Burchard's *Liber decretorum* and accordingly in 19 'books' is found in several MSS of Gratian, cf. Kuttner, 'De Gratiani opere noviter edendo,' *Apollinaris* 21 (1948) 120 n.9.

14 W. Holtzmann 'Über eine Ausgabe der päpstlichen Dekretalen des 12. Jahrhundsrts,' *Nachrichten der Akademie der Wiss. in Göttingen*. Phil.-hist. Kl. 1945. pp. 15–36; Kuttner, 'Notes on a Projected Corpus of Twelfth-Century Decretal Letters,' *Traditio* 6 (1948) 345–51; for the English material see Nos. 12–26 of Dr. Holtzmann's list, p. 22, of twenty-six (twenty-seven: *Trad.* 6, 348) primitive collections.

15 Canterbury: London, Brit. Mus. Royal MS 10.B.iv, fol. 42v-58v; 59v-65v (Holtzmann's No. 14, *Coll. Cantuar. I et II*). For collections no longer extant see e.g. Nos. 1048, 1050, 1056, 1081, 1317, 1318 in James, *Ancient Libraries* 99ff.; but entries in the old inventories are of course to be judged with caution (cf. e.g. James' No. 628, from Prior Eastry's catalogue: 'Casus decretalium secundum Johannem Hispanum. In hoc volumine continentur: Constituciones Romanorum Pontificum et decretales epistole.' The book is today MS D.11 [Y.8] of Christ Church, Canterbury, and contains after Johannes de Deo, *Casus decretalium*, 58 leaves of Bernard of Parma's *Glossa ordinaria* on the Decretals. Prior Eastry's misleading description is based on two passages of the prologue [beg. 'In huius libri principio quinque sunt prenotanda']: '... Intentio domini Gregorii ... diuersas constitutiones et decretales epistolas ... in unam compilationem ... reducere; ... materia in hoc

important collections, the *Wigorniensis,* is in a codex connected with Baldwin, bishop of Worcester and later archbishop of Canterbury — who had been earlier a fellow-student of Urban III and Stephen of Tournai; tutor, by appointment of Eugene III, to Innocent II's nephew, Gratian (the Cardinalis of the glossators). Archdeacon of Exeter under Bartholomew, until his retirement to the abbey of Ford where, as abbot, he was often a judge delegate;[16]—or that another collection (Brit. Mus. MS Royal 15.B.iv) consists largely of papal letters addressed to West Country prelates: Baldwin's predecessor, Roger of Worcester, and Bartholomew of Exeter, whom Alexander III called the twin lights of the English clergy.[17]

The canonist Cardinalis was not a nephew of Pope Innocent II, but he was the French canonist Raimundus de (H)arenis – cf. my additions to p. 97 (Retractationes). (P.L.) Baldwin, abp. of Canterbury. He was appointed Legate to the Canterbury province by Urban III in the letter 'Divine sapiencie inscurtabilis altitudo' (18. XII. 1185), ed. P. M. Baumgarten, EHR 9 (1894) 331–41, at p. 339 (S.K.)

Connections such as these with a group of prelates who ranked among the most frequently commissioned papal judges delegate show the practical value of the early decretal compilations. But there is more than this. A number of primitive collections reveal efforts to organize, at least tentatively, the new material. This was done, at times, by prefixing topical rubrics to the individual letters and particularly to the individual paragraphs of letters dealing with a variety of subjects;[18] at times, by grouping the decretals, still undivided, roughly into books or *partes.* This latter procedure (occasionally combined with the insertion of guiding rubrics) was chosen in the *Wigorniensis,* mentioned before, and a group of collections related to it.[19]

Such methods, however, must appear crude if compared with the intellectual achievement of the 'systematic' collections which, more often than not at the cost of cutting apart individual rescripts, endeavored to fit the papal texts methodically into an elaborate framework of juridical concepts.[20] The Anglo-Norman collections of this type, though perhaps fewer in number than those of the French schools, were nevertheless of great historical significance. For,

---

opere sunt ipse constitutiones et decretales epistole sub singulis titulis collocate ...'). — Worcester: Brit. Mus. Royal MSS 10.A.ii, fol. 5–62v (Holtzmann's No. 22, *Coll. Wigorn.;* cf. H. E. Lohmann, 'Die Collectio Wigorniensis,' *Zeitschrift der Savigny-Stiftung für Rechtsgeschichte* [=ZRG], Kan. Abt. 22 [1933] 36–187); 11.Bii, fol. 97–102 (Holtzmann's No. 12, *Coll. Wigorn. II;* cf. Kuttner, *Repertorium* 283–5); 15.B.iv, fol. 107v-118v (Holtzmann's No. 18. *Coll. Royal).*

16 Cf. Lohmann, *op. cit.* 53 n.1 and R. L. Poole, 'The Early Lives of Robert Pullen and Nicholas Breakspear ...,' in *Essays in Medieval History Presented to T. F. Tout* (Manchester 1925) 69.
17 Giraldus Cambr. *Opp.* VII, 57.
18 Cf. Holtzmann, *Über eine Ausgabe* 26; cf. Nos. 19, 20 of his list, p. 22.
19 *Ibid.* Nos. 21–26. Additional fragments of one of these, *Coll. Peterhusensis* (No. 26; cf. *Traditio* 6, 348) have been found in the meantime. The collection can now be reconstructed (Bks. 1–4.52) as follows: Cambridge, Peterhouse MS 193, fol. 223–230v; MS 114, fol. i-viii, 219–224v; MS 193, fol. i-viii; MS 203, fol. 258–263v; MS 180, fol. i-viii; 225–232v. (Information kindly supplied by Dr. Holtzmann and by Mr. Charles Duggan of Trinity College, Cambridge. Mr. Duggan hopes to publish shortly a detailed study of this and some related collections.)
20 Cf. Juncker, 'Die Collectio Berolinensis,' ZRG Kan. Abt. 13 (1924) 344 n.3.

among the several families of systematic collections of the twelfth century, it was the so-called *Appendix Concilii Lateranensis* (c. 1181–5) which became the fountainhead of the main decretal tradition—: the ancestor, by way of the French collection known as *Bambergensis* and other texts derived from the latter, of Bernard of Pavia's all-important *Breviarium extravagantium*.[21] The English origin of the *Appendix*, which has recently been questioned, can be established by the fact that for reference and interpretation this collection was used in the writings, not of the Bolognese, but of the Anglo-Norman school alone.[22] Another interesting group of English collections appeared in the decade following the publication of the *Appendix*. It is characterized by an amalgamation of continental models — especially of the *Bambergensis* (as in the collection of Bodleian MS Tanner 8) and, in a later stage, also of the compilation of Bernard of Pavia (as in the *Collectio Sangermanensis*) — with materials from the country's own decretalist tradition.[23] And again, it can be shown that such collections served as working tools to Anglo-Norman legal and canonistic writers[24] — at a time when Bernard's *Breviarium* was already established in Bologna as the recognized text for teaching on the decretals.

II. Bolognese and French Connections

The history of the English collections raises serious doubts as to the correctness of the widespread assumption that whatever canonical learning existed, in the late 1100's, in the dominions of the English king, must have come from Bologna, just as the study of Roman Law had been imported from there two generations earlier by Vacarius. But even aside from the decretal collections, the current view, according to which all science of canon law in England is ascribed, directly or indirectly, to the activities of men returning from the schools of Italy,[25] is no longer

---

21 Cf. E. Friedberg, *Quinque compilationes antiquae* (Leipzig 1882) xi ff.; F. Heyer, ZRG Kan. Abt. 3 (1913) 625ff.; W. Holtzmann, 'Die Register Papst Alexanders III. in den Händen der Kanonisten,' *Quellen und Forschungen aus italienischen Archiven* ... 30 (1940) 15.
22 Kuttner, *Traditio* 6, 349, citing the evidence from Honorius, the *Summa In nomine,* and the *Summa De iure canonico tractaturus.*
23 Cf. Holtzmann, *Die Register* 64; 'Die Dekretalen Gregors VIII.' *Mitteilungen des Instituts für österr. Geschichtsforschung* 58 (1950) 115 n.4. On *Coll. Abrincensis* cf. references in Kuttner, *Repertorium* 299. — Paris, B. N. MS lat. 3922A from Rouen, with its several, successive supplements (*Coll. Rotomagensis* etc.) to the *Coll. Francofortana,* affords an interesting example of the working methods of an Anglo-Norman collector, Holtzmann, *Die Register* 66; *Über eine Ausgabe* 23, 35; and in *Zeitschrift für Schweizer. Geschichte* 29 (1949) 152. An index of rubrics and chapters of a collection of the *Bambergensis* group, with marginal references to additional decretals, is found in Brit. Mus. MS Royal 2.D.ix, fol. 11–22r, probably from Pershore Abbey; the references in the margin are given by arabic number (!), inscription, and incipit, evidently from an English primitive collection. The MS represents the preparatory stage of a compilation of the type MS Tanner 8.
24 The evidence from the Caius glosses on the Decretum, the Royal *Quaestiones,* the glosses of the Vacarian school, and the *Ordo Baltimorensis* is given below, Appendix A.
25 Cf., e.g., H. G. Richardson, 'The Oxford Law School under John,' *Law Quarterly Review* 57 (1941) 322f., 336.

acceptable. To be sure, one may point to the well-known afflux of English students to Bologna, from the early years of Thomas Becket to the beginning of the thirteenth century, when the Englishmen Richard, Gilbert, and Alan, the Welshman John, and others, are found among the *magistri* active in the Bolognese school, while at the same time a good many more repaired thither to freshen up their legal knowledge — as did Thomas of Marlborough[26] — or to prepare themselves for careers at home. But these facts prove only the great attraction which the queen of law schools possessed throughout the western world, even as the early presence of Bolognese works in English monastic and cathedral libraries demonstrates the far-reaching authority of the Italian glossators' doctrines: all this, however, does not make the Anglo-Norman study of canon law a mere seedling of Bologna.

Of the twelfth-century celebrities who went from England to study in Italy, none seems to have embarked on a career of teaching and writing upon his return. We do not know how thorough a formation in canon law young Thomas Becket received at Bologna;[27] at any rate, to credit him with the introduction in England of the first copies of Gratian's *Decreta*[28] remains a guess unsupported by any evidence. The archbishop's later intensive canonistic studies under the guidance of Master Lombard of Piacenza during the exile at Pontigny[29] would seem, rather, to indicate that his earlier stay in Bologna did not suffice for a full course.

Again, Peter of Blois became archdeacon of Bath, and later of St. Paul's London, without ever having finished the legal studies he had begun in his early years at Bologna.[30] References to civil law are occasionally found in his letters,[31] and his

26 *Chronicon Abbatiae de Evesham* (ed. W. Dunn Macray, Rolls Series; London 1863) 147, 168; cf. Pollock and Maitland I, 121; Kantorowicz, *Bractonian Problems* 18; Richardson, in *Engl Hist. Rev.* 59 (1944) 41 n.4.
27 William Fitzstephen speaks of *leges* only: 'per annum studuit in legibus Bononiae,' *Materials for the History of Thomas Becket* (ed. J. C. Robertson, Rolls Series: London 1875–85) III, 17; John of Salisbury, of *ius civile* and *sacri canones*, cf. *ibid.* II, 304.
28 Cf. R. Foreville, *L'église et la royauté* (*supra*, Introd. n.1) 21.
29 Herbert of Bosham, in *Mat. Becket* III, 523; John of Salisbury, *ep.* 168 (*ibid.* V, 163). On the use of the Decretum in the letters of the archbishop's later years see Brooke, *The English Church and the Papacy* 111, 209; Foreville, *op. cit.* 146ff., 265–8 etc.; an interpretation given by St. Thomas of C.11 q.1 c.45 is quoted in the glosses of the French school on Stephen of Tournai's *Summa* (Berlin, Staatsbibliothek MS lat. qu. 193), printed by F. Thaner, 'Zwei anonyme Glossen ...,' *Sitzungsberichte der kais. Akademie der Wiss.* Philos.-hist. Klasse [=*SB Vienna*] 79 (1875) 231, 221, n.1: '... Sanctus Thomas volens facere autenticum consonare sic exponebat quod hic dicitur "competentes iudices" i.e. clericus clericum et laicus laicum iudicem ...' (Thaner mistook this for a reference to St. Thomas Aquinas).
30 Cf. Petr. Bles. *ep.* 26 (PL 207, 91; also in *Chartularium Universitatis Parisiensis* ed. Denifle and Chatelain I [Paris 1889] 32 No. 27). On his career see now C. R. Cheney, *Bishops' Chanceries* (I n.6 *supra*) 9 n.1, 24, 33–5.

For Petrus Blesensis cf. now also my article „Bürgschaft und Darlehen im Dekretalenrecht des 12. Jahrhunderts. Zugleich zur Biographie des Peter von Blois und des Stephan von Tournai, In: V. Beuthien et. al. (ed.), Festschrift für Dieter Medicus zum 70. Geburtstag (Köln etc. 1999) 297–316. Also in: *P. Landau*, Europäische Rechtsgeschichte und kanonisches Recht im Mittelalter (Badenweiler 2013) 783–804. (P.L.)
31 *Epp.* 26, 71, 115 etc.

practical skill in handling canonical matters must have been considerable if two successive archbishops had him represent the see of Canterbury in important law suits at the Roman Curia: he appeared in 1178 as procurator for Archbishop Richard, with Gerard Pucelle, against Robert, abbot-elect of St. Augustine's Canterbury; and in 1187 he argued the case for Archbishop Baldwin against the monks of Christ Church.[32] All this, however, does not warrant the designation of *iurisperitus* which chroniclers have given Peter of Blois.[33] In the one letter in which the archdeacon of Bath tried his hand at the solution of an intricate canonical *quaestio* on marriage and religious vows, the protestation of incompetence at the beginning[34] is not merely a rhetorical flourish: for he discusses the proposed problem intelligently enough, but in a manner which betrays a marked difference from the technical style of the contemporary, professional decretists.[35]

A third name to be mentioned in this context is that of Master David of London,[36] a graduate of Bologna who was repeatedly employed as agent at the Curia by Bishop Gilbert Foliot and other English prelates. His student years he had spent at Paris, Clermont, and Bologna before 1170; it remains therefore uncertain whether we can attribute to him the glosses with the siglum *d.* that appear in Bolognese gloss strata belonging to the 'eighties[37] when David's pursuits were no longer in the academic field. But even if these glosses be his, they testify to the author's activities in Italy, not in England.

David of London: he was agent in Rome, not only for Gilbert Foliot and other prelates, but also for the monasteries of St. Pancras and Glasburne; his studies in Bologna were in particular centered on *quaestiones disputate* (both these facts were supplied to me by the late Eleanor Rathbone in a letter of 1948). – At some time David became a *familiaris* of Bishop Roger of Worcester and might have

---

32 William Thorne, *Chronica*, in Twysden, *Historiae anglicanae scriptores X* (London 1652) 1821f.; Thomas of Elmham, *Hist. monast. S. Augustini* (ed. C. Hardwick, Rolls Series; London 1859) 420–3; cf. JL 13039–40. — Gervase of Canterbury, *Opp.* I, 367ff.; cf. Stubbs, Introd. to *Epp. Cantuar.* p. xlvii and Index s.v. Blois. Roger, Abbot-elect of St. Augustine's, Canterbury vs. Abp. Richard (1178), monks of Faversham vs. King John (1201) and vs. Abp. Hubert Walter (1202): see um. Thorne in Twysden, 1848 ff. (S.K.)
33 Wm. Thorne, *loc. cit.* — Cf. Savigny's censure, *Gesch. des röm. Rechts* IV, 436: '... gibt von dem Stand seiner juristischen Bildung eben keinen hohen Begriff.'
34 *Ep.* 19: 'Verumptamen cum sis in scolis, ego autem in castris, et cum iam biennium in legibus et canonibus expenderis, vereor ne temptative hoc facias, ut sic me in simplicitate mea callide comprehendas' (*Chart. Univ. Par.* I, 35; PL 207, 69).
35 Peter refers to the canons of the Decretum mostly by their inscription alone (*ex octava synodo, ex synodo Eugenii papae* etc., cf. PL 207, 70f.), which corresponds neither to the Bolognese nor to the early French style (on the latter, cf. *Repertorium* 171, 173). It is perhaps characteristic that he solves the first part of the proposed question ultimately 'assertione iuris civilis,' i.e. by paraphrasing *Dig.* 2.1.15, and the second part, without giving any argument of authority at all. Whether he ought to have discussed the pertinent decretal JL 14061 (X 3.32.3) of Alexander III (cf. Goussainville's note, PL 207, 71 n.50) remains an open question as long as the date of *ep.* 19 is unsettled.
36 Z. N. Brooke, 'The Register of Master David of London,' in *Essays in History Presented to R. L. Poole* (Oxford 1927) 227–45.
37 Kuttner, *Repertorium* 19, 51; *Traditio* 1, 281 n.15. For a reference in the *Summa Permissio quedam* (French school) cf. *Repertorium* 193; W. Ullmann, *Medieval Papalism* (London 1949) 11 n.6.

compiled the material used in Part II (cap. 70–125) of the *Collectio decretalium Alcobacensis prima*; see M. G. Cheney, Roger, Bishop of Worcester 1164–1179: An English bishop of the age of Becket (Oxford 1980) 206–208. (S.K.)

To date only one of the masters who were actually teaching in England towards the end of the twelfth century, the hitherto little noticed Simon of Southwell (of whom more later), can be said positively to have been for some time connected with the school of Bologna.

Still, a strong case could be built for the traditional view if the growth of the English school of canonists were to be linked with the Italian civilian whom Archbishop Theobald had brought to Canterbury not long after 1139 and to whom we owe the introduction of formal legal instruction in England. Master Vacarius' career as a teacher of Roman Law need not be reexamined here.[38] It seems certain that the range of his lecturing went beyond the portions of the Digest and the Code which he had abstracted and fitted with cross-references, *authenticae,* and glosses in his *Liber pauperum*: for, opinions are quoted from Vacarius in Hugolinus' *Dissensiones dominorum,* in two glosses on Bulgarus' *De regulis iuris,*[39] and in a recently discovered lemmatic commentary on the Institutes in Royal MS 10.B.iv, fol. 203–219, from Worcester.[40] Of his several theological treatises two are extant,[41] but exaggerated claims have been made on the achievements of Vacarius as a canonist. The active part he played in ecclesiastical affairs can be traced from the time when he was sent to York in 1154, with the newly appointed archbishop, Roger of Pont l'Evêque (who had been Theobald's archdeacon), until almost the end of the century. No specialized canonistic learning, however, is implied by the commissions Vacarius had to carry out as Roger's agent on several occasions during the Becket controversy, and later repeatedly as papal judge delegate.[42]

---

38 See F. de Zulueta, *The Liber pauperum of Vacarius* (Selden Soc. 44; London 1927) xiii–xxiii. For traces of lost MSS of the *Liber pauperum* (in addition to those listed by de Zulueta pp. xxiv ff.) cf. e.g. W. Senior, *Law Quart. Rev.* 47 (1931) 337 (Glastonbury), 339 (Lanthony), 341 (Durham).

39 De Zulueta pp. 299, xxii, xxiv (*b*); perhaps also in glosses on the *Ordo Olim edebatur,* cf. *ibid,* xxii n.36; E. Caillemer, 'Le droit civil dans les provinces anglo-normandes au XIIe siècle,' *Mémoires de l'Academie nationale ... de Caen* (1883) 192.

40 To be discussed on another occasion (E. R.). Cf. also ch. VII n.247 *infra.*

41 The *Tractatus de assumpto homine,* of which Maitland, *Law Quart. Rev.* 13 (1897) 142–3, published the prologue (a full edition is now being prepared at the Gregorian University in Rome, cf. J. de Ghellinck, *Revue d'histoire ecclésiastique* 44 [1949] 173 n.1); and the *Liber contra multiplices et varios errores,* ed. Ilarino da Milano, *L'eresia di Ugo Speroni nella confutazione del maestro Vacario* (Studi e testi 115; Città del Vaticano 1945). In the latter treatise, Vacarius alludes to several other theological writings of his, p. 583: 'in quibusdam aliis meis opusculis' (cf. Introd. 95).

42 The following decretals are addressed to, or make mention of Vacarius: Alexander III, JL 11908 (1171).

Decretals mentioning or addressed to Vacarius: JL 11908 (1171) mentions him with Mag. Amgerus as compurgators of the archbishop of York – ed. PL 200, 735c. JL 11908 is addressed to the archbishop of Rouen and the bishop of Amiens. Printed also in: *Robertson,* Becket Materials, 7, 498–501. (S.K.)

The Vacarian gloss on the *Liber pauperum* offers nothing to justify the assumption that the master lectured also on canon law,[43] and this impression is confirmed by a perusal of those sections of his theological tract *Contra multiplices et varios errores* which we should expect to contain arguments from canon law. Writing as late as the seventies of the twelfth century,[44] only an author for whom canonistic science had no interest at all could treat, e.g., of the sacramental power of unworthy priests, yet completely bypass the presentation of this thorny problem in terms of canon law as given in Gratian and passionately discussed among decretists:[45] Vacarius, however, merely introduces a number of rather ill-fitting civilian similes.[46] The only treatise he dedicated ex professo to a canonical problem is his *Summa de matrimonio*, written — since we have to conclude with Maitland that he knew the *Summa* of Rufinus — shortly after c. 1157–59.[47]

The Summa de matrimonio from Vacarius was dated by Gouron in 1164 – cf. A. Gouron, Sur les sources civilistes et la datation des Sommes de Rufin et d'Etienne de Tournai, BMCL 16 (1986) 55–70; also in: A. Gouron, Droit et coutume en France au XIIe et XIIIe siècles (Ashgate 1993), no. X. (P.L.)

This work shows again the author's practice of applying to questions of canon law analogies drawn from purely civilian concepts: in this case, both the Bolognese theory of the *copula* and the French theory of the *sponsalia de praesenti* are dismissed and the juridically relevant moment of marriage is placed in an act borrowed from the Roman law of transfer of ownership, the mutual delivery (*traditio*) of man and woman.[48] Even more revealing is the doctrine of the flexibility and historical relativity of canon law which Vacarius develops in this unorthodox

---

JL 13937 (1177 iun. 30, cf. *Repertorium* 280 as against the conjectural date 1165–8 proposed by F. Liebermann, *Engl. Hist. Rev.* 11 [1896] 312 n.62); 14224 (undated); a decretal of 22 July 1179, ed. W. Holtzmann, *Papsturkunden in England* I (Abhandlungen der Gesellschaft der Wiss. zu Göttingen, Phil.-hist. Kl. N. F. 25; 1930–31) 440 No. 169 and an otherwise unknown fragment in the collection of Bodleian MS Tanner 8 (p. 595b, between the canons of the Council of Tours and those of the Third Lateran Council), addressed to the abbots of Rufford and Leicester and Master Vacarius.— Urban III, JL 15740–41 (undated); Innocent III, Potthast 347 (1198).

JL 11908 = WH 383a. It is also in 1 Par. c. 171. (P.L.)

The decretal edited by *Holtzmann*, Papsturkunden in England I, no. 169 (p. 440) is addressed to the abbot of Vaudey and Mag. Vacarius, inc. 'Conquestus est nobis Ordericus quod cum ecclesiam de Cumba', Date Segni 22.7.1179. (S.K.)

43 Cf. de Zulueta, *Lib. paup.* xxiii; of the glosses referring to canon law (cf. Index VI, p. 318; most of them from Wenck's lost codex or from the secondary strata of the other MSS) none can be considered as being by Vacarius himself (cf. Index VI, pp. 310–14).

44 Ilarino da Milano, *op. cit.* 74, 345f.

45 Gratian D.32 p.c.6; C.1 q.7; 9 q.1; 24q.1. Cf. L. Saltet, *Les réordinations* (Paris 1907).

46 *Contra multipl. errores* pp. 486 §1 No. 3, 489.2.1, 494.5.2, 503.11.1, etc. Cf. Padre Ilarino's Introd. 135–83. Similarly, in the discussion of baptism (511.13.3; cf. Introd. 92 n.1, 223f.) Vacarius introduces the concept of possession at civil law.

47 F. W. Maitland, 'Magistri Vacarii Summa de matrimonio,' *Law Quart. Rev.* 13 (1897) 133–43 (introd.) and 270–87 (text; not reprinted in *Collected Papers* III, 87ff.); he puts the *terminus a quo* (basing himself on Schulte's dates for Rufinus) at 1156 (p. 139f.).

48 *De matr.* §§ 12, 17, 30 (pp. 274, 283) etc. Cf. Maitland, *op. cit.* 136f.; de Zulueta, *Lib. paup.* xxiii.

treatise, together with a violent attack on Gratian's dialectical method[49]—not realizing, evidently, that this very method would become eventually the most efficient instrument of the scientific development of canon law by the glossators. It is, therefore, certainly not through Vacarius — who, after all, had left Bologna when the school of Gratian was yet in its first beginnings — that we can expect the canonistic tradition of this school to have been transmitted to England.

Considerable evidence exists, on the other hand, of canonistic learning in English ecclesiastical circles which definitely points to other than Bolognese connections: mostly with the school, or schools, of France. There Gerard Pucelle, on whose importance for the English school more will be said presently, spent most of his teaching career. The correspondent who put before Peter of Blois the *quaestio* mentioned above was a student of *leges et decreta* in Paris, and Paris is the proper place, Peter wrote back, for a solution to such questions.[50] Had not Henry II, at the height of the Becket controversy, thought of requesting the opinion of the Parisian canonists on the burning issue of criminous clerks?[51] It was in Paris, too, that Peter of Blois, as he writes elsewhere, had purchased the legal books for his nephew[52] and that Gerald of Wales studied the *decreta* under Master Matthew of Angers and himself delivered the lectures of which he was later to give so grandiloquent an account; one of his auditors being Master Roger the Norman, who had been a student of civil law in Bologna, taught the arts in Paris, and was to become dean of Rouen cathedral toward the end of the century.[53]

English canonists in France: For some early English *magistri*, however, it remains uncertain where they had studied. This is, for instance, the case of Mag.

---

49 *De matr.* §16 (p. 276f.); cf. J. de Ghellinck, 'Magister Vacarius: Un juriste théologien peu aimable pour les canonistes,' *Rev. d'hist. eccl.* 44 (1949) 173–8, at p. 177. A similar contempt for canon law was expressed by Peter the Chanter and Master Ivo (the Younger) of Chartres, whom he quotes, cf. *Verbum abbreviatum* c. 53 (PL 205, 162–5, esp. 164C; on Master Ivo see B. Smalley, *Engl. Hist. Rev.* 50 [1935] 680–6; A.M. Landgraf, *Einführung in die Geschichte der theologischen Literatur der Frühscholastik* [Regensburg 1948] 135f.). Their strictures, however, differ from those of Vacarius the civilian in that they measure the positive law of the Church against the divine law.
50 *Ep.* 19 (*Chart. Univ. Par.* I, 35; PL 207, 69).
51 *Chart. Univ. Par.* I, 21–3; cf. S. E. Thorne, *op. cit.* (above, Introd. n.2) 500.
52 *Ep.* 71 (*Chart. Univ. Par.* I, 33; PL 207, 219). This nephew was not his namesake, the canonist and chancellor of Chartres, cf. *Traditio* 2 (1944) 492 n.2.
53 *Gir. Camb. Opp.* I, 46–8. Master Roger and Peter of Blois were the only survivors of thirty-seven who went to Sicily with Stephen of Perche in 1167; Pet. Bles. *ep.* 46 (PL 207, 133). He was perhaps the Master Roger who disputed with Peter the Chanter whether Thomas Becket had died a rebel or a martyr, cf. S. Gutjahr, *Petrus Cantor Parisiensis: Sein Leben und seine Schriften* (Graz 1899) 16 n.4, quoting Caesarius of Heisterbach, *Dialogus miraculorum* 8.69 (ed. J. Strange, Cologne 1851; II, 139). Roger was a member of the chapter of Rouen before 1181, cf. L. Merlet, *Cartulaire de l'abbaye de la Sainte-Trinité de Tiron* (Chartres 1883) II, 98 (1171–82); J. H. Round, *Calendar of Documents Preserved in France* ... (London 1899) No. 11 (1173–81; cf. *ibid.* No. 41); cf. also PL 207, 134, n.100. (But the letter of the Cardinal Legate Peter [Steph. Torn. *ep.* 69 in Du Molinet's ed.], referred to in *Histoire littéraire de la France* 15 [1820] 327f. is not to Dean Roger the Norman, cf. J. Desilve, *Les lettres d'Etienne de Tournai* [Paris 1893] ep. 83, p. 97 n.3.).

Walter of London, archdeacon of York, who played an important role in the York election dispute 1140, as shown by D. Baker, Viri religiosi and the York election dispute, S C H 7 (1991) 87–100, at p. 96, citing John of Hexham, *The Priority of Hexham*, ed. J. Rayne (Surtees Society 44, Durham 1865) 133. (S.K.)

Several other English teachers of law in France are known: John of Salisbury's friend, the Londoner, Master Philip de Calne, clerk to Archbishops Theobald and Thomas Becket, had studied at Tours for two years before the exile and was learned in *humanum ius*.[54] Recommended by Becket to Fulk, dean of Reims, as a clerk worthy of preferment, he was teaching law, presumably civil law, for a time in that city.[55] Another of St. Thomas' household in exile, Gilbert de Glanville, later bishop of Rochester, was learned in both laws and taught at some unspecified school.[56]

Clerks of Thomas Becket: add Mag. Arnulphus (Ernulphus), his chancellor; see *Petrus Cantor*, PL 205, 132 A-B. (S.K.)

Some time after 1192 Master P. of Northampton, who had been lecturing in Paris on canon law, sought the licence of the *scholasticus* of Reims to teach in that city.[57] Later than these,[58] Benedict of Sawston, clerk to Prince John, royal treasurer, precentor of St. Paul's and from 1215–1226 bishop of Rochester, was lecturing in law at Paris, where he was living in 1214, and his opinions were quoted in Langton's *Quaestiones*.[59]

Historians would probably have made more of these data, had not the important share which the French schools of decretists held in the development of twelfth-century canonistic science been underrated for a long time. Today we know that ever since Stephen of Tournai introduced the methods of Gratian's school in his native country, French canonists — basing themselves of course on a thorough study of Bolognese work — produced in their glosses, *summae, distinctiones, quaestiones,* etc. an impressive literature of their own.[60] It is in the substantial influence of this literary production, far more than in the personal contacts of individual Englishmen, that the main interest of Anglo-Norman relations with France

---

54 *Mat. Becket* III, 101, 527.
55 *Ibid.* V, 166. J. R. Williams, in *Speculum* 6 (1931) 406, quoting Peter the Chanter, *Summa de sacramentis,* MS Paris, B. N. lat. 14521, fol. 78rb. Cf. London, Brit. Mus. MS Harl. 3596, fol. 128.
56 *Mat. Becket* III, 52. One of his pupils was Ralph de Sully, Abbot of Cluny (1173–?), cf. J. Thorpe, *Registrum Roffense* ... (London 1769) 51.
57 Gervase of Prémontré, *ep.* 57 in C. L. Hugo, *Sacrae antiquitatis monumenta* ... (Etival 1725) I, 55. For the reading Northampton see C. R. Cheney, 'Gervase, Abbot of Prémontré ...,' *Bull. John Rylands Library* 33 (1950) 40 n.9.
58 As for others, such as Warin of St. Alban's (cf. below, ch. VIII n.299), a connection with the schools of France remains uncertain.
59 M. Gibbs, *Early Charters of the Cathedral Church of St. Paul, London* (Camden Third Series 58; London 1939) 187; A. Gregory, 'The Cambridge MS of the Quaestiones of Stephen Langton,' *The New Scholasticism* 4 (1930) 189 and n.
60 S. Kuttner, 'Les débuts de l'école canoniste française,' *Studia et Documenta historiae et iuris* 4 (1938) 192–204. MSS of Gratian with glosses of the French school (much more numerous than was assumed in this paper, p. 200) will be discussed elsewhere (S. K.).

must be sought. The influence of French teaching became apparent as a determining factor at the moment when English canonistic learning turned from the receptive stage into that of productive scholarship, i.e. when an English school properly speaking began to take shape. Without going into details at this point one may recall the impact of French training, traceable both in doctrine and local coloring, on so outstanding a commentary as the *Summa Omnis qui iuste* (*Summa Lipsiensis*),[61] to which in turn a number of other early Anglo-Norman treatises and glosses are linked. Criteria of style and formulation show as a rule a marked affinity between French and English decretists: evidence that outweighs in its historical implications the extensive knowledge these men display of writings of the leading Bolognese glossators—which, after all, were so widely circulated, read, and recopied that a student would not necessarily have to travel to Italy to acquire or to become acquainted with them.

III. On the So-called Practical Outlook of the English School

The customary over-emphasis on the connections of English canonists with the school of Bologna is paralleled by another misconception, which concerns the character of their work. The few twelfth-century writings that are relatively well known as products of the Anglo-Norman school are nearly all concerned with Roman and canonical procedure: the so-called *Ulpianus de edendo*;[62] the *Ordo Bambergensis* (*c.* 1182–85);[63] a cento of minor pieces in a manuscript from Citeaux for which Caillemer, none too aptly, coined the name of *Summa Bellinensis*;[64] the *Practica legum et decretorum* (*c.* 1183–89) written by William Longchamp before his chancellorship;[65] and probably the *Ordo Olim edebatur,* although the authorship of the Bolognese civilian, Otto Papiensis cannot be entirely excluded.[66]

The Ordo 'Olim edebatur' was written by the English canonist Rodoicus Modicipassus – cf. *A. Gouron*, Qui a écrit l'ordo "Olim edebatur"?, Initium 8

---

61 *Ibid.* 197; Schulte, in *SB Vienna* 68 (1871) 37ff.
62 *Incerti auctoris Ordo iudiciarius* ed. Haenel (Leipzig 1836). Cf. M. Conrat, *Geschichte der Quellen und Literatur des römischen Rechts im früheren Mittelalter* (Leipzig 1891) 615; Caillemer, *Le droit civil* etc. (above, II n.39) 170–4.
63 Schulte, *SB Vienna* 70 (1872) 285–326. Cf. Caillemer, *op. cit.* 178–81; E. Seckel, 'Distinctiones glossatorum,' *Festschrift ... F. von Martitz* (Berlin 1911) 330; J. Juncker, ZRG Kan. Abt. 15 (1926) 466 n. (discussing interpolated references, cf. *Traditio* 6, 349 n.43). A second copy of the *Ordo* is found in the miscellaneous codex Brit. Mus. Royal 2.D.ix (cf. above I n.23).
64 *Op. cit.* 175f. A set of proof-sheets of Caillemer's abortive edition is now in the library of the University of Minnesota Law School.
65 Edited by Caillemer, *op. cit.* 204–26 and discussed *ibid.* 197ff.
66 Cf. Caillemer, *op. cit.* 185–7; Seckel, 'Über neuere Editionen juristischer Schriften aus dem Mittelalter,' ZRG Rom. Abt. 21 (1900) 306–22 (citing MSS and editions, p. 307f. and maintaining Otto's authorship 'trotz einiger nicht leicht wiegender Zweifel,' p. 107); de Zulueta, *Lib. paup.* xxii n.36; Genzmer (-Seckel), 'Über die dem Pillius zugeschriebene Summa de ordine iudiciorum "Invocato Christi nomine",' *Sitzungsberichte der Preuss. Akad. der Wiss.* Phil.-hist. Kl. (1931) 413 n.2 No. 8. Among the MSS to be added to Seckel's list, we find again (cf. n.63) the Royal MS 2.D.ix.

(2003) 65–84; also in: *A. Gouron, Pionniers du droit occidental au Moyen Âge* (Ashgate 2006), no. XIII. (P.L.)

Another curious, if disorderly, little composition made up at Oxford *c.* 1202–9 of portions of an *Ordo iudiciarius* and a number of forensic forms, both secular and ecclesiastical, has recently come to light in a manuscript now at Baltimore and has been analyzed by Mr. Richardson.[67] All these works[68] seem to suggest an overwhelming concentration of English writers on matters of practical interest: procedure, actions, formularies, and the like. This supposition seems confirmed by the voluminous, unfinished treatise on procedure which that Oxford celebrity of the mid-thirteenth century, William of Drogheda, published under the title *Summa aurea.*[69] It is perhaps significant, in this connection, that modern writers on the role of canon law in England rarely fail to make express mention of the *Ordo iudiciarius* (*c.* 1196) of Ricardus Anglicus — although reference to a work admittedly composed in the school of Bologna is certainly not warranted unless it were for showing traces of Richard's previous English training — but almost never take notice of his numerous and excellent canonistic writings on subjects other than procedure.

The picture of an English school primarily bent upon satisfying the practitioner's needs is quite mistaken and based on one-sided evidence. An undue predilection on the part of many nineteenth-century scholars and editors of medieval legal writings for monographs on procedural law has given far greater prominence to this type of literature than it actually had in either the Italian, French, or English schools.[70] With the English masters, no less than with their continental colleagues,

---

[67] H. G. Richardson, "The Oxford Law School under John,' *Law Quart. Rev.* 57 (1941) 319–38; 'The Schools of Northampton in the Twelfth Century,' *Engl. Hist. Rev.* 56 (1941) 595f. For the decretal collection used by the author of the *Ordo* see below, Appendix A (IV). — The forms have been in part edited by H. E. Salter, in *Formularies Which Bear on the History of Oxford c. 1204–1420* (Oxford Historical Soc. n.s. 4–5; 1942) II, 271–7, and are discussed in Cheney, *Bishops' Chanceries* (above, ch. I n.6) 124–8.

[68] Two early treatises of a similar type, written in a hand of the twelfth century, are found in MS Brit. Mus. Royal 10.B.iv (from Christ Church, Canterbury) fol. 33–41: 'Iudicandi formam in utroque iure,' and fol. 59r-v: 'Iudicium est trinus personarum trium actus,' with several other civilian and canonistic treatises (including Peter of Blois' *Distinctiones, cf. Repertorium* 220, and an extract *de praescriptionibus* from Stephen of Tournai's *Summa,* cf. below, IV n.78), two decretal collections (cf. *Repertorium* 282; Holtzmann, *Über eine Ausgabe* 22) and the Lateran Decrees of 1179 (fol. 62ra). The treatises on procedure will be discussed elsewhere.

The two early procedural treatises 'Iudicandi formam' and 'Iudicium est trinus personarum' were edited by L. Fowler-Magerl, Ordo iudiciorum vel ordo iudiciarius. Begriff und Literaturgattung (Ius commune. Sonderhefte 19, Frankfurt/M. 1984): 'Iudicandi formam', p. 273–280 (Appendix III), 'Iudicium est trinus personarum', p. 297–300 (Appendix VI). (P.L.)

[69] Ed. L. Wahrmund, *Quellen zur Geschichte des römisch-kanonischen Processes im Mittelalter* II, 2 (Innsbruck 1914); cf. F. de Zulueta, in *Mélanges G. Cornil* (Paris 1926) II, 639–57; H. G. Richardson, 'Azo, Drogheda, and Bracton,' *Engl. Hist. Rev.* 59 (1944) 38ff.

[70] H. Kantorowicz, *Studies in the Glossators of the Roman Law* (Cambridge 1938) 72, listing editions of twelfth-century *Ordines,* speaks of 'unusual, even excessive attention.' In the case of Ricardus Anglicus, for example, two modern editions are available of his *Ordo,* but his other works have remained unprinted to this day. — It is certainly correct that the study of law in Bologna was closely

the composition of formularies and *ordines iudiciorum* remained but one among their manifold literary pursuits, subordinate to the main concern which underlay all teaching and writing in the age of the glossators: to raise the knowledge of law from a professional technique to a scholastic science.

A few decades ago, the *Summa Omnis qui iuste* (c. 1186) seemed to be the only monument of Anglo-Norman origin that was not confined to the practical-procedural outlook. Today, however, a considerable number of glosses, *summae, quaestiones, distinctiones, notabilia*, and miscellaneous minor treatises have come to light — an array of writings which may easily be enlarged by further research but which even at the present state of our knowledge shows that the English contribution to canonistic science in the late twelfth century, quite apart from the important field of systematizing the decretal law, affected every branch of the literature.

IV. The Beginnings of Anglo-Norman Writing on Canon Law

The beginnings of this literary activity are quite uncertain. It would be tempting to claim English origin for such early treatises as the two fragments on different parts of the Decretum, both presumably antedating the *Summa* of Rufinus (c. 1157–9), which occur, in association with the writings of Paucapalea and Rolandus, in two twelfth-century manuscripts in the libraries of Worcester Cathedral (MS Q.70, fol. 1–40v) and Cambridge University (MS Addit. 3321, vol. I, fol. 4–35V).[71] Yet neither manuscript has so far been examined in detail, and at present one can only say that the Worcester fragment provides early evidence for English copying of Bolognese work, since it is in part closely dependent on Paucapalea,[72] whereas the Cambridge manuscript is not even written in an English hand and was only recently brought from the Continent; the fragment in question, described by the author as *glosule*,[73] closely follows Rolandus, who is frequently cited,[74] and in the discussion on marriage mentions at various points the *legiste,* Bulgarus in particular, Jacobus and the little known Metellus;[75] moreover, only one of the additional items in the miscellaneous codex shows criteria of style which may point to an origin outside Bologna.[76]

---

bound up with *ars notaria* and *dictamen* (Richardson, *Oxford Law School* 331ff.), but it is very debatable whether one can lay all the stress (p. 336) on the 'intensely practical' nature of the school.
71 Kuttner, *Repertorium* 129–31; cf. G. Barraclough, *Engl. Hist. Rev.* 53 (1938) 493 n.3.
72 E.g. to D. 29–31, 32–35 (fol. 4ra-va, 5va). Another codex from Worcester, Brit. Mus. Royal MS 11.B.ii, contains the works of Paucapalea and Rolandus together with *Notabilia* on excommunication and penance, a primitive collection of decretals (*Repertorium* 126, 128, 240, 283; cf. above I n.15), and a fragment of glosses of a very early type to D.1 c.1–9 (fol. 85v; not properly determined *loc. cit.* 128).
73 Fol. 19r.
74 E.g. fols. 10r, 10v, 11r, 13r, 13v, 30r, 31v, 32v, 34r, 34v.
75 Fols. 11r, 13v, 14r, 18v, 19r. Cf. *Repertorium* 129 n.2. For Metellus see also *Quaestiones Stuttgardienses* q.29 (ed. Thaner, *Die Summa Magistri Rolandi* ... [Innsbruck 1874] 283).
76 *Distinctiones*, vol. I fol. 36–59; cf. *Repertorium* 213, 214 n.2.

The earliest treatise on Gratian for which an English origin can be asserted with a fair degree of certainty is the *Summa De multiplici iuris divisione,* a systematic textbook written c. 1160–70, largely based on Stephen of Tournai's *Summa,* and extant in three manuscripts which are all of English provenance.[77] For all its lack of originality the work would seem to be important as the first instance of the orientation characteristic of the insular canonists.[78] Stephen, the principal link between the Bolognese and the early French schools, was definitely responsible for the spread of the new science in the Western countries. The *Summa De multiplici* thus fulfilled the same function for England which in France can be assigned to the two similar paraphrases of Stephen's *Summa* preserved in MSS lat. 16538 and 16540 (Sorbonne) of the Bibliothèque nationale.[79]

In the same period Master Odo de Doura wrote his *Decreta minora,* of which only charred portions survive in Cotton MS Vitell. A. iii. of the British Museum (from Canterbury?), and which also shows the strong influence of Stephen of Tournai's teaching.[80] The combination of epitomizing and expository elements in the *Decreta minora* as well as other criteria of style and diction point to Odo's training in France; but since his surname should be referred to Dover (*Doura-Dovra*) and not to the Belgian town of Dour (*Durnum*),[81] he represents in all likelihood another early link between the French and the English schools. Odo of Dover might well be the Magister Odo to whom John of Salisbury turned in 1168 for advice on a problem of scriptural interpretation, for the letter contains a strong hint that the addressee was well trained also in law.[82]

---

77 *Repertorium* 139–41; cf. Barraclough, *loc. cit.* 493; see also Ullmann, *Med. Papalism* 59 n.2, 64, 66 ('Summa Lambethana').

78 To the single English MS of Stephen's *Summa* listed in *Repertorium* 135 (Worcester MS Q.44) may now be added the fragment (to D.30 c.17-D.39 c.11) in Queen's College, Oxford, MS 317 (fol. 140ra-142va) from Reading (I should like to thank Dr. R. Klibansky for drawing my attention to this codex. E. R.). An extract *de praescriptionibus* from Stephen's *Summa* to C.16 q.3 is found in Cambridge, Trinity College MS O.7.40 (fol.176v-177r; cf. *Repert.* 135 n.7) from St. Augustine's, Canterbury, and in Brit. Mus. Royal MS 10.B.iv (fol. 42) from Christ Church.

The extract de prescriptionibus from Stephen's Summa has the Incipit 'Quod autem prescriptio' in the Cambridge manuscript and the Incipit 'Quoniam in hac questione de prescriptione multa dicuntur' in the British Library manuscript; the B. M. manuscript lacks the lemma § Quod autem .... (S.K.)

79 *Repertorium* 136–41. The evidence for French origin (cf. *ibid.* 136 n.2) will be discussed elsewhere.

80 *Repertorium* 172–7. The provenance of the MS is doubtful, cf. Brooke, *The Engl. Church and the Papacy* 244; N. Ker, *Medieval Libraries of Great Britain* (London 1941) 25 rejects Canterbury.

81 For *Durnum*=Dour, cf. e.g. the charter in MGH *Dipl.* 3, 492 lin. 26, 28. This disposes of the suggestion made in *Repert.* 172.

82 Jo. Sar. *ep.* 284 ('... scienti legem loquor': PL 199, 320B); but the term might also denote the *lex mosayca.* — This Odo is not to be confused with Odo, prior of Canterbury (1167) and later abbot of Battle, cf. C. Schaarschmidt, *Johannes Saresberiensis nach Leben und Schriften* ... (Leipzig 1862) 273 and C. J. Webb's note in his edition of the *Policraticus* (Oxford 1909) I, 7 line 17; Webb suggests (*ibid.* II, 205) that he may be the Odo whose letter to Gilbert Foliot is wrongly prefixed to the *Ysagoge in theologiam* in Cambridge, Trinity College MS B.xiv.33 (on which see A. Landgraf, *Ecrits théologiques de l'école d'Abélard* [Spicilegium sacrum Lovan. 14; 1936] xlivf.)

Further material for future investigation of possible English work is presented by a number of manuscripts not yet sufficiently examined:[83] glosses on the *Summa* of Rufinus in Hereford Cathedral MS O.6.xiv; the glosses on Gratian of an unidentified master *b.* which occur in conjunction with glosses of Rufinus in a codex from Durham, now MS 101 of Sidney Sussex College, Cambridge, and similarly in MS 46, from Citeaux, of the Chester Beatty Collection,[84] and in Douce MS 218 of the Bodleian Library.[85] He was probably the same *b.* who is found repeatedly quoted in the *Summa Omnis qui iuste* and who, since his teaching seems to antedate that of John of Faenza, cannot be identified with John's famous pupil, Bernard of Pavia.[86]

For master b., mentioned in English manuscripts, cf. now also R. *Weigand*, Bazianus und B.-Glossen zum Dekret Gratians, Mélanges G. Fransen II, Stud. Grat. XX (1976) 453–495; also in: R. *Weigand*, Glossatoren des Dekrets Gratians (Bibliotheca Eruditorum 18, Goldbach 1997) 285–325 with Addenda p. 429s. Here on p. 430 Weigand assumes Bernhard of Pavia as author of the b.-Glosses in MS Cambridge, Sidney Sussex College 101, whereas Kuttner had excluded this hypothesis. (P.L.)

If the gloss composition of the Sidney Sussex manuscript should turn out to be of English provenance, then the same origin is to be assumed for the *Notabilia Clericus apud civilem,* which are here appended to the Decretum and precede it in another Durham codex, MS C.iv.1 of the Cathedral Chapter Library;[87] this is the more probable because the unusual beginning of this little collection of rules,

Clericus apud ciuilem iudicem conuictus ab episcopo suo degradandus est, ut sic puniatur a ciuili iudice, nisi ecclesiasticum sit crimen, ut C.xi. q.i. Si quis (c.18),

fits nowhere better than in the climate of the Becket controversy.[88]

---

83 The list given above is selective. English work might also be represented by certain transformations (*Repertorium* 269–71) and abbreviations (*ibid.* 261f.) of the Decretum in English MSS, as e.g. the *Abbreviatio Lex alia divina est* (Brit. Mus. MS Harley 3842, based on Omnibonus) or the *Abbreviatio Matrimonium est* (London, Lambeth MS 139, from Lanthony). For an unusual copy of the Decretum from Lanthony, in Lambeth MS 449, cf. *Repert.* 30.
84 *Repertorium* 131, 24, 29.
85 Fols. 4ra, 4vb, 5ra-b, 6ra, etc.
86 Kuttner, *Traditio* 1, 295 n.24; cf. Schulte, 'Die Summa Decreti Lipsiensis,' *SB Vienna* 68 (1871) 45f. Not connected with the tradition of these MSS are the interesting glosses of the French school in MS Heiligenkreuz 44, although two of them are signed as follows: (i) to D. 54 diet. a.c. 9: 'Peculium est substantia ... secundum r. p.' (fol. 46, based on Rufinus and Paucapalea); (ii) to C.11 q.3 c.3: 'Sententiam omnimodo iustam faciunt ... B.' (fol. 132, not identical with any of the texts on *sententia iusta* and *iniusta* discussed by F. Gillmann, *Archiv für katholisches Kirchenrecht* [=AKKR] 104 [1924] 5ff.).
87 *Repertorium* 234.
88 Barraclough, *Engl Hist. Rev.* 53, 494.

Even if some of these possibilities should have to be discarded upon closer examination, a work like the *Summa De multiplici* alone leaves no doubt that a new generation of canonists was coming up in England, for whom occupation with canon law meant essentially doctrinal elaboration on Gratian's work. By comparison with this novel approach, the contemporary writing of the older generation, such as the *Poenitentiale* of Bartholomew of Exeter,[89] must needs appear old-fashioned. Bartholomew had received his training at Paris in the early 'forties,[90] i.e. before the *Concordia discordantium canonum* eclipsed the older canonical collections, and, according to Gerald of Wales, he was more learned in the *leges* than in the *canones*.[91] His sparing personal dicta in the Penitential[92] show that he was not entirely unaware of the more recent teaching of the glossators on the Decretum,[93] but on the whole their searching analysis of canonical concepts seems to have been of small interest for his purpose,[94] and he preferred to make his book in the main a recompilation of old *auctoritates*. What is more, he used as sources from which to draw his quotations (so far as we can judge from Dom Morey's tentative edition) the outdated collections of Ivo of Chartres and Burchard side by side with, and at times even in preference to, the 'modern' texts of Gratian and Peter Lombard:[95] for him they all remained equally books of authority. To be sure, the Penitential became a successful handbook for confessors[96] and its author, a renowned practical jurist. But this should not obscure the fact that canonistic scholarship properly speaking took root in England rather by the efforts of the men who, in the 'sixties and early 'seventies, let themselves be guided by the aims and techniques of the continental glossators.

---

89 A. Morey, *Bartholomew of Exeter, Bishop and Canonist* (Cambridge 1937).
90 Morey, *op. cit.* 4f.
91 Gir. Camb. *Opp.* VII, 57.
92 They are not set off in Dom Moray's edition from the canons quoted and therefore not always easy to recognize. Some dicta are of importance for understanding the structure of the work, e.g., cc.5–7 (p. 177 lin. 23–178.9), cc.10–11 (181.27–182), c.22 (191.32–192.22); others contain *summulae*, e.g., c. 25 (194.6–16), c.26 (195.2–14); others again, interpretations.
93 E.g. c. 58, where the distinction 'qui non omnem quam debuit ... diligentiam adhibuit' (223. 14–19), follows Rufinus (to D. 50 c.37; ed. Singer, *Die Summa Decretorum des Magister Rufinus* [Paderborn 1902] 126); in c.117 the restrictive interpretation of C. 33 q.2 c.12 (279.25–31) is based on Rufinus *ad loc.* (500 Singer).
94 Compare, e.g., the *summulae* on excommunication (c. 118, p. 280) and perjury (c. 73, **p.** 241) with the contemporary commentaries to C.11 q.3 and C.22 q.2. By contrast, note the reference in c.73 to English law, 'iudicia uero que uulgo leges aperte uocantur,' (241.34; cf. Liebermann, *Die Gesetze der Angelsachsen* [Halle 1903–16] I, 583 and references; *ibid.* Index s.v. *lex*.). Cf. above, note 91.
95 Cf. Morey 173f. and notes to the edition, *passim*. E.g. c.24 (192.34–194.4), c.47 (214.21–32), c.71 (240.13–29; the source is Ivo, *Decr.* 6.397), c.72 (240.31–241.14; the source is Burch. *Decr.* 19.42), c.73 (241.37–242.21; Burch. 12.14, 8, 9 or Ivo 12.71, 65, 66), c.117 (279.32–280.4), c.128 (286.28–287.15) etc.
96 For its influence on Robert of Flamborough and the treatise *De iniungendis penitentiis* cf. Morey, *op. cit.* 171; P. Anciaux, *La théologie du sacrement de pénitence au XIIe siècle* (Louvain 1949) 129–30. Its relation to the *Notabilia* on excommunication and penance (above, n.72; *Repertorium* 240) needs to be investigated.

Full light is thrown on the literary production of the Anglo-Norman school in the 'eighties with the important group of writings belonging to the circle of the *Summa Omnis qui iuste,* the most elaborate of all commentaries on Gratian prior to Huguccio. The work has come down in two complete manuscripts, and it is characteristic for its reputation that in a third codex (Luxembourg MS 144) portions of it were used to complete the *Summa* of Huguccio for those sections of the Decretum which the Bolognese master had left out in the first edition of his great commentary.[97]

The Summa Lipsiensis, according to Kuttner 'the most elaborate of all commentaries on Gratian prior to Huguccio', is now being edited by *R. Weigand/P. Landau/W. Kozur/K. Miethaner-Vent* (ed.), Summa 'Omnis qui iuste iudicat' sive Lipsiensis (MIC, Ser. A, Vol. 7, Tom. I-III, Città del Vaticano 2007–2014). The author was Rodoicus Modicipassus – cf. my article 'Rodoicus Modicipassus – Verfasser der Summa Lipsiensis?', ZRG Kan. Abt. 92 (2006) 340–354. (P.L.)

Two other *Summae,* the fragment *In nomine* in MS 53 of Oriel College, Oxford (from St. Andrew's, Northampton)

For the fragment 'In nomine' cf. also *R. Weigand,* Die Naturrechtslehre der Legisten und Dekretisten von Irnerius bis Accursius und von Gratian bis Johannes Teutonicus (Münchener Theologische Studien, III. Kanonistische Abt. 26, München 1967) 196–200. (P.L.)

and the voluminous commentary *De iure canonico tractaturus* in Laon MS 371*bis* are closely related to *Omnis qui iuste;*[98] the teaching of the group is further represented in the glosses on Gratian of MS M.13 of the Museum Plantin-Moretus in Antwerp; of MS 162 of Pembroke College, Cambridge; of MSS C.ii.1. and C.iii.1 of Durham Cathedral;[99] in the *Ordo Bambergensis,*[100] and in marginal glosses to the *Summa De iure canonico.*[101] We may add to this impressive list the most successful piece of English canonistic writing in the twelfth century, the *Summa decretalium quaestionum* of Master Honorius, to be discussed later in this paper.[102] Finally, we may note here, also, that Ricardus Anglicus in his early years,

---

97 *Repertorium* 156, 197.
98 *Ibid.* 198–204. To the evidence for the English origin of the *Summa In nomine* the passage '... hinc argumentum precipue commendandam esse ecclesie anglicane institutionem' (fol. 363r) may be added. (An error in the original foliation of Oriel MS 53, thus far unnoticed, makes the following corrections of references necessary: *Summa In nom.* fols. 356r-363v, *Quaest. Oriel.* 338r-339v, *Coll. Oriel. I* and *II,* 340r-349v, 353r-354v [cited as fols. 256, 238 etc. in *Repert.* 199, 249, 295 and elsewhere].)
99 *Repert.* 13, 24, 26. The glosses of Olmütz, Cathedral Chapter MS 266 (set iv, added to three earlier, Bolognese strata) are related at, least to the *Summa Et est sciendum* (*Repertorium* 195), one of the chief sources of *Omnis qui iuste.*
100 Caillemer, *Le droit civil* etc. (above, II n.39) 182. Schulte, *Die Geschichte der Quellen und Literatur des canonischen Rechts von Gratian bis auf die Gegenwart I* (Stuttgart 1875) 233 believes that the Ordo and the *Summa Omnis qui iuste* may even be written by the same author.
101 These glosses are found particularly in the section on marriage (fol. 155ff.); like the *Summa* itself (cf. *Traditio* 6, 349 n.38) they cite decretals from the *Appendix Conc. Lat.*
102 Below, ch. VI.

181

before he went to make himself a reputation at Bologna, seems to have been associated with this group of eager and enterprising canonists.[103]

V. Gerard Pucelle and the Schools of Paris and Cologne

It was to be expected that English work in canon law should have begun as an echo of Stephen of Tournai's teaching; it is equally typical of the period that the first English master of canon law of whose career and activities substantial data are at hand should have spent most, if not all, of his teaching career in France. Gerard Pucelle, bishop of Coventry in 1183–84, has been long familiar to historians of the University of Paris as the friend of John of Salisbury who was teaching there in the first decades of the reign of Henry II.[104] But although John's letters refer to his friend as a lecturer in both laws and, as do other documents, as a person of note in political as well as in learned circles,[105] Gerard remained less than a name to historians of canon law until 1907, when Saltet identified him with the *magister G. Coventrensis episcopus* whose opinion is quoted in a discussion of the status of deposed prelates by the author of the *Summa Omnis qui iuste*.[106] It is therefore necessary to bring together at this point the main facts bearing on his career as a canonist.[107]

Born in England, probably about 1115–20, Gerald Pucelle spent several years as a fellow-student of John of Salisbury studying philosophy in the schools of France,[108] where he became a teacher some time before 1156 when his pupil, Lucas of Hungary, was made bishop of Erlau.[109] Of his other pupils we know Walter Map, the historian Ralph Niger, Master Richard (a relative of John of Salisbury), and probably a certain Gervase who later retired to Durham.[110] The master, who lectured in theology as well as in canon and civil law, was at home

---

103 Below, ch. IX.
104 Cf. *Hist. litt. de la France* 14 (1817) 301; *Chart. Univ. Par.* I, 9–10.
105 References below, nn. 108ff., 139ff.
106 L. Saltet, *Les réordinations* (Paris 1907) 355, quoting the text from Schulte, *SB Vienna* 68 (1871) 43f. Cf. J. de Ghellinck, *Le mouvement théologique du XII*^e *siècle* (2nd ed. Bruges etc. 1948) 348 n.4 (1st ed. Paris 1914: p. 224 n.5). Saltet, *op. cit.* 355 n.2 says that also *Glos. ord.* on Dist. 19 c.8 refers to him: 'Variis modis ponitur casus huius capituli. G. inducit quasi sit abrogatum, et Melendus sentit cum eo et omnes qui dicunt ueritatem sacramentorum non esse apud hereticos …'. But *G.* is here Gratian who rejects c.8 in the dictum that follows; cf. also dict, ante c.8 and the *Nota correctorum*.
107 Until recently the only substantial account of Gerard Pucelle's activities was that of H. Reuter, *Geschichte Alexanders des Dritten* (Leipzig 1860–64) III, 216–21, which, however, treats but one aspect of his career. In 1949 Father A. Gabriel brought together the known material about various aspects in 'English Masters and Students in Paris during the XIIth Century,' *Analecta Praemonstratensia* 25 (1949) 38–40. A fuller account will be given by E. Rathbone in *English Cathedrals and the Schools* (cf. above, I n.6).
108 Jo. Sar. *ep.* 199 (PL 199, 220B).
109 Walter Map, *De nugis curialium* 2.7 (ed. M. R. James, Anecdota Oxoniensia 14; Oxford 1914) 69. Lucas became later archbishop of Esztergom.
110 W. Map *ibid.* — G. B. Flahiff, 'Ralph Niger,' *Medieval Studies* 2 (Toronto 1940) 106 n.13, 107; for Ralph's views on the study of law see H. Kantorowicz and B. Smalley, 'An English

both in the schools of Paris and at the court where he enjoyed the special favor of Louis VII.[111]

He received first orders and his first preferment from Archbishop Thomas of Canterbury before the latter left England,[112] and during the exile he was considered a member of Becket's *familia*, was kept informed of events promptly, and consulted on various occasions. At the end of 1165 or early in 1166, however, at the height of the controversy, Gerard, to the consternation of his friends, announced his intention of going to Germany on a mission to the Emperor, apparently with the approval of the Pope, and later asked John of Salisbury to join him.[114] Refusing the invitation with horror, John warned his friend of the danger to the Church when one well-known to have studied and taught both laws should be seen dealing with the schismatics, and, while affirming his own belief in Gerard's loyalty, pointed out the moral and political dangers he would be incurring by his actions.[115]

John's fears appeared to be justified. With Frederick Barbarossa and his circle Gerard was accorded a position even higher than he had enjoyed in France. Everything he said was regarded as 'sacrosanct.'[116] He accepted not only acclaim but also benefices from the schismatics and further incriminated himself by returning to England in 1168 without first visiting his patron, the exiled Archbishop, and taking the oath to Henry II which Becket's followers had stubbornly refused.[117]

Later in the same year, however, Gerard was reconciled with Becket on the understanding that he would renounce the benefice he had received in Germany unless the church concerned, after its return to the fold, wished to retain him, and took an oath declaring ordinations made by the schismatics to be invalid.[118] The Archbishop interceded for him with the Pope, who in turn obtained permission from Louis VII for the master to resume residence in France.[119]

Theologian's View of Roman Law: Pepo, Irnerius, Ralph Niger,' *Medieval and Renaissance Studies* 1 (London 1941) 244ff. — Jo. Sar. *ep.* 238 (PL 199, 269, on Richard); *Libellus de vita et miraculis s. Godrici ... auctore Reginaldo monacho Dunelmensi* (ed. W. Stevenson, Surtees Soc. 20; 1845) 452–4.

111 Jo. Sar. *ep.* 185, cf. *epp.* 238, 295 (PL 199, 195 and 268f., 340f.). Gerard's discussion of the term *persona* is quoted by Prepositinus, cf. *Chart. Univ. Par.* I, 9 No. 10, note; Gabriel, *loc. cit.* 39 n.173.
112 Herbert of Bosham, in *Mat. Becket* III, 525; Jo. Sar. *ep.* 239 (PL 199, 271).
113 *Mat. Becket* III, 525; V, 478.
114 Jo. Sar. *ep.* 168 (PL 199, 160D; *Mat. Becket* V, 351).
115 Jo. Sar. *loc. cit.* and *ep.* 189 (PL 199, 199C).
116 *Ibid*, and *ep.* 197 (PL 199, 216D-217B). Cf. W. Giesebrecht, *Geschichte der deutschen Kaiserzeit* V, 2 (Leipzig 1888) 518f. and VI (1895) 457; R. Knipping, *Die Regesten der Erzbischöfe von Köln im Mittelalter* II (Bonn 1901) No. 856; J. Spörl, 'Rainald von Dassel in seinem Verhältnis zu Johann von Salisbury,' *Historisches Jahrbuch der Görres-Gesellschaft* 60 (1940) 250–57.
117 *Ibid*, and *ep.* 239 (PL 199, 271; *Mat. Becket* VI, 453). Alexander III, JL 11400–01.
118 *Mat. Becket* VI 433–6.
119 *Ibid.* 436.

For Gerard Pucelle cf. also *J. Fried* Gerard Pucelle und Köln, ZRG Kan. Abt.68 (1982) 125–135; and *Ch. Donahue,* Gerard Pucelle as a Canon Lawyer: Life and the Battle Abbey Case, in: *R. H. Helmholz* et al. (ed.), Grundlagen des Rechts. Festschrift für Peter Landau zum 65. Geburtstag (Paderborn etc. 2000) 333–348. (P.L.)

Gerard's stay in Cologne is of interest for the history of canon law as well as for its political and biographical implications. During the late 'sixties and early 'seventies so many canonistic works were composed in Cologne or nearby that we are entitled to postulate the existence of a school of canon law in the ecclesiastical metropolis of the Rhineland, if only for a short time during the schism. These writings include the outstanding *Summa Elegantius in iure diuino* (1169, the so-called *Summa Coloniensis*), the *Distinctiones Monacenses* (after 1170), whose author was a native of Westphalia, and a short treatise on procedure beginning *Hactenus magister Gratianus egit de personis.*[120] The author of the *Summa Antiquitate et tempore* (after 1170), who also wrote *Notule super libello de significationibus uerborum* (and may be responsible for the glosses on the *Summa Elegantius* in the Paris and Vienna manuscripts),[121] was teaching at Cologne for some time.[122] Still another *Summa,* on the second part of Gratian, written *c.* 1167 and beginning 'Quoniam omissis centum distinctionibus,' recently found in MS 35 of Verdun, points definitely to the Cologne archdiocese as its place of origin.[123] All these works are offshoots of

---

120 Kuttner, *Repertorium* 170–2, 178f., 215f., 168 n.6 (121). In the *Summula Hactenus* the form for a bill of complaint is made out in the name of 'ego Remgerus canonicus sancti Andree ... sancte Coloniensi ecclesie sedi presidente Philippo ...,' cf. H. Singer, 'Beiträge zur Würdigung der Decretistenlitteratur,' AKKR 69 (1893) 443 n.244; a canon and school master of St. Andrew's named Renerus is mentioned by Caesarius of Heisterbach, *Dialogi miracul.* 4.50 (ed. Strange I, 217). — For connections of at least one treatise of civil law, a commentary *de regulis iuris,* with Cologne and Mayence, see G. Haenel, 'Zu Bulgarus' Commentar ... de regulis juris,' *Sitzungsberichte der sächsischen Akademie der Wiss.* Phil.-hist. Cl. 27 (1875) 244f., 255 (Leipzig, Universitätsbibl. MS Haen. 12, fol. 25ff.).

121 Vienna MS lat. 2125; Paris, B. N. MS lat. 14997. These glosses, beginning with a *divisio* of the system of moral sciences ('Moralis sapientia [est que *add. Par.*] in libris utriusque iuris. hec diuiditur in ratiocinatiuam et amministratiuam, hec [que *Par.*] in amministratione officiorum continetur et in echonomicam politicam [et ethicam *add Par.*] subdiuiditur ...'; cf. also Ullmann, *Med. Papalism* 26 n.1) will be discussed elsewhere.

122 *Repertorium* 168, 179, n.3; cf. Singer, 'Beiträge ... II,' AKKR 73 (1895) 82 n.248, 97ff. (also pp. clviii *n.* and clxxii-iii of his edition of Rufinus).

123 Cf. the various forms for appeals etc. at C. 2 q.6: '... Ego R. sancte col(oniensis) ecclesie episcopus te W. bon(nensis) ecclesie canonicum ad apostolicam sedem quam appellasti ab obseruatione mei iudicii hiis apostolis dimitto; ... Ego G. sancte bon(nensis) ecclesie filius licet indignus ...; Ego G. contra sententiam domini R. col. archiepiscopi iniuste in me illatam *(corr.* latam) idus febr. anno incarnationis domini M.c.lxviii. feria ii. rem. *(corr.* Romanam) sedem appello et apostolos peto; ... Nos G. et b. sindici (idest defensores *inter lin.*) canonicorum sancte bon(nensi)s ecclesie ...' (Verdun MS 35, fol. 13v-14r). Archbishop Rainald died on 14 August 1167; the date in form iii must be emended (also on computistic grounds) to Monday, 13 February 1167. The *Summa,* based on Paucapalea and Stephen of Tournai, will be discussed

the French school:[124] we may remember, in this connection, that a compilation of Bolognese *formulae*, by one Master Bernard, reached Cologne c. 1167–69 by way of Paris,[125] and that both Archbishop Rainald of Dassel and Philip of Heinsberg, who succeeded him in 1167, had been trained in France.[126] We learn from Caesarius of Heisterbach that Philip, when he was a young student in Reims, before 1153, had as his tutor (*magister et paedagogus*) one Godfrey who later became an Augustinian canon and master of the schools at St, Andrew's of Cologne until in his old age he entered the Cistercian order.[127] This Godfrey may well have been the *frater Godefridus* who is given as the author of the *Summa Elegantius in iure divino* in a contemporary codex from another Augustinian abbey, St. Victor's in Paris (now MS lat. 14997 of the Bibliothèque nationale);[128] one might, of course, be tempted to connect the entry with Godfrey of St. Victor, who is known as the author of philosophical and theological writings,[129] but an Augustinian Master Godfrey of Cologne would seem to have a better title to the foremost work of the Rhenish school.

Already Maitland thought it a coincidence worthy of note that Vacarius professed a doctrine on marriage which otherwise occurs only in the *Summa Elegantius*

elsewhere. (I should like to thank the Rev. Dr. P. J. Kessler for drawing my attention to this codex. S. K.)

124 *Repertorium* 168f. For the dependence of the *Summa Elegantius* on Peter Lombard see Saltet, *Réordinations* 332 n.1; A. Landgraf, in *Zeitschrift für katholische Theologie* 63 (1939) 167–9, 175 n.118. The *Summa Antiquitate et tempore* was probably composed in Paris, after the author's stay at Cologne, cf. Singer *loc. cit.* (n.19). For French influences on the judicial organization of the archdiocese of Cologne see F. Gescher, 'Um die älteste Satzung des erzbischöflichen Offizialats von Köln,' *Annalen des Historischen Vereins für den Niederrhein* 130 (1937) 1–21.

125 C. H. Haskins, 'An Italian Master Bernard,' *Essays in history presented to A. L. Poole* (Oxford 1937) 220.

126 J. Ficker, *Reinald von Dassel* (Cologne 1850) 5; H. Koeppler, 'Frederick Barbarossa and the Schools of Bologna,' *Engl. Hist. Rev.* 54 (1939) 583; Martens, 'Philipp von Heinsberg,' *Allgemeine deutsche Biographie* 26 (1888) 3; Lauchert, LThK 8 (1936) 230 s.v.

127 Caes. Heist. *Dial.* 2.16, 4.49 (ed. Strange I, 84f. and 215). Master Godfrey is not to be confused with Godfrey, notary of the dean of the Cathedral *(Dial.* 6.5, 11.43–44; cf. Strange I, 9 n.1). His stay at Rheims antedates the death of St. Bernard (1153), cf. *Dial.* 2.16; he was succeeded as *scholasticus* of St. Andrew's by Master Renerus (cf. n.120 above).

128 Cf. Repertorium 171. A. Teetaert, 'Commentationes historiae iuris canonici,' *Collectanea Franciscana* 14 (1944) 238, considers the entry on the fly-leaf as being written by the same hand as the text of the *Summa.*

129 Earlier studies on Godfrey of St. Victor (cf. M. Manitius, *Geschichte der lateinischen Literatur des Mittelalters* III [Munich 1931] 779) have now been largely superseded by the researches of Ph. Delhaye; cf. *Revue du moyen âge latin* 3 (1947) 225–41; *Revue bénédictine* 58 (1948) 93–109, and particularly his two volumes, *Le Microcosmus de Godefroy de Saint-Victor. Edition — Etude théologique* (Mémoires et travaux ... des Facultés catholiques de Lille 56–7; Lille-Gembloux 1951). Delhaye has refuted the traditional identification of Godfrey of St. Victor with Geoffroy de Breteuil; on the possibility of assigning to the Victorine master the *Summa Elegantius* he expresses himself with the greatest reserve (*op. cit.* II, 196–8). One might add that the one passage on *moralis sapientia* and law in which Delhaye finds a vague similarity with some verses of Godfrey's *Fons philosophiae* (p.198) does not even belong to the author but to the glossator of

(*Coloniensis*), at about the same time Henry II 'was carrying on a flirtation with the Calixtines.'[130] If we add that the English Master Gerard was in Cologne while this *Summa* and other works on canon law were being written in that city, then the hypothesis of a special connection between the school of Cologne and the early English canonists becomes very suggestive. In view of this possibility, some passages of the often underrated *Summa Antiquitate et tempore* in particular acquire a greater significance than has been heretofore recognized. This commentary, in one place, illustrates the concept of *mala consuetudo* by an English example;[131] in another, it offers an elaborate discussion of a computistic problem which, as we are told in the slightly earlier *Summa Magister Gratianus in hoc opere* (*Summa Parisiensis, c.* 1170), had puzzled 'm. Girardus.'[132] Finally, in all the canonistic literature of the twelfth century there seem to be only two writers who claim a knowledge of Cresconius, that elusive African canonist of the sixth or the seventh century whose *Concordia canonum* had never played a very conspicuous role in the history of canonical collections:[133] one being the author of *Antiquitate et tempore*, who refers to Cresconius three times, perhaps only from hearsay;[134]

Kuttner comments three references to Cresconius only from hearsay: In his NR he is adding: "*P. Landau*, Vorgratianische Kanonessammlungen bei Dekretisten und in frühen Dekretalensammlungen, Proceedings San Diego (MIC, Subsidia 9; 1992) 93–116 at p. 116 – without referring at all to the present article – says there is no reason to assume ("unterstellen") that the author of *Antiquitate et tempore* cited Cresconius 'from hearsay'. he omits, however, our 'perhaps'." (S.K.)

The other, according to the report of an otherwise unknown master Egidius — of whose *Lucubratiunculae* on the Decretum a brief fragment was discovered by F. Patetta in 1892[135] — being none but Gerard Pucelle. He is credited by Egidius with a remark on the opening words of the Decretum (more probably

the *Summa* (cf. n.121 above), and that elsewhere Godfrey shows a certain contempt for canonists: 'nullus erit nisi sit loquax decretista' (*Fons phil.* 24.2. ed. A. Charma, in *Mémoires de la Societé des Antiquaires de Normandie*³ 7[1869] 15).

130 *Law Quart. Rev.* 13 (1897) 137.
131 D.4 c.2 v. *mala consuetudo*: 'ut in Anglia, si aliquis naufragium passus fuerit, si qua retinuit, eadem confiscantur et auferuntur ei' (Singer, AKKR 73, 69 n.199). Cf. the passionate denunciation of the English law of wreck by Gerald of Wales, *De principis instructione* 1.20 (*Opp.* VIII, 117–20).
132 D.18 c.4; cf. Singer *loc. cit.* 82–4 and n.252. The quotation in *Sum. Par.* reads *ad loc.* v. *iperberiti*: 'idest septembris. secundum hoc quomodo idus sit decimus dies dubitat m. Girardus. vel possumus dicere ...'. (Our thanks are due to Father G. B. Flahiff for collating Bamberg MS Can. 36 with Schulte's reading in *SB Vienna* 64 [1870] 127.)
133 For MSS see F. Maassen, *Geschichte der Quellen und Literatur des canonischen Rechts ...* (Graz 1870) 806ff. and 846; H. Wurm, *Studien und Texte zur Dekretalensammlung des Dionysius Exiguus* (Bonn 1939) 37–9; for the occasional use made of Cresconius by early medieval collections, Fournier-Le Bras, *Histoire des collections canoniques en occident ...* (Paris 1931–2) I, 331, 343, 425; II, 117.
134 The three passages are quoted in Schulte, *Geschichte der Quellen und Lit.* I, 44 (as from Rufinus); for corrections and observations see Singer, AKKR 73 (1895) 53, 84, 89, 111; *Rufinus* clxix f.
135 Rome, Biblioteca Vittorio Emanuele MS 1369 (Sessor. 43) fol. 75ra; (photostats obtained through the kindness of Professor G. Levi Della Vida); cf. Patetta, 'Sull'introduzione del Digesto

it was a gloss on the rubric, *Concordia discordantium canonum*) to the effect that Gratian's words were taken from Cresconius: '... ita enim in breuiatione cresconii continetur, sicut retulit se legisse magister Girardus pul.'[136] Patetta's little discovery (he did not identify the master quoted by Egidius) seems to have passed unnoticed,[137] but together with the other clues just mentioned it strongly supports the assumption that the author of *Antiquitate et tempore* at one time studied under Gerard Pucelle.

After his position in France had been restored, Gerard presumably taught there again for several years after 1168. He returned to active affairs, it appears, about 1174–5 when he witnessed a charter as principal clerk to Becket's successor, Archbishop Richard,[138] a post he retained until 1183. In this capacity his legal knowledge and diplomatic skill were frequently in demand, for both the archbishop and others,[139] as, for example, in the suit between Battle Abbey and Godfrey de Luci, son of the justiciar, when Gerard's pleading, based on several well-made points of canon law and the argument that *salva pace Domini regis* the secular power has no authority *in rebus ecclesiasticis,* turned the tide in favor of Abbot Odo, his former associate at Canterbury.[140]

Although Gerard appears constantly in the service of Archbishop Richard between c. 1174 and 1183,[141] his career in the schools was not forgotten. In a

---

a Bologna,' *Rivista italiana per le scienze giuridiche* 14 (1892) 66–7. The title, 'lucubratiuncule egidii' (in cipher, cf. Patetta *loc. cit.*) is certainly recherché and may have been suggested by classical or patristic reminiscences, cf. Fronto, *Epp. ad Marcum Caes.* 1.4(3); Pliny, *N.H.* praef. 24; St. Jerome, *epp.* 117.2, 119.1; the text begins (ad v. *Humanum genus*) 'Recentes auditorum animi ...'As far as one can judge from the brief fragment, which covers only D.1 pr.-c.7, the work was to contain *quaestiones decretales*. Egidius depends very much on the *Summa* of Simon of Bisignano (c. 1177–9); in addition, he cites *ste.* (probably Stephen of Tournai), Master Aldric (on whom cf. Savigny, *Geschichte* IV, 231–6; Johannes Bassianus called him 'aliquis utpote subtilissimus,' cf. Kantorowicz, *Studies in the Glossators* 54), an unidentifiable Master *blā.* (cf. the text below, Appendix B) and Gerard Pucelle. This suggests that Egidius may have belonged to one of the Western schools rather than to that of Bologna; the literary type (cf. below, ch. VI on *quaestiones decretales*) would seem to point in the same direction.

136 The full quotation is printed and discussed below, Appendix B. — One of the two marginal notes added by another hand to Egidius' fragment is signed 'secundum bazianum' (d. 1197) and reads (to D.1 c.7): 'Set fertur M. G. sic dixisse quia sicut facilius possum tibi ostendere quod non sit deus quam quod sit, ita facilius possum ostendere quod non sit ius naturale quam quod sit.' This observation is certainly characteristic of the spirit of intellectual adventure among the twelfth-century scholastics, but whether *G.* here refers to Gerard remains very doubtful.

137 It is not mentioned by other scholars (Seckel, Kantorowicz, Meijers) who have studied the codex Sessorianus after 1892 for the miscellaneous civilian writings it contains. We may add here that among its various unrecorded items (fol. 75ff.) there is a fragment of the *Summa* of Sicardus (fol.78r-79v).

138 J. H. Round, *Ancient Charters* (Pipe Roll Soc.; London 1888) 72.

139 Cf. for example William Thorne and Thomas of Elmham as cited above, II n.32; Gir. Camb. I, 48f. Further details will be given elsewhere (cf. above, n.107).

140 *Chron. monast. de Bello* (above, I n.7) 172–8. Of Gerard's pleading (pp. 176–8) the author says: 'cum ... perorasset et allegationem suam legum et decretorum, quae hic inserere longum erat, auctoritatibus comprobasset ...' (p. 178).

141 D. C. Douglas, *The Domesday Monachorum of Christ Church Canterbury* (London 1944) 45 n.4, 109.

collection of letters of Alexander III, Louis VII, and their contemporaries which seems to have been put together at the Abbey of St. Victor,[142] is a group of three, dating from about 1178, referring to his learning.[143] In the first Peter, Cardinal of St. Chrysogonos — who was in France on a mission relating to the schools, and whose award to the Abbey of Sainte-Geneviève in settlement of a difficult suit Gerard Pucelle witnesses first after the high ecclesiastical dignities[144] — recommends the master to the Pope as a clerk worthy of promotion. In the second, dated 7 February 1178, Alexander III, praising Gerard's knowledge of the *artes* and his success with his students, grants him the privilege of retaining the income from his English benefices for four years if he is teaching. The third letter, dated 15 March 1178, which is also incorporated in an English collection of decretals,[145] permits him as a special favor to recover the revenues of his German benefice, which he had lost through his association with the schismatics, adding that he is to suffer no hurt, financial or other, on account of his mission to the Emperor, a striking testimony to Gerard's loyalty on that occasion.

Although Master Gerard had to wait till 1183, when he was made bishop of Coventry, for the preferment recommended by Cardinal Peter, he is twice found intervening on behalf of masters whom he considered good clerks suitable for the episcopate. In 1176 he proposed Master John of Cornwall (of whom more later) to the English royalist prelates for the vacant see of St. David's,[146] and at the Third Lateran Council he urged the Pope to recognize the election of Master Bertold (= Bertram) to the bishopric of Bremen,[147] his arguments being overruled in both cases by purely secular considerations. He continued, as bishop-elect, for a short time in the archbishop's service,[148] but eventually went to his cathedral where, a few months later, he died in circumstances which led to the belief that he had been poisoned.[149] It is indicative of the affection and respect which Gerard evoked throughout his life that the monks of Canterbury, who had

---

142 Vatican MS Reg. lat. 179, ed. A. Duchesne, *Historiae Francorum scriptores* IV (Paris 1641) 567–762; cf. A. Luchaire, *Etudes sur quelques manuscrits de Rome et de Paris* (Université de Paris, Bibliothèque de la Faculté de lettres 8; 1899) 31ff.

143 PL 200, 1370f.; Mansi 21, 963; *Chart. Univ. Par.* I, 9f. Nos. 10–11 (JL 13023, 13032).

144 Paris, Bibl. Ste.-Geneviève MS 1651 (E.1.25) fol. 221; cf. *Chart. Univ. Par.* I, 45 n.1.

145 *Coll. Cottoniana* (No. 25 in Dr. Holtzmann's list [above, I n.14]) 5.21: JL 13032 (London, B. M. Cotton MS Vitell. E.xiii, fol. 256; cf. K. Hampe, in *Neues Archiv der Ges. für ältere deutsche Gesch.* 22 [1896] 391).

The decretal JL 13032 = WH 633 is only found in Collectio Cottoniana (Cott. 5.21). (P.L.)

146 E. Rathbone, 'John of Cornwall: a Brief Biography' *Recherches de Théologie ancienne et médiévale* [=RTAM] 17 (1950) 49.

147 For this episode see the *Annales Stadenses* and *the Catalogus episcoporum Bremensium,* Mansi 22, 236 (better in MGH *Script.* 16, 348) and 240. It seems highly probable that *magister Gherardus* (*quidam magister Gerardus* Mansi) was Gerard Pucelle, who was at the Council as Archbishop Richard's deputy (Gir. Camb. *Opp.* I, 48), the more so in view of his intervention on behalf of John of Cornwall.

148 He witnesses a charter as bishop-elect, Oxford, MS Bodl. 423, fol. 95rb.

149 Gervase of Canterbury, *Opp.* I, 307–8.

known him well for several years, celebrated his obit with the rites usual for that of an archbishop.[150]

From this brief outline of Gerard Pucelle's career it is clear that he was, as lawyer and teacher, in Herbert of Bosham's phrase, *nomine et fama celebris* to his contemporaries.[151] We should expect therefore to find some record of his teaching in canonistic literature apart from the references already noted.[152] It is reasonable to identify with Gerard Pucelle the *Ger.* cited in glosses in an early codex in Durham Cathedral Library;[153] the Master Gerard whose opinion on the punishment of plaintiffs who fail at their complaint in criminal cases is given in a work of the French school, recently discovered in a manuscript at Liège;[154] and the Gerard whose *Summa super decretalia* is listed in the Rochester catalogue of 1202.[155] With these clues as a starting point we may hope that further research may bring to light enough of his teaching to leave no doubt why Gerard Pucelle was such an imposing figure in France, the Rhineland, and his own country.

VI. Honorius and the Summae Quaestionum

The years after the death of Gerard Pucelle witnessed the eager productivity of the circle of canonists around the *Summa Omnis qui iuste*. Among their writings the *Summa decretalium quaestionum* of Master Honorius is of particular interest for more than one reason: it is the only work of the group whose author can be definitely identified, the name of Honorius being attested by two of the extant seven manuscripts;[156] it must have been widely appreciated since the number of copies preserved surpasses by far that of any other work of the Anglo-Norman

---

150 Obit list in London, B. M. Cotton MS Nero C.ix, fol. 3v.
151 *Mat. Becket* III, 525.
152 *Sum. Lips,* (above n.106), *Sum. Par.* (n.132), Egidius (n.136).
153 Durham MS C.iii.1, fol. 68; cf. *Repertorium* 26 and n.1.
154 Liège, Séminaire MS 6.N.15, *Summa Quid sit symonia* (fol. 135r-145v), to C.2 q.3, *Qua pena feriendi sint qui in accusacione defecerint*: 'Refert utrum accuset in scriptis uel sine scriptis ... Magister Gerardus tamen distinxit utrum sit necessarius accusator an uoluntarius. Necessarius, ut heres pro morte testatoris et filius de morte patris. Necessarius non timet penam talionis; de uoluntario predicta intelliguntur' (fol. 173rb-va). We wish to thank Abbé G. Fransen, who plans to publish a study on this *Summa* of the French school, discovered by him, for his kind permission to quote the passage on Gerard from his transcript.
   The Summa 'Quid sit symonia' was discussed by *G. Fransen,* Stud. Grat. I (1953) 296–298. Another commentary on procedure in Gratian's Decretum is the *Summa Elnonensis,* written around 1165/1168 and preserved in MS Valenciennes, Bibl. Munic. 193, fol. 111rb-115rb. It had probably Gerard Pucelle as author. Cf. *G. Fransen,* Colligite fragmenta: La Summa Elnonensis, Stud. Grat. XIII (1967) 85–108. (P.L.)
155 W. B. Rye, 'Catalogue of the Library of the Priory of St. Andrew, Rochester, A.D. 1202,' *Archaeologia Cantiana* 3 (1860) 60 No. 205.
156 Six MSS are listed in Kuttner, *Repertorium* 424 and *Traditio* 1 (1943) 321 n.4; add Paris, B. N. MS lat. 14591, fol. 50–83ra (from St. Victor). Honorius' name appears in the *explicit* of Douai MS 640 (fol. 42va) and the *incipit* of Zwettl MS 162 (fol. 179r).

school; moreover, it has considerable literary merits because of the innovations it introduced in the methods and form of canonical writing.

Yet the work has been unduly neglected by historians of canon law. Schulte, who published in 1870 a summary account of the unusual structure and a few pages of text from the anonymous manuscript of Bamberg, wrongly assumed on the strength of the opening words, 'De questionibus decretalibus tractaturi ...,' that he had to do with *quaestiones* from the early Bolognese school of decretalists after Bernard of Pavia, written in illustration of the *Compilatio I*. In his *Geschichte der Quellen* he all but passed over the work in silence.[157] Saltet was the first to recognize (in 1907) that the *quaestiones* of the Bamberg codex belong to the orbit of the French school and, more specifically, to that of the *Summa Lipsiensis;* but this important observation remained generally unnoticed.[158] What is more, it escaped everyone's attention that as early as 1845 a brief description had been given of our treatise from the Douai manuscript, with its important clue to the identity of the author in the subscription, 'Explicit summa M. Hon.'[159]

For Master Honorius of Kent and his works – Summa questionum decretalium and Summa decreti 'De iure canonico tractaturus' – cf. now mainly the survey by *R. Weigand*, Bemerkungen zu den Schriften und Lehren des Magister Honorius, Proceedings of the Fifth International Congress of Medieval Canon Law, Salamanca 1976 (MIC Ser. C, Vol. 6, Città del Vaticano 1980) 195–212. Parts of the Summa questionum on marriage doctrine were edited by *B. Grimm*, Die Ehelehre des Magister Honorius. Ein Beitrag zur Ehelehre der anglonormannischen Schule, Stud. Grat. XXIV (1989) 231–387. A complete edition of this Summa is in preparation by *P. Landau/W. Kozur* et al. in Würzburg. (P.L.)

It is this colophon, meanwhile corroborated by the inscription of the Zwettl manuscript, 'Incipiunt questiones ueneriales secundum magistrum Honorium,' which enables us to assign the work to a man whose name is not entirely unfamiliar to English historians: a master Honorius is mentioned by Thomas of Marlborough as one of his teachers *in scolis,* and Roger of Hoveden recounts in detail this master's long struggle (1198–1202) for the archdeaconry of Richmond.[160] In the

---

157 Schulte, 'Literaturgeschichte der Compilationes antiquae,' *SB Vienna* 66 (1870) 58–64; briefly mentioned in *Geschichte der Quellen und Lit.* I (1875) 234 n.2 ('Interessante Quaestiones zu den Dekretalen weist nach meine Lit. Gesch. S.8–15'), but not at all in the chapter on 'Systematische Schriften' (p. 231).

158 Saltet, *Réordinations* 318–21, 338 and n.1; cf. de Ghellinck, *Mouvement théologique* 200 n.2 (2nd ed. 322 n.5).

159 Eugène F. J. Tailliar, *Notice de manuscrits de la bibliothèque de Douai concernant la législation du moyen âge* (Douai 1845; reprinted as appendix to H. R. Duthilloeul, *Catalogue déscriptif et raisonné des manuscrits de la bibliothèque publique de Douai*, 1846) 48ff. quoting from MS 584 (now 640). Cf. also the description of MS 640 by C. Deshaisnes in vol. 6 (in-4°) of the *Catalogue général des manuscrits ... des départements* (Paris 1878).

160 *Chronicon Abbatiae de Evesham* 126; Roger of Hoveden, *Chronica* (ed. W. Stubbs, R. S.; London 1868–71) IV 44f., 52, 89, 158ff., 176ff. Some aspects of Honorius' ecclesiastical career have been treated by Stubbs, Introd. IV, lxxi ff.; A. H. Thompson, 'The Register of the Archdeaconry of Richmond,' *Yorkshire Archaeological Journal* 25 (1920) 131–5; C. T. Clay, *Early Yorkshire*

course of this complex litigation, Pope Innocent III issued a considerable number of judicial mandates, several of which eventually found their way into the official compilations of decretals.[161]

Of Honorius' early years little is known save that he was a native of Kent.[162] The church of Willesborough in the same county seems to have been his first benefice, if we may surmise that he was the Honorius — not yet styled *magister* — for whom Lucius III in 1184 or 1185 issued a mandate of provision to the abbot and monks of St. Augustine's, recommending the grantee on account of his learning and because he had no wherewithal while staying at the schools.[163] The identification, however, remains doubtful, for the mandate also contains a clause of dispensation from which it appears that the beneficiary of Pope Lucius' letter was a priest's son,[164] whereas the taint of irregularity *ex defectu natalium* was never pointed out against Master Honorius in the Richmond case — though his adversaries did not hesitate to tax him with murder, sacrilege, arson, *et alia multa gravia et enormia*.[165]

At any rate, the scholastic career of Honorius must have filled the decennium *c*. 1185–95. In 1192 he witnessed, among other *magistri*, a judgment delivered by John of Cornwall and Robert of Melun at Oxford.[166] Three years later, in 1195, we find him as *officialis* in the service of Archbishop Geoffrey Plantagenet of York;[167] for some time he was also the latter's vicar general (*procurator spiritualium*).[168] As the archbishop's man, however, Honorius could not fail to come into conflict with the all-powerful dean of York, Simon of Apulia. Master Simon, himself an able lawyer, chancellor of York since 1190, and perhaps the author of a (canonistic?) *Summa*,[169] had led the chapter in constant litigation with

---

Charters IV (Yorkshire Archaeol. Soc. Record Series, extra series I; 1935) xxv f.; S. Painter, *The Reign of King John* (Baltimore 1949) 166f. and 236f.; Cheney, *Bishops' Chanceries* 12f. His identity with the author of the *Summa quaestionum* was briefly stated by S. Kuttner, in *Traditio* 1, 321 n.4; cf. also 'Zur neuesten Glossatorenforschung,' *Studia et docum. hist. et iuris* 6 (1940) 305 n.43; see further W. Ullmann, 'Honorius III and the Prohibition of Legal Studies,' *Juridical Review* 60 (1948) 179; *Med. Papalism* 11; E. Rathbone, RTAM 17 (1950) 52 n.39.

161 Potthast, *Regesta Romanorum pontificum* I [=Po.] (Berlin 1874) Nos. 1190–91, 1260–62, 1285 (X 3.7.6), 1311, 1338 (X 2.20.30), 1692 (X 3.8.7) 1693–94, 5035 (X 1.10.3). Two other mandates are referred to in Po. 1190, 1191, 1261, cf. note 179 below. — Another decretal addressed to Honorius (Po. 1402: X 2.25.2 archidiacono Richemundie, but cf. 3 Comp. 2.16.1 and several primitive collections [cited *Repert.* 302; MS Vat. Pal. 652 c.7] for fuller address) is not concerned with the Richmond case.
162 Po. 1338: '... dilectus filius magister Honorius de Kent (*al.* Rent', Bent', Berent'; cf. Friedberg, *Corp. iur. can.* II, 326 n.10 to X 2.20.30) qui archidiaconus Richemundie nominatur ...'.
163 Holtzmann, *Papsturkunden* in England I, 510 No. 228.
164 *Ibid.*: '... non praeiudicante eo quod pater eius in eadem ecclesia ministret' etc.
165 Po. 1692 (PL 214, 1022B).
166 H. E. Salter, *The Cartulary of Oseney Abbey* (Oxford Historical Soc.; Oxford 1929–36) IV, 431; cf. E. Rathbone, RTAM 17, 52 and 50 n.28.
167 Rog. Hov. III, 298; IV, 9, 44.
168 Po. 1692 (PL 214, 1023B). Cf. E. Fournier, *Les origines du vicaire général* (Paris 1922) 91f.
169 Gir. Camb. *Opp.* IV, 383 ('copiose litteratum et jurisperitum'); Stubbs, *Rog. Hov.* IV, Introd. li. Lanthony Priory owned a 'Summa magistri symonis de Apuleya, quaternus ligatus,' No. 281 of the

Archbishop Geoffrey ever since he had been made dean, after a disputed election, by Pope Celestine III in 1193.[170] It seems that during the 'nineties the *decanus Eboracensis* was widely talked of: one of his law suits is referred to, evidently as a matter of common knowledge, in the glosses of the Vacarian school.[171] More quarrels with the archbishop were to follow,[172] and Master Simon's ambition was eventually satisfied only in 1214, when he obtained the bishopric of Exeter (d. 1223).[173]

The Richmond case began as part of the general antagonism between the archbishop and his chapter. When Geoffrey, in 1198, conferred the vacant archdeaconry upon Master Honorius, he had just obtained from his royal brother a promise of non-interference with appointments in the diocese.[174] But through able maneuvering on the part of Simon and the canons, King Richard presently changed his mind and nominated one of his own clerks, Roger of St. Edmunds, to the archdeaconry.[175] While Honorius received the obedience of the clergy of Richmond, the archbishop's request for his installation in the chapter was rejected at York: the mandate, Simon alleged, was addressed to the chapter alone instead of bearing the proper address to Dean and chapter. Honorius promptly appealed to Rome, whereupon the canons proceeded to install Roger and to invest

---

fourteenth-century catalogue in R. W. Williams, 'Gloucestershire Medieval Libraries,' *Transactions of the Bristol and Glos. Archaeol. Soc.* 31 (1908) 153. Cf. K. Edwards, *The English Secular Cathedrals in the Middle Ages* (Manchester 1949) 181, 190; cf. 187 n.3. The nature of the *Summa* remains, however, uncertain, since the codex was kept at the library in *arm.* IV *grad.* 3, which contained almost no legal books (for a few exceptions see Nos. 287–8, 304–6), while the proper shelves for books of canon and civil law were *arm.* IV *grad.* 1 and 2 (see Nos. 229–48, 250–71 of the catalogue).

170 *The Historians of the Church of York and its Archbishops* (ed. J. Raine, Rolls Series; London 1879–94) III, 92–4, 99–104; Rog. Hov. III, 170, 230f., 278–85; Celestine III, JL 16829, 17108, 17121, 17300–02, etc. Cf. Stubbs, *loc. cit.* lvii–lxxiv.

Master Simon of Apulia was Dean and Chancellor of York 1190–1213 and later bishop of Exeter 1213–1224. Simon was most probably Simon of Bisignano – cf. *M. Bertram*, Simon of Apulia. Randbemerkungen zu der Edition der Dekretsumme des Simon von Bisignano, https:mittelalter.hypotheses.org/10240. (P.L.)

171 *Vac.* 1.14 n.6 (*Cod.* 1.23.5): 'arg. pro decano eboracensi.' (De Zulueta, *Lib paup.* Introd. lxxxv, rightly expresses 'considerable doubts' as to Wenck's interpretation, which referred this gloss to the controversy on primatial rights between the sees of Canterbury and York.) The passage of Justinian's Code on which the gloss was written reads: 'Sacrilegii instar est divinis super quibuscumque administrationibus vel dignitatibus promulgandis obviare beneficiis.' Among the complaints of Dean Simon and the chapter against the archbishop, adjudicated by Celestine III on 8 June 1194 (JL 17121), there is one for which this *lex* could well be cited as an *argumentum*: Geoffrey, the chapter claimed, had refused to reinstate disseized canons and clerks, spurning every mandate of restitution (cf. Rog. Hov. III, 280). Or perhaps the gloss refers to the incident when Simon on his return from Rome, in February 1195, was forcibly prevented by the archbishop's *familiares* from making his entrance as dean in the Cathedral (*ibid.* 283f.).

172 Rog. Hov. III, 298 (case of the West Riding, 1195), IV, 158 (case of Cleveland, 1201), 174f. (case of Beverley, 1201; cf. Gir. Camb. *Opp.* I, 435).

173 Eubel, *Hierarchia catholica medii aevi* I (2nd ed. Münster 1913) 242.

174 Rog. Hov. IV, 44f.

175 *Ibid.* 52. For Roger as a witness in royal acts cf. e.g. *Epp. Cant.* 549, 551 (1196–97).

him with the possession of the archdeaconry.[176] Honorius was forcibly ejected from Richmond, but returned the next year and again received the local clergy's oaths of obedience; Dean Simon retorted with excommunication.[177] The sequence of events thereafter becomes blurred:[178] at some point, a settlement out of court must have taken place, but Roger of St. Edmunds nonetheless managed to elicit favorable letters to judges delegate from Innocent III — which the pope promptly revoked in December, 1200.[179] It turned out that Roger had been encouraged in his course of action by the archbishop himself, for matters had in the meantime become further involved by Geoffrey's change of heart: he had made his peace with the chapter[180] and a violent quarrel had broken out between him and Honorius over certain franchises and privileges of the archdeacons of Richmond.[181] A second law suit was now pending in Rome, where Honorius, since 1201, had been pleading his cause in person,[182] and it became at times difficult even for the pope to keep the two cases apart.[183] He finally issued an interlocutory decision in the suit Honorius vs. Geoffrey, protecting the former in his possession of the franchises, while leaving a number of points to be cleared by delegates.[184] In the main

176 Rog. Hov. IV, 52; Po. 1692 (PL 214, 1022B).
177 Rog. Hov. IV, 89.
178 *Ibid.* 176: '... propter appellationes hinc inde factas et propter testium varietatem.
179 Po. 1190 (20 December 1200), 1191, 1261: *ibid.* 181, 184, 177. The mandates which Innocent III revoked are lost; there was one addressed to the abbots of St. Edmund's and Sibton and the prior of Norwich (cf. Po. 1190, 1261), and another, to the abbots of St. Edmund's and St. Benet of Holme and the prior of Monk's Toft (cf. Po. 1191).
180 Rog. Hov. IV, 126 and 177 (Po. 1261).
181 *Ibid.* 158f.; Po. 1260 (3 February 1201, wrongly dated *anno quarto* by Stubbs, *ibid.* 160). The liberties at issue were chiefly: (1) freedom from episcopal censures against the clergy of the archdeaconry (cf. Po. 1260); (2) the archdeacon's right of institution to benefices and (3) his *custodia* of vacant churches in the archdeaconry (cf. Po. 1260, 1285). Geoffrey insisted that all these had been conceded only as personal privileges to one of Honorius' predecessors (William de Chemillé [Chimely], archd. 1189–96; cf. Rog. Hov. III, 16; IV, 12, 37, below, VII n.246); that in conferring the archdeaconry upon Honorius he had expressly reserved the said rights; and moreover, that the latter had renounced them formally in writing. Honorius maintained that the franchises belonged to the archdeaconry as such; that the archbishop had reserved them only after the conferral; and that he, Honorius, had renounced these *libertates* under duress and for tactical reasons, after having been dispossessed by the archbishop; the act of renunciation on the part of a *spoliatus* being invalid at canon law (cf. Po. 1285: Rog. Hov. IV, 177ff. and X 3.7.6; cf. also Po. 1692 [PL 214, 1023C] for his denial that he had renounced the archdeaconry itself). Stubbs' unfavorable opinion of Honorius in this matter (Rog. Hov. IV, lxxii) is unjustified.
182 Rog. Hov. IV, 158; Po. 1260–62 (*ibid.* 159, 177, 181). Also the mandate Po. 1311 (fragment, without address or date; *ibid.* 181) belongs to this phase of the struggle; it is probably the letter addressed to the bishop of Ely and the abbot of Waltham, mentioned in Po. 1260.
183 Cf. Po. 1338 (X 2.20.30), which must be dated before Po. 1285.
184 Po. 1285, *anno quarto* (the date 22 February–March 1201 in Potthast is too narrow). The textual transmission of the letter (transl. A. H. Thompson, *loc. cit. supra* n.160) is very unsatisfactory both in Roger of Hoveden (IV, 177ff.) and the decretal collections *(Alan.* 3.6.3, *Bern. Compost.* 3.9.4, *3 Comp.* 3.7.3, X 3.7.6.). Quite apart from the cuts in the latter, there are many divergencies; thus the name of William de Chemillé (cf. note 181 above; Friedberg, *Corp. iur. Can.* II, 485

issue, however, against Roger and the canons, Honorius was ultimately upheld: on June 1, 1202, papal sentence was pronounced in his favor.[185]

It is understandable that by this time Honorius no longer felt any attachment to the fickle Archbishop Geoffrey. Even while prosecuting his own suit, he had already worked occasionally as an agent for Hubert Walter in Rome.[186] He was a member of the primate's *familia* at the latest in 1203:[187] in this year his former student, Thomas of Marlborough, met him as *clericus archiepiscopi Cantuariensis*,[188] and about the same time Honorius helped in negotiating the reconciliation between Hubert Walter and Gerald of Wales.[189] After the archbishop's death, King John sent him to Rome (20 December 1205) as one of his proctors in the great Canterbury election dispute, which found more than one celebrated jurist pleading for one or the other side in the pope's court.[190] Master Honorius' hard-won dignity as *archidiaconus Richemundiae* was by now expressly acknowledged also in the royal letters,[191] but his triumph cost him dear. From the year 1201, the time when he first betook himself to Rome, he owed the king 300 marks for letters of protection, 'et ut possit uti iure suo super archidiaconatu Richemundie.' The debt runs through the Pipe Rolls till 1208[192] and a laconic entry in the Annals of Dunstable for that year says that he was deprived of all his possessions and

---

n.15 *ad loc.*) is missing in Hoveden's text, and the passage 'cui archidiaconus ... competebat' (Rog. Hov. IV, 178.15–18; cf. Friedberg *ibid.* between nn. 16 and 17) is rertainly corrupt, etc.

185 Po. 1692 (PL 214, 1021–5; X 3.8.7), 1693–4. Some time before reaching this final decision, Innocent seems to have been annoyed with both parties and contemplated applying the rule of escheat, Po. 5035 (X 1.10.3; a fuller text in the collection of Alanus, *app.* 55 [2nd ed. 1.9.3], cf. R. von Heckel, in ZRG Kan. Abt. 29 [1940] 319f.).

186 Po. 1695 (PL 214, 1027B; a shorter text in X 1.9.6).

187 *Reg. Antiquis. Lincoln* (cf. above, I n.10) I, 254 (c. 1200–05, probably not before 1203); more documents cited in K. Major, 'Episcopal Acta ...,' *Bull. Inst. Historical Research* 10 (1932–3) 148; Cheney, *Bishops' Chanceries* 12 nn. 5–6.

188 *Chron. Evesham 126.*

189 Gir. Camb. *Opp.* III, 323. — Honorius' reputation as a lawyer outside his immediate circle is evident also from the quotation, in Geoffrey of Coldingham, of his opinion in the dispute between Bishop Philip (1197–1208) and the monks of Durham: '... dominus Honorius, vir discretus, Richemundiae archidiaconus, immanitatem impiorum arguens, et populum manifeste docens, quod in his omnibus episcopus graviter deliquisset, nulla auctoritate suffultus, cum prior ecclesiae a jurisdictione episcopali se per appellationem absolvisset,' *Historiae Dunelmensis scriptores tres* (ed. J. Raine, Surtees Soc. 9; 1839) 22. For the dispute see F. Barlow, *Durham Jurisdictional Peculiars* (Oxford 1950) 22–7.

190 *Rotuli litt. patentium* I, 57; cf. Stubbs, Introd. to Walter of Coventry's *Memoriale* (Rolls Series; London 1873) II, l-li; Clay, *Early Yorks. Charters* IV, xxvi; Painter, *Reign of King John* 166f. For Honorius' motions at the Curia see Innocent III, Po. 2732 (PL 215, 836C, 837B): he was not pleading for the monks of Christ Church (as Cheney, *Bishops' Chanceries* 13 n.1 holds) but for the minority among the monks that had been won over by the king for John de Grey's candidacy. As to other lawyers active in the proceedings cf. *Traditio* 1, 301f. and 326 n.30.

191 *Rot. pat.* I, 57.

192 Pipe *Roll 3 John* (Pipe Roll Soc. New Series 14; London 1936) 160; a similar entry for Roger of St. Edmunds, *ibid.* 248. Cf. the Pipe Rolls for the following years (N.S. 15–24; London 1937–45): *4 John* 58, *6 John* 205, *6 John* 198, *7 John* 46, *8 John* 195, *9 John* 82, *10 John* 54. A

thrown into prison at Gloucester.[193] This is the last we hear of the unhappy master: five years later the archdeaconry of Richmond was held by Richard de Marisco.[194] History would have it that the interlacing cases of Master Honorius against Roger of St. Edmunds and the archbishop of York could be read by generations of canonists in four different places of the Gregorian Decretals,[195] while his work as a scholar of canon law was soon forgotten. There is no evidence that he wrote anything beside the *Summa decretalium quaestionum,* which belongs to the earlier period of his life, before he emerged as Archbishop Geoffrey's *officialis.*

'There is no evidence that he (Honorius P. L.) wrote anything beside the Summa decretalium quaestionum.' But R. Weigand could prove that Honorius wrote also the Summa decreti 'De iure canonico tractaturus' – cf. *R. Weigand,* Bemerkungen (Proceedings Salamanca) at p. 190. (P.L.)

This chronology is established by the close relations which tie Honorius' treatise to the circle of the *Summa Omnis qui iuste* (c. 1186). Saltet has demonstrated how much the two works have in common in their discussion of the celebrated controversy between Johannes Faventinus and Gandulph (if the siglum *G.* has been rightly interpreted) concerning orders conferred by heretics and schismatics;[196] an observation which can be corroborated by numerous other points of contact in the substance or formulation of doctrines.[197] Within the group of canonists belonging to this circle, connections are often particularly striking between Honorius and the *Summa De iure canonico tractaturus* of Laon MS 371*bis* (where, incidentally, a fragment from Honorius follows immediately upon the *Summa*). Compare for instance, the discussion of *reparatio clericorum lapsorum* in the three works:[198]

second debt, one palfrey, dates of 1205 and runs from *Pipe Roll 7 John* 58 to *11 John* 133. Cf. also *Rotuli litt. clausarum* I, 115; Clay, *loc. cit.*
193 *Annales Dunstapliae,* in *Annales monastici* (ed. H. R. Luard, Rolls Series; 1864–9) III, 31. Cheney, *op. cit.* 13 n.1 and Painter, *op. cit.* 236f. assume that he was imprisoned perhaps not only for financial reasons.
194 *Clay, loc. cit.*
195 Cf. notes 161, 181, 183–185.
196 Saltet, *Réordinations* 320f., 338 n.1. Honorius ultimately sides with *G.* (p. 338), the Summa *Omnis qui iuste,* with *Jo.* (p. 334 n.3). Since Gandulph did not treat of this matter in his *Sententiarum libri IV* (ed. J. von Walter, Vienna 1924), the attribution to him of the opinion of Master G. on *ordinatio ambulatoria* (Saltet 318ff.; cf. Walter, Introd. xxxvi ff.; de Ghellinck, *Mouvement théol.* 322 n.5) remains but an attractive conjecture, whereas *Jo.* is certainly John of Faenza (cf. e.g. the quotations in *Glos. ord.* to C.9 q.1). Gandulph's name is nowhere given in full in the texts relating to the controversy (see also the Bolognese glosses quoted by Saltet 354; in the text of *Sum. Omnis qui iuste* quoted p. 320 n.1, '... contra sententiam Gandulphi.' the name has been expanded by the editor; cf. p. 335 and the MSS). On the other hand, *G.* cannot stand for Gerard Pucelle, who held the opposite opinion (*ibid.* 355); and Dr. Ullmann's suggestion, *Jurid. Review* 60 (1948) 179, to refer the siglum to Willielmus Vasco (Gulielmus Guascus, *fl. c.* 1210–30) must be rejected on paleographical as well as chronological grounds; for William's career and writings cf. *Traditio* 1, 336–40; *Engl. Hist. Rev.* 60 (1945) 105.
197 E.g. below n.237. To cite only one other example, the discussion of six meanings of the term *ius naturale* (cf. *Repertorium* 201–4) recurs almost verbatim in Honorius, dist. 3 tit. 1.
198 Leipzig, Universitätsbibliothek MS 986, fol. 42v; Laon MS 371*bis.* fol. 95rb (*Summa De iure can.*) and 173va (Honorius). For another example see below, Appendix C.

Omnis qui iuste, D. 50 pr.: ... in homicida etiam dispensauit Alex. iii. ut in extra. Tanta §Presbiterum (JL 13912, *App. Conc. Lat.* 26.13) ...[199] *De iure can. tract. D. 50 pr.*: ... in homicidio autem non dispensatur circa reparationem nisi in casu, ut j(nfra). e(adem). di. De hiis clericis (c.36), nunquam autem circa promotionem. Alex. tamen circa promotum — ut in ex. de deposit. Presentium, Presbiterum (*App.* 26.6, 13) — et circa promouendum — ut in ex. tit. eod. Lator (*App.* 26.14) — dispensauit, de cuius facto non est disputandum.

Honorius, dist. 2, tit. 8, q. 4: Item queritur an papa cum homicida possit dispensare. Et non uidetur, nam contra prohibitionem domini faceret dicentis ad Dauid: 'Non edificabis michi domum quia uir sanguinis es,' vt de cons. di. i. (c.2; cf. 1 *Paralip.* 28.3, 17.4, 22.8 etc). At hoc non licet, vt. xxv. q.i. Sunt qui (c.6). Econtra uidetur, nam hodie restituuntur, vt di. L. De his clericis, j. ex. de deposit. Presbiterum. Immo promouentur, vt j. ex. de depo. Lator. Solutio: non uidetur eos qui semel post baptismum occiderunt, siue septennes et infra, siue furiosos, ex aliqua dispensatione posse promoueri, licet secus factum ab Alexandro tertio reperiatur, de cuius facto non est disputandum.

The source which Honorius employed consistently for his references to papal decretals is the so-called *Appendix Concilii Lateranensis* (c. 1181–85) and not, as Schulte assumed, the *Compilatio I*.[200] This fact in itself would not necessarily imply that the work was written before 1191/2, since in the Western schools Bernard's compilation became an accepted text much later than in Bologna. What is decisive, however, for dating Honorius' treatise not later than c. 1190 is the absence of any reference to, or knowledge of, Huguccio's great *Summa*, published between 1188 and 1190; in fact, no Bolognese glossator after Simon of Bisignano is quoted.[201]

One of the chief points of interest of the treatise lies in its original literary form, which combines the characteristics of a systematic *summa* with the dialectical technique of *quaestiones*. Honorius proposes to discuss three major fields of

---

199 According to the *Summa*, the decretal JL 13912 *Presbyterum* (addressed to Bartholomew of Exeter) would seem to be part of Alexander III's famous response to Bartholomew on the legitimation of natural children, JL 13917 *Tanta est vis*. This is also asserted, in the same context, by Ricardus Anglicus: '... Alex. enim quendam sacerdotem post homicidium commisum qui annis .xii. penitentiam agunt (*sic*) sacerdotio restituit in capitulo illo quod incipit Tanta est uis, uocatque eos inperitos qui sacerdotem reparari non posse opinantur post dignam penitentiam ...' (*Summa quaestionum* [cf. below, ch. IX] Montecassino MS 396, p. 199b). But the actual opening section of JL 13917 (*Meminimus*, cf. *App.* 33.1, *Sang.* 9.32) must have remained unknown to the two canonists.

200 Cf. *Traditio* 6, 349 n.39; additional evidence may be found even in the text printed by Schulte, *SB Vienna* 66, 60–4; e.g. p. 62 'extra. de ordinat. fi(liorum) sa(cerdotum)' (*App.* tit. 19); p. 64 'extra. de iure patr. Dilectus' (*App.* 47.2; not in *1 Comp.* but *2 Comp.* 3.24.1).

201 See e.g. Hon. *de iure patr.* 2.15 q.1: '... Vel secundum S' ius patronatus merum (mixtum?) est spirituale nec de mero iure set dumtaxat ex dispensatione canonum est ...' (Laon MS *371bis*, fol. 176r; the text of Bamberg, printed by Schulte *loc. cit.* 61 lin. 5–6 is corrupt). Cf. Simon de

canon law in as many parts (which he calls distinctions): procedure, orders and offices, marriage. Each *distinctio* consists of a number of *tituli* arranged according to the author's own system;[202] it will be noted that the opening title of each distinction deals with a general topic, prefixed, as it were, by way of an introduction to the respective field: rescripts are discussed at the beginning of the first part, a title on simony introduces the second, and two lengthy and remarkable titles on natural law are presented, surprisingly, as prolegomena to the section on marriage law.[203]

In his radical departure from the traditional order of Gratian, Honorius goes far beyond earlier decretists such as the author (Godfrey of Cologne?) of the *Summa Elegantius in iure divino* or Sicard of Cremona, both of whom loosened up the formal divisions of Gratian's text but strictly adhered to the sequence of his topics.[204] Again, by devising a system of his own, Honorius differs from Peter of Blois, the only other contemporary writer of a general treatise on canon law to abandon the legal order of the *Decreta*, who preferred to forego a systematic approach altogether.[205]

So much for the framework of the *Summa* which Honorius proceeds to fill by the abundant *quaestiones* that make up the main body of each title. As a rule, he begins a new *titulus* with a *continuatio* and *summula* in which the pertinent basic

---

Bisignano on C.16 q.7 in Schulte, *SB Vienna* 63, 322f. For a passage of doubtful reading, which only at first sight seems to quote Huguccio, cf. Appendix C.

202 Preface: '... utile duximus sub tripartita colligere distinctione, quarum (*om. Schulte*) prima continet questiones ad ordinem iudiciarium pertinentes, secunda metas (meras *Sch.*) decretales ad ministros altarisque ministeria spectantes, tertia matrimoniales ...' (Douai MS 640, fol. Ira; Schulte, *SB Vienna* 66, 58). The term 'titulus' is not used in the preface, but frequently in cross-references, e.g. 1.8 *de confessione*: '... contraria capitula habes supra t. de accusatione' (Douai fol. 7rb); 2.4 *de potestate ligandi et solvendi*: '... quere supra t. de notoriis' (fol. 16va), etc. — A list of titles is given by Schulte, *loc. cit.* 59f., but there seem to be variations in the MSS.

203 In the Douai MS these two titles (*de iure naturali, de prohibitionibus*) occupy nearly twelve columns (fol. 26rb-29rb), one-seventh of the whole codex. — It may be observed here that at the end of part III several MSS contain various additions. The last title, *de errore conditionis*, is followed in the Douai MS, fol. 42vb, by a *quaestio reportata*, 'Cuidam coniugato dampnato ad mortem donatur uita si intret monasterium ... Magister adhesit huic parti, quicquid uideatur theologis.' In Leipzig, Universitätsbibliothek MS 984, the following question is appended: 'Queritur si Lazarus resurgeret an posset uxorem repetere ...'; this problem belonged to the traditional stock of scholastic discussions, cf. the *Summa Et est sciendum* (*Glos. Stuttg.* as quoted in Gillmann, AKKR 107 [1927] 220), Huguccio (*ibid.* 221 n.1), and a collection of *quaestiones reportatae* from the school of Bazianus in Montecassino MS 396 (p. 84b-112b) q.3 (p. 86a). — Such accretions prove the use made of Honorius' work in the schools, as does also the addition of marginal notes by later hands, e.g. in MS Douai 640 (quoting decretals of Innocent III from *Comp. III*).

204 *Repertorium* 151f. 171. For the system of the *Summa Elegantius*, fifteen *partes* subdivided in *tituli*, see Gillmann, AKKR 106 (1926) 533–41, and particularly the table of contents prefixed to the Vienna codex (MS 2125, fol. 1–10r), which is authentic, as stated in the epilogue: '... Tytulatim autem opos (*sic*) hoc distinximus tytolosque omnes cum sua numerorum adiectione prenotare curauimus, ut lectori per hanc diligentiam quid quesierit sine difficultate occurat' (fol. 154).

205 *Repertorium* 221. Occasionally there is a certain topical coherence among Peter's *distinctiones*, e.g. cc. 34–42 on *coactio*; cf. also Reimarus, *Petri Blesensis opusculum de distinctionibus ...* (Berlin 1837) Introd. xxi.

concepts, definitions, and distinctions are stated; sometimes, however, the first question is proposed immediately or preceded by the *continuatio* alone.[206] In the preface, Honorius announces the literary genus of his work as *quaestiones decretales,* and in so doing, he makes use of a technical term[207] for *quaestiones* which in some way discuss problems pertaining to the interpretation of the *decreta,* i.e., of canon law, even as the *quaestiones legitimae* of the civilians pertain to the interpretation of the *leges* (a theological counterpart would be the twelfth-century *quaestiones de sacra pagina).*[208] The questions vary in type, length, and form. They are very often concerned with problems of construction and interpretation presented by the law itself, especially by antinomies in the sources; with problems of clarifying the juridical nature of or the specific rules governing a particular institute; but sometimes also with practical problems presented by a case or a hypothetical situation.[209] In most instances, the questions contain matter that admits of doubt or controversy and requires dialectical argumentation — the only type which the medieval schoolmen considered a *quaestio* in the proper sense;[210] but we find also questions which are merely a catechetical device of teaching, i.e., stating a given rule of law in the form of query and answer: 'questiones aliquando fiunt causa dubitationis, aliquando causa docendi,' as Robert of Melun observed in the parallel field of theology.[211] In the questions of the controversial type, Honorius sometimes gives alternative solutions by referring to the contrasting opinions of other authors, but more frequently he takes a stand himself. Formal variations can also be found in his way of connecting the individual questions: in most cases they are proposed, discussed, and solved one after another, but at times a series of questions is first presented each with its pro's and con's, with all the solutions postponed to the end of the section (*ad primum dicatur ..., ad secundum dicatur ...,* etc.).[212]

---

206 *Repertorium* 425. The title *de crimine* (2.8), for example, has a very long *summa;* tit. 2.4 begins without any *continuatio:* 'De potestate ligandi et soluendi queritur utrum heretici hanc habeant ...'; for various *continuationes* cf. Schulte, *SB Vienna* 66, 59f.

207 Cf. the glosses (wrongly attributed to Peter of Poitiers, cf. Landgraf, *Einführung* [above, II n.49] 99f.) to the Sentences of Peter Lombard, quoted by Saltet, *Réord.* 350, 356; 'hec questio magis est decretalis quam theologica ...'; '... hec questio decretalis est.'

208 Kantorowicz, *Studies in the Glossators* 129ff.; Kuttner, in *Studia et docum. hist. et iuris* 6, 304–8; *Traditio* 1, 320f.; Landgraf, 'Quelques collections de "Quaestiones ...",' *RTAM* 7 (1935), 122ff.; *Einführung* 41; J. de Ghellinck, Pagina et sacra pagina ...,' *Mélanges Auguste Pelzer* (Louvain 1947) 53–5.

209 E.g. *de crimine* 2.8 qq. 5, 6, 10; *de iure patr.* 2.15 qq. 3–6, 9–12 (cf. below, Appendix C).

210 R. M. Martin, *Les oeuvres de Robert de Melun* (Louvain 1932–8) I, xxxvi; Kantorowicz, 'The Quaestiones disputatae of the Glossators,' *Tijdschrift voor Rechtsgeschiedenis* 16 (1937–8) 4 and 21f., citing Boethius (cf. e.g. PL 64: 1048Dff; 1176Dff.).

211 *Quaestiones de epistolis Pauli,* prol. (*Oeuvres* II, 3.18). Cf. Grabmann, *Geschichte der scholastischen Methode* II (Freiburg 1911) 328; Kantorowicz, *Studies* 129 ('catechismal type'). For example: 'Set quid si hereticus uel excommunicatus presentet, numquid tenetur (episcopus) admittere? Resp. nequaquam, arg. xvi. q.vii. Pie, Trigentius' (Honorius, *de iure patr.* q.11, cf. Schulte, *SB Vienna* 66, 63).

212 See the question on *violentie repulsio* below, Appendix C.

This variety of matter and form shows that an attempt to define the genus of *quaestiones decretales* by more specific characteristics would do violence to the elasticity of the literary type in its actual use, although the *quaestiones decretales* and *legitimae* were certainly meant by the glossators to be distinct from the *quaestiones disputatae.* The difference, then, can be stated only approximately in terms of objectives: as a rule, *quaestiones decretales* (and *legitimae*) are more concerned with doctrinal interpretation, *enodatio*,[213] *solutio contrariorum,* while *quaestiones disputatae* undertake primarily the solution of cases. But just as cases are found in the *quaestiones decretales,* so also the *quaestiones disputatae* often include theoretical problems.[214]

What distinguishes the two species is rather the difference in origin. *Quaestiones disputatae* grew out of the students' actual classroom exercises held under the direction of their masters; the *quaestio decretalis,* on the other hand, was developed as a special glossatorial technique in the *lectio* (and in the corresponding literary production), along with the other formal styles, such as *summulae, casus, notabilia, distinctiones,* etc., to which the masters were prompted by their text. As the occasion arose, the glossator would introduce a new problem by the word *queritur, dubitatur,* or *solet queri,* then argue and solve it.[215] When the Bolognese authors in their *Summae* freely interspersed the systematic exposition and lemmatic commentary with such questions, they were following, in a way, the example of Gratian himself who — not to mention the formal organization of his second part into *causae* and *quaestiones* — had frequently employed this device in his dicta.[216]

But the incidental use of a technique is one thing, its development into the distinctive feature of a literary genus, another. Treatises composed with studied consistency of *quaestiones decretales* appeared first in the schools of the West, during the 'eighties. Apart from the probable influence of the forms of writing current among French theologians,[217] a certain impulse may well have come from the *Summa* of Sicard of Cremona, with its novel arrangement (especially of part II) into *quaestiones principales* and *incidentes.*[218] Whatever the Cremonese

---

213 The term is used by Rogerius and other civilians (cf. Kantorowicz, *Studies* 192), following perhaps the *Auctor ad Herennium* 2.10.15; also by Robert of Melun ('Questiones de epistolis Pauli ... enodate').
214 Cf. Kantorowicz, *Tijdschr.* 16, 16 (Hugolinus); Genzmer, ZRG Rom. Abt. 55 (1935) 329 (Pillius); Kuttner, *Repert.* 427 (Damasus).
215 Examples may be found in Rufinus, Stephen of Tournai, etc.; for Simon de Bisignano and the *Summa Omnis qui iuste* cf. the texts printed by J. Juncker, ZRG Kan. Abt. 15 (1926) 326–500, *passim.*
216 D. 6 pr.; D. 14 pr.; D. 19 pr.; D. 20 pr.; D. 23 p.c.11, p.c.13; D. 27 pr.; D. 33 pr.; D. 34 p.c.12; D.37 pr.; D. 39 pr.; D. 50 pr.; D. 54 p.c.21; D. 63 p.c.34, p.c.35; D. 65 p.c.8; D. 68 pr.; D. 74 pr.; D. 92 p.c.3 (§1); D. 95 p.c.2 (§1); D. 99pr. — to cite examples from pt. I only.
217 For theological *quaestiones* originating in the *lectio* cf. Landgraf, RTAM 7, 124f.; *Einführung* 41; P. Glorieux, 'Sentences,' DThC 14 (1941) 1873; 'Sommes théologiques,' *ibid.* 2341ff.
218 *Repertorium* 152. For incidental *quaestiones* in pt.I see e.g. the section *de continentia* (=D. 26ff.): 12 questions.

master's own scholastic affiliation — and we have every reason to doubt that he belonged at any time to the school of Bologna[219] — it is significant that one of the first writings in the new style was composed on the model of his work by a Parisian student: the *Summula decretalium quaestionum* of Evrard of Ypres, monk of Clairvaux, who simply epitomized Sicard's treatise by way of the catechetical query-and-answer method.[220] A number of such superficial transformations of existing *summae* into 'questiones que fiunt causa docendi' can be found in the orbit of the French school;[221] the mature stage of the *quaestio decretalis,* however, was to be reached only where all the didactic and dialectical possibilities of the new form were put to use for a lively, searching exposition of canon law.

Such *quaestiones decretales* seem to have been not merely published in writing but also delivered orally on a day set aside for this purpose every week, as was customary for *quaestiones disputatae.* Thus the work of Honorius is described in one manuscript[222] as 'questiones ueneriales', and this designation appears credible if we consider that, preceding Honorius by a few years only, Gerald of Wales used to discuss *causae decretales* in Paris on Sundays before an overflowing and enthralled audience (as he boasts),[223] whereas his regular lectures on the Decretum were given twice daily throughout the week.[224]

Of the full grown type of *quaestiones decretales,* the work of Honorius remains the leading representative, its closest counterpart being the *Summa quaestionum* 'Circa ius naturale uarie solent fieri questiones,' ascribed to Ricardus Anglicus, which will be discussed below.[225] As further examples of this class of writings we may list the following:[226]

219 Cf. Kuttner, 'Réflexions sur les brocards des glossateurs,' *Mélanges Joseph de Ghellinck* (Gembloux 1951) II, 767–92, esp. 783ff., where the question of Sicard's French connections is discussed.
220 *Repert.* 187–90.
221 E.g. several fragments ('Questio si iure naturali'; 'Dubitatur a quibusdam') in Arras MS 271, cf. *Repertorium* 181, 154 (French connections are also to be assumed for the prologue 'Omnia poma vetera et nova,' ibid. 154; cf. the beginning of Peter Comestor's glosses on St. John's Gospel, Landgraf, *Einführung* 103). See further the *Lucubratiunculae* of Egidius (above, V n.135) and, for a later period, a set of glosses in Paris, B. N. MS 3886A, with queries and answers based on Huguccio's *Summa.*
222 Zwettl MS 162, fol. 179r, as cited above.
223 Gir. Camb. *De rebus a se gestis* 2.1 (*Opp.* I, 45f.). His description makes it clear that these were not *quaestiones disputatae*: it was he himself, not the *auditores,* who argued the *causae decretales,* using *legum et canonum rationes* and *rhetoricae persuasiones.* Gerald has preserved the inception, 'Proposueram prius audire ...' (p. 46f.) and the topic of his first *quaestio* (p. 47): 'utrum iudex secundum allegata iudicare debeat an iuxta conscientiam,' which was one of the most widely discussed problems for civilians and canonists alike; cf. references in Kantorowicz, *Studies in the Glossators* 21 n.19; *Glos. ord.* ad C.3 q.7 c.4 v. *audit*; ad C.30 q.5 p.c.9 v. *credenda*; ad X 1.31.1 v. *quod canones censent,* etc.
224 *Opp.* I, 48.
225 Ch. IX.
226 The *quaestiones* of Angers MS 312, fol. 129r-136v (*Repertorium* 251) are, however, to be eliminated: the fragment can be identified as q.5-q.10 c.15 of Robert Courson's *Summa.*

(1) Munich MS lat. 16083, fol. 52va-73va: *Summa quaestionum* in the order of the Decretum, beg. 'Queritur utrum quicquid est contra ius naturale sit peccatum mortale,' incomplete, related in parts to the teachings of Honorius and his group, c. 1185–90;[227]
(2) Paris, Bibliothèque nationale, MS lat. 3934A, fol. 102r-v and 103vb: fragment of systematic *quaestiones* on marriage (Grat. C.27, qq.1 and 2), beg. 'Queritur utrum diuisi ponantur hec tria,' written between 1179 and *Comp. I*, with references to a Master G.;[228]
(3) Avranches MS 149, fol. 129–130v: *Summa quaestionum*, beg. 'In lege sic describuntur sponsalia' (rubr. *De sponsalibus et matrimonio*), perhaps of Norman origin, after *Comp. I*;[229]
(4) Douai MS 649: loosely connected *Summulae quaestionum,* scattered over a miscellaneous and misbound volume (fol. 26–28v, 43–59 [with a series of *quaest. disputatae* inserted fol. 54v-57v],[230] 149v–152v, 153–155v, 166–169v), probably collected by several students of a French master, not before 1205;
(5) Vienna MS lat. 2163, fol. 52–74v: *Summa quaestionum*, beg. 'Videndum est quid sit constitutio' (rubr. *De constitutionibus*), probably Bolognese, c. 1205–1206, on select titles of the Decretals in the order of *Comp. I*.[231]

Thereafter, at Bologna, the style of the *summa quaestionum decretalium* would occasionally leave its mark also on the literary elaboration of cases and problems that had originally been disputed in class (*quaestiones redactae* as distinct from *reportatae*), as can be observed first with Damasus, and later, e.g., with Johannes de Deo and Johannes Andreae.[232] Treatises on procedure with an admixture of the form of the *summa quaestionum* — a type which occurs for the first time in the *Summa de ordine iudiciorum* of the civilian Johannes Bassianus[233] — were to become more frequent during the thirteenth century: we may cite, e.g., the

---

227 Our thanks are due Abbé G. Fransen for contributing this interesting discovery.
228 The MS has been reexamined after the first mention made in *Repert.* 255. (The fragment fol. 103ra-va belongs to a treatise on procedure.)
229 The codex, from Mont-Saint-Michel, contains the *Collectio decretalium Abrincensis*, the *Comp. I* and miscellaneous other canonistic material (cf. e.g. *Traditio* 1, 299 n.40, 312 nn.19–20, 323 n.17 [ii]). Immediately preceding the *Summa quaestionum* is a group of *quaestiones disputatae*, of French origin, after 1210 (beg. 'Dominus papa contulit cuidam monasterio tale priuilegium').
230 These may belong together with other *quaest. disp.* in the same codex, fol. 143–148v ('Papa scribit episcopo parisiensi ...'), fol. 156r. Cf. *Trad.* 1, 324 n.22a.
231 *Ibid.* 323 n.17 (vii); followed by *quaest. disputatae* discussed *ibid.* 323ff.; cf. Ullmann, *Med. Papalism* 210f.
232 *Repert.* 427 (Damasus; a *summula* precedes e.g. his *quaestio de causa propr. et poss.*: 'Hec materia difficilis est et bene et diligenter exposita circa litteram ...,' MS Vat. Borgh. lat. 261, fol. 27va); *Traditio* 1, 322 n.9 (Johannes de Deo); the *Quaestiones mercuriales* of Johannes Andreae are disputations and at the same time a commentary on the *Regulae iuris* of the *Liber Sextus*.
233 Seckel, 'Ueber neuere Editionen ...,' ZRG Rom. Abt. 21 (1900) 289 n.1; Kuttner, in *Studia et docum. hist. et iuris* 6, 307.

fragment 'Nota quod quicumque agit in iudicio,' from the school of Tancred;[234] the *Libelli* of Roffredus Beneventanus; the *Summa aurea* of William of Drogheda; the *Summula quaestionum* of Albertus Galeottus; the *Tractatus de maleficiis* of Albertus Gandinus, etc.[235]

It can reasonably be assumed that Master Honorius at the time he wrote his treatise (c. 1186–90) was staying in the schools of France. Like the author of the *Summa Omnis qui iuste,* he was in the habit of using the names of French dioceses in examples illustrating a point under discussion;[236] and Paris is suggested as the actual place of his teaching by a *quaestio* on the usurious character of a certain type of loan practiced among Parisian students.[237] But soon after publication of his *quaestiones decretales,* and before October 1192,[238] Honorius must have returned to England and associated there with other masters of canon law who were definitely teaching in that country. Thomas of Marlborough, in his account of the interview he had in 1203 with Hubert Walter and three of his clerks, viz. Honorius, John of Tynemouth, and Simon of Southwell, calls the three without any distinction *magistri mei in scolis.* Obviously Thomas is referring in this context, not to the time when he studied theology in Paris under Stephen Langton, but to his canon law studies in England.[239] It is to the other two masters named by him in connection with Honorius, and to the canonistic production of the English school in the 'nineties that we shall now turn our attention.

VII. The Circle of John of Tynemouth:

The Caius Glosses and the Royal Quaestiones

One of the principal records of the Anglo-Norman school is a late twelfth-century copy of the Decretum containing a wealth of contemporary glosses, now MS 676

234 Rome, Biblioteca Casanatense MS 1910, fol. 73r-v; Avranches MS 149, fol. 135rb-va.
235 For Drogheda see Wahrmund and de Zulueta *loc. cit.* (above, III n.69); for Gandinus and Galeottus, cf. Kantorowicz, in ZRG Rom. Abt. 44 (1924) 277, 294; for Roffredus, Schulte, *Gesch.* II, 78.
236 Paris and Chartres: Hon. 1.4 *de occultis;* 2.5 *de clavibus;* cf. Saltet, *op. cit.* 319 n.3.
237 Hon. 2.10 *de usuris*: '... Item queritur de culcitis que parisius a scolaribus suscipiuntur mutuata certa pecunia sub hac conuentione ut singulis mensibus de mutuo remittatur unus denarius quasi in precium locationis, utrum scolares sint usurarii? ... nec excusantur ex dispensatione episcopi parisiensis, set nec ex pape indulgentia possent excusari cum utriusque testamenti pagina sit usura detestata, ut xxv. q.i. Sunt qui (c.6),' Laon MS 371*bis*, fol. 174va. Cf. *Sum. Omnis qui iuste* to C. 14 q.4 *in fine:* '... Item de clericis qui in scolis sunt solet queri an usurarij sint; hac enim conditione x. uel xii. solidos commodant pro culcitis ut quolibet mense denarius de sorte remittatur ...; set quid de episcopo parisiensi qui hoc aprobat et dispensat cum clericis qui parisius sunt ... nec maior eo, quia contra ius naturale non potest dispensare,' Rouen MS 743, fol. 83rb. — The students in the hospices at Paris had to rent or to provide their own matresses, as Father A. Gabriel has kindly pointed out to us by letter; cf. e.g. Jacques de Vitry: 'Audivi cum essem Parisius de quodam scolari quod in morte culcitram suam dimisit in manus socii sui ...' (*Exempla* ed. Th. F. Crane, London 1890; no.115).
238 Note 166 above.
239 *Chron. Evesh.* 126; for his studies under Langton see *ibid.* 232f.

(283) of Gonville and Caius College, Cambridge. So many of the glosses are ascribed to *Jo. Ti.* or *Jo. de Ti.* that we may assume they were based on lectures given by this master.[240] Often the same gloss cites *Jo. Ti.* and *S. de S.*,[241] a master whose opinion is referred to in a large number of other glosses in this codex and once or twice in the glosses to an abbreviation of Peter of Poitiers' Sentences in MS Lambeth Palace 142 (from Lanthony).[242] There can be no question that we have here Thomas of Marlborough's masters, John of Tynemouth and Simon of Southwell.[243] It would be interesting, moreover, if some of the frequent quotations *secundum al.* should prove to refer to early lectures in England of Alanus — his first work in Bologna cannot be dated before 1206, considerably later than the glosses of the Caius manuscript — but it must be conceded that in nearly all cases the context makes the reading *secundum alios* equally, or even more probable.[244] However, there are other English canonists quoted. Twice at least we find the theologian John of Cornwall,[245] and once a gloss is signed by Master Nicholas de Aquila, presumably the dean of Chichester (*c.* 1197–1217) who was elected bishop of that see in 1209 though apparently never consecrated.[246]

The glosses reveal the varied influences characteristic of works of the Anglo-Norman canonists in their connection with teachings of the *Summa Omnis qui iuste* and of the School of Vacarius;[247] in their references to Placentinus and

---

240 *Repertorium* 22f.
241 E.g. fols. 64r, *193ra, *194ra, *198ra and below, note 261. (The asterisk denotes glosses printed below, in Appendix D.)
242 Fol. 88va, where 'Simon de suū.' is quoted on *pollutio nocturna*. (These glosses will be discussed on another occasion. E. R.)
243 E. Rathbone in an unpublished lecture (Oxford 1939) and 'John of Cornwall,' RTAM 17 (1950) 51f. and nn.33–37. The identification of *Jo. ti.* has been suggested independently by C. R. Cheney, *Bishops' Chanceries* 13f. and by Professor J. C. Russell in a letter dated 24 April 1945.
244 Fols. 2va, 31ra, 80vb, 134ra, 136va, *138va, *178va, *181ra (iii), 183rb, *187va (ii) *et passim*.
245 Fols. 99rb, 196rb (on marriage), printed in RTAM 17, 51, where John's career and writings are discussed.
246 Fol. *129va. Master Nicholas de Aquila occurs as dean in several Chichester charters, cf. *Chichester Chartulary* (ed. W. D. Peckham, Sussex Record Soc. 46; 1946) Nos. 28, 194, 196, 197, 201 (cf. 407), 302, 341; *The Chartulary of the Priory of St. Pancras of Lewes* (ed. L. F. Salzmann, Sussex Rec. Soc. 38; 1932) I, 110; cf. *ibid.* I, 65: 'Nicholas son of Walter de Aquila' (*c.* 1170). For his election to the bishopric see Dunstable Annals s.a. 1209, in *Annales monastici* III, 31; Oseney Annals, *ibid.* IV, 54. On the Norman family L'Aigle cf. G. M. Cooper, 'Some Accounts of Michelham Priory in Arlington,' *Sussex Archaeological Collections* 6 (1853) 129f. — Nicholas would seem to have been a pluralist if he, and not another master of the same name was the schoolmaster of Avranches who opposed, *c.* 1197–8, any new election to fill that see while the case of the bishop-elect, William de Chemillé (who had been uncanonically transferred to Angers), was pending in Rome, cf. Innocent III, Po. 457, 454, 630 (PL 214, 419f. and 630; *Coll. Gilb.* 1.61, cf. Heckel, ZRG Kan. Abt. 29 [1940] 182f.; for William's case see Po. 108, 575; for his antecedents as archdeacon of Richmond see above, VI n.181).
247 For *Omnis qui iuste* cf. *Repert.* 23, also fol. 1r on natural law. A gloss quoting Vacarius on custom (fol. 4va, D. 11 c.4: '... Vac. dicit quod consuetudo populi in contrarium nitentis [?] tollit legem set non uincit ...,' cf. *Vac.* 1.8 n.35; n.32 [p.18] de Zulueta lxxvii) will be discussed elsewhere.

several of the Bolognese civilians, Bulgarus, Martinus and Johannes Bassianus;[248] to Bolognese canonists, Rolandus (as master and pope),[249] Rufinus,[250] Huguccio and his school,[251] Cardinalis,[252] Albertus (as master and pope),[253] Bazianus,[254] and especially to John of Faenza[255] and Gandulphus;[256] to theologians of the French school, Gilbert de la Porrée and his followers,[257] Peter the Chanter,[258] and the English masters Robert Pullen[259] and Bartholomew.[260]

Opinions drawn from such diversified sources lent color and life to the discussions. John of Tynemouth and Simon of Southwell frequently took issue with one another and it is clear that the two were rivals.[261] At one point the gloss reads: 'Master Simon of Southwell boasts that he debated this matter at Bologna. Master John of Tynemouth concedes the question is difficult but he solves it thus.'[262] Evidently John had not enjoyed the same advantages as his colleague.

The glosses are in the form of a *reportatio*. Citations are usually in the third person but often a direct quotation is given with the attribution to John of Tynemouth at the end.[263] In the solution of the questions the master shows a wide knowledge and a discriminating use of the sources and of earlier commentators. His illustrations are drawn from a variety of sources, ranging from geometry and the classical *auctores* to feudalism,[264] as well as the legal and theological works already noted. The discussions are full of topical interest. Events and protagonists of the Becket controversy crop up frequently,[265] special customs of the English or French Church occasionally.[266] The validity of papal rescripts, or of a custom

---

248 Placentinus fols. 137r, 137rb; Bulgarus, Martinus, Joannes Cremonensis fols. 107va, 137r, rb; Jo. Bassianus (Cremonensis) fol. 115vb.
249 Fols. *178vb, *187va (i, as pope); 183rb, *187va (ii-iv, Rolandus).
250 Fols. *187va (ii), *194rb, 215vb.
251 Fols. 31ra, 52rb, 80vb, 93vb, 133va, 140ra, *178vb. 'scole H(uguccionis?)' fol. 140rb.
252 Fols. 134ra, 136va, 181ra, 184va, *187va (ii, iii), *194rb.
253 Fol. 134ra: 'arg. contra Cardinalem et papam Gregorium 8 (*sic*) antequam esset papa, qui dicebant omnes decimas dari intuitu personarum'; fol. *187va (ii-iv, 'Albertinus'). For the use of arabic numerals cf. *Repertorium* 205 n.3.
254 Fol. 185r ('secundum Bazan.').
255 Fols. 31rb, 43vb, 48vb, 80va, 81ra, 94rb, 95va, 112va, 113vb, 121va, 122va, 123ra, 140va, 168va, *169vb, *187va (ii-iv), *194rb.
256 Fols. 31rb ('contra Jo. Fauentinum'), 32ra, 43vb, 48vb, 81ra, 113vb, 115vb, 122va, 128ra, 140ra, *165vb, 168va, *178vb, 196rb, 215vb ('Rufinus aliter').
257 Fols. 115ra, *154rb.
258 Fols. 165vb, *167ra. 217rb.
259 Fol. *165vb (with Gandulph).
260 Fols. 126rb, *201va.
261 Fols. 99va, 116ra, 131ra, 140va, *193ra, *194ra.
262 Fol. *198ra.
263 E.g. fols. 181ra 'nec ego audeo concedere,' contradicting Cardinalis; *181ra (ii), *184va. The gloss fol. *187va (i) says 'Malo ergo dicere ...' but is not signed.
264 Geometry fol. 216ra; classical authors fols. 2ra, 46ra (Cicero), 113ra (Horace), 23vb (Juvenal), 162va (Seneca) etc.; feudalism fol. *138va.
265 Fols. 71rb, *101rb, *164rb.
266 Fols. *44rb, *123rb, *138va, *173rb.

opposed to a statement in the Decretum,[267] the relative severity of *leges* and *canones*,[268] the definition of what constitutes simoniacal practices, with reference for example to ecclesiastical judges or to notaries,[269] the relations between Christians and Jews,[270] the whole field of marriage law,[271] are the subject of careful analysis.

Even more topical are the discussions in a series of canonistic *quaestiones disputatae* in a manuscript from the Abbey of St. Augustine's, Canterbury, now British Museum, Royal 9.E.vii.[272] Here we find debates on current problems: references to a bishop who was at once papal legate and royal chancellor,[273] who can be no other than William Longchamp;[274] to problems arising out of the Crusade and capture of Richard Coeur de Lion;[275] to the imprisonment of the bishop of Beauvais in 1196, which seems to have been a standing joke to his contemporaries;[276] to the relative authority of the powers of a legate as against those of a royal official in Normandy carrying out the instructions of his master who, absent on the Crusade, was under the pope's protection.[277]

In the discussion and solution of the cases a number of masters are named. Master Nicholas,[278] whose disputations seem to be the core of the *reportatio*, may well be Nicholas de Aquila; master *Jo. de Thi.*[279] is certainly John of Tynemouth. Master Simon of Derby, cited in the solutions to one or two of the *quaestiones*, seems to be the master of that name who witnessed several Lichfield charters;[280] and if the surname should be meant to distinguish him from the more frequently

---

267 Fols. *44rb, 123rb, *129va (custom), *173r, *173v (rescripts).
268 Fol. *169vb.
269 Fols. 69rb, *129va.
270 Fol. *184va.
271 Fol. *178va *et seqq.*
272 Fols. 191–99; cf. G. F. Warner and J. P. Gilson, *Catalogue of Western Manuscripts in the Old Royal and King's Collections* I (London 1921) 295; Kuttner, *Repertorium*, 251f.; Ullmann, *Med. Papalism* 191–3, 200f. (and Index s.v. *Quaest. London.*); Cheney, *Bishops' Chanceries* 13.
273 Fol. 197v: 'Cancellarius legatus a domino papa per totam Angliam constitutus ...'.
274 Cf. *Repertorium* 252 n.3. Dr. Ullmann (*op. cit.* 153 n.4, 200) refers this to Archbishop Hubert Walter; but when Hubert became chancellor in 1199 he held no longer legatine authority, since Innocent III did not want to see the cumulation of the two politically incompatible offices repeated, cf. Brooke, *Engl. Church and the Papacy* 221.
275 Fol. 195rb: 'Rex Anglie cum a peregrinatione Ierosolimitana rediret ab imperatore Alemanie captus est ...' and n.277.
276 Fol. 195rb-va; cf. Ullmann, *op. cit.* 191; Rog. Hov. IV, 16, 21–3, 40f.; Matthew Paris, *Historia Anglorum* (ed. F. Madden, Rolls Series; London 1866–9) II, 59f.; *Chronica maiora* (ed. H. R. Luard, R. S.; 1872–83) II, 421–2.
277 Fol. 195v; cf. *Repertorium* 252 and n.3 for the date (1192) of the incident referred to.
278 Fols. 193va, 195va, vb, 196ra, 197ra, rb.
279 Fols. 191ra, 195rb.
280 Fol. 191va (S. de derebi), probably also 191rb (S. de rebi). For Simon of Derby cf. H. E. Savage, *The Great Register of Lichfield Cathedral Known as Magnum Registrum Album* (William Salt Archaeological Society, Collections for a History of Staffordshire, 1924 [1926]) Nos. 173 (c. 1193), 114, 356 (before 1208); *Registrum Antiquiss. Lincoln* (above, I n.10) III, 400; V, 36; *Oseney Cartulary* (above, VI n.166) V, 66; London, B. M. Harleian MS 3650, fols. 38r, 38v, 39r, 43v; Harl. 3868, fol. 15ra.

cited Master *Si.*,²⁸¹ the latter is probably to be identified with Simon of Southwell rather than with Simon of Apulia,²⁸² whom we have met before as the chief antagonist of Master Honorius. Master John of Kent is presumably the clerk of Archbishop Hubert Walter who was chancellor of St. Paul's (in 1204), a royal justice, and perhaps the author of a lost work on the Decretum and a *Summa de poenitentia*.²⁸³ There is finally one reference to Master Gregory,²⁸⁴ who may possibly be Master Gregory of London, author of the *Mirabilia Romae*, who betrays some interest in legal antiquities,²⁸⁵ or the as yet unidentified *Gre.* quoted in the *Summa Quamvis leges seculares*.²⁸⁶

The English masters cited in these two manuscripts²⁸⁷ are virtually unknown in the history of canon law. Their teaching careers must belong to the period c. 1188–98, for the lectures recorded in the Caius glosses were given after the pontificate of Gregory VIII, at a time when the work of Huguccio and his school was already known; the *Quaestiones* discuss events of the years 1192–6; and both the glosses and disputations antedate the pontificate of Innocent III. The fact, already noted, that the masters used an English collection of decretals compiled during

281 Fols. 191vb, 196rb, 195ra 'ut in bro(cardo) magistri Simonis.'
282 Cf. above, ch. VI at n.169ff. At the time the disputations of the Royal MS were held, the dean of York would not have been active in the schools.
283 Fols. 195ra, rb, 196ra. Cf. S. Kuttner, in *Traditio* 2, 494 n.9. A Master John of Kent witnesses a charter of Geoffrey, bishop-elect of Lincoln, c. 1173/82 (*Reg. Ant. Linc.* II, 33). He or another of the same name was a justice at Northampton in June 1190 (B. M. Cotton MS Claud. D.xii. fol. 88). As clerk of Hubert Walter he was given the church of Appledore by Felix, prior of Dover (Lambeth MS 241, fol. 227v-228) and witnessed a number of the archbishop's charters (*ibid.* fol. 189v; Canterbury, Dean and Chapter Muniments, Reg. A, fol. 157v; Cambridge, University Library MS Ll.ii.15, fol.7r-v; B. M. Harleian MS 391, fol. 105*) and three charters of Bishop William of London (B. M. Cotton MSS App. xxi, fol. 56v [twice] and Vesp. F. xv, fol. 185v). As chancellor of St. Paul's he attests two charters, cf. M. Gibbs, *Early Charters ... of St. Paul* (above, II n.59) No. 58 and Historical Manuscripts Commission, *Ninth Report* (London 1883) Appendix p. 42a, No. A 1521. He received a prebend from Stephen Langton in 1214, cf. K. Major, *Acta Stephani Langton Cantuariensis archiepiscopi A.D. 1207–1228* (Canterbury and York Soc. 50; Oxford 1950) 17, but whether he ever belonged to Langton's household (K. Major, pp. xxxvii, 19, 47) remains uncertain.

For John of Kent cf. J. Goering, The 'Summa de penitentia' of John of Kent, BMCL 18 (1988) 13–31. (P.L.)
284 For Master Gregory of London cf. R. Weigand, Art. Gregory of London, Lex MA 4 (1989) 1683. (P.L.)
285 G. Rushforth, 'Magister Gregorius de mirabilibus urbis Romae ...,' *Journal of Roman Studies* 9 (1919) 18, 58, cf. M. R. James, in *Engl. Hist. Rev.* 32 (1917) 554; Manitius, *Geschichte der lat. Lit.* (above, V n.129) III, 250, 252.
286 *Repertorium* 206 n.1 and below, ch. IX n.343.
287 Future studies will tell whether other writings can be attributed to them, especially to Simon of Southwell and John of Tynemouth. Cf. *Repert.* 25 for the siglum *S.* occurring in glosses of the Anglo-Norman school on the Decretum, Durham MS C.ii.1; *ibid.* 251 for *gl. Vac.* 4.36 n.5 ('secundum Simonem'); and *Traditio* 6, 349 n.40, for glosses of an English Master *Jo.* on the *Appendix Conc. Lat.* in Leipzig, Univ. MS 1242. As to the Decretum in Paris, B. N. MS 3905B, the glosses of Master *tv.* (*ty., tu.*, cf. *Repert.* 40) prove upon reexamination to belong to a somewhat earlier canonist of the French school.

this period, a copy of which is found in the present MS Tanner 8 of the Bodleian Library,[288] and the evidence from charters to be given in the next chapter point to the same conclusion.

VIII. Centers of Legal Study in England

In recounting his interview with Hubert Walter and the three clerks who had been his masters in the schools,[289] Thomas of Marlborough gives no indication of the place where he studied under Honorius, John of Tynemouth and Simon of Southwell. To which schools was he referring? He himself, we learn elsewhere, had lectured in both laws before his profession, in Exeter and Oxford.[290] *A priori*, therefore, one should be tempted to place the three masters in the schools of Oxford. Nevertheless, for the sake of completeness, let us first consider other possible centers.

There is some evidence concerning the study of law at the cathedral schools of Exeter and Lincoln.[291] At Exeter, Bartholomew — like his friend Baldwin, the future archbishop, a frequent papal delegate — composed his widely read Penitential, and Thomas of Marlborough taught for some time in the city. At Lincoln, students interested in law seem to have gathered c. 1160–75, and Bishops Walter and Hugh patronized such men as John of Cornwall, Simon of Southwell and John of Tynemouth,[292] to name only masters we have met above.

Walter, bishop of Lincoln: This was Walther of Coutances (de Constantiis), archdeacon of Oxford 1175–1182, bishop of Lincoln 1183, archbishop of Rouen from 1184 or 1185, who died in 1207. He addressed to the bishop of Exeter 'super quibusdam negociis iuris librum unum', see *John Bale*, Index Britanniae scriptorum, ed. *R.L. Poole* (Oxford 1902) 103 [A second edition, by Poole and M. Bateson, was published in Cambridge 1990]. I shall give fuller bibliography and discuss the possibility of other writings by Walther of Coutances in an article planned for a Festschrift to appear in 1994. (S.K.) – I discussed this commentary by Kuttner in my note, Stephan Kuttner's last discovery on Walter of Coutances. A commemoration 110 years after Kuttner's birthday, in: BMCL 33 (2017) 229s. (P.L.)

But it must be remembered that Bartholomew's treatise is very old-fashioned in method and betrays no technical canonistic training on the part of its author;[293]

---

288 Above, ch. I at n.23; cf. below, Appendix A.
289 *Chron. Evesham* 126.
290 *Ibid.* 267. The late Hermann Kantorowicz, *Bractonian Problems* (Glasgow 1941) 17 n.2 challenged the reading 'apud Exoniam *et Oxoniam*,' but see F. M. Powicke and A. B. Emden in their revised edition of H. Rashdall, *The Universities of Europe in the Middle Ages* (Oxford 1936) III, 18 n.1; H. G. Richardson, 'Azo, Drogheda and Bracton,' *Engl Hist. Rev.* 59 (1944) 41 n.3.
291 For the English cathedral schools cf. K. Edwards, *op. cit.* (above, VI n.169) 187ff., 187 at n.3. Further details will be given in E. Rathbone's forthcoming book (above, I n.6).
292 Cf. E. Rathbone, RTAM 17, 50f. and below, nn.320, 330.
293 Above, ch. IV nn.89–95.

and the school of Lincoln, towards the end of the century, the period of the works under discussion, was renowned for theology rather than law.[294]

'The school of Lincoln, towards the end of the century...was renowned for theology rather than law.' But we have many sources for the study of law in Lincoln already in the second half of the twelfth century. A survey is given in my article, The Origins of Legal Science in England in the Twelfth Century: Lincoln, Oxford and the Career of Vacarius, in: *M. Brett/ K.G. Cushing* (ed.), Readers, Texts and Compilers in the Earlier Middle Ages. Studies in Medieval Canon Law in Honour of Linda Fowler-Magerl (Ashgate 2009) 165–182. (P.L.)

Latterly the claims of Northampton to be the chief center of learning in England for a brief period have been emphasized,[295] and to the evidence already produced one may add that Vacarius in his recently published theological treatise *Contra multiplices errores* refers to a stay in Northampton *causa studendi*,[296] which we must probably interpret as meaning, to teach. An interesting manuscript from the priory of St. Andrew's, which includes fragments of at least one work of the Anglo-Norman school and of collections of decretals,[297] shows that canon law was not neglected. But the majority of the references to the schools of Northampton concern the *artes* and science, Daniel of Morley stating specifically that he chose this city rather than any other because there the preponderance of law had not swamped other branches of learning.[298]

Although one would hesitate to suggest lectures on canon law in a monastery as early as the twelfth century, this possibility cannot be entirely ruled out for St. Alban's, where some time after 1183 Master Warin, *in decretis lector nominatissimus*, succeeded Alexander Nequam as master of the schools.[299] He was the nephew of Abbot Warin (1183–95), known himself as a man of great learning and, with his brother Matthew, a former student of medicine at Salerno. It is difficult to establish where the younger Warin acquired his fame as reader in canon law. All we know is that he had turned to the study of *leges et decreta* at the time his uncles left the world to enter the monastery. Du Boulay has claimed him for the

---

294 Gir. Camb. *Opp.* I, 93; cf. R. W. Hunt, 'English Learning in the Late Twelfth Century,' *Transactions of the Royal Historical Soc.*[4] 19 (1936) 21.
295 H. G. Richardson, 'The Oxford Law School under John,' *Law Quart. Rev.* 57 (1941) 327f. and 'The Schools of Northampton in the Twelfth Century,' *Engl. Hist. Rev.* 56 (1941) 595ff. Cheney, *Bishops' Chanceries* 126f. is, however, not convinced that the Baltimore formulary (above, III n.67) is based on a collection made at Northampton, as Mr. Richardson suggests.
296 Ed. Ilarino da Milano (above, II n.41) 527 §19, cf. Introd. 89.
297 Oxford, Oriel College MS 53; cf. *Repertorium* 199ff., 295; Holtzmann, 'Die Register Papst Alexanders ...' (above, I n.21) 19ff.; 'Über eine Ausgabe ...' (above, I n.14) 23 Nos. 29, 30c; Kuttner, *Traditio* 6, 347 n.25; above, IV n.98. The origin of the Oriel *Quaestiones* (*Repert.* 249) will be discussed elsewhere.
298 Hunt, *loc. cit.* 24 and 27.
299 *Gesta abbatum monasterii sancti Albani* (ed. H. T. Riley, Rolls Series; London 1867–9) I, 194–6. For Alexander Nequam's views on the sources of civil and canon law see H. Kantorowicz, 'A Medieval Grammarian on the Sources of Law,' *Tijdschrift voor Rechtsgeschiedenis* 15 (1936–7) 25–47.

school of Paris, but his only evidence is a letter of recommendation, written by the elder Warin (then prior) to Richard of St. Victor (d. 1173) on behalf of an unnamed *nepos meus*, its bearer.[300] At any event, we are told in the *Gesta abbatum* that during the tenure of Master Warin the school of St. Alban's flourished, and the library was augmented. But no trace of his lecturing has been recovered thus far, unless we are permitted to refer to him a quotation, 'et gar. ibi glosat ...,' in an early thirteenth-century apparatus of glosses on Gratian.[301]

While Exeter, Lincoln and Northampton undoubtedly enjoyed some reputation as centers of legal study at one time or another, there can be no question that Oxford retained its position as the chief school of law. That Vacarius taught there in Stephen's reign appears certain.[302]

'That Vacarius taught there (in Oxford P. L.) in Stephen's reign appears certain.' New research since 1976 had the result that Vacarius probably never taught in Oxford, but that legal studies in Oxford in civil and canon law using Vacarius' Liber pauperum started only with Vacarius' students probably between 1185 amd 1190 (so-called 'pauperiste'). Master Vacarius himself might have taught mainly in Lincoln; cf. *R.W. Southern*, Master Vacarius and the beginning of an English academic tradition, in: *J.J.G. Alexander* (ed.), Medieval learning and literature. Essays presented to Richard William Hunt (Oxford 1976) 257–286; *P. Stein*, Vacarius and the civil law, in: *Ch. Brooke* et al. (ed.), Church and government in the middle ages. Essays presented to C. R. Cheney (Cambridge 1976) 119–137; *L. E. Boyle*, The beginnings of legal studies at Oxford, Viator 14 (1983) 107–131; and my summary 'The origins of legal science in England' – here at p. 208. (P.L.)

Whether he resumed teaching, there or elsewhere than at Northampton, at a later date, we do not know. But it seems probable that masters established themselves as teachers of canon law in Oxford during the pontificate of Alexander III, since Robert Blund repaired there frequently about 1175 to debate legal questions.[303] Some years later such discussions were enlivened by the feud between the followers of Vacarius, nicknamed *pauperistae* from their reading of the *Liber pauperum*, and Martin, a clerk who had studied civil law for a time at Bologna — presumably the same Master Martin who witnessed, with Master Honorius, the award of John of Cornwall and Robert of Melun in October 1192.[304] Constantly in opposition to the other masters, Martin, who had received a thorough grounding in the liberal arts before beginning law, taunted them, at a gathering of scholars where cases were being heard before the justices, with having jumped from the

---

300 C. E. Bulaeus, *Historia Universitatis Parisiensis* II (Paris 1665) 304f. The letter is in *Chart. Univ. Par.* I, 40 No. 38. — A Master Warin, *officialis* of the archdeacon of Bedford, witnessed acts of St. Hugh of Lincoln c. 1193–8, cf. Cheney, *op. cit.* 145, n.6.
301 Douai MS 592 (cf. *Repert.* 36) fol. 93r, to C.2 q.6 c.29. But since this canon is taken from civil law (*Dig.* 49.4.1 and 3), *gar.* may also stand for Garnerius (Irnerius).
302 De Zulueta, *Liber paup.* xvi f.
303 Petr. Bles. *ep.* 62 (PL 207, 185).
304 *Oseney Cartulary* IV, 431; cf. above, VI n.166.

study of the Disticks of Cato to that of the Institutes,[305] as on another occasion he made fun of Hubert Walter's Latin.[306]

Toward the end of the century, students from overseas were to be found in the schools of Oxford: Nicholas of Hungary, whom the king supported there for several years;[307] Emo of Friesland and his brother Addo, who sat up through the night copying the Decretum, the Decretals, and the *Liber pauperum* as well as other books of civil and canon law.[308]

Emo of Friesland: More should have been said on Emo in this paper. He became the first abbot of Bloomkamp (+ 1237). In his *Chronicon* he often inserted moral, canonistic and theological observations, thus on vocation for the priesthood, on tithes; on simony (see pp. 491 s. of the edition cited in the next entry here [n. 20]). Menko began his continuation (see *ibid.*) with the remark 'Cronica ista cum moralibus opusculis que ad ingenium exacuendum, vitam et mores informandos inseruntur', ed. cit. (n. 308) p. 523. (S.K.)

Senatus, prior of Worcester, writing to Clement, prior of Oseney, refers his correspondent to 'the city that lies close to you, in which there are many eloquent orators and men who can weigh the words of the law and who bring forth from their treasure things new and old for every one who asks.'[309] It was to Oxford that Gerald of Wales went not long after Easter 1186[310] to find an appreciative audience for the reading of his immortal works and again, about 1198–99, in search of advocates in his suit with the Archbishop of Canterbury, but with less success: for his opponent had been there before him and had taken all the leading lawyers, leaving only a few just out of school and without experience.[311] In the course of his long account of this dispute Gerald mentions by name several of the agents acting for Hubert Walter, and conspicuous among them are all three of Thomas of Marlborough's masters, John of Tynemouth being the principal both at home and abroad, with Simon of Southwell sometimes as co-proctor, and Honorius as his fellow-deputy to bring about a reconciliation.[312] Since the Archbishop turned

---

305 Gerald of Wales, preface to *Speculum ecclesie*. This anecdote occurs in the damaged part of the preface and has hitherto been known only from the somewhat misleading paraphrase of Antony Wood, cf. T. E. Holland, *Collectanea* (Oxford Hist. Soc. 16; 1890) II, 177; Rashdall, *Universities* (2nd ed.) III, 21 n.2 and App. II, 476f.; de Zulueta, *Lib. paup.* xviii. We wish to thank Dr. R. W. Hunt for the permission to use the correct text which he has been able to establish from transcripts of extracts in various MSS in the Bodleian Library, and hopes to publish shortly, with a discussion of the implied allusion to Cato and Justinian.

306 Gir. Camb. *Opp.* II, 344f. On Hubert's Latin see also *ibid.* III, 254.

307 *Pipe Rolls 5–8 Ric. I* (Pipe Roll Soc. N. S. 3; 5–7; 1927–30) pp. 122, 88f., 142, 70, respectively.

308 *Menkonis Chronicon* (ed. L. Weiland, MGH *Script.* 23; 1874) 524, 531. Cf. de Zulueta, *Lib. paup.* xvii f.

Menkonis Chronicon: this is actually a continuation of Emo's own *Chronicon*, ed. *ibid.* p. 454–523. (S.K.)

309 Rashdall, *Universities* III, 33 and n.1; Hunt, *Engl Learning* 30.

310 *Opp.* I, 72–3, cf. I, 413.

311 *Ibid.* III, 228.

312 *Ibid.* III, 218, 265–98 *passim*, 307, 323. Cf. Cheney, *Bishops' Chanceries* 12–14.

to Oxford when he wanted help in legal matters, there is a strong presumption that some of the clerks who are known to have been in his employ may have spent some period of their lives as lecturers in that city, and there is evidence to substantiate this hypothesis.

To begin with, in describing how Emo of Friesland and his brother studied and copied the *Liber pauperum* and the books of canon law, the Bloomkamp Chronicle gives another interesting detail: the students at Oxford used to take down the glosses *ex ore magistrorum*,[313] that is, in the form of *reportatio* — a practice of the Western schools not used at Bologna in the twelfth century[314] — which is precisely the way in which the glosses of John of Tynemouth and his group have come down to us in the Gonville and Caius manuscript. A close association between the Oxford glossators of the *Liber pauperum* and the masters referred to in the Caius glosses and the Royal *Quaestiones* is further indicated by the fact that canonists and civilians alike, although they had a choice of a number of almost contemporary English compilations, made use of the same collection of decretals.[315] Again, when in the Royal manuscript one *quaestio* takes for its topic a papal commission issued to the bishop of Lincoln and the prior of St. Frideswide's, Oxford, and another *quaestio* discusses a mandate to the same prior and the archdeacon of Exeter,[316] the specific local coloring appears unmistakable.[317]

Certain clues may be found in monastic annals which also point to the connection of several of the canonists with Oxford. It is worth noting, for example, that the election of Nicholas de Aquila to the bishopric of Chichester is recorded only in the annals of Oseney and of Dunstable[318] and that the author of the latter, whose importance in the history of canon law in England will be discussed in the next chapter, is our sole authority for the date of John of Tynemouth's death (1221).[319] The inference to be drawn from the annals is borne out by the evidence of the charters and of other documents and narrative sources which bear on the careers of the masters.

John of Tynemouth witnessed an award made at Stanton, a few miles from Oxford, and confirmed at St. Frideswide's in 1188 by judges delegate of the

---

313 *Menkonis Chron.* 524: '... Parisius, Aurelianis et Oxonie audierunt et ex ore magistrorum glosaverunt ... Oxonie etiam Decreta, Decretales, Librum Pauperum necnon alios libros canonici iuris et legalis, vigilias dividendo scripserunt, audierunt et glosaverunt.'
314 At Bologna, the *lectura reportata* was in the form of a lemmatic commentary, cf. e.g. E. M. Meijers, 'Sommes, lectures et commentaires,' *Atti del Congresso Internazionale di diritto romano, Bologna 1933* (Pavia 1934) I, 463, 466ff.
315 *Coll. Tanner*, cf. above I n.23, VII n.288. The references to decretals in the glosses of the Vacarian school, which puzzled the learned editor of the *Liber pauperum* (cf. Introd. xxvii, lxxxvi, xci n.11), are discussed below, Appendix A (III).
316 B. M. Royal MS 9.E. vii, fol. 196vb (cf. *Repert.* 251 n.2); fol. 198ra.
317 Professor Cheney, however, who stresses the fact that the prior of St. Frideswide's was well known as a delegate in other parts of England (*Bishops' Chanceries* 126), would perhaps not admit the argument.
318 *Ann. monast.* IV, 54; III, 31.
319 *Ibid.* III, 66 s.a. 1221.

bishop of Lincoln.[320] A few years later, John became clerk to the archbishop, attesting a number of his charters, at least from 1198 if not earlier, and acting as his agent at the Curia.[321] The *Os claudens* (as Gerald of Wales jestingly translates his name),[322] surviving his misadventures when he stooped to intrigue against the quick-witted archdeacon of Brecon and found himself the victim of his own plot,[323] was made canon of Lincoln (1206?–15).[324] He was a papal judge delegate about 1210.[325] As archdeacon of Oxford (1215–21)[326] John of Tynemouth appears to have had a clerk Master Robert of Clipstone,[327] presumably the same who formerly as proctor of Bishop Malger of Worcester against the monks of Evesham at Rome had been chaffed by Innocent III for basing his arguments on the doctrines of English canonists concerning prescription and episcopal rights.[328]

Master Honorius, as we have seen, was a member of a court held in Oxford in October 1192 by John of Cornwall and Robert of Melun, as judges delegate of the bishop of Lincoln. Honorius' co-signatories included no less than eight other masters, making a total of eleven masters in all forming the court. We shall not be far wrong in assuming that several among them, in particular Honorius himself, were, like John of Cornwall, lecturers in the schools of the city.[329]

Simon of Southwell was canon of Lincoln, possibly as early as 1184 and witnessed several documents, including some Oxford charters, from the early years of St. Hugh's episcopate.[330] Then he joined the household of Archbishop Hubert, one of whose *acta* he witnesses in, or very soon after 1193.[331] As clerk to the

---

320 *The Cartulary of the Abbey of Eynsham* (ed. H. E. Salter, Oxford Hist. Soc. 49; 1907) I, 72; Cheney, *op. cit.* 13.
321 Cheney, *op. cit.* 14 (cf. pp. 20, 158) gives 1198 as the earliest date, but there are several charters which might be earlier. A study of Hubert Walter's *acta* (John witnessed at least twenty of them, Cheney *loc. cit.*) is desirable.
322 *Opp.* III, 274.
323 *Ibid.* 292, 295f.
324 *Oseney Cartul.* IV, 22 (1206); *Reg. Antiquiss. Lincoln* II, 311–12 (1215); III, 52 (before 1208); IV, 136 (*c.* 1210), 202 (1206–14). Cf. Cheney, *op. cit.* 14 n.3.
325 A. W. Goodman, *The Chartulary of Winchester Cathedral* (Winchester 1927) 208.
326 *Rotuli Hug. de Welles* (above, I n.10) I, 129, 147, 170, 172, 175; II, 2; *Ann. monast.* III, 66; Cheney, *loc. cit.* n.4. John's successor, Master Matthew, appears first on 2 August 1221, *Rot. Hug.* II, 192.
327 Oxford, Bodleian MS Laud. lat. 17, fol. 224vb. In his account of this formulary, Professor Cheney (*op. cit.* 129) does not mention the connection between Robert and John indicated in the text.
328 *Chron. Evesham* 189f. ('adversarius') and 151f. ('vir facundissimus et in utroque iure, civili videlicet et canonico, apprime eruditus'): Cf. Pollock and Maitland, *Hist, of Engl. Law* I,116; Ullmann, *Med. Papalism* 13 (the identification, suggested *ibid.* 12 n.1, with Master Robertus de Anglia, one of the founders of the school of Vicenza [cf. *Trad.* 1, 326 n.32] is not warranted). The pope's quip on that occasion, about Robert and his masters having drunk too much beer, does not necessarily imply a reflection on the quality of English learning but repeats only a standing Bolognese joke; cf. e.g. Ricardus Anglicus, preface to the *Distinctiones*: '... resistentes atramento uelut anglicus inebriabo' (MS Vat. lat. 2691, fol. 1).
329 Cf. E. Rathbone, RTAM 17, 50–53.
330 The principal references are given by Cheney, *op. cit.* 13, cf. 79 n.2.
331 *Lichfield Magnum Registrum Album* (above, VII n.280) No. 252.

archbishop, Simon represented Hubert's chapter of Lambeth at Rome in the long suit against the Canterbury monks, and the archbishop himself against Gerald of Wales; he also acted as his *officialis generalis* (vicar general) while Hubert was out of England.[332] In 1198 he reported to Innocent III details concerning a case in which he had been appointed judge delegate by the Pope's predecessor.[333] In 1202 a suit of novel disseisin brought against him was handled by his bailiff.[334] In 1203 he became treasurer of Lichfield[335] where he held a canonry in 1209.[336] Soon after this date his name no longer occurs in the records. So much for his administrative career; for his activities in the school we must turn to the Caius glosses. Here Simon appears as a former lecturer in Bologna[337] and Paris where, on one occasion, he converted the great Petrus Cantor to his point of view,[338] and as the rival of John of Tynemouth in the schools from which the glosses derive.[339] Since evidence from various sources points to Oxford as the place of their origin and the scene of John's teaching, and since Marlborough refers so casually to his masters in the schools as if the reader would know to which schools he was referring, it seems clear that he had studied with Hubert Walter's three clerks in the city where he was to succeed them as a lecturer in both laws.

IX. An English Canonist at Bologna

Shortly after the time when John of Tynemouth, Simon of Southwell, Nicholas de Aquila and their colleagues were lecturing at Oxford, there is a marked change in the production of the English schools which brings them more definitely in line with Bologna. Bernard of Pavia's *Breviarium* replaces the English collections as the standard text of papal decretals, and the great commentary of Huguccio becomes, as elsewhere, the chief guide for English writing on Gratian. This new

---

332 *Epp. Cant.* 407; Gir. Camb. *Opp.* III, 218, 300; *ibid.* 203, 216–7. Cf. Cheney, *op. cit.* 13. Gerald's text, 'generalis eiusdem officialis in Anglia relictus' (III, 203) can be added to the instances, quoted by P. Fournier, *Les officialités au moyen âge* (Paris 1880) 23–4, for *officiales* acting also as vicars general; such instances do not invalidate, however, the observations of Chanoine Edouard Fournier, *Les origines du vicaire général* (Paris 1922) 72ff., 129, on the different origin of the two offices.
333 Po. 395 (PL 214, 381; *Bern. Compost.* 5.13.3; shortened in X 5.20.9).
334 D. M. Stenton, *The Earliest Lincolnshire Assize Rolls* (Lincoln Record Soc. 22; 1926) 8 No. 51.
335 Cheney *loc. cit.* and B. M. Harleian MS 391, fol. 105*; Le Neve, *Fasti Eccl. Anglic.* (2nd ed. Oxford 1854) I, 581, citing Cotton MS Tib. C.ix (Waltham Register) fol. 143 for c. 1205. The dates of two acts witnessed by Simon as treasurer of Lichfield are given as ?1200 and c. 1200–5 respectively by the editors (Cheney, *op. cit.* 257–8, and Canon Foster, *Reg. Antiquiss. Linc.* I, 254; cf. Cheney 11); but in 1202 he was still canon of Lincoln (see preceding note) and between 1201 and 1203 two of his co-signatories, Master Honorius and John of Tynemouth, were frequently out of the country, cf. above, VI nn.182ff.; Gir. Camb. *Opp.* III, 265ff. — Cf. further below, IX n.415.
336 *Lichfield Magn. Reg. Alb.* No. 464, p. 222; cf. K. Major, *Acta Steph. Langton* (above, VII n.283) No. 61.
337 Cf. above, VII n.262 and below, Appendix D (fol. 198ra).
338 Below, Appendix D (fol. 167ra).
339 *Ibid.* (fols. 193ra, 194ra); above, VII, n.241.

development is unmistakable in two works which will have to be examined more closely in future studies: the *Summa Prima primi* of the Royal MS 11.D.ii in the British Museum and the intimately related *Summa Quamuis leges seculares* (on part I of the Decretum only) in a codex from Caen, now at Paris, Bibliothèque Sainte-Geneviève MS 342.[340] For the provenance of the two *Summae* it is probably significant that both refer to the *lex anglicana* in the same context[341] and that the opening words of the first, 'Prima primi uxor Ade post primam hominis creationem ...' etc., which recur at the beginning of the second paragraph of the prologue in the Paris manuscript, echo a passage in Walter Map's *De nugis curialium*.[342] Again, one would like to know to whom the *Summa Quamuis leges* refers when, after reporting Huguccio's doctrine on self-defense in almost the same words as the *Summa Prima primi*, it registers the opposition of a certain *Gre*.[343] Was he the Master Gregory of the Royal Quaestiones, or perhaps Master Gregory of London to whom we referred above?[344]

The reception of the *Compilatio I* is clearly reflected in the *Collectio Abrincensis*, but no certain instance of English glossing on Bernard's compilation can be adduced thus far,[345] the little Baltimore *Ordo iudiciorum* being the only other writing of this period that may be safely assigned an English or Norman origin.[346] We are in the realm of mere conjecture with such writings as the *Summa quaestionum Abrincensis*,[347] the fragment of an apparatus on Gratian in Évreux MS 106,[348] or the *Inceptio* 'Missurus in mundum' of a *m(agister) Willehmus*, who certainly belonged to one of the Western schools but for whom English connections could be argued only from the fact that the text is transmitted in the codex from Weingarten, now at Fulda, which contains the first

---

340 *Repertorium* 204–6. The Paris MS belonged to the *paroisse de Sainct-Jehan de Caen* in 1438, cf. Ch. Kohler, *Catalogue des manuscrits de la Bibliothèque Sainte-Geneviève* (Paris 1893–8) I, 206. For its glosses on Gratian see *Traditio* 1, 286. Caillemer, *op. cit.* (above, II n.39) 195 n.3 believes that Caen may have been a center of legal studies in the 12th cent.

341 *Repert.* 206 (*Sum. Prima primi*); Ste.-Genev. MS 342, fol. 186ra: '... lex tamen anglicana punit si interficiatur non hostis' (collated by Mlle. Vielliard).

342 Ed. James (Oxford 1914) p. 145. *Sum. Quamvis leges* has the better reading '... post primi hominis creationem.'

343 *Repert.* 205 n.1. *Gre.* is certainly not Gregory the Great, cf. the quotation from the *Summa Animal est substantia* (*Sum. Bamb.*) in Kuttner, *Kanonistische Schuldlehre von Gratian bis auf die Dekretalen Gregors IX.* (Studi e Testi 64; Città del Vaticano 1935) 351 n.1; on Huguccio's opponents *ibid.* 353 n.1.

344 Above, VII nn. 284–85.

345 The possibility of English origin of the gloss compositions in Worcester MS F.122 and Lambeth MS 105 (cf. *Traditio* 1, 313 n.22) needs further investigation; the Lambeth MS contains in its second layer of glosses frequent references to the teaching of Master Petrus Brito, in the third person ('p. B¹ dicit'; 'p. B¹ intelligit'), cf. Ullmann, *Med. Papalism* 209; possibly a *reportatio* of glosses of this master, even as in the *Apparatus In quibusdam libris* of Paris, B. N. MS lat. 15398, fol. 204–279 (cf. *Trad.* 1, 317 n.54).

346 Above, ch. III n.67.

347 Above, ch. VI n.229.

348 Cf. *Repert.* 36 for the Western origin of the glosses (set *b*).

draft of Alanus' collection of decretals.[349] It has been suggested recently that the Cambridge manuscript of the *Apparatus Ecce vicit leo* (Trinity College 0.5.17, from Bradenstoke Priory) represents a separate English reworking rather than a copy of this important French commentary.[350] If this view be correct, and if the Cambridge version should not be merely another instance of the medieval attitude of which Professor Schulz pointedly says that 'juristic literature was treated with no more respect than we nowadays show for cookery books,'[351] we should have to assume a return of the English school of the early thirteenth century to the merely reproductive stage of the decade *c.* 1160–70.

Be this as it may, there is no doubt that shortly before and after the turn of the century, the best canonistic talent of the British Isles was no longer to be found at home but had taken the road to Bologna. It is not within the scope of this paper to discuss the numerous English canonists who, as is well known, studied or taught at Bologna during this period and thus helped to give the foremost law school of Europe the truly international color which characterizes it from the time of Innocent III. For the present inquiry only those masters are of interest whom we can show to have been connected with the English schools before they were active in Italy. This connection, we believe, can be established in the case of Ricardus Anglicus; as for other masters,[352] the present state of research would allow no more than conjectures.

The identity of Master Richard has long intrigued historians. He has been dubbed, quite arbitrarily, *Adagonista*, and confused with such masters as Richard Grant, St. Richard de Wych, Richard of Middleton, and, most persistently, Richard Poore, dean of Salisbury (1197–1214) and successively bishop of Chichester (1215), Salisbury (1217), and Durham (1228–37).[353] We know Poore as a fellow

---

349 *Repert.* 166f.; for Western origin cf. F. Gillmann, *Zur Inventarisierung der kanonistischen Handschriften aus der Zeit von Gratian bis Gregor IX.* (Appendix to the reprint of his 'Des Johannes Galensis Apparat ...' [AKKR 118, 174–222]; Mainz 1938) 64–6; for the inscription, 'Inceptio m. Willehelmi,' cf. Heckel, in ZRG Kan. Abt. 29 (1940) 121 n.1. A Master *Wil.* or *Gwil.* is repeatedly quoted by Gilbertus Anglicus in the glosses to his own collection, cf. *Repert.* 327 n.2; *Trad.* 1, 337 n.42.

350 Ullmann, *Med. Papalism* 208 ('Summa Cantabrigiensis').

351 F. Schulz, *History of Roman Legal Science* (Oxford 1946) 142f. — In the passages quoted by Dr. Ullmann from the Cambridge MS (*op. cit.* 146, 180, 196) the textual differences from other MSS of *Ecce vicit leo* are not greater than, e.g., the variations among the MSS of the *Summa* of Rufinus (cf. pp. xii, xxxiv, xxxviii-xl and the *apparatus criticus* of Singer's edition), or of the glosses of Ricardus Anglicus on *Comp. I* (cf. Gillmann, in AKKR 107 [1927] 618).

352 Thomas of Marlborough, who, after having taught at Oxford, upon the pope's advice attended classes at Bologna in 1205 between hearings of the Evesham case (cf. above, II n.26), cannot be counted in the same category.

353 For the various attempted identifications see L. Wahrmund, in his edition of Richard's *Ordo* (Quellen zur Gesch. des römisch-kanon. Processes ... II, 3; Innsbruck 1915) xiii-xvi: 'blosse Vermutung oder gar ... Fabel'; but Richard Grant (Wethershed), chancellor of Lincoln (1221–9) and archbishop of Canterbury (1229–31) is still mentioned as a possibility by P. Glorieux, *Répertoire des maîtres en théologie de Paris au XIIIe siècle* (Paris 1933–4) I, 1280f. The origin of the confusion with Richard of Middleton has been traced by R. Hocedez, *Richard de Middleton, sa vie, ses oeuvres, sa doctrine* (Spicilegium sacrum Lovaniense 7; 1925) 14, 16f.

student of Thomas Marlborough in theology under Stephen Langton, and as a friend of Robert of Flamborough, the canon penitentiary of St. Victor's, but we have no evidence to indicate that he had any special concern with legal studies.[354] In fact, among the score of Richards with the master's title in English historical and literary sources, only two can be singled out as possible lecturers or writers on canon law: first, an otherwise unknown master R. *de laci anglicus*, who is quoted as the author of a gloss ('notauit') on 's(upra) de cohabit. cler. et mul. c. Vestra' in the fragment of a commentary on the Gregorian Decretals, discovered by the late Hermann Kantorowicz on a fly-leaf of the Karlsruhe MS Aug. XXX (fol. 251v, written before 1266);[355] and second, Master Richard de Mores (Morins), Augustinian canon of Merton and prior of Dunstable from 1202 to 1242, who, as Professor Josiah C. Russell has pointed out, is described by the *Gesta abbatum* of St. Alban's as a former regent master 'in iure et canonum sanctionibus' at Bologna and elsewhere, and in MS 275 of Trinity College, Dublin, as the author of a work with the subscription, 'Explicit summa breuis magistri Ricardi de mores super decreta graciani.'[356]

What evidence have we on which to base a decision between these two possibilities? The argument in favor of R. de Lacy, suggestive as it seems on first sight, presupposes a chain of rather precarious inferences. First, since the quotation in the Reichenau codex refers *per se* to a gloss on the Gregorian Decretals ('supra'), it could be assigned to Ricardus Anglicus only on the assumption that this master published glosses on one of the pre-Gregorian collections containing the chapter *Vestra* (Lucius III, JL 15178) — that is, either the collection of Gilbert (1202) or the *Compilatio II* (*c.* 1210)[357] — which is improbable since all of his known writings can be dated before the accession of Innocent III; or, still more unlikely, on the surmise that he glossed the decretal *Vestra* before it became part of a collection accepted at Bologna. Second, we should have to assume further that these glosses, while remaining entirely unknown to the early thirteenth-century decretalists, were read, identified, and adapted to the Gregorian compilation by the anonymous author of the *fragmentum Augiense* about the middle of the century. Finally,

---

354 C. R. Cheney, *English Synodalia of the Thirteenth Century* (Oxford 1941) 52ff. J. C. Russell, *Dictionary of Writers of Thirteenth Century England* (London etc. 1936) 112, 136 suggests with good reason that the identification of the canonist with Richard Poore rests on a confusion of the latter with St. Richard de Wych, who had had legal training before he became chancellor of Oxford (*c.* 1235), chancellor of Archbishop Edmund (*c.* 1237–40), and bishop of Chichester (1244–53; cf. Ralph Bokyng's *Vita* of *c.* 1270 in *Acta Sanctorum Apr.* I, 286), and to whom later legend ascribed years of study in exemplary poverty at Bologna and Paris (John Capgrave's *Vita, ibid.* 278b); the legend being thereafter transferred to Master Richrd 'the poor,' bishop of Chichester 1215–7.
355 Cf. *Repertorium* 223 n.1; the identification has since been widely accepted.
356 *Gesta abbatum mon. s. Alb.* 307, naming as Richard's companion a Master Thomas of Tynemouth; Dublin, Trinity College MS 275, pp. 169–183. Cf. Russell, *Dictionary* 111ff. and, with hesitation, Richardson, in *Law Quart. Rev.* 57, 323; Kuttner, in *Traditio* 1, 284 n.25.
357 *Gilb.* 3.1.1; *2 Comp.* 3.1.1 (X 3.2.7).

we should have to prove that *R.* de Lacy stands for Richard, and not for Robert, Ralph, or another name.[358]

The *Summa brevis* attributed in the Dublin manuscript to Richard de Mores occurs, anonymously, in at least two other copies: Royal MS 11.A.ii (fol. 195–203v) of the British Museum and MS 86 (fol. 1–5v) of the Cistercian monastery in Rein, Styria.[359] It consists of a summary outline of the topics treated in each section (*distinctio, quaestio*) of the Decretum, offering sometimes the barest descriptive statement, sometimes brief discussions of the subject matter and, in part II, frequently uses the didactic query-and-answer style.[360] A curious trait of the *Summa brevis* is the author's delight in versification. Prefixed to the opening words, 'Tractaturus igitur Gratianus de iure canonico orditur ab altiori ...' is a prologue of twelve hexameters,

> Plus quam posse meum possit me posse iubetis,
> Cum uestram cogor in iure docere Mineruam.

> ... sicque mea cum uestro uelle uoluntas
> Incipit ut tandem cupiat quodcumque necesse est,

borrowed from the *Anticlaudianus* of Alain de Lille.[361] In part II, nearly all Gratian's original *quaestiones* have been molded into hexametric monostichs, frequently not without violence to the meter, and the responses occasionally affect the language of rhymed prose.[362] Short verses precede both the second and the third part, and two of the manuscripts conclude with an epilogue composed of three distichs, the author's birthplace being named in the last line:

> Si lira delirat, ueniam deposco liture,
>   Dum rude de uena paupere serpit opus.
> Uas figulum, scriptum scriptorem, fabrica fabrum
>   Auctoremque suum uiuificabit opus.
> Principium sine principio, sine fine maritet
>   Fini legitimo lincolniensis[363] opus.

358 Cf. e.g. *Trad.* 1, 326 n.32 for Rodulphus Anglicus and Robertus de Anglia; the obit list of S. Maria del Reno in Bologna (cited *ibid.*) contains still another Robert (d. 1254) and one Rainaldus Anglicus.
359 The first of these was cited in *Repert.* 231, but with wrong classification.
360 Examples below, Appendix E: Dist. 1–3, C. 16 qq. 4–5 (descriptive); Dist. 75, C. 18 q.2 (discussions), and *passim* for query and answer style.
361 *Anticlaud.* 2.1.7–21 (PL 210, 498f.), cf. Warner and Gilson, *Cat. Royal MSS* I, 336. The *Summa* omits vv. 9, 14–15 of the original and changes 'indocta docere' (v.8) to 'in iure docere' (v.2 above). Slight variants in the MSS of the *Summa* have not been noted here.
362 C.1 q.1: 'Queritur an possint bona spiritualia uendi ...,' D(ublin MS 275, p.) 171b; q.2: 'An sit ob ingressum fas ecclesie dare quicquam ...'; q.4: 'Criminibus patris maculetur an inscia proles ...'; q.5: 'An patris ob munus promotus iure minister ...' *(ibid.)* etc. Further examples in the following notes and below, Appendix E, also for rhymed prose (C.25 q.1).
363 'lincoliensis' D 183b; 'lineosis' Rein MS 86, fol. 5v; 'linconensis' Zwettl MS 162, fol. 70r (for the separate tradition of the distichs in this MS see below, at n.405).

Richard de Mores often supports his statements by references to individual canons in Gratian or to decretals. The latter he cites consistently by *extra*, title and chapter, from the *Compilatio I*; twice only there are direct citations of the Third Lateran Council.[364] No later decretals are used, and the only other canonist quoted by name is Huguccio.[365] The treatise must therefore be assigned to the 'nineties, i.e. to the period before Richard was elected prior of Dunstable. The most revealing feature of the work is, however, the author's habit of citing himself. Nearly every time the canonical problem in hand calls for a more detailed discussion — well over sixty times — Richard de Mores refers to *distinctiones* which he has written elsewhere on the subject.

For Ricardus Anglicus, Distinctiones, cf. G. Silano, The "Distinctiones Decretorum" of Ricardus Anglicus (Ph. D. dissertation, Toronto 1982). (P.L.)

At first sight the frequent use of the adverbial term *extra* in this context ('quod extra plene distinxi' etc.)[366] is confusing, since it seems to imply a work on *decretales extravagantes*. It soon becomes clear, however, that the author always employs this unusual expression to designate distinctions written on Gratian's text, but 'outside' the present, summary treatise. In every case these references can be conveniently verified in the *Distinctiones* of Ricardus Anglicus.[367] The problem of identification is therefore solved: the English master Richard who taught at Bologna before the end of the twelfth century was Richard de Mores of Lincoln.

The *Summa brevis* is obviously the hitherto missing work of which Ricardus Anglicus speaks in the prologue to his *Distinctiones*:[368]

... sciat me ... continentiam distinctionum et continuationes causarum et solutiones questionum et seriem paragraforum congessisse, quibus

---

364 Dist. 92: 'Additur quod cantandum sit plus corde quam ore, vt ... in con. later. Cum in sacris (c.3)'; C. 10 q.3: 'Quanta dari debet sinodalis summa per annum? Resp. duo solidi nomine cathedratici, vt ... in con. later. Cum apostolus (c.4) extra, tit. de censibus (*1 Comp.* 3.34.6).' D 171a, 174a. The references to *Comp.* I are never given as 'extra I.' (the statement to the contrary in *Repert.* 231 was based on a misunderstanding, see note 366).

365 C. 15 q.1: 'Queritur an quod agit furibundo sit reputandum (*leg.* imputandum). R(espondeo) cum magistro hugone simpliciter quod non, nec admitto quorumdam distinctionem ...,' D 175b. For Huguccio's doctrine cf. *Kanonistische Schuldlehre* (above, n.343) 107f.

366 Also 'dic ut distinxi ex. j(nfra) e(adem) ...' (D 175a), misinterpreted as reference to 'extra I,' in *Repert.* 231.

367 E.g. Dist. 17: 'Cuius auctoritate fiant concilia distingue ut eadem distinctione scripsi sufficienter' (D 169; cf. Richard's *Distinctiones*, MS Vat. lat. 2691, fol. 1v: 'Concilium generale uel uniuersale quod fit speciali auctoritate domini pape ...; particulare uel speciale ...; episcopale uel singulare ...'); Dist. 19: 'Quam uim optinent decretales soluo per distinctionem hic extra. positam' (D 169; cf. *Dist*. MS Vat. *ibid.*: 'Decretalis epistola specialis, que dirigitur ad unam prouinciam ... hec non trahuntur ad consequentiam, nisi prouincia uel persona exempli causa apponatur; generalis, que omnibus dirigitur tenenda. hec trahit ad consequentiam ...'). More examples below, App. E.

368 *Repert.* 224f. — A. Teetaert, 'Commentationes ...' (above, V n.128) 241 notes that in Paris, B. N. MS lat. 14859, fol. 390v (a penitential book from St. Victor) there is a quotation, 'Ricardus dicit in summa decretorum ...'; but we find that over the R a small S has been written as if by correction (=Sicardus).

si negotiorum fluctuationes ystorias me apponere paterentur, quod nullus negat esse facillimum, opus esse tam continuum quam perfectum presumerem predicare ...

Our treatise is here correctly described as consisting of the contents of Gratian's *distinctiones* (pts. I and III; C.33 q.3 *de poen.*), *continuationes* of the *causae*, solutions of Gratian's *quaestiones*, and summaries of the incidental matters introduced in Gratian's dicta (*paragraphi*).[369] It may be asked, however, whether Richard does not take too much pride in the elementary, if somewhat pretentious little *Summa* by advertising it in many more words than, e.g., his far more important works on the *Compilatio I*, and by claiming that it would become an *opus perfectum* if he only were to find time to insert *ystorie*, i.e. an elaboration of bible stories touched upon by Gratian.

The rather puzzling observation that the *Summa brevis* cites the *Distinctiones* in the past tense and is in turn listed in the prologue to the latter as a work already published, has its parallel in the cross-references running back and forth between the *Distinctiones* and some of Ricardus Anglicus' other works (e.g. the glosses and the *Brocarda*) and makes the chronological relations difficult to establish. The possibility that the *Distinctiones* were published in two successive redactions cannot be ruled out; the absence of the prologue from certain manuscripts[370] and a passage in the prologue mentioning *multas novitates*[371] invite further investigation of this question.

In any event, one has to conclude that the *Summa brevis* was composed at Bologna, during the same period in which Richard was occupied with his writings on the *Compilatio I*, his *Ordo* (c. 1196), and the *Distinctiones* (1196–8).[372] Nevertheless his writings show certain traces of a previous connection with the Anglo-Norman schools and thus bear out what the *Gesta abbatum* have to say about Richard de Mores 'qui et Bononiae et alibi ... rexerat.'[373] To be sure, the allusion to Lincoln in the last verse of the *Summa* can hardly be taken as a proof of affiliation with the schools of that city[374] (tempting as it may be to draw a parallel between the didactic verses and outline method of the *Summa brevis* and the work of William de Monte, chancellor of Lincoln c. 1190–1213, who summarized the theological learning of the day and wrote a collection of glossed verses on topics in theology and Scripture in alphabetical order[375]); nor is the use of an English place-name, in one of the forms of complaint discussed in the *Ordo iudiciorum*,[376]

---

369 See App. E, for example C. 25 (*continuatio*), C.18 q.2 (*paragraphi*).
370 Oxford, Bodleian MS Selden supr. 87, fol. 159r-181v; Douai MS 649, fol. 7r-25v; add B. M. Royal MS 10.C.iii, fol. 4r-48v.
371 *Repert.* 224 n.1.
372 *Ibid.* 225f.
373 *Loc. cit. supra* n.356.
374 This would require the reading 'lincolniense opus,' an emendation which is ruled out by the meter.
375 R. W. Hunt, 'English Learning ...' (above, VIII n.309) 21.
376 *Ordo* c.6: 'Deo et vobis B. et C. conqueror ego R. de G. qui iniuste detinet ecclesiam sancti Petri de Collig. (*al.* Collingna, Coll'.) mihi assignatam' (ed. Wahrmund p. 4, cf. xx n.1). Similar Latin

indicative of anything but Richard's nationality. The convincing proofs of his scholastic antecedents are such facts as the influence of the *Summa Omnis qui iuste* on certain passages in the *Distinctiones*,[377] and of the French civilian treatise known as *Brachylogus* and the *Ordo Olim edebatur*, on Richard's *Ordo*.[378]

Influence of the Ordo 'Olim edebatur' on Richard's Ordo iudiciarius. Olim edebatur was written by Rodoicus Modicipassus – cf. A. Gouron, Qui a écrit l'ordo "Olim edebatur"?, Initium 8 (2003) 65–84; also in: *A. Gouron*, Pionniers du droit occidental au Moyen Âge (Ashgate 2006), no. XIII – as well as the Summa Omnis qui iuste iudicat (Summa Lipsiensis) – cf. above my article at p. 181. (P.L.)

The formal method employed in this procedural work, viz. the mixture of doctrinal exposition and texts abstracted from the legal sources — 'ad instar cuiusdam compilationis,' as Tancred described it[379] — also calls to mind a feature characteristic of the early French *summae* and of Odo of Dover.[380] Above all, the *Ordo* contains an express mention of the Vacarian glossator, Ascelinus — a name so strange to anyone unfamiliar with the English schools that medieval copyists as well as the modern editor of the *Ordo* mistook it for a reference to Azo.[381]

The pre-Bolognese associations of Richard de Mores appear to have been primarily with the group of Honorius and the author of the *Summa Omnis qui iuste* — at least, if we may rely on the attribution to *magister Ricardus* of a work not listed in his own retrospective catalogue: the *Summa quaestionum* beginning 'Circa ius naturale uarie solent fieri questiones,' which has come down anonymously in MS 396 of Montecassino, but is subscribed, 'Explentur questiones ueneriales magistri ricardi super tota decreta' in MS 162 of the Cistercian Abbey of Zwettl.[382] The qualification of these interesting *quaestiones* as *veneriales* — the same term as used for the work of Honorius in this codex[383] — implies that they were orally delivered in a special class on Fridays. As in the case of Honorius'

---

forms occur for several places, e.g. Cooling, Kent; Collingham, Notts.; Cowling, Yorks. West Riding.

377 E.g. Rich. *Dist*. D. 1 pr. (on natural law), D. 19 pr. (on decretals, cf. n.367), etc.

378 Cf. Caillemer, *op. cit*. (above, II n.39) 189; Wahrmund, *ed. cit*. xxii-iii; H. Fitting, *Ueber die sogenannte Turiner Institutionenglosse* (Halle 1870) 73f.

379 The passage from Tancred's *Ordo* has been frequently quoted, cf. Wahrmund, *loc. cit*.; the method of *quaedam compilatio* which Richard imitated was of course that of the Decretum, not of the *Liber pauperum*, as de Zulueta (p.li) suggests.

380 Above, IV at n.80. The same method is found in the *Summa Elegantius*, the *Summa Quoniam omissis* (above V, n.123), the *Rhetorica ecclesiastica* (cf. E. Ott, in *SB Vienna* 125 [1891] 95), the *Ordo Olim*, etc.

381 *Ordo* c. 37 '... secundum Ascelinum' (ed. Wahrmund p. 86, variants in n. 25; interpreted as reference to Azo in the Introduction, p. xxiv). On Ascelinus see de Zulueta, *Lib. paup*. xx n.29, xxxiii, cxiii.

382 M(ontecassino MS 396, p.) 191a-247a; Z(wettl MS 162, fol.) 145ra-173ra. Cf. Kuttner, in *Traditio* 1, 321 n.4 and 323 n.18 (xii); Ullmann, *Med. Papalism* 211–5. (Z reads at the beginning: '... uarie quest, sol. Fieri'.)

383 Above, VI n.222.

treatise, we have to do with a *Summa* composed of *quaestiones decretales*, in the sense discussed in a previous section of this paper. The resemblance between the two works is striking as regards scope, form, method, style, and doctrinal elaboration. One marked difference, however, will be found in their organization: Honorius arranges his *quaestiones decretales* according to a system of his own, whereas the *Summa Circa ius naturale* adheres more closely to the traditional order of Gratian, grouping its *summulae* and *quaestiones* in thirty-seven chapters or titles (though there are no formal headings in the Montecassino codex and only a few in that of Zwettl), which represent a selection of Gratian's topics.[384] One may observe, further, that among the questions treated in each 'title' the number of those directly concerned with difficulties and antinomies in the sources — *quaestiones decretales* in the literal sense — is often greater in this *Summa* than in Honorius' work.[385] Moreover, *magister Ricardus* frequently incorporates questions borrowed directly from the *Summa* of Simon of Bisignano — whose influence on the Anglo-Norman writers of the 1180's is well established — but which are not found in Honorius.[386] Still, the differences between the two *Summae quaestionum* are only such as one would normally expect among members of the same family: they do not invalidate the dominant traits the two have in common. Many identical questions, of interpretation as well as of casuistry, recur in both, although the solutions are not necessarily the same.[387] Within the circle to which both of them belonged, a collation of parallel passages reveals at times a special affinity between the *Summa quaestionum* ascribed to Richard and the *Summa Omnis qui iuste* on the one hand, between Honorius and the *Summa De iure canonico tractaturus*, on the other.[388] This affinity extends to the style of citing contemporary decretals, for which the two latter authors consistently refer to the *Appendix Concilii Lateranensis*[389] while the two former cite from a collection not arranged in titles.[390]

---

384 See the list below, Appendix E (II).
385 E.g. *de continentia* tit. 8 qq.3–5, *de lapsis* 9.6, *de iure patronatus* 23.8–11 (*ibid.*)
386 E.g. *de iure naturali* 1.1; *de iure patr.* 23.1–3 (*ibid.*). For Simon's influence on the *Summa Omnis qui iuste* cf. *Repert.* 149, 197.
387 For opposition see e.g. *de iure patr.* 23.11 (below, App. E).
388 For example, above, VI nn.198–199. On the renting of matresses by the students in Paris, the question is formulated in *Sum. Circa ius nat.* almost verbatim as in *Sum. Omnis qui iuste* (above VI, n.237; M 215b, Z 156va). On a problem of marriage, 'magister h(ugo) de sancto victore' is quoted by both authors in the same words (Schulte, *SB Vienna* 68 [1871J 46; M 235b). Cf. also n.393 below; examples could be given from almost every title.
389 *Traditio* 6, 349 nn.38–9.
390 For *Omnis qui iuste* this was already recognized by Schulte, *SB Vienna* 68, 50f.; for *Circa ius nat.* see examples below, nn. 391, 400, and App.E. Sometimes the references are helpful for the reconstruction of the original papal letters, e.g. tit. 32 *de enormitate delicti*: '... quod non debet uir conuerti nisi uxor similiter conuertatur, ... aliter autem si factum fuerit, si et consensu mulieris ingressus fuerit, reuocatur ad thorum illius, vt in ex. Intelleximus' (M 235a, Z 168ra), which shows that X 3.32.1 (JL 13946+13948–9; cf. Lohmann, *ZRG Kan. Abt.* 22 [1933] 73) is part of JL 13950, thus confirming a marginal note to *App.* 26.24 (JL 13948) in Mansi 22, 372.

The latest decretal mentioned in the *Summa Circa ius naturale* is one of Pope Lucius III (1181–5),[391] and the work may have been completed before Master Albertus de Morra ('Albertinus') became Pope Gregory VIII in 1187.[392] As one would anticipate, given the author's scholastic affiliation, the local coloring of the treatise points to Paris as the place of writing; except for one reference to Canterbury cathedral as the scene of the martyrdom of St. Thomas (but this was known to every one),[393] examples are taken from the diocese and the academic life of Paris.[394] One *quaestio* in the chapter on rescripts is concerned with a papal mandate addressed to G. *archidiaconus parisiensis ecclesie*: what, the author asks, if there are three archdeacons in Paris whose name begins with G.? If the proper addressee can be ascertained, he decides, the mandate will be valid.[395] Now, unless the letter G. is chosen at random, it must be meant to designate Girardus, one of the archdeacons of Paris at the time our *Summa quaestionum* was being written; and during his long tenure (*c.* 1166–91)[396] there had in fact been other archdeacons in the chapter of Notre Dame whose name began by the same letter.[397]

All these details which permit us to date and to localize the *Summa Circa ius naturale* at Paris, about or after 1186, are derived from the anonymous codex Cassinensis. In the Zwettl manuscript the evidence has been tampered with in several places.[398] In one *quaestio* the scribe (or his exemplar) substituted the dioceses of Bologna and Modena for Paris and Chartres;[399] in other instances

---

391 M 208b (*de appell.* tit.11): '... nam et ordinarius recusari potest, ... et deligatas (*sic*) eodem modo potest recusari, vt in ex. Ad aures.' Lucius III, JL 14965–6 (X 2.28.36).

392 *De perplexitate* (tit.3): '... Albertinus solebat dicere' (M 195a, Z 147ra). Cf. *Kanonist. Schuldlehre* (above, n.343) 267 n.1.

393 *De ecclesiis de nouo edificandis* (tit.35): '... Item quid si in ecclesia aliquis uirum (?) occidat, ut contigit in cantu<a>riensi? Et dicunt quod huiusmodi sanguinis effusio ecclesiam non polluit set consecrat' (M 239a). Cf. Sum. *Omnis qui iuste* to *De cons.* D.1 c.19 v. *homicidio*: 'Quid si in ecclesia martir occidatur ut in cantuariensi ecclesia contigit? Dicunt quod talis ecclesia non est consecranda quia huiusmodi ...' (Rouen MS 743, fol. 134rb).

394 *De excommunicatione* (tit.20): '... si enim parisiensis solus nouit aliquem esse excommunicatum ...' (M 214a); and cf. nn.388 (*culcitre*), 395, 399.

395 *De rescriptis* (tit.26): '... Item quid si causa committatur G. archid. parisiensis ecclesie et sunt tres in eadem quorum quilibet uocatur g.: numquid expirat iurisdictio ...? Ad primum dicimus quod si possit de persona <de>legati constare cui scil. sit demandatum, mandatum erit ualidum ... (M 224b).

396 Jo Sar. *epp.* 182 and 174 (PL 199, 182 and 165; *c.* 1166); *Cartulaire de l'église de Notre-Dame de Paris* (ed. Guérard, Paris 1850) III, 439 (1168); I, 45 (1191), and I, 397–8; II 9, 176, 198, 293, 311, 339, 503; III, 358, 386 (for years in between); *Chart. Univ. Par* I, 50 No. 50 (1180).

397 Guermundus, c. 1147–73 (*Cartul. N.D.* I, 40, 389; II, 9, 176, 339, 360, 503; III, 358, 439); Gratianus, c. 1177–78 (*ibid.* II, 293, 503).

398 The following observations are based on collations kindly supplied by Dr. Ullmann, who has examined Z in detail and generously put at our disposal an unpublished note of his. We are also indebted to Abbé Fransen for several collations.

399 *De perplex.* (tit.3); '... in ecclesia parisiensi ... in ecclesia caporiensi' (*sic*; M 194b); '... in ecclesia bononiensi ... in ecclesia mutinensi' (Z 146vb).

he replaced the original references to *extravagantes* or Lateran constitutions by citations from the *Compilatio I*, without any attempt, however, at consistency in such changes;[400] and in the title on elections a new *quaestio* was interpolated and solved by reference to a decretal of Innocent III, cited from the collection of Gilbert (1202).[401]

It is obvious that such 'cookery book' alterations should not be taken for an authentic second redaction, supposedly published by the author at Bologna after an interval of more than fifteen years. But if the Zwettl codex is unreliable as regards the text of the treatise, the question arises whether we are allowed to give credence to its colophon, i.e., to accept the asserted authorship of *magister Ricardus*. The fact that Richard does not list the *Summa quaestionum* as one of his works in the *Distinctiones*, and that only slight textual similarities with his known writings can be discovered in the Parisian treatise, would tend to increase our misgivings.

Yet these doubts are not necessarily justified. First, the Zwettl manuscript must be given credit for being correct in the only other instance in which it assigns an author's name to one of its many miscellaneous items, viz. the work of Honorius. Second, the person who planned the contents of the codex, certainly had access to a much fuller *corpus ricardianum* than can be found in any other single known manuscript.[402] Not counting the *Summa quaestionum* and a lemmatic commentary on the *Compilatio I*, largely based on glosses by Richard,[403] this manuscript offers no less than three of his writings (*Distinctiones, Brocarda, Ordo*,[404] and betrays traces of a fourth, on fol. 70r, where the concluding distichs of the *Summa brevis* precede, quite incongruously, a collection of *Notabilia* on Gratian (beg. 'Greg[orius]. Qui multum emungit sanguinem elicit')[405] which may eventually

---

400 *De elect.* (tit.7) '... sicut ergo tenet electio ab omnibus uel a maiori parte facta, vt in con(cilio) l(ateranensi) Cum in cunctis, ... expresse hoc colligitur ex quodam c(apitulo) alex. iii. Causam' (M 197b); the references (*3 Conc. Lat.* 3 and JL 14070) changed to 'ut ex. de elect. Cum in cunctis ... ex quodam cap. alex. iii. de elect. et el. pot. Causam' in Z 148ra (*1 Comp.* 1.4.16,17). — *De lapsis* (tit.9): '... etiam si conuicti fuerint uel confessi, poterit dispensari, vt c. alex. iii. Licet preter' (M 199b; JL 14091); changed to 'ex. de iudiciis, Aut (*sic*) si clerici' in Z 149ra (*1 Comp.* 2.1.6). — *De conuictis* (tit.12): '... item alex. iii. dicit laicos non posse admitti ... vt in ex. Licet preter' (M 204b); changed to 'ex. de iudic. De cetero' in Z 151rb (*1 Comp.* 2.1.7). — *De spoliatis* (tit.14): '... restitutionem petere potest, vt in ex. In litteris' (M 206b); reference (JL 14219) changed to 'ex. de restit. exspol. Ex litteris' in Z 152rb (*1 Comp.* 2.9.5). Elsewhere M and Z agree in their references.
401 Z 148ra: 'Item queritur si patronus alicuius ecclesie semet elegerit an possit. Dicitur quod non, ut ex. t. de iure patronatus, Per nostras' (Po. 275; *Gilb.* 3.24.3). Dr. Ullmann points this out.
402 The contents of Zwettl MS 162 are listed in *Traditio* 1, 323 n.18. Of other MSS, only the following contain more than one work: Vat. lat. 2691 (*Dist.* and *Ordo*, cf. *Repert.* 223, 225), Douai 644 (the same, *ibid.* 222, 225), Avranches 149 (*Brocarda* and *App. Comp. I*, cf. *Trad.* 1, 299 n.40 and 312 n.20)
403 *Trad* 1, 323 n.18 (i); beg. 'Materia auctoris in hoc opere.'
404 *Ibid*, (vii, viii, x).
405 *Ibid.* (v). The opening *notabile* is *Prov.* 30.33 as quoted by St. Gregory to Augustine of England (D. 4 c.6); another collection of *Notabilia* (B.M. MS Addit. 18325, cf. *Repert.* 235) begins with

prove to be a fifth work, namely, the hitherto missing 'singula argumenta per ordinem decretorum usque ad ultimum capitulum' of Richard's catalogue.[406] If the 'patron' of the manuscript was so intimately conversant with the works of the English master, we may well believe that he had good authority for assigning to him the *Summa quaestionum*.

The absence of the treatise from the list of works in the *Distinctiones* is perhaps less astonishing than it would first appear, since Richard's *Casus* on the *Compilatio I* are also omitted[407] and even one of his most important writings, the *Apparatus* of glosses on this compilation, is mentioned there only in the most indirect manner.[408] In the case of the *Summa quaestionum* Richard may have been loath to put on a level with his mature Bolognese production a work written approximately ten years earlier in a foreign school. A transfer from the schools of France and England to Bologna could not but effect a change in outlook and style. Making a fresh start, as it were, under the impact of the contemporary Bolognese teaching, Richard would soon have found himself detached from his earlier, almost meticulous dependence upon the terminology and opinions of the *Summa Omnis qui iuste*, and as often as not this led him to revise his doctrinal position. While his teaching on certain questions, for example on the powers of emperor and pope, remained basically the same,[409] he abandoned some of his early opinions, such as that on papal dispensation for murderous clerks.[410] But the point should not be overstressed, since Richard reversed himself occasionally also in writings of his Bolognese period.[411]

From the foregoing observations and the previously known data the following biographical outline emerges: Richard de Mores of Lincoln began his

---

the same proverb, and Simon of Apulia quoted it in his quarrel with Honorius (Rog. Ho v. IV, 53; the text as printed, 'Vehementer emungit qui sanguinem ejicit,' would seem to be corrupt).

406 The terms *argumenta* and *notabilia* were used interchangeably for the same literary species (cf. *Repert.* 3, 233) as distinct from *casus*; the emendation proposed for Richard's text in *Repert.* 224 ('argumenta decretalium,' interpreted as a reference to his *Casus Comp. I*) cannot be defended.

407 See preceding note; MSS of the *Casus* are listed in *Repert.* 398. Abbé Fransen kindly informs us that the MS of Munich (MS lat. 16083, fol. 36rb-52va) has a contemporary rubric, 'Casus mag(ist)ri Ricardi,' and concludes with distichs in which the author admits his weakness for versification (cf. above, at n. 361ff.): 'Ad solitum suspiro metrum, ne deserat ortum/Ortolanus, equus prelia, mergus aquas/ ...' etc.

408 *Repert.* 225.

409 *Sum. quaest.* tit.3 'Queri solet utrum summus pontifex utrumque gladium habeat, scil. materialem et spiritualem' (M 196–197a, Z 147vb-148ra) has been discussed by Ullmann, *Med. Papalism* 211ff. The answer is in the negative, even as in Richard's *generale* 'arg. de iurisdictione distincta' to *1 Comp.* 4.18.7 (printed from the *Apparatus* of Tancred — who wrongly assigns it to Laurentius Hispanus — by Schulte, *SB Vienna* 66 [1870] 85 and Gillmann, AKKR 105 [1925] 541 n.2; cf. *ibid.* 107 [1927] 647 n.2, also Ullmann, *op. cit.* 145). Richard published this both in the *Apparatus* and the *Brocarda*.

410 *Sum. quaest.* 9.3 *de lapsis*; *contra* gl. to *1 Comp.* 4.6.7, *Sum. brev.* and *Dist.* to D.50 (see below, Appendix E).

411 E.g. on the release from the oath of fealty, *Sum. brev.* C.15 q.6; *contra* gl. to *1 Comp.* 5.6.7 (*ibid.*).

career, 'praecognita ad plenum logica,'[412] at Paris as a student and lecturer in canon law with a group of other Anglo-Norman canonists, publishing his *quaestiones decretales* when he was about twenty-five years old, c. 1186–7. Between that time and his appearance in Bologna in the mid-nineties, he may or may not have taught somewhere in England, but was most probably in touch with the Vacarian school at Oxford.[413] From Bologna, where he completed within a brief span of years (c. 1194–7) a surprising number of canonistic writings — some of them of lasting value — he returned to his own country about 1198. It was perhaps only then that he entered the Augustinian house of Merton. Still a deacon, he was elected prior of Dunstable in 1202 and ordained to the priesthood on 21 September.[414]

Ricardus Anglicus 'elected prior of Dunstable in 1202'. In 1202 he travelled with the papal legate, the abbot Giraldus de Casamari, from England to France, returning to England in 1203: see Ann. Dunstapl. p. 28 (cf. n. 414 of the article). (S.K.)

He ruled the priory for forty years, busy all the time with visitations, commissions, judicial affairs,[415] and the compilation of the Dunstable Annals. His continued intellectual interests are recorded in the Annals: on his way back from the Fourth Lateran Council — he must by then have been in his fifties — Richard stayed for a year in Paris to attend formal courses in theology.[416] If our conclusions are correct, Ricardus Anglicus could look back at the age of eighty (d. 9 April 1242)[417] on a career less brilliant perhaps, by standards of preferment, than that of many a fellow canonist, but rich in scholastic and practical accomplishments.

So much for Richard de Mores; it remains to be seen whether in the case of other English Masters at Bologna earlier activities in their own country can be established. The question is of especial interest for Alanus Anglicus, who in many

---

412 *Gesta abbat. s. Alb.* I, 307.
413 Cf. n.381 above. When older bibliographers have Ricardus Anglicus teaching for some time at Oxford (references in Wahrmund's ed. of the *Ordo*, p.xv) this is part of the confusion with the career of St. Richard of Chichester (*Acta Sanct. Apr.* I, 286, cf. above, n.354).
414 *Ann. Dunstapl.* in *Ann. monast.* III, 28; cf. Russell, *Dict, of Writers* 112.
415 References in Russell, *ibid.* 112f.; also K. Major, *Acta Steph. Langton* No. 37 (where Richard de Mores and Simon of Southwell, treasurer of Lichfield, are among the witnesses of an act of Hubert Walter), No. 54 (cf. Russell 113a n.2); one may note further Richard's law suit with Moses the Jew, *Select Pleas ... from the Exchequer of the Jews A.D. 1220–1284* (ed. J. M. Rigg, Selden Soc. 15; London 1902) 4–5, and his activity as 'magister et procurator' of a certain Leodegarius Piparde, before 1219, *Rotuli Hug. de Welles* I, 109.
416 *Ann. monast.* III, 44. Since he was back in England by 1217, he cannot be identified with Ricardus Anglicus, a regent master in theology at Paris in 1218, *Chart. Univ. Par.* I, 85.
417 *Ann. monast.* III, 158. This excludes identification with the 'magister Ricardus anglicus' entered under 15 September (no year) in Trombelli's obit list of S. Maria del Reno, Bologna (reprinted in Sarti and Fattorini, *De claris archigymnasii Bononiensis professoribus* [2nd ed. Bologna 1888–96] II, 287).

respects can be considered one of the leading professors in the decade preceding the Fourth Lateran Council.[418] His collection of decretals (c. 1206)[419] points to English affiliations, since for the pre-Innocentian texts Alan frequently appears to have relied on the tradition of the collections belonging to the *Sangermanensis* group.[420] Concerning these and other possible antecedents[421] of the *compilatio Alani*, the impending researches of Professor Holtzmann may soon allow us to formulate definite conclusions. Even more intriguing are the problems raised by the frequent quotations *secundum al.* in the glosses on Gratian of the Caius manuscript. As we stated above,[422] in most cases the reading *secundum alios* suggests itself more readily, but with all due caution one should not exclude a *priori* the possibility of a reference to Alanus in each and every instance. Once the glosses have been collated in detail with the *Apparatus Ius naturale*, which Alanus published on the Decretum over ten years later as a regent master in Bologna,[423] we may be in a position to judge whether or not he was originally connected with John of Tynemouth and his associates in the English schools.

The Catholic University of America
and Palmer, Mass.

Appendix A

On the Use of Collectio Tanner and Related Texts in the English Schools

(The numbers of books, titles, and chapters of *Coll. Tanner* [Bodleian MS Tanner 8] are cited according to Professor Holtzmann's unpublished analytical description. The present writers are very much indebted to Professor Holtzmann and to

---

418 For a list of his writings cf. Traditio 1, 289 n.52.
419 On the two redactions see *ibid.*; also Kuttner, in *Miscellanea Giovanni Mercati* (Studi e Testi 121–6; Città del Vaticano 1946) V, 619–20 and nn. 11, 12; *Traditio* 6, 350 n.52.
420 Cf. for example *Sang.* 5.4.7: *Alan.* 2.3.1; *Sang.* 5.11.2–3: *Alan.* 2.3.2–3 (same order); *Sang.* 9.5 ('Idem' i.e. Alexander III; actually Ps.-Hormisda JK+867): *Alan.* 4.9.2 ('Alexander iii.'); *Sang.* 7.147: *Alan.* 6.12 [6.3.2; 2nd. ed. 6.6.1] (cf. Kuttner, 'La réserve papale du droit de canonisation.' *Rev. hist. de droit franc. et étr.*[4] 17 [1938] 179f., 213f.), etc.
421 Cf. e.g. the hypothesis advanced by W. Ullmann, 'A Scottish Charter and Its Place in Medieval Canon Law,' *Juridical Review* 61 (1949) 232, regarding the collection of Durham MS C.iii.3, fol. 123r-158r.
422 Ch. VII, at n.244.
423 Trad. 1, 289. Dr. Ullmann, in denying Alan's authorship (*Med. Papalism* 150 n.1), must have misunderstood the conclusive arguments set forth in *Trad. loc. cit.* n.52. If further arguments were needed, one may point to the fact that in a gloss on his own compilation (*Alan.* 1.20.1 [1.16.1] v. *non intendimus*, MS Vercelli lxxxix, fol. 65rb) Alan refers precisely to the doctrines of *App. Ius nat.* which Dr. Ullmann discusses: '... quod papa est iudex ordinarius omnium hominum de omni negotio, et sufficienter probauimus .xcvi. Si duo in glosa. Alii tamen contra ...'. For Alanus as decretist cf. also *Repert.* 43, 53.

Dr. R. W. Hunt, Keeper of Western Manuscripts at the Bodleian Library, for their generous assistance.)

I. Glosses on the Decretum of Cambridge, Gonville and Caius College MS 676.

(1) fol. 173rb (C. 25 q.2 c.3): 'extra de preminencia Eboracensis et Cantuariensis archiep. Cum certum sit' (JE 1829; X 1.33.1): *Coll. Tanner* 6.7.1 alone has this rubric; in *App.* 44. 1, *Bamb.* 47. 1 etc. (*Cass., Lips., Oriel. 1*) it runs de *preemin. Londin. et Eborac ...*' in *Sang.* 7.141 no rubric is given (as is the case throughout Bks. 7–10), but even as in most instances (cf. Singer, 'Neue Beiträge über die Dekretalensammlungen ...' *SB Vienna* 171, I [1914] 95) it can be reconstructed from the corresponding title of *Abr.* 7.14.1: *de preminentia ecclesiarum et prelatorum.* In *1 Comp.* 1.25.1 the decretal appears in the title *de maioritate et obedientia.*

(2) fol. 178vb (C.27 q.1 pr.): 'extra de habitum religionis suscipientibus Consuluit' (JL 14005; X 4.6.4): *Tann.* 7.1.5, tit. *de habitum religionis suscipientibus uel professis seu monasterium ingressis matrimonium postea contrahere uolentibus.* — *App.* 45.4 *de sponsalibus secundo; Bamb.* 50.33 etc. *de matrim. contrahendo; Sang.* 8.4, no rubric *(de nuptiis voventium et conversorum:* cf. *Abr.* tit. 8.1); *1 Comp.* 4.6.7 *qui clerici vel voventes matrim. contr. possunt.*

(3) fol. 181r (C.27 q.1): 'extra de sponsa in futuro cognita Veniens' (JL 13902; X 4.1.15): *Tann.* 7.4.1 and *Abr.* 8.2.1 *de sponsa de futuro cogn.; Sang.* 8.23, no rubric (but cf. *Abr.*). — *App.* 45.1 *de sponsalibus secundo; 2 Comp.* 4.1.2 *de spons. et matr.*

(4) fol. 194ra (C. 32 q.5 c.18): 'extra de leprosis Leprosis' (JL 13773; cf. X 4.8.2); *Tann.* 7.11.3 *de leprosis; Sang.* 9.19, no rubric (no corresponding title in *Abr.*; the rubric may have been *de lepr.* as in *Tann.* or *de coniugio leprosi* as in *1 Comp.* 4.8.2). — The section *Leprosi(s)* of JL 13773 occurs elsewhere as a separate chapter only in *Francof.* 3.4 *que non impediunt uel dissoluunt ...*; otherwise usually as second paragraph of the decretal *Quoniam sicut:* thus *App.* 37.3 *de leprosis, Bamb.* 52.2 etc. *de lepr. coniugatis, 1 Comp. loc. cit.* and also, duplicated, in *Tann.* 7.11.2. (In *Bamb.* 50.15 etc. *de matrim. contrahendo* it appears also as second paragraph of the section *Super hoc vero* of the same decretal).

(5) fol. 140r (C.17 q.1 c.1): 'Votum ... expressum simplex obligat, infra eadem q. ca(pitulo) 5. ad obseruationem non compellit, In extra l(ibro) 6. ti.1 Meminimus' (JL 13162; X 4.6.3): this is a reference to *Coll. Tanner* by book, title, and chapter, numbered as *Tann.* 7.1.1 (see No.2 above for rubric) by Dr. Holtzmann, since he counts the Councils of Tours and the Lateran at the beginning of the collection as Bk.1; but reckoned as 'libro 6.' by the glossator, who counts, in accordance with the Bodleian MS (cf. Kuttner, *Repertorium* 294), Bk. 1 from the first title after the conciliar matter. — Cf. *Sang.* 8.(1.)1. — *1 Comp.* 4.6.6 and all collections not arranged by book and title are out of the question.

These references are fully convincing for *Coll. Tanner* and eliminate the *Appendix-Bambergensis* group; only for (3), and perhaps for (4), *Coll.*

Sangermanesis — in another copy — could have served as well. On the other hand the following references (cf. Kuttner. *Repertorium* 23) present difficulties:

(6) 'in quodam extrau(aganti) i(dest) Cum quisque, quod quidam habent super illu(m? illud?) ca(sum? capitulum?) ...': the wording indicates that this unidentifiable text is not cited from a collection current in the schools.

(7) 'extra de clericis homicidis Lator' (JL 14216; X 5.12.9): no such title is found in the known collections; the decretal is given under the title *de homicidio voluntario vel casuali* in *1 Comp.* 5.10.10, and *de depositione clericorum et dispensatione circa eosdem* in *App.* 26.14, *Bamb.* 11.13 etc. In *Sang*, the end of Bk. 2, where this title would have had its place (cf. *Abr.* tit.2.11), is missing. *Tann.* 2.8.10 has the decretal in the title *de illis qui incidunt in canonem date sententie*, but incorrectly so, since the papal decision does not deal with excommunication for assault against clerics (which is the proper matter of this rubric, cf. *App.* 14; *Bamb.* 7 etc.; *Sang.* 2.8) but with a question of irregularity for accidental homicide. It is therefore possible that another copy of *Coll. Tann.* had a marginal notation 'de clericis homicidis' in this place, to indicate that the rubric de *illis qui* etc. is not pertinent here.

(8) 'in extra tamen An liceat monacho Ex parte tua' (JL 11872; X 5.1.11): a title *an liceat monacho (accusare abbatem suum?)* is nowhere found. The decretal occurs (cf. Holtzmann, *Die Register* pp. 32, 64f.) in *App.* 50.16 and *Oriel. 1* 57.17 as part of a supplement without rubrics; *Cass.* 45.3 *de restitutione spoliatorum*; *Sang.* 10.13 (no rubric, probably *de accusationibus* as in *1 Comp.* 5.13.; cf. *Abr.* tit.9.1); likewise without rubric in *Tann.* 7.15.11. But we have to consider that the rubricator of the codex ceased working towards the end of Bk. 7 (thus *Tann.* 7.15.1–5=*Sang.* 7.59–63 should bear the rubric *de secundis nuptiis*, cf. *Abr.* tit. 8.12) and that *Tann.* 7.15.6–16 is a miscellaneous supplement, largely taken from the same source as *App.* 50 (cf. Holtzmann, *loc. cit.* 64f.). Another copy of the collection may have supplied individual rubrics for these chapters. In the light of the conclusive evidence given above (Nos. 1–5) for *Coll. Tanner* it needs hardly to be said that its use for reference implied the existence, at the time, of many more copies than the one now extant among the Bodleian MSS.

II. *Quaestiones* of London, Brit. Mus. Royal MS 9.E.vii; fol. 191–199 (cf. Kuttner, *Repertorium* 252).

(1) fol. 195v: 'extra quid sit officium eius a quo appellatur Sicut Romana ecclesia' (JL 12293; X 1.3.1): the distribution of the *extravagantes* on appeals under several elaborate headings is peculiar to *Coll. Tanner* and its descendants (cf. the rubrics of *Sang.* 6.8–15; Singer, *Neue Beitr.* 268 n.1). The title *quid sit officium* etc. is *Tann.* 5.12, *Sang.* 6.13, but *Sicut Romana* appears only in the subsequent title, *Tann.* 5.13.5, *Sang.* 5.14.5 *de appellationibus non recipiendis*. A mistake such as in the Royal *Quaestiones* could always be easily explained by straying of the eye;

but by a curious coincidence the rubricator of the Bodleian MS forgot to fill in the rubric of *Tann.* 5.13 so that the wrong reference would fit precisely this MS.

(2) fol. 197v: 'extra de excessibus archidiaconorum Cum satis' (JL 13898; X 1.23.4): *Tann.* 3.1.2 *de excessibus archidiaconorum contra suos episcopos et episcoporum contra suos archidiaconos*, while the title is reversed in *App.* 24.2, *Bamb.* 12.2 etc. (*de exc. ep. Contra ... et archid. contra ...*). — *1 Comp.* 1.15.4, *Sang.* 3.1.5 *de officio archidiaconi*.

III. Glosses of the Vacarian school on the *Liber pauperum* (from de Zulueta's edition).

(1) *Vac.* 1.3. n.25 (*Cod.* 1.3.32, *auth.* 'Clericos quoque' [*Nov.* 123.21]): 'Haec autent. innovata est et illa similiter "si clericum" per decretales tit. de clericis ante secularem iudicem c.i et iii.' The title is *Tann.* 4.6 *de clericis ante secularem iudicem non trahendis et de causis sanguinis in locis religiosis non exercendis*, which in *Sang.* 5.5 and *Abr* 5.6 became combined with the rubric of *1 Comp.* 2.2 so as to read *de foro competent et de clericis ante* etc. — *Tann.* 4.6.1 'Quanto circa' (JL—): *Sang.* 5.5.1, *Abr.* 5.6.1, cf. *Par.* I 151. — *Tann.* 4.6.3 'Relatum est' (JL 14047): *Sang.* 5.5.7; cf. *1 Comp.* 2.1.4 *de iudiciis*; *Lips.* 22.4 *de decimis* etc.

(2) Vac. 1.17 n.14 (*Cod.* 10.1.7 pr.): 'In extra ut lite pendente uxores etc. c.i Contra in extra Significaverunt.' A similar title occurs only in *Abr.* 8.14 *ut lite pendente coniugate maneant in potestate* (*viri*) and must be restored before *Sang.* 9.81=*Abr.* 8.14.1. But this decretal (JL 13735; X 2.13.8) does not fit the rule of the Code to which the gloss was written ('defensionis ... facultates ... adhuc controversia pendente inquietari describique fas non sit') which is implied rather in *Sang.* 9.83, *Abr.* 8.14.2 (Singer p. 344–6). The entire title *ut lite etc.* is missing at the end of Coll. Tanner, where one should expect it between *Tann.* 7.15.1–5 *de secundis nuptiis* (*Abr. tit.* 8.12) and the miscellaneous supplement, *ibid.* 6–16 (cf. above, on Caius Glosses, No. 8). Only a fuller copy of *Coll. Tanner* could give the solution. — The second reference, 'extra Significaverunt,' probably means either *Tann.* 5.7.6 (JL 13799; *Sang.* 6.8.7, *1 Comp.* 2.20.35 etc.) or *Tann.* 5.3.3 (JL—; *Sang.* 6,3.3, *Abr.* 6.3.1; *Brug.* 44.7), both of which deal with problems of possession *controversia pendente*; but the reference without title can give no definite clue.

(3) *Vac.* 2.11 n.13 (*Dig.* 3.2.11.1): 'Omnia ista innovantur per decretalem tit. de secundis nuptiis c. Super illa vero questione' (JL 14219; X 4.21.4): *Tann.* 7.15.2 (as for the rubric see above, on Caius Glosses, No. 8), *Sang.* 9.60 (rubric to be supplied from *Abr. tit.* 8.12), *App.* 9.2, *Bamb.* 55.2, *1 Comp.* 4.22.2. The title is common to all collections.

As in the case of the Caius glosses, we may conclude that *Coll. Tanner* must have been used by the Vacarian glossators, though in a copy different from the Bodleian MS.

IV. *Ordo iudiciarius* of Baltimore, Walters Art Gallery MS W.15 (cf. Richardson: *Law Quart. Rev.* 57, 321).

(1) 'in extra. decretali epistola, titulo qui filii sunt legitimi, c. Causa<m> que inter nobiles' (JL 13932; X 1.29.17, 2.14.3, 4.17.4): *Tann.* 7.13.4, *Sang.* 9.29 (no rubric, but cf. *Abr.* tit. 8.11), *Lips.* 63.4, *1 Comp.* 4.18.4 *qui filii sint legitimi.* — *Bamb.* 53.6 *de filiis coniungendis* etc.

(2) 'extra Alexandri iii. cantuariensi episcopo Cum te consulente (consulere MS) c. de appellationibus Si super causam' (JL 13967; X 1.29.18): *Tann.* 5.13.2, *Sang.* 6.14.2 *de appellationibus non recipiendis.* — *Brug.* 47.17 *quibus appellationibus est vel non est deferendum ...; App.* 46.2 *de potestate iudicum* (where the beginning of JL 13967, *Cum te consulente*, precedes as c.1 while the other collections place it elsewhere; cf. *Tann.* 4.2.9, *Sang.* 5.2.14, *Brug.* 35.3 etc.); *Gilb.* 1.13.1, *2 Comp.* 1.12.1 *de officio et pot. iud. delegati* (under this last named rubric, the section *Si super causam* is also duplicated in *Tann.* 4.3.33, *Sang.* 5.3.34).

While for No. 1 several collections could have been used, No. 2 shows that *Coll. Tanner* or *Coll. Sangermanensis* served as source for both references.

Appendix B

Gerard Pucelle on Cresconius and Gratian

Master Egidius writes at the beginning of his *Lucubratiunculae* (above, V n.135):

Humanum genus etc. Recentes auditorum animi in huius operis uestibulo plures eructuant questiones. Nam in primis querunt utrum hec uerba 'humanum genus' usque ad illum locum 'hinc etiam ysidorus' sint uerba magistri an alterius, puta alicuius sancti. Dicunt quidam quod sunt uerba fulgentii, nam is fecit breuiationem canonum, vt in di. lxiii. § Ex his (p.c.34). Alii dicunt quod sint uerba cresconii: ita enim in breuiatione cresconii continetur, sicut retulit se legisse magister Girardus pul. Alii dicunt quod sint uerba ysidori. Set M. Si. et M. blā. dicunt uerba Magistri esse: nam si uerba ysidori essent, non diceretur 'hinc' set 'item' uel 'idem.' Set et cresconii quomodo sint, cum non habeamus nisi ex uerbis illius Magistri? Fulgentii uero non sunt, quia licet is breuiationem canonum fecerit, non tamen ideo sequitur quod sint uerba ipsius. Item si alicuius sancti uerba essent, ... (Rome, Bibl. Vitt. Em. MS 1369 [Sessor. 43] fol. 75ra).

The whole problem of the authorship of Gratian's opening words is taken from the Summa of Simon of Bisignano (cf. the text in Schulte, *SB Vienna* 63, 319), whose opinion Egidius follows also for the rest of the argument, not printed here. Simon's opinion was adopted by the *Summa Dubitatur a quibusdam* of Arras MS

271 (fol. 162, cf. *Repertorium* 154) and the Anglo-Norman *Summa In nomine* (cf. *ibid.* 200) — which may prove a clue for the identification of 'M. blā.'

The other two opinions reported by Egidius are not mentioned elsewhere. The following interpretation suggests itself. Gerard Pucelle is said to have positively stated that he had read the *breviatio cresconii,* but cannot have claimed in good faith to have found there the words 'Humanum genus duobus regitur, naturali uidelicet iure et moribus' etc. (the closest approach to this would be the passage, '... unde pervidens mundanis ac divinis legibus humanae vitae regimen consistere' etc. in Cresconius' preface, PL 88, 829). In all likelihood he would have remarked that the title of the Decretum is very similar to the rubric of the *breviatio cresconii* ('Hic habetur concordia canonum conciliorum infrascriptorum et praesulum romanorum' etc. PL *loc. cit.*); Egidius, who admittedly had not seen a copy of Cresconius ('cum non habeamus nisi ex uerbis illius Magistri'), must have misunderstood Gerard's observation 'uerba sunt Cresconii' — probably a gloss to the title, *Concordia discordantium canonum* — and referred it to Gratian's opening sentence.

It is equally understandable how *quidam,* who likewise knew nothing of a *breviatio cresconii,* would have tried to improve on Gerard's statement by substituting a *breviatio* of which they did know something, the 'breuiatio canonum Fulgentii Cartaginensis ecclesie diaconi' quoted in Gratian *loc. cit.* It is true that in Egidius' account the opinion of *quidam* precedes that of Gerard, but the context suggests that it originated in a discussion of Gerard's gloss: the argument 'nam is fecit breuiationem canonum' makes no sense otherwise, as indeed it made no sense to Egidius: 'nam licet is breuiationem canonum fecerit, non tamen ideo sequitur ...' etc. Of the actual relation between the works of the two ancient African canonists the glossators will hardly have been aware.

The parallel between the title of the Decretum and that of the collection of Cresconius was later to occupy the minds of the humanists; cf. Antonio Agustín's *De emendatione Gratiani dialogorum libri duo* 1.1 (Tarragona 1587).

Appendix C

Excerpts from the Summa quaestionum of Honorius

Dist.2. tit.1 *de symonia* (the following passage has been collated in four MSS, with the kind assistance of Abbé Fransen and Mlle. Vielliard, to show the extreme caution which is needed in the interpretation of sigla and abbreviations): ... Suspensio ergo inflicta non potest redimi; set quid de infligenda? R(esponsio). secundum s. quelibet infligenda[a] potest redimi, ar. di. L. Clerico (c.37). Secundum s̃. et h. iniusta suspensio infligenda potest redimi,[b] secus de iusta ... § Item queritur utrum super decimis liceat transigere ... Solutio. Secundum s̃. in eo solo casu[c] ...

a) MS Laon 371*bis*, fol. 171ra; 'R. secundum G. (*on erasure*) quelibet infligenda' Paris, B.N. lat. 14591, fol. 61ra; 'R. secundum quemlibet infligenda' Zwettl 162, fol. 189vb; *om.* Douai 640, fol. 14vb (*homoeotel.*).

b) L; 'secundum S. et h' nulla suspensio potest redimi infligenda' D; 'secundum ñ et iniusta suspensio infligenda potest redimi' P; 's. ft' in hunc iusta suspiccio infligenda potest redimi' Z.

c) L; 'secundum G. in eo solo casu' D; 'secundum S̃. in eo solo casu' P; 'secundum quod in eo solo casu' Z.

Dist. 2 tit.8 *de crimine* (L fol. 173rb-vb): Premisimus de continentia que promouendis principaliter est necessaria. Sequitur ergo ut de singulis capitulis apostolice regule dispiciamus que omnia in personis non solum promouendorum in perpetuum, uerum etiam in quolibet ecclesie promouendo <in?> prepositum debent conuenire, vt di. lxxxi. Apostolus (c.1). Et primo de illo capitulo, 'oportet episcopum esse sine crimine' uideamus, prenotantes quibus modis crimen accipiatur in hoc casu. Dicitur autem crimen iiii^{or} modis. Primo modo dicitur ... (a long discussion follows, corresponding to that of *Sum. Omnis qui iuste* [*Lips.*], cf. Kuttner, *Kanonistische Schuldehre*, Città del Vaticano 1935, pp. 9ff.).

(q.1) His ergo prelibatis queritur an criminalia ante baptismum commissa promouendum impediant ...

(q.2) Item queritur an propter quodlibet criminale a promotione aliquis repellendus ...

(q.3) Item queritur an lapsis post penitentiam de iure competat reparatio an ex dispensatione eis indulgeatur ...

(q.4) Item queritur an papa cum homicida possit dispensare ... (cf. above, ch. VI at n.198)

(q.5) Item de aduocato qui semel prestitit patrocinium in causa sanguinis reo contra actorem solet queri an possit promoueri ...

(q.6) Item de clerico iurisperito queritur a quo dum querat iudex an reus mori debeat, respondet eum mori debere, an talis debeat a promotione repelli ...

(q.7) Item solet queri de episcopis qui temporalem habent iurisdictionem, quorum procuratores occidunt, an ipsi ut homicide irregulares debeant reputari ...

(q.8) De crimine commisso uel infamia contracta ante baptismum, an imputetur post baptismum, motum et solutum infra tit. de infamia inuenies.

(q.9) Item queritur an de enormibus peccatis possit hoc intellegi quod dicitur di.L. De his uero (c.34), quod scil. si occulta fuerint, seruato gradu possit penitere ...

(q.10) Item queritur de clerico an licitum sit coram iudice, qui impositurus est ultimum supplicium, furem super rebus sibi furtim sublatis conuenire ...

(q.11) Item solet queri [qr] baptizatus in infirmitate an possit promoueri ...

Dist.2 tit.15 *de iure patronatus* (printed in full from MS Bamberg Can. 45 by Schulte, *SB Vienna* 66, 60–4; but the Laon MS, fol. 176rb-va, obviously offers better readings): Premisimus de electione episcopi, cuius electio libera cleri est, cum in episcopali ecclesia nemo ius habeat patronatus. Ceterum cum in monasterio ius patronatus habeatur, poterit patronus uacante abbatia cum fratribus eligere, vt xviii. q.ii. Abbatem (c.3). In ecclesia uero parrochiali patronus solus eligit, vt xvi. q.ii. Decreuimus (q.7 c.32). Videamus ergo de hoc iure patronatus.

(q.1) Primo (scr.j⁰) queritur utrum ius patronatus sit spirituale uel corporale uel mixtum ... quid ergo? Solutio Jo. Dicatur quod est mixtum ecclesiasticum ... (quoting Johannes Faventinus, who is repeating the doctrine of Rufinus, *Summa* C.16 q.7, ed. Singer p. 370) uel secundum S' ius patronatus merum (mixtum?) est spirituale ... (cf. above, VI n.201)

(q.2) Item queritur utrum ius patronatus possit uendi, et uidetur, quia si uniuersitas uendatur et ius patronatus transit, vt ex de iure patr. Cum scculum (JL 13960, *App. Conc. Lat.* 15.13) ...

(q.3) Item queritur: filio patroni instituto ad presentationem patroni — quod licite fit, arg. xii q.ii. Quisquis (c.19), di. lxxxvi. Non satis (c.14) — si ad ipsum deuoluatur ius patronatus patre mortuo cum bonis hereditariis, utrum utrumque sibi possit retinere, et ecclesiam et ius patronatus? Et uidetur ...

(q.4) Set posito ipsum, dum esset minoribus ordinibus, de legitimo matrimonio patre uiuente suscepisse filium, et uxore mortua, ut dictum est, ad presentationem patris fuisse institutum, et mortuo patre ipsum habere bona hereditaria cum iure patronatus et ecclesiam, queritur utrum resignata ecclesia possit episcopus filium dignum et meritum ad eius presentationem instituere? Et uidetur ... Solutio. <Ad primum> dici potest ... ad secundum dici potest ... vt in ex. de ordinatione filiorum sacerdotum (*App.* tit. 19).

(q.5) Item queritur si duo ditauerint, utrum alter plus iuris quam alter in iure patronatus habere possit ...

(q.6) Sic dicatur de eo quod queritur si ciuitas ecclesiam fundet quod ibi nullus ciuis est patronus, set tota uniuersitas, arg. xii. q. ii. Qui manumittuntur (§1 p.c.58).

(q.7) Item queritur utrum ius patronatus inter heredes possit diuidi, puta si plures sint ecclesie, ut singuli singularum ecclesiarum sint patroni ...

(q.8) Item queritur utrum clericus de manu laici beneficium adipisci possit ecclesiasticum. Non uidetur ... E contra uidetur quod talis se tueri possit, si longa fuerit p(rescriptione) munitus, vt in ex. de iure patr. Cum pastorali (JL 13893, *App.* 15.9) ... Solutio. Dici potest quod tueri se possit non momento longe prescriptionis, set pretextu diuturne taciturnitatis episcopalis, qua episcopus uidebatur consensisse et negotium ratihabuisse; uel legatur illud 'aut' quod in eadem decretali sequitur pro 'et', et planum erit.

(q.9) Item queritur si unus in sua possessione ecclesiam fundauerit et alius eam ditauerit, quis eorum pa tron[at]us censeri debeat ...

(q.10) Item posito quod ecclesia ad alium locum transferatur, queritur utrum is esse debcat patronus nove qui fuit patronus ueteris ...

(q.11) Set quid si hereticus uel excommunicatus presentet, nunquid tenetur episcopus admittere? Resp. nequaquam, arg. xvi. q.vii. Pie. Trigentius (cc.26, 27). Quid ergo faciet episcopus? Elapsis duobus uel tribus mensibus, set quid si (*leg.* secundum quod) melius prelato uisum fuerit; poterit eum ordinare, vt in ex. ex Ro(mano) con(cilio) Quoniam (c.17).

(q.12) Item queritur utrum, si non dominus presentet et episcopus instituat aliquem, ex post facto conperto quod ille dominus fit (? siue? fundi?) patronus non fuerit, possit amoueri ...

Dist. 3 tit.2 de *prohibitionibus* (MS Douai 640, fol. 28vb-29ra): ... § Item queritur de uiolentie repulsa utrum licita sit. Et uidetur, quia a iure naturali est, a quo nullum illicitum, vt. di.i. Ius naturale (c.7). E contra quod se defendentes non promouentur, vt di. xlvi. Seditionarios (c.8). Item in euangelio, 'Si quis te percusserit' etc. (Mt. 5.39) xxiii. q.i. §i et ii. Item apostolus, 'non uos uindicantes' etc. (Rom. 12.19) vt xi. qiii. Ira (c.68).

Item quod dicitur <in> continenti posse repelli uiolentiam, queritur quod tempus ibi contineatur, cum in continenti dicatur fieri quod scil. <infra> triduum fit uel infra x. dies, vt infra ii.q.vi. Anteriorum (c.28), uel infra mensem, vt i.q.i. Constat (c.111), uel infra annum et diem, vt xx.q.ii. Puella (c.2).

Item queritur utrum <h>is qui iter perfectionis arripuerunt liceat uim repellere. Et uidetur, quia omnia iura hoc permittunt, vt in ex. de his qui inci(dunt) in ca(nonem) Si uero (*App.* 14.9–10, JL 12180). Si ergo omnia hoc permittunt, ergo et illa que perfectis proposita uel prodita?[a] E contra non uidetur, quia penitentia taliter occidentibus uidetur et (*leg.* iniungitur) biennis, vt d. L. de his clericis (c.36). Ergo mortale est uel saltem ueniale. Set perfecto pro uita conseruanda non licet uenialiter peccare, vt xxii. q.ii. Ne quis arbitretur (c.14); ne quidem ergo [non] licet monacho occidere ne occidatur.

Solutio. Ad primum dicatur licitum uim repellere in continenti, scil. flagrante maleficio, cum moderamine inculpate tutele, causa defensionis, non ultionis, quod prohibetur in canone 'Seditionarios' et in apostolo. Illud euangelicum de perfectione consilium propositum.

Ad secundum dicatur tunc fieri in continenti, quando sine interuallo fit uel post modica interualla, dum actu contrario interueniente non aboleri uideatur iniuria. Hoc tamen credimus locum habere cum res aliqua corporalis adimitur, non cum corpori tantum iniuria infertur. Tunc enim post interualla non licet; non enim esset defensio set pocius ultio.[b]

Circa tertium dissentio est: placet quibusdam perfectos posse uim repellere ui occidendo, si alias euadere non possint, et quod dicitur c. Ne quis arbitretur, de uita alterius loquitur, non propria; uel forte nec etiam ueniale est quod iubetur penitentia imponi — hec ad cautelam — et quod dicitur in euangelio, in perfectis consilium est et citra ordinem. Aliis placet in contrarium, exemplo domini dicentis paratos <esse> debere ad omnem iniuriam tolle<ra>ndam.[c]

a) Cf. *Sum. De iure canonico* D.1c.7 (MS Laon 371bis, fol. 83ra-b): '... Item queritur an uiolentie repulsio competat perfectis; et hoc quidam concedunt, quia dicitur quod omnia iura permittunt uim repellere, quare ideo non iura que perfectis sunt proposita? Aliis uidetur contra ...' (continued below, note c).

b) Cf. *ibid*, (preceding the text in note a): '... Et nota quod in continenti dicitur fieri quod sine interuallo fit uel cum interuallo, continuata ad hoc opera. Hoc tamen credimus locum habere cum res corporalis adimitur, non <cum> corpori iniuria anfertur (*leg.* infertur). Tunc enim post interualla, continuata ad hoc opera, non liceret; non enim esset defensio set potius ultio.'

c) Cf. *ibid,* (note a, continued): '... Aliis uidetur contra, et hoc uerius, cum perfectus ad iniuriam tollerandam paratus esse debeat, vt xxiii. q.i. Paratus (c.2).'

Appendix D

Select Texts from the Glosses on Gratian, MS 676 (283) of Gonville and Caius College, Cambridge

(fol. 44rb) D.70 c.2 v. *quilibet titvlatus*: Quidam intelligunt hoc de canonicis secularibus per hoc quod sequitur, alii autem soluunt ex his uerbis, 'episcopi dispensatione,' set male, quia nec etiam una ecclesia sine episcopali auctoritate alicui concedi potest. Alii dicunt nimii rigoris esse, quod falsum est; quia(?)[a] in concilio lateranensi, Quia nonnulli (*3 Lat.* c. 13). Solutio. Iste canon non est admissus in anglicana uel gallicana ecclesia. Videtur etiam tacito consensu pape et contraria consuetudine abrogari. Multa autem excipiuntur ex hoc canone, de quibus infra 16 q. ult. Per laicos (c.20).

a) Here and elsewhere in the glosses of this MS the usual abbreviation for *quia* is found where one would normally expect the word *arg (umentum)*. Cf. below, fol. 138va, 169vb. 173rb, etc.

(fol. 101rb) C.7 q.1 c.47 v. *proretam*: idest nauis gubernatorem, a prora. — Hoc modo respondit beatus Thomas cantuariensis archiepisopus londoniensi episcopo eum literis suis sepius hortanti ut regis uoluntati obsequium daret, dicens: 'Dubia nauem meam concutit procella, ego clauum teneo. Tu me in sompnum uocas?'

(fol. 129va) C.15 q.2 c.1 v. *Observandum quoque*: Nota hoc capitulum legi potest de aduocatis et tunc omnino abrogatum est, tum per contrariam consuetudinem, tum per illud in conc. later. Clerici in (*3 Lat.* c.12). Vel loquitur de iudicibus ecclesiasticis, qui non debent uendere iusticiam, ut seculares faciunt de facto. Nec obuiat quod dicitur 'pro impensis patrociniis,' quia ipsi sunt quasi patroni utrique parti. Vel non debent accipere sportulas, ut faciunt seculares iudices, uel promittere aliquid se ad dignitatem eligentibus, quod licet et facere secularibus, qui si ad honores eligerentur causa rei publice promittere possunt, D. de pollicitationibus l. Si quis ob honorem (*Dig.* 50.12.11). Et tunc 'pro impensis patrociniis,' idest suffrages, ut 1 q.6 Si quis autem (c.l); uel 'impensis,' idest impendendis. N. de Aqi.

(fol. 132rb) C.16 q.1 c.20 v. *officia*: Arg. monachum uel canonicum regularem decanum uel archidiaconum fieri non posse, (D.) 58 Si quis de alterius (c.2). Fit (?*scr.* In{^{a}}) tamen in monasterio sancti Albani et in ecclesia metropolitana burdegalensi, ubi nullus est decanus nisi habitum canonici regularis suscipiat.

(fol. 138va) C.16 q.7 pr. v. *de manu laicorum*: ... Solutio: illud de inuestitura temporalium, ut baronie alicuius, istud autem de spiritualibus; uel illud iam desoleuit.

(fol. 138va) C.16 q.7 c.1 v. *sacrilegii*: Queritur de militibus gallie, num sacrilegi sint quia decimas percipiunt? Responsio. etiam, si impenitentes fuerint, uel parcitur multitudini; quia 1.D. (50) Ut constitueretur (c.25).

(fol. 138va) C.16 q.7 c.4 v. *de negotio*: iusto scil. (*interlin.*) Vel secundum al. de omni negotio ubi dominium rei adquiratur, et ita de prostibulo set non de furto. (*marg.*)

(*ibid.*) Arg. aduocatos debere decimas dare de salario iusto quidem, set num magistri de collecta sua?

(fol. 154rb) C.23 q.4 c.21 v. *predestinata*: Homini saluando quinque sunt necessaria: predestinatio, gratia preuia (operans *interlin.*), gratia superaddita (cooperans *interlin.*), meritum et premium. Predestinationis triplex est effectus, infra de cons. 4 Nemo tollit (c.141). Horum quelibet causa est suorum sequentium. Gilebertus tamen Porret. dicit meritum non esse causam premii, cum nemo possit sufficienter uitam eternam promereri, set quandam occasionem. Alii concedunt contrarium.

(fol. 164rb) C.23 q.8 c.21 v. *gratis immolabor*: Hoc etiam beatus Thomas dixit.

(fol. 165vb) C.24 q.1 c.35: Due sunt claues, una ligandi et soluendi, altera discernendi inter lepram et lepram, 20 D. §1. Set obicitur: utramque contulit dominus Petro, et si due collate sunt ei et loquens Petro locutus est omnibus prelatis, ergo omnes habent eas. Quod falsum est, quia nec monachi claustrales uel presbiteri sine titulo ordinati uel excommunicati. Set nec soli presbiteri habent, quia et laici uidentur eas habere, arg. de cons. 4 Sanctum (c.36), ibi 'dedit ergo quod accepit' etc. Solutio: secundum quosdam omnes habent eas, non in actu set in habitu. Econtra non soli habent, quia et boni clerici non presbiteri habent eam. Set si boni clerici habent, non tamen habent ut clauem, quia accidentale est claui non esse clauem. Set pari ratione nec presbiter suspensus eam habet, quia non habet quem liget uel soluat.

Solutio secundum Gan. et Rob. Pulein: potestas ligandi et soluendi est quasi lamina cultelli, scientia discernendi inter lepram et lepram est quasi manubrium. Lamina per se sine cultello incidit manum; sic et potestas ligandi et soluendi sine discretione ledit, ligat tamen. Et dicunt quod unica est clauis, set dicuntur due propter duplicem effectum.

Set contra hoc illud euangelij: 'ue uobis legisperitis qui tulistis clauem scientie et ipsi non introiistis' (Luc. 11.52) et 40 D. Sicut (c.8) et (D.) 38 Omnes (p)sallentes (c.6). Cantor parisiensis dicit quod una clauis est obnoxietas quedam siue auctoritas ligandi et soluendi, alia est auctoritas discernendi inter lepram et lepram, quam habent soli sacerdotes. Multi ergo sunt habentes scientiam, nec tamen habent auctoritatem illam. Prescisus quidem ab ecclesia utramque amittit. Jo. Ti. sequitur Precentorem.

(fol. 167ra) C.24 q.1 c.25 v. *cathedre*: Hinc arg(uit) S. de S. mandatum pape posse durare mortuo papa etiam re integra, et ita persuasit Precentori parisiensi.

(fol. 168ra) C.24 q.1 c.35 v. *ex quo*: Hoc contra Jo. Ti. qui dicit extra ecclesiam non esse claues. Set secundum eum hic 'ex quo talia predicare ceperunt,' maxime; hoc autem hic dicitur quia non prius constat ecclesie sicut et in c. sequenti.

(fol. 169vb) C.24 q.3 c.6 v. *predicta crimina*: Secundum Io. Fa. et omnes fere reus accusatus absens contumaciter non solum ob contumaciam, set etiam de crimine sibi obiecto condempnari potest. Hic et 9 q.3 Decreuimus (C.3 q.9 c.10) arg. xi. q.1 Christianis (c.12) arg.

Ergo leges clementiores sunt quam canones; quia D. de penis 1. Absentem § Aduersus (*Dig.* 48.19.5 pr.). Ad hoc respondent dicentes canones esse clementiores, quia xi. q.3 Rursus (c.36).

Secundum Io. Ti. aliter: semper enim pro contumacia a suspensione incipiendum est et ita procedendum in pena, iuxta illud supra (Dist.) 81 Dictum (c.8), ita quod si reus tandem excommunicatus per annum persistat in excommunicatione contumaciter, tunc demum irreparabiliter deponatur. Et ita intelligitur illud 'intra annum' xi. q.3 Rursus.

(fol. 173r) C.25 q.1 p.c.16 v. *contra generalia decreta*: Solutio: si rescriptum sit
⎡ iuri naturali contrarium: ei non obtemperatur, s. eod. Sunt quidam (c.6), x.
⎢ Non licet (D.10 c.2), saluo tamen eo quod ius naturale a iure positiuo recipit
⎢ interpretationem, ut illud 'Non occides' a iure naturali est, '<in>iuste scil.' a
⎢ iure positiuo.
⎣ iuri positiuo contrarium:
　　⎡ nulli obest: ei parendum est ...
　　⎣ alicui obest ⎡ parum: ei parendum est ...
　　　　　　　　 ⎣ multum si ⎡ exprimatur: ubi non obstet ius contrarium presumendum ...
　　　　　　　　　　　　　　 ⎣ non exprimatur: non ualet donec secundum mandatum uenerit ...

(fol. 173rb) C.25 q.2 c.3 v. *Brittanorum*: maioris scil. britannie, quia 3 q.6 Hec quippe (c.10).

uero omnes episcopos: Arg. omnes episcopos anglie cantuariensi esse subiectos, quod non est uerum. Non enim dicitur hic 'submittimus' set 'committimus.' De hoc in ex. de preminencia eboracensis et cantuariensis (archiep.) Cum certum (sit). (*Coll. Tann.* 6.7.1, see above, App. A.)

(fol. 173v) C.25 q.2 c.15: Quidam tamen meticulosi iudices seu simplices omnino exequuntur mandatum pape, etiam licet iuri contrarium, arg. supra (D.) 19 In memoria, Nulli (cc.3,5); arg. C. Di. (100) Contra morem (c.8). Solutio: si iuri naturali fuerit contrarium, non est sequendum, quia ius naturale papa non potest immutare, supra eod. q.1 Sunt quidam (c.6), licet illud determinare potest, 33 q.2 Quos deus (c.18). Si autem iuri positiuo fuerit contrarium, et hoc expresse, scil. 'non obstantibus etc.', omnino sequendum est mandatum, quia illud ius bene

237

potest immutari. Set si non expresse, expectandum est secundum mandatum, ut in distinctione supra eo. q.1 ult. in media (cf. above, gl. C.25 q.1 p.c.16)

(fol. 178va) C.27 q.1 pr.: Secundum Io. Ti. in omni matrimonio significatur (Hec distinctio locum habet infra eod. q.2 Cum societas [c.17]):

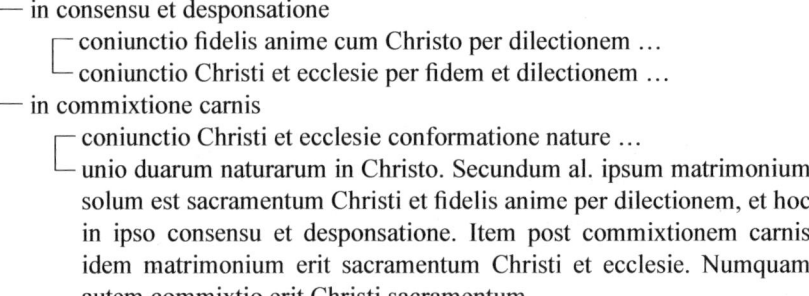

Secundum al. ipsum matrimonium solum est sacramentum Christi et fidelis anime per dilectionem, et hoc in ipso consensu et desponsatione. Item post commixtionem carnis idem matrimonium erit sacramentum Christi et ecclesie. Numquam autem commixtio erit Christi sacramentum.

(fol. 178vb) C.27 q.1 pr. v. *Quod voventes*: Votum est conceptio melioris boni animi deliberatione firmata[a] deo sponte oblata. Ex hac descriptione colliguntur 3. gradus uoti, secundum quod primum dicitur propositum, postea desiderium, tandem uotum. Set quia fere omnibus capitulis huius questionis contraria sunt supra 27.D. Quidam, Si uir (cc. 2, 3), quidam sic: Votum aliud publicum, aliud priuatum; secundum Gan. uotum aliud de presenti, aliud de futuro; secundum Alex. uotum aliud simplex, idest sine sollempnitate: istud impedit contrahendum, set non dirimit contractum, ut ibi; aliud sollempne, quod sollempnizatur in crucis susceptione, in ordine, in habitu, in manu episcopi: istud impedit contrahendum et dirimit contractum, <ut> hic.[b] Item uotum secundum quosdam aliud necessitatis, sine quo salus non est, ut in hiis que exprimuntur in baptismo, ubi tamen improprie dicitur uotum; aliud supererogationis, et proprie, quia quis sponte offert quod quidem deus non exigit offerendum, set oblatum requirit.

Secundum H. omne uotum, et solum, perpetue continencie proprie acceptum, siue simplex siue sollempne, impedit et dirimit matrimonium postea contractum.[c] Sollempnitas enim quoad uoti substantiam nihil operatur, set quoad probationem, ut in matrimonio. Et de huiusmodi uoto loquuntur omnia capitula hic usque Nuptiarum (c.41).[d] Si autem improprie accipiatur uotum, ut cum proposito dicitur uotum — 17 q.2 Nos nouimus (c.2), infra ead. q. Proposito (c.21), Nuptiarum (c.41) prope medium — post tale uotum non dirimitur matrimonium. De huiusmodi uoto infra ead. cap. penult. et ult. (cc.42, 43) et 27.D. Quidam, Si uir (cc.2, 3) intelliguntur. Set in extra, de habitum religionis suscipientibus, Consuluit (*Coll. Tann.* 7.1.5, cf. above, App. A) in fine contra.[e]

Solutio: Alexander ibi non ut papa set ut magister distinxit; uel ibi sollempne, idest de presenti; simplex, idest de futuro.[f] Quod potest colligi ibidem et capitulo Meminimus (*Tann.* 7.1.1) in fine. Vel ibi 'non dirimit,' quia non potest probari. Non enim deficit ius set probatio, D. de testamentaria tutela, Duo sunt Ticii (*Dig.* 26.2.30).

a) Cf. the gloss of the French school to Stephen of Tournai's *Summa*, Berlin MS lat. qu. 193 fol. 86, as published by Thaner, *SB Vienna* 79 (1875) 216–8: '... Votum conceptio melioris boni animi deliberatione firmati (*sic*) ...'

b) Cf. *ibid.*: '... Solempne votum et impedit matrimonium contrahendum et dirimit contractum ... simplex votum impedit matrimonium contrahendum sed non dirimit contractum. In hac opinione fuit Gratianus, Rufinus, Johannes (Faventinus), Alexander III et Bassianus.'

c) *Ibid*, (continued): 'Ugucio vero praemissam distinctionem sub sensu assignato non recepit ... dicit ergo Uguicio praescise quod omne votum perpetuae continenciae et solum impedit matrimonium contrahendum et dirimit contractum ...'

d) *Ibid*. 218: 'Omnia ergo capitula huius quaestionis a principio usque ad capitulum Nuptiarum intelliguntur de voto de praesenti, exinde usque ad finem quaestionis de voto de futuro. Hac distinctione utitur Uguicius et sequaces eius.'

e) *Ibid.* (continued): 'Alexander vero III et fere tota ecclesia utitur praedicta distinctione, quae est de voto solemni et simplici, et quidem Alexander ponit eam in decretalibus Qui clerici vel voventes etc. in capitulo Consuluit' (*1 Comp.* 4.6.7).

f) *Ibid.* (continued): 'Sed Ugucio respondet quod non loquitur ut papa sed ut magister; vel dicit quod ipse vocat votum simplex, votum de futuro; votum solempne, votum de praesenti.'

(fol. 181ra) (i) C.27 q.2 pr.: Sponsalia sunt mentio futurarum nuptiarum seu repromissio, Dig. de sponsal. l(ege) 1 (23.1.1). Que si contrahantur inter aliquos, ut solet fieri, per uerba de futuro, sponsus et sponsa inde dicuntur; set inter hos non est matrimonium, nisi uelimus dicere spe futurorum, non re presentium. Si autem sequitur copula carnalis, necdum est matrimonium ibi, set tantum ecclesia presumit esse, in extra. de sponsa in futuro cognita, Veniens (*Tann.* 7.4.1, cf. above, App. A), que secundum Io. Ti. formata est ex illa lege Dig. pro socio 1. Merito (17.2.51), et admittitur probatio in contrarium. Potest autem probari copulam carnalem non interuenisse affectu maritali set motu fornicario ... matrimonium autem neque actio neque passio neque qualitas dici potest, set quedam res per se existens ...

(fol. 181ra) (ii) C.27 q.2 c.3: Ad hoc uerbum 'indiuiduam' obicitur de Jacob. Responsio. Tempori (*sic*) Jacob eius coniunctio cum Lia fuit indiuidua, inspecta prima institutione qua dictum est 'Erunt duo in carne una' (Gen. 2.24) et fuit uerum matrimonium inter ipsum et Lyam, uerum quoque inter ipsum et Rachel. Set consilio familiari spiritus sancti fuit hoc contra primam institutionem matrimonii. Eadem igitur fuit tunc substantia matrimonii que et nunc, set non idem effectus matrimonii uel potestas erat in illis: neutra enim earum habuit plenam potestatem in Jacob. Jo. Ti. uel prima erat uxor, alie fornicarie set excusate, 32 q.4 Obiciuntur (c.7) in media.

(fol. 181ra) (iii) *ibid.* v. *fide*: Que fides mutue castitatis est; est et alia fides in primo cohitu que mutue seruitutis est, j.eod. Sunt qui dicunt (c.19) arg.; uel utraque fides oritur in ipso contractu matrimonii, set una suspensa secundum al. usque ad tempus traductionis; de quo tamen plenius infra eod. Desponsatam (c.27) in media.

(fol. 184va) C.28 q.1 c.13: Quidam dicunt tantum azima prohiberi, quia superstitionem continent et certis tantum temporibus sumuntur. Set ego generaliter idem de omnibus cibis eorum intelligo, infra eod. cap. proximo (c.14) arg. Nec est hoc prohibitum propter cibi immunditiam set in odium iudaice superstitionis, et quia ipsi cibis nostris non indistincte utuntur. Set numquid christiano fame pereunti licet uti eorum azimis? Resp. uidetur quod non, quia generaliter est prohibitum nec est nostrum excipere (C.31 q.1 c. ult. [13] *interlin.*), de cons. 1 Sicut (c.11), item 32 q.4 Sicut (c.8). Set infra de cons. 5 Discipulos (c.26) arg. contra. Solutio: necessitas legem non habet; unde si aliter non patet aditus euadendi mortem, tunc licet, xi. q.3 Quoniam multos etc. (c.103). Item nonne possum emere uinum uel cibaria eorum uel alio contractu accipere et ita comedere? Resp. ita, quia omnia munda mundis*; non enim tam prohibetur huiusmodi comedere quam cum eis comedere. Illicita est enim eorum familiaritatis communio. Similiter quod christianus eger medicinam a iudeo emere potest et potest per se uel ab alio christiano dante sumere, si non aliter possit mors euadi. Set num iudeo languenti possumus medicinam dare? Resp. et uendere et dare ei possumus, set alius porrigat. Set et eam exibere possumus pietatis intuitu, xi. q.3 Quoniam multos (c.103). Jo.t'. (*82 Proposuisti [D.82c.2] in medio *interlin.*)

(fol. 187va) (i) C.30 q.3 c.5 rubr. v. *Pascalis vero secundus*: Si hoc uerum est, tunc dicemus Alexandrum papam errasse in decretali de filiis coniungendis ante uel post compaternitatem, Utrum (JL 14091; *Tann.* 7.12.1),[a] ubi dicitur hoc capitulum esse correctum per capitulum hic proximum supra, Super quibus (c.4). Pascalis enim secutus est Urbanum, ut in cronicis. Malo ergo dicere literam hic falsam, et est litera uerior 'Pascalis primus,' quam dicere Alexandrum male dixisse, quod est absurdum; quia C. de leg. et constit. 1. ult. (*Cod.* 1.14.12) et 19 Sic omnes (D.19. c.2).

a) We may conclude from *Coll. Bamb.* 53.1 etc. that de *filiis coniungendis* was the original rubric for *Tann.* 7.12; but the rubricator left off before this title and another hand supplied the rubric *de cognatione spirituali* from *Comp. I.*

(fol. 187va) (ii) C.30 q.4 pr.: Querit Gratianus an aliquis possit ducere commatrem uxoris sue, et primo improbat, deinde probat, tandem soluit. Hunc conflictum quidam euitant proferentes posteriora prioribus. Alii dicunt 'commatres' cuius altera alterius filium de sacro fonte suscepit: tales ducere non licet. Item sunt commatres que eundem puerum de fonte suscipiunt: tales ducere licet. Alii distinguunt inter directam commaternitatem et indirectam siue emergentem: directas non licet ducere, indirectas licet, et ita Rollandus.[a] Alii distinguunt an matrimonium precesserit commaternitatem, et de hac priora capitula, an econtra, et ita posteriora; et ita Albertinus et Io. fa. et Ruffinus.[b] Secundum al. (Alanum? alios?) refert an post commaternitatem uxor sit cum uiro una caro effecta, et sic priora capitula, uel non sit, et ita posteriora; et ita Gratianus. Secundum al. refert an uxor mea susceperit filium alterius, uel alia filium eius, ut in primo casu non possim illam aliam ducere, in secundo bene; et ita sentit Car. et bene, quia nunquam prohibeor contrahere cum commatre uxoris mee, nisi et ipsa mihi sit effecta commater, quod fit ubi uxor mea, postquam cognouero eam in matrimonio, alterius filium suscipit de fonte.

a) Rolandus, *Stroma* ad loc. (ed. Thaner p. 148f.).
b) Rufinus, *Summa* ad loc. (ed. Singer p. 465).

(fol. 187va) (iii) C.30 q.4 v. *assumpta uxor commater*: in carnalem copulam post contractam commaternitatem, secundum Gr.
idest ubi matrimonium precessit commaternitatem, secundum R. et al.[a] et Io. fa. directa, secundum Rol. suscipiendo, C. directa, Rol.
(fol. 187va) (iv) C.30 q.4 v. *ejus uxor commater non est*: directa, Rol. quia nondum fuit cognita post compaternitatem contractam, secundum Gra. quia nondum fuit ducta in matrimonium tempore susceptionis nec ante, secundum R. Io. et al.[a]

a) Albertus, cf. gl. ii above: 'Albertinus et Io. fa et Ruffinus.'

(fol. 193ra) C.32 q.4 c.14 v. *voluptates*: ... Sol.: S. de S. dicit ex hoc uerbo 'dampnate' mortale peccatum esse huiusmodi in propria uxore, set leui satisfactione purgandum. Io. de Ti. dicit esse ueniale, et exponit 'dampnate,' idest reprobate, supra i.q.ult. Saluberrimum (q.7 c.21), uel 'dampnate,' idest punite, 13 q.2 Tempus (c.23) in fine.
(fol. 194ra) C.32 q.5 c.18 v. *pro societate fideque*: ergo et lepram ... arg. in extra, de leprosis, Leprosi (*Tann.* 7.11.3, cf. above, App. A) arg.; set ibidem Peruenit (7.11.1) contra arg. Solutio: S'. de S'. distinguit si ita sit leprosus quod expellatur, uel quod timeatur infectio, non tenetur eum sequi coniunx.[a] Set forma contrahendi matrimonium contra, ubi dicitur 'siue sanus siue eger.' Item quod hic dicitur Quicquid (c.22) contra; supra eod. § Cum ergo (dict, p.c.16) contra in fine. Set et ita ibi tribueretur occasio malignandi cuilibet. Set et idem esset in aliis morbis.
Unde J. de Ti. dicit: quantumcumque sit leprosus, tenetur eum sequi, et tamen cogi non potest. Ad multa enim tenemur ad que non cogimur, ut est 'Pasce fame morientem' (D.86 c.21), dare omnia pauperibus (Mt.19.21, etc.). Item supra eod. Qui uiderit (c.13).

a) Lincoln Cathedral MS 121 has the following gloss to *App. Conc. Lat.* 37.2 *Pervenit* (=*Tann.* 7.11.1; JL 13794): 'Arg. contra. Set hic ubi de locis inhabitatis expelluntur ad loca solitaria, illud ubi non; uel hic quando tanta apparet macula quod ex contactu timetur infectio, illud quando non ita' (communication from Professor W. Holtzmann). A similar gloss is printed in Mansi 22, 394 to the same decretal. Huguccio does not accept the decretal *Pervenit* and says the healthy person should follow the leprous, cf. the text in Gillmann, AKKR 107 (1927) 249 n.3.

(fol. 194rb) C.32 q.5 c.33 v. *non facile*: Io. Fa. Gra. Ruf. legunt 'non facile' idest non; et tunc arg(uitur) quod difficile fit, nullo modo fit, supra 2 q.6 Biduum (c.29), Cod. de testib. Iurisiurandi (4.20.9). Car. Io. de Ti. aliter legunt. Dicunt enim facilius uxores a uiris quam uiros ab uxoribus accusari, et secundum eos quod difficile fit, aliquo modo fit, ut Cod. de penis 1.6 (9.47.6), supra 1 q.1 Principatus (c.25), et hic ubi dicitur 'uiri autem liberius.'

(fol. 198ra) C.33 q.2 c.19 v. *Antiqui et sanctissimi patris*: Hoc capitulum iactat S'. de S'. se docuisse bononie. Est enim aliquantulum difficile, set Io. de Ti. intelligit de marito qui commisit adulterium incestuosum manifestum insidians personis tantum, uel etiam matrimonio, set consanguinitate longinqua.

(fol. 201 va) *De poen.* D.1 c.66 v. *ingrediatur ecclesiam*: Arg. pro Barthol. qui dicit neminem qui est in mortali debere ingredi ecclesiam ...

Appendix E

Excerpts from Two Writings of Richard de Mores (Ricardus Anglicus)

I. Summa brevis super decreta

(D.1) Tractaturus igitur gracianus de iure canonico orditur ab altiori, a iure uidelicet naturali, multipharie distinguens tam ipsum ius naturale quam positiuum, quod facit distinctione prima.

(D.2) Tandem subdistinguit ius ciuile.

(D.3) Post distinguit ius canonicum adiciens quid sit eius officium. (Dublin, Trinity College MS 275, p. 169).

(D.74) An fieri possit cui uis ut promoueatur.

Quod extra eodem loco distinxi.[a]

(D.75) Subiungitur quibus temporibus ordines conferantur.

Hic nota quod ordo episcopalis omni dominica bene confertur, vt c.i; sequentes tres ordines tantum vi. temporibus anni, quod dic vt j(nfra) e(adem) c. ult. (c.7); accolitatus autem et minores ordines in aliis festis etiam conferuntur, vt ex. de temporibus ordin. Subdiaconus (*1 Comp.* 1.6.1). (D p.170).

a) Ric. *Distinctiones* D.74: 'In principio circa promotionem inspicitur: promouens, utrum hoc faciat celo caritatis ...; promouendus, utrum iustam habuerit excusationem uel non ...; ecclesie necessitas ... utilitas ...; promotus ...' (MS Vat. lat. 2691, fol. 4r).

(C.2 q.1) Quere an officio notoria iudicis obstent.
R(espondeo) obseruandum ordinem iudicarium exceptis v. casibus extra notatis.ᵃ
(q.2) Iudicium dici non debet in expoliatum.
Quod bene distinctum est/ca. iii. q.i. In principio.ᵇ ...
(q.8) Qualiter fiat accusatio? R. ut ex. eodem loco distinxi.ᶜ Hic adde quod supra defuit. (D 171b-172a).

> a) Ric. *Dist.* C.2 q.1 §1: 'Omittitur ordo iudiciarius: propter euidentiam sceleris ...; propter defectum iudicis ...; propter scandalum ...; propter dilapidationem ...; propter contumaciam ...' (V 5v).
> b) *Ibid.* C.3 q.1 §1: 'Spoliatur quis: rebus uel beneficio ...; officio ...; communione fraterna ...' etc. (V 6v).
> c) *Ibid.* C.2 q.8 §1: 'Videamus quid sit accusare ..., quot sint species ...' etc. (V 6v).

(C.5 q.6) Qualiter obiectum qui non probat est feriendus.
R. ut distinxi ii.q.iii in prin.ᵃ (D 173b)
(C.14 q.4) Clericus aut laicus non debet sumere fenus.
R. non debet nisi uelud fideiussor pro alio soluerit sortem uel usuras, vt/ ex. de fideius. Institutus (*1 Comp.* 3.18.5). Item ut redimatur proprium predium ecclesie accipi potest usura, vt ex. de usuris, Plures (*1 Comp.* 5.5.1). Verumptamen est usura bona que accipi potest, vt di. xlvi. Sicut non suo distinxi.ᵇ (D 175a-b).

> a) Ric. Dist. C.2 q.3 §1: 'Accusator peccat cum aut errore decipitur aut ...' etc. (V 5v).
> b) *Ibid.* D.47 c.1 (following immediately upon D.46 c.10 *Sicut non suo*): 'Est usura: elemosine, ut que reliquerit pater aut mater ...; sacre scripture ...; pecunie ...' (V 2v).

(C.15 q.6) An liceat quicquam extorqueri cruciatu.
Quod dico vt ex. eodem loco distinxi.ᵃ Incidit an excommunicato domino absoluatur uassallus. Respondent quidam simpliciter quod ita, arg. j. e. q. c. Iuratos (c.5). Ego autem dico eos non aliter absolui nisi hoc exprimatur in sentencia; pro me facit xi. q.iii. Quoniam multos (c.103).ᵇ (D 176a).

> a) Ric. *Dist.* C.15 q.6 is missing in V.
> b) Richard reversed himself in his glosses on *1 Comp.* 5.6.7 *De brabantionibus*: 'Set nonne iurauerunt ... Set domino excommunicato ipso iure suspenditur fidelitas. Dicunt quidam quod non, nisi secunda et specialis super hoc emanauerit sententia: set eorum opinionem exaudio tantum in speciali familia, ut xi. q.iii. Quoniam (c.103). Alios autem ipso iure dico suspensos ...'; *ibid. v. abiuratis*: 'Nota uasallos excommunicatorum a fidelitate relaxatos, vt ...; arg. contra ...; Solutio: Hec contraria

intelliguntur de speciali familia, qui ab anathemate excipiuntur ibi, hic autem de uasallis.' The full text is found in Gillmann, 'Richardus Anglikus als Glossator ...,' AKKR 107 (1927) 654f.; the second gloss recurs in Richard's *Brocarda* (MS Vat. Chis. lat. E.VII.218, fol. 79vc).

(C.16 q.4) Ecclesie que contra quas prescribere possint?
R. quelibet potest prescribere contra quamlibet, vt. s(upra) e. q.iii. Per singulas (c.1).
(q.5) Proprietasne soli donet tollatue capellam?
R. non, vt j. e. c. Possessio (c.2). (D 176a).
(C.18 q.2) Fratribus a solis sine presule an fiat abbas.
R. Monachis est abbas eligendus consentiente domino fundi / vt j. e. Abbatem (c.3), ab episcopo instituendus et consecrandus, vt hic c.i. Excipiuntur priuilegiata monasteria, in quibus abbates per monachos eliguntur et per eosdem instituuntur, que quoad legem diocesanam omnino sunt libera, vt j.e. Quam sit (c.5). Set non quoad legem iurisdictionis, vt xvi. q.i. Interdicimus (c.10), j.e. Si quis abbas (c.15), nec quoad seruicium, si quod prestare consueuerunt episcopo, j.e. c.ult. (31). Est tamen casus in quo permittitur episcopo abbatem eligere, scil. quando omnes uolunt aliquem minus ydoneum habere, vt j.e. Si quis abbas. Nam sicut per (*leg.* propter?) maliciam episcoporum nonnulla monasteria sunt exempta, <ita> et episcopis subiecta, vt j.e.q. Si quis abbas. — Additur autem de dupplicibus monasteriis prohibitis, vt j.e. § Non solum (dict. a.c.21). — Accedit etiam ne clerici sint honerosi monasteriis, vt c. Peruenit et Dudum (cc. 26–27). — Apponitur etiam qualiter monasteria pacta possunt inire cum episcopis, vt c. penult. (c.30). (D. 176b–177a).

(C.25) Supra dictum est de ea dignitate ecclesie quam habet in ligando et soluendo. Nunc uideamus de ea quam habet in dispensando.
(q.1) Queritur an recte peto quod dederat mihi papa.
R. Quantum ad tema presens in exceptione decimarum, dic ut distinxi xvi. q.i. Questi (c.46).[a] De prerogatiua autem sedis apostolice, de qua hic subditur, que erit meta? R. Cum petentibus nil sit positum finitum, vt in aut. de referendariis in princ. (*Auth.* 2.5 pr.=*Nov.* 10 pr.), quascumque metas preelegerit discretio, easdem uelud emula amplectatur dispensatio,[b] arg. i. q.v. Presentium (c.3), vt iudice libante iusticiam nil aliud estimetur dispensatio quam iuris mitigatio, cum iusta succedit necessitatis uel pietatis uel utilitatis conpensatio.[b] Nec enim, cum hoc fit, neruus ecclesiastice seueritatis frangitur, set incuruatur.

Incuruatur enim heliseus, incuruatur herodes.
Nec humilitatis meritum propheta perdidit,
Nec deitatem deus incarnatus amisit.

Nota igitur quod aliud est dispensare, aliud legem statuere. Dispensare potest ut supra, legem autem statuere non potest contra generalem statum ecclesie, / vt j.e. Que sunt (c.3), Quidam (c.6). Set si illud posse attendamus quod in facto consistit, eo usque extendetur statuendi potentia, quo usque manifesta dei ecclesie fiat iniuria. Set ex tunc uelut fractor murorum fidei tanquam hereticus repelletur, vt di. xxii. Omnes (c.1), di. xl. Si papa (c.6). (D 179a-b).

a) Ric. *Dist.* C.16 q.1 c.46: 'Religiosorum predia: propria ...; conducta ...' etc. (V 10v).
b) Rhymed prose.

II. Summa quaestionum

(List of topics according to Montecassino MS 396, pp. 191–247; in Zwettl MS 162, fol. 145r-173r, some titles are subdivided according to information kindly supplied by Dr. Ullmann.)

1. De iure naturali (cf. Gratian, D.1). 2. De nocturna pollutione (cf. D.6). 3. De perplexitate (cf. D.13). 4. De consuetudine (cf. D.11). 5. De decretalibus epistolis (cf. D.19). 6. Utrum summus pontifex utrumque gladium habeat (cf. D.22, D.96). 7. De electione (cf. D.23, D.63). 8. De continentia clericorum (cf. D.26–34). 9. De lapsis (cf. D.50). 10. De servis (cf. D.54). 11. De simonia (cf. C.1). 12. De convictis (cf. C.2 q.1). 13. De eo quod legitur in evangelio 'Si peccaverit ...' (Mt. 18.15; cf. C.2 q.1 c.19). 14. De spoliatis (cf. C.2 q.2). 15. De purgatione vulgari (cf. C.2. q.5). 16. De appellationibus (cf. C.2 q.6). 17. De testibus (cf. C.3 q.5). 18. De induciis (cf. C.3 qq.2–3). 19. De infamatis (cf. C.3 q.4). 20. De excommunicatis (cf. C.4, C.9, C.11 q.3). 21. De usura (cf. C.14). 22. De praescriptione (cf. C.16 q.3). De iure patronatus (cf. C.16 q.7). 24. De iuramento (cf. C.22). 25. De hereticis (cf. C.24). 26. De rescriptis (cf. C.25 q.1). 27. De voto (cf. C.27 q.1). 28: De matrimonio in genere (cf. C.27 q.2). 29. An matrimonium sit inter infideles (cf. C.28). 30. De errore (cf. C.29). 31. De propinquitate spirituali (cf. C.30 q.1). 32. De enormitate delicti (cf. C.31 q.1). 33. De frigidis et maleficiatis (cf. C.33 q.1). 34. De consanguinitate (cf. C.35). 36. De ecclesiis de novo aedificandis (cf. *De cons.* D.1). 36. De sacrificio altaris (cf. *De cons.* D.2). 37. De baptismo (cf. *De cons.* D.4).

Tit.1 (M 191a-193b): Circa ius naturale uarie solent fieri questiones. Inprimis queri solet quid ipsum sit. Secundo an eo omnia sint communia, et si hoc, utrum leges et iura alia per que libet (*sic*) habere propria sint ei contraria. Tertio an precepta iuri <s> naturalis dispensationem admittant. Quarto de his que in capitulo ysidori continentur in dist. i. Ius naturale (c.7). V° an omnium una libertas sit; item an quelibet coniunctio maris et femine sit de iure naturali, uel aliqua non.

(q.1) Ad primum diuersi uario modo respondent. Dicunt enim quidam quod ius naturale sit liberum arbitrium, set horum sententia, ut uidetur, ex eo infirmatur quod libero arbitrio homo ad bonum et malum flectitur. Ius uero naturale malum semper prohibet et detestatur. Alii dicunt quod sit caritas, per quam homo facit bonum uitatque contrarium. Set hoc non uidetur, quia caritas in solis bonis est. Alii dicunt quod ius naturale est superior pars anime, ratio scil. que nec in caym potuit extingui teste scriptura. Cum enim sit natura, i.e. naturale bonum, delictorum meritis obfuscari poterit, nunquam tamen extingui.[a] Nullorum sententiam reprobamus. Sic enim accipi potest ius naturale secundum uarias acceptiones iuris naturalis, quarum notitia plena reddet que sequuntur; et ideo eas premittere uidetur necessarium.

Dicitur enim ius naturale ordo quidam et instinctus nature ... id cuiquam nil (*leg.* non) facere quod sibi nolit fieri.[b] His modis accipitur ius naturale.

(q.2) Nunc ad <secundum> membrum accedamus, an scil. de iure naturali sint omnia communia ...

a) Cf. Simon de Bisignano, *Summa* D.1, as printed by Schulte, in *SB Vienna* 63 (1869) 319f. and O. Lottin, *Le droit naturel chez saint Thomas d'Aquin et ses prédécesseurs* (2nd ed. Bruges 1931) 106f. Richard slightly shortened Simon's text and changed the sequence of the three opinions: Simon reports first ('dicunt enim quidam') on those who identify natural law and charity, second ('alii uero dicunt') on those who identify natural law and free will, and then gives his own opinion ('nobis itaque uidetur') on natural law as the *superior pars anime* or *synderesis*.

b) Richard here enumerates the six meanings of the term, natural law, slightly abridged from the *Summa Omnis qui iuste*, as printed in Lottin, *op. cit.* 108; Kuttner, *Repertorium* 201ff.

Tit.8 (M 198b-199a): De continentia clericorum inprimis queritur, si aliquis fuit ordinatus inuitus, an teneatur continere ratione ordinis sic suscepti ...

(q.2) Item queritur de licentia apostoli omnibus data qua concessit ut unusquisque suam habeat propter fornicationem, quomodo sit ei derogatum ...

(q.3) Item queritur quomodo sancti patres niceni concilii, statuentes ne quis uxorem ducat in tribus gradibus, potuerint aliquem obligare ad continentiam seruandam, si eam in ordinis susce<p>tione non exprimat ...

(q.4) Item queritur in quo casu loquitur cap. xxviii. di. Diaconi (c.8) ubi dicitur ...

(q.5) Item queritur de eo quod habetur (dist.) lxxxii. Apposuisti (c.2) ...

(q.6) Item queritur si clericus orientalis est (*leg.* ecclesie) ad partes istas uenerit, an posset uxori adherere et celebrare ...

(q.7) Item quid si clericus occidentalis ecclesie uenerit ad orientalem, [p] possetne ei uxorem habere sicut alii ...

(q.8) Item quid si clericus illius ecclesie ordines hic susciperet et post ad propriam redit ecclesiam ...

(q.9) Item queritur si impuberes promoueantur ad ordines sacros, utrum, cum perueniant ad annos discretionis, teneantur continere ...

Tit. 9 (M 199a-200a): De lapsis queritur an post actam penitentiam de iure communi possint promoueri ...

(q.2) Item queritur de eo quod dicitur (dist.) L. Hii qui altario (c.52), ubi dicitur quod si lapsi fuerint ...

(q.3) Item queritur an papa possit dispensare cum homicida. Quod non uidetur, nam post perpetratum homicidium quantacumque secuta penitentia in sacerdotio ministrare non poterit qui[a] homicidium commisit, vt di. L. Miror (c.4). Item contra preceptum domini non potest quis dispensare uel contra prohibitionem. Dominus enim dixit: 'Non edificabis mihi domum quia uir sanguinum es.'[a] Videtur ergo <quod> contra hoc dictum non potest quis dispensare, vt xxv. q.<i> Sunt quidam (c.6). Econtra uidetur quod possit: [aliud] alexander enim quendam sacerdotem post homicidium commisum qui annis .xii. penitentiam agunt (*sic*) sacerdotio restituit in capitulo illo quod incipit Tanta est uis, uocatque eos inperitos qui sacerdotem reparari non posse opinantur post dignam penitentiam.[b] Vnde uidetur quod possit dispensare, non obstante eo quod dominus dixit 'Non edificabis' etc. Nam in penis contra constitutionem domini uel apostoli potest rigor temperari, vt di. lxxxii. Presbiter (c.5) .[c]

(q.4) Item queritur si aliquis ante baptismum homicidium commiserit, an post baptismum possit promoueri ...

(q.5) Item queritur de eo qui baptizatur instante articulo mortis ...

(q.6) Item queritur de causa constitutionis illius cap. Is qui di. L. (c.57) ubi dicitur quod si aliquis in ultimis peccatum suum confessus fuerit et communionem acceperit, si post conualuerit et publice non penituerit nec alio modo fuerit criminosus, admitti potest ad clerum. Set quis fecit hanc questionem? Nullus de hoc dubitare posset ...

a) Cf. *1 Paralip.* 28.3; 17.4 etc.; Honorius, *Sum. quaest.* 2.8.4 (above, VI at n.198).

b) JL 13912; cf. above, VI n.199.

c) Richard reversed himself on this in his later writings. Cf. *Summa brevis* D.50: '... uerumtamen nota quod excepto corporali homicidio papa potest cum quolibet peccatore post penitentiam dispensare, nisi scandalum impediat ...' (Dublin, Trinity College MS 275, p. 170); *Distinctiones* D.50 pr.: 'Crimen ...: maximum, ut homicidium sponte commissum, incestus, simonia. Isti penitentia peracta per dispensationem quedam recuperant, homicida tamen nunquam exequetur sacerdotium, i. q.vii c.ii. ...' (MS Vat. lat. 2691, fol. 3r); *Apparatus* ad *1 Comp.* 4.6.7 v. *ad sacerdotium*: 'Nec credo papam dispensare posse sine peccato in sacerdotio cum homicida, vt de cons. di.i. ...' (Gillmann, AKKR 107, 646). This is connected with the fact that Alexander III's decretal JL 13912 (*App.* 26.13) was not accepted in *Comp. I* or any later Bolognese collection.

Tit. 23 (M 217a-218b): Solet queri utrum ius patronatus sit spirituale uel corporale, et quidem si spirituale est, non est successorium ...

(q.2) Item queritur cum plures sint patroni ei<us>dem ecclesie, an equaliter uel inequaliter habeant ius patronatus ...

(q.3) Item cum ius patronatus acquiratur per ditationem, vt xvi. q.ult. Filiis (c.31), queritur an quicumque dat aliquid ecclesie, puta xl. uel lx. solidos, an dicatur ius patronatus acquisiuisse ...ᵃ

(q.4) Item solet queri utrum ius patronatus possit diuidi inter heredes ...ᵇ

(q.5) Item queritur an ius patronatus habeatur in ista ecclesia, que tamen necessitate uel alia de causa in alium locum transfertur ...ᶜ

(q.6) Item queritur an is qui omnia uendidit ius patronatus uendere intelligatur ...

(q.7) Item queritur quod si ciuitas basilicam constituat, eritne quilibet de ciuitate patronus? ...ᵈ

(q.8) Item solet queri de contrarietate duarum decretalium, inprimis de illa que dici<t> patronum qui possidet, non tamen uerus patronus est, si [re]presentauerit et alius postmodum ius patronatus eui[n]cerit, quod possit infirmare presentationem factam a priore. Hoc dicitur in extrau(aganti) Dilectus (JL 13764), cui contrarium dicit illa, Consultationibus (JL 12636). Set dici potest quod si credatur esse patronus et possideat, presentatio ab eo facta non infirmabitur, quo casu loquitur illud c. Dilectus.

(q.9) Item [so.] de illa decretali queritur, que dicit ecclesias non uacantis monasterii (*leg.* uacantes monasterio) concedi posse, vt in ex. Consultationibus; cui obloquitur alia que dicit concessiones factas non uacantium ecclesiarum locis religiosis non ualere, vt in ex.u(ag). Quamuis (JL 14156) ...

(q.10) Item ratio (merito?) queritur de eo quod dicitur, quod si unus eligat presentationem domini fundi, alter concessionem episcopi ...ᵉ

(q.11) Item queritur de eo quod dicitur in decretali illa, Cum pastorali (JL 13893), quod scil. se tueri possit clericus tantum <in> donatione laici si longa prescriptione fuerit munitus. Quid est ergo quod dicitur alibi quod si quis per laicos obtinuerit beneficium, adeo deponi debet et excommunicari, vt xvi. q. ult. Si quis deinceps, Quoniam, Si quis clericus (cc.12, 13, 16) ? Quidamᶠ respondent sic dicentes silentium episcopi equipollere auctoritati que ab initio debuit interuenisse; eo enim ipso quod tacet, ratam uidetur habere concessionem factam a laico. Set nonne debet deponi, quia suscepit ab initio de manu laici, ut dicunt predicta capitula?

(q.12) Item queritur de heretico uel excommunicato presentante ...ᵍ

(q.13) Item queritur quomodo monachi potestatem habeant instituendi ...

(q.14) Item de archidiaconis queritur an longa consuetudine sibi possint uendicare ius instituendi clericos ...

(q.15) Set queri potest utrum alius quam sacerdos curam animarum habere posset, cum nullus alius habeat potestatem ligandi uel soluendi ...

(q.16) Item queri potest utrum personalis uicarius uel episcopus habeat curam animarum, scil. an unus eorum an simul omnes ...

(q.17) Item queritur de monasteriis illis que non sint priuilegiata ...

(q.18) Item cum ius patronatus acquiratur tribus modis, queritur quis presentare debeat, uel illi (*sic*) qui fundauit, uel illi qui di[c]tauit, uel illi in cuius possessione posita est ecclesia ...ʰ (q.19) In fine notare potes specialem casum in quo aliquis eligere sibi successorem potest, ut si ad eum deuolutum fuerit ius patronatus ...[423]

a) Qq. 1–3 from Simon, *Summa* C.16 q.7 c.26, as printed in Schulte, *SB Vienna* 63, 322f. ('... Unde primo queritur an ius patr. sit spirituale ...'; 'Item queritur cum plures sint ...'; 'Item cum ius patr. per ditationes ...'); for qq.1–2 cf. also Honorius, *Sum. quaest.* 2.15 (above, Appendix C).
b) cf. Honorius, *ibid.* q.7.
c) From Simon, *loc. cit.* 323 ('... Item queritur de eo qui ius patr. habet in aliqua ecclesia, que tamen ...'); cf. also Hon. *loc. cit.* q.10.
d) Qq.6–7: cf. Hon. *loc. cit.* qq.2, 6.
e) Q. 9: cf. Simon *loc. cit.* ('... Item queritur an sine consensu episcopi patronus possit religioso loco concedere ...'); q.10: cf. Hon. *loc. cit.* q.12.
f) 'Quidam' refers to Honorius, *loc. cit.* q.8 .
g) Cf. *ibid.* q.11.
h) Cf. *ibid.* q.9.
i) Cf. *ibid.* qq.3–4.

RÉFLEXIONS SUR LES BROCARDS DES GLOSSATEURS

This essay by Kuttner, published in 1951, is his survey for the literary genus of *Brocarda* or *Generalia* defined by him as 'énonciation de principes d'ordre général.' He had only referred to this type of canonistic literature in a few sentences of his 'Repertorium' (p. 239). He sees the origin of the brocarda in 'un arsénal pour la discussion' without 'la solutio contrariorum' (p. 253s.) (P.L.)

I

On sait que les *generalia* ou *brocarda* doivent leur existence au désir des glossateurs, légistes ou canonistes, de rattacher l'explication des décisions particulières qu'ils trouvaient dans les sources du droit à l'énonciation de principes d'ordre général. L'établissement de *generalia* répond donc au besoin d'une science systématique du droit: par voie d'induction et d'abstraction on dérive de tel canon ou de telle *lex* particuliers une certaine pensée normative qu'on exprime, pour la plupart, par une brève maxime et dont, á l'aide de références parallèles (*concordantiae*) et opposées (*contraria*), on éprouve la solidité, c'est-à-dire si et dans quelle mesure elle peut servir de règle générale. C'est par la possibilité d'une telle considération dialectique — possibilité indiquée soit par une antithèse expresse, soit par un simple *contra*, accompagnés des allégations appropriées — que se distingue, dans la terminologie des glossateurs, le *generale* du simple *notabile* ou *argumentum*.[1]

D'après une ingénieuse hypothèse de Hermann Kantorowicz le terme, autrement inexplicable, de *brocarda*, *brocardica*, pourrait bien avoir trait à ce caractère distinctif des *generalia* et reposer sur la déformation, en guise de jeu de mots,

---

1 E. GENZMER, *Die iustinianische Kodifikation und die Glossatoren*, dans les *Atti del Congresso Internazionale di Diritto Romano, Bologna, 1933*, t. I, p. 424, Pavia, 1934; S. KUTTNER, *Repertorium der Kanonistik: Prodromus corporis glossarum*, t. I, dans les *Studi e Testi*, t. LXXI, pp. 3, 239, Città del Vaticano, 1937. Par contre, cfr la définition du simple *argumentum* par le canoniste Richard l'Anglais, *glossa ad Comp. I*, 5.36.10 v. *invenit*: «Nota quod argumentum est quod sola investigatione invenit veritatem», imprimée chez F. GILLMANN, *Richardus Anglikus als Glossator der Compilatio I.*, dans l'*Archiv für katholisches Kirchenrecht*, t. CVII, 1927, p. 623.

de *pro-contra*[2]. Le fait est que le mot se trouve quelquefois épelé *procard(ic)a*; et l'adjonction *vulgo, vulgariter* dont le terme est plus d'une fois accompagné[3] démontre qu'il s'agit bien d'une expression de jargon. La dérivation de *brocarda* du nom de l'évêque Burchard de Worms (dont la collection canonique ne contient pas de *generalia* du tout) a été reléguée déjà par Savigny dans le domaine de la légende[4]; elle ne s'en trouve pas moins encore çà et là dans les traités de droit.

L'hypothèse de Kantorowicz s'accorderait bien avec le fait que Pillius, qui a introduit le terme *brocarda* dans la langue écrite, n'entendait pas s'en servir pour désigner les *generalia* de son *Libellus disputatorius*, mais bien plutôt ses *Quaestiones*[5], ainsi donc un genre littéraire qui a en commun avec les *generalia* la discussion à l'aide d'arguments pour et contre[6]. Ce n'est qu'après Pillius que

2 H. Kantorowicz, *The Quaestiones disputatae of the Glossators*, dans la *Tijdschrift voor Rechtsgeschiedenis*, t. XVI, 1937–38, p. 4; cfr A. van Hove, *Prolegomena*, 2ᵉ éd., dans le *Commentarium Lovaniense in Codicem iuris canonici*, v. I, t. I, p. 449, n. 7, Malines-Rome, 1945.

3 Cfr la rubrique du ms. de Bruxelles, 131–134 (2558), fol. 1: «Incipiunt generalia que vulgo brocarda dicuntur, a domino Otone composita, et eorumdem discordantium concordia», citée par W. M. d'Ablaing, *Zur Bibliothek der Glossatoren*, dans la *Zeitschrift der Savigny-Stiftung für Rechtsgeschichte*, Roman. Abt., t. IX (1888), p. 16; E. Seckel, *Distinctiones Glossatorum*, dans la *Festschrift der Berliner Juristischen Fakultät für Ferdinand von Martitz*, p. 407, n. 4, Berlin, 1911. La même rubrique dans le ms. de Worcester, F. 14, n° 4. Cfr aussi la définition donnée par la *Materia ad Pandectam*, citée plus loin, p. 263:«quae... vulgariter brocarda appellantur».

4 C. F. von Savigny, *Geschichte des römischen Rechts im Mittelalter*, 2ᵉ éd., t. III, p. 568 et suiv., Heidelberg, 1834–51. — Tout au plus peut-on dire que pour la permutation *procontra <*procarda* <*brocarda* l'association phonétique avec la collection de l'évêque de Worms, fréquemment citée sous la forme *in Brocardo* par les décrétistes du XIIᵉ siécle, ait pu jouer un certain rôle.
Ce n'est qu'à titre de curiosité que nous mentionnons ici l'étymologie proposée par M. W. Spargo, *The Etymology and Early Evolution of Brocard*, dans *Speculum*, t. XXIII, 1948, pp. 472–76: le mot serait un dérivé du vieux celtique *broc*, «of a mixed color», «grey, speckled», «variegated, not distinctly shaded», qui se trouverait aussi à la base du nom irlandais pour blaireau, mais auquel dans notre cas aurait été adjoint, du vieux français, le suffixe péjoratif *-art, -ard*, pour caractériser «juridical forms which are of composite origin» (p. 475); car les brocards auraient été des «pretty miscellaneous compilations... the quality of which... remained steadily at the low level of the 'every man his own lawyer' type of textbook misused today.» On se demande si M. Spargo a jamais lu des *brocarda* de l'époque des glossateurs, vu qu'il conclut son article ainsi qu'il suit: «The older brocards were awkward, homely, unskillful general statements of canon law, made by persons who understood that type of law rather poorly and were at the same time so unversed in Latin that they did not make up their generalizations in good Latin».

5 Seckel, *Ueber neuere Editionen juristischer Schriften aus dem Mittelalter*, dans die *Zeitschr. der Sav.-Stift.*, Roman. Abt., t. XXI, 1900, p. 289; Genzmer, *art. cit.*, p. 420, n. 328; p. 426; U. Nicolini, *Pillii Medicinensis Quaestiones sabbatinae, Introduzione all'edizione critica*, p. 25, Modena, 1933.

6 Il est à remarquer que dans les *Quaestiones* de Pillius un certain nombre de thèmes sont formulés non comme cas particuliers, mais comme théorèmes abstraits sous forme interrogative, et pourraient donc tout aussi bien être présentés comme propositions; c'est précisément à des thèmes de ce genre que Pillius paraît se référer de préférence comme se trouvant *in brocardis nostris* (cfr la liste des citations chez E. Genzmer, *Seckel und Ugo Nicolini über die Quaestionen de Pillius*, dans la *Zeitschr. der Sav.-Stift.*, Roman. Abt., t. LV, 1935, p. 329). D'autre part plus d'une fois des *generalia* (dans le *Libellus disputatorius*) et des *distinctiones* du même maître revêtent la forme de questions, *Cum queritur utrum...*, cfr Seckel, *Distinct. Glossat.*, p. 362.

brocardum est usité tout simplement comme synonyme de *generale*. Mais encore aux XIIIe et XIVe siècles notre terme était parfois appliqué à toute *materia quae est contrariarum opinionum rationibus involuta*[7]: en fait, les *Distinctiones* de Pierre de Belleperche — qui se présentent presque toutes sous forme de questions didactiques (*cum queritur...*, *si queritur...*)[8] — furent connues aussi, par exemple de Balde, sous le nom de *brocarda*[9].

Quant aux *generalia* ou brocards proprement dits, le *contrarium* est dès l'origine un élément caractéristique de ce genre littéraire; la solution des antinomies présentées ne l'est pas. Au premier degré de l'évolution les auteurs se contentent d'aligner les arguments contradictoires qu'ils ont décelés dans les sources: les brocards de ce genre ne forment qu'un arsenal pour la discussion, comme le *Sic et non* d'Abélard[10]. Ce n'est qu'à une étape ultérieure que vient s'y ajouter, par application conséquente de la méthode scolastique, la *solutio contrariorum*, qui établit des distinctions ou d'autres délimitations. Pour l'histoire des doctrines juridiques c'est là la partie la plus intéressante des brocards, lorsque par les *solutiones* les glossateurs ont mis le moyen heuristique des maximes générales au service de la connaissance systématique du droit. La *solutio* se trouve ajoutée, soit par l'auteur des *generalia* lui-même (tel Pillius dans la deuxième édition de son *Libellus disputatorius*)[11], soit par d'autres qui prennent la suite de son ouvrage, comme l'a fait Azon dans sa revision des *Brocarda* d'Otto Papiensis[12]. C'est aussi le cas du canoniste Richard l'Anglais: en parlant de ses brocards il dit seulement avoir composé des *generalium solutiones*[13]: il ne revendique pas, comme en étant l'auteur, les *generalia* eux-mêmes.

De même que presque tous les types littéraires et méthodes didactiques des glossateurs, les *brocarda* apparaissent au XIIe siècle sous deux formes: ou bien, disséminés parmi d'autres genres de gloses, à la marge des livres de droit canon et romain, ou bien réunis dans des collections distinctes. D'après l'opinion courante le genre prend son origine dans les gloses, par un développement logique des

---

7 Définition donnée par le *Vocabularius iuris utriusque*, cfr Savigny, *op. cit.*, t. III, p. 569, note e. La définition «brocardicum in iure dicitur quando ex vtraque parte racionibus fortibus pro et contra argumentatur» se trouve dans le *Vocabularius Quia in libris*, éd. par Seckel, *Beiträge zur Geschichte beider Rechte im Mittelalter*, t. I, p. 363, Tübingen, 1898.
8 E. Steffenhagen, *Beiträge zu Savigny's Geschichte des römischen Rechts im Mittelalter*, p. 20, Königsberg, 1859; F. Lajat, notice sur Pierre de Belleperche, dans l'*Histoire littéraire de France*, t. XXV, p. 378, Paris, 1869; E. M. Meijers, *De universiteit van Orleans in de XIIIe eeuw*, dans la *Tijdschr. voor Rechtsgesch.*, t. II, 1919, p. 484.
9 Cfr Steffenhagen, Meijers, *loc. cit.* Thomas Diplovatatius connut un ms. de Pierre de Belleperche, intitulé *Distinctionés seu brocarda*, cfr Savigny, *op. cit.*, t. VI, p. 33, note *i*.
10 Parallèle souligné par Genzmer, *Die iustinianische Kodifikation...* (art. cit. plus haut, n. 1), p. 427.
11 Seckel, *Distinct. Glossat.*, p. 327, n. 1; Genzmer, *loc. cit.*
12 On ne sait pas exactement si toutes les solutions sont dues à Azon, ni combien de degrés de rédaction (en tout cas plus de deux) il y a lieu d'admettre dans les Brocards d'Otto-Azon; cfr Seckel, *op. cit.*, p. 384, n. 2.
13 Cfr notre *Repertorium*, p. 417; voir plus loin, p. 263 et suiv.

notabilia, qui comptent parmi les plus anciens types bolonais de gloses[14]. Dans le sens primitif la *nota* marginale est destinée à diriger l'attention du lecteur sur tel ou tel passage remarquable du texte (des *notae* de ce genre se trouvent bien avant l'âge des glossateurs[15]); parfois la *nota* consiste dans la répétition, en marge du texte, d'u passage important. Au moment où la *nota* sert à exprimer une pensée dérivée de la loi, nous avons le *notabile* dans le sens plus étroit et qui peut s'identifier avec *l'argumentum*, lequel suppose toujours un processus d'abstraction[16]. Bien entendu les *notabilia* que les glossateurs introduisent par les mots *Nota quod..., Arg. quod..., Hinc collige...,* ne se prêtent pas tous à être amplifiés en *generalia*, vu que souvent il s'agit ici d'un *speciale* trouvé dans tel on tel passage des sources. Et même parmi les *notabilia* qui ont été formulés comme des règles de droit en termes généraux, il s'en trouve beaucoup qui ne sont jamais devenus de véritables *generalia*[17].

II

Or, ces derniers temps, il a été découvert, quant aux origines des *brocarda*, d'autres connexions historiques, qui permettent de se rendre compte des influences que les disciplines rhétoriciennes, la topique notamment, ont exercées sur le développement de notre genre littéraire. Nous sommes redevables de ces nouveaux résultats aux remarquables recherches de M. Albert Lang, publiées pendant la guerre, sur la structure de deux parmi les plus anciennes collections de brocards[18]: I° l'ouvrage dit *Perpendiculum*, inconnu jusque récemment, et qui fut composé par un canoniste anonyme, probablement peu aprés 1180[19].

---

14 GENZMER, *art. cit.*, p. 423; cfr notre *Repertorium*, p. 3.
15 Cfr M. CONRAT, *Geschichte der Quellen und Literatur des römischen Rechts im früheren Mittelalter*, t. I, p. III, n. 5; p. 120, n. 9, Leipzig, 1891.
16 Sur les différentes espèces de *notabilia* voir surtout G. PESCATORE, *Die Glossen des Irnerius*, pp. 52–54, Greifswald, 1888; pour les canonistes cfr notre *Repertorium*, pp. 3, 232 et suiv., 408; G. M. DÉNES, *I notabili di Paolo Ungaro*, pp. 41–52, Rome, 1944 (renseignements utiles, mais à corriger dans plusieurs points de détail).
17 On peut observer toutefois que çà et là un *notabile* exprimant un principe d'ordre général, mais sans aucun développement dialectique, a été inséré dans des collections de *brocarda*. C'est pourquoi Savigny dans la Ire éd. de sa *Geschichte* (t. III, p. 525 et suiv., Heidelberg, 1822) refusa de considérer les *contraria* comme un trait distinctif des brocards. Le passage en question a été modifié dans la 2e éd. (t. III, p. 568 et suiv., 1834), où Savigny parle d'un double usage du terme, *brocarda* signifiant parfois simplement des règles générales, mais le plus souvent des règles qui se prêtent aux arguments contradictoires. Dans le même sens cfr B. BRUGI, *Per la storia della giurisprudenza e delle università italiane, Nuovi saggi*, p. 48, Turin, 1921.
18 A. LANG, *Rhetorische Einflüsse auf die Behandlung des Prozesses in der Kanonistik des 12. Jahrhunderts*, dans la *Festschrift Eduard Eichmann zum 70. Geburtstag dargebracht*, pp. 69–97, Paderborn, 1940; *Zur Entstehungsgeschichte der Brocardasammlungen*, dans la *Zeitschr. der Sav.-Stift.*, Kanon. Abt., t. XXXI, 1942, pp. 106–141. Comme il m'a été impossible de me procurer aux États-Unis la *Festschrift* citée, je dois m'en rapporter aux notes que j'ai prises en 1946 dans l'exemplaire de la Bibliothéque Vaticane.
19 Décrit pour la première fois dans notre *Repertorium*, pp. 241–42. Aux 5 mss. qui s'y trouvent énumérés, Lang a ajouté le ms. de Munich, lat. 8013, fol. 115v-117v (*Rhetor. Einfl.*, p. 73, n. 17);

The 'Perpendiculum' (or Summula de presumptionibus) was planned to be edited by Rudolf Motzenbäcker and Norbert Brieskorn, but the edition was not published. For the date of the 'Perpendiculum' cf. *A. Gouron*, Aux racines de la théorie des présomptions, Rivista internazionale di diritto comune 1 (1990) 99–109, here p. 106–108; also in: *A. Gouron*, Droit et coutume en France au XIIe et XIIIe siècles (Ashgate 1993), no. VII, and cf. *A. Gouron*, Une école de canonistes anglais à Paris: maître Walter et ses disciples (vers 1170), Journal des Savants (2000) 47–72, here p. 64s., also in *A. Gouron*, Pionniers du droit occidental au Moyen Âge (Ashgate 2006), no. VI. (P.L.)

2° Le *Libellus disputatorius* de Pillius (1re édition), d'une date un peu plus rapprochée, qui n'était connu des anciens historiens de la littérature du droit romain au moyen âge que par ouï-dire et que Seckel a redécouvert en 1892[20].

A la différence des collections proprement dites — c'est-à-dire des *generalia* réunis sans un plan cohérent; ou ramenés à l'ordre légal des sources où ils ont été puisés — les deux ouvrages sont, en partie du moins, des monographies systématiquement ordonnées. Ils prennent leur point de départ, l'un et l'autre, dans la théorie des présomptions, qu'ils nous présentent dans le cadre d'une Somme sur cinq différentes possibilités d'incertitude judiciaire: *incerta (incertitudo)* concernant ou la *substantia* ou la *qualitas*, de faits tant externes (n°s 1–2) qu'internes (n°s 3–4), ou bien concernant l'interprétation du texte d'une loi ou d'un document (n° 5). Pour chacune des incertitudes il se trouve établi un nombre de titres typiques de présomptions (*loci* dans le *Perpendiculum; modi* chez Pillius), accompagnés des allégations respectives *pro* et *contra*, à la manière de *brocarda* sans solutions (= *Perpend.*, 1re partie; *Lib. disp.*, livre 1er)[21].

Chez Pillius, cette partie est suivie d'un deuxième livre systématique dans le même style sur le procès, tandis que le troisième livre de Pillius et la seconde

---

un septième se trouve à Grenoble, ms. 626 (391, 1), fol. 161^v-163. Une brève mention du ms. de Leipzig (*Repert. loe. cit.*) déjà chez Th. A. REIMARUS, *Petri Blesensis opusculum de distinctionibus... sive... Speculum iuris canonici...*, p. XXXII, Berlin, 1837, qui, se fondant sur une communication de Richter, pensa y voir un ouvrage apparenté aux Distinctions de Pierre de Blois (même indication dans le catalogue des mss. de la Bibliothèque de la Ville de Leipzig, par R. G. R. NAUMANN, 1838, p. 80). — Pour la date approximative cfr LANG, *Rhetorische Einflüsse...*, p. 88; *Zur Entstehungsgeschichte...*, pp. 110, 135.

20 Liste des mss. (deux fragments et deux mss. complets de la première, un ms. de la deuxième rédaction) avec les indications bibliographiques nécessaires chez LANG, *Zur Entstehungsgeschichte...*, pp. 108–109; cfr p. 106, n. 1 (d'après KANTOROWICZ, *Eine Gesamtausgabe des Pillius in Vorbereitung*, dans la Zeitschr. der Sav.-Stift., Rom. Abt., t. L, p. 473) sur la simultanéité des premières communications faites en 1900 par Seckel d'une part et Gaudenzi de l'autre. La priorité de Seckel (1892) résulte de la note dans ses *Distinctiones Glossatorum* (ouvrage cité plus haut, n. 3), p. 327, n. 1. — Malheureusement tous les travaux préparatoires pour une édition du *Libellus disputatorius*, commencés par Seckel et continués par M. Genzmer, ont péri pendant la guerre dans l'incendie de Hambourg.

21 LANG, *Rhetorische Einflüsse...*, pp. 73–84; *Zur Entstehungsgeschichte...*, pp. 111, 113, 125–134 (voir p. 127 pour la table des incertitudes; pp. 128–129 pour l'usage des termes *locus* chez l'un et *modus* chez l'autre auteur). Cfr aussi les renseignements préliminaires dans notre *Repertorium*, p. 241–242; GENZMER, *Die iustinianische Kodifiliation...*, p. 428 (sur Pillius).

partie du *Perpendiculum* nous donnent des *brocarda* généraux non ramenés à un système et ne se bornant pas à des matières juridiques déterminées. Dans les manuscrits du *Perpendiculum* la deuxième partie[22] contient des variations considérables dans le nombre, le choix et la suite des *generalia*; dans certains mss, se sont infiltrés de simples *notabilia* et autres pièces étrangères[23]. Les allégations relatives aux différentes énonciations varient elles aussi dans les mss. (c'est ainsi par ex. que çà et là dans le ms. Borgh. 287 se trouvent citées des décrétales[24], ce qui n'est jamais le cas dans la partie systématique *de presumptionibus*); parfois se trouvent même ajoutées des solutions[25]. Tout cela démontre que le *Perpendiculum* a été répandu sans que la deuxième partie en fût considérée comme un ouvrage littéraire terminé. Nous ne savons guère si ces changements et additions sont dus à l'auteur lui-même ou à d'autres qui ont remanié son ouvrage. La question n'est d'ailleurs que d'une importance secondaire.

Afin de préciser la place qui revient aux deux ouvrages dans l'histoire médiévale des méthodes et de la littérature juridiques, il faut, ainsi que l'a démontré M. Lang, étudier de plus près leur commun point de départ, à savoir le cadre général de la théorie des présomptions. Il se trouve en effet que la première partie du *Perpendiculum*, dans la structure des *incerta* et dans l'établissement des différents titres de présomptions (*ex persona, ex tempore, ex loco*, etc.) suit de très près les distinctions systématiques que le décrétiste Sicard de Crémone avait établies en cette matière dans sa *Summa* (vers 1179-81), à propos de la *Causa* 6, q. 5, de Gratien[26]. Or le système de Sicard repose sur la théorie cicéronienne des *status* rhétoriciens (*controversiae*) et des modes ou lieux d'argumentation (*loci*) de la démonstration rhétorique[27]. Abstraction faite de quelques transpositions et de

---

22 Parmi les sept mss. cinq (Cambridge, Pembroke College ms. 101; Leipzig, Bibl. de la Ville ms. 247; Grenoble ms. 626; Bibl. Vaticane, mss. Borgh. lat. 287 et Pal. lat. 653) contiennent les deux parties, le ms. Munich 8013 seulement la première, et le ms. Fulda D. 10 seulement la deuxième (cfr *Repertorium loc. cit.*, LANG, *Zur Entstehungsgeschichte...*, p. 110, n. 15).

23 LANG, *art. cit.*, p. 111, n. 17. Quant à la pièce *Delicto coram iudice*, qui est attachée à la 2e partie dans le ms. Borgh. et celui de Leipzig, voir plus loin, note 31.

24 Par ex.: «Jn decretis al'(exandri). iii. consuluit. religiosi. peruenit ad audientiam» (fol. 7rc); «Jn decr. alex. iii. Sicut ex litteris», «Jn co(ncilio) roma(no) al' iii. quod a predecessore» (fol. 8rb), etc. Notre remarque sur l'absence totale de telles citations, *Repertorium*, p. 242, est donc à corriger.

25 Par ex.: «Consuetudinis auctoritate defenditur quod alias illicite fieri diceretur...; contra...; (solution:) In his postremis capitulis nota carissime quod quesiuisti...» (ms. Borgh. fol. 3ra; Pal. fol. 115rc), etc.

26 LANG, *Rhetorische Einflüsse...*, pp. 73, 85 et suiv.; *Zur Entstehungsgeschichte...*, pp. 111, 127-129. Il s'agit bien de Sicard C. 6, q. 5 et non pas de q. 4 ni de C. 2, q. 4, ainsi qu'on lit p. 73 du premier ou p. 123 du deuxième article.

27 *Rhetorische Einflüsse...*, pp. 74 et suiv., 81 et suiv., 90 et suiv. — Les *status* cicéroniens (*quaestio facti, nominis*, etc.) étaient connus des glossateurs déjà avant Sicard et les autres auteurs cités par M. Lang (*art. cit.*, p. 95: *Brachylogus*, 4.14 et *Ordo Tractaturi de iudiciis*, éd. Gross). La première discussion paraît s'en trouver chez Bulgarus, *Materia Codicis* § 4, cfr H. KANTOROWICZ, *Studies in the Glossators of the Roman Law*, p. 42, Cambridge, 1938. Quant à l'*Ordo Tractaturi* la question d'une influence de Sicard ne se pose pas, puisque cet ouvrage a paru en France vers 1170.

quelques variations[28], la contribution essentielle du *Perpendiculum* consiste dans le développement des différents titres de présomptions, que Sicard avait rédigés en catalogue schématique, par l'addition des arguments *pro* et *contra* pour chacun d'entre eux[29]. Ainsi donc notre auteur réunit les formes de la *summa* et du brocard en une Topique détaillée (il persiste à parler de *loci*) des preuves par probabilité employées dans les controverses juridiques. Tous ces titres de présomptions avec leurs concordances et *contraria* nous fournissent non pas des *vera*, comme s'exprime l'auteur, mais *et probabilia et apparentia*; car, pour constater et apprécier les faits dans un procès (*substantia et qualitas facti*), de même que pour interpréter des textes incertains de la loi ou d'un document[30], il ne s'agit pas de démonstration logique, mais de persuasion par des syllogismes et des arguments probables. Le but de l'ouvrage consiste donc à enseigner l'art de la dispute (*propter exercitium disputandi*) et de la plaidoirie (*oratorem potius quam iudicem instruat*)[31].

De même que le *Perpendiculum*, et de toute probabilité par l'intermédiaire de celui-ci, le premier livre de Pillius dépend dans sa disposition générale de Sicard, C. 6, q. 5[32]. Mais Pillius — outre que naturellement il développe les différents brocards tout autrement que le canoniste — amplifie dans maints endroits le système par de nouveaux points de vue et par des digressions, qui risquent presque

---

The ordo 'Tractaturi de iudiciis' was written for its major part already in Paris around 1165 by Walter of Coutances – cf. *A. Gouron*, Une école de canonistes anglais à Paris (above at p. 255) and P. Landau, Walter von Coutances und die Anfänge der anglo-normannischen Rechtswissenschaft, in "Panta rei". Studi dedicati a Manlio Bellomo III, ed. *O. Condorelli* (Roma 2004) 188–204. (P.L.)

28 Pour la transposition dans le système des *incerta* voir LANG, *Zur Entstehungsgeschichte* ..., p. 127; la variation matérielle la plus importante se trouve dans la section de l'*incertitudo circa interpretationem*, cfr *ibid.*, pp. 134, 140.

29 *Rhetorische Einflüsse*..., pp. 73, 88; *Zur Entstehungsgeschichte*..., pp. 118, 123.

30 Dans la section *circa interpretationem* le *Perpendiculum* traite de l'harmonisation des textes en développant les méthodes couramment proposées depuis Yves de Chartres, Bernold et Abélard (LANG, *Zur Entstehungsgesch.*, p. 140). On a observé justement qu'à l'origine ces méthodes sont d'un caractère plutôt rhétoricien et ne se réunissent à la dialectique qu'à une seconde phase; cfr G. PARÉ, BRUNET et TREMBLAY, La renaissance du XIIe siècle, Les écoles et l'enseignement, pp. 267 et suiv., Ottawa-Paris, 1933; R. MCKEON, Rhetoric in the Middle Ages, dans *Speculum*, t. XVII, 1942, p. 21.

31 Épilogue de la 1re partie: «...nec tamen uera continet hoc perpendiculum, set et (*om. cod. Borgh.*) probabilia et apparentia propter exercitium disputandi, ut presentis instructionis. (instructoris *cod. Fuld.*) beneficium oratorem potius quam iudicem instruat». L'intention d'instruire l'avocat dans l'art de l'argumentation inspire également les *Notabilia Delicto coram iudice*, qui dans le ms. Borgh. sont placés à la suite du *Perpendiculum*, tandis que dans le ms. de Leipzig ils se trouvent dans la 2e partie de l'ouvrage. Ils commencent: «Delicto coram iudice manifestato (manifeste *Lips.*) aliquando (*om.Lips.*) allegantes delinquenti uolumus implorare ueniam, aliquando uolumus contra ipsum exasperare vindictam, aliquando assidentes (existentes *Lips.*) iudici iustitie ordinem <et?> equitatis suadere uolumus normam (formam *Lips.*), aliquando lesum inducere ut remittat (emittat *Borgh.*) gratis offensam. In primo casu...» (Borgh. fol. 8[v]; Lips, d'aprés LANG, *Rhetor. Einfl.*, p. 84). Bien que la méthode de cet écrit soit entièrement différente de celle du *Perpendiculum*, il n'est pas exclu qu'ils soient du même auteur.

32 LANG, *Zur Entstehungsgeschichte*..., p. 139 et suiv. Pour les variations communes au *Perpendiculum* et au *Lib. disputatorius* mais s'écartant de Sicard, voir les textes *ibid.*, pp. 127–129, pour les

de rompre la continuité du plan d'ensemble, tandis que d'autre part il oublie au cours de son exposé certains des sujets dont, au commencement de son livre, il s'était proposé de traiter[33].

L'importance centrale du traité des présomptions pour l'un et l'autre ouvrage est évidente. Le canoniste n'a même pas donné au sien un titre d'ensemble, la deuxième partie n'ayant pas reçu de forme littéraire définitive. *De presumptionibus* est la seule suscription qui se trouve dans les mss.; et en parlant de *hoc perpendiculum* dans l'épilogue de la première partie, l'auteur entend non pas donner un titre, mais caractériser son ouvrage[34]. Par conséquent, quand notre canoniste dans un autre écrit, les *Notabilia* avec l'incipit *Argumentum quod religiosi*, se réfère à un passage de la première partie de ses Brocards, il parle simplement de *Summula de presumptionibus*[35], comme s'il s'agissait d'un ouvrage indépendant[36]. Chez Pillius le livre premier occupe plus de la moitié de tout le *Libellus*; aussi l'ouvrage était-il connu au moyen âge par antonomase sous le nom *De presumptionibus*. Le feudiste Alvarottus écrit: «... et tandem quia est via brocardica, remisit se ad libellum disputationum Py. qui alias appellatur de presumptionibus[37]». Il est en effet manifeste que le domaine des présomptions se prêtait tout particulièrement à l'établissement de règles générales d'argumentation et à l'examen de la portée de ces règles à l'aide de *contraria*.

On ne peut toutefois se ranger à l'opinion de M. Lang, quand il veut en tirer la conclusion historique que le type littéraire des *brocarda* dans l'école de Bologne serait issu de la manière de traiter la doctrine des présomptions, par l'application analogue de cette méthode aux *notabilia* généraux[38]. A notre avis cette hypothèse se heurte à deux objections: *a*) elle ne tient pas compte du fait que l'histoire des *brocarda seu generalia* en tant que genre littéraire indépendant (collections et ouvrages systématiques) ne s'identifie point avec l'histoire du *brocardum seu generale* en tant que type méthodique ou forme du penser juridique; *b*) sans preuves à l'appui elle considère le *Perpendiculum* et le *Libellus disputatorius* comme produits caractéristiques de l'école de Bologne.

---

raisons démontrant que Sicard ne peut être que la source médiate et que le *Perpendiculum* ne peut dépendre de Pillius cfr *ibid.*, p. 139.
33 D'après Lang, *art. cit.*, p. 137, «wirkt die zugrundegelegte Gliederung wie ein fremdes, schlecht angepasstes Kleid».
34 Cfr le texte cité plus haut, note 31.
35 Cfr le texte dans notre *Repertorium*, p. 236. Le passage en question se réfère à la discussion *circa interpretationem*, mentionnée plus haut, note 30.
36 C'est autre chose si Pillius dans le *Lib. disp.* désigne parfois la brève introduction au livre 1er comme *presumcionum summula*, cfr Lang, art. cit., p. 114 et suiv.
37 Texte cité par Savigny, *Geschichte* (ouvrage cité plus haut, note 4), t. IV, p. 330, note *d* ; on comprend que pour lui cette désignation devait rester inexplicable.
38 Lang, *Zur Entstehungsgeschichte...*, pp. 116 et suiv., 118 et suiv., et surtout p. 123: «...die letzte Bestätigung für unsere Behauptung..., dass die Entstehung der Brocarda mit der Behandlung der Praesumptionen in ursächlicher Beziehung steht»; avec un peu plus de précaution p. 119: «...dass die Literaturform der Brocarda wenn nicht überhaupt den Anstoss, so doch einen mächtig fördernden Anreiz vom Traktat de praesumptionibus erhalten und in ihm ihr methodisches Vorbild gefunden hat».

III

Pour ce qui est du premier point, il y a lieu de remarquer que parmi les formes littéraires employées par les glossateurs c'est seulement pour les *quaestiones disputatae*, issues d'exercices pratiques[39], qu'on n'en peut retracer l'origine dans des gloses particulières. Les *distinctiones*, les *solutiones contrariorum*, les *notabilia*, les *casus*, les *summulae*, etc., furent employés pour l'explication des livres de droit dans l'enseignement oral et dans les gloses écrites, avant que les genres littéraires correspondants aient trouvé une existence indépendante[40]. Or il semble permis d'affirmer *a priori* qu'il en a été de même des *generalia*, c'est-à-dire que dans les manuscrits glosés les *notabilia* qui exprimaient un principe général furent déjà munis d'arguments *contra*, avant que les deux ouvrages spéciaux, le *Perpendiculum* et le *Libellus disputatorius*, aient été écrits. Encore ne sait-on pas avec quelque exactitude si ce sont réellement les deux ouvrages se fondant sur la théorie des présomptions, et non plutôt les Brocards du légiste Otto de Pavie — collection de *generalia* d'une tout autre nature — qui se trouvent chronologiquement au début du genre littéraire[41].

En tout cas, des *notabilia* amplifiés en *generalia*, sans aucun rapport méthodique avec la doctrine des présomptions, forment non seulement le point de départ de la collection d'Otto, mais se laissent retracer positivement dans les mss. des livres de droit dont les gloses remontent à une période antérieure au *Perpendiculum*. Quant aux gloses des légistes, je ne suis pas familier avec la tradition manuscrite, de sorte que je ne peux rien dire de précis sur la date des différents brocards dans les gloses du XIIe siècle[42]. Mais parmi les canonistes bolonais, il s'en trouvé déjà chez Jean de Faenza[43] (vers 1170) et, en nombre considérable, dans les gloses et

---

39 KANTOROWICZ, *The Quaestiones disputatae* (*art. cit.* plus haut, note 2), *passim*; cfr notre étude *Bernardus Compostellanus Antiquus*, dans *Traditio*, t. I, 1943, p. 320 et suiv., avec des indications sommaires sur les différences entre les *quaestiones disputatae* et les autres types de *quaestiones* tels qu'ils furent développés par les glossateurs dans la *lectio* ou dans des ouvrages littéraires. Les problèmes analogues qui existent dans l'histoire des questions théologiques sont beaucoup mieux connus; cfr surtout A. LANDGRAF, *Quelques collections de Quaestiones de la seconde moitié du XIIe siècle*, dans les *Recherches de théologie ancienne et médiévale*, t. VII, 1935, pp. 113–128; *Einführung in die Geschichte der theologischen Literatur der Frühscholastik*, p. 41, Regensburg, 1948.

40 C'est là un point acquis dans l'histoire littéraire de la jurisprudence médiévale. Citons seulement, pour le droit canonique, les travaux de J. JUNCKER, *Summen und Glossen*, dans la *Zeitschr. der Sav.-Stift.*, Kanon. Abt., t. XIV, 1925, pp. 384–474; *Die Summa des Simon von Bisignano und seine Glossen*, *ibid.*, t. XV, 1926, pp. 326–500.

41 Cfr GENZMER, *Die iustinianische Kodifikation...*, pp. 425, 428; cfr aussi p. 426, n. 359 (collection de brocards de Johannes Bassianus?).

42 Par ex. dans les gloses signalées par SAVIGNY, *Geschichte*, t. III, p. 567, note *a*.

43 Par ex. la glose à D. 50, c 18, v. *non fuit*: «Hinc colligere potes fauorabiliorem esse delictorum emendationem et animi constantiam propter que canones interpretantur non esse quod est uel esse quod non est, ut hic et j(nfra) xxxii. q. i. quod autem... Ex diuerso quoque in odium culparum interpretantur canones contra ipsos criminosos non esse quod est et esse quod non est, ut j. vii. q. i. Factus est... Jo.» (Bibl. Vaticane, mss. lat. 2494, 2495; Paris, Bibl. nationale, ms. lat. 3888;

la *Summa* de Simon de Bisignano, introduits pour la plupart par les mots *Hinc collige...*[44]. L'auteur du *Perpendiculum* reprend donc une méthode déjà en usage; d'ailleurs il s'en est servi aussi en dehors de cet ouvrage, vu que certains parmi ses *notabilia* dans la collection *Arg. quod religiosi* sont déjà accompagnés d'un *contra*[45].

Le développement de brocards dans le cadre d'une théorie systématique des présomptions représentait une contribution originale et importante, mais il est resté la marque individuelle de deux auteurs. Lorsque Pillius, vers 1195, publia la deuxième édition, augmentée des *solutiones*, du *Libellus disputatorius*, il songeait même à l'éventualité qu'un jour son ouvrage remplacerait les *apparatus* traditionnels de gloses comme fondement d'un enseignement systématique du droit[46]. La tradition générale de l'école n'a pas suivi nos deux auteurs: pour elle, la voie qui conduisit aux collections de brocards était directement et tout naturellement donnée par une méthode usitée dans les gloses. S'il en était autrement, il faudrait que dans les collections de *generalia* postérieures au *Perpendiculum* et au *Libellus disputatorius* il se trouvât tout au moins une trace indiquant les présomptions comme point de départ. Tout au contraire les *Generalia* canoniques de Richard l'Anglais, qui ont paru à peu près en même temps que la deuxième édition de Pillius[47], se rattachent à l'ordre légal de la *Compilatio I*; et Richard traite du schéma des titres de présomptions non pas dans cet ouvrage, mais dans ses *Distinctiones decretorum*, avec un *pro* et un *contra* pour chaque membre.[48]

Trèves, ms. 906, etc.). Cfr aussi la glose citée par JUNCKER, *Summen und Glossen* (*art. cit.* plus haut, n. 40), p. 471, n. 2.

44 On trouve des exemples chez JUNCKER, *Die Summa des Simon von Bisignano*, pp. 367, 401–406, 457–458, etc. Sur l'arrangement graphique spécial employé pour les brocards dans les mss. de la Somme de Simon, à savoir la subdivision des colonnes du texte pour mieux placer les rangées d'allégations, cfr *ibid.*, p. 368, n. 3. Quelques mss., par ex. Rouen 710, indiquent toujours ces passages dans la marge par les lettres *ar*(*gumentum*), de même que les *notabilia* et les questions, insérés çà et là au cours de l'exposition, sont marqués à la marge par les signes *No.* et *Q.*

45 Par ex.: «Nota licita permitti, ut di. iii. cap. omnis autem. Ar. contra xxxi. q. i. hac ratione.» (Cambridge, Pembroke College, ms. 101, fol. 56^r). Il reste à rechercher s'il existe des rapports, et lesquels, entre ces *notabilia* et la 2e partie du *Perpendiculum*.

46 Cfr GENZMER, *art. cit.*, p. 427 et suiv. Pour la date cfr SECKEL, *Distinctions Glossatorum*, p. 377, n. 2.

47 Cfr notre *Repertorium*, p. 416. —Peut-être l'ouvrage de Richard n'est-il pas la première collection de brocards canoniques. Dans le ms. D. 10 de Fulda il se trouve à la suite du *Perpendiculum* un recueil (fol. 82–87^v) que je ne connais que par les notes de Seckel. Il a paru vers 1185 et commence par les mots *Arg. a minori per negationem*. Seckel le désigne comme *Argumenta s. Brocarda* (cfr *Repertorium*, p. 235), mais sans indiquer s'il s'agit seulement d'*argumenta* avec un alignement d'allégations ou de véritables *brocarda* sans solutions. Dans ses communications sur le ms. de Fulda M. Lang ne s'est pas prononcé sur cet ouvrage.

48 Ms. Vat. lat. 2691, fol. 11^v, à C. 18, q. 2, c. 21: «Presumitur: ex causa, j. xxiii. q. viii. occidit; contra j. xxxii. q. iiii. origo. — ex persona, d. lxxxix. decenter; contra j. xxiii. q. iii. sicut ex. — ex loco... — ex tempore...» etc., en tout 17 titres de présomptions. Encore au XIVe siècle Jean d'André, dans ses additions au *Speculum* de Guillaume Durand (lib. II, pars II, tit. *de praesumpt.*, § *Praesumptio est arg.*) fera mention de cette distinction de Richard.

A plusieurs égards la genèse des *Generalia*, ou plutôt des *Generalium solutiones*, de Richard est très instructive pour l'histoire de ce genre littéraire dans la dernière décade du XIIe siècle. Ils nous sont transmis sous deux formes: ou bien comme faisant partie de son *Apparatus* à la *Compilatio I*[49], ou bien rédigés en collection continue, séparément publiée[50]. Les différents brocards proposés consistent pour la plupart en maximes explicites, parfois aussi en un simple terme lemmatique (par exemple *pro bona consuetudine; pro vulgari purgatione; de iurisdictione distincta*)[51]. Ils sont toujours introduits, au cours des gloses, par les mots *argumentum...* ou *nota...*[52], tandis que dans la collection indépendante les différents brocards se trouvent écrits à la manière de rubriques, en rouge,

---

49 Pour les mss. cfr notre *Repertorium*, p. 325; *Bernardus Compostellanus* (*art. cit.* plus haut, n. 39) pp. 312, n. 20; 313, n. 22; en ce qui concerne le ms. de Lambeth Palace 105 (un *apparatus* de composition mixte) cfr aussi les observations de W. ULLMANN, *Medieval Papalism*, pp. 208–10, London, 1949, surtout au sujet d'une couche plus récente qui contient un bon nombre de gloses de Pierre le Breton.

50 Mss.: Vat. Chis. E. VII. 218, fol. 74–80^r; Avranches 149, fol. 139–147^v (ce ms. contient aussi, fol. 7–77^V la *Comp. I* avec *l'Apparatus* de Richard dans la deuxième couche de gloses; il offre donc les brocards deux fois); Bamberg, ms. can. 45 (P. II. 4), fol. 40, 1–7; Zwettl 162, fol. 73–82^r; cfr *Repertorium*, p. 417; *Bernardus Compostellanus*, pp. 299, n. 40 et 312, n. 20. Quant au ms. de Nuremberg, Cent. V. 95, fol. 1–6^v, cité dans notre *Repertorium* d'après SECKEL, *Distinctiones Glossatorum*, pp. 345, n. 6, 386, le regretté Dr. R. Most me communiqua dans une lettre (15 mars 1939) que ce ms. ne donne de chaque *generale* que l'énoncé principal, suivi d'une seule allégation. Il serait difficile de déterminer s'il s'agit d'un extrait de l'ouvrage de Richard (comme on pourrait conclure de Inexplicit... *generalia argumenta decretalium* et de l'usage constant du mot initial *Rubrica*) ou plutôt d'un écrit précurseur (*Notabilia* ?).

Une collection de brocards qui ne s'identifie pas avec l'ouvrage de Richard mais qui en dépend, se trouve à Saint-Florian, ms. XI.346, fol. 156rb-180^v, 155^r–156ra: «Incipiunt procardica decretorum. § Ar. quod nullus priuetur iure suo sine culpa sua...» (une reférence expresse à Richard, fol. 179^v: «...Solutio: dicit R/ constitutionem illam 'si quis in tantam' [C.1, q. 4, c. 13] etc. non habere locum...»). Encore une autre collection, dans la même bibliothèque, ms. XI. 720, fol. 73–81, commence: «*a*) § Nullus iure suo priuandus erit sine culpa sua. Per sex iure suo loca persone spoliantur. *b*) xvi. q. vi. per totum. q. vii. inuentum... *c*) § Ar. quod nullus priuetur iure suo absque culpa sua. Absque culpa sua: paupertas. odium fauor et uitium. scelus ordo.» Les trois sections de chaque *generale* sont écrites d'abord en deux colonnes (*a, bc*), ensuite en trois (*a, b, c*) par deux mains différentes (d'abord *ab, c*; ensuite *a, bc*). Les solutions assez primitives n'ont rien à voir avec Richard.

For the Brocarda Florianensia in Sankt Florian Stiftsbibliothek XI. 346 (Brocarda Florianensia I) see now W. *Stelzer*, Gelehrtes Recht in Österreich (Mitteilungen des Instituts für österreichische Geschichtsforschung, Ergänzungsband XXVI, Wien/Köln/Graz 1982) 119. (P.L.)

51 Cfr les trois textes chez GILLMANN, *Richardus Anglikus...* (*art. cit.* plus haut, note 1) pp. 628–29; 643. n. 3; *Johannes Galensis als Glossator*, dans l'*Archiv für kath. Kirchenr.*, t. CV, 1925, p. 541, n. 2. Dans ce dernier endroit la glose *arg. de iurisdictione distincta* (sur le pouvoir indépendant de l'empereur) est imprimée d'après la citation dans l'*Apparatus* de Tancrède (ainsi déjà chez J. F. VON SCHULTE, *Literaturgeschichte der Compilationes antiquae*, dans les *Sitzungsberichte* de l'Académie de Vienne, *phil.-hist. Cl.*, t. LXVI, 1870, p. 85), qui l'attribue faussement à Laurent d'Espagne. Cfr la correction implicite chez GILLMANN, *Richardus Anglikus*, p. 647, n. 2.

52 Parfois la même règle se trouve exprimée par une *nota* dans un endroit (p. ex. gl. à *Comp. I*, 3.37.2: «Nota sub pretextu boni uel conpensatione non est malum faciendum...», chez GILLMANN, *art. cit.*, p. 611), et par un *argumentum* dans un autre (gl. à *Comp. I*, 5.15.3: «Arg. pretextu boni malum non esse faciendum...», *ibid.*, p. 612).

à la tête des colonnes respectives d'allégations, et commencent par le sigle ℟ (*rubrica*)⁵³.

Il nous faudrait encore une étude détaillée avant qu'on puisse établir sous laquelle des deux formes Richard a publié son travail pour la première fois⁵⁴. En tout cas, semble-t-il, son ouvrage est éclos des *Notabilia* de Bernard de Pavie, qui apparaissent déjà parmi les gloses primitives de la *Compilatio I* et qui se trouvent eux aussi comme collection détachée (avec une allégation pour chaque *notabile*), dans le ms. Melk 333⁵⁵. Bernard lui-même a pourvu quelques-uns de ses *notabilia* de citations parallèles, parfois aussi de *contraria*, enfin même de brèves solutions⁵⁶. Dans quelques mss. glosés de la *Comp. I* où la couche richardienne est inscrite d'une autre main que le matériel plus ancien, comme par exemple dans Modène, Bibl. Estense, ms. a. R. 4. 16, les *generalia* se présentent souvent avec leurs *concordantiae* et *contraria* dans l'une, les solutions de Richard dans la seconde couche⁵⁷,

---

53 On lit donc, p. ex., les deux brocards cités dans la note précédente comme « ℟ sub pretextu boni... » et « ℟ pretextu boni... » (ms. Chis. fol. 78ᵛᵃ et 79ᵛᵈ).

54 M. Lang se prononce (*Zur Entstehungsgeschichte*..., p. 109, n. 12) en faveur d'une priorité des gloses, en supposant par erreur que celles-ci ne présenteraient pas encore de solutions. Mais on pourrait fort bien tirer argument en faveur des gloses comme étant la forme originale, de ce que nous allons dire sur les relations entre Bernard de Pavie et Richard, comme aussi de ce que nous savons en général des méthodes de travail chez les Bolonais. D'autre part on peut faire valoir dans le sens opposé (outre ce qui a été déjà observé dans notre *Repertorium*, p. 418 avec n. 3) certains autres arguments; p. ex. Richard donne souvent aux maximes elle-mêmes, soit dans les gloses, soit dans la collection, le nom de *rubrica*, *prima rubrica*, et aux antithèses le nom de *rubrica contraria* (cfr les exemples, d'ailleurs mal expliqués, chez GILLMANN, *Richardus Anglikus*, pp. 596, 635 et suiv., et dans l'*Archiv für kath. Kirchenr.*, t. CXII, 1932, p. 485 et suiv.), ce qui s'accorderait seulement avec la graphie de la collection.

55 Cfr notre article *Bernardus Compostellanus*, p. 299, n. 39. On trouve des exemples de *notabilia* parmi les gloses choisies de Bernard; imprimées par LASPEYRES, *Bernardi Papiensis... Summa decretalium*, p. 323 et suiv., Ratisbonae, 1860, et, en grand nombre, pris dans le ms. Ye. 52 de Halle, par GILLMANN, dans l'*Archiv für kath. Kirchenr.*, t. CVIII, 1928, pp. 486–501. — La collection de Melk, ms. 333 (F. 33), fol. 252ᵛ-254ᵛ, commence: «Arg. quod nullus iure suo priuatur sine culpa...»; cfr Vincent d'Espagne, gl. à *Comp. I*, s. I.I.I.«<Hic> signatur ber. argumentum quod nullus iure suo priuetur sine culpa sua...» (Leipzig, Bibl. de l'Université, ms. 983, fol. 1). Ce premier *argumentum* prend chez Richard la forme suivante: «...quod nullus suo priuetur beneficio sine culpa sua»; mais parfois il se trouve une variante qui se rapproche du texte de Bernard, ainsi ms. Avranches 149, fol. 139 («Quod nullus priuetur iure suo...»). Cfr aussi les deux recueils de brocards à Saint-Florian, cités plus haut, note 50.

56 On trouve des exemples de solutions chez LASPEYRES, *loc. cit.*, n° 22 (mais le n° 3 *ibid.* est en réalité une glose de Richard, cfr GILLMANN, *Richardus Anglikus*, p. 602) et chez GILLMANN, *art. cit.*, p. 642, n. 1 (gl. *Nota secundum bulgarum*); *Archiv für kath. Kirchenr*..., t. CVIII, p. 491 et suiv. (gl. *Arg. ad ea que frequentius*); cfr aussi plus loin, note 58. — Dans l'*Apparatus* de Richard un bon nombre de *notabilia* avec leurs *concordantiae* se trouvent signés par le sigle *b*. et ensuite amplifiés en brocards, p. ex. les textes chez GILLMANN, *Richardus Anglikus*, pp. 578 (*Arg. ad communem*), 591 (*Arg. quod non tenet*), 609 (*Arg. quod ordinarius*), 637 (*Arg. quod sine diminutione*). Enfin un *generale* dont les allégations pour et contre furent recueillies par Bernard, mais dont Richard a donné la solution, dans *Archiv*..., t. CVIII, p. 495 (*Nota attestationes*).

57 Pour la stratification du ms. a. R. 4.16 (lat. 968; XII.L.8), fol. 1–76ᵛ, voir notre étude *Bernardus Compostellanus*, p. 312 et suiv.: parfois les gloses de Richard se présentent comme une couche

ce qui s'accorde très bien avec la remarque de Richard: «sciat me... generalium solutiones in commento decretalium addidisse». Parfois il paraît aussi avoir retouché une solution proposée par un autre[58].

Toutefois la démonstration par M. Lang du rapport existant entre la rhétorique et les *brocarda* garde sa valeur, quand bien même on n'admet pas que le traité des présomptions soit un chaînon nécessaire dans le développement de ce genre littéraire à l'école de Bologne. La connaissance des méthodes et notions apprises dans le *trivium* est reflétée dans beaucoup d'autres gloses et distinctions des glossateurs[59]; et c'est ainsi qu'on trouve à côté des principes juridiques aussi l'un ou l'autre des *loci* rhétoriciens énoncés comme *notabile* ou bien discutés comme *generale*[60] ou encore que les auteurs répartissent parfois par *loci* d'argumentation les séries d'allégations employées pour un seul *generale* juridique[61]. De plus, les glossateurs se rendaient compte de ce que dans le raisonnement du juriste les *generalia* exercent la fonction de lieux communs, ainsi que cela se trouve exprimé dans la définition donnée par la *Materia ad Pandectam* de l'école de Johannes Bassianus: «argumenta ad causas de facto adnotamus, quae loci generales vel generalia vel vulgariter brocarda appellantur[62]».

---

distincte, parfois elles sont réunies à la couche plus ancienne ou à la couche plus récente (Bernard de Compostelle et autres) des gloses. — Dans le ms. Lambeth 105 les *solutiones* de Richard font partie de la même couche que les *argumenta* et les allégations *pro* et *contra*, mais souvent le scribe les a séparées de celles-ci, de sorte que la solution se trouve transcrite à un autre endroit de la page, et n'est rattachée au *generale* primitif que par un signe de renvoi. Il a probablement copié dans un exemplaire ayant plusieurs couches de gloses.

58 Nous croyons avoir découvert la trace d'un tel procédé pour le brocard «Arg. iudicandum potius secundum allegata...; arg. contra...; Solutio: dicunt omnes quod contra conscientiam nemo est condempnandus...», identique dans la glose à *Comp. I*, 1. 23.1 et dans la collection de Richard; cfr GILLMANN, *Richardus Anglikus*, p. 655 et notre *Repertorium*, p. 418, n. 2. Or parmi les gloses de la plus ancienne couche dans le ms. de Modène, ce brocard se trouve signé *ber.*, mais avec les mots *dicunt omnes* écrits d'une main plus récente. Il est donc bien possible que la solution originale ait commencé par *dicimus* (ou un terme équivalent) et que ce mot ait été remplacé plus tard par la version richardienne, qui du reste se présente comme résumé d'une opinion d'autrui.

59 BRUGI, *op. cit.* (plus haut, note 17), pp. 24–35, 38–40; GENZMER, *Die iustinianische Kodifikation...*, pp. 385–88, et *Vorbilder für die Distinctionen der Glossatoren*, dans les *Acta Congressus Iuridici Internationalis, Romae, 12–17 Nov. 1934*, t. I, 1935, pp. 343–58. Pour Richard l'Anglais, cfr par ex. ses *Distinctiones decretorum*, à C. 3, q. 4, c. 9: «Aliquando argumentamur: a minori ad maius, d. xxxviii. si in laicis; — a maiori ad minus...» etc., en tout 9 membres (ms. Vat. lat. 2691, fol. 6^v), ou sa distinction sur les figures rhétoriques, gl. à *Comp. I*, 5.36.10 (chez GILLMANN, *art. cit.*, p. 625).

60 Cfr LANG, *Rhetorische Einflüsse...*, p. 83, n. 43; voir aussi le commencement des *Notabilia Fuldensia/*, plus haut, note 47.

61 Ainsi dans le brocard *Honerosas et malas consuetudines...* de Richard (ms. Chis., fol. 74^{vc}; Bamb., fol. 1), où les arguments sont divisés en groupes *a minori, a maiori, ...ab oppositis*, correspondant aux membres de la distinction à C. 3, q. 4, c. 9.

62 Citée par SAVIGNY, *op. cit.*, t. III, p. 553, note *a*; la définition se trouve attribuée à Azon dans une addition au Vocabulaire dit *Epitome alphabetica Basiliensis*: «brocardica sunt loci generales quibus argumenta ad causas de facto adnotamus. Az.», cfr SECKEL, *Beiträge...* (*op. cit.* plus haut, note 7), p. 408, n. 107.

IV

Le second point d'importance pour préciser la place du *Perpendiculum* dans l'histoire des *brocarda* concerne la question de savoir à quelle école l'ouvrage se rattache. M. Lang n'hésite pas à lui attribuer une origine bolonaise, en raison de sa dépendance de Sicard[63]. Or il est bien vrai que jusqu'à présent il n'a pas été contesté que le canoniste crémonois ait fait partie de l'école de Bologne; mais il n'est pas moins vrai que personne n'a jamais donné des raisons pour cette assignation. Elle remonte à une époque d'historiographie où, pour le XIIe siècle, les notions «canoniste» et «bolonais» étaient encore considérées comme synonymes. Tout au plus s'est-on demandé si, temporairement, Sicard pourrait avoir transféré son enseignement à Mayence, où il était incardiné à l'époque de la publication de sa *Summa*, ainsi qu'en témoigne l'épilogue (*Apologia*)[64].

En réalité l'assignation traditionnelle se heurte à de sérieuses objections. Par son style, sa méthode, sa structure[65], l'ouvrage de Sicard se distingue nettement des Sommes des décrétistes bolonais. Il n'a pas écrit de gloses; et ses opinions ne sont ni citées ni prises en considération par les glossateurs de Bologne. Par contre un certain nombre de critères semblent indiquer un rapport avec l'école française: l'ouvrage a été terminé en Rhénanie[66]; il se sert abondamment de la *Summa Codicis* de Placentin, rédigée à Montpellier[67], et de plusieurs *Summae* de maîtres décrétistes français: telles la Somme *Imperatorie maiestati* (où Sicard a pris par exemple quelques tournures caractéristiques de son prologue, y compris le terme *iustitia positiva*)[68], et la Somme parisienne *Magister Gratianus in hoc opere* (où

---

63 Zur Entstehungsgeschichte..., pp. 123, 135.
64 Cfr M. SARTI et M. FATTORINI, *De claris Archigymnasii Bononiensis professoribus*, t. I, p. 285, Bologne, 1769; F. KUNSTMANN, *Zur Geschichte des Gratianischen Dekrets*, dans l'*Archiv für katholisches Kirchenr.*, t. X, 1863, p. 342 et la bibliographie ultérieure citée dans notre note *Zur Biographie des Sicardus von Cremona*, dans *la Zeitschr. der Sav-Stift.*, Kan. Abt., t. XXV, 1936, pp. 476–78; VAN HOVE, Prolegomena (op. cit. plus haut, note 2), p. 435. — Le fait que Sicard a bien enseigné à une école ressort des mots *sociorum tamen utilitatem feruenti animo cupientes* dans le prologue (SARTI, *loc. cit.*), ce que SCHULTE, *Geschichte der Quellen und Literatur des canonischen Rechts*, t. I, p. 145, Stuttgart, 1875, conteste sans raison.
65 Discutés dans notre *Repertorium*, pp. 151–53.
66 Pour la dépendance des canonistes rhénans de Paris, cfr *Repertorium*, pp. 171, 179, n. 3, 216. On reviendra sur cette question à propos de la. carrière scolaire de Gérard Pucelle,dans un article sur les débuts de l'école canoniste anglaise, à publier en collaboration avec Mlle Eleanor Rathbone.
67 Cfr E. OTT, *Die Rhetorica ecclesiastica*, dans les *Sitzungsberichte* de l'Académie de Vienne, t. CXXV, 1891, p. 28.
68 .Prologue de Sicard: «Diligite iustitiam... Sane imperatorie maiestati, que uentis imperat et mari, cedit ad gloriam talium complicum habere cateruam qui in sua regenda republica positiuam sapiant seruare iustitiam...»; *Summa Imperatorie* (*Monacensis*): «Imperatorie maiestati cedit ad gloriam, si ministros habeat eruditos... Quocirca imperator noster Christus Jesus, uentis imperans et mari, tales sibi elegit...»; et à D. 1, pr. v. *ius naturale*: «i. e. iustitia naturalis. Idem (item?) est iustitia positiua et ius consuetudinarium...» (Munich, ms. lat. 16084, fol. 1^{r-v}). Cfr H. SINGER, *Beiträge zur Würdigung der Decretistenliteratur, I*, dans l'*Archiv für kath. Kirchenr.*, t. LXIX, 1893, qui a fort bien observé l'influence exercée par la *Summa Monacensis* sur Sicard (cfr p. 380, n. 21 au sujet du prologue; cfr aussi pp. 382, n. 30, 407, 434, 439; en ce qui concerne Pierre le

il a emprunté par exemple — peut-être par l'entremise de la Somme *Antiquitate et tempore* — la qualification des matières traitées par Gratien comme *doctrina sacramentalis, moralis* et *iudicialis*[69]. La préférence pour la discussion de matières juridiques d'après les principes de la rhétorique[70], l'intérêt que prenait Sicard à la systématique et à la combinaison de différentes formes littéraires (*summa, quaestio, distinctio*)[71] sont caractéristiques pour l'école française[72]; les *disputationes theologiae*, telles qu'il les a rédigées[73] en dehors de sa Somme et d'autres ouvrages[74], font formellement partie depuis Odon d'Ourscamp de l'enseignement parisien[75]. Enfin, une influence immédiate de Sicard ne peut être démontrée que dans des ouvrages français (Évrard d'Ypres; Somme *In eadem civitate*)[76]. La

Mangeur comme étant le modèle du prologue de la Somme anonyme, voir notre *Repertorium*, p. 180, n. 8). Sur *iustitia positiva* chez Sicard cfr aussi GILLMANN, *Zur Inventarisierung der kanonistischen Handschriften aus der Zeit von Gratian bis Gregor IX.*, appendice du tirage à part de son article *Des Johannes Galensis Apparat zur Compilatio III...* (paru sans l'appendice dans l'*Archiv für kath. Kirchenr.*, t. CXVIII, 1938), p. 66, Mayence, 1938, qui pourtant ne fait pas mention du rapport avec l'école française.

69 Cfr les textes parallèles chez SCHULTE, *Die Summa magistri Rufini zum Decretum Gratiani*, p. LXIX et suiv., Giessen, 1892 (Sicard et Somme *Antiquitate*); p. LXI et suiv. (Sommes *Magister Gratianus* et *Antiquitate); observations critiques chez SINGER, *Die Summa decretorum des Magister Rufinus*, p. CLXII, n. 97, Paderborn, 1902. Le texte de la Somme *Magister Gratianus (Parisiensis)* sur *doctrina sacramentalis* etc. se trouve chez GILLMANN, dans l'*Archiv für kath. Kirchenr.*, t. CVI, 1926, p. 524, n. 1. On ne lit rien de semblable chez Étienne de Tournai, qui est considéré à tort par Gillmann comme source de la trichotomie en question (p. 554).

70 Sur les bases rhétoriciennes de sa doctrine du procès cfr LANG, *Rhetorische Einflüsse...*, p. 90 et suiv. L'importance que Sicard attachait à la formation, rhétoricienne du juriste ressort du passage suivant: «...Iudici facienda est probatio, non aduersario, licet in dialectica disputatione aduersario probetur, ubi aduersarius quasi iudex. Unde et causidici nostri peccant, in scolis docti potius disputare quam continue perorare...» (ms. Rouen 710, fol. 28ᵛ-29ʳ, à C. 6, q. 5).

71 Cfr *Repertorium*, p. 152 et suiv.

72 Les rapports voulus des auteurs français avec les *artes* (cfr notre article *Les débuts de l'école canoniste française*, dans *Studia et documenta historiae et iuris*, t. IV, 1938, p. 202, avec les indications bibliographiques dans n. 58 ibid.) ne sont pas à confondre avec la connaissance, qui va de soi pour tous les glossateurs (cfr plus haut, note 59), des matières enseignées dans le *trivium*. — Quant au penchant des canonistes français pour les formes mixtes, il suffit de rappeler les combinaisons *summa-abbreviatio* (Somme *Elegantius in iure diuino*, Somme d'Odon de Doura), *summa-distinctio* (Somme *Imperatorie maiestati* et son groupe), *summa-quaestio* (maître Honorius), etc.

73 J. DE GHELLINCK, *Le mouvement théologique du XIIᵉ siècle*, 1ʳᵉ éd., p. 310, n. 3, Paris, 1914 (2ᵉ éd., p. 462, 1948); cfr notre note *Zur Biographie...* (citée plus haut, n. 64), p. 477; GILLMANN, *Zur Inventarisierung...* (plus haut, n. 68), p. 62. L'ouvrage, cité dans le *Mitrale*, n'a pas été retrouvé.

74 *Liber mythologiarum* (perdu), *Mitrale* (MIGNE, *Patr. lat.*, t. CCXIII), *Chronique* (éd. O. HOLDER-EGGER, *Monumenta Germaniae historica, Scriptores*, t. XXXI, 1903).

75 On sait que quelques-uns des canonistes bolonais ont rédigé des *Sententiae*, cfr DE GHELLINCK, *op. cit.* (2ᵉ éd.), p. 462; VAN HOVE, *op. cit.*, p. 456. Par contre nous ne connaissons pas de *quaestiones disputatae* théologiques de l'école de Bologne du XIIᵉ siècle.

76 Cfr notre *Repertorium*, p. 187 et suiv.; *Bernardus Compostellanus* (art. cit. plus haut, n. 39), p. 282, n. 20. La Somme *In eadem civitate* consiste, à part le premier prologue, qui repose sur Étienne de Tournai, presque uniquement en extraits de Sicard (le deuxième prologue p. ex. commence *Diligite iustitiam...* ms. Boulogne-sur-mer 119, fol. 3ʳ); on pourrait bien parler d'un *Sicardus abbreviatus*:— C'est par erreur que VAN HOVE, *op. cit.*, p. 435, n. 3 compte aussi la Somme

transmission répétée de sa Somme avec les Distinctions de Pierre de Blois dans le même ms.[77] et la mention de certaines coutumes de la *Gallicana ecclesia* comme étant opposées au *ius scriptum*[78] acquièrent, ajoutées à toutes ces observations, une signification renforcée.

Ce que nous savons de la biographie du canoniste crémonois s'accorde fort bien avec ces observations. Le peu de dates certaines que nous possédons sur ses débuts sont les suivantes: Il reçut les ordres mineurs de l'évêque Offredus de Crémone (1168–85). Il écrivit la *Summa* entre 1179 et 1181. En 1183 Lucius III l'ordonna sous-diacre et l'envoya en mission politique en Allemagne, pour préparer l'entrevue du Pape avec Frédéric Barberousse à Vérone (1184). En 1185 il fut élu évêque de sa ville natale comme successeur d'Offredus. De cette chronologie[79] et de la supposition que la *Summa* aurait pour base des cours tenus à Bologne, on a déduit que le séjour à Mayence (attesté dans l'épilogue) aurait eu lieu en 1183[80]. Mais cette conclusion se heurte à l'invraisemblance qu'un sous-diacre papal pendant les quelques mois de sa mission diplomatique ait pu être incardiné dans un diocèse allemand, et que dans un témoignage littéraire écrit à cette époque il ait pu mentionner sa ville natale et sa *translatio* à Mayence[81], sans faire la moindre allusion à son emploi au service du Pape.

Tout s'explique beaucoup plus simplement si l'on suppose que le jeune clerc de Crémone s'est rendu vers 1170[82] en France (à Paris?) pour y faire ses études, et qu'ensuite il y a exercé les fonctions de maître en théologie et en droit canon jusqu'à ce que vers 1180 il reçut une prébende à Mayence[83]. L'archevêque Chrétien de Mayence est connu pour avoir patronné aussi d'autres maîtres parisiens[84]. Avec cette explication il n'est plus nécessaire d'intercaler un espace de temps entre la rédaction de la Somme (1179–81) et sa publication, avec addition de l'*Apologia*, à Mayence[85]. Quant à la suite de la carrière de Sicard, nous savons

---

Dubitatur a quibusdam, le Prologue *Omnia poma vetera*, et un fragment *Queritur cuius sint hec verba* (tous énumérés dans notre *Repertorium*, p. 154) parmi les écrits influencés par Sicard.

77 *Repertorium*, p. 153.
78 C. 15, q. 7; texte imprimé chez Schulte, *Zur Geschichte der Literatur über das Dekret Gratians, Erster Beitrag*, dans les *Sitzungsberichte* de l'Académie de Vienne, t. LXIII, 1869, p. 348.
79 Pour la Somme cfr *Repertorium*, p. 151, pour les autres dates cfr la Chronique de Sicard, *éd. cit.*, pp. 168 et 24.
80 Kunstmann, *loc. cit.* (plus haut, note 64); déduction universellement acceptée (à l'exception de Holder-Egger, qui nie l'identité de l'évêque-chroniqueur et du canoniste), cfr *Repertorium*, p. 153.
81 «...ego uero Sychardus Cremone filius et moguntine ecclesie filius spiritualis translatione...»
82 Après le *terminus a quo* pour sa réception des ordres mineurs (1168).
83 Probablement avant l'automne de 1179, puisque l'archevêque de Mayence était prisonnier pendant quinze mois depuis la Saint-Michel de cette année, cfr les *Gesta Henrici II*, ed. W. Stubbs (Rolls Series), t. I, pp. 243, 250.
84 C'est par son entremise — *interventu quoque ven. fratris nostri Maguntini archiepiscopi*, écrit Alexandre III (Jaffé-Loewenfeld, n° 13032) — que Gérard Pucelle en 1178 fut réintégré dans ses bénéfices.
85 Si quelques mss. de la Somme ne contiennent pas l'*Apologia* (tel le ms. de la Bibliothèque Ambrosienne à Milan, M. 64) ou si elle s'y trouve ajoutée d'une autre main (tel le ms. 226 de

que Lucius III (1181–85) était l'obligé de Chrétien de Mayence pour l'assistance qu'il en avait reçue à plusieurs reprises contre les Romains rebelles. L'archevêque allemand resta jusqu'à sa mort (25 août 1183) dans l'entourage intime du Pape[86]: il est donc facile à comprendre qu'en 1183, lors des délibérations de la Curie, un canoniste d'origine italienne qui se trouvait au service de Chrétien fût choisi pour la mission auprès de l'Empereur, et que le Pape, en l'ordonnant sous-diacre, l'ait attaché à la famille pontificale.

Sicard of Cremona was recognized by Kuttner to have been a member of the French school of canonists, correcting the traditional classification as a Bolognese canonist. He wrote his Summa decretorum mainly in Mayence where he stayed with some interruptions form 1179 to 1185– cf. now *P. Landau*, Simon von Bisignano, Sikard von Cremona und die Mainzer Kanonistik der Barbarossazeit, Zur Biographie des Simon von Bisignano und zur Forschungsgeschichte, BMCL 28 (2008) 119–144, here p. 138–140; and *I. Riedel-Spangenberger*, Der Kanonist Sicardus von Cremona (1155–1215) in Mainz (1178–1183), in: Recht-Bürge der Freiheit, Festschrift für Johannes Mühlsteiger SJ zum 80. Geburtstag, ed. *K. Breitsching/ W. Rees* (Kanonistische Studien und Texte 18, Berlin 2006) 437–452. (P.L.)

S'il est donc plausible au point de vue de l'histoire littéraire aussi bien qu'au point de vue biographique que Sicard doit être rangé au nombre des décrétistes français, il n'y a plus aucune raison de considérer le *Perpendiculum* comme un produit de l'école de Bologne. Encore beaucoup plus consciemment que Sicard l'auteur du *Perpendiculum* place le traité des présomptions dans le cadre de la doctrine rhétoricienne des *loci*[87]. Et la combinaison ingénieuse des formes du brocard et de la *summula* s'accorde aussi bien avec la tendance caractéristique, mentionnée plus haut, de l'école française à créer de nouveaux genres littéraires hybrides que par exemple la combinaison de *distinctiones* et de *brocarda* dans le *Speculum* de Pierre de Blois, qui a paru vers la même époque[88]. Il n'a pas été

---

l'Hôpital de Cues), c'est là un fait aussi habituel que la fréquente absence du prologue dans certains mss. d'ouvrages du moyen âge.

86 Cfr les *Gesta Henrici, ed. cit.*, t. I, p. 308 et suiv.; Lucius III, lettre du 2 septembre 1183 aux évêques d'Allemagne (Jaffé-Loewenfeld, n° 14909).

87 Non seulement il commence par les mots: «Hic locus in iudiciis frequens est et pernecessarius...» (à comparer Sicard, à C. 6, q. 5: «... et attende quod presumptionis locus necessarius est quociens de incerto disputatur...»), mais il introduit aussi dans chaque section les différents titres de présomptions par les mots: «...presumitur ex his locis».

88 Pour le caractère de l'ouvrage de Pierre de Blois cfr notre *Repertorium*, p. 222; LANG, *Zur Entstehungsgeschichte...*, p. 123 et suiv.; DE GHELLINCK, *op. cit.*, pp. 479–80, 495–97. Pierre regarde comme but de ses distinctions la concordance (cfr cc. 2, 9, 11, etc., dans l'éd. de REIMARUS, Berlin, 1837), comme sujet il traite des propositions qu'il désigne tantôt comme *generale* (cc. 38, 46, etc.), tantôt comme *regula, regulare* (cc. 3, 13, 15, 24, 26, 28, etc.), tantôt comme *quaestio* (cc. 5, 20, 27, 40 [où il faut lire *quaestio* au lieu de *quomodo*, éd. cit., p. 72], 41, etc.). Dans tous les mss. les allégations sont placées à la marge, en dehors du texte, ce qui correspond à l'intention de l'auteur: cfr cc. 42, 53, où il parle de *extra signati canones* (pp. 76, 98). — A ajouter aux mss.: Exeter Record Office, 4 feuilles, fragment de c. 14 (v. *eo enim ipso*, p. 37, ligne 2 de l'éd.) à c. 22 (v. *sed accessit*, p. 50, ligne 6).

possible jusqu'à présent de percer l'anonymité de notre auteur. Il est vrai que dans ses *Notabilia*, qui nous sont transmis dans le seul ms. de Cambridge, Pembroke College 101 (provenant de Bury Saint-Edmund's), il fait une fois allusion à saint Thomas Becket[89]; mais cela ne suffit guère pour voir en lui un Anglais.

D'autre part on ne peut pas trouver une objection contre l'assignation de notre auteur à l'école française dans le fait que le *Perpendiculum* a inspiré l'ouvrage d'un légiste italien. C'est bien à Modène que Pillius, venu de Bologne vers 1182, a composé son *Libellus disputatorius*[90]; mais il a été prouvé qu'à plusieurs égards Pillius a subi des influences françaises — ce qui n'a rien d'étonnant chez un élève de Placentin — et qu'il a eu même des relations personnelles avec le clergé parisién[91]. D'ailleurs il n'est pas sans intérêt d'observer que même chez son adversaire Johannes Bassianus l'habitude d'insérer des *generalia* dans un traité systématique (le *Libellus de ordine iudiciorum*) pourrait bien être due à des influences françaises[92].

V

Quand on recherche les causes et les courants intellectuels qui ont amené les glossateurs du XIIe siècle à formuler des *generalia* et à les réunir en collections, il y a lieu enfin de ne pas perdre de vue qu'il existe un parallèle historique entre l'œuvre des auteurs du moyen âge et les *regulae iuris* des juristes romains[93]. De même que

---

L'ouvrage anonyme commençant *Breuiter quid contrarietatis*, cité dans notre étude *Bernardus Compostellanus...*, p. 99, n. 29 (Boulogne-sur-mer, ms. 119, fol. 73–81ᵛ) n'est autre chose qu'un extrait de Pierre de Blois, de c. 1, § 9 jusqu'à la fin, dans lequel certains chapitres sont abrégés (p. ex. cc. 21, 58), retranchés (cc. 24, 28, 56) ou divisés (c. 58), mais où avant tout sont omises toutes les rubriques contenant les *brocarda* proprement dits, ainsi que toutes les allégations marginales.

89 C. 24, q. 1: «...c. audiuimus (c. 4). arg. pro papa Alexandro v(sque) c. alienus (c. 19). arg. sume de beato Thoma.» La note vise le martyr de Cantorbéry comme champion de l'unité de l'Église, dont il est question dans les canons cités.

90 H. KANTOROWICZ, *Kritische Studien*, dans la *Zeitschr. der Sav.-Stift.*, Rom. Abt., t. XLIX, 1929, pp. 75–78; indications bibliographiques ultérieures chez LANG, *Zur Entstehungsgeschichte...*, p. 135, n. 50; à ajouter E. GENZMER, *Eine anonyme Kleinschrift de testibus...*, dans la *Festschrift Paul Koschaker*, t. III, p. 387 et suiv., Weimar, 1939.

91 GENZMER, *Seckel und Ugo Nicolini...* (*art. cit.* plus haut, note 6), p. 329 et suiv. L'archidiacre parisien Osmond, à qui est dédiée la *Summula de reorum exceptionibus* (cfr *ibid.*), a signé plusieurs actes du chapitre de Notre-Dame comme *canonicus Parisiensis* depuis 1163 (*Gallia Christiana*, t. VIII, *instr.*, p. 338; *Cartulaire de l'église de Notre-Dame de Paris*, éd. GUÉRARD, t. I, p. 43, Paris, 1850) et comme *archidiaconus Parisiensis* entre 1185 (*Cartulaire* cité, t. II, p. 311) et 1193 (*ibid.*, p. 468; cfr t. I, p. 398 et t. III, p. 386 [1186]; I, 47 [1187]; I, 397 [1189]; I, 45 [1191]).

92 Cfr SECKEL, *Ueber neuere Editionen...* (*art. cit.* plus haut, note 5), p. 289.

93 Parallèle souvent discuté, mais plutôt du point du vue doctrinal qu'historique, chez les juristes du XVe au XVIIe siècles. Parmi les auteurs modernes, cfr entre autres P. DE TOURTOULON, *Les principes philosophiques de l'histoire du droit*, t. II, pp. 380 et suiv., Paris, 1919; B. BRUGI, *Nuovi saggi* (*op. cit.* plus haut, note 17), p. 48 et suiv.; *Le regulae juris dei giureconsulti romani*, Modène, 1930; P. VINOGRADOFF, *Les maximes dans l'ancien droit anglais* (1923), dans les *Collected Papers*, t. II, p. 244, Oxford, 1928; Ch. LEFÈBVRE, *Les pouvoirs du juge en droit canonique*, pp. 144, 151, 153–55, París, 1938; cfr aussi DÉNES, *op. cit.* (plus haut, note 16), p. 45 et suiv.

les *generalia* les *regulae iuris* ne sont pas des dispositions indépendantes, mais des abstractions de principes généraux, qui ont été trouvées à la base de décisions juridiques particulières, par voie d'induction, en recherchant, comparant, et délimitant des idées normatives similaires: *non ex regula ius sumatur, sed ex iure quod est regula fiat*[94]. Il peut être aujourd'hui considéré comme acquis que l'établissement de telles règles repose sur la pénétration dans la jurisprudence romaine de la dialectique hélléniste depuis le dernier siècle de la république[95]. De même que les *generalia* les *regulae iuris* ne sont pas d'une application absolue: elles sont sujettes à des restrictions et des exceptions qui nécessitent des interprétations dialectiques.

Dans l'appendice à son *Ordo iudiciorum* Bulgarus, un des plus anciens glossateurs, a déjà discuté d'après la méthode des *solutiones contrariorum* une série de *regulae iuris*, prises non seulement dans le titre 50.17 des Digestes[96]. La tendance dialectique n'est pas aussi prononcée dans son *Apparatus* à Dig. 50.17[97], où il s'occupe surtout d'analyser et de commenter les différentes règles; toutefois, là aussi, il trace aux glossateurs qui le suivront la voie pour la solution de toutes les difficultés d'interprétation en expliquant, dès le commencement, le rapport entre règle et exception par les notions de genre et d'espèce[98]. Cela donnera lieu plus tard à une controverse d'écoles: les exceptions sont-elles

---

[94] Paul, *Dig.* 50.17.1.

[95] F. Schulz, *History of Roman Legal Science*, p. 66 et suiv., Oxford, 1946.

[96] Édition de L. Wahrmund, dans ses *Quellen zur Geschichte des römisch-kanonischen Processes im Mittelalter*, t. IV, fasc. 1, pp. .10–17, Innsbruck, 1925; cfr comptes rendus critiques de Kantorowicz, *Kritische Studien*, pp. 85–93; F. de Zulueta, dans la *English Historical Review*, t. XLII, 1927, p. 468. La méthode appliquée par Bulgarus, difficile à reconnaître par suite de l'insuffisante technique éditrice de Wahrmund, se montre dans les exemples suivants: § *Actore non probante... Negantis factum...* (deux règles, cfr Cod. 2.1.4 et 4.19.23), *His obloquitur...* (opposition, prise dans Cod. 4.1.3), *Interdum pro actore...* (solution). — § *Quod nullius in bonis... At divinae res... Cum ergo...* ; *Quid ergo de homine...* (autre opposition), *Sed de his tantum* (Wahrmund lit *enim*) *regula loquitur...* (solution). — Ou encore: § *Cum quid contra leges... Sed homicidium... Respondeo...* ; *Filius familias contra ius... Respondeo...* (la solution, avec une distinction entre prohibition absolue et relative, va jusqu'à la fin de la page. Au sujet du problème difficile posé par la règle *Cum quid contra leges fit, pro infecto habeatur* [Cod. 1.14.5.1], cfr Rogerius, *Enodationes quaestionum super Codice*, éd. Kantorowicz, *Studies in the Glossators*, pp. 286–93, Cambridge, 1938). — § *Sequitur alia regula... His contrarium invenitur... Respondeo... etc.* — On trouve dans le petit traité encore d'autres *solutiones contrariorum*; on y voit même une certaine anticipation de la forme des *quaestiones legitimae* (cfr *ed. cit.*,p. 12, ligne 4; p. 13, lignes 11–17).

[97] Édition de F. G. C. Beckhaus, *Bulgari ad digestorum titulum de diversis regulis iuris antiqui commentarius...*, Bonn, 1856. D'autres mss. chez Kantorowicz, *Kritische Studien*, p. 93; à ajouter Ann Arbor, University of Michigan, ms. 52, fol. 37ra-43^{vc}, 45ra-48^{vc}, cfr notre note dans *Traditio*, t. II, 1944, P. 497, n. 30. Les rapports chronologiques ne sont aucunement certains. D "apres Wahrmund, *ed. cit.*, p. xxvi, et Kantorowicz, *art. cit.*, p. 88, le petit traité attaché à l'*Ordo iudiciorum* serait antérieur au commentaire.

[98] A la suite des mots de Dig. 50.17.1 ...*simul cum* (*regula*) *in aliquo vitiata est, perdit officium suum*, Bulgarus cite Dig. 50.17.202 (le fameux *omnis definitio in iure periculosa*) et continue: «...ei enim quod regulariter traditur, per exceptionem saepius contradicitur, ut in hoc exemplo: ...

contenues dans la règle, *de regula* (Placentin), ou sont-elles *extra regulam* (Johannes Bassianus)[99]?

Nous ne prétendons nullement en conclure qu'il existe un rapport génétique entre la discussion dialectique des *regulae* chez Bulgarus et la création des brocards. Aussi bien les glossateurs ont-ils la plupart du temps[100] maintenu une distinction terminologique entre les catégories *regula-exceptio* et *generale-contrarium*[101]. Et cela à juste titre, vu que dans beaucoup de *generalia argumenta* les *contraria* s'avèrent d'un si grand poids que ni la proposition ni la contre-proposition ne peut être posée en règle générale[102], ou que c'est même au *contrarium* que revient l'application plus générale[103]. De plus, beaucoup de *brocarda* ne sont pas formulés en maximes complètes mais se présentent comme simples lemmes pour l'argumentation[104].

Mais dans les nombreux cas où le *generale* contient une maxime qui en fait peut être démontrée comme étant un principe général de droit, il devient, bien qu'exprimé *per verba incerta*, une proposition universelle — dans le même sens dans lequel une *regula iuris* contient une *affirmatio* (ou bien une *negatio*) *universalis*[105] —, et de même que les exceptions des *regulae*, les *contraria* sont alors déclarés comme n'étant que de simples *diversa, specialia, in casu, casus speciales*[106]. La ressemblance entre de tels brocards et les régles des anciens n'aura

---

Cum enim officium sit regulae ut singula complectatur, quod autem excipitur non complectitur, dici potest et uiciari et eius officium non exerceri, ac sic per speciem uiciatur genus, quoniam per speciem derogatur generi...» (*ed. cit.*, p. 2). Pour l'importance qui revient au commentaire de Bulgarus dans l'histoire de la glose au titre *de regulis iuris* des Digestes, cfr GENZMER, *Die iustinianische Kodifikation*..., pp. 394–96; LEFÈBVRE, *op. cit.* (plus haut, note 93), pp. 140–45. Sur les gloses d'un canoniste anonyme au commentaire de Bulgarus cfr G. HAENEL, dans les *Berichte über die Verhandlungen der kgl. sächsischen Gesellschaft der Wissenschaften* phil.-hist. Classe, t. XXVII, 1875. pp. 239 et suiv., 247 et suiv.

99 Cfr la *Glossa ordinaria* d'Accurse à Dig. 50.17.1 et 202; le résumé de la controverse chez Dinus dans son commentaire aux *regulae iuris* du Sexte, *prooem.*, § *Circa quintum* (ed. in-16°, Venise, 1585, pp. 7–10); LEFÈBVRE, *op. cit.*, p. 146 et suiv.

100 Pas toujours: cfr plus haut note 88 pour Pierre de Blois, ou p. ex. le brocard de Richard l'Anglais imprimé chez GILLMANN, *Richardus Anglikus*, p. 591 (*Arg. quod non tenet appellatio*).

101 Voir surtout Azon, cité par GENZMER, *Die iustinianische Kodifikation*, p. 425.

102 Exemples dans Richard (GILLMANN, *art. cit.*): pp. 641, n. 5, 649.

103 *Ibid.*, pp. 584 (*Arg. quod rebus nondum habitis*), 610 (*Arg. non dici factum*), 642 (*arg. ecclesiam non debere*), 644, n. 7, 655.

104 Voir plus haut, p. 261.

105 Selon Bernard de Pavie, *Summa* (ed. LASPEYRES, p. 282) la *regula* est une «diffinitio... rerum conplectens universitatem.» Cfr aussi Genzmer, *Die iustinianische Kodifikation*..., p. 425, n. 350, LEFÈBVRE, *op. cit.*, p. 145. Les glossateurs ont plus d'une fois fait observer que dans les règles de droit une proposition universelle peut être exprimée *per signa indefinita* (tel Azon et Accurse, gl. a D. 50.17.1, Dinus, etc.). Richard l'Anglais relève que c'est là un trait distinctif du langage juridique, cfr son brocard *Arg. generale verbum* (chez GILLMANN, *art. cit.*, pp. 595–96): «...quod autem dicitur infinita (Gillmann lit: in fi[ne]) uniuersali equipollere, regulare est in iure, quamuis distinguatur in artibus».

106 P. ex. Simon de Bisignano, gl. à Dist. 21, c. 9; C. 1, q. 4, c. 1, chez JUNCKER, *Simon...* (*art. cit.* plus haut, note 40), pp. 398–99, 406; Richard, chez GILLMANN, *art. cit.*, pp. 591, 644, n. 7, etc.

pas échappé aux glossateurs. Ici on peut en effet comparer la forme, la création *a posteriori* (*ex iure quod est*)[107], la fonction; et il ne reste comme trait distinctif qu'un critère technique: la *regula iuris* se trouvait déjà formulée dans les sources, tandis que le *generale* ne fut formulé que par les glossateurs[108], ce qui ne comporte toutefois qu'une différence quantitative dans l'*auctoritas* de l'une et de l'autre.

Au cours de l'histoire ultérieure de la jurisprudence médiévale, cette dernière différence pouvait elle aussi disparaître. On sait que le *Liber Sextus* de Boniface VIII (1298) se termine par un titre composé de 88 nouvelles *regulae iuris*. La commission chargée de la rédaction de l'œuvre législative pontificate[109] a puisé la plupart de ces maximes générales directement dans les sources des deux droits. Mais un bon nombre des *regulae* bonifaciennes, comme par exemple la fameuse règle d'interprétation, *odia sunt restringenda et favores ampliandi*[110], sont en effet issues des brocards des glossateurs.

---

107 Point vivement discuté pour les *regulae* depuis Bulgarus; cfr le résumé chez Jean d'André, gl. *Non est novum* au Sexte, rubr. *de R. J.*

108 Différence soulignée par tous, de Azon (cfr GENZMER, *loc. cit.*) à Reiffenstuel (cfr LEFÉBVRE, *op. cit.*, p. 151).

109 La légende bibliographique, remontant aux chroniqueurs florentins du XIVe siècle, d'après laquelle le pape aurait confié la rédaction des *regulae iuris* comme travail spécial au légiste Dinus, s'est maintenue dans la plupart des manuels de droit canon, malgré sa réfutation par B. HAURÉAU, *Quels sont les auteurs du sixième livre des décrétales ?* dans le *Journal des savants*, 1884, pp. 271–75; *Notices et extraits*, t. II, pp. 121–27, Paris, 1891. Bon exposé chez L. FALLETTI, art. *Dinus Mugellanus*, dans le *Dictionnaire de droit canonique*, t. IV, 1949, col. 1252 et suiv.

The authorship of the legist Dinus for the Regulae Iuris of the Liber Sextus is no 'légende bibliographique', but can be proved by contemporary sources around 1300 – cf. P. Landau, Dinus Mugellanus und die Regulae Iuris des Liber Sextus, in: *B. Basdevant-Gaudemet* et al. (ed.), Plenitudo Iuris. Mélanges en hommage à Michèle Bégou-Davia (Sceaux 2015) 329–342. (P.L.)

110 R. J. 15. Cfr p. ex. la *Glose ord.* à *Dig.* 28.2.19, v. *adiuvandas*: brocard d'Azon à la base d'un *notabile* de Johannes Bassianus. Un cas caractéristique de la méthode employée par les rédacteurs du Sexte se trouve dans la juxtaposition, de R. J. 43, *Qui tacet consentiré videtur* (brocard, cfr p. ex. Richard l'Anglais, chez GILLMANN, *art. cit.*, p. 644, n. 7) et 44, *Is qui tacet non fatetur, sed nec utique negare videtur* (puisée dans Dig. 50.17.142).

Here Kuttner had written that the Regula iuris 'Qui tacet consentire videtur' in the Liber Sextus (c. 43) had its source in Richardus Anglicus, referring to Franz Gillmann. He corrected it in his copy with the handwritten note: "Rich. Angl. apud Gillmann p. 644, n. 7 has this as 'Arg. taciturnitatem pro consensu haberi', not 'Qui tacet, consentire videtur' (p. 75, n. 7 in Gillmann's erweiterter Sonderabdruck, Mainz 1928)." (S.K.)

PAPST HONORIUS III. UND DAS STUDIUM DES ZIVILRECHTS

Kuttner's article, published in 1953 in a 'Festschrift' for the famous German jurist *Martin Wolff*, who had emigrated to Oxford in the years of the Nazi regime in Germany, lays stress upon the motivation of Pope Honorius III to support the study of theology in Paris instead of secular sciences like law and medicine. He rejects a political interpretation of the constitution 'Super speculam', which saw in the papal law an instrument for the struggle between sacerdotium and imperium. Pope Honorius III was no enemy of imperial civil law. (P.L.)

In der Konstitution *Super speculam* vom 22. November 1219[1] traf Papst Honorius III. eine Reihe von Bestimmungen, deren Bedeutung für das Verhältnis der mittelalterlichen Kirche zum Zivilrecht oft erörtert worden ist. Die Konstitution hat drei dispositive Teile, deren jeder durch allgemeine, motivierende Erörterungen pastoraler Natur eingeleitet ist. Der erste Teil befaßt sich mit Maßnahmen zur Förderung und wirtschaftlichen Sicherstellung des Studiums der Theologie; der zweite erneuert die von Alexander III. auf dem Konzil von Tours (1163)[2] dekretierten Strafen für Ordensgeistliche, die ihre Klöster verlassen, um Medizin oder Zivilrecht zu studieren, gibt in einigen strittigen Punkten eine authentische, verschärfende Interpretation des Konzilsschlusses und dehnt das Studienverbot nebst Strafen auf gewisse Kategorien des Weltklerus aus. Im dritten Teil endlich wird aller Unterricht und alles Studium des Zivilrechts an der Universität Paris verboten.

---

1 *P. Pressutti*, Regesta Honorii Papae III (Romae 1888–95) no. 2267; vgl. *A. Potthast*, Regesta pontificum romanorum (Berlin 1874) no. 6165. Nach dem Register (mit Adresse an den Patriarchen von Antiochia) ediert von *J. B. Card. Pitra*, in Analecta novissima (Spicilegii Solesmensis altera continuatio) I (1885) 570–73; aus verschiedenen Empfängerüberlieferungen von *Savigny*, Über die Decretale Super specula des Pabstes Honorius III., in Zeitschrift für geschichtliche Rechtswissenschaft 8 II (1833) 225–37 (= Vermischte Schriften 3, 412 ff.; Adresse an den Patriarchen von Grado etc.); *Liljegren*, Diplomatarium Suecanum I (Stockholm 1829) 199 ff. (an die Bischöfe Schwedens); *Martène*, Amplissima collectio I 1146 (Chartular von St. Emmeram); *Denifle* und *Chatelain*, Chartularium Universitatis Parisiensis I (Paris 1889) 90–93. no. 32 (aus der Hs. Lissabon, Alcob. 263 [jetzt Hs. 12] fol. 221, mit der Adresse *capitulo Parisiensi*, datiert 16. Nov. 1219). *Denifles* Ausgabe ist am leichtesten zugänglich; auch im Nachdruck bei *M. Fournier*, L'église et le droit romain au XIIIe siècle, in Nouvelle Revue historique de droit français et étranger 14 (1890) 115–18; gegenüber der vielfach akzeptierten Datierung im Kopialbuch von Alcobaça ist aber an dem Datum des Registers festzuhalten.

2 *Mansi* 21, 1179 (c. 8); Comp. I 3. 37. 2; X 3. 50. 3.

Super speculam war eine *constitutio* im technischen Sinn, d. h. ein *motu proprio* ergangenes, allgemeines Kirchengesetz[3]; die Ausfertigungen wurden nach damaligem Brauch einzeln an die jeweiligen Empfänger adressiert[4]. Bald nach ihrem Erscheinen von Tancred und anderen Bolognesern zitiert und erörtert[5], wurde die Konstitution öfters Handschriften der rezipierten Dekretalensammlungen als Anhang beigeschrieben[6]; besonderes Interesse verdienen einige Handschriften, in denen die Konstitution bereits eine redaktionelle Bearbeitung erfahren hat, indem sie unter Streichung der Arenga und der pastoralen Zwischenerwägungen auf ihre juristisch erheblichen Partien reduziert und in drei selbständige, mit Sachrubriken versehene Kapitel zerlegt wurde[7]. In zwei dieser Handschriften sind die drei Kapitel mit einem ausführlichen Glossenapparat versehen, der Willielmus Vasco zum Verfasser hat, aber auch mehrere unsignierte und einige mit der Sigle des Johannes Teutonicus versehene Glossen umfaßt[8].

Die drei Trennstücke entsprechen ungefähr den Ausschnitten, die Honorius III. sodann in seine offizielle Dekretalensammlung (Compilatio V) aufnahm, die, vermutlich von Tancred redigiert, am 2. Mai 1226 publiziert wurde[9], aber nur kurze Zeit in Geltung blieb. Die endgültige Fassung erhielten die drei Stücke von *Super speculam* in den Dekretalen Gregors IX. (5. September 1234), wo St. Raymund von Penyafort teils weitere Kürzungen vornahm, an einer wichtigen Stelle aber einen in Comp. V gestrichenen Passus wiederherstellte[10]. Zur Veranschaulichung diene die folgende Tabelle:

---

3 Zur Definition von *constitutio* (im Gegensatz zu *decretalis*) vgl. *Gloss. ord.* X proem. ad v. *constitutio; Hostiensis,* Summa, tit. de const. (1. 2).

4 Originalausfertigungen sind nicht erhalten; für verschiedene Empfängerüberlieferungen vgl. Anm. 1.

5 Für Tancreds Apparate zu den Compilationes I–III vgl. *Kuttner,* Repertorium der Kanonistik 1140–1234 (Cittá del Vaticano 1937) 358 n. 2; *G. Post,* in Anniversary Essays in Mediaeval History by Students of Chas. H. Haskins (Boston-New York 1929) 263 n. 30; *F. Gillmann,* Zur Inventarisierung der kanonistischen Handschriften ... (Mainz 1938; Anhang zum Sonderabdruck von: Des Johannes Galensis Apparat zur Comp. III ... aus Archiv für kath. Kirchenrecht 118, 174 ff.) 85. Für Raymund von Penyaforts Summa iuris (ed. *Rius,* Barcelona 1945) und die anonymen Quaest. Borghesianae vgl. *Kuttner,* in Miscellanea Giovanni Mercati (Città del Vaticano 1946) V 628 n. 29 und in Seminar 8 (1950) 65.

6 Z. B. in den Dekretalenanhängen zur Comp. IV der Hss. *Rouen 706, fol. 298v (vgl. *Kuttner,* Repertorium 303), Bamberg Can. 19, fol. 77va–78vb (*Gillmann,* Zur Inventarisierung 69), Florenz, Laurenziana *S. Croce V sin. 4, Vorsatzblatt (*Kuttner,* in Traditio 1 [1943] 337 n. 43), Paris, B. N. *lat. 14 321, fol. 241; Anhang zur Comp. III der Hs. Lissabon, *Alcob. 381 (ol. 305) fol. 224 (Traditio loc. cit.; vgl. Misc. Mercati V 618 n. 5); in der Hs. *Wien 2183, fol. 106—108 folgen Press. 2267 und 2268 auf die Konstitutionen des vierten Laterankonzils (vgl. Seminar 8, 65). – Der Asteriskus bezeichnet Hss., die der Verf. selbst eingesehen hat.

7 Hss. Bamberg, S. Croce, Alcob.

8 Inc. 'Nota in causis ecclesiasticis' (Hss. Alcob. und S. Croce); vgl. Traditio loc.cit., Misc. Mercati loc.cit. und *W. Ullmann,* in Juridical Review 60 (1948) 178.

9 Vgl. Repertorium 382. Die Angabe des Johannes de Deo über Tancred als Kompilator (vgl. *H. Kantorowicz,* in Zschr. der Savigny-Stiftung, Kan. Abt. 12 [1922] 435) wird durch das anonyme Dekretalenprincipium der Hs. Vat. *Borgh. 45 gestützt, vgl. Misc. Mercati V, 625, 633.

For Tancred as compiler of the Compilatio V cf. now the fundamental study by *L. E. Boyle O. P.,* The Compilatio quinta and the registers of Honorius III, BMCL 8 (1978) 9–19. (P.L.)

10 X 3.50. 10 § *Quia vero;* vgl. unten S. 279.

Original	Private Dekretalen-anhänge	Comp. V	Dekr. Greg. IX.	Rubriken
(Arenga) Super speculam – – – – vitis vere.	–a)	–a)	–a)	
(c. 1) Cum itaque – – – – fulcimenta, volumus et mandamus – – operantes. Hoc autem – – – – transgressores.	3b)	5. 2. 1	5. 5. 5	De magistris
(c. 2) Sane licet fallax – – – – populorum, contra huiusmodi presumptores – – nuntientur. Quia vero theologie – – observari.	2	3.27.1	3.50.10 c)	Ne clerici vel monachi secularibus negotiis se immisceant.
(c. 3) Nam cum sint multi – – filiis prophetarum. Sane licet sancta – – – – innodetur. Vos autem fratres – – – – curaveritis promovere.	1 –e)	5.12.3	5.33.28 d)	De constitutionibus (Privatanh.); De privilegiis (Comp. V, Greg. IX.)

a) 'Super specula. et infra' am Anfang jedes Kapitels. b) 'Vos autem fratres et filii etc.' add. Cod. S. Crucis (cf. orig. c. 3 in fine); Cod. Bamb. expl. 'noveritis' (so Gillmann loc. cit.; corr. 'curaveritis' = c. 3 i. f.?). c) 'Contra religiosas personas' inc. X.
d) 'et discipuli Elysei – – pedes suos' om. X (vgl. unten S. 283) e) Vgl. Anm. b.

Lassen sich die in der Konstitution verordneten Einschränkungen des zivilistischen Studiums aus innerkirchlichen, disziplinären und pastoralen Gründen erklären, oder sind eher rechtspolitische, vielleicht gar weltpolitische Motive für ihren Erlaß und die Aufnahme in die Dekretalensammlungen bestimmend gewesen? Die Frage ist in der neueren Forschung vor allem gegen Ende des 19. Jahrhunderts lebhaft diskutiert worden. Der Auffassung von *Savigny* und *Hinschius*, die sich im wesentlichen für die erstgenannte Interpretation ausgesprochen hatten[11], traten

11 *Savigny*, Geschichte des römischen Rechts im Mittelalter² III (Heidelberg 1834) 364–74 (unstimmig freilich die gegenteilige Äußerung p. 90, sowie die Vermutung p. 367, die Eifersucht Bolognas

mehr und mehr Autoren entgegen, die den politischen Charakter von *Super speculam* betonten und teils aus allerlei Gründen Feindseligkeit der Kurie gegen das römische Recht überhaupt in der Konstitution ausgedrückt fanden[12], teils das Hauptgewicht auf ihren letzten, Paris betreffenden Teil legten und darin eine von König Philipp August veranlaßte, bewußte päpstliche Unterstützung französischen Widerstandes gegen eine Romanisierung des *droit coutumier* erblickten[13]. Das eine wie das andere Motiv würde der Konstitution, durch die dem Mittelalter geläufige Gleichsetzung von römischem Recht und Kaiserautorität, eine antikaiserliche Spitze geben; und von da ist man mit einem Schritt in der großen Politik, so daß *Super speculam* zu einem kurialen Instrument im Kampf zwischen *sacerdotium* und *imperium* wird.

Die sorgfältige Widerlegung all solcher Theorien in *Georges Digards* eingehender Analyse (1890) der Konstitution und ihrer historischen Zusammenhänge[14] ist für einige moderne Kanonisten maßgebend geblieben[15]. Aber die herrschende Meinung unter Rechtshistorikern hält an der politischen Auslegung in der einen oder anderen Schattierung fest – Veranlassung durch den König von Frankreich[16],

---

oder anderer Legistenschulen auf Paris möge mitgewirkt haben); *Hinschius*, System des kath. Kirchenrechts I (Berlin 1869) 139 f., bes. 140 n. 4.

12 *C. A. Schmid*, Die Rezeption des römischen Rechts in Deutschland (Rostock 1868) 114 ff.; *E. Caillemer*, Le Pape Honorius III et le droit civil (Lyon 1881); ders. in Nouv. Revue hist. de droit franç. et étr. 3 (1879) 599 ff.; *M. Fournier*, ibid. (vgl. Anm. 1) 14, 102 ff., 110 ff.; Abbé *G. Péries*, La Faculté de droit dans l'ancienne Université de Paris (Paris 1890) 93 ff; *Schulte*, Geschichte der Quellen und Literatur des Canonischen Rechts I (Stuttgart 1875) 105; II (1877) 72 f. Selbst *Denifle*, Die Universitäten des Mittelalters bis 1400 (Berlin 1885) ist von dieser Vorstellung nicht frei (vgl. pp. xxiv f., 209 f., 253 f. etc.). Die geplante *Introduction générale* zu *M. Fourniers* und *L. Dorez'* La Faculté de décret de l'Université de Paris au XVe siècle (3 v. Paris 1895–1913) ist nie erschienen.

13 *A. Tardif*, in Nouv. Revue hist. etc. 4 (1880) 291; Histoire des sources du droit français: Origines romaines (Paris 1890) 324–32; *E. Chénon*, Le droit romain à la Curia regis de Philippe-Auguste à Philippe le Bel, in Mélanges Fitting I (Montpellier 1907) 197–212, bes. 198 ff.; Histoire générale du droit français I (Paris 1926) 508 f.

14 *G. Digard*, La papauté et l'étude du droit romain au XIIIe siècle, in Bibliothèque de l'Ecole des chartes 51 (1890) 381–419, bes. 393 ff.

15 Vgl. etwa *B. C. Kuhlmann*, Der Gesetzesbegriff beim Hl. Thomas von Aquin (Bonn 1912) 23 ff., 37 f.; *B. Kurtscheid*, De utriusque iuris studio saec. XIII, in Acta Congressus iuridici internat. Romae 1934 II (1935) 339 ff.; *A. Van Hove*, Prolegomena² (Commentarium Lovaniense in Codicem iur. can. I 1, Mechliniae–Romae 1945) 466; ders. in Miscellanea historica in honorem Leonis van der Essen (Brussel 1947) I 260, 267 ff. (vgl. aber p. 268, wo der Zusammenhang mit einer Démarche Philipp Augusts als 'conjecture vraisemblable' bezeichnet wird).

16 So *E. M. Meijers*, De universiteit van Orléans in de XIIIe eeuw, in Tijdschrift voor Rechtsgeschiedenis 1 (1918) 115; *Rashdall-Powicke-Emden*, The Universities of Europe in the Middle Ages² (Oxford 1936) I 322 n. 2; *H. Kämpf*, Pierre Dubois und die geistigen Grundlagen des französischen Nationalbewußtseins (Leipzig-Berlin 1935) 12 f.; *H. Mitteis*, Die germanischen Grundlagen des französischen Rechts, in Zschr. Sav.-Stift. Germ. Abt. 63 (1943) 159 f.; *Olivier-Martin*, Précis d'histoire du droit français² (Paris 1934) 94 no. 247; *P. Koschaker*, Europa und das römische Recht (München 1947) 76 f.; *H. E. Feine*, Kirchliche Rechtsgeschichte I (Weimar 1950) 325 n. 3.

Antagonismus zwischen kanonischem und römischem Recht[17]; selbst von päpstlichem Weltherrschaftsstreben und Dunkelmännertum ist neuerdings wieder die Rede gewesen[18]. Für die Fortdauer der angeblichen Tendenzen des Papsttums unter Honorius' Nachfolgern verweist man gelegentlich auch heute noch darauf, daß Innozenz IV. in der Bulle *Dolentes* das für Paris erlassene Unterrichtsverbot auf Frankreich, England, Schottland, Wales, Spanien und Ungarn ausgedehnt habe, obwohl *Dolentes* längst unzweifelhaft als Fälschung erwiesen ist[19].

Liest man die drei Dekretalenkapitel in ihrem ursprünglidien Zusammenhang im Rahmen des Originaltextes, so tritt deutlich hervor, daß die Hauptsorge Honorius' III. der Hebung des Studiums der Theologie galt. Die einzelnen Maßnahmen, Förderung wie Abwehr, sind in umfangreiche, einleitende und überleitende Erörterungen eingebettet, die dieses Grundmotiv in einer mit biblischen und anderen Allegorien gesättigten Sprache immer wieder eindringlich machen wollen. Aber auch in den dispositiven Abschnitten wird stets auf die Vordringlichkeit der theologischen Ausbildung Bezug genommen, und diese Bezugnahmen blieben bei der Zerlegung und Verteilung in drei Dekretalenkapitel stehen[20]. Die Glossatoren[21] haben das durchaus erkannt; daher vertritt z. B. Hostiensis in seinem Kommentar zu c. 2 die Auffassung, das Kapitel müsse nicht strikt, sondern weit ausgelegt werden; denn unter dem Prinzip 'odia sunt restringenda et favores ampliandi' sei es nicht als 'odiosum' (gegen die Legisten), sondern als 'favorabile' (für die Theologen) zu verstehen[22].

---

17 *A. Koeniger*, Grundriß einer Geschichte des katholischen Kirchenrechts (Köln 1919) 39; *G. Sarton*, Introduction to the History of Science II (Baltimore 1931) 528, 688; *Koschaker* loc.cit.; *W. Ullmann*, Honorius III and the Prohibition of Legal Studies, in Jurid. Rev. 60 (1948) 177–86.
18 *Ullmann*, loc.cit. 180 ff., 186 ('narrow-minded and illiberal'); Medieval Papalism (London 1949) 97.
19 Eingehende Begründung der Unechtheit bei *Digard*, loc.cit. 383–92 (gegen *M. Fournier*, Nouv. Rev. hist. 14, 98 f., der die schon von *Denifle* in seiner Edition der Bulle ausgesprochenen Zweifel [Chart. Univ. Par. I 262, zu no. 235] für unerheblich erklärt hatte). Digards 'démonstration péremptoire' (so *Chénon*, Hist. gén. I 509) ist sowohl *Koschaker* (loc.cit. 77) wie *Ullmann* (Jurid. Rev. 60, 183 n. 22) entgangen.
20 c. 1 (X 5.5.5.) passim; c. 2 (X 3.50.10): ' ... § Quia vero theologiae studium cupimus ampliari...'; c. 3 (X 5. 33. 28): '... ut plenius sacrae paginae insistatur ...'
21 Eine erschöpfende Behandlung der kanonistischen Glossatorenschriften zu *Super speculam* und anderen in dieser Studie erörterten Texten ist dem Verfasser gegenwärtig, ohne Handschriften und ausreichende Handschriftenphotographien, nicht möglich. Außer dem Apparat des Willielmus Vasco (oben Anm. 8) und den Apparaten zur Comp. V (Jacobus de Albenga und Zoën, vgl. Repertorium 383) wären zahlreiche ungedruckte Glossenapparate, Summen, Kommentare und Lecturae des 13. Jahrhunderts zum Liber Extra (Übersicht bei *Van Hove*, Prolegomena 473, 474–80) heranzuziehen. Selbst wichtige gedruckte Werke, wie die Summa Gottfrieds von Trani und die Lectura des 'Abbas antiquus' Bernhard von Montmirat (vgl. Zschr. Sav.-Stift. Kan. Abt. 26 [1937] 485 n. 2) waren zur Zeit nicht zugänglich.
22 *Hostiensis*, Lectura zu X 3. 50. 10 ad v. *ampliari*: 'Non est ergo haec pena seu prohibitio odiosa, ut quidam somniaverunt, sed favorabilis, cum non in odium transgredientium sed in favorem theologiae et fidei, ut sequitur, sit inducta ...' (ed. Venet. 1581 III fol. 183ra).

Des Papstes Klage über den Mangel an geschulten Theologen und den Schaden, den die Kirche dadurch leidet, daß so viele Kleriker einträglicheren Wissenschaften nachlaufen[23], darf nicht als wortreicher Gemeinplatz beiseitegeschoben werden. Die Katharerbewegung und verwandte Häresien stellten eine sehr ernste Bedrohung der Christenheit im 13. Jahrhundert dar; der größte Gefahrenherd war Südfrankreich, wo unter einem vielfach laxen Episkopat das Katharertum sich ständig ausbreiten und fest organisieren konnte. Die mannigfachen Metaphern, in denen Honorius von den Feinden des Glaubens und dem weitgehend vernachlässigten Apostolat des Glaubensschutzes durch Lehre und Predigt spricht, sind zum großen Teil Briefen seines Vorgängers Innozenz III. über die Zustände in der Provence entnommen[24]; der Ruf nach Theologen war damit in einen für die Zeitgenossen sehr realen Zusammenhang gestellt.

Der Wirksamkeit dieses Rufes standen Hindernisse im Wege, die es zu beseitigen galt[25]. Für weite Kreise des Klerus boten die *scientiae lucrativae* einen größeren materiellen Anreiz; das ließ sich zunächst dadurch ausgleichen, daß mit dem Studium der Theologie gewisse wirtschaftliche Vergünstigungen verbunden wurden. Daher verordnete *Super speculam* c. 1 Stipendien und benefizialrechtliche Sicherungen für Dozenten und Studenten der Theologie, die den Weltgeistlichen den Aufenthalt an Universitäten fern vom Sitz ihrer Benefizien ermöglichen sollten[26]. Diese Vorschriften schufen erst die materielle Voraussetzung dafür, daß in c. 2 gewissen Klassen des Weltklerus das zivilistische und das medizinische Studium mit der Begründung 'quia vero theologiae cupimus studium ampliari' verboten werden konnte[27]. Im Anschluß an diesen Satz betont der Papst noch einmal in bilderreicher Sprache die Notwendigkeit von Kämpfern zur Verteidigung des Glaubens.

Die Studienbeschränkungen des c. 2 beruhen auf einer Gegenüberstellung von geistlichen und weltlichen Wissenschaften, die auch in der Einordnung des Kapitels unter die Rubrik 'ne clerici vel monachi saecularibus negotiis se immisceant' zum Ausdruck kommt. Wenn man hier nach einem Antagonismus zwischen kanonischem und römischem Recht sucht, ist die Frage falsch gestellt. Denn

---

23 Die zwei Aussagen: 'quod modica est in terra scientia domini' und 'quia plures ... currunt ad scientias lucrativas' bilden den Kern der Arenga, auf den sich die ganzen biblischen und rhetorischen Allegorien beziehen.

24 Vgl. die Nachweise bei *Digard*, Bibl. éc. ch. 51, 394 n. 2 (wo Inn. III Reg. 3. 24 statt 3.26 zu lesen ist), nn. 3–4, 397 n. 2; vgl. auch n. 4 zu dem Irrtum *M. Fourniers*, der einige der starken bildlichen Ausdrücke auf die Zivilrechtslehrer statt auf die Irrlehrer bezogen hatte (Nouv. Rev. hist. 14, 103).

25 Schluß der Arenga: '... quosdam obices amovere cupimus huic itineri obsistentes ...'

26 Alle Prälaten und Kapitel sollen geeignete Kleriker für das Studium der Theologie auswählen und notfalls unterhalten; wer an theologischen Fakultäten lehrt oder studiert, soll sein Benefizialeinkommen unverkürzt, ohne Rücksicht auf entgegenstehende gemein-oder partikularrechtliche Beschränkungen beziehen (gesetzliche Befreiung von der Residenzpflicht), und zwar Dozenten für die Dauer ihrer Lehrtätigkeit, Studenten für fünf Jahre.

27 Vgl. *Innozenz IV*. Apparatus zu X 1.1.1: '... et bene videtur quod semper plus deberent intendere circa cognitionem praedictorum (d. h. der Glaubensartikel) quam circa cognitionem iuris, postquam expensas habent ab ecclesia, nisi in contrarium eos iusta causa moveat' (ed. Venet. 1570 p. 2a).

c. 2 befaßt sich nicht mit der Geltung oder Unterdrückung von Rechtssystemen, sondern mit klerikalen Studien, und schon die Tatsache, daß hier die medizinische und die zivilistische Wissenschaft zusammen (*leges vel physica*) der Theologie gegenübergestellt werden, sollte den Gedanken an kuriale Feindschaft gegen eine der beiden Disziplinen unmöglich machen. Daß die Gegenüberstellung ein für *leges* und *physica* unvorteilhaftes Werturteil einschließt, liegt auf der Hand; aber dies Werturteil ist durchaus relativ: nur im Verhältnis zur *scientia domini* und nur in ihrem Wert für den Klerus[28], dessen eigentliche Aufgabe eben eine geistliche ist, werden die Profanwissenschaften mit leeren Hülsen, trockenen Zisternen, trügerischem Glanz, eitler Schönheit, beifallsüchtigen Dienerinnen verglichen[29].

Die Konzilien des 12. Jahrhunderts hatten die Unvereinbarkeit des Studiums der Medizin und des weltlichen Rechts mit dem Ordensstande hervorgehoben und die Motive der Gewinnsucht und des Ehrgeizes getadelt; daß insbesondere die Ausübung der Advokatur für Mönche unschicklich sei, hatte man sogar mit einem Zitat aus dem justinianischen Codex belegt[30]. Honorius hielt es für geboten, das Verbot von Tours auszudehnen, aber eben doch nur auf bestimmte Klassen des Weltklerus[31], bei denen solche *saecularia negotia* der Erfüllung ihrer kirchlichen Pflichten unzuträglich waren und aus deren Reihen der Papst ganz besonders eine intensivere Beschäftigung mit der Theologie erwartete. Die Konstitution nennt Archidiakone, Dekane, Pröpste, Kantoren und Inhaber von Personaten, d. h. von Kapitelspfründen, die mit irgendwelcher Jurisdiktion, Seelsorge oder sonstigem Vorrang vor den einfachen Kanonikaten verbunden waren[32]; ferner aus der Pfarrgeistlichkeit die *plebani*, schließlich alle Priester.

Selbst für diese Personengruppen hatte Honorius nachträglich Bedenken. Denn in der Compilatio V ist der ganze die Ausdehnung enthaltende Absatz

---

28 Vgl. *Hostiensis*, Lect. zu X 3. 50.10 ad v. *theologiae*: 'nam haec scientia favorabilis est ad omnes, legalis vero et physicalis odiosa est quoad religiosos et presbyteros et personas, et ideo favores ampliantur et odia restringuntur ...'(fol. 183ra).

29 So in der Arenga: '... accepta non modica portione Jesu Christi comparant sibi de ipsa siliquas vacuas et sonoras que non satiant; ... fodientes sibi cisternas que aquam non prevalent continere ...'; in der Einleitung zu c. 2: 'Sane licet fallax sit gratia ceterarum scientarum et vana etiam pulchritudo; ... et illicite se convertunt ad pedissequas amplectendas que plausum desiderant populorum ...'

30 Reims 1131 c. 6 = II Lat. 1139 c. 9 (*Mansi* 21, 459; 528); darin'... attestantur vero imperiales constitutiones absurdum, imo opprobrium esse clericis si peritos se velint esse disceptationum forensium' (C. 1. 3. 40). Tours 1163 c. 8 (oben Anm. 2). Vgl. auch III Lat. c. 12 (Mansi 22, 225; gekürzt in Comp. I 3. 37. 3, X 3. 50. 4), Paris 1212 c. 1. 6 (*Mansi* 22, 820) usw. und Honorius III. selbst an den Bischof von Poitiers, Comp. V 3. 1. 1.

31 Hinsichtlich des Ordensklerus behandelt *Super speculum* c. 2 § 1 die Strafbestimmung von Tours c. 8: '... sicut excommunicati ab omnibus evitentur', und gibt 'propter quorumdam opiniones diversas' (vgl. *Hostiensis* ad loc. fol. 182vb) die amtliche Auslegung, daß es sich um *ipso facto* eintretende, öffentlich zu verkündende Exkommunikation handelt.

32 Eine scharfe Abgrenzung zwischen *dignitates* und *personatus* besteht im Dekretalenrecht nicht, vgl. z. B. *Glos. ord.* X 3. 5.13 ad v. *singula officia*. Man kann nicht sagen, daß Personate bloßen Ehrenvorrang hatten (so Feine, Kirchl. Rechtsgesch. 320). Vgl. auch *Kathleen Edwards*, The English Secular Cathedrals in the Middle Ages (Manchester 1949) 136 n. 1.

'Quia vero' *rell.* gestrichen; er wurde erst im Liber Extra wieder hergestellt, bereitete aber auch dann noch Auslegungsschwierigkeiten. Unter Berufung teils auf das Prinzip des Dekretalenrechts, 'idem est iudicium de personatibus et de beneficiis curam animarum habentibus' (X 1.6. 54, vgl. 3. 5. 28), teils auf die Vorschrift, daß der Inhaber eines Pfarrbenefiziums gehalten ist, den nötigen Weihegrad zu erwerben (X 3. 5. 30), wollte die Glossa ordinaria das Verbot von *Super speculam* auf alle Kuratbenefizien angewendet wissen[33], und so verstand es auch Gregor IX. in einem Reskript an den Bischof von Orléans[34]. Zudem war der Begriff *plebanus* nicht eindeutig[35]. Er meinte in *Super speculam* (im Sinn vor allem oberitalienischer Verhältnisse) den Rektor einer kollegialen Taufkirche (*plebs*) mit einzelnen bepfründeten Kapellen, also den Land-archipresbyter[36]. Aber erst eine authentische Definition Clemens' IV., von Bonifaz VIII. im Liber Sextus wiederholt[37], hat diese Auslegung endgültig fixiert und damit alle noch

---

33 *Bernhard von Parma*, Glos. ord. X 3. 50. 10 ad v. *presbyteros;* so auch Hostiensis und Innozenz IV. ad loc. Die entgegengesetzte Meinung vertraten Gottfried von Trani, Pierre Sampson und Bernhard von Montmirat. Vgl. den Bericht über die verschiedenen Interpretationen bei *Johannes Andreae*, Glos. ord. Sext 3.24.1 ad v. *declaramus.*

34 *L. Auvray*, Les registres de Grégoire IX (Paris 1890 ff.) no. 2399 = Chart. Univ. Par. I 156 no. 106. Zu diesem Reskript vgl. unten S. 288 f. Die vom Studium der *leges* ausgeschlossenen Klassen werden dort als 'archidiaconis, decanis, archipresbyteris et aliis personis ecclesiasticis curam animarum habentibus dumtaxat exceptis' aufgezählt. Der Vergleich mit der Liste Honorius' III. ('archidiaconos, decanos, prepositos, plebanos, cantores et alios clericos personatus habentes necnon presbyteros') ergibt, daß den *plebani* bei Gregor IX. die *archipresbyteri*, und den Pröpsten, Kantoren und Inhabern anderer Personate die 'personae ecclesiasticae curam animarum habentes' entsprechen.

35 In den von *H. Schäfer*, Pfarrkirche und Stift im deutschen Mittelalter (Stuttgart 1903) untersuchten Quellen bezeichnet *plebanus* zuweilen den Stiftspräbendar, dem die Pfarrechte zustehen (meist Custos oder Thesaurar), oder überhaupt den Rektor der Pfarrkirche, zuweilen aber auch den ständigen Vikar des die Seelsorge selbst nicht ausübenden Inhabers der Pfarrpfründe, den „Leutpriester". Vgl. *Schäfer* 53–56, 150 n. 3, 186 f.; *Feine*, Kirchl. Rechtsgesch. 338.

36 Über diese Einrichtung vgl. vor allem G. *Forchielli*, La píeve rurale (Roma 1931; 1938); *Feine* 156 f., 175. Zu *plebanus* = *archipresbyter* s. Anm. 34, zum Gebrauch des Ausdrucks in der päpstlichen Kanzlei in diesem Sinn vgl. etwa die Urkunden, die bei *E. Berger*, Les registres d'Innocent IV (Paris 1884 ff.) im Index s. v. *plebanatus, plebes, plebanus* verzeichnet sind, z. B. no. 5638: 'plebanus et canonici plebis de Greppano'.

37 Sext. 3. 24. 1: '... piae memoriae Clementis papae quarti praedecessoris nostri vestigiis inhaerentes declaramus'. Die Dekretale Clemens' IV, *Habito cum fratribus* ('quam non habemus', sagt *Joh. Andreae*, Glos. ord. ad loc.) kommt nur in Extravagantensammlungen des 13. Jhdts. vor, z. B. in den Hss. Preßburg, Domkapitel 13 (vgl. *Denifle*, Chart. Univ. Par. I 93 n. 2 zu no. 32) und Reims 699 (vgl. *P. J. Kessler*, in Zschr. Sav.-Stift. Kan. Abt. 31 [1942] 283). In der Sammlung der Hs. Prag, Nationalmuseum XVII. A. 5 (ol. I. B. 4) ist *Habito* Gregor IX. zugeschrieben; *Friedberg*, Corp. iur. can. II 1064 (ad Sext. 3. 24.1) hat diese Inskription akzeptiert, so auch *Tardif*, Hist, des sources 286; *Digard* loc.cit. 406 f. Dagegen schreibt *Bernhard von Montmirat*, Lect. X 3. 50.10 die authentische Interpretation von *Super speculam* einer Dekretale Gregors IX. zu 'quam nescio esse veram, et incipit *Sabbato proximo*' (vgl. Studia et documn. hist: et iuris 6 [1940] 426 n. 1). In der Tat ist es höchst fraglich, ob Gregor IX. sich je im Sinn von *Habito* geäußert hat; denn für Orléans hielt er ja gerade das Studienverbot hinsichtlich aller Seelsorgsgeistlichen aufrecht (Anm. 34; ungenau Stud. et doc. loc.cit.).

nicht zu Priestern geweihten Inhaber einfacher Pfarrbenefizien[38] gegen die Anwendung von *Super speculam* gesichert. Wie weite Kreise des Weltklerus im 13. Jahrhundert von dem Verbot erfaßt wurden, läßt sich statistisch kaum sagen. Die Verhältnisse der Neuzeit, unter denen die Priesterweihe das normale Ziel für den Regular- und Diözesanklerus ist, dürfen nicht irreführen[39]: gerade für die akademische Laufbahn war der Erwerb höherer Weihen im Mittelalter durchaus nicht das übliche, und die Mehrzahl der Studenten aus dem Weltklerus wurde wahrscheinlich von dem Verbot überhaupt nicht betroffen[40].

Aber auch für die Ordensleute, Priester und obengenannten kirchlichen Dignitäre darf das Verbot des 'exire ad audiendas leges vel physicam' nicht dahin verstanden werden, daß Honorius III. ihnen jegliche Beschäftigung mit diesen Disziplinen hätte verbieten wollen. Der Punkt war von großer Bedeutung für das in der Konstitution überhaupt nicht berührte Studium der *decreta*, des kanonischen Rechts[41]. Ganz abgesehen von der Frage der subsidiären Geltung des römischen Rechts im kirchlichen Rechtssystem (worüber Honorius sich in c. 3 äußert) war in der kanonistischen Glossatorenschule die Auslegung und wissenschaftliche Behandlung der *canones* unter ständiger Heranziehung der römischen Rechtsquellen und Rechtsbegriffe festbegründete Methode. Auch über die Gebiete hinaus, die (wie z. B. Prozeß, Testamente, Verträge usw.) ohne Kenntnis des Zivilrechts überhaupt nicht verstanden werden konnten[42], darf man schon für das späte 12. Jahrhundert von einer fortschreitenden Romanisierung der kanonistischen Wissenschaft reden: das lehrt ein Blick in die Fülle der zivilistischen Allegationen auf jeder Seite der Dekretisten- und Dekretalistenschriften. Daran ist durch *Super speculam* nichts geändert worden und sollte auch nichts geändert werden. Mit den Ideen derer, die am liebsten die Kanonistik ganz von der zivilistischen Begriffswelt emanzipiert gesehen hätten[43], hat *Super speculam* sich gar

---

38 Clem. IV: 'illi qui habent simplices curas animarum'; Bonif. VIII: 'qui parochiales ecclesias obtinere noscuntur'.

39 Manche Autoren sprechen irrtümlich von einem Verbot für den ganzen Weltklerus; so *Caillemer*, Le Pape Honorius etc. (Anm. 12) 13, *M. Fournier*, loc.cit. 97, 101 *Ullmann*, Jurid. Rev. 60, 177.

40 Vgl. die Erörterungen Innozenz' IV. über die Erlaubtheit des Rechtsstudiums für *clerici*, App. zu X 1.1.1.

41 Die Annahme, daß in *Super speculam* dem Sinne nach das kanonische Recht unter der Theologie miteinbegriffen sei (so *Fournier* 108, 111, *Digard* 399 n. 2, *Koschaker*, Europa und das röm. Recht 76 f.) ist irrig.

42 Eine Liste solcher kanonischer Rechtsinstitute gibt *Hostiensis*, Lect. zu X 3. 50.10 ad v. *ampliari*; vgl. auch *Guil. Durantis*, Speculum 2. 2 de disput. et allegat. advocatorum § 5 n. 4 (ed. Venet. 1577 fol. 753).

43 Vgl. die bei *Koschaker* 77 zitierte Pariser Predigt (13. Jhdt.): 'quondam ecclesia consuevit regi in pace per canones, modo regitur per advocatos ... et student in legibus dicentes quod canones non possunt scire sine legibus'; ferner *Roger Bacon*, Opus tertium c. 24: '... sed nunc (ius canonicum) principaliter tractatur et exponitur et concordatur per ius civile; ... si etiam ius canonicum purgaretur a superfluitate iuris civilis et regularetur per theologiam, tunc ecclesie regimen fieret gloriose et secundum propriam eius dignitatem' (ed. Brewer p. 84 ff.; zitiert bei *M. Fournier* 91 n. 2, *Digard*

nicht befaßt, und insofern ist es müßig, darüber zu spekulieren, ob Honorius III. sich bewußt war, daß für jeden Kanonisten eine gründliche Kenntnis der *leges* unerläßlich blieb. Jedenfalls ist die oft zitierte, bissige Bemerkung Roffreds von Benevent[44] über „saure Kirschen" unberechtigt.

Für die Dekretalisten war es ausgemacht, daß Studenten des kanonischen Rechts, soweit sie zu einer der von der Konstitution betroffenen Gruppen gehören, sich die notwendigen Zivilrechtskenntnisse durch Privatstudium verschaffen müssen[45]. Ob ein solches Studium die Form von Vorlesungen für einen geschlossenen Hörerkreis in Privat- oder Klosterräumen annehmen darf, wurde schon in den um 1220 entstandenen Quaestiones Borghesianae diskutiert[46]. Unter den Kommentatoren der Dekretalen Gregors IX. verneint Hostiensis die Frage, während Innozenz IV. sie ohne weiteres bejaht[47].

Darüber hinaus blieb individuelle Dispensation[48] von dem formellen Studienverbot immer möglich; aber das gehört nicht zur Frage der Beurteilung von *Super speculam*. Nur sollte man sich angesichts der Beschränkung der Konstitution auf bestimmte Personenklassen kein übertriebenes Bild von der Notwendigkeit solcher Dispensationen machen. Viele der großen Dekretalisten des 13. Jahrhunderts hatten die Vorlesungen bekannter Legisten gehört[49]; nichts zwingt dazu anzunehmen, daß sie in ihren Studienjahren bereits Priester waren oder eins der dishabilitierenden Benefizien besaßen[50].

---

418). Eine gewisse Vorstufe solcher Klagen findet sich im 12. Jhdt. in der Gegenüberstellung von *lex Justiniani* und *lex Domini*, etwa bei *Bernhard von Clairvaux*, De considerat. 1. 4 (PL 182, 732); *Peter von Blois*, epp. 26, 140 (PL 207, 91; 416).

44 Libelli in iure can. 6.1: '... sed, si audeo dicere, tam lator canonis illius quam et duo consiliarii, qui fuerunt pure theologi, fecerunt sicut vulpes quae, dum non posset gustare de cerasis, cepit illa publice vituperare ... .' (zitiert nach *Savigny*, Gesch.² III 365).

45 *Hostiensis*, Lect. zu X 3. 50. 10 ad. v. *student;* ad v. *theologiae:* '... Solutio: non obstat quod oppositum est de iuribus legalibus, quia et sine principali studio, lectione et auditu legum per libros legales qui haberi possunt et glossas suas et illas quae in dictis iuribus apponuntur sufficiens notitia de ipsis haberi potest, ... dummodo ibi principaliter non studeat.'

46 *Quaest. Borgh.* (oben Anm. 5) q. 22: 'Archidiaconi et plebani audiunt leges in camera. Queritur an incidant in penam illius const. Super specula ...' (Hs. Vat. *Borgh. 261, fol. 109rb).

47 *Hostiensis* loc.cit.; *Innozenz IV*, App. zu X 3. 50. 10 ad v. *exeuntes*: 'de claustris suis; si enim ibi audirent vel legerent, secus' (ed. Ven. p. 552a). Hostiensis' gegenteilige Entscheidung (der z. B. *Guido de Baysio*, Rosarium zu C. 1 q. 3 c. 8 ad v. *vel extra* folgt) beruht auf seiner Auffassung von *Super speculam* als einer weit auszulegenden *lex favorabilis*, vgl. oben Anm. 22, 28.

48 Vgl. *Joh. Andreae*, Quaest. Mercuriales, ad reg. iur. 39 no. 3, 6; *Digard*, loc.cit. 406 n. 2; *Chénon*, Mél. Fitting I 200 f.; *Van Hove*, Proleg.² 466 n. 4; *Rashdall*, Universities² I 322 n. 2.

49 Vgl. die Listen bei *Kurtscheid*, loc.cit. (Anm. 15) 334, 336, aus denen aber Johannes de Deo gestrichen werden sollte: der ihm stets zugeschriebene Kommentar zu Johannes Bassianus' Arbor actionum (*Savigny*, Gesch.² V 474 f.; *Schulte*, Gesch. II 106) hat einen portugiesischen Legisten Johannes, Kanonikus von Idanha, zum Verfasser, vgl. Seminar 8 (1950) 55 n. 10.

50 So waren z. B. Gottfried von Trani und der jüngere Bernhard von Compostella noch Subdiakone, als sie bereits hohe Kurialämter bekleideten; Hostiensis sagt im Epilog seiner Summa (vgl. *Kuhlmann*, Der Gesetzesbegriff ... 32 n. 1), er habe das Werk *in officio minori* begonnen (zur Zeit der Veröffentlichung, c. 1250–53, war er Erzbischof von Embrun).

Für die Interpretation des letzten Kapitels der Konstitution ist es noch einmal nötig, an die Katharerwirren zu erinnern. Die umfangreiche Einleitung zu c. 3 wiederholt die Warnung vor den Gefahren der Häresie, preist Paris als die Hochburg der gelehrten Streiter für den Glauben und beklagt den Vorwitz[51] derer, die mit den 'traditiones saecularium principum' den Schmieden der Glaubenswaffen den Platz streitig machen wollen, ihre Ware zur Anlockung ausbreiten und so, obwohl sie 'in locis plurimis habeant sui studii professores', an einer ohnehin zu engen Stätte die 'filii prophetarum' noch weiter beengen. Und nun beginnt der dispositive Teil mit der vielerörterten Begründung:

> Sane licet sancta ecclesia legum secularium non respuat famulatum, que satis equitatis et iustitie vestigia imitantur; quia tamen in Francia et nonnullis provinciis laici romanorum imperatorum legibus non utuntur, et occurrunt raro ecclesiastice cause tales, que non possent statutis canonicis expediri,

um mit dem Finalsatz,

> ut plenius sacre pagine insistatur et discipuli Elysei liberius iuxta fluenta plenissima resideant ut columbe, dum in ianuis scolas non invenerint ad quas divaricare valeant pedes suos,

zu dem Gesetzesbefehl 'firmiter interdicimus et inhibemus ne Parisius' *rell.* und den Strafklauseln überzuleiten.

Von der ganzen kunstvoll aufgebauten Einleitung des Verbots allen Unterrichts und Studiums des *ius civile* in Paris 'vel in civitatibus seu aliis locis vicinis' ist in der endgültigen Fassung der Dekretalen nur die juristisch erhebliche Trias der Klauseln 'Sane licet ...[52], quia tamen ..., ut plenius..., (unter Streichung der allegorischen Anspielung auf die Enge der Verhältnisse, 'et discipuli' *rell.*[53]) stehen geblieben. Daß von diesen dreien die letzte den Zweck (*causa finalis*) des Gesetzes ausspricht, steht grammatisch fest und folgt gedanklich aus dem Gesamttenor des Kapitels[54]. Eine analytische Interpretation des Textes muß darum stets zu dem Ergebnis kommen, daß der Kausalsatz 'quia tamen' *rell.*, mit *Savigny*[55] zu reden, „nicht der Grund des Verbots seyn, sondern die Unschädlichkeit desselben beweisen" soll, in scholastischer Terminologie also eine *causa materialis per accidens* (*sc. removens impedimentum*) ausdrückt.

---

51 'improbi' darf an dieser Stelle nicht als „böse, moralisch schlecht" verstanden werden, da ja wenige Zeilen später von der *equitas* und *iustitia* der weltlichen Gesetze die Rede ist.
52 'satis' om. X.
53 Vgl. 4 Reg. 6. 1–2: 'Dixerunt autem filii prophetarum ad Eliseum: Ecce locus in quo habitamus coram te angustus est nobis. Eamus usque ad Jordanum ...'; Cantic. 5. 12: 'Oculi eius sicut columbae super rivulos aquarum quae lacte sunt lotae et resident iuxta fluenta plenissima.'
54 *Chénon*, Mél. Fitting I 199 (vgl. auch Hist. gén. I 509) spricht zu Unrecht von 'raison visée en passant'.
55 Gesch.² III 369 Anm. g.

Das hindert freilich nicht, daß erstens der ganze Passus 'Sane licet – – expediri' im Dekretalenrecht, unabhängig von seiner Beziehung auf das spezielle Lehrverbot, die Bedeutung eines allgemeinen Rechtssatzes erhalten mußte, und daß es zweitens dem Rechtshistoriker unbenommen bleibt nachzuforschen, ob sich nicht hinter der offiziellen Formulierung der Verbotsgründe eine andere psychologische Wirklichkeit verbirgt. An diesem Punkt setzen die politischen Deutungen ein, die teils eine Mißbilligung der subsidiären Geltung des römischen Rechts im kirchlichen Bereich, teils eine Stützung des *droit coutumier* gegenüber den *leges* im weltlichen Bereich als das eigentliche Gesetzmotiv betrachten.

Dogmengeschichtlich gehört der umstrittene Passus in einen Problemkreis, mit dem die Glossatoren sich seit Gratian beschäftigt haben: Geltung und Umfang der Verbindlichkeit des römischen Rechts in der Kirche und Staatenwelt des Mittelalters[56].

Für das Verhältnis von *leges* und *canones* war es unbestrittene Doktrin, daß dem römischen Recht subsidiäre Geltung zur Ausfüllung von Gesetzeslücken zukommt, soweit es nicht im Widerspruch zu Prinzipien des kanonischen Rechts steht[57]. Die Verbindlichkeit der *leges* für den Klerus und den kirchlichen Richter beruht in diesem Fall nicht auf der ihnen eigenen Gesetzeskraft, sondern auf ihrer (stillschweigenden oder ausdrücklichen) Anerkennung durch den kirchlichen Gesetzgeber[58]. Die Lehre vom römischen Recht als *lex suppletoria* war in einer Dekretale Lucius' III. offiziell kanonisiert[59] und von Honorius III. selbst in einem Responsum an den Kardinallegaten Johannes Colonna angewandt worden[60]. Ihre Wiederholung in *Super speculam* lehnt sich sprachlich bewußt

---

56 *Maassen* veröffentlichte und besprach in den Sitzungsberichten der Wiener Akademie 24 (1857) 79 ff. erstmals die interessanten Erörterungen Huguccios (Summa ad D. 1 c. 12) zu dieser Frage. Die neueste Darstellung des gesamten bisher veröffentlichten (und einigen bisher unveröffentlichten) Quellenmaterials findet sich bei *S. Mochi Onory*, Fonti canonistiche dell'idea moderna dello Stato (Milano 1951).
57 Vgl. *Van Hove*, Prolegomena² 461 ff. und in Misc. van der Essen I 258 ff.
58 *Huguccio*, Summa loc.cit.: '... Item quid de clericis? numquid et ipsi ligantur legibus romanis? Sic, illis quae approbantur ab ecclesia et non obviant canonibus. Sed non ideo quia sint promulgatae ab imperatoribus, sed quia sunt confirmatae a domino papa ... (zitiert nach *Maassen*, loc.cit. 80). Eine etwas ältere Lehre sah den Rechtsgrund der Verbindlichkeit für den Klerus darin, daß Kleriker als *latini* „Römer" seien; so *Simon von Bisignano*, Summa zu D. 1 c. 12 v. *in eos solos constituta:* 'hinc collige in causis ecclesiasticis uel aliorum hominum ro(bur) leges non habere ... Responsio: forte romanos hic omnes latinos intelligit ... (Hs. Rouen *710, fol. 64va). Ihm folgt die *Summa Omnis qui iuste* (Lipsiensis: 'hinc collige quod leges romane solos romanos ligant, non clericos, ut hic et d. xcvi. Cum uerum (c. 6); dici tamen potest hic appellari romanos omnes latinos...' (der abweichende Text bei *Schulte*, Wiener SB 68 [1871] 53, dem *Van Hove*, Misc. van der Essen I 269 n. 24 und *Mochi Onory* 135, 174 n. 1 folgen, ist entstellt).
59 JL 15 189: Comp. II 3. 26. 3, X 5. 32. 1; für 'nisi ab ecclesia fuerit approbatum' beriefen sich die Kanonisten auch oft auf Innozenz III. X 1. 2. 10 (Comp. III 2. 2. 5).
60 *Pressutti* 1586 (18. Aug. 1218): Comp. V 1. 20. 1, vgl. *Digard* 393 n. I; *Van Hove* loc.cit. 261 n. 9; *R. L. Wolff*, in Traditio 6 (1948) 42. In X 1. 36. 11 fehlt der Teil der Dekretale, der sich auf die bestehenden 'iura canonica et civilia' bezieht.

an die Formulierung Lucius' III. an[61]. Sie will weder eine Unterordnung[62] des römischen Rechts als solchen (d. h. im Zivilbereich) unter das kanonische Recht statuieren, noch überhaupt Neues lehren, sondern dem möglichen Mißverständnis vorbeugen, als ob mit der Schließung der Pariser Legistenfakultät das anerkannte Prinzip der Subsidiarität des Zivilrechts auch nur teilweise von der Kirche aufgegeben würde[63]. Denn auch der weitere Satz von der Seltenheit kirchlicher Prozesse, die nicht schon durch die *canones* allein erledigt werden könnten, enthält keine Einschränkung und Zurückdrängung[64] der subsidiären *leges*, sondern eine tatsächlidie Feststellung (und damit ein Argument der Praktikabilität des Verbots), die angesichts der ständigen Vervollkommnung des Dekretalenrechts in den Jahrzehnten seit Lucius III. nicht ganz unberechtigt war[65]. Die Glossatoren haben es denn auch nicht anders verstanden. Allenfalls konnte man sich fragen, ob der Ausdruck 'raro occurrunt' nicht vielleicht doch eine rhetorische Übertreibung darstellte[66].

Die Frage der Ergänzung des kanonischen durch das römische Recht war von unmittelbarem Interesse für die Kirche; die Frage der (weltlichen) Geltung des römischen Rechts in den einzelnen Staaten war das nicht. Dennoch haben sich die Kanonisten schon seit dem 12. Jahrhundert theoretisch oft mit diesem Problem beschäftigt, und zwar zunächst deshalb, weil das Decretum Gratiani eine Reihe von Stellen enthielt, in denen von *reges* und *civitates*, *reges et principes*, einzelstaatlicher Gesetzgebung und *consuetudines patriae* die Rede ist[67]; andererseits aber auch Texte, die sich auf die Universalität des *imperium romanum* und die Einzigartigkeit der Kaiserwürde beziehen[68]. Dazu kommt, daß die sich immer

---

61 JL 15 189: 'Quia vero, sicut humanae leges non dedignantur sacros canones imitari (vgl. Nov. 83.1), ita et sacrorum statuta canonum priorum principum constitutionibus adiuvantur ...; vgl. die Wendungen 'sicut ... non respuat famulatum', 'vestigia imitantur' in *Super speculam*.
62 So *Ullmann*, Jurid. Rev. 60, 182.
63 Die Kontroverse, ob Landesrecht oder römisches Recht als subsidiäre Quelle des kanonischen Rechts zu gelten habe, gehört einer viel späteren Epoche an und bewegte vor allem spanische Autoren im 17. Jhdt. Zur Sache vgl. *Van Hove*, Proleg.² 107–115, 462 f., 523 f., 568 f. und in Misc. van der Essen I 265–69, der aber zu Unrecht annimmt, schon der Glossator Laurentius Hispanus habe die subsidiäre Geltung des römischen Rechts für die Kirche in Frankreich und Spanien bestritten (Proleg.² 463 n. 1, 523), vielleicht unter dem Einfluß von *Super speculam* (Misc. v. d. Essen I 269). Die Glosse des Laurentius (unten Anm. 73) befaßt sich nur mit Geltung der *leges romanae* in der weltlichen Rechtsordnung dieser Länder und ist außerdem vor 1215 zu datieren.
64 So *Schulte*, Gesch. I 105; *M. Fournier*, loc.cit. 105; *Ullmann*, loc.cit. 180.
65 Dagegen meint *Ullmann*, loc.cit., da es damals außer Comp. III keine offizielle Sammlung gegeben habe, sei es 'a euphemism on the part of Honorius III to speak of existing canon law'.
66 Nicht ohne Ironie sagt *Hostiensis*, Lect. ad loc. v. *raro*: 'tamen occurrunt, ut supra de novi operis nuntiatione et in materia testamentorum, tutorum, servitutum et in multis aliis de quibus etiam non habemus speciales rubricas, et hae quas habemus non sufficiunt ad omnia quae occurrunt ...' (ed. Ven. V fol. 88vb). *Bernhard von Parma* hielt es nicht einmal für nötig, in der Glos. ord. zu dem obenerwähnten Kapitel Lucius' III. (X 5. 32. 1 ad v. *adiuvantur*) die Konstitution *Super speculam* unter den möglichen Gegeninstanzen gegen seine These 'et ita in causa ecclesiastica leges possumus allegare' aufzuzählen.
67 Vgl. *Mochi Onory* 132 ff. und passim.
68 Der klassische *locus* ist C. 7 q. 1 c. 41 *In apibus*.

deutlicher abzeichnende Vielfalt der europäischen Staatenwelt, der 'reges qui non subsunt imperatori'[69], den Glossatoren ebenso bewußt war wie die universale Bedeutung des Kaisertums[70], in dessen eigentümlicher, alle Fürstenwürde überragender Autorität sich die kirchliche Einheit des christlichen Abendlandes auf weltliche Weise verkörperte. Dazu kommt ferner, daß die scholastische Mentalität sich von dem historischen Unterschied zwischen dem mittelalterlichen Kaiser und dem *dominus mundi,* dem byzantinischen Autokrator, der das Corpus iuris erlassen hatte, keine Rechenschaft gab und daß die aufkommende staufische Reichs- und Kaiserideologie den Unterschied wirkungsvoll verwischte[71]. So kann es einen nicht verwundern, daß die Kanonisten mit dem Problem der weltlichen Rechtsordnungen im Grunde nicht fertig wurden. Man sollte aber auch nicht vergessen, daß es ihnen gar nicht darum ging, abgerundete staatsrechtliche Theorien zu verkünden[72], sondern einzelne, für das kanonische Recht selbst unerhebliche Quellenantinomien zu interpretieren.

Zu einer *communis opinio* ist es in diesem Punkt nicht gekommen. Die Tatsache, daß in den meisten Ländern justinianisches Recht keine praktische Geltung hatte, war nun einmal gegeben; sie wurde von manchen Autoren als durchaus Rechtens angesehen[73], während andere die ideelle Universalität des römischen Rechts mit allerlei Konstruktionen retten wollten, vor allem mit der Distinktion, daß zwar nicht *de facto,* aber *de iure* alle Länder dem römischen Imperium unterständen oder doch wenigstens unterstehen sollten[74]. Zur Begründung mußten dabei

---

69 Huguccios Formulierung, bei *Mochi Onory* 155. Vgl. ferner die Glossen der Engländer Richardus (bei *Gillmann,* Arch. kath. KR 107 [1927] 626) und Alanus (bei *Schulte,* Wiener SB 66 [1870] 89 f.); dazu *Ullmann,* in Engl. Historical Rev. 64 (1949) 4; *Mochi Onory* 68, 238, 253.

70 Zur neueren Literatur über den mittelalterlichen Kaiserbegriff vgl. die Darstellung bei *Koschaker* 51 ff.; *F. L. Ganshof,* in Le Moyen Age 55 (1949) 164 ff.

71 *Koschaker* 39 ff. 54; freilich ist das von ihm gewählte Beispiel für „scholastisches Denken" (p. 49 f.) unglücklich. Denn in Gratian D. 8 c. 5 '... Dominus dixit: ego sum veritas; non dixit: ego sum consuetudo, sed veritas' ist es nicht „der mittelalterliche Jurist", der „bedenkenlos die ihn interessierende Frage nach der Geltung des Gewohnheitsrechts in das Bibelzitat hineinträgt "– sondern der Kirchenvater Augustinus (De baptismo contra Donatistas 3. 6. 9, vgl. D. 8 c. 6).

72 Eine Begründung für diese, von der herrschenden Meinung über die „politischen Theorien" der Kanonisten abweichende Auffassung soll im Rahmen dieses Aufsatzes nicht versucht werden. Vgl. aber z. B. Hostiensis, der über das Verhältnis von Kaiser und Papst durchaus guelfisch, über das von Kaiser und Einzelstaaten hingegen ghibellinisch denkt. Vgl. auch die Bemerkungen von *A. Stickler,* in Traditio 7 (1951) 458 f. (bei Besprechung von *Ullmanns* Medieval Papalism).

73 So vor allem *Laurentius,* in Glossa Palatina (Hs. Vat. *Pal. 658, fol. 50 rb = P, c. 1210–15) zu C. 12 q. 2 c. 8 ad. v. *novies;* bisher nur aus dem Referat in *Guido de Baysio,* Rosarium ad loc. (= G, vom Jahre 1300) bekannt: '... et ita quelibet regio potest sibi ponere (imponere G) legem (om. P), et ita franci (Francigenae G) et hyspani non obligantur romanis legibus (leg. om. P). Romana ecclesia non confirmat eas nisi circa eos quibus (circa eos circa quos G) prodite sunt. Prodite sunt autem illis tantum qui sub imperio romano sunt ... unde non circa gallicos uel hyspanos ...' (vgl. *Maassen,* Wiener SB 24, 81; *Mochi Onory* 245; *Van Hove,* oben Anm. 63). Der Satz 'Romana ecclesia non confirmat' *rell.* richtet sich gegen Huguccios Lehre von der *subiectio ratione pontificis* (nächste Anm.). Zur Glos. Pal. vgl. *Kuttner,* Repertorium 81 ff. und in Taditio 1 (1943) 290 f.

74 *Huguccio,* Summa ad D. 1 c. 12 gibt auf die Frage, 'sed quid de Francis et Anglicis et aliis ultramontanis, numquid ligantur legibus romanis ...?' eine bejahende Antwort aus drei Gründen:

die *loci* vom **unus imperator in orbe** und **dominus mundi**[75] herhalten. Solcher Schulweisheit blieb es meist gleichgültig, daß in der Gegenwart das römische Recht nicht einmal in des Kaisers deutschen Landen Gesetzeskraft besaß[76]. Ohne sich zu den akademischen Spekulationen über Kaisergewalt und Kaiserrecht positiv oder negativ zu äußern, stellte Honorius III. in *Super speculam* fest, daß „in der Ile-de-France[77] und manchen anderen Provinzen die Laien die *leges* der römischen Kaiser nicht anwenden". Der neutrale Ausdruck 'non utuntur' war ausreichend, um klarzumachen, daß es sich hier um *pays coutumier* handelte[78], vom Standpunkt der weltlichen Gerichtsbarkeit also kein praktisches Bedürfnis für eine Zivilrechtsschule in Paris und somit kein Bedenken gegen die Reorganisation der Universität vorlag. Hätte der Papst 'legibus non ligantur' oder 'leges respuunt', 'non recognoscunt' gesagt, so hätte darin freilich schon eine Stellungnahme gelegen. Aber er vermied es, von Unverbindlichkeit oder Protest gegen die Verbindlichkeit des Kaiserrechts zu sprechen; er vermied vor allem jede Bezugnahme auf den Satz in der Dekretale *Per venerabilem*[79] seines Vorgängers Innozenz III., daß der König von Frankreich 'superiorem in temporalibus non recognoscit'. Dieser enthielt in der Tat eine Aussage von unmittelbar staatstheoretisch-politischem Charakter, deren Tragweite unter den Dekretalisten lebhaft diskutiert wurde und die eine gewisse Rolle in der Entstehungsgeschichte des Axioms 'rex imperator in regno suo' zu spielen bestimmt war[80].

'Utique, quia subsunt vel subesse debent romano imperio ... .'; zweitens 'praeterea quicunque utuntur lingua latina dicuntur Romani...' (vgl. Simon, oben Anm. 58); drittens 'item saltem ratione pontificis subsunt romano imperio: omnes enim Christiani subsunt apostolico et ideo omnes tenentur vivere secundum leges romanas, saltem quas approbat ecclesia' (zitiert nach *Maassen*, loc.cit. 79 f.; vgl. *Van Hove*, Misc. v. d. Essen I 266; *Mochi Onory* 174 ff.). Von diesen Theorien ist die dritte die interessanteste, aber nur die erste hat erhebliche Verbreitung erlangt: aus ihr entwickelte sich im 13. Jhdt. die *de iure – de facto*-Theorie. Vgl. auch *Koschaker* 75.

75 C. 7 q. 1. c. 41; Dig. 14. 2. 9 vulg. '... ego sum dominus mundi' (ἐγώ μέν τοῦ κόσμου κύριος); auch Cod. 7. 37. 3 'cum enim omnia principis esse intelligantur' wird zitiert, d. h. der Passus, zu dem Accursius die Geschichte von Martinus und Bulgarus auf dem ronkalischen Reichstag (*Savigny*, Gesch.² IV 181) erzählt.
76 Eine Andeutung immerhin bei *Hostiensis* (unten Anm. 82); auch schreibt schon die *Glosse Ecce vicit leo* (französische Schule, nach 1202) zu D. 1 c. 12: '... immo omnes latini istis legibus debent uti, quia cum unus tantum debet esse imperator, ut vii. q. i. In apibus, omnes subesse debent illi imperatori et suis legibus uti. Hodie tamen non fit quia non sunt omnes sub imperatore' (Hs. St. Florian *XI. 605, fol. 2rb).
77 Mittellat. *Francia* ist Ile-de-France, nicht Frankreich (*Gallia*).
78 Vgl. *Will. Vasco*, gl. (oben Anm. 8) ad v. *legibus:* 'bene dicit ad differentiam lombarde qua utuntur. Utuntur etiam iure consuetudinario sive generali sive speciali quod pro lege accipitur' (zitiert nach Ullmann, Jurid. Rev. 60, 183).
79 Potth. 1794: Comp. III 4. 12. 2; X 4. 17. 13.
80 Vgl. aus der neueren Literatur etwa *F. Schulz*, Bracton on Kingship, in Engl. Hist. Rev. 60 (1945) 149 f.; *Ullmann*, The Development of the Medieval Idea of Sovereignty, ibid. 64 (1949) 4 f.; *Mochy Onory* passim (s. Index s. v. *Per venerabilem*), besonders 271 ff. wo das von *Gillmann, G. Post* u. a. veröffentlichte Glossenmaterial des frühen 13. Jhdts. zusammengestellt ist. Die von *Mochi Onory* 271 in der Titelüberschrift gegebene Formulierung 'rex imperator in regno

Nun haben zwar diejenigen Glossatoren, welche die Theorie von der fortdauernden Universalität des Kaisertums vertraten, sowohl bei *Per venerabilem* wie bei *Super speculam* mit der distinguierenden Auslegung *de facto – de iure* operiert[81]; aber daraus einen Schluß auf den gedanklichen Zusammenhang der beiden, nachträglich so umgedeuteten Texte zu ziehen, ware unzulässig.

Eine prinzipielle Stellungnahme zu der Frage des Gegensatzes zwischen den praktisch angewandten einheimischen Rechten und dem akademisch betriebenen *ius civile* lag überhaupt nicht, auch politisch nicht, im Interessenkreis der Kurie. Der Gegensatz bestand ja fast überall[82], ohne daß die Kurie daran gedacht hätte, in ihn einzugreifen oder sich ihn politisch nutzbar zu machen. Es hieße die Bedeutung der zweifellos vorhandenen Gedankenassoziation zwischen römischem Recht und Kaiserideologie in der mittelalterlichen Mentalität überschätzen, wenn man es anders erwartete. Honorius' Nachfolger Gregor IX. trug keinerlei Bedenken, das Verbot für Paris durch Aufnahme von *Super speculam* in seine Dekretalensammlung aufrechtzuerhalten und andererseits nur wenige Monate später, am 17. Januar 1235, den Unterricht und das Studium des Zivilrechts in Orléans (außer für die kanonisch verhinderten Personenklassen) für zulässig zu

---

suo, superiorem in temporalibus non recognoscit' ist aber in dieser Form nicht quellenmäßig, sondern aus verschiedenen Glossatorentexten – vgl. etwa p. 253 f. – kombiniert; ferner beruht die Behauptung, schon Innozenz' Lehrer Huguccio habe den Satz 'rex in regno suo dicitur imperator' vertreten (164 ff.) auf Fehlinterpretation zweier Stellen. *Huguccio*, Summa zu C. 7 q. 1 c. 41: '... alibi videtur quod alius sit iudex provintie et alius rex, ut xxiii. q. iiii. Duo (c. 35). Set rex ibi dicitur imperator ...' heißt lediglich, daß „dort", d. h. im canon *Duo*, der Ausdruck *rex* auf den Kaiser zu beziehen ist; ebenso meint zu D. 2 c. 4 der Satz '... vel idem est rex et imperator ...' nur, daß in diesem canon die zwei Ausdrücke synonym gebraucht werden, und zwar für den Kaiser, wie der Zusatz 'set rex antequam coronetur' zeigt. (Mit den vorstehenden Bemerkungen deckt sich die [erst während der Drucklegung dieses Aufsatzes erschienene] Kritik von *E. M. Meijers*, in Tijdschr. voor Rechtsgesch. 20 [1952] 123 n. 2.)

81 Zu *Per venerabilem* vgl. die bei *Ullmann* loc.cit. 4 f. und *Mochi Onory* 276 ff. besprochenen Glossatoren (wobei wiederum manches zu korrigieren bleibt: z. B. die falsche Zuschreibung der Glossen des *Bernhard von Parma*, Gl. ord. zu X 1. 6. 34 und 4. 17. 13 an den Zeitgenossen Innozenz' III., Bern. Compostellanus Antiquus; oder Mochis gezwungene Auslegung einer angeblichen 'de facto'-Glosse des Laurentius, die in Wahrheit von Johannes Galensis stammt [vgl. *Gillmann*, in Arch. kath. KR 118, 179 f. und 199], u. a. m.). – Zu *Super speculam* vgl. vor allem *Bernhard von Parma*, Gl. ord. zu X. 5. 33. 28 ad v. *non utuntur:* 'cum tamen ab omnibus debeant observari ... et licet ab omnibus de facto non servantur, quia non subsunt imperatori, de iure tamen debent subesse ... .'; *Hostiensis, Lect.* ad. loc. Vgl. *Van Hove* Proleg.² 462 n. 3. Die Apparate zur Comp. V ad loc. bleiben zu prüfen.

82 *Hostiensis*, Lect. zu 5. 33. 28 ad v. *nonnullis provinciis:* 'aliis quam in Francia iacent. Melius dixisset magister (!) „quasi in omnibus aliis", sicut est Hispania tota, Anglia, Scotia, Wallia, Hybernia, Alamannia, Dacia, Suecia, Norveia, Hungaria, Boemia, Polonia, Bulgaria; et breviter excepta Italia et regno Arelatensi nullae aut paucae provinciae sunt quae iure civili regantur, licet utantur argumentis ipsius (ipsarum *ed.*) propriis deficientibus consuetudinibus et statutis ...'(ed. Ven. fol. 88). Auf die Andeutung der Lehre vom *ius commune* im letzten Satz kann hier nicht näher eingegangen werden.

erklären⁸³. Diese päpstliche Approbation einer zukunftsreichen Legistenschule 'en plein pays de coutume'⁸⁴ kann man nur dann als eine Inkonsequenz oder ein Aufgeben von Positionen bezeichnen⁸⁵, wenn man Prinzipien voraussetzt, zu denen sich Honorius III. in Wahrheit niemals bekannt hatte.

Aus dem bisher Gesagten ergibt sich die Unwahrscheinlichkeit der Hypothese, nach der das päpstliche Verbot für Paris auf Betreiben König Philipp Augusts erfolgt sein soll, um die Unabhängigkeit des *droit coutumier* vom kaiserlichen Recht zu demonstrieren. Ganz abgesehen davon, daß es dem Kurialstil widersprochen hätte, die Beantwortung eines königlichen Antrags anhangsweise, und ohne ausdrückliche Erwähnung, in einer für die Gesamtkirche bestimmten Konstitution zu erledigen, ruht alles, was für die Hypothese an Beweis vorgebracht worden ist, auf sehr fragwürdigen Grundlagen⁸⁶. Das einzige Quellenzeugnis, fast hundert Jahre jünger als *Super speculam*, ist die Ordonnance Philipps des Schönen vom Juli 1312 für die Universität Orléans, worin es heißt⁸⁷:

> ... ut autem liberius ibidem (d. h. in Paris) studium proficeret theologie, progenitores nostri non permiserunt legum secularium seu iuris civilis studium ibidem institui, quinimo id etiam interdici sub excommunicationis pena per apostolicam sedem procurarunt.

Mit den 'progenitores nostri' ist nach dem Zusammenhang Philipp August gemeint, dem freilich hier ausdrücklich nur das theologische Motiv von *Super speculam* unterlegt wird; das „nationale" ergibt sich erst indirekt, wenn man auf dem Umweg über Papst Honorius' Formel 'quia tamen in Francia' rell. auch die weiteren Ausführungen der Ordonnance von 1312 (über den Vorrang der *usages* und *coutumes* vor dem *droit écrit* und die Geltung des letzteren nur kraft örtlicher, vom König anerkannter *coutume*)⁸⁸ in Philipp Augusts angebliches 'procurare' hineinliest.

---

83 *Auvray* no. 2399, Mandat (*Digard* loc.cit. 402 n. 2 spricht ungenau von einem Responsum) an Bischof Philipp Berruyer von Orléans: '... mandamus quatenus scolares praefatos, archidiaconis ... (vgl. Anm. 34) exceptis, libere leges ibidem audire ac docere permittas'.

84 So *Glasson*, Hist, du droit et des instit. de la France IV (Paris 1891) 238; vgl. schon *Savigny*, Gesch.² III 401; ferner *Meijers*, in Tijdschr. voor Rechtsgesch. 1 (1918) 111; 14 (1936) 249. *Koschaker* 143 rechnet Orléans irrig zum *pays de droit écrit*.

85 So *Digard* loc.cit. und 404 f. über Gregor IX.

86 So schon *Caillemer* (Anm. 12) 22–26, *M. Fournier* 106 f., *Péries* 93 (die freilich nur einen Einwand gegen ihre These von der Feindseligkeit der Kurie gegen das römische Recht beseitigen wollen) und *Glasson* IV 234 f.

87 Text nach *M. Fournier* 105 n. 3.

88 Dieser Abschnitt bei *Tardif*, Hist, des sources 333 f.; *Chénon*, Mél. Fitting I 209 f. (in französischer Übersetzung); *P. van Wetter*, Le droit romain et Beaumanoir, ibid. II 544 (lat.). Vgl. dazu *H. Mitteis*, Zschr. Sav.-Stift Germ. Abt. 63 (1943) 155 f. 164 f. (mit Literaturangaben). Der mögliche Anteil der kanonischen Lehre von der Verbindlichkeit des Zivilrechts kraft päpstlicher Anerkennung (oben S. 284; für die späteren Dekretalisten vgl. *Van Hove*. Proleg.² 525 f.) an der Entstehung der französischen Doktrin bleibt zu untersuchen.

Mit dieser von *Tardif* und *Chénon* entwickelten Konstruktion[89] mag der Sinn der Aussage Philipps des Schönen vielleicht gut getroffen sein. Deren historische Glaubwürdigkeit ist aber damit nicht erwiesen[90], ohne Zirkelschluß auch unerweisbar. Umgekehrt läßt sich vieles gegen die Glaubwürdigkeit des von keiner älteren Quelle gestützten Berichts der Ordonnance vorbringen. Für Philipps des Schönen eigene Universitäts- und Staatskirchenpolitik war es höchst unbequem anzuerkennen, daß einst ein Papst *motu proprio* in französische Universitätsverhältnisse eingegriffen haben sollte[91]. Philipp hatte soeben (1311–12) in zwei von ihm betriebenen Angelegenheiten – Vernichtung des Templerordens und Kassation aller gegen ihn selbst ergangenen Maßnahmen seines toten Gegners Bonifaz VIII. – den würdelos schwachen Papst Clemens V. zum Werkzeug seines Willens gemacht[92]. Auf der Höhe seines Triumphes konnte er sich darin gefallen, die Willfährigkeit des Heiligen Stuhls gegenüber dem König von Frankreich als eine historisch gegebene Einrichtung erscheinen zu lassen. Wenn es galt, zu diesem Zweck eine kleine Entstehungsgeschichte für *Super speculam* zu erfinden, so konnte das Philipps des Schönen Gewissen nicht sehr belasten: die königliche Kanzlei war aus der Zeit des Konflikts mit Bonifaz VIII. an kühnere Fälschungen[93] gewöhnt.

Man sollte es also aufgeben, für *Super speculam* nach politischen Gründen zu forschen. Honorius III. war so wenig wie sein Vorgänger oder seine Nachfolger ein Feind des „kaiserlichen" Zivilrechts. Die Gründe, aus denen er das Studium der *leges* gewissen personalen und örtlichen Beschränkungen unterwarf, hat er im Text der Konstitution mit aller Deutlichkeit selbst ausgesprochen.

---

89 *Tardif*, Nouv. rev. hist. 4, 291; Hist. des soucres 328 f.; *Chénon*, Mél. Fitting I 199 f.
90 *Digard* 399 f. läßit die Frage offen (vermutlich aus Respekt vor 'notre éminent maître M. Tardif', vgl. 399 n. 5) und begnügt sich mit der Annahme, daß Philipp jedenfalls mit *Super speculam*, vor allem aus religionspolitischen Gründen, recht zufrieden gewesen sein müsse. Das ist möglich, aber reine Spekulation und nimmt der Theorie Tardifs ihre Pointe.
91 *M. Fournier* loc.cit. 107.
92 Clemens V, Bulle *Rex gloriae* vom 27. April 1311; Bulle *Vox clamantis* vom 22. März 1312.
93 Z. B. die bekannte Veröffentlichung des päpstlichen Mahnschreibens *Ausculta fili* vom 5. Dezember 1301 in aufreizend entstellter Form (*Deum time*, vgl. *Potthast* † XIV nach no. 25097 = *Digard* et al. Registres de Boniface VIII no. 4424).

RETRACTATIONES

I. The Scientific Investigation of Mediaeval Canon Law

p.3 (and n.6) 'the progress achieved in the last eighty-odd years': This paper represents the state of research and the need for new editions and coordinated investigations as seen in 1949. One could not attempt to bring it up to date for the points here discussed, taking into account the many international congresses and the new institutes and periodicals founded since those days. A general reference to books, papers, and editions of recent decades will be found in my contribution, 'The revival of jurisprudence', to the Haskins memorial conference of 1977, published as *Renaissance and renewal in the twelfth century* ed. R.L. Benson and G. Constable (Cambridge, Mass. 1982) 299–323.

III. Zur Frage der theologischen Vorlagen Gratians

p.25 n.l: This note was written and signed by the Editor of 'diese Zeitschrift', i.e. the *Zeitschrift der Savigny-Stiftung für Rechtsgeschichte*, Kan. Abt., U(lrich) St(utz).

p.27 n.10: The identity of Master Rolandus, author of the *Stroma* and the Sentences, with Rolandus Bandinelli, the future Alexander III, can probably no longer be maintained, see 'Retractationes' to No. VII below, 'Bernardus Compostellanus antiquus' 281 (–82) n.17.

p.27ff.: 'Magister A.' has been identified as Prior Elmer (Ailmerus) of Canterbury by H.J.F. Reinhardt, 'Die Identität der Sententiae Magistri A. mit den Compilationes Ailmeri...', *Theologie und Philosophie* 50 (1975) 381–403, cf. his *Die Ehelehre der Schule des Anselm von Laon* (Beiträge zur Gesch. der Philos. und Theol. des Mittelalters N.F. 14; Münster 1974) 4 n.20; Reinhardt edited the part of the Sentences dealing with matrimony in an appendix, pp.135–263 (see, however, some critical observations in G. Fransen's review in *Revue théologique de Louvain* 9 [1978] 186–88).

Elmer of Canterb.: see now P. Landau, 'Gratian and the Sententiae Magistri A.', in: Aus Archiven und Bibliotheken. Festschrift für Roymund Kottje zum 65. Geburtstag, ed. H. Mordek (Frankfurt M./Bern etc. 1992) 311–26, at. p. 313 – also in: *idem*, Kanones und Dekretalen (Bibliotheca eruditorum 2, Goldbach 1997) 161–176. (S.K.)

p.34 n.49: The authorship of the *Summa sententiarum* is now commonly assigned to Odo of Lucca, with the exception of Book 7, which incorporates Walter (not Hugo) of Mortagne's *tractatus de coniugio.* See A.M. Landgraf, *Introduction à l'histoire de la litérature théologique de la Scolastique naissante* as revised by A.-M. Landy and translated by L.-B. Geiger (Montréal-Paris 1973) 98–102. See also F. Petit, Gautier de Mortagne, DHG ɛ 20. 14 (1982) 100–02. (S.K.)

p.34 n.51: On the Palea C.27 q.2 c.51 'Duobus modis' and its origin in the school of Anselm of Laon (not Ivo) see R. Weigand, *Die bedingte Eheschliessung im kanonischen Recht* (Münchener theologische Studien, Kan. Abt. 16; Munich 1963) 246–47 n.17; F. Ganshof, 'Note sur deux textes de droit canonique dans le "Liber Floridus",' *Études de dr. can. dédiées à Gabriel Le Bras* (Paris 1965) I 99-115, at 106ff.

IV. New Studies on the Roman Law in Gratian

This article, published in 1953, was supplemented in the following year by 'Additional notes...' (*Seminar* 12.68-74), reprinted here as No. V. Since then, J. Gaudemet has gone over the same ground with additional observations in 'Das römische Recht in Gratians Dekret', *Österr. Archiv für Kirchenrecht* 12 (1961) 177–91 (unfortunately the German translation is often inadequate and marred by many slipshod references), and Mme. J. Rambaud-Buhot has summed up and expanded her previous findings in the section she contributed on Gratian to Le Bras, Lefebvre, Rambaud, *L'Age classique* (Histoire des Institutions et du Droit de l'Église en Occident 7; Paris 1965), at pp. 119–29.

One aspect, however, of my paper calls for a substantial *retractatio*. Conclusive evidence presented by G. Rabotti, 'Le interpolazioni dei testi romanistici nel Decretum Gratiani secondo Diomede Brava: Storia d'una falsificazione', *Studia Gratiana* 8 (1962) 117–58, makes it certain that the Gratian manuscript formerly of Besançon which Guido Grandi, writing under the pseudonym of Brava in 1730, asserted to have seen and which I considered lost but real, never existed but was a piece of fiction, produced to fortify certain hypotheses of Grandi's concerning the codex Pisanus (Florentinus) of the Digest. Thus, wherever my discussion of texts in Gratian refers *inter al.* to Brava's manuscript (*Br*), such references should be canceled—or rather, be reinterpreted as indicating critical conjectures which Grandi hid under the mask of manuscript evidence.

Whatever one may think of his unscrupulous methods, Grandi-Brava's forgotten pamphlet deserved to be brought back to the attention of the modern student of Gratian's book. His open criticism of a substantial number of Roman law texts in Gratian (cf. p.53 of this paper), together with the oblique criticism in the guise of a fictitious codex, anticipated by more than two centuries many results of modem inquiry and should secure him a lasting place in the history of canonistic scholarship (see also Rabotti, 'Le interpolazioni' 149).

Besides the ample bibliography in Rabotti's article, see also F. Lanzoni, 'A proposito dei falsi del padre Guido Grandi', in his *Storia ecclesiastica e agiografia faentina* ... (Studi e testi 252; Città del Vaticano 1969) 429–33; E. Garms-Cornides, 'Rivalutazione del Settecento', *Römische hist. Mitteilungen* 12 (1970) 197–278, at pp. 218–19 and nn. 95, 96. To the reprints of the *Disquisitio critica* (cf. p.53) add Nikolaus Leszkoczy, *De Decreto Gratiani dissertatio* (Vindob. 1760; not seen, but cf. G. Phillips, *Kirchenrecht* IV [1851] 160f. and n.38; Rabotti 148). For Grandi's largely unedited correspondence (p.55) see L. Tenca, 'Epistolario manoscritto del padre Guido Grandi', *Archivio storico lombardo*[8] 4 (1953) 273–80.

p.47 Tabulation of *paleae* not a safe guide to the 'original' shape of the Decretum: see examples in J. Rambaud, *L'Age classique* 110f.

p. 48 Transmission of the *tract. de poenitentia* and the *tract. de cons.*: This was already discussed in 1877 by G. Haenel in reporting on the Gratian MS he owned; se my 'Additional notes ...' (reprinted here as No. V) 77 n.24. L. Guizard's paper, cited as forthcoming in n.16, appeared as 'Manuscrits du "Decretum Gratiani" conservés à l'Université de Paris', *L'Année canonique* 2 (1953) 77–161; also in *Studia Gratiana* 3 (1955) 17–50. See further Karol Wojtyła [Pope John Paul II], 'Le traité "de penitentia" de Gratien dans l'abrégé de Gdansk Mar. F.275', ibid. 7 (1959) 355–90; J. Rambaud-Buhot, in *L'Age classique* 82–99.

pp.56–70: For Roman law texts or clusters of texts here analyzed, explicit reference to their discussion in the writings by J. Rambaud-Buhot and J. Gaudemet, indicated at the beginnings of these notes, will be made only where needed in specific cases. This also applies, of course, to the material in my 'Additional notes' of 1954, reprinted No. V infra.

p.58 (No.5) C.1 q.4 p.c.9 § Crimen (*al.* c.6): Some manuscripts copy it in both places— Vetulani p.17; Rambaud, *L'Age classique* 123 n.3; and see Friedberg n.57 ad loc., whose observation on textual differences between the two places has never been followed up.

p.61 (No.31) C.6 q.4 c.1 fin. (*al.* c.4 fin. *al.* q.5 c.2): CJ 4.19.23: See also J. Kejř, on Bratislava (Pressburg) MS 14, 'Bratislavský rukopis Dekretu Gratianova', *Pravnicke Studie* 8 (1960) 264–94 at 279–81 (p.293 of German summary); also the photos of Madrid B.N. 87 and Barcelona MS Ripoll 78 in P. Pinedo, 'Decretum Gratiani, Dictum Gratiani', *Jus canonicum* 2 (1962), plates x, xi after p.164.

p.61 (No.18) C.3 q.3 p.c.4: The concluding §7 (*palea*) is a duplication of C.3 q.6 p.c.2, discussed in 'Additional notes' (reprinted No. V infra) 71–72.

pp.61–65 Transcriptional disturbances: Future investigation should be extended to the Roman law texts which entered the Decretum by way of intermediary collections and were therefore excluded from Vetulani's critique. Thus C.2 q.7 c.26 came from the *Epitome Juliani* 41.2 (c.172) by way of Ivo, *Pan.* 5.28. Friedberg designated it as *palea* for the sole reason that it was absent from four of his eight MSS (n.204 ad loc.); no known MS, edition, glossator, or medieval list of *paleae* classifies it as such. J. Rambaud dropped it, without any discussion, from her list in *L'Age classique* 109; it is not discussed by H. Zapp, 'Paleae-Listen', ZRG Kan. Abt. 59 (1973) 83–111. But its absence from, or later insertion into, a considerable number of Gratian MSS is shown in the tabulations of M. Boulet-Sautel (n.62 above), *Studia Gratiana* 1.156-57; also W. Ullmann (n.8 above), ibid. 208: 5 out of 9 MSS in Cambridge. We have obviously another instance of multiple recension.

p.63 nn.87, 88: The manuscripts G.71 and G.7 of the Law Library of Congress have now the shelfmarks D401 and D402 respectively.

p.63 n.90: The sentence 'Sed melius dicitur...' in C.10 q.2 c.10 §10 (No.32) was first recognized as part of *Auth. Qui res iam dictas* in twelfth-century glosses, see those quoted by J. Juncker in ZRG Kan. Abt. 15 (1926) 351.

p.64f.: For the composition of the *summula de prescriptione* in C.16 q.3 p.c.15-p.c.16 (No.39) by double interpolation see N. Vilain, 'Prescription et bonne foi du Décret de Gratien (1140) á Jean d'André (†1348)', *Traditio* 14 (1958) 121–89, at 179–85.

p.65f. (Nos.42,43) C.25 q.2 cc.14-15, p.c.16: J. Erickson, 'The Collection in three books and Gratian's Decretum', BMCL 2 (1972) 67 n.4 and table p.75, has determined the direct derivation suggested by Vetulani—pp.35, 37—of this cluster of texts from 3L. (For C.36 q.2 c.3 [No.46, see p.65], differences of inscription make a direct relation, suggested by J. Gaudemet, 'Das römische Recht ...' 189, less likely.)

Erickson p. 67 n. 3 must be corrected. Additions to Erickson see G. Motta, Testi di sant' Ambrogio ... Nota documentaria, Atti del Congresso ... (Milano 1976) II 82.93 at p. 93: D86 cc. 19, 20. (S.K.)

p.66: The Justinianic model for Gratian D.5 pr. on Natural law should have been discussed by G. Garancini, 'Razionalismo e volontarismo nella concezione del diritto naturale nel *Decretum* di Graziano', *Aevum* 47 (1973) 6, 15f.

p.67f.: In this attempt at explaining the genesis of Gratian's 'mulier apud pretorem pro alio non intercedat', C.15 q.3 pr., the conjecture based on CTh. 9.1.3 (Brev. 9.1.2) in 'Brava's manuscript' must of course be dropped.

V. Additional Notes on the Roman Law in Gratian

p.74 Omnebene (Omnibonus, Ognibene) and his so-called *Abbreviatio*: Add J. Rambaud-Buhot, 'Les divers types d'abrégés de Gratien: De la table au commentaire', *Receuil de travaux offert à M. Clovis Brunei* (Paris 1955) 397–411 at 406ff. (cf. 69 n.7), and her paper 'L'Abbreviatio decreti d'Omnebene' to be published in the *Proceedings of the Sixth International Congress of Medieval Canon Law, Berkeley 1980*; A. Vetulani and W. Uruszczak, 'L'oeuvre d'Omnebene dans le MS 602 de la bibliothèque municipale de Cambrai', *Proceedings of the Fourth International Congress ... Toronto* (Monum. iur. can. Ser. C.5; Città del Vaticano 1976) 11–26.

p.74 n.8 MS Vat. Reg. lat. 1039: Among the misattributions one may also note P. Kehr, 'Papsturkunden in Rom ...', *Nachr. Akad. Göttingen* 1903 p.59 (Polycarpus).

p.74 n.9: Medieval writing on the trichotomic division of *lex divina* in the New Law needs a comprehensive study. The fundamental importance of Hugh of St. Victor as cited in this note (see also the *Didascalicon* 4.2, ed. Buttimer p.72.10) is certain; for possible antecedents see R. Baron, *Science et sagesse chez Hugues de Saint-Victor* (Paris 1957) 104–5. Among canonists note also the *Summa Elegantius in iure diuino* 1.28 (ed. Fransen and Kuttner p.7f), or the *Prologus Omnia poma uetera* on 'sanctorum patrum apostolis succedentium constitutiones et decreta', cited by P. Legendre, *La pénétration du droit romain dans le droit canonique classique* (Paris 1964, *ex* 1957) 55 n.3.

Summa Sicut uetus testamentum: The fragment in MS Madrid B.N. 87 is to be cancelled as a different work. On the *Summa* itself see also infra, No. VII, 'Retractationes' to p.97 n.18.

p.76: Another example of Gratian's insecure grasp of technicalities in Roman law is found in his reference to the *S.C. Turpillianum*, C.2 q.3 p.c.7; cf. the criticism of *Gl. ord.* ad loc. v. *infamem*. But his implicit quotation, ibid. §1, 'Cum enim leges seculi ... sacros cánones sequi non dedignentur', from Auth. 6.11 (Nov. 83) 1 is to the point.

Concerning the five Roman law passages not recorded by Mme. Rambaud as missing in Omnebene, examination of the MSS available (Paris lat 3886 and Vat. Reg. lat. 1039) shows that actually two of these, Nos. 28 and 29, are absent from *O* while Nos. 22 and 27 are present. As for No. 19, the long *summula* on infamy (C.3 q.7 p.c.1-c.2), *O* presents only a paraphrase of, or rather a substitute for, the distinction, 'Porro infamia multipliciter irrogatur' (Grat. c.2 §20) tacking it immediately onto c.1 ('Infamis persona – cognitor'): 'Infamia autem irrogatur quandoque ...'. Further study is needed to establish the sources of the fourfold (c.2 §20) and the threefold (*O*C.3 q.7 p.c. 1) distinctions, both of which apparently were modeled upon the writing of civilian glossators, perhaps from the school of Martinus. P. Landau, *Die Entstehung des kanonischen Infamiebegriffs von Gratian bis zur Glossa ordinaria* (Köln-Graz 1966)

30, considers the fourfold distinction in c.2 §20 to be identical with that of Placentinus, *Summa Codicis* 2.12 (ed. Mogunt. 1536, p.54f.). However, the text of Omnebene and a brief comment by Stephen of Tournai ad loc. (*Porro infamia*: 'Istud paragraphum Plene intelliges ...' p.197 Schulte) are evidence for a much earlier intrusion of this material into the original train of Gratian's thought.

p.76 n.21: The pseudo-etymology *palea* < gr. *palin* for doublets in Gratian is still considered 'durchaus vertretbar' by H. Zapp, 'Paleae-Listen' ZRG Kan. Abt. 59 (1973) 86n.

VI. *Les débuts de l'école canoniste française*

Given the general nature of this survey, which was originally presented as an oral communication, the notes that follow will be limited to essential corrections and references. Much new bibliographical and manuscript information could be added from work done after 1938, but since this is to a large extent provided elsewhere in this volume, it will suffice in most instances to refer to these articles, always to be consulted, however, with their respective 'Retractationes' below, (i) 'Anglo-Norman canonists' (No. VIII) p.175f.: *Ordines* and procedural treatises (here p.86); pp.195f. and 202f.: *Summa Omnis qui iuste* (here p. 83); 184–186: *Summa Elegantius*, *Summa Antiquitas et tempore* (here p.81, 82); 300: *Summa Magister Gratianus in hoc opere* (here p.82); 314: Evrard of Ypres (ibid.); 205–207: *Quaestiones Londinenses* (here p. 86). — (ii) 'Bernardus Compostellanus antiquus' (No. VII) pp.140–148: *Quaestiones* (here p.86).

See also in general A.L. Gabriel, 'Les origines de la Faculté de Décret de l'ancienne Université de Paris', *L'Année canonique* 17 (1973) 507–31. An older and at times still useful book by G. Péries, *La Faculté de Droit dans l'ancienne Université de Paris* (Paris 1890) contains nothing of significance for our topic.

p. 81 Odon de Dour: rather Odo of Dover, see 'Anglo-Norman canonists' 293 (in this vol. p. 178).

p. 81 *Summa* 'Imperatorie maiestati': It was not the author but the 'patron' of the Munich MS, from St. Nicola in Passau, who had relations with Carinthia, as W. Stelzer has recently shown in 'Die Summa Monacensis ("Summa Imperatorie maiestati") und der Neustifter Propst Konrad von Albeck', MIÖG 88 (1980) 94–112. See also the observations I made on the genesis of the *Summa* in 'A forgotten definition of justice', SG 20 (1976) 87 (= *The history of doctrines and ideas of canon law* ... [London 1980] No. V).

p. 84 *Animal est substantia*: Rather an *Apparatus* than a *Summa*. For MSS see the 'Interim checklist(s)' in *Traditio* 11 (1955) 447; 12 (1956) 564; 13 (1957) 470; 'Varia', ibid. 14 (1958) 509. See further A.M. Stickler, 'Zum Apparat "Animal est substantia",' BMCL 1 (1971) 73–75. There exists a partial edition by E.M. de Groot, *Doctrina de iure naturali et positivo humano in Summa Bambergensi* (*DD.1–20*) (Nijmegen 1970).

p. 85: Pierre de Blois le jeune was neither a nephew of his better known namesake nor his junior, see S. Kuttner, 'Pierre de Roissy and Robert of Flamborough', *Traditio* 2 (1944) 492 n.2; for MSS and bibliography see C. Lefebvre, DDC 6 (1957) 1472 s.v.

p. 86: Cancel the *Quaestiones Andegavenses*, actually a fragment of Robert Courson's *Summa*, see 'Anglo-Norman canonists' 200 n.226; cancel *Quaestiones Laudunenses*, actually an incomplete copy of Honorius, *Summa quaestionum*, see 'Bernardus Compostellanus antiquus' 141 n.279.

p.87 Glosses on Gratian before the *Ordinaria*: This is superseded by later research, so already 'Bernardus Compostellanus antiquus' 96 n.15 and bibliography in the 'Retractationes'; on apparatuses of glosses preceding *Ecce uicit leo* see 'Retract.' to pp.102–109 of that article.

pp.89f.: I would no longer defend the historical conjectures expressed in the concluding pages. At present, we know more on French decretalists of the early thirteenth century, such as the *Apparatus Militant siquidem patroni* (cf. n.65; bibliography in G. Dolezalek on a MS fragment of this text, BMCL 5 [1975] 130–32) and the works from the school of Petrus Brito, see 'Bernardus Compostellanus antiquus' 137 n.258 with 'Retractatio' (below) for bibliography. French recensions of the *Compilationes antiquae* show considerable changes of the texts received at Bologna, see G. Fransen, 'Les diverses formes de la Compilatio prima', *Scrinium Lovaniense: Mélanges historiques Étienne van Cauwenbergh* (Louvain 1963) 235–53, and 'La tradition manuscrite de la Compilatio prima', *Proceedings Boston* (MIC, Subsidia 1; Vatican City 1965) 55–62; K. Pennington, 'The French recension of Compilatio tertia', BMCL 5 (1975) 53–71.

VII. Bernardus Compostellanus Antiquus

At the time this paper was written in the early 1940s, nobody knew whether and when the days would come to continue investigating the antecedents of the *Glossa ordinaria* on Gratian's Decretum. For this reason (as I then said, p.95 above), I packed the paper full of all sorts of information that had not previously been published on the early glossators of canon law. When it appeared in 1943, it demonstrated that much progress had already been made beyond the state of learning recorded in the *Repertorium der Kanonistik* (1937).

This, however, was very little as compared with the great strides taken by new research in the thirty-seven years since the end of the second World War, which saw the great *Convegno* commemorating Gratian's eighth centenary at Bologna in 1952; the foundation of the Institute of Medieval Canon Law in 1955 at Washington (now resident in Berkeley); the *Proceedings* of six international congresses sponsored by the Institute jointly with other academic institutions, from 1958 to 1980 (here cited for short as *Actes Louvain, Proceedings Boston* etc.); the new outlets for publishing canonistic research such as *Studia Gratiana* (since 1953) and the *Bulletin* of the Institute (published in *Traditio* from 1955 to 1970, and as a periodical of its own [=BMCL] since 1971). New information on manuscripts has been collected by scholars travelling to libraries and recording what they found—in the time-honored fashion of the great Maurists and of the nineteenth- century historians of medieval Roman and canon law. But even more important than the steady increase in our knowledge of manuscripts, the continued and ever-broadening analysis of manuscript texts has led to a thorough revision of earlier assumptions concerning the development of the Bolognese glossators' production in the twelfth century and at the beginning of the thirteenth.

All this would make it necessary for me to rewrite much of the historical outline which I attempted on pages 95–109 of this paper and of the supporting information assembled in the pertinent footnotes. Those pages, however, must stand as they are: a summing up of what we knew by 1943. The notes that follow here can only sketch the road travelled in the last forty years: even a mere bibliographical list of published research in the field would fill several pages. It seems advisable, therefore, to limit this 'Retractatio' to (1) general information on new manuscripts, (2) substantial articles or selected new findings on individual glossators and anonymous writings, (3) the new insights into the development of *apparatus glossarum*, from the late twelfth century to Johannes Teutonicus.

The following additional abbreviations will be used:

BMCL   *Bulletin of medieval canon law, New series*
DDC   *Dictionnaire de droit canonique*
LThK² *Lexikon für Theologie und Kirche* (ed. 2)
MIC   *Monumenta iuris canonici*
MIÖG   *Mitteilungen des Instituts für österreichische Geschichtsforschung*
NCE   *New Catholic Encyclopedia*
REDC   *Revista española de derecho canonico*
RSDI   *Rivista di storia del diritto italiano*
RDC   *Revue de droit canonique*
RHE   *Revue d'histoire ecclésiastique*
SG   *Studia Gratiana*
TRG   *Tijdschrift voor Rechtsgeschiedenis*
ZRG   *Zeitschrift für Rechtsgeschichte der Savigny-Stiftung*

No further reference will be made to the summary notices on Bernard of Compostella by S. Kuttner in NCE 2.339 and by A. García y García in 'Canonistas gallegos medievales', *Compostellanum* 16 (1971) 108–10. García's three surveys, 'La canonística ibérica medieval posterior al Decreto de Graciano' in the *Repertorio de Historia de las ciencias eclesiásticas en España* 1 (1967), 2 (1971), 5 (1976), will be cited as 'Canonística ibérica (I) [or (II), (III)]' with appropriate page references. Much of this material is now included in García's 'La Canonística Ibérica (1150–1250) en la investigación reciente', BMCL 11 (1981) 41–75.

As for the biography of Bernardus, his traditional identification with the archdeacon of that name whom one can trace in documents at the archives of Santiago from 1183 until his death, before May 1232 (see A. López Ferreiro, *Historia de la Santa A.M. Iglesia de Santiago de Compostela* V [1902] 41–42, 350–51; García y García, 'Canonistas gallegos' 108–9), is open to serious doubt since in the inscription of his *Collectio Romana* (1208) he calls the work 'breuiarium ... per Bernardum Compostellanum *canonicum* fideliter compilatum'. This, however, must be left to a separate study.

p.96 n.14: New MSS of pre-*Ordinaria* glosses. As of 1963, thirty-seven MSS had been added to this list; see my report, 'Some Gratian manuscripts with early glosses', *Traditio* 19 (1963) 532–36. Since then, the following were recorded: Biberach an der Riss, Spitalarchiv B.3515; Bremen, Univ. Ms.a.142; Burgos, Cath. Chapter 4 (?); Hamburg, State and Univ. Libr. Cod. jur. 2231; Leningrad, Public Libr. MS lat. F.II vel. 23; Madrid, Facultad de Ciencias Políticas MS 1137; Fundación Lázaro Goldiano MS490; Nürnberg, Stadtbibl. Cent. 11.41; Paris, B. N. lat. 3895. Previous guesses (see *Repert.* pp. 18, 51,

104 n.3) were confirmed for Cologne, Cath. Chapter 128; Einsiedeln, Monast. 193 (66); Marburg, Univ. 33 (*ol.* C.l). The unnumbered manuscript of the Law Library of Congress, Washington D.C. is now D401; it was, in between, G.71 and was so cited in 'New Studies on the Roman Law ...', *Seminar* 11 (1953; = No. IV in this volume) 63 n.87.

Bibliography: G. Fransen, 'Manuscrits canoniques conservés en Espagne (III)', RHE 51 (1956) 937; A.M. Stickler, 'Iter helveticum', *Traditio* 14 (1958) 463; J. Rambaud-Buhot, 'L'étude des manuscrits du Gratien', *Actes Louvain* (1959) 63; A. García y García, 'Nuevos manuscritos del Decreto ...', *Études d'histoire de droit canonique dédiées à Gabriel Le Bras* (Paris 1965) 126–28; A. Vetulani, 'Trois manuscrits canoniques ... de Leningrad', SG 12 (1967) 191–201; R. Weigand, book reviews, ZRG Kan. Abt. 54 (1968) 405–6; ibid. 56 (1970) 401–5; 'Die Dekrethandschrift B.3515 ...' BMCL 2 (1972) 76–81; M. Bertram, 'Some additions to the "Repertorium der Kanonistik",' BMCL 4 (1974) 10–12. The Marburg MS had long ago (probably in the 1920s) been recognized by the late Friedrich Heyer in his unpublished papers, now at the Institute of Medieval Canon Law in Berkeley.

pp.96–101: New MSS of major decretist writings here surveyed. RUFINUS: Leipzig, Univ. Libr. Rep. I.4°,47 (*ol.* Stadtbibl., catal. Naumann No. 78), fol. 41r-56v: a fragment ending in D.23 a.c.21, identified in Heyer's unpublished notes; Lucerne, Zentralbibl. P.MS 21; Vatican Libr. MS Barb. lat. 1413, fol. l-106vb; also short fragments on fly-leaves and paste-downs in Cues, Hospital 269 and Oxford, St. John's Coll. 235. — JOHANNES FAVENTINUS: Barcelona, Arch. Corona de Aragón, MS Ripoll 34; Madrid, B N. 399 (*ol.* C.12, C.48) and 421 (C.41); Salamanca, Univ. 2077 and 2399 (*ol.* Madrid, Palacio 11.735 and 163); Tarazona, Cath. Chapter 41 (G.17) and 77 (G.12); Zurich, Zentralbibl. Rh.42(409); also fragments in Bordeaux, Bibl. Municipale MS 37, fol. 1–5, 174–175 (C.l q.l c.17-C.2 q.3 p.c.7, communicated by H. Van de Wouw); Oxford, Bodl. MS Laud. misc. 112, fol. 426 (Prologue); Vatican Libr. MS Vat. lat. 4954 (fly-leaves). MSS lost in the second World War: Chartres 173 (200); Münster 603 (notes and collations are among the Heyer papers). A full copy made of the lost Munich MS lat. 3873 (cf. *Repert.* 144) by H.M. Gietl (d. 1918) exists at the Staatsbibliothek. — For Stephen of Tournai, Huguccio, and Ricardus Anglicus revised lists of MSS are found in my 'Interim checklists' (1955–57; see bibliography below). Add to these, for STEPHEN OF TOURNAI: fragments in Dublin, Trinity Coll. H.2.15a, pp. 89–90 (from C.l q.2 and q.3; communication by G. Mac Niocaill) and Leningrad Lat. F.II vel. 23, fol. 2 (beginning of prologue); for HUGUCCIO: Barcelona, Univ. 504; Madrid, B.N. 11962 and Fundación Lázaro Galdiano 440 (written as set iv of glosses on Gratian, incomplete); for RICARDUS ANGLICUS: Hereford, Cath. Chapter P.II.3, fol. 58vb-164v (identified by G. Silano in an unpublished Toronto Ph.D. thesis), Paris, BN lat. 4276, fol. lr-52v; Toledo, Cath. Chapter 24–9, fol. 255ra-275r; Warsaw, National Libr. BOZ 63, fol. 240r-308v. — BENENCASA: Olomouc, State Archives C.0.48 [all MSS formerly of the Cathedral Chapter are now at the Archives under their old shelfmarks, preceded by the letters C.O.]; also fragments in Heverlee (Louvain), Abbaye de Parc (fly-leaves) and Lindau, Stadtarchiv P.I.49, fol. 1–7 (D.51 c.5-C.1 q.l c.115, communicated by G. Dolezalek). Plock MS 80 was destroyed during the second World War.

Bibliography: A. Scharnagl, necrology of Gietl, AKKR 98 (1918) 447; G. Fransen, 'Manuscrits canoniques conservés en Espagne', RHE 48 (1953) 230–32; 49 (1954) 153; 51 (1960) 940; S. Stelling-Michaud, *Catalogue des manuscrits juridiques ... conservés en Suisse* (Genève 1954) p.30 no.21; A.M. Stickler, 'Iter helveticum', *Traditio* 14 (1958) 466, 468; S. Kuttner, 'Interim checklist(s) of manuscripts', *Traditio* 11 (1955) 440–41; ibid. 12 (1956) 563; 13 (1957) 469; see also 15 (1959) 498–99; 17 (1961) 534; 19 (1963)

534; M. Boháček, 'Le opere delle scuole medievali nei manoscritti ... di Olomouc', SG 8 (1962) 355 (p.37 in the original Czech publication, *Rozpravy Československe Akademie věd*, Social Sciences 70 [1960] no.7); A. García y García, 'Los manuscritos jurídicos ... de Toledo', *Traditio* 21 (1965) 512–13; also *Études ... Le Bras* (see above, to p.96 n.14) 125; 'Canonística Hispanica (IV)', BMCL 1 (1971) 71–72; E. Van Balberghe, 'Fragmenta Parcensia', *Archives et bibliothèques de Belgique* 41 (1970) 593; A. Vetulani, 'Trois manuscrits canoniques ...' SG 12 (1967) 194; M. Bertram, 'Some additions ...', BMCL 4 (1974) 14, 16.

p.97 n.18 Paucapalea: See T.P. McLaughlin, s.v. in NCE (1967) 11.1. Recently the *Summa Sicut uetus testamentum* (see p.95 n.10) has been proposed, but unconvincingly, as 'The true Paucapalea?' by J.T. Noonan in *Proceedings Salamanca* (MIC, Subsidia 6; Vatican City 1980) 257–86. See now R. Weigand, 'Paucapalea und die frühe Kanonistik', AKKR 150 (1981) 137–57. — MS Alençon 134, fol. 163r-196r, should be canceled from the list of Paucapalea MSS, see the brief note in *Traditio* 15 (1959) 452.

p.97 n.19: See R. Benson, 'Rufin', DDC 7 (1965, *ex* 1961) 779–84, with bibliography.

p.97 n.20: See A.M. Stickler, 'Jean de Faenza', DDC 6 (1954) 99–102.

p.97 (before n.21): The identity of the master called 'Cardinalis' remains uncertain. The latest suggestions are the cardinals Raymond of Arènes, see A. Gouron, 'Le cardinal Raymond des Arènes: *Cardinalis?*', RDC 28.2-4 (1978) 180–92; cf. S. Kuttner in BMCL 9 (1979) 103; or Hermannus, see R. Weigand in AKKR 149 (1980) 5 n.14.

The magister called 'Cardinals' was definitely identified by Weigand to have been Rainmundus de (H)arenis – cf. *R.Weigand*, Die Glossen des Cardinalis – Raimundus de (H)arenis, in: *H. Lüdicke/H. Paarhammer/D. Binder* (ed.), Recht im Dienste des Menschen, Fetgabe Hugo Schwendenwein zum 60. Geburtstag (Graz 1986), 267–285, also in: *R. Weigand*, Glossatoren des Dekrets Gratians (Bibliotheca Eruditorum 18, Goldbach 1997) 149–165.

p.98 n.24 David of London: see S. Kuttner and E. Rathbone, 'Anglo-Norman canonists,' (No. VIII in this volume) 170.

p.98 n.25 (i): The correct name of the master addressed in JL 13854 is Fidantia, canon of Città Castellana, see W. Holtzmann, *Kanonistische Ergänzungen zur Italia pontificia* (Tübingen 1959) p.28f. No.21 (=*Quellen und Forschungen* 37 [1957] 82f.). — (ii): Philip of Aquileia was a pupil of Johannes Teutonicus, according to Guido de Baysio, *Rosarium* D.100 c.10 — (iii): The siglum Φ in the glosses of *Coll. Cassellana* might be merely a distortion of majuscule *M*.

p.98 (–99) n.26: The glossator *Ro.* could well be the other master Roland at Bologna (not Rolandus Bandinelli, the future Alexander III) for whom documentary evidence exists in 1154 and 1159, and who was probably the author of the *Stroma* and the Sentences, until recently considered to be writings of Bandinelli; see J.T. Noonan, 'Who was Rolandus?', *Law, Church and Society*, edd. K. Pennington and R. Somerville (Philadelphia 1977) 21–48; R. Weigand, 'Magister Rolandus und Papst Alexander III.', AKKR 149 (1980) 3–44.

For Rodoicus (Rodoricus? Rotbertus?) Modicipassus see S. Kuttner s.v. in DDC 7 (1965, *ex* 1961) 701–2, with bibliography; J. Brundage, 'The quaestiones of Rotbertus Modicipassus in a Barcelona manuscript', *Studies in medieval culture* 5 (1975) 87–95.

p.99 n.28: The glosses signed *Al.* cannot be attributed to Adalbert (Vojtěch) Ranconis of Prague, see J. Kejř, 'Les manuscrits du Décret de Gratien dans les bibliothèques tchécoslovaques', SG 8 (1962) 27–28.

p.99 n.29: See Ph. Delhaye, 'Étienne de Tournai', *Dictionn. d'hist. et de géogr. ecclés.* 15 (1963) 1274–78, with bibliography. In 'The third part of Stephen of Tournai's Summa',

Traditio 14 (1958) 502–5, I have shown that the commentary on Gratian's *De cons*, is not authentic. For the works contained in Boulogne-sur-Mer MS 119, see 'Réflexions sur les brocards des glossateurs' (No. IX in this volume) 265 n.76, 267, n.88.

p.99 n.30: On Huguccio's work as a grammarian and for full bibliography see A.M. Stickler s.v. in LThK² 5 (1960) 521–22, DDC 7 (1965, *ex* 1963) 1355–62, NCE (1967) 7.200-01; G. Cremascoli, 'Uguccione da Pisa: saggio bibliografico', *Aevum* 42 (1968) 123–68. Several of the minor among these writings were published by Cremascoli in *Studi Medievali* 14 (1973) 353–442, and again as a volume in the *Biblioteca di Studi Medievali* 10 (Spoleto 1978); also by N. Häring, who was unaware of Cremascoli's work, in SG 19 (1976) 355–416. Thus, the *Expositio de symbolo apostolorum* (unquestionably his) has now been edited four times (1755, 1973, 1976, 1978). The date of the great *Derivationes* remains controversial, see my remarks in *The history of ideas and doctrines of canon law in the Middle Ages* (London 1980), 'Retractationes' p.7.

p.100 n.31: The commentaries on *tract. de poen.* and *tract. de cons.* in Milan, Ambros. A.238 inf. are part of the *Lectura* of Petrus de Salinis, with Bartholomaeus Brixiensis's glosses on C.33 q.4-C.36 inserted in between. See *Traditio* 12 (1956) 601 n.24; 'Interim Checklist (III)', ibid. 13 (1957) 469.

p.100 n.32: Concerning the stages of composition of the *Summa* and certain substitute parts, see my Interim Checklists cited above for pp.96–101; also L. Prosdocimi, 'La "Summa decretorum di Uguccione ...",' SG 3 (1955) 349–74, and 'Iter Germanicum', SG 7 (1959) 251–72, whose hypothesis on the *extraordinariae*, i.e. the earliest supplement for C.23-26, as lecture notes of the master himself or his *reportator* (SG 3.364ff) remains, however, unconvincing. But Prosdocimi is correct in observing that in Huguccio's own belated fragment on C.23 (pr.- q.4 c.33) the explicit reference to a decretal of 1201, 'ut in extra innocentii tertii Litteras tuas' (Po. 1560) cannot be dismissed as an interpolation (so F. Gillmann in AKKR 94 [1914] 244, n.1 to p.243). It is found to my knowledge in at least five of the seven MSS containing the fragment.

p.100 n.33 *Summa Reginensis*: A.M. Stickler, 'Vergessene Bologneser Dekretisten', *Salesianum* 4 (1952) 481–503, and revised Italian version in SG 3 (1955) 375–410, suggests Petrus Beneventanus as possible author. For the influence of the Anglo-Norman *Summa De iure canonico tractaturus* (Honorius) on *Sum. Reg.* see K.W. Nörr, *Zur Stellung des Richters im gelehrten Prozess der Frühzeit* (München 1967) 42 n.27, 44, 47; R. Weigand in AKKR 149 (1980) 10 n.31.

p.100 n.34 Ricardus Anglicus (Richard de Mores): see 'Anglo-Norman canonists ...' (No. VIII of this volume) 213–26, 242–49; and my articles s.v. in DDC 7 (1965, *ex* 1960) 676–81; NCE 12.481-82.

p.101–102 n.39, 40: The most recent, revised list of MSS for these (and other) collections is in *Decretales ineditae saeculi XII*, from the papers of the late W. Holtzmann edd. S. Chodorow and C. Duggan (MIC, Corpus Collectionum 4; Vatican City 1982) xixff. My remark on 'some scanty glosses' (n.21) is obsolete, cf. *Traditio* 6 (1948) 349 n.40. P. Landau, 'Studien zur Appendix und den Glossen in frühen systematischen Dekretalensammlungen', BMCL 9 (1979) 1–21, has shown that these glosses represent a substantial apparatus based on the teaching of English canonists before Comp. I, especially John of Tynemouth.

p.102 n.40 Correct references: *Repertorium* pp. 291 (*Appendix*), 292 (*Bamb.*), 293 (*Lips. Cass.*), 294 (*Bodl.* [*Tann.*]), 296 and pp. 13, 17, 23, 25...

pp.102–109: As stated above, these pages on the development of Bolognese apparatuses of glosses are no longer adequate. The work of Jiři Kejř, Alfons Stickler, and especially Rudolf Weigand has established the existence of a formal though flexible apparatus of glosses on Gratian as early as the eighties of the twelfth century. It can be safely assumed that the *Apparatus Ordinaturus magister* in its first redaction was completed about 1180, perhaps in the school of Bernard of Pavia, the second about 1190, probably in the school of Huguccio. (Several of the MSS listed p.102 n.42 represent one or the other recension of *Ordinaturus magister.*)

Bibliography (in selection): J. Kejr, 'La genèse de l'apparat "Ordinaturus" ...,' *Proceedings Boston* (MIC, Subsidia 1; Vatican City 1965) 45–53; see also SG 12 (1967) 143–53; A.M. Stickler, 'Zur Entstehungsgeschichte und Verbreitung des Dekretapparates "Ordinaturus ...", ibid. 111–41; R. Weigand, *Die bedingte Eheschliessung im kanonischen Recht* (München 1963) 229ff., esp. 231 n.97; idem, 'Welcher Glossenapparat zum Dekret ist der erste?', AKKR 139 (1970) 459–81; see further ZRG Kan. Abt. 61 (1975) 394f., ibid. 64 (1978) 73–94; BMCL 1 (1971) 31–41; ibid. 5 (1975) 35–51; 'Zur Handschriftenliste des Glossenapparats "Ordinaturus magister",' ibid. 8 (1978) 41–47, and several articles on individual glossators.

p.105 n.59: On the apparatus in Douai MS 592 see now A.M. Stickler, 'Die "Glossa Duacensis" zum Decret Gratians', *Speculum iuris et ecclesiarum: Festschrift für Willibald M. Plöchl* (Vienna 1967) 385–92.

p.106 Apparatus of Alanus: The first recension should be dated about 1192, see A.M. Stickler, 'Alanus Anglicus als Verteidiger des monarchischen Papsttums', *Salesianum* 21 (1959) 371–72; the second was completed c. 1205 (communication from P. Landau), see my note in *Traditio* 22 (1966) 476. A revised list of 13 MSS is found in Stickler's article, 348–49; see also SG 12 (1967) 129 n.56. Three of these, however, contain only part III (*de cons.*) beg. 'Expleto de matrimonio tractatu', which is transmitted with Alanus in four MSS altogether, but occurs elsewhere as part of other gloss compositions, and is ascribed to a magister 'R. de parui passu' (=Rodo(r)icus or Robertus Modicipassus?) in Seo de Urgel MS 2882 [Beer 8], fol. 159–168rb; see G. Fransen, 'Un commentaire au "De consecratione",' *Traditio* 13 (1957) 508–9. Thus it remains rather doubtful whether this 'commentaire passepartout' belongs to Alanus.

Separate traditions of Alanus's prologue 'Ius naturale tres habet acceptationes' exist in Bamberg Can. 13 (P.I.16), fol. 272va, together with the first gloss of rec. 2 (Weigand, 'Neue Mitteilungen ...', *Traditio* 21 [1965] 482); Escorial ç.1.5, fol. 482r (Fransen in RHE 48 [1953] 227); Stuttgart HB VI.95, fol. 267r/v (paper, an. 1457: photographs kindly supplied by J. Autenrieth). As for the enlarged tradition of the Apparatus in Paris BN lat. 15393 (*Repert.* 67, 70f., 75) see now S. Kuttner, 'Universal pope or servant of God's servants', RDC 32 (1981) 140: it proves to be the normal text of rec. 2 with the *Casus* of Benencasa inserted.

On Alanus as a decretalist (cf. n.61) see my paper, 'The collection of Alanus: A concordance of its two recensions', RSDI 26 (1953) 37–53.

pp.106–108 on Laurentius and the *Glossa Palatina* are largely superseded by the fundamental study of A.M. Stickler, 'Il decretista Laurentius Hispanus', SG 9 (1966) 461–549, who has traced the development of the Spaniard's glosses into what would be their ultimate form as represented by *Glos. Pal.* (revised list of MSS pp.502–3) — left, however, in an imperfect and not quite satisfactory shape when the author departed from Bologna in 1214 (p.544ff.). On many of its inconsistencies (see e.g. A. Padoa

Schioppa, 'Sul principio della rappresentanza diretta', *Proceedings Toronto* [MIC, Subsidia 5; Vatican City 1976] 130–31) the last word has not been said; this applies also to the prologue 'Ex ore sedentis in throno', which is found in only two out of fourteen MSS (Douai 590 and Munich lat. 28174) and exists separately, though signed *Ia.*, on the same page as the prologue of Alanus in Bamberg Can. 13, fol. 272va (Weigand, *Traditio* 21 [1965] 482).

For recent bibliography see also A. García y García, 'Canonística Ibérica (I)' 406–7; (II) 203–5; idem s.v. 'Lawrence of Spain', NCE 8.569-70.

p.107: line 15, read 'is not as yet unravelled ...'.

p.108: Another apparatus was composed at Bologna *c.* 1204–1209 (1207?) by Willielmus Vasco, more than a decade before his gloss additions (see pp.158ff. below) to the *Ordinaria*. No complete text exists: in the MSS Beaune 5 and Grenoble 62 (482, set ii) most of William's glosses were erased; a fuller version, without Gratian's text, is MS Poznan 28, fol. 105r-22lv (first analyzed as 'Summa Poznanensis' by K.W. Nörr in *Traditio* 17 [1961] 543–44). Willielmus's prologue 'Missurus in mundum', of which only the concluding part is given in the Grenoble MS, exists separately in Fulda MS D.14. — Bibliography: A.M. Stickler, 'Der Dekretist Willielmus Vasco', *Études ... Le Bras* (Paris 1965) 705–28; idem in BMCL 1 (1971) 76–78; S. Kuttner, 'Another copy of Willielmus Vasco's Apparatus ...', *Traditio* 22 (1966) 476–78. Tier Virginio Aimone Braida, Il proemio 'Missurus in mundum', BMCL 13 (1983) 27–38. (S.K.).

pp.108–09 Johannes Teutonicus: See my article s.v. in *Neue Deutsche Biographie* 10 (1974) 571–73, with bibliography. Since then, the first volume appeared of K. Pennington's edition, Johannis Teutonici *Apparatus glossarum in Compilationem tertiam* (MIC, Corpus Glossatorum 3.1; Vatican City 1981); likewise A. García y García's edition of the *Apparatus in quartum Concilium Lateranense*, in *Constitutiones Concilii quarti Lateransis una cum commentariis glossatorum* (MIC Corp. Gloss. 2; 1981).

p.108 n.86: Additional MSS of the *Glossa ordinaria* have been recorded in Grenoble 72; Ivrea, Arch. Capitolare 72 (C), with major lacunae (communication by G. Fransen); Lublin, Catholic Univ. MS 1; Munich lat. 14024 (set ii); Saint-Mihiel 5 (set ii); Tarazona 93 (10; fragments). To be cancelled: Frankfurt, Barth. 7 (wrong shelfmark 1 in *Repert.* 95; actually Barth. Brix.); Madrid, B.N. 12790 (Ee.2; Barth. Brix.). — Bibliography: A. Vetulani, 'Les manuscrits du Décret ... dans les bibliothèques polonaises', SG 3 (1953) 255f.; G. Fransen, 'Manuscrits canoniques conservés en Espagne', RHE 48 (1953) 226–27; A.M. Stickler, 'Decretistica Germanica adaucta', *Traditio* 12 (1956) 594; S. Kuttner, 'Some Gratian manuscripts ...', *Traditio* 19 (1963) 534, 535; J. Sydow, 'Die Dekret-Handschriften der Bayerischen Staatsbibliothek', SG 7 (1959) 204.

The late F. Gillmann (†1941) in a posthumous article published by E. Rösser, 'Der Prager Codex XVII A 12 (früher I B I) und der Dekretapparat des Laurentius Hispanus', AKKR 126 (1953/54) 3–43, interpreted some references in Guido de Baysio's *Rosarium* such as 'in antiquo apparatu Johannis', 'antiqua glossa Johannis' as evidence of an earlier and a later redaction made by Johannes of his apparatus (pp.38–41). But Guido had merely Johannes's original work in mind, as distinguished from its revision by Bartholomeus Brixiensis (cf. also Rösser's editorial note, p.38 n.148). The main purpose of Gillmann's paper was to show that the Prague MS does not contain the apparatus of Laurentius; this agrees with my observations, p.106 n.65 above (cf. Rösser's concluding note 188, p.43).

pp.109–29: Bernard of Compostella's apparatus on Gratian—or at least its major part—has meanwhile been found by R. Weigand in Gniezno, Cathedral Chapter MS 28 in the youngest layer of glosses, which frequently bear the siglum *b.* (which Vetulani, in his survey of Gratian MSS in Poland, SG 1 [1953] 228, 232, believed to represent Bernard of Pavia); the date of completion is about 1205. See R. Weigand, 'Neue Mitteilungen aus Handschriften', *Traditio* 21 (1965) 482–84; A.M. Stickler, 'Der Kaiserbegriff bei Bernardus Compost. Ant.', SG 15 (1972) 103–24 at 109ff.; for comparison of some glosses in Munich lat. 28175 see M. Bertram, 'Die Abdankung Cölestins V.', ZRG Kan. Abt. 56 (1970) 83–85.

p.110f. Bazianus: References by him to Comp. I have in the meantime found in his *quaestiones*, see A.M. Stickler, 'Sacerdotium et regnum nei decretisti ...', *Salesianum* 15 (1953) 607 n.47.

pp.112–13: More is now known on Bernard of Pavia as glossator of Gratian; perhaps he was the master in whose school the first redaction of the *App. Ordinaturus magister* originated, see R. Weigand, 'Frühe Glossen ...', BMCL 5 (1975) 49; 'Zur Handschriftenliste ...', BMCL 8 (1978) 45; 'Bazianus und b. —Glossen ...', SG 20 (1976) 453–95 at 477ff.

In Bernard's *Summa de matrimonio* the reference to 'doctor meus Vg.' (not 'magister ...' as I wrote in n.111) is considered by Weigand a genuine part of the first redaction, dropped later in the second, see *Die bedingte Eheschliessung im kanonischen Recht* (Munich 1963) 242–43 (=241 n.2), whereas F. Cantelar suggests that Bernard may have referred to Hugh of St. Victor, see 'Bernardus Papiensis: "Doctor meus Hugo"': Huguccio de Pisa o Hugo de San Victor?', ZRG Kan. Abt. 55 (1969) 448–57. — Additional MSS: Würzburg Mp.th.fol.122, fols. 26v-31r (F. Gillmann in AKKR 116 [1936] 115); Paris, B.N. lat. 3454, fols. 49–52 (G. Fransen in ZRG Kan. Abt. 55 [1969] 439). The treatise was not written before 1174, since the decretal JL 13970 which Bernard cites (see n.113) was issued in Ferentino, October 1174/1175, see W. Holtzmann, *Kanonistische Ergänzungen* (cf. *supra*, note to p.98 n.25) p.83f. no.115 (=QF 38 [1958] 101f.).

Bernard's authorship of the *Coll. Parisiensis secunda* (p.113 n.113) has been challenged by J.M. Hanenburg, 'Decretals and decretal collections in the second half of the XIIth cent.', TRG 34 (1966) 522–99, at 697f., but see P. Landau, 'Die Entstehung der systematischen Dekretalensammlungen', ZRG Kan. Abt. 65 (1979) 120–48, at 126.

Summa de electione (p.113 n.115): additional MSS in Amiens 377, fols. 148v-151ra (*Repert.* 292 n.l) and Ivrea 67 (VIII), fols. 46ra-47vb (incomplete; communication from G. Fransen); for the date, see P. Landau, 'Zum Ursprung des "ius ad rem" ... *Proceedings Strasbourg* (MIC, Subsidia 2; Vatican City 1971) 89 n.35: between 21 July 1177 and 19 March 1179.

p.112 n.112: The Chester Beatty MS is now at Baltimore, Walters Art Gallery, W.777. See D. Miner on provenance and illuminations in *Journal of the Walters Art Gallery* 31/32 (1968/69) 48–56.

p.117 *Generalia* (*Brocardica*) of Ricardus Anglicus: more in 'Réflexions sur les brocards des glossateurs' (No. IX of this volume) 260–263; see also DDC 7.680f.

p.116 n.126: The former Vollbehr MS (Washington) of Bernard of Pavia's *Summa titulorum* is now at the University of California, Berkeley, School of Law, Robbins MS 7; it was once Phillipps MS 6331. The MSS of Seo de Urgel 2030 (Beer 124) and Madrid, B.N. S.242 (now 1136), listed with question marks in *Repertorium* 387 n.2, 388, are to be cancelled.

p.117 n.127: Melk MS 333 should now be cited as Melk 190 (*ol.* 333; F.33).

p.117 n.128: New MSS of Bernard's *Casus*: Alba Julia, Bibl. Batthyanyana 292, see M. Bertram and S. Kuttner in BMCL 4 (1974) 10; Oxford, Bodleian Libr. Lat. misc. 60, fragment of 14 leaves, from books 3 and 4 (examined by R.M. Fraher).

p.118: For positive evidence of Bernard of Compostella as a decretist glossator (§11) see also Gillmann-Rösser, 'Der Prager Codex XVII A 12 ...' (cited above to p.108 n.86) 34–35.

p.119f.: For glosses of Melendus on Comp. I see also Weigand, *Bedingte Eheschliessung* 283–86.

p.121: The gloss 'In iure ueteris testamenti' on C.16 q.1 pr. which Bernard cites as his own is found in Gniezno MS 28, fol. 147rb (communication from R. Weigand).

p.122 Willielmus Vasco: see above to p.107. Another set of additions to the *Ordinaria* of Johannes Teutonicus in Pommersfelden MS 142 includes glosses by Bern. Compostellanus, see H. Müller, *Der Anteil der Laien an der Bischofswahl* (Kanonistische Studien und Texte 29; Amsterdam 1977) 149 n.43.

p.129: Bernardus on Comp. I is often cited in glosses of Erlangen MS 349, see R. Weigand, 'Mitteilungen aus Handschriften', *Traditio* 16 (1960) 559; see also below, to p.132 n.224 for Freiburg (Br.), Univ. MS 361a.

p.129: Silvester's glosses on the decretal *Pastoralis* are also found in Zwettl MS 162, fol. 213va; for a comparison of the two MSS, see S. Kuttner in *Traditio* 22 (1966) 474–76. More material on Silvester's biography and glosses in J. da Rosa Pereira, 'Silvestre Godinho, un canonista protuguês', *Lumen* 26 (1962) 691–98; see also A.D. de Sousa Costa, *Mestre Silvestre e Mestre Vicente* ... (Braga 1963 [publ. 1967]); and A. García y García, *Estudios sobre la Canonística portuguesa medieval* (Madrid 1976) 106–8.

p.130 n.218: This pre-Gratian collection has since been edited by M. Fornasari, 'Collectio canónica Mutinensis', SG 9 (1966) 246–356 (also separately, Bologna 1965 [*sic*]).

p.132 n.223: Of Bernard of Pavia's glosses printed by Laspeyres, No.3 has to be cancelled, see F. Gillmann in AKKR 107 (1927) 602 n.2 (not by Bernard but by Richard). More on his *notabilia* and *argumenta* in my 'Réflexions sur les brocards des glossateurs' (No. IX of this volume) 262. — Another MS of the early gloss composition here mentioned (incomplete and contaminated) is in Florence, Laurenziana MS S. Croce IV sin.2, fol. 1–47.

p.132 n.224 Ricardus Anglicus, *Apparatus* on Comp. I: More in my article on Richard, DDC 7.680 (with bibliogr.) and C. Lefebvre, 'Les gloses à la "Compilatio Ia" et les problèmes qu'elles soulèvent', *Proceedings Boston* (MIC, Subsidia 1; Vatican City 1965) 63–70; 'Les gloses à la "Compilatio Ia" du ms. Pal. lat. 652 de la Bibl. Vaticane', SG 20 (1976) 135–56. Additional MSS in Munich lat. 8302 (see Weigand in *Traditio* 16.560) and Freiburg (Br.), Univ. 361a, which includes also some glosses by Bern. Compostellanus (communication from G. Fransen).

p.133 Pelagius: For biography and bibliography see D. Mansilla, 'El cardenal hispano Pelayo Gaitán (1206–1230)', *Anthologica annua* 9 (1961) 417–73; cf. A. García y García, 'Canonistas gallegos medievales', *Compostellanum* 16 (1970) 118–21; 'Canonística ibérica (III)' 386–87. But among the forms of his siglum in the Modena MS, *p.* must be eliminated: as A.M. Stickler, 'Vergessene Bologneser Dekretisten', *Salesianum* 14 (1952) 485f. (Italian version, SG 3 [1955] 389f.) has shown, the glosses so signed belong to Petrus Hispanus since they agree with the latter's *Apparatus* in Würzburg Mp.th. fol. 122. Thus, e.g. the gloss cited in the note to p.135, below.

p.132 n.226: The folio reference for Klosterneuburg MS 1045 should read l-7v, 9r-32v.

p.135 and n.243: Bernard was taught Roman law not by Azo but by Cacciavillanus. For, the original author of the gloss that refers to Azo's lectures ('ut audiui') was Petrus Hispanus:

see Stickler in *Salesianum* 14.486 n.53 (=SG 3.389 n.55). In his Apparatus on Gratian, however, Bernardus Compostellanus writes, D.95 c.1 *Peruenit* v. *debeant*: '...id enim quod solet dici, "ea que cause cognitionem desiderant per libellum non expediuntur", sic intelligo: idest non de plano, secundum quod didici a cachiavillano, aliter tamen exponitur a plerisque ...' (Gniezno MS 28, fol. 60ra, communicated by G. Fransen).

p.136: Another gloss to Comp. I with the signature of Azo is found in Vat. lat. 1377, fol. 67r, *De despons. impub. Continebatur* (4.2.8), v. *proxima*: 'supple pubertati. acco.' But in both instances (as also in the case of Vat. lat. 1367 on C.3 q.6 pr. discussed p.157) this does not prove actual lecturing by Azo on the canonistic texts.

p.136 n.251: Bazianus is also quoted as 'bal.' in a gloss of Gniezno MS 28 on C. 13 q.2 c.5, which corresponds to the one printed above, p.118f. (communication from R. Weigand).

pp.137–38: The problem of identifying the master *p.* of the interlocking glosses by *p.* and *b.* here printed remains unsolved. In view of the strong arguments against Pelagius (see the notes to pp.133, 135 above), the second Petrus Hispanus (Portugalensis) seems the least unlikely of the candidates. A time span between 1205/6 for the glosses on Comp. I (the date of Bernard's glosses, see p.138) and 1223 or 1229 (so the documentary evidence for the younger Petrus in Bologna and Padua, see p.137 n.51) is not too long for an academic career. — But if Petrus Hispanus Portugalensis was the P. Yspanus whom Johannes de Petesella in 1235/36 cited as deceased (which is very likely), he could not be identical with Bishop Pedro Salvadores of Porto (d.1247, see p.137 n.256), as I. da Rosa Pereira has pointed out; 'O canonista Petrus Hispanus Portugalensis', *Arquivos de historia da cultura portuguesa* 2 (1968), 18 pp. [offprint]. See also García y García, *Estudios ... Canonística portuguesa* (cited above, to p.129) 104–6.

p.137 n.254: The authorship of the two procedural treatises remains uncertain also according to the most recent investigation in the first installment of Antonio Pérez Martín's 'El Ordo iudiciarius "Ad summariam notitiam" y sus derivados: Contribución a la historia de la literatura procesal castellana, I: Estudio', *Historia institucións documentos* 8 (1982) 1–72, at 43–49 with list of MSS p.43 n.141 (cf. the preliminary list by García y García, *Estudios* 105). An edition followed as part II. Pérez Martín is inclined to distinguish two authors, *Ad summariam notitiam* being probably written by a civilian rather than a canonist. The other treatise has been edited from four MSS by M.T. Napoli, 'L'Ordo iudiciarius "Quia utilissimum fore" ...', ZRG Kan. Abt. 62 (1976) 58–105, at 87ff. (without mention of the variant incipit 'Quoniam utilissimum').

p.137 n.258 Petrus Brito: He should be counted among the French canonists (W. Ullmann, *Medieval Papalism* [London 1949] 109–10: 'Western, perhaps even English'); see in particular R. Weigand, 'Neue Mitteilungen ...', *Traditio* 21 (1965) 485–91 on the *Apparatus Quia brevitas amica est audientie* (Comp. I) from his school, and 'Glossenapparat zur Compilatio prima aus der Schule der Petrus Brito', *Traditio* 26 (1970) 449–57 on the *Apparatus Bernardus Papiensis prepositus.* However, since P. Brito did not know the decretal *Pastoralis* (see *Traditio* 22 [1966] 476), his teaching on Comp. I must be dated before 1205, instead of after 1216: in none of the texts printed by Gillmann (as cited n.258) do the references to Compp. II-III come from his pen: in particular the gloss citing 4 Comp. 2.12.4 (see *Zur Inventaris.* 59) is signed *p.*, not *p.b'*. and probably belongs to the younger Petrus Hispanus (Portugalensis).

Magister Petrus Brito was one of the three arbiters, with *magister Radulphus* of Reims and Bernard, chancellor of Paris, who were elected by litigants in Soissons sometime before October 1212, i.e. the date at which the former chancellor Bernard, then already bishop of Geneva, was transferred to Embrun by Innocent III (Po. 4618–20). Before 4 March 1218, when Honorius III appointed judges delegate to terminate the case, Petrus Brito had gone 'uiam uniuersi carnis'. See X 2.20.50 (5 Comp. 2.12.3; Pressutti 1132) and Hostiensis, *Lectura* ad loc. vv. *et cancellarium, unus ipsorum, et alius* (ed. Venice 1581, II fol. 104va). This disposes of my assumption (n.258) that Brito could be the *magister Petrus Prepositi* from the diocese of Le Mans, to whom Honorius III wrote in April 1218 (Pressutti 1270). (Hostiensis's remarks just cited have also some autobiographical interest.)

p.137: Petrus de Cardo is not 'otherwise unknown', but was the Catalan master Petrus de Cardona, who died as cardinal before 1185; see H. Kantorowicz, 'A Greek Justinian contribution ...', *Seminar* 3 (1945) 55 (with bibliogr. in note 25) = *Rechtshistorische Schriften* (Karlsruhe 1970) 195 and n.25; A. Gouron, 'Autour de Placentin à Montpellier: Maitre Gui et Pierre de Cardona', SG 19 (1976) 337–54, at 347ff.; also in: *idem*, La science du droit dans le decidi de la France au Moyen Age (London 1984) no. VII.; also P. Freedman, 'An unsuccessful attempt at urban organization in ... Catalonia', *Speculum* 54 (1979) 479–89, at 488. Petrus de Cardona: two persons of the same name? *A.Gouron*, Un assaut à deux vagues. La diffusion du droit romain dans l'Europe du XIIe siècle, in: El dret comú i Catalunya, Actes del Simposi Barcelona 1990, ed. A. Iglesia Ferreirós (Barcelona 1991) 47–63 at p. 51 – also in: *id.*, Droit et coutume en France an XIIe et XIII siècles (Ashgate 193) no. XVI.

pp.140–148 Bernard's *Quaestiones*: Much of the general observations on *quaestiones disputatae* and *quaestiones decretales* were resumed and revised in 'Anglo-Norman canonists' (No. VIII of this volume) 197–202; moreover, this whole chapter is now superseded by the score of articles in which G. Fransen over the years has analyzed many collections of *quaestiones* in preparation of a comprehensive *Corpus quaestionum* These articles contain substantial new information on the MSS here discussed and many others: thus it would be futile to attempt a detailed list of *addenda* and *corrigenda* to the present paper. — G. Fransen, 'Les "questiones" des canonistes (I)-(IV)', *Traditio* 12 (1956) 566–92; 13 (1957) 481–501; 19 (1963) 516–31; 20 (1964) 495–502; 'Deux collectiones de 'questiones', *Traditio* 21 (1965) 492–510 (esp. on Bernardus Compostellanus, 493ff.); also 'Varia ex manuscriptis', ibid. 519–20; 'La structure des "quaestiones disputatae" et leur classement', *Traditio* 23 (1967) 516–34; 'Les "Questiones" des canonistes: Bilan provisoire et plan de travail', *Actes Louvain* (1959) 129–34; 'Tribunaux ecclésiastiques et langue vulgaire d'après les "questiones" des canonistes', *Ephemerides theol. Lovanien.* 40 (1964) 391–412; '"Utrumque ius" dans les "Questiones Andegavenses"', *Études ... Le Bras* (Paris 1965) 2.897-911; 'Quaestiones' (with Ch. Lefebvre), DDC 7 (1965) 407–18, at 413–15; 'Quaestiones Vaticanae, Urgellenses et Lemovicenses', ZRG Kan. Abt. 55 (1969) 437–48; 'Les Quaestiones Cusanae: Questions disputées sur le mariage', *Festschrift A. Dordett* (Vienna 1976) 209–21; 'Les Questiones Neapolitanae', BMCL 6 (1976) 29–40; 'Les canonistes médiévaux et les problèmes de leur temps: quelques "quaestiones disputatae"', *Mélanges offerts à Jean Dauvillier* (Toulouse 1979) 307–17.

Gérard Fransen's numerous studies on canonistic questions are now collected in: *G. Fransen*, Canones et Questiones I, 2. La Littérature des "Questiones" des Canonistes et Civilistes, Bibliotheca Eruditorum 25 (Goldbach 2002). (P.L.)

A survey on research concerning the collections of quaestiones from canonists was given by me in a colloquy of the Historisches Kolleg in Munich 1995 – cf. *P. Landau*, Kanonistische Quaestionenforschung, in: *M. Bellomo* (ed.), Die Kunst der Disputation (Schriften des Historischen Kollegs. Kolloquien 3, München 1997) 73–84. In my article I also mention desiderata in this field of research (p. 84). (P.L.)

For the Summa questionum, written by the English master Honorius circa 1188–1190, cf. now W. *Kozur*, Die Dekret- und die Quaestionensumme des Magister Honorius im Lehrbetrieb des 12. Jahrhunderts, in: Proceedings of the Thirteenth International Congress of Medieval Canon Law, Esztergom 2008, MIC, Ser. C, Vol. 14 (Città del Vaticano 2010), 419-429, and W. *Kozur/K. Miethaner-Vent*, Titel in der Questionen- und Dekretsumme des Magister Honorius. Neues zu Aufbau und Abfassung der beiden Summen, in: Proceedings of the Eleventh International Congress of Medieval Canon Law Catania 2000, MIC, Ser. C, Vol. 12 (Città del Vaticano 2006), 153–168. Portions of the Summa quastionum, bearing on marriage doctrine, have been edited by B. *Grimm*, Die Ehelehre des Magister Honorius. Ein Beitrag zur Ehelehre der anglo-normannischen Schule, Stud. Grat. 24 (Romae 1989), 231–387. A complete critical edition is planned with support by the Deutsche Forschungsgemeinschaft (DFG). (P.L.)

The series of articles by Gérard Fransen enumerated in these Retractationes can be supplemented now by essays from *André Gouron* on the subject of Quaestiones – cf. 1.) A. *Gouron*, Note sur les collections de quaestiones reportatae chez les civilistes du XIIe siècle, in: "Houd voet bij stu". Xenia iuris historiae G. van Dievoet oblata (Leuven 1990) 55–66 – also in: *Id.*, Droit et coutume en France aux XIIe et XIIIe siècles (Ashgate 1990), no. VI; 2.) *Id.*, La diffusion des premiers recueils de questions disputées: des civilistes aux canonistes, in: R. J. *Castillo Lara* (ed.), Studia in honorem eminentissimi Cardinalis Alphonsi M. Stickler (Studia et textus historiae Iuris Canonici 7, Roma 1992) 152–169; 3.) *Id.*, Observations sur le Stemma Bulgarcium, in: C. *Alzati* (ed.), Cristianità ed Europa. Miscellanea di studi in onore di Luigi Prosdocimi I (Roma/ Freiburg/Wien 1994) 485–495 – 2.) and 3.) also in: *Id.*, Juristes et droits savants: Bologne et la France médiévale (Ashgate 2000), no. IV and VI; 4.) *Id.*, Maître Jean et les « Questions disputées » de Grenoble, in: B. *d'Alteroche* et al. (ed.), Mélanges en l'honneur d'Anne Lefebvre-Teillard (Paris 2009), 463–471. (P.L.)

Several *quaestiones* from *Quaest. Londinenses* in B.L. (B.M.) MS Royal 9.E.vii. have been printed and discussed by J.A. Brundage in *Mediaeval Studies* 24 (1962) 153–60, *Speculum* 38 (1963) 443–52, and *Manuscripta* 19 (1975) 86–97; also from the *Quaest. Barchinonenses* of the Archivo de la Corona de Aragón, MS San Cugat 55 in *Manuscripta* 15 (1971) 67–76, and *Studies in medieval culture* 5 (1975) 87–95 (see to p.98–99 n. 26 above).

p.143 n. 290: The *Quaestiones* of Bamberg MS Can. 45 begin 'Vocatus (not 'Veniens') quidam ad regimen ciuitatis' and end fol. 56v (not 56r).

p.144 n. 292(vii): The *Summa quaestionum* in Vienna 2163 cites once at least 'ex. iiii', and thus was completed after 1216.

p.144 n. 293(iii): The same treatise on penance apparently in Poznan, Metropolitan Chapter MS 28, fol. 190r-200v, cf. A. Vetulani, 'Les manuscrits du Décret ... dans les bibliothéques polonaises', SG 1 (1953) 275.

p.144 n.293(ix): On Jacobus Columbi's *Summa feudorum* (ends fol. 104r, not 104v) see also E.M. Meijers, 'Les glossateurs et le droit féodal', TRG 13 (1934) 129–49, at 137–41 = *Études d'histoire du droit* III (Leiden 1959) 267–70.

p.144 n.293(xiv): There follows (xv) Silvester, glosses on *Pastoralis*, see note to p.129 *supra.*

p.145: In the Vienna MS (W) the solutions of *ber.* begin fol. 86va (not 87r).

p.146: In the case beg. 'Episcopus ulixbonensis bona fide possidebat ...' (which is also in Z) the solution should read: 'M. aufert ei, b' assentit' (not 'asserit'); see Fransen in *Traditio* 21.497. Hence Melendus and Bernard were in agreement on the boundary conflict.

p. 146 n.299: The reading is *hu.* in Z, hence Huguccio is meant.

p. 146 n.302: On Vincentius's career and writings, the book by J. Ochoa Sanz, *Vincentius Hispanus, canonista boloñes del siglo XIII* (Rome-Madrid 1960) is unfortunately blemished by special pleading and misinformation. I corrected some points in 'Notes on MSS: Vincentius Hispanus', *Traditio* 17 (1961) 537–41, and '"Wo war Vincentius Hispanus Bischof?",' ibid. 22 (1966) 471–74. See also A.D. de Sousa Costa, *Mestre Silvestre e Mestre Vicente* (Braga 1963 [publ. 1967]). While these 'Retractationes' were readied for going to press, Ochoa has reopened the controversy in 'El glosador Vincentius Hispanus y titulos comunes "de foro competenti" canonico', *Miscellanea in onore dei Professori Anastasio Gutiérrez e Pietro Tocanel* (Rome 1982) 429–88, at 444–66.

p. 148 n.307 correct the foliation: W 86v-87ra, Z 173r/v.

p. 148–54 Bernard's 'Compilatio Romana': Concerning Bernard's stay at the Roman Curia, Johannes Andreae was probably right when he rejected Willielmus Duranti's contention that Bernardus Compostellanus, according to Vincentius, had once delivered a judgment 'in curia' (*Speculum iud.* III *de inquis.* §1: '...Vincentius tamen notat in eod. tit. Qualiter lo secundo [X 5.1.24] quod B. Compostell. in curia contrarium iudicauit'). This, Jo. Andreae says, is a misunderstanding of Vincentius's words: '... non enim dixit quod Ber. Compostell. sententiauerit *in curia*, sed dixit quod sententiauit *in causa* episcopi Fauentini illam [*scil.* inquisitionem] faciendam ...' (i.e. Vincentius merely cited Bernardus as having given an opinion on a case); but, Jo. Andreae continues, Duranti probably had the younger Bernardus Compostellanus in mind, who was a 'curialis' (of Innocent IV), 'et ideo addidit "in curia"' (ed. Venet. 1577, III fol. 28vb, gl. *k*). Savigny, *Geschichte* V 575n and Schulte, QL II 114n, in quoting Duranti (for B. Comp. junior) overlooked Johannes Andreae's remarkable piece of literary criticism.

p. 148: The ratio of 277 decretals from Gilbertus/Alanus to 154 from the papal registers must be changed to 278 and 153, since Heckel overlooked one more piece: Bern. 5.16.4 = Alan. 1.15.1+2.1.2 (1.19.2+2.2.2), while rightly recognizing a third section of the same decretal (Po. 919), Bern 4.10.2 = Alan. 4.11.2 (4.11.2).

p. 148 n.309: On Bernard's discussion of the authenticity of certain decretals in the Epilogue, see C.R. Cheney, 'Three decretal collections ..., Additional note', *Traditio* 15 (1959) 480–83.

p. 150 Manuscripts: A small fragment (1.8.12-14) can be added from a fly-leaf in Douai MS 598 (fol. 1r/v). — Singer p.5f. mentioned the *ms. cod. doctissimi ... Nic. Fabri* (Nicolas Lefèvre, 1544–1612) from which the first two *tituli* were published in Antonio Agustín's *Compilationes antiquae* — though not by Agustín, as Singer believed (he did not know the *ed. princeps*, Lérida 1576), but by Charles Labbé in the revised Paris edition of 1609; see S. Kuttner, 'Antonio Agustín's edition of the Compilationes antiquae', BMCL 7 (1977) 10. Labbé's codex can be identified through common errors and variants as the Harleian MS 3845 of the British Library (provenance: library of the chancellor Philippe Séguier, d. 1672).

p. 149 n. 314: Paris MS lat. 3922A, fols. 235ra-242rb is not a full Rainier of Pomposa, but a selection made by the unknown Rouen canonist, see W. Holtzmann (†)-C.R. and M.G. Cheney, *Studies in the collections of twelfth-century decretals* (MIC, Corpus Collectionum 3; Vatican City 1979) 140–41 159.

The 'unknown Rouen canonist' mentioned by kuttner as responsible for MS Paris lat. 3922 A was *Walter of Coutances*, archbishop of Rouen 1185–1207, cf. P. *Landau*, Walter von Coutances und die Anfänge der anglo-normannischen Rechtswissenschaft, in: *O. Condorelli* (ed.), "Panta rei". Studi dedicati a Manlio Bellomo III (Roma 2004) 183–204, here p. 200. (P.L.)

p.150: The glosses of the Modena MS are not from Tancred's Apparatus but from a mixed composition that includes Vincentius (see e.g. Stickler as cited above, to p.133, *Salesianum* 14.481 n.2; SG 3.384 n.20), Laurentius, and others.

p.152 n. 336: The calendar of rubrics in Theiner's unnamed MS of Halle is Ye.52, part ii, fol. 8r/v.

p.152 (Theiner' calendo) *suma*: corr. *summa*.

p.153: A significant new area of Bernard's influence was discovered by K. Pennington, 'The French recension of Compilatio tertia', BMCL 5 (1975) 53–71, who showed that the *Comp. Romana* was the chief source for interpolated chapters and for variant readings in this family of MSS. This throws an interesting sidelight on the French canonists' attitude towards the pope's authentication of Comp. III. The 'French version' includes Bernard's Epilogue (Pennington p.60 n.25).

p.153 n. 345: In four cases, however, no other sources are known for Comp. IV than the corresponding chapters of Bernard's collection; see Kuttner, 'Johannes Teutonicus ... und die Compilatio quarta', *Miscellanea Giovanni Mercati V* (Studi e Testi 125; Vatican City 1946) 619 with n.9.

p.153 Salzburg collection: Another excerpt or abbreviation from Bernard is found in St. Florian MS XI.346, fols. 131r-154r, after an abbreviated Comp. IV; see *Miscellanea Mercati* V 630 n.34. As Winfrid Stelzer has pointed out to me, this MS is connected with the learned activities of Altmann of St. Florian (on whom see Stelzer's article in MIÖG 84 [1976] 60–104).

p. 154 n. 352 Ambrosius: see now A. Martín-Avedillo, 'La "Summa super titulis decretalium" del canonista Ambrosius', ZRG Kan. Abt. 54 (1968) 57–94, and 'Influjo del canonista Ambrosius en San Raimundo de Peñafort', REDC 26 (1970) 329–55.

p.154 n. 353: The Plock MS was destroyed in World War II, see *Traditio* 12 (1956) 565f.

p.154 n. 354: Vincentius's *Apparatus* is now edited: A. García y García, *Constitutiones Concilii quarti Lateranensis una cum Commentariis glossatorum* (MIC, Corpus Glossatorum 2; Vatican City 1981) 271–384.

p.154 n. 355: Melk MS 518 should now be cited as Melk 289 (*ol.* 518; 1.37).

p.154 n. 356: Use of Bernard's compilation in the *Glossa Palatina*: other examples in A.M. Stickler, 'Il decretista Laurentius Hispanus', SG 9 (1966) 512; S. Kuttner, 'Universal Pope or Servant of God's Servants ...', RDC 32 (1981) 109–49, at 123–24, 142.

p.155 n. 364: One might think of the other Stephanus Provincialis at Bologna, author of an Apparatus on the Clementines, whom Johannes Andreae cited as 'dominum stefanum cancellarium legati in lombardiam'; see N. Zacour, 'Stephanus Hugoneti and his Apparatus on the Clementines', *Traditio* 17 (1961) 527–30; S. Kuttner, 'The Apostillae of Johannes Andreae on the Clementines', *Études ... Gabriel Le Bras* (Paris 1965) I 198–99. But he seems too late to be considered here: he came to Italy with the legate Bertrand du Poujet in 1320, became bishop of Bologna in 1330, and died in 1332.

p.155 f. nn. 366–369. Ricardus de Senis: see my article in DDC 7 (1965, *ex* 1960) 681–84. The date of his will was 13 (not 27) January 1314.

p.156 Jacobus de Albenga: see also J. Lips and H. Wagnon in DDC 6 (1957, *ex* 1954) 77–78. Jacobus was not the teacher of Pierre de Sanson; E.M. Meijers, *Responsa doctorum Tholosanorum* (Haarlem 1938) vii n.6 (=*Études d'histoire du droit* III [Leiden 1959] 171 n.20). gloss additions to Comp. IV (cf. *Repert.* 373 n.6) in Córdoba, Cathedral

MS 10, see A. García y García, 'Canonistica Hispanica (IV)', *Traditio* 23 (1967) 507–8; cf. García et al., *Catálogo de los manuscritos e incunables de la catedral de Córdoba* (Salamanca (1974) p.17.

p.157 Martin of Zamora: More on biography (against the identification here proposed) and writings in A. García y García, 'Canonística ibérica (I)' 407, 412.

p.157 Pelagius and Vincentius: See above, notes to p.133 and 146 n. 302.

p.159 and n.398 *Ordo Scientiam omnes naturaliter appetunt*: The name of the master whose *vestigia* the author proposes to follow was Petrus Peuerel according to the spelling of the best MSS and the papal registers. He was a canon in Paris whom Innocent III in January 1209 commissioned with Mr. Richard Poore to hear a case (Po. 3590; 3 Comp. 1.3.7 = X 1.4.8), and again in two cases, 1211 and 1213; he was elected to the see of Agde in 1214 but apparently died before consecration; see John W. Baldwin, *Masters, princes and merchants*: The social views of Peter the Chanter and his circle (Princeton 1970) II 11 n.27, 21 n.150, and J.-M. Carbasse, 'L'ordo iudiciorum "Sapientiam affectant omnes",' *Confluence des droits savants et des pratiques juridiques*: Actes du Colloque de Montpellier ... 1977 . (Milan (1979) 13–33 at 24–28, who suggests that Petrus Peuerel probably was the author of that *Ordo* ('Sapientiam') and discusses the different form of his name (Puluerellus) in the letter announcing his election as printed in *Gallia Christiana* 6, *instr.* p.332.

As for the Walter (Gualterus) who wrote the *Ordo Scientiam*, I believe it is possible tentatively to identify him with Master Walter Cornut (or Cornuti), who was a canon, and became dean, of the chapter of Paris in the times of Petrus Peuerel, was said to be a canonist, and became archbishop of Sens in 1222 (see Baldwin II 11 n.27).

p.159 n. 401: For glosses of Willielmus Vasco on Compp. I-IV in Córdoba MS 10 see García as cited to p.156 above on Jacobus de Albenga; cf. *Repert.* 33 n.1 (for Comp. I).

VIII. Anglo-Norman Canonists of the Twelfth Century

In the notes that follow, I have made no attempt at completing the bibliographical information on every aspect of canon law in England during the twelfth century or the early part of the thirteenth. Scanning the published research of the past thirty years we find more and more space given to matters of canon law in biographies of churchmen and biographical dictionaries, in editions of collected letters, in studies of church administration, court procedures, cases, wills, councils and synods, anglo-papal relations, as well as in recent work on the texts of Glanvill and Bracton. This amounts to a remarkable harvest of new research and writing since the days when we published this joint paper. Reference, however, in these notes must be limited to those new materials or interpretations that have a direct bearing on the history of Anglo-Norman canonists and their teaching in the period we discussed. (Abbreviations other than those used in the article will be the same as those listed in the 'Retractationes' for No. VII of the present volume, *q. v.*)

We failed in this paper to discuss *Brocarda* of English origin, and mentioned only briefly those of Ricardus Anglicus (de Mores) on pp. 337, 338 n. 70. But there exists a short set in the British Library, MS Royal 9. C. VI, fol. 2ra–3vc. It begins, after the last line of a preceding *brocardum* ... 'hoc ergo nec pro se', with the words, 'Argumentum testes non esse cogendos' (see infra IX 788–792 NR [7]) and is completed at the end. (S.K.)

p.164 n.5: The distribution of labor in composing this paper did not follow any prearranged lines; there was no division between biographical (E.R.) and canonistic (S.K.) material as the late W. Holtzmann assumed in his otherwise very perceptive review, ZRG Kan. Abt. 39 (1953) 465–69, at p.466.

p.165 Canterbury litigation: For a recent account, see C.R. Cheney, *Pope Innocent III and England* (Päpste und Papsttum 9; Stuttgart 1976) 208–20.

p.165: Peter of Paxton was vice-archdeacon of Lincoln, see Cheney, *Bishops' Chanceries* (p.165 n.6) 144, hence not merely a 'country parson'.

p.166 Decretal collections: Much more information is now available in the two volumes published thus far from the papers of the late Walther Holtzmann preserved in Berkeley: *Studies in the collections of twelfth-century decretals*, edited, revised, and translated by C.R. Cheney and M.G. Cheney; *Decretales ineditae saeculi XII*, ed. and revised by S. Chodorow and C. Duggan (MIC, Corpus Collectionum 3-4; Vatican City 1979, 1982). The Canterbury collections (see note 15) have been analyzed by C. Duggan, *Twelfth century decretal collections and their importance in English history* (London 1963) 73–76, 162–71; *Coll Wignorniensis altera* (previously called *Wigorn. II*) is analyzed ibid. 152–54; for another member of the Worcester family in Cambridge, Trinity College R.14.9, fols. 82r-87v, see Duggan, 'The Trinity Collection ...', *Traditio* 17 (1961) 506–26; cf. *Twelfth-century decretal collections* 191–92; also in *id.*, Canon Law in Medieval England (London 1982), no. VII, with Addenda at Corrigenda p. 4f.. H. Mayr-Harting, 'Master Silvester and the compilation of early English decretal collections', *Studies in Church History* 2 (1965) 186- 98, has argued that this clerk of Bishops Roger and Baldwin at Worcester was the principal compiler of *Coll. Wigorn.* Important new observations on this whole cluster of English collections and continental links are presented by M.G. Cheney, *Roger, Bishop of Worcester 1164–1179. An English bishop of the age of Becket* (Oxford 1980) 197–206.

p.167f. Baldwin's appointment by Eugene III as tutor for the papal nephew (later cardinal) Gratian: J.T. Noonan interprets this passage in John of Salisbury's letter 532, ed. Robertson, *Materials* V p.3 (=edd. W.J. Millor and C.N. Brooke II [Oxford 1979] ep. 289 p.603), which reads 'Gratianum, cuius tu ... a sanctae recordationis papa Eugenio Ferentini decretus es institutor', as rather indicating that the pope in 1150/51 decreed the 'teaching of Gratian', i.e. of the Decretum, making it thereby an official book: 'Was Gratian approved at Ferentino?' BMCL 6 (1976) 15–27. The hypothesis was refuted by the late P. Classen, 'Das Decretum Gratiani wurde nicht in Ferentino approbiert', BMCL 8 (1978) 38–40. However, the generally accepted designation of Cardinal Gratian as a nephew of Innocent II (so also here, p.167) instead of Eugene III is based on an error by R.L. Poole (cited p.167 n.16); see Noonan p.24 n.47 and Classen p.40.

p.167: For Bishop Roger of Worcester and the letters of Alexander III addressed to him, see M.G. Cheney, 'Pope Alexander III and Roger, Bishop of Worcester, 1164–79: the exchange of ideas', *Proceedings Toronto* (MIC, Subsidia 5; Vatican City 1976) 207–27; and her book on Roger (cited above), especially pp. 113–65 and 317–73 (calendar of papal letters).

p.168f. *Appendix Concilii Lateranensis*: More evidence for its English origin in S. Kuttner, 'The decretal "Presbiterum" (JL 13912)—a letter of Leo IX', BMCL 5 (1975) 133–35. The lines of relationship between the systematic collections in general have been thoroughly reexamined by P. Landau, 'Die Entstehung der systematischen Dekretalensammlungen und die europäische Kanonistik,' ZRG Kan. Abt. 65 (1979) 120–48.

p.168 Collection of the Bodleian MS Tanner 8: A full analysis was published by Holtzmann in *Festschrift zur Feier des 200jährigen Bestehens der Akad. der Wiss. in Göttingen* (1951) 83–145.

p.168 n.23: For the collections of MS Paris lat. 3922A from Rouen, see now Holtzmann-Cheney, *Studies* (cited above to p.166), also C.R. Cheney on decretals of Innocent III in *Traditio* 11 (1955) 149–62. — Concerning B.M. (now British Library) MS Royal 2,D. ix, fols. 11-22r, our interpretation of the marginal references was wrong: they all can be traced in the *Bambergensis* group, though the style of citation is unusual; hence there was no attempt here at amalgamating two traditions (communication by W. Deeters to W. Holtzmann, 13 June 1954).

p.168: Further evidence of Englishmen's learning in Roman law in E. Rathbone, 'Roman law in the Anglo-Norman realm', SG 11 (1967: *Collectanea S. Kuttner* I) 253–71.

p.169 Thomas Becket in Bologna: G. Barbetta, 'Sull'introduzione a Verona del culto di S. Tommaso Becket', *Studi storici Veronesi Luigi Simeoni* 20/21 (1970/72) 107–38, discusses his friendship with Ognibene (Omnibonus) the canonist and later bishop of Verona [not seen; cf. the notice in DA 30 [1974] 309.

p.169 First copies in England of Gratian's *Decreta*: W. Holtzmann in his review of this article suggested very convincingly, on the showing of quotations in the *Policraticus*, that John of Salisbury was probably instrumental in introducing Gratian's book to England: ZRG Kan. Abt. 39 (1953) 466–67. With regard to a later copy (c. 1180), the Dyson Perrins MS 2, it has been speculated that this may have been one of the books which Herbert of Bosham brought from the abbey of Ste.-Colombe-lès-Sens to Canterbury, see C.H. Talbot in H.P. Kraus, *Thirty-Five Manuscripts* (Catalogue 100; New York [1967]) pp. 7–8; R. Schilling. 'The Decretum Gratiani formerly in the Dyson Perrins collection ...', *Journal of the British Archaeological Assn.* 26 (1963) 27–39. the manuscript is now in the collection of Dr. P. Ludwig, Aachen, see my note in *Traditio* 19 (1963) 535–36. — While this volume is readied for going to press, the acquisition of Dr. Ludwig's medieval MSS by the J. Paul Getty Museum in Malibu, California has been announced.

p.169 Peter of Blois: For his career see D.E. Greenway in the new edition of Le Neve's *Fasti ecclesiae anglicanae, 1066–1300*, I: St. Paul's London (London 1965) 10; on his intellectual stature, R.W. Southern, 'Peter of Blois: a twelfth-century humanist', *Medieval Humanism and other studies* (Oxford 1970) 105–32.

p.170: Archbishop Hubert Walter is sometimes counted among the English students at Bologna because his obit occurs in the Necrology of S. Salvatore; but this is not evidence for his having studied there, see C.R. Cheney, *Hubert Walter* (London 1967) 18f.; 'Hubert Walter and Bologna', BMCL 2 (1972) 81–84. — On David of London, see M.G. Cheney, 'Pope Alexander III and Roger ...' (cited above to p.167) 215f; and her book on Roger, pp. 177, 207f. (also Index s.v.). It seems that in the French *Distinctiones Consuetudo* references to 'm.d.' and to 'David' indicate two different canonists (Bamberg MS Can. 17, fols. 100vb, 102rb). p. 170, David of London: he was agent in Rome, not only for Gilbert Foliot and other prelates but also for the monasteries of St. Pancras and Giseburne; his studies in Bologna were in particular centered on *quaestiones disputatae* (both these facts were supplied to me by the late Eleanor Rathbone in a letter of 1948). – At some time David became a *familiaris* of Bishop Roger of Worcester and might have compiled the material used in Part II (cc.50–125) of the *Collectio decretalium Alcobasensis prima*; see M.G. Cheney, *Roger, Bishop of Worcester 1164–1179: An English bishop of the age of Becket* (Oxford 1980) 206–08.

pp.171–73: The traditional views on Vacarius's having introduced the formal teaching of Roman law in England and particularly at Oxford have been seriously challenged by R.W. Southern, 'Magister Vacarius and the beginning of an English academic tradition,' *Medieval learning and literature*: *Essays presented to Richard W. Hunt* (Oxford 1976) 257–86, as a 'patchwork of facts and fancy' (p.282): in his view, Vacarius would have ceased to be a master of the schools when he left Bologna; and whatever teaching on the contents of his *Liber pauperum* he did in his later years was that of a country parson, without academic institutional framework (pp.262, 282). But Southern underrates the evidence of secondary English glosses on the *Liber pauperum* and of other learned writings in which Vacarius's views are cited: thus, the glosses on Gratian in Cambridge, Gonville and Caius MS 676 (see this article, p.203 n.247 and C. Duggan, 'The reception of canon law in England ...', *Proceedings Boston* [MIC, Subsidia 1; Vatican City 1965] 359–90, at 376 n.111), also in: *id.*, Canon Law in Medieval England (London 1982), no. XI, with Addenda et Corrigenda p. 7f.; the glosses added to Bulgarus, *De regulis iuris* in B.L. MS Royal 11.B.xv from Rochester (ed. Beckhaus pp. v, 54, 56; de Zulueta 299f.); the *quaestio* in B.L. MS Addit. 24659, fol. 2r on *actiones negatoriae*; the marginal notes on a set of *quaestiones* in Oxford, Oriel College MS 53 from Northampton, fol. 355r; glosses on the *Ordo Olim edebatur* in Paris B.N. lat. 3922A (Bethmann-Hollweg, *Geschichte* VI 68 n.35); a set of civil law definitions by a canonist in B.L. MS Harley 4967, fol. 3r; the fragment of a commentary on the *Digestum vetus* in Vienna MS 2436, fol. 1r/v, and a *Summa de dilatoriis* in Cambridge, Trinity College B.i.29 (bibliographical references in my paper 'Dat Galienus opes et sanctio Justiniana', reprinted in *The history of ideas and doctrines of canon law in the Middle Ages* [London 1980] No. X, 2 ed. Ashgate 1992. p.241f. and 'Retractationes' p.19). In all these writings, terminology such as 'huic solutioni obuiat magister in notis suis' (gl. Vac. 1.8, de Zulueta p. 18 n.32), 'Vac. aliter soluit in N (ota) sua "Sed neque scripta"' (ibid., cf. *Lib. paup.* C.8.52[53]2, v. *rationem*, de Zulueta p. 15); 'set mag. Va. soluit sic et melius' (Oriel MS cit.); 'solutio dominorum bononiensium ...; magister sic soluit' (gl. Vac. 2.4, de Zulueta p.36 n.8) clearly indicate formal lecturing, formal glosses ('notae') and formal discussion of the opinions of Bolognese masters. These are not the unstructured, leisurely observations of a country pastor.

The long-lost Wenck manuscript of the *Liber pauperum* with its important glosses was rediscovered in Leningrad by P. Stein, see his 'Vacarius and the civil law', *Church and government in the Middle Ages: Essays presented to C.R. Cheney* (Cambridge 1976) 119–37, at 120f. This is one of the five MSS from Wenck's library, sold to St. Petersburg in 1830 after his death, see A. Vetulani, 'Les oeuvres d'Accurse dans les bibliothèques de Leningrad', *Atti del Convegno di Studi Accursiani* (Milan 1968) III 1308. It is now at the University Library, MS lat. 4. For smaller fragments recovered from bindings etc. see the bibliographical note in Southern's article, p.272 n.3. — Legendre's suggestion of more Vacarian material in Oxford, Magdalen College 258 ('Miscellanea Britannica', *Traditio* 15 [1969] 491 n.2) was abandoned in his analysis of the MS, 'Recherches sur les commentaires pré-accursiens', TRG 33 (1965) 353–429.

Future research should not neglect the generally overlooked paper by A. Stölzel, 'Glossenapparat des Vacarius Pragensis ...', *Festschrift für Heinrich Brunner* (Berlin

1914) 1–35, as H. Kantorowicz had already pointed out in his review of de Zulueta's edition, ZRG Rom. Abt. 49 (1929) 63–73, at 66.

I'm not able to verify 'a note s.xii [quoting Vacarius] in a copy of Dig. from Reading' which in Eleanor Rathbone's papers is mentioned without further details; nor can I verify the suggestion that Bracton may have used a glossed copy of the *Liber pauperum*, which H. Kantorowicz (again, according to E.R.'s notes) advanced in a seminar held at Oxford, 1937.

For the biography of Vacarius cf. now also my article, The Origins of Legal Science in England in the Twelfth Century: Lincoln, Oxford and the Career of Vacarius. In: *M. Brett/K.G. Cushing* (ed.), Readers, Texts and Compilers in the Earlier Middle Ages. Studies in Medieval Canon Law in Honour of Linda Fowler-Magerl (Farnham 2009) 165–182. (P.L.)

p.171 n.40: The commentary on the Institutes, beg. 'Sacrosancte ac saluberrime euangelice discipline', will be edited by P. Stein for the Selden Society.

p.171 n.41: The *De assumpto homine* was edited by N.M. Haring in *Mediaeval Studies* 21 (1959) 147–75.

p.171 n.42: For a calendar of documents bearing on the career of Vacarius and the papal commissions he received, see Southern's article, pp.282–85; the fragment from Tanner MS 8 p.595b (not 895b) is printed in Holtzmann, 'Coll. Tanner' p. 105. See also G.V. Scammel, *Hugh du Puiset, bishop of Durham* (Cambridge 1956) 84 for a case in which Vacarius and the bishop sat as arbitrators in a suit involving the canons of Bridlington.

p.173 n.49: For Vacarius's low opinion of Gratian see also the gloss of the Gonville and Caius MS 676, fol. 142vb quoted by Stein, art. cit. p.135: 'hanc opinionem Gratiani deridet Vacarius'. Another English critic of Gratian was Ralph Niger: '[decreta Gratiani] in quibus dimidiata iura male contrectabantur' (*Moralia regum* c.19, ed. B. Smalley in Kantorowicz and Smalley, 'An English theologian's view of Roman law ...', *Medieval and Renaissance Studies* 1 [1941] 252).

p.173 n.52 read: ... the canonist and canon prebendary (not: chancellor) of Chartres.

p.173 Roger the Norman: See further J.W. Baldwin, 'A debate at Paris over Thomas Becket', SG 11 (1967) 121–32; J. Ramackers, *PU Frankreich* 2 (1937) 407–8 No.323; JL 17646, ed. S. Chodorow, *Decretales ineditae* 36–38 No.20.

p.175: For bibliography on the *Ordines* here mentioned see K.W. Nörr, 'Die Literatur zum gemeinen Zivilprozess', in Coing's *Handbuch der Quellen und Literatur* ... I (Munich 1973) 388. The *Ordo Bambergensis* had better be called by its incipit, *Ordo Quia iudiciorum quedam* than by the library housing one of its three manuscripts. For the third, in Cambridge, Trinity College B.i.29, see P. Weimar, 'Tractatus de violento possessore ...', *Ius Commune* 1 (1967) 65. The so-called *Ulpianus de edendo* should be cited as *Ordo Quoniam ea que in ciuilibus.*

William of Longchamp, *Practica legum et decretorum*, beg. 'Iuris scientia res quidem sanctissima est': The part which Caillemer missed in his edition was completed from fol. 55va of the MS (Paris lat. 3454) and some readings were corrected by G. Fransen and P. Legendre in RHD 44 (1966) 115–18; see also the description of the Paris MS by Fransen in ZRG Kan. Abt. 55 (1969) 438–39.

p.176 and n.67: Cheney, *Bishops' Chanceries* 126 questions the Oxford origin of the Baltimore *Ordo* and formulary; still, the evidence for Oxford is rather strong, see J. Sayers, *Papal judges delegate in the province of Canterbury 1198–1254* (Oxford 1971) 48f. — For two English *Summae quaestionum* on procedural matters see below to p.201.

p.177: This master Rolandus is not to be identified with Rolandus Bandinelli; see R. Weigand, *Die bedingte Eheschliessung im kanonischen Recht* (Munich 1963) 116–26; 'Quaestiones aus der Schule des Rolandus und Metellus', AKKR 138 (1969) 82–94; and especially 'Magister Rolandus und Papst Alexander III.', AKKR 149 (1980) 3–44; G. Fransen, 'La structure des 'quaestiones disputatae ...', *Traditio* 23 (1967) 519–20.

p.178 *Summa De multiplici.* Closely related, in part identical, is the *Summa De iure naturali* discovered by P. Legendre, 'Miscellanea Britannica', *Traditio* 15 (1959) 494, in Durham MS Cosin V.iii.3, fols. 30ra-70vb; see K.W. Nörr, 'Die Summen "De iure naturali" und "De multiplici iuris diuisione",' ZRG Kan. Abt. 48 (1962) 138–63. — The author of *De multiplici* was familiar with the English sokage ('eorum qui socum gerunt') as Msgr. D. Shanahan has kindly pointed out to me (Lambeth MS 139, fol. 152rb). The influence of Stephen of Tournai is also seen in the definitions of *canon, decretum*, and *decretalis epistola* (from Stephen's preface, pp.2–3, ed. Schulte) given by the small collection of definitions (B.L. MS Harley 4967) mentioned above in the note on Vacarius.

p.178 n.79 French origin of the *Summa Quoniam status* (Paris lat. 16538): See e.g. the full quotation (fol. 11va/b) of a decretal of Alexander III to Bishop Boso of Châlons (†1162) as mentioned by W. Holtzmann, 'Über die vatikanische Handschrift der "Collectio Brugensis",' *Collectanea Vaticana in honorem A.M. Card. Albareda* (Studie e Testi 219–20; Vatican City 1962) I 405, on *Brug.* 45.9.

p.179: The Chester Beatty MS is now at Baltimore, Walters Art Gallery, W.777. See 'Retractatio' to No. VII above, p.180 n.94.

p.180 Bartholomew of Exeter's *Poenitentiale*: Add Uppsala, MS C.60, fols. 34r-71r.

p.181 *Summa De iure canonico tractaturus*: R. Weigand, 'Bemerkungen über die Schriften und Lehren des Magister Honorius', *Proceedings Salamanca* (MIC, Subsidia 6; Vatican City 1980) 195–212, has shown this to be probably a work of the master discussed in ch. VI below.

p.182 Gerard Pucelle: See C. Lefebvre s.v. Pucelle, DDC 7 (1965, *ex* 1959) 402–4.

p.183: John of Salisbury addressing Gerard as 'in utroque iure peritum', *ep.* 185, PL 199.195C (=ep. 184, ed. Millor and Brooke II 220), has been interpreted by G. Miczka, 'Utrumque ius—eine Erfindung der Kanonisten?', ZRG Kan. Abt. 57 (1971) 127–49, at p.144f., as meaning rather, 'in divine and human law'.

p.184–187 on the school of Cologne: The edition of the *Summa Elegantius* by G. Fransen, with the collaboration of the present writer, is now finished (MIC, Corpus Glossatorum 1 I–IV; Vatican City 1969, 1978, 1986, 1990). One of its sources was pointed out long ago by G. Ott, 'Die Rhetorica ecclesiastica (SB Akad. Vienna 125.8; 1892) 40–41. Dr. Linda Fowler-Magerl called this generally overlooked relationship to the editors' attention. Dr. Fowler has also established that the *Rhetorica* probably originated in Hildesheim c. 1161; her findings were briefly communicated by Dr. W. Stelzer in a paper read at the Sixth Medieval Canon Law Congress in Berkeley (1980). Published in: L. Fowler-Magerl, *Ordo iudiciorum vel ordo iudiciarius* (Ius commune. Sonderhefte 19, Frankfurt/M. 1984) 45–56.

The commentary in Haenel's MS on the *De regulis iuris* (p.184 n.120) was written by Bertram of Metz, see my paper in *Traditio* 13 (1957) 501–05, and now the edition, from three MSS, by S. Caprioli, *Bertrandus Metensis de regulis iuris* (Perugia 1981). He is the same as the Master Bertoldus mentioned p.188. The suggestion by P. Gerbenzon, 'Bertram of Metz the author of the Summa "Elegantius in iure diuino" (Summa Coloniensis)?', *Traditio* 21 (1965) 510–11 needs further study.

For the *Summa Antiquitate et tempore* see now my paper, 'Gratian and Plato', republished in *The history of ideas and doctrines of canon law* (London (1980 2 ed. Ashgate 1992) as No. XI, at pp.95–98, on the author's interpretation of the *Timaeus*. The well-read author also quoted verses of the poet Hugo Primas (the passage, on D.18 c.8, was completely misunderstood by Singer, 'Beiträge II' 84 n.284, as a reference to an Archbishop Hugo of Reims); on the other hand, the author was able to remark on D.1 c.1 that the *regia strata*, i.e. the King's Highway (in England) is not an *ager alienus* (Msgr. D. Shanahan pointed this out to me). Of his three references to Cresconius (see p.186 at n.134), one was repeated by the *Distinctionés Monacenses* D.18 c.3, the other is paralleled by *Summa Elegantius* 2.111 (ed. Fransen I 94).

Another MS of the *Summa Quoniam omissis* was discovered in Gent, University MS 1429, fols. 43va-72rb (with an appendix, 72vb-73ra), by Dr. Dirk Van den Auweele; see 'Annual Report', BMCL 9 (1979) xii, and his paper, 'Le codex Gandavensis 1429: un Parcensis précieux', RTAM 49 (1982) 205–21, at 217–19.

Finally, a collection of exercises in pleading from Liège should be added to the writings from the circle of Cologne, see H. Silvestre, 'Dix plaidoiries inédites du XIIe siècle', *Traditio* 10 (1954) 373–97, at 386 n.10.

For the school of Cologne see now my survey: P. Landu, Die Kölner Kanonistik des 12. Jahrunderts. Ein Höhepunkt der europäischen Rechtswissenschaft (Kölner Rechtsgeschichtliche Vorträge, H.1), Badenweiler 2008. This school of canon law existed at least from 1165 to 1190. The author of the Summa 'Antiquitate et tempore' was probably *Geoffrey (Gottfried)* of St. Andrew in Cologne – cf. P. Landau, Die Dekretsumme Fecit Moyses Fecit Moyses tabernaculum – ein weiteres Werk der Kölner Kanonistik, ZRG kan. Abt. 96 (2010) 602–608. (P.L.)

p.185 n.129: There is a new edition of Godefroy de Saint-Victor, *Fons philosophiae* by P. Michaud-Quantin (Analecta mediaevalia Namurcensia 8; Louvain-Lille 1958).

p.186 *Summa Magister Gratianus in hoc opere*: T.P. McLaughlin in his edition, *The Summa Parisiensis on the Decretum Gratiani* (Toronto 1952), dates the work ten years earlier, about 1160 (Introd. pp.xxxi-iii); see also C. Lefebvre, DDC 6 (1957) 1230f. s.v. 'Parisiensis (Summa)'. But such an early date is contradicted by the author's quoting from Placentinus's *Summa Codicis* 4.19 (ed. Mogunt. 1536 p. 149; see G. Fransen, 'Colligite fragmenta', SG 13 [1967] 106–7) and by the influence of Stephen of Tournai, which McLaughlin p.xxviii-ix wrongly denies (the evidence cannot be discussed here). The *Summa* was known to the author of *Elegantius in iure diuino*; it should thus be dated slightly before 1170, in the late 'sixties.

p.186 Egidius: See also A. Rota, 'Il decretista Egidius e la sua concezione del diritto naturale', SG 2 (1954) 211–49, published without the author's being aware of the present paper. Rota 244 n.28 misreads the reference to 'M.G.' (here 187 n.136) as M. S(imon de Bisignano).

p.187 n.137 *Summa* of Sicardus: The Codex Sessorianus (Rome, Bibl. Naz. 1369) contains more than the photostats then at our disposal showed: fols. 78ra-86vb, 88ra-117vb, see A. Petrucci et al., 'Censimento dei codici dei secoli xi-xiii', *Studi medievali*[3] 9 (1968) 1167–68; actually pr.-D.63, D.48 (*sic*)-C.30.

p.187 Godfrey de Luci *vs.* Battle Abbey: Several of the points at issue were discussed by J.W. Gray, 'The *ius praesentandi* in England from the Constitutions of Clarendon to Bracton,' EHR 67 (1952) 481–509, at 484f.

p.187: A Magister Ivo of Cornwall, canon of Exeter, appeared in this suit for Godfrey of Luci. see *Chronicon monasterii de Bello* (cited supra 165 n.7) 174.

p.189: Further references to Gerard's teaching are found in glosses on the *Summa Elegantius* 2.138 ('mag. Geherardus' in the Vienna MS, fol. 32va); in the first redaction of the *Summa* of Sicardus (MS Ambros. M 64 sup. as communicated by Professor P.J. Kessler); in the *Distinctiones Monacenses* on D. 28 c.17 ('magr. Gerhardus'); in the *Summa Elnonensis* of Valenciennes MS 193 ('M. Ge.' repeatedly, see G. Fransen, 'Colligite fragmenta', SG 13 [1967] 83–108, at 92–96); and may be intended by the initial G. in glosses of the French school in Berlin MS lat. qu. 193 of Stephen of Tournai, published by Thaner, art. cit. p.169 n.29 above, at pp. 225, 226 (cf. *Repertorium* 41 n.1), or by the marginal attribution to 'M(agister) G.' of the prologue 'Videndum que materia que intentio' in the same MS (*Repert.* 184). But here we reach the borderline of mere conjecture. On the other hand, the late Friedrich Heyer took notes from glosses on Johannes Faventinus's *Summa* quoting G. and once 'Magister Ger.', in Münster MS 603 [130]; the Heyer papers are now at Berkeley, but the Münster MS was lost in the second World War.

p.189: For Honorius add the notice by A.B. Emden, *A biographical register of the University of Oxford to A.D. 1500* (3 vols., Oxford 1957–59) II 956–57 s.v.

p.191 Honorius as *officialis* (of Geoffrey of York): Alanus in his gloss on 1 Comp. 3.7.1 v. *officialium* stated: 'Officiales dicuntur in Anglia quibus episcopus uices suas committit' (Munich lat. 3879, fol. 41vb), which Tancred ad loc. changed to 'Officiales dicuntur in Francia ... committit. ala.' adding another definition of his own; see F. Gillmann, 'Romanus pontifex iura omnia in scrinio pectoris censetur habere', AKKR 106 (1926) 159n.

p.191 Simon of Apulia: See also Emden, *Register Univ. Oxford III* 2144–45 s.v. Apulia.

pp.192–194: For the papal letters referred to on these law suits see the material calendared by V. Pfaff, 'Der Vorgänger: Das Wirken Coelestins III. in der Sicht von Innozenz III.' ZRG Kan. Abt. 60 (1974) 121–67, at 134 n.39 and 165; and especially C.R. Cheney and M.G. Cheney, *The letters of Pope Innocent III (1198–1216) concerning England and Wales*, Nos. 111 (Po. 678, not mentioned in our paper), *249*, *250*, *270*, *271*, 272–73, 283, *284*, 303–05, 330, 365, 382, 415–16, *417*, *418*, 419, *420*, 421, 699. (Numbers here printed in italics designate letters that are mentioned only in others and not listed in Potthast.) — The unnamed archdeacon of Richmond who during a visitation descended on a church belonging to Bridlington Priory with ninety-seven horses, twenty-one hounds, and three falcons, and thereby prompted the letter of Innocent III 'Gravem nec silentio transeundam', printed in W. Dugdale, *Monasticon Anglicanum: A history of the abbies and other monasteries...*, 6 vols. in 8 (London 1846), 6.1 No. XIII p. 288. calendared as no. 1101 (if it is genuine), does not seem to have been Master Honorius.

The letter of Innocent III 'Gravem nec silentes transeundam' was printed in: W. Dugdale, Monasticon Anglicanum: A history of the abbies and other monasteries, vol. 6.1 (London 1846) 298 (no. XVII). (S.K.)

p.194: Honorius paid his debt to the exchequer by Michaelmas 1210 (*Pipe Roll 12 John*, p. 153).

p.195: On *dispensatio cum homicida*, the *Summa Omnis qui iuste*, D.50 c.4 (Rouen MS 743, fol. 23rb) also provides a strong parallel to Honorius's *Sum. quaest.* and to the *Summa De iure canonico tractaturus* (for authorship see the note to p.181 above).

The decretal *Presbyterum* JL 13912 here invoked by Honorius actually was a much earlier letter: Leo IX to Archbishop Eadsige, see S. Kuttner as cited above to p.168f.

p.196: For Honorius and Huguccio see below to p.231.

p.199: On these different types of *quaestiones* see also A. Padoa Schioppa, 'Le Questiones super Codice di Pillio ...', *Studia et docum. hist. et iuris* 39 (1973) 239–80, at 256–61.

p.200 Evrard of Ypres: Add N.M. Haring, 'A Latin dialogue on the doctrine of Gilbert of Poitiers', *Mediaeval Studies* 15 (1953) 243–89; 'The Cistercian Everard of Ypres and his appraisal of the conflict between St. Bernard and Gilbert of Poitiers', ibid. 17 (1955) 143–72.

p.200 *Quaestiones decretales* delivered in the classroom: See also Barcelona, Archives MS S.Cugat 55, fols. 54v-57v, beg. 'Queritur quare uotum sollempne ...', which bears the rubric *Disputationes*, see G. Fransen, 'Manuscrits canoniques ... en Espagne II', RHE 49 (1954) 154f., and the detailed analysis by J.A. Brundage, 'Some canonistic quaestiones in Barcelona', *Manuscripta* 15 (1971) 67–76.

p.201 *Summa quaestionum* of Munich MS lat. 16083 (cancel *Repertorium* 430): The first five *quaestiones* are also in Cues MS 226, fol. 4r/v, in a different order, see my note in *Traditio* 13 (1957) 508.

p.201 n.228: The fragmentary treatise on procedure in Paris lat. 3934A, fol. 103ra/va is Placentinus, *Sum. Inst.* 4.10–17, see P. Legendre, 'Fragment d'un manuscrit perdu ...', RHD 34 [33] (1956) 436–47.

This list of *quaestiones decretales* could be expanded, see e.g. the Barcelona MS just cited, the two procedural *Summae quaestionum* of English origin in the Bodleian MS Selden supr. 87, fols. 140r-148v, 150v-158ra which I briefly mentioned as a future editorial project in 'Zur Entstehungsgeschichte der Summa de casibus ...', ZRG Kan. Abt. 39 (1953) 422 n.18; or Bamberg MS Can. 17, fols. 182rb-183rb, beg. 'Vtrum liceat iuramentis paganorum', in part the same as Arras 271, fol. 187v, beg. 'Interrogatus quis an super decimarum ...'

p.202 n.234: This treatise from Tancred's school exists also in Montecassino MS 136, p.234; see my 'Notes on manuscripts', *Traditio* 17 (1961) 51, and see R.M. Fraher, 'Tancred's "Summa de criminibus",' BMCL 9 (1979) 23–35 on the whole cluster of texts in the Casanatense MS; with an edition of the *summula de criminibus*, which has six *quaestiones*.

pp.202–05: More material of glosses from the Gonville and Caius MS 676 was discussed by C. Duggan, 'The reception of canon law in England ...', cited above to pp.171–73. Biographical notices on the masters discussed in the present chapter are given in Emden, *Register Univ. Oxford* (cited above to pp.189ff.) I 560 s.v. de l'Aigle, 571 s.v. Derby, II 817 s.v. Gregory, 1037 s.v. Kent, III 1704 s.v. Siwelle, 1923 s.v. Tynemouth.

p.203 Glosses of Simon of Southwell to an abbreviation of Peter of Poitiers' sentences in Lambeth MS 142: E.R. discussed these (cf. her remark in n.242) much later in 'Peter of Corbeil in an English setting', *Medieval learning and literature* (the Festschrift for R.W. Hunt cited to pp.171–73 above) 287–306. For the spelling and interpretation of the toponym see the note to p.212 below.

p.203: Alanus's first work in Bologna, his apparatus on the Decretum, in the original version, is of a much earlier date, about 1192, see A.M. Stickler and further bibliography as cited above, 'Retractationes' to 'Bernardus Compostellanus Antiquus' (No. VII of this volume) p.106.

p.203: J.C. Russell has suggested that Nicholas de Aquila was the same as Nicholas of Guildford, one of 'The patrons of "The Owl and the Nightingale",' *Philological Quarterly* 48 (1969) 178-85.

p.203 n.247 'consuetudo populi in contrarium nitentis': For this phrase cf. Cod. 1.14.5.

p.204 Rolandus as master and pope: The commonly accepted identity of Rolandus Bandinelli (Alexander III) with the Bolognese master who wrote the Sentences and the *Stroma* can probably no longer be maintained: see J.T. Noonan, 'Who was Rolandus?,' *Law, Church and Society*, edd. K. Pennington and R. Somerville (Philadelphia 1977) 21-48, and R. Weigand, 'Magister Rolandus und Papst Alexander III.', AKKR 149 (1980) 3-44. It is, however, a strange misunderstanding when Noonan charges, pp.29-32, that E.R. and I took the passage 'Alexander iii. ibi non ut papa set ut magister distinxit' (printed in the appendix of this paper from fol. 178vb of the Caius glosses and referred to at p.204 n.249) as evidence for the pope's *earlier activities in the schools* — as if we had not been able to see that 'ibi' in this gloss refers to the decretal *Consuluit* cited in the immediately preceding *contrarium*, and that it simply means 'Alexander in *Consuluit* made his distinction not (officially) as pope but (speaking privately) like any magister'. A closer reading of our footnote 249 would have shown that it cites fol. 178vb and fol. 187va(i) for references to Alexander 'as pope', and fol. 187va(ii-iv) as 'Rolandus'.

pp.205-07: The *Quaestiones* of the Royal MS have been discussed at length by J.A. Brundage, 'The crusade of Richard I: Two canonical *quaestiones*', *Speculum* 38 (1963) 443-48, with the two texts, qq. 38 and 39, printed pp.448-52 (a number of readings and source references stand in need of correction); see also 'A twelfth century Oxford disputation concerning the privileges of the Knights Hospitallers', *Mediaeval Studies* 24 (1962) 153-60 (text of q.1 printed pp. 158-60), and 'The treatment of marriage in the *Quaestiones Londinenses*', *Manuscripta* 19 (1975) 86-97. For a list of the masters represented and the *quaestiones* which bear their sigla see *Speculum* 38.447 n.13 (for Simon of Derby add q.6, 's̄. de dere').

p.206 Master John of Kent: C.R, Cheney, *Hubert Walter* (London 1967) 166 doubts the identity with the later chancellor of St. Paul's, London; but the latter is styled *magister* in Gibbs, *Early Charters* ... No.58 (cited 206 n.283), and see D.E. Greenway, *Fasti* ... (cited above to p.169) 26, 49; Emden, *Register Univ. Oxford* II 817.

Master Gregory: By the printer's oversight the footnote n.44 with the appropriate references to fols. 192vb and 194ra dropped out; cf. Brundage, *Speculum* 38.447 n.13 No.6. For possible identifications see Emden, *Register Univ. Oxford* II 320.

p.206 n.287 Glosses of Master Jo. on the *Appendix Conc. Lat.*: On John of Tynemouth as an influential glossator of English decretal collections see now P. Landau, 'Studien zur Appendix und den Glossen in frühen systematischen Dekretalensammlungen,' BMCL 9 (1979) 1-21, at 19-21; 'Die Glossen der Collectio Cheltenhamensis', BMCL 11 (1981) 9-27, at 23f.; and my 'Anhang', ibid. 27-28.

For the Collectio Cheltenhamensis see now G. Drossbach, Die Collectio Cheltenhamensis: Eine englische Decretalensammlung (MIC, Ser. B, Vol. 10, Città del Vaticano 2014).

p.208 Vacarius at Northampton *causa studendi*: R.W. Southern reads this as a reference only to his theological studies at a mature age (p.261 of his article cited to pp.171-73 above) and doubts that Vacarius taught there. It is, however, worth noting and perhaps more than a coincidence that the manuscript from St. Andrew's, Northampton here mentioned quotes 'mag. Va.' in a marginal entry (see the notes to pp.171-73).

p.209 n.300 Master Warin: See also the letter 'magistri Warini de Hubaldeston' (Hibaldstow, Lincs.?), No.8 p.16f. in C.R. Cheney, 'Harrold Priory: A twelfth century dispute', *Bedfordshire Historical Record Society* 32 (1952) 1–26.

p.209: As mentioned above, Southern rejects the tradition of Vacarius's teaching at Oxford. — For Robert Blund as canon and prebendary of Lincoln 1185–86 see Emden, *Register Univ. Oxford* I 207.

p.210 n.305 Gerald of Wales: See now R.W. Hunt, 'The preface to the *Speculum ecclesie* of Giraldus Cambrensis', *Viator* 8 (1977) 189–213, text reestablished at p.205 lin. 27–28: '... sed saltum quem uos fecistis a *Cum animaduerterem* ad *Imperatoriam maiestatem*,' and comments pp. 194, 197. Cf. Ralph of Beauvais as quoted by Gerald, *Gemma ecclesiastica* 2.37 (*Opp.* II 349).

p.210 n.306 Hubert Walter's Latin: C.R. Cheney, 'Hubert Walter and Bologna' (cited above to p.170) 83f. observes that the passage of the *Gemma ecclesiastica* on an illiterate archbishop speaking in poor Latin before Alexander III (*Opp.* II 344f.) cannot refer to Hubert. There remain, however, the three amusing stories Giraldus Cambrensis told Pope Innocent III of Hubert Walter's blunders in speaking at a synod, at a meeting with lawyers in Oxford, and in 'correcting' the Latin of King Richard I: *Libellus inuectionum* 1.5 (*Opp.* III 29–30; cf. III 254).

p.210 Senatus of Worcester: See further P. Delhaye, 'Deux textes de Senatus de Worcester sur la pénitence', *Recherches de théol. anc. et médiév.* 19 (1952) 203–24, and E. Rathbone, 'Roman law in the Anglo-Norman realm', SG 11 (1967) 265–66, with a fuller text of the first letter, pp.270–71.

p.210: The material on Gerald's suit with Canterbury is assembled in E.C. Davies, *Episcopal acts and cognate documents relating to Welsh dioceses 1066–1272* (Cardiff 1946) I, D.277–378 (pp.300–29) and discussed ibid. 208–32; see also the review by C.R. Cheney, EHR 64 (1949) 101.

p.211: For John of Tynemouth's career see also Emden, *Register Univ. Oxford* III 1923; F.A. Cazel, 'Norman and Wessex charters of the Roumare family', *A medieval miscellany for Doris M. Stenton* (Pipe Roll Society n.s. 36; London 1960) 83f. and 88; Historical MSS Commission, *Calendar of the Manuscripts of the Dean and Chapter of Wells* 1 (London 1907) 54–55, 489.

p.212 Simon of Southwell: Spellings of the toponym vary greatly: e.g. Sudwella, Sutwele, Siwelle, Suelle, Suū (see p.203 n.242), Suwelle (Register of Innocent III 1.404 [Po. 395] ed. Hageneder-Haidacher I p.603). It was understood by earlier historians and in this paper as referring to Southwell in Nottinghamshire, but (as Lady Stenton first pointed out to us) Sywell, Northamptonshire seems to be preferable; the form 'Simon of Sywell' is now used by C.R. Cheney, *Hubert Walter* pp.164, 168; Cheney and Cheney, *Letters of Pope Innocent III concerning England* ... No.55 (=Po. 395); E.R. in the paper cited to p.203 above, at pp.288, 297. Emden, *Register Univ. Oxford III* 1704 s.v. Siwelle leaves the alternative open.

p.214: The *Summae Prima primi* and *Quamuis leges seculares* are being edited by R. Benson and J. Van Engen for the *Monumenta iuris canonici*. The edition was not finished. (P.L.)

Editions of the Summa 'Prima primi' and the 'Summa Quamvis leges seculares' were not published until now. (P.L.)

p.214 n.342: The reading in *Summa Quamuis* ('Prima primi uxor Ade post primi hominis creationem') is not the better one: Walter Map's text has '... post primam ... creationem' like the other *Summa.* This passage is part of the section entitled 'Dissuasio Valerii ad Ruffinum ne uxorem ducat', *De nugis cur.* 4.3-5 (pp.153–58 ed. James), actually an earlier piece of Map's which he incorporated here (see p. 158 lin. 7–10). For the medieval commentaries on the *Dissuasio Valerii* (often inscribed as a work of St. Jerome; PL 30.262-69 among the *spuria*) see M.R. James's introduction to W. Map, pp.xxx-xxxviii; R.J. Dean, 'Unnoticed commentaries on the "Dissuasio Valerii",' *Medieval and Renaiss. Studies* 2 (1950) 128–50.

p.214: The *magister Willehelmus* of the Prologue 'Missurus in mundum' did not belong to one of the western schools, but was the Bolognese canonist Willielmus Vasco, on whom see above, 'Retractatio' to p.108 of No. VII in this volume.

pp.215–226: Some additional material on Ricardus Anglicus in S. Kuttner s.v., DDC 7 (1965, *ex* 1960) 676–81, and NCE 12.481-82 s.v.

p.215 St. Richard de Wych: see E.F. Jacob, 'St. Richard of Chichester', JEH 7 (1956) 174–88. For Richard Poore, especially his return to Paris during the interdict and six times judge delegate between 1209 and 1213, 'docens Parisius sacram paginam' (Po. 4700, 10 April 1213), see J.W. Baldwin, *Masters, princes and merchants* (Princeton 1970) I 31, II 21 nn.149, 150.

Adagonista (Ricardus): perhaps Brocardista (ex 'Antagonista') – cf. *Jo. Balens*, Scriptorum illustrium majoris Britanniae Catalogus (Basileae 1551) II, 152, citing ex Philippo Vuolphio (?). (S.K.)

pp.216 R. de Lacy and the fragment in Karlsruhe: While *Traditio* vol. 7, including this paper, was in the press, the late E.M. Meijers showed in a brief note, 'Ricardus Anglicus et R. de Lacy', TRG 20 (1952) 89–90, that the author of the gloss reported in the Karlsruhe fragment was Robert de Lacy, active as *professor iuris civilis* and *officialis* of the bishop of Winchester in the 1280s, and that he should not have been taken to be our Ricardus Anglicus. (Meijers could not be aware that the identification made in *Repertorium* 223 had been withdrawn in the present article; but this might have deserved an editorial note in the posthumous reprint, *Études d'histoire du droit III* [Leiden 1959] 278–79.)

p.217: A fourth MS of the *Summa brevis*, with the inscription, 'Hic est introitus magistri Ricardi peritissimi in iure diuino et humano seu canonico' was found by M. Boháček in Olomouc, State Archives C.O.209 (formerly Cathedral Chapter 209), fols. 267r-268v, 270r-271v; see my 'Interim checklist of manuscripts (III)', *Traditio* 13 (1965) 470 and Boháček, 'Le opere delle scuole medievali di diritto del Capitolo di Olomouc', SG 8 (1962) 307–421, at 353f. = p.36 of the original published [in Czech] in the *Rozpravy Československe Akademie věd*, Social Sciences 70 [1960] no.7).

p.217 lines 16–17: read 'nearly all of Gratian's original *quaestiones* ...'

p.217, n. 363: The verses occur also at the end of Richard's *Distinctiones* in the Bodleian MS Selden supr. 87, fol. 181v.

p.219 William de Monte: See also his work on penance, discussed by H. MacKinnon, 'William de Montibus: a medieval teacher', *Essays in medieval history presented to Bertie Wilkinson* (Toronto 1969) 32–45.

p.220 n. 380: The same method is used in the *Ordo Iudicandi formam in utroque* mentioned p.176 n. 68.

p.220 n. 381: Ascelinus is also cited in a fragment of glosses on Gratian, B.L. MS Addit. 34391, fols. 39–40: '... dominum Acelinum', together with 'mag. Galt.', see P. Legendre, 'Miscellanea Britannica', *Traditio* 15 (1959) 491–97, at 493.

p.223 *Notabilia* on Gratian in the Zwettl MS: An argument against our tentative attribution was pointed out to me in a letter by G. Fransen (1959): These *Notabilia* lack Gratian's part III, while Richard's catalogue of writings speaks of 'singula argumenta ... usque ad ultimum capitulum'. Other *Notabilia* beginning with Prov. 30.33 (or Gregory's quotation of it, D.4 c.6) are extant in Utrecht, Univ. 3.B.2, fol.? (communication from Professor Gerbenzon); Paris, B.N. lat. 4288, fols. 146v-152v. Later material with the same incipit in Bruges, Grand Séminaire 45–144, fols. 191rb-197va (saec. xiv; communication from Professor Fransen), and Colmar, Bibl. de la Ville 509, fols. 85v-? (saec. xv; M. Bertram, 'Some additions ...', BMCL 4 [1974] 11).

p.225: A passage in the *Quaestiones* of Nicholas de Aquila reported in the Royal MS discussed above (pp.205ff.) reads, '... renuntiari potest secundum magistrum ricc.^{ar} et iudicium per has auctoritates ...' (fol. 193rb) and thus may indicate English academic connections of Richard de Mores before or after his Bolognese years.

On a passage in the Questiones of Nicholas de Aquila: 'renuntiari potest secundum magistrum ricc. et iudicium per has auctoritates' – cf. *C.E. Lewis*, Ricardus Anglicus: A "familiaris" of archbishop Hubert Walter, Traditio 22 (1966) 469–471 (=Bulletin 1966), at p. 471 n. 15, referring to a communication by letter of S. K. on this quotation. (S.K.)

For Richard's judicial activities see J. Sayers, *Papal judges delegate* (cited above to p.176) 414–18 and the calendar of his cases, 296–301.

p.225 n. 417: The obit for 'magister Ricardus anglicus' in Trombelli's list is entered under 15 August (xviii. kal. Sept.).

p.226 and nn. 421, 422 English antecedents of the *compilatio Alani*: see also S. Kuttner, 'The collection of Alanus: A concordance of its two recensions', *Rivista di storia del dir. ital.* 26 (1953) 37–53, at 52f., and W. Holtzmann, 'Die Sammlung Tanner', *Festschrift ... Göttingen* (cited above to p.168) 97 n.30.

pp.226–30 Use of the *Collectio Tanner* in the English schools: More material from the glosses of Gonville and Caius MS 676 has been collected by C. Duggan, 'The reception of canon law ...', *Proceedings Boston* (cited above to pp.171–73) 376f. and 388–90. One may add the gloss on C.27 q.2 c.18: 'hic deest palea, que tamen est in ex. de sponsis aliis adherentibus, Lex diuine', quoted by W. Ullmann, 'The paleae in Cambridge manuscripts of the Decretum', SG 1 (1953) 161–216, at 212; this can be identified as *Tann.* 7.5.14. One should further add the decretal references in an unpublished set of *Brocarda*, beg. 'Leges uel decretales epistole, licet ad certas personas directe, generalium constitucionum habent effectum', at the end of a fragment from the *Digestum novum*, four bifolia in Durham Cathedral, Dean and Chapter Muniments, 'Endpapers and Bindings' No. 30 (N.R. Ker, *Medieval manuscripts in British libraries* II [Oxford 1977] p.508: 'legal dicta' fols. 3v-6r). See e.g. 'jn extra, de taciturnitatibus que literas inpetr(atas uiribus carere efficiunt) ex parte et c. cum ordinem c. ueniens et multis aliis' (fol. 3va) = *Tann.* 6.2.3, 5, 7); 'jn extra, de sententiis retractandis c.ii. (fol. 3vb) = *Tann.* 4.5.2. (Photostats had been provided by Mr. Ker before his death.)

p.231: The uncertain siglum 'h'. (or $\bar{h}, \tilde{n}$.) used for an author cited by Honorius in *Sum. quaest.* 2.1 might refer to an early gloss of Huguccio—i.e. prior to his *Summa*—as Weigand, 'Bemerkungen über ... Honorius', *Proceedings Salamanca* (cited above to p.181) 202–4 suggests.

p.232 Honorius 2.8: The text in the first line should read: 'Premisimus de continentia que promotioni clericorum (... est necessaria)'.

p.236: The opinion of Robert Pullen quoted fol. 165vb is also reported in two glosses on Peter Lombard's Sentences published by L. Hödl, *Die Geschichte der scholastischen Literatur und der Theologie der Schlüsselgewalt* (Beiträge zur Gesch. der

Philos. und Theol. des Mittelalters 38.4; Münster 1960) 136–37; for Petrus Cantor see ibid. 312.

p.242: The opinion of Bartholomaeus (fol. 201va) is also discussed by Huguccio and the *Glossa ordinaria* on C.11 q.3 c.42, and by the *Apparatus Ecce uicit leo* on C.33 q.4 c.7 ('magister barth. theologus'), see P. Huizing, *Doctrina decretistarum de excommunicatione* (Pont. Univ. Gregoriana, Excerpta ex diss. ad lauream jur. can.; Rome 1952) 24–25. In the Roman edition of the gloss C.11 q.3 c.42 v. *arceri* the reference is misprinted as 'Baz(ianus) tamen intelligit …' The identity of this Master Bartholomew remains uncertain. It is very unlikely that the bishop of Exeter was meant by these glosses, as Huizing (p.24 n.25) assumes.

p.244 *Summa brevis* C.18 q.2: The reading of the first line of the *responsio*, 'A monachis est abbas eligendus …' in the Olomouc MS (noted above to p.217) seems preferable.

In C.25 q.1, the argument 'Cum petentibus nil sit positum finitum' from Auth. 2.5 (Nov. 10) 1 is one which Richard was to use also later, in his *Apparatus* on Comp. I regarding petitions for dispensation, see my paper 'Pope Lucius III and the bigamous archbishop of Palermo' (1961), reprinted as No. VII in *The history of ideas and doctrines of canon law in the Middle Ages* (London 1980, 2ed. Ashgate 1992) p.425 n.71.

IX. Réflexions sur les brocards des glossateurs

In the analysis of the conceptual framework and dialectic function of *argumenta brocardica* or *generalia*', in testing their affinity to, and differentiation from, universal propositions, *regulae, notabilia*; and in retracing the history of *brocarda* collections before they gave way to the *Modi arguendi* of a later period, Peter Weimar's paper on 'Argumenta brocardica', in *Studia Gratiana* [=SG] 14 (*Collectanea Stephan Kuttner IV*; Bologna 1967) 89–123, has considerably expanded and deepened the scope of these *réflexions*. See also his paper 'Die legistische Literatur …' *Ius commune* 2 (1969) 43–83, at 60f; the relevant pages in his chapter on the Glossators, in Coing's *Handbuch der Quellen und Literatur …* I (Munich 1973) 237–41, and his notice on 'Brocarda, Brocardica', in *Lexikon des Mittelalters* 2.4 (1982) 707–8.

As for the term itself, H. Kantorowicz's etymology (*procontra), which I accepted, was shown to be linguistically impossible by Leo Spitzer, 'Latin médiéval *brocard(ic)a* > français *brocard*', *Modern Language Notes* 70 (1955) 501–6: he traced derivations in the *volgare* of lat. *broccus*, 'with sharp (protruding) teeth' which include the 'forked' (argument), the 'raillerie piquante', and the lance in tournament; see also Weimar, SG 14.106-9.

p.251 n.1: The definition by Ricardus Anglicus of *argumentum* is in fact taken from Isidore, *Etymol.* 18.15.5, as copied in the glossed text, 1 Comp. 5.36.10.

p.252: Before Pillius (*Libellus disputatorius*, 2nd ed. c. 1195), Huguccio first used the term 'in brocardo' in connection with an adversative argument, see K.W. Nörr, *Zur Stellung des Richters im gelehrten Prozess des Frühzeit: Iudex secundum allegata non secundum conscientiam iudicat* (Munich 1967) 60, quoting from the *Summa* C.3 q.7 c.4. In the beginning the noun seems to have been of masculine gender (*brocardus*), see Weimar, SG 14.107. So also in the Avranches MS 149 of Ricardus (p.261 n.50 below), inscribed fol. 139r, 'Brocardi super decretales' (unidentified in *Repertorium* 422).

p.252 n.3: This rubric for Otto's *Brocarda* (with Azo's solutions) is found in several other manuscripts; its inversion in Vienna MS 2077, fol. 92ra, 'Incipit concordia discordantium generalium que uulgo brocarda dicuntur ...' (cf. Genzmer, art. cit. note 6 supra), underscores the parallel with Gratian's method.

p.252 n.4: The old alliterative derivation from the name of Burchard was again proposed by E. Meyer, 'Brocardica', ZRG Kan. Abt. 38 (1952) 453–73.

p.253 n.7: See also, among the humanists, Udalricus Zasius (Zäsy, †1533) *In títulos aliquot Digestí veteris commentaria*, Dig. 1.2.2.4 (med.) *Datumque est* v. *alias duas*: 'Accur(sius) hic colligit accidens origini preualere ... adducit tam arg. contra ... [cf. *Gloss, ord.* ad hoc. v. *et ita ex accidente*]. Eius perplexi, quod barbari brocardum uocant, dissolutio uulgo est cognita' (*Opera* [Lugduni 1550–51, repr. 1964] I 281); quoted as 'Barbaris quod Brocardum uel Brocardicum dicitur ... hoc Latinis perplexum dici' by Caspar Hervag in the 'Epistola nuncupatoria' for the Basel edition (1567) of Azo's *Brocarda*, fol. α3-α3v, where he also claims that Azo in his *Summa* on Dig. 3.4. [i.e. the collection of *summulae* from the school of Johannes Bassianus which is often inscribed as 'Materia ad Pandectam'] called 'doctrinam brocardicam in ambas partes perplexam'. The quotation is not verifiable; Hervag may have slipped, intending to refer to Zasius's *Paratitla* ad loc.: '... sed est doctrina brocardica, in ambas partes implexa' (*Opera* I 96 num. 22), cited also by Weimar, SG 14.99 n.36.

p.253 n.12: On the stages of redaction of Azo's *solutiones* see S. Kuttner, 'Analecta iuridica vaticana', *Collectanea vaticana in honorem Anselmi M. Card. Albareda* I (Studi e Testi 219; Città del Vaticano 1962) 415–52, at 446–49; Weimar, SG 14.121. On 'salicta' = thicket of willours, wicker name from Azo's *Brocarda*. See P. Weimar in Coing's Handbuch I 239: so subscr. in Vatic. MS Chis. E. VII. 218. But only there, says M. Schwaibold in Rechtshist. Journ. 4 (1985) 214 n. 49. (S.K.)

p.254 'l'ouvrage dit *Perpendiculum*': The name is indeed convenient for a work that lacks a general title, since the authentic title, (*summula*) *de presumptionibus*, covers only its first part (see p.258). But it should be used with reservations: the author clearly meant the expression 'this plumb line' in the epilogue of Part I as a descriptive image, not as a title for his *brocardica*. This is quite different from two tenth-century writers: *Volumen perpendiculorum* is actually the alternative title of Ratherius of Verona's *De contemptu canonum* (PL 136.485; see E. Meyer, 'Nachtrag zur Quaestionenlehre', ZRG Rom. Abt. 72 [1955] 358); and the last work of Atto of Vercelli (†961) was the *Polipticum quod appellatur perpendiculum* (PL 134.859; also ed. G. Goetz [Abhandl. Akad. Leipzig 37.2, 1922]). Neither is mentioned by P. Lehmann, *Mittelalterliche Büchertitel* (SB Akad. Munich 1948.4 and 1953.3).

p.254 n.19: Six more MSS recorded in my checklists and notes, *Traditio* 11 (1955) 447; 13 (1957) 470; 19 (1963) 511; see further H. van de Wouw, BMCL 3 (1973) 100, on the MS Aschaffenburg, Hof- und Stiftsbibl. Perg. 26, fol. 214va-217va (and p.98 on eight *brocardica* from part II inserted in a collection of *questiones* fol. 197ra-207v, between qq. 10 and 11); and add Paris, B.N. lat. 4720A (from St. Martial, Limoges), fol. 30vb-36v, discovered by G. Fransen (letter of September 1971); Paris, B.N. lat. 14606, fol. 166v-167v, beg. 'Qui occasionem damni dat.', identified by R. Motzenbäcker (letter of December 1974) as a series of *brocarda* from part II (recorded separately as *Notabilia* in *Repertorium* 233); and Oxford, University College 117, fol. 145(bis)ra-vb, beg. 'Introductis publica auctoritate': a series of rubrics, without arguments pro and contra, from part II, in an order of its own. (For other material in this MS see P. Legendre, 'Miscellanea Britannica', *Traditio* 15 [1959] 494 n.11, and my note ibid. 16 [1960] 533.)

p.256f. Influence of Sicard of Cremona on the *Brocarda* (*Summula*) *de presumptionibus*: R. Motzenbäcker, *Die Rechtsvermutung im kanonischen Recht* (Münchener theol. Studien 3.10; Munich 1958) 93(-95) n.l, argues for priority of the latter, c. 1170–77. The matter needs fresh investigation. A. *Gouron*, Un assaut en deux vagues. (cited supra VII, 137 R) considers this treatise *De presumptionibus* dating of 1173/1177 and having been used by Sicard of Cremona. This seems unlikely since the treatise closely follows the categories and distinctions established by Sicard. (S.K.)

p.257 n.31: The text beginning 'Delicto coram iudice manifestato' should be more adequately described: (1) *Notabilia* (so *Repertorium* p.234) is a misnomer for this brief instruction in pleading (*allegare*) in criminal cases under the significant rubric 'Ad mouenduum uarie iudicem' (which was occasionally miscopied as 'Admonendum uarie …'; so also in Lang, 'Rhetorische Einflüsse' 84). (2) It is best characterized as a *distinctio* with appropriate references to be used in each of four ways of pleading; as such it appears in at least four MSS that have a second, unsystematic and variable series of *generalia* after the *De presumptionibus* (MS references from the unpublished tabulations by Dr. Motzenbäcker: Grenoble 626, fol. 163rb/c; Munich lat. 7622, fol. 50rb; Leipzig, Univ. Rep. II (4°) 117, fol. 5ra (*ol.* Stadtbibl. Naumann 247]; Vatican, Borgh. lat. 287, fol. 6vc). (3) It appears again in Borgh. lat. 287, fol. 8va/b, after the series of *generalia* and followed by another set of *distinctiones*, which begin 'Hec sunt que suadent ne spoliatus restituatur …' and are often presented in the form 'Tria (or 'quattuor' etc.) sunt que faciunt quod …' (cf. *Repertorium* 234, where they are wrongly considered part of 'Delicto coram').

p.258 'la deuxième partie n'ayant pas reçu de forme littéraire définitive': The tabulations of Dr. Motzenbäcker (cf. the preceding note) show that 'part II' is actually made up of two series, of which the first, beg. 'Introductis publica auctoritate renuntiare non licet', is fairly uniform in the MSS while the second, usually beg. 'Principium spectandum', varies greatly and ought to be labeled as part III. (Details must be left to the future edition.)

p.259 Otto of Pavia: The earliest version appears to be that of the *Brocardica Dolum per subsequens purgari*, in Stockholm, Royal Libr. B.683, fol. 58r-104v: Weimar, SG 14.120. It so happened that I was able to indicate to Professor Weimar three further MSS from earlier correspondence (1953, 1954) with Francis de Zulueta, whose interest in *Dolum* reached back for over twenty-five years before his death. See also P. Legendre, *La pénétration du droit romain dans le droit classique de Gratien à Innocent IV* (Paris 1964) 34 n.3; Weimar, in Coing's *Handbuch* I 239. These are Cambridge, Gonville and Caius College 327 (527), pp. 85–165; Lincoln, Cathedral 121, fol. 129r-166r; and London, Lambeth Palace 139, fol. 58r-93v. Another copy exists in Worcester, Cathedral F 14 (communication from P. Weimar, April 1973), and a scattered series of *brocarda* in Durham, Cathedral C.III.3, between fol. 67v and 74v (see C.R. Cheney on this MS in SG 11 [1967] 39, and P. Legendre as cited by Weimar in *Handbuch* I 238), may be related to *Dolum*; so also a shorter series in the same MS, fol. 161ra-162vc, without the *pro-contra* references but with solutions.

The Brocardica 'Dolum per subsequentia (or 'subsequens') purgari', preserved in five English manuscripts and a Swedish manuscript, were probably not written by Otto Papiensis, but had perhaps an English author. Cf. *M. Schwaibold*, Brocardica "Dolum per subsequentia purgari", Ius commune, Sonderhefte 25 (Frankfurt/M. 1985), and *Id.*, Wer sucht, der findet, Rechtshistorisches Journal 4 (1985) 202–214; also *H. Lange*, Römisches

Recht im Mittelalter I: Die Glossatoren (München 1997) 145 and 239. A later redaction written by Otto Papiensis is found according to Schwaibold in a Vatican manuscript. (P.L.)

p.260 'Hinc collige ...' glosses in Simon of Bisignano: For a collection of *solutiones* in MS Vat. lat. 10754, fol. 83r-85r, mostly based on these arguments assembled by Simon, and attached to selected lemmata of Gratian's Decretum pt. I, see my note to M. Bertram, 'Some additions to the "Repertorium der Kanonistik",' BMCL 4 (1974) 9ff., at p. 16.

p.260 n.47: The collection beg. 'Argumenta a minori per negationem' is to be classified as containing mostly *brocardica*; see Nörr, *Zur Stellung* (cited in the note above to p.252) 51 n.2; Weimar, SG 14.127.

p.261 n.50 Ricardus Anglicus: The reference to the fragment of his *generalia* in Bamberg Can. 45 should be corrected, fol. 45ra/vc, continued lra-7vb. For Munich lat. 8032, fol. Ora/vb, 3rb and lr-2r (two versions, both with only one *allegatio* as in Nurnberg, Cent. V.95) see R. Weigand, 'Mitteilungen aus Handschriften', *Traditio* 16 (1960) 562-3. For more MSS see my checklists and notes in *Traditio* 13 (1957) 470; 16 (1960) 533; Bertram, 'Some additions ...' BMCL 4 (1974) 11. Of these, MS Bruges, Ville 366 also gives two versions as already noted by G. Fransen (see Bertram loc. cit.). Random examination of some texts in the second, fol. 51ra-54vb, shows changes and abridgments made in Richard's *allegationes* and *solutiones*; they are definitely inferior to the original work. The latter was indicated by Bertram for fol. 27va-50va, but actually occupies fol. 27va-40vc, 49ra-50va, interrupted by the quire fol. 41va-48vc, a thus far unnoticed copy of the *Brocarda* of Damasus, in a different hand and incomplete at the end; it breaks off in the solution of No. 120, 'Nemo plus iuris in alium transfert ...' (cf. Barth. Brixiensis's recension = *Tract, univ. iuris* [Venice 1584] 18.512 num.21), with the last eleven missing.

p.262 and n.55: MS Melk 333 should now be cited as Melk 190 (*ol.* 333; F 33). The reading 'arg. quod nullus iure suo' (rather than '... beneficio suo') is also that of the older version (fol. O) in the Munich MS just mentioned, see Weigand loc. cit., and in the second version at Bruges and Avranches.

p.265 n.69: The trichotomy *moralis, iudicialis, sacramentalis* in describing Gratian's threefold doctrinal purpose does actually occur in Stephen of Tournai as edited by Schulte (p.261), prologue to part III *de cons.* But this whole part of the *Summa* is not authentic; see my paper in *Traditio* 14 (1958) 502-5, where also more examples from writings of the French school for the above-mentioned trichotomy are cited, p.505 n.16.

The so-called part III of the Summa, attributed by Schulte to Stephen of Tournai (Summa 'Fecit Moyses Tabernaculum'), was written by Geoffrey (Gottfried) of St. Andrew in Cologne – cf. *P. Landau*, Die Dekretsumme Fecit Moyses Tabernaculum – ein weiteres Werk der Kölner Kanonistik, ZRG kan. Abt. 98 (2010) 602–608. (P.L.)

p.266: For the presence (ten times) or absence (twelve times) of the clause 'et Moguntine ecclesie filius spiritualis translatione' in the manuscripts of the *Summa* containing Sicard's *Apologia* see checklists and notes in *Traditio* 12 (1956) 562–63; 13 (1957) 470, 503; 15 (1959) 499–500; this facilitates, of course, a preliminary classification of recensions; see also P.J. Kessler, 'Wiener Novellen', SG 12 (1967) 92 n.5, where he refers to fuller discussion in the *prolegomena* of his planned edition (cf. ibid. n.4). — The reference above in note 85 to the Milan MS should read Biblioteca Ambrosiana M.64 sup.

pp.268–71: Much work remains to be done in exploring the glossators' and their successors' thought—what I have called here 'les courants intellectuels'—concerning that area between philosophy, dialectic, and rhetoric in which *generalia* and *regulae* developed, and in which we notice a sharpening differentiation between 'universal' and 'general' propositions, or between their counterparts labeled, as the case may be, *exceptiones* or *specialia*. See e.g. the observations of S. Caprioli, 'Tre capitoli intorno alla nozione di "regula iuris" nel pensiero dei glossatori', *Annali di storia del diritto* 5–6 (1961–62) 221–374, at 221–26; Weimar, SG 14.102f., and P. Stein, *Regulae iuris* (Edinburgh 1966) 144–45, 150–52. We should beware, however, of the temptation to find in medieval lawyers the conceptual perfection of the philosopher's discourse.

Further study of collections of *Brocardica* from the glossators' period will show us in detail how the devices of the *artes* were judiciously employed in teaching the techniques of arguing a case. The following texts, selected from a much larger list of jottings from manuscripts, may deserve particular attention:

(1) 'Argumentandum ex superficie litere': Oxford, University College 17, fol. 152va–157vc; briefly noted by P. Legendre, 'Miscellanea Britannica', *Traditio* 15 (1959) 494 n.11. Without solutions; references to Digest, Code, and Gratian.

(2) 'Argumentum quod uoluntas pro facto reputatur': Luxembourg MS 139, fol. 279va–281rb; see Weimar, SG 14.122. Decretals are cited in an unusual form from *Comp. prima*, e.g. 'dec(retalis) l(ib.) iii. t(it.) xxxiiii. Cum apostolus' = 1 Comp. 3.34.6.

(3) 'In quibus casibus ordo seruetur': Madrid, B.N. 421, fol. 13ra–24vc, mostly civilian, appended to a copy of the *De presumptionibus*.

(4) 'Leges uel decretales epistole, licet ad certas personas directe, generalium constitutionum habent effectum': Durham, Dean and Chapter Muniments, Endpapers and Bindings, fragm. No.30, fol. 3v–6r; see above, 'Retractationes' to 'Anglo-Norman Canonists' (No. VIII) 340–42.

In the Retractationes for his article Kuttner lists four more collections of Brocardica. In his personal copy he made six further additions:

(5) 'Initium esse spectandum': Edinburgh, National Library MS 6122, fol. 135r–141v. (letter R. Somerville 19. X. 71). But this may be Azo.

(6) 'Quem non posse facere iure suo': Lincoln, MS 121. fol. 179va–183vd. (given as blank folio in *Holtzmann/Cheney* p.121).

(7) 'Argumentum testes non esse cogendos': London, British Library, MS Royal 9. C. VI, fol. 2rb–3vc.

(8) 'Iuris positivi ignorantia excusat': Vat. MS Pal. Lat. 667, fol. 8v–19r; Freiburg/Br., MS 163, fol. 362v–372v; with the variant beginning "Ignorantia iuris positivi excusat", cf. for MS Pal. 667 also *Kuttner*, Repertorium, p.421, n. 2. Both manuscripts are saec. XV.

(9) 'Argumentum (Argumenta cod.) a minori, ex. De parrochia nullus episcopus', Paris B.N., MS lat. 14, fol. 128r–143r – cf. *J. Tarrant* (ed.), Extravagantes Johannis XXII, (MIC, Ser. B, Vol. 6, Città del Vaticano 1983) Prolog p. 60.

(10) Paris, B.N. MS 4378, fol. 187–189v. Fragments of Roman law – cf. *H. Singer* (ed.), Rufinus, Summa decretorum, p. XXXVII. (S.K.)

Outside the sphere of the two laws, see e.g. the *Brocardica de vitiis et virtutibus* in Paris, B.N. lat. 14947, fol. 386: M.W. Bloomfield et al., *Incipits of Latin works on the virtues and vices, 1100–1500 A.D.* (Cambridge, Mass. 1979) p.289 No.3375 = Bloomfield, 'A preliminary list …', *Traditio* 11 (1955) 318 No.537.

X. Papst Honorius III. und das Studium des Zivilrechts

p.273 n.1: The new edition from the papal Register by V.J. Koudelka in *Monumenta diplomatica s. Dominici* (Monum. Ordinis Fratrum Praedicatorum historica 25; Rome 1966) No. 104, pp. 107–11, should at least have mentioned, and preferably collated, the several originals despatched that are on record; we may add one more addressed to the archbishops and bishops 'in Prouincia constitutis', on which the copy in the appendix to Comp. IV, MS Córdoba 10, fol. 305va-306va, is based (description by A. García y García in *Traditio* 23 [1967] 506).

p.274 '*Constitutio* im technischen Sinn': E. Pitz, *Papstreskript und Kaiserreskript im Mittelalter* (Bibliothek des Deutschen Historischen Instituts in Rom 36; Tübingen 1971) 171–91, has argued that *Super speculam* was a rescript issued upon the petition of St. Dominic, presented with the support of reform-minded friends at the Curia, and largely drafted by him upon previous understanding with the masters of theology in Paris; a rescript which was only outwardly given the appearance of a general *constitutio*. The real original would have been the letter addressed to the cathedral chapter of Paris which we know through its copy in the Alcobaça MS (note 1 above); its date of November 16 (instead of 22) would be the actual day of issue, and all other recorded recipients would be identifiable as friends or admirers of St. Dominic.

Only some flaws of this unconvincing hypothesis may be pointed out: it leaves unexplained such recipients as the bishops of the Provence (Córdoba MS, cited above) or the *prelati universi* or *universarum ecclesiarum* (Florence MS cited p.274 n.6; Beaune MS 19, fol. 295v after Comp. IV, communicated by G. Fransen); it presupposes a great blunder in the Chancery if we ought to believe that the original which was enregistered for 22 November as despatched to 'the Patriarch of Antioch' and his suffragans had been impetrated by Cardinal Peter of Capua, former master of theology and cathedral canon of Paris, and thus presumably involved in drafting the text. Cardinal Peter had never been more than patriarch-elect, and a new patriarch of Antioch had been consecrated three days earlier, on 19 November. Nor could the original 'rescript' have been issued to the *capitulum Parisiense*, since the text in the Alcobaça manuscript as elsewhere concludes with a mandate addressing 'uos autem *fratres* et filii …' (I do not know where Pitz [p. 181] read the final words 'Lugduni similiter faciatis' in this text; it is not in the edition of the Chartularium from the Alcobaça MS.)

It is another matter that behind a far-reaching *constitutio* such as *Super speculam* there always lie suggestions and proposals made by competent advisers and discussed with them; but this does not make the papal counselors into petitioners for a rescript, and technically the pope still decrees *motu proprio* (the term is misunderstood by Pitz). On the *consiliarii* in this case see p.282 n.44 and the additional observations below.

p.274 n.6: Add the Beaune and Córdoba MSS cited in the preceding notes. In the latter, the *constitutio* is undivided, while Beaune 19 presents it shortened and in three chapters, like the MSS cited in note 7.

p.275, tabulation, note a): The variant 'Super specula' in the decretal collections is based on the construction, frequent in medieval Latin, of *super* with the ablative, here of *specula*, 'watch tower'. The censure of Mitteis (cited p.276 n.16) p.159 n.72, as though this variant indicated the plural accusative of *speculum*, 'mirror', is beside the point.

p.276 Political interpretation: Some authors have tried to keep to a middle ground by combining Honorius's pastoral and disciplinary motives with a papal wish to support the aims of Philip Augustus; thus P. Fournier in his inaugural lecture at Paris, *Revue historique de* *droit fr. et étr.*⁴ 1 (1922) 250; G. Le Bras, 'La Faculté de Droit au moyen âge', *Aspects de l'Université de Paris*, ed. L. Halphen et al. (Paris 1949) 83–100, at 90f.; F. Calasso, *I glossatori e la teoria della sovranità* (2nd ed. Milan 1951) 57–59; also, but with greater emphasis on the political side, P. Legendre, *La pénétration du droit romain dans le droit canonique classique de Gratien à Innocent IV* (Paris 1964 ex 1957) 35–50. More strongly, W. Ullmann, *Principles of government and politics in the Middle Ages* (London and New York 1961; 2nd ed. 1966) 199 n.4, in repeating his earlier uncompromisingly political assessment of *Super speculam* (see above, 277 n.17 and 84 n.18) rejects the present paper as written 'in spite of the overwhelming evidence' and as 'somewhat naive'.

It is therefore reassuring to read an *obiter dictum* in Pollock and Maitland's *History of English law before the time of Edward I*, which parallels Henry III's prohibition of teaching *leges* in London with that of Pope Honorius (Cambridge 1895, p.102; 2nd ed. 1898, p.122): 'Theology was to be protected against law …' and 'it is by no means certain that we ought not to connect this with a movement in favour of ecclesiastical reform, rather than with that "Nolumus leges Angliae mutari" which the barons were about to utter'.

p.277 'mit biblischen … Allegorien gesättigte(n) Sprache': None of the editions has a satisfactory scriptural apparatus. For some helpful indications see R. Hausherr, 'Eine Warnung vor dem Studium von zivilem und kanonischem Recht in der Bible moralisée', *Frühmittelalterliche Studien*: Jahrbuch der Universität Münster, ed. K. Hauck 9 (1975) 380–404.

p.279 n.30: Add the council of Clermont 1130 c.5 and see R. Somerville, 'Pope Innocent II and the study of Roman law', *Revue des études islamiques* 44 (1976, publ. 1978) 107–14 (a paper read at the first Colloque International de la Napoule on Islam and the Occident in the Middle Ages). Somerville discusses the intriguing question why II Conc. Lat. c.9 is omitted from the Lateran decrees of 1139 that are found in Gratian's Decretum. — One may also add a letter of Celestine III to the bishop of Sigüenza concerning canons regular who had requested permission to study *legum scientia*: They should be told to study theology (*Coll. Seguntina* c.117, ed. W. Holtzmann in RHE 50 (1955) 450; see also p.420). — The decree of the legatine Council of Paris (1212) should have been cited as pt.2 c.20 (Mansi 22.831). — The decretal 5 Comp. 3.1.1 is Pressutti 5505 (Po. 7780).

p.280 n.37: The decretal *Habito* (with the variant incipit 'Habito communi cum fratribus') is attributed to Gregory IX also in Porto, Bibl. Municipal MS 48, fol. 13v-14r, see I. da Rosa Pereira, 'Manuscritos de direito canónico existentes em Portugal', *Arquivo Histórico de Madeira* 11 (1959) 196–242, at p.7 of the offprint (Funchal 1960).

p.282 Roffredus Beneventanus: His remark about 'duo consiliarii' presupposes some personal knowledge about the making of *Super speculam*; his personal connections with the Curia were already documented by H. Denifle, *Entstehung der Universitäten* (note 12 above) 424 note 846. For his appointment in 1218 as *iudex ordinarius* in his home town by Honorius III see Pressutti 1303; in a judgment of Cardinal Sinibaldus (the later Innocent IV) under Gregory IX (Auvray 2491, 17 Jan. 1235) he is styled 'advocatus curie domini pape'. As Professor Leonard Boyle has pointed out to me by letter, there is reason to believe that one of the two *consiliarii* of whom Roffredus speaks was Master William of Auxerre, proctor of the University of Paris 'tempore Honorii III' (*Chartularium Univ. Par.* 1.162-63). The passage from the *Libelli de iure canonico* was quoted before Savigny, in 1769, by Sarti, *De claris Archigymnasii Bononiensis professoribus* I (2nd ed. Bologna 1888) 137 n.2; it needs fresh examination in its context concerning *rectores ecclesiarum parochialium*. A rapid collation of fol. xixrb/va in the edition Avignon 1500 (pp.369b-370a of the reprint in *Corpus Glossatorum iuris civilis* vol. 6, Turin 1968) with some Vatican manuscripts shows considerable discrepancies, of which only one ought to be mentioned here: '(consiliarii) qui fuerunt pure theologi'] 'qui fuerunt parisius theologi' MS Borgh. 250, fol. 20ra. (Could Cardinal Peter of Capua, former master of theology at Paris—see the notes above to p.274, on Pitz's hypothesis—have been the second adviser?)

p.282 n.48: this *quaestio* of Johannes Andreae (ed. Venet. 1581, fol. llra-12rb) was originally debated on 3 April 1311; edited with an introduction from MS Cesena, Bibl. Malatestiana II sin.3, fol. 100rb-101rb by C. Mesini, 'De clericorum doctoratu et professoratu ...', *Antonianum* 32 (1957) 109–46 on dispensations. See further the *Quaestiones Andegavenses* of Paris, B.N. lat. 11724, ed. H. Fitting, in *Nouv. Revue historique de droit franç.* 29 (1905) 709–36, at p.724 (q.5).

p.284 n.58: More material, especially from early writers of the French school, in A.M. Stickler, 'Imperator vicarius Papae', MIÖG 62 (1954) 165–212, at 172ff. For the use of Roman law 'ubi non est contraria legi canonum' see already Gratian D.10 p.c.6; Stephen of Tournai D.10 pr.; Alexander III to the archbishop of Uppsala, JL 12117 '... Romanorum imperatorum leges ... quae tanquam canones, ubi canonibus non obuiant, sunt obseruandae' (PL 200.258C-D).

p.285 n.61: Before Lucius III, an implicit quotation of the passage from Nov. 83 c.1 was already given by Gratian C.2 q.3 p.c.7 §1: 'Cum enim leges seculi ... sacros canones sequi non dedignentur', and see explicitly *Summa Elegantius in iure diuino* 1.63 (ed. Fransen-Kuttner p. 19.6-7).

p.285f. Imperial authority and ideology: However, H. Krause, *Kaiserrecht und Rezeption* (Abh. Akad. Heidelberg 1952, No.l) has shown that 'Kaiserrecht' and Roman law were not simply considered interchangeable by the glossators. See also R. Feenstra's review in *Tijdschr. voor Rechtsgesch.* 22 (1954) 363–75.

p.286 n.71: St. Augustine actually quotes here from St. Cyprian's Seventh Council of Carthage, 'Sententiae episcoporum numero lxxxviii' (see PL 3.1103B; CSEL 3.1.345).

p.286 n.73 Roman law not applied in France and Spain: See also Raymond of Peñafort, *Summa iuris can.* 1.11 (ed. J. Rius Serra [Barcelona 1945] pp.40- 41, and cf. Legendre, *La pénétration du droit romain* [cited above to p.276] 36 n.6), who based this on *prescriptio longissimi temporis*. The *Lex Visigothorum* (*Fuero juzgo*) was cited in this context by Zoën, gloss to *Super speculam* 5 Comp. 5.12.3 v. *non utuntur*: 'Immo audiui quod lege Ispanorum seu Gothica cautum est quod qui legem allegauerit Romanam capite puniatur' (quoted from MS Tours 565 by Legendre 62 n.4), and Vincentius X 5.33.28 v. *non utuntur*. 'In Yspania excellentissima prouinciarum prima lex in libro iudiciorum Legionum hec est: quicumque recep<er>it leges Romanas capite punitur, et ita de pari contendit cum imperio' (Paris MS lat. 3967, fol. 197vb), who continued in a chauvinistic, anti-French and anti-Basque vein:

> etiam cum Francia, quia in eo tempore quo non erant in Yspania nisi gentiles, in ipso introitu Franchi perierunt cum paribus suis, et residui cum rege suo retrocedentes dimiserunt ioculatores suos in Vasconia qui nec locuntur gallicum nec yspanum.

He was quoted verbatim by Johannes Andreae, *Novella* ad loc. (ed. Venet. 1581, V, fol. 110ra). See also J. Ochoa Sanz, *Vincentius Hispanus: Canonista boloñes del siglo XIII* (Rome 1960) 16f. and n.38. The 'lex Gothica' or 'prima lex in libro iudiciorum' of León would be *Lex Visig.* 2.1.10-11 (*al.* 8–9) ed. Zeumer (MGH Leges nat. Germ. 1; Hannover

1902) p.58f. But the penalty there is thirty pounds of gold (p.59.2-3) which, though enormous, is not capital punishment.

What may be the earliest reference to this prohibition is found in the letter of Pope John VIII to the bishops of Gallia Narbonensis and Spain which requested an insertion on sacrilege in the *liber legis Gothice*, since 'in eisdem legibus scriptum est ut cause quas ille leges non habent non audirentur a iudicibus illius patrie' (JE 3180; unfortunately excluded with many others by the editors from the 'epistolae passim collectae', i.e. outside the Register, of John VIII in MGH Epp. 7.2 [Berlin 1928; repr. Munich 1978] as 'non ad res Germanicas spectantes', see p.313).

p.286 n.74: See also *Summa Reginensis* ad loc. quoted by Legendre, *La pénétration* 37 n.2.

p.288 n.81: For the *de facto/de iure* distinction see also Jacques de Révigny: '…et si hoc non recognoscit rex Francie, de hoc non curo' quoted by M.E. Meijers, 'De universiteit van Orléans …' *Tijdschr. voor Rechtsgesch.* 1 (1918) 115 *n.*1 = *Études d'histoire du droit* III (Leyden 1959) 9 n.19.

p.289 'das einzige Quellenzeugnis': There exists one text before Philip the Fair which could be (but has never been) cited against my interpretation, *Li livres de Jostice et de Piet* (ed. Rapetti 1850) 20.15.10:

> Por ce que en France et en moult de leus n'use l'en pas des lois de Rome … por ce deffant li papes Honoires et li rois de France que celes lois ne soient leues a Paris ne iqui environ; et qui encontre ce fera, ne soit pas oiz en cause et soit escomeniez.

Mitteis, 'Die germanischen Grundlagen …' (note 16 above) 161 n.75 has quoted this passage in a somewhat different context, though with a (!) after 'li rois de France'. The book itself, from the Orléanais, about 1259, exists in a single manuscript. It presents a strange mixture of *coutumes* with Roman law and Decretals in translation. However, the author ascribes imperial laws to kings of France, texts from the Digest to *baillis* of his own day, papal texts to the bishop of Orléans and also to secular authorities; see Chénon, *Histoire générale* (note 13 above) I 554–55; F. Olivier-Martin, *Histoire du droit français des origines à la Révolution* (Paris 1948 and 1951) 116; G. Sicard, 'Observations sur quelques chapitres du "Livre de Jostice et Plet" …', *Mélanges d'histoire du droit privé offertes à Pierre Petot* (Paris 1959) 519–29, esp. 529 n.7. Those observations should caution us against giving any historical value to the assertion on joint action of 'li papes Honorius et li rois de France' which the author interpolates in his paraphrase of *Super speculam* from X 5.33.28.

INDEX 1: GENERAL INDEX

Three special indices follow below. Index 2: Papal letters, Index 3: Initia operum, Index 4: Manuscripts. All items in the *Retractationes*, printed here after the last article, are indexed by the page(s) to which they refer, followed by the symbol R and the page of R in the index.

Abaelard: 26 n.8, 33 n.45 and 46, 34 n. 52, 35 n. 54, 37–41, 43–44 – *Sic et Non*: 19, 21, 253, 257 n.30
Abbas antiquus: see Bernard of Montmirat
Abbreviatio Decretorum: Humanum genus: 144 n.292 – *Lex alia divina*: 74 n.9, 179 n.83 – *Matrimonium est*: 179 n.83 – *Quoniam egestas*: 80 – in Paris, B. N. lat. nouv. acq. 1761 n.73–75.
Abbreviation of the *Compilatio Romana*: 153
Accursius: 76 n.17, 270 n.99 – 272 n.110, 287 n. 75
Adagonista (Ricardus): 215 & R (p. 319)
Adalbert (Vǒjtěch) of Prague (Albertus Ranconis) 99 n.28 & R (p. 299), 106 n.65
Addo of Friesland: 210.
Agustín, Antonio, *Compilationes antiquae*: 150 R (p.307).
Ailmerus: see Elmer
Al.: 99 n.28 & R (p. 299)
Alain de Lille, *Anticlaudianus*: 217.
Alanus (Anglicus): 169, 191R (p. 315), 203, 226, 286 n.61 – *Apparatus Ius naturale*: 106 & R (p. 301), 203R (p. 317), 226 – *Apparatus* on Comp. I: 106 n. 61 – *Collectio decretalium*: 106 n.61, 106R (p. 301), 130, 133, 138–40, 148 & R (p. 307), 153 f. n. 349, 193 n. 184, 225–26 & R (p.320) – cited in English glosses: 203, 226 – other glosses: 106 n.61, 108 n.83, 156
Alanus ab Insulis: see Alain de Lille

Albericus: 134 n.244
Albertus (Albertinus) Beneventanus (de Morra: Gregory VIII): 99, 204, 206, 222
Albertus Galeottus, *Summula quaestionum*: 202.
Albertus Gandinus, *Tractatus de maleficiis*: 202.
Albertus Ranconis: see Adalbert of Prague
Aldricus: 187 n.136
Alexander III, pope (Rolandus Bandinelli): 23, 98 n.25, 113 n.114, 167 & R (p. 310), 188, 204 & R (p. 317), 209, 238, 266 n. 84, 273, 284 n.58 R (p. 327); see Rolandus – and magister Rolandus: 98 (–99) n. 26 R (p. 299) – and see papal letters between JL 10584 and 14424.
Alexander Nequam: 208
Alger of Liège (Luik, Lüttich): 26 n.5, 26–7 n.8, 27, 79
Alvarottus: 258.
Ambrose saint: 37–8, 42
Ambrosius, *Summa titulorum*: 154 & R (p. 308)
Amgerus (Angerus): 171 n.42
Anglo-Norman schools: 83–4, 86–7, 101–2 n.39, 40 (p. 300), 163–249; and see Exeter, Lincoln, Northampton, Oxford, St. Albans
Anonymi: see *Abbreviatio, Apparatus,* Commentaries etc. Anselm, saint, abp. of Canterbury: 17
Anselm of Laon: 32 ff., 34 n. 51 & R (p. 291)

GENERAL INDEX

Anselm of Lucca: 16, 64 n.93, 70.
Antioch, Patriarch: 273 n.1, 274 R (p. 325).
Apparatus glossarum
– *Animal est substantia*: 84, 84 R (p. 295), 89.
– *Bernardus prepositus* (Comp. I): 137 n.258 R (p. 305)
– *Ecce vicit leo*: 89, 91, 96 n.14, 105 n.50, 215, 242 R (p. 321), 287 n. 76.
– *In quibusdam libris* (Comp. I): 137 n.258, 214 n. 345
– *Ius naturale*: see Alanus.
– *Militant siquidem patroni* (Comp. I): 89R (p. 296)
– *Ordinaturus magister*: 88, 102–09 R (p. 300), 112–13 R (p. 303)
– *Quia brevitas amica est audientie* (Compilatio I): 137 n. 258 (p. 305)
– *Servus appellatur* (Comp. III): 104 n.55, 108 n.82, 115 n.120, 126 n.182, 140 n.275
– on the Decretum: 95 f., 105–09, 102–09 R (p. 300)
– on the Decretum in MS Evreux 106: 214
– on Comp. I: 104 n.55
– on const. 'Super speculam': 159 n.402
– on the *De regulis iuris*: 184 n.120
– on Ricardus Anglicus, *Ordo*: 144 n. 292
Appellatio ante sententiam: 134
Argumenta, argumentum: 251 n.1 & R (p. 321), 254, 260 n.47.
Arnulphus (Ernulphus), chancellor of Thomas Becket: 174
Ascelinus: 220, 220 n.42 & R (p. 320)
Atto of Vercelli: 254 R (p. 322)
Augustine, saint: 38–9, 286 n.71 & R (p. 327); see *Liber de vera et falsa poenitentia*
Authenticae: 47, 50–51, 59
Authenticum: 50, 59
Azo: 119 n. 142, 123 n. 167, 128, 135 n. 243 and n. 244, 135 n. 243 R (p. 304), 136R (p. 305), 157 n. 389, 220, 263 n.62, 270 n.101 – *Brocardica*: 253 n.7R (p. 322), 253 n.128 R (p. 322).

b. *(ber)*: 98, 108–19, 109–29 R (p. 302 f.), 112 n. 108, n. 109 and n. 112, 145R (p.307), 146 R (p. 307), 179

bal. (Bazianus?): 136 n. 251
Baldus: 253
Baldwin, bp. of Worcester, abp. of Canterbury: 147, 167–70, 166 R (p. 310), 167 R (p.310), 207
Bartholomew, bp. of Exeter: 167, 180, 196 n.199, 207, 242 R (p. 321) – *Poenitentiale*: 180 & R (p. 314)
Bartholomew, mr. of theology: 242 R (p. 321)
Bartholomew of Brescia (Brixiensis): 62 n.85 – *Glossa Ordinaria*: 96 n.14, 100 n.31 & R (p. 300), 106 n.65, 107 n.72, 109, 124 n.170, 128, 155 – *Quaestiones*: 124 n. 170
Basianus: see Bazianus
Battle Abbey: 165f., 187
Bazianus (*baz., bar., bal.*, Basianus): 187 n.136, 197 n.203, 204, 242 R (p. 321) – *consilium*: 110 n.100 – Glosses: 99, 110–11, 113–16, 129 – *Quaestiones*: 110 n. 97, 111 n.105 – siglum: 111, 136 n.251 & R (p. 305)
Benedict, abbot of Peterborough: 166
Benedict of Sawston, bp. of Rochester: 174
Benencasa Aretinus: 62 n.85 – *Casus*: 100f., 96–101 R (p. 298), 106 n. 65, 106 R (p. 301)
ber.: see *b*.
Berengaria, queen: 137 n.258.
Bernard, chancellor of Paris, bp. of Embrun: 137 n. 258 (p. 305)
Bernardus (*magister dictaminis*): 185
Bernard of Clairvaux, saint: 33 n. 45, 123, 282 n. 43.
Bernardus Compostellanus antiquus, Additions to the *Glossa Ordinaria*: 122–25, 158 – *Compilatio (Collectio Romana)*: 93 f., 121, 125 n.174, 131–33, 148–52 & R (p. 307), 193 n.184; calendar of rubrics: 152 n. 336 & R (p. 308); see also Abbrevation, Glosses – Glosses on Comp. I: 118, 121, 129–40. – Glosses (*Apparatus*) on the Decretum: 109–29 & R (p. 302 f.), 156 – Glosses on the IV Lateran Council?: 155 n.359. – *Quaestiones*: 140–48 and R (p. 306), 145 R (p. 307), 146 R (p. 307) – siglum: 109–19, 109–29 R (p. 302 f.) – Spanish and Italian matters: 118–19, 135, 146, 148

Bernardus Compostellanus iunior: 94 n.4, 148–54 R (p. 307), 282 n.50
Bernard of Montmirat (Abbas antiquus): 156 n. 380, 277 n.21, 280 n.33, 280 n.37
Bernard of Parma: 166 n.15, 280 n.33, 285 n.66, 288 n.81 – *Casus*: 117 n.129
Bernard of Pavia (Papiensis): 112–13, 116–18, 146, 166–68, 179, 196, 213 – *Argumenta (Notabilia)*: 116 f. – *Breviarium extra vagantium* (Comp. I): 101–02 – *Casus*: 117 – *Collectio Parisiensis secunda*: 113 & 112–13 R (p. 303) – Glosses on Comp. I: 132–35, 132 n.223 R (p. 304) – Glosses on the Decretum: 98, 102–09 R (p. 300 f.), 112–13 & R (p. 303), 118 – *Notabilia*: 262, 263 n. 58 – siglum: 116–18 – *Summa de electione*: 113 – *Summa de matrimonio*: 113, 112–13 R (p. 303), 116 n.121, 117 n.130, 144 n.293 – *Summa titulorum*: 116, 116 n.126 R (p. 303), 118 n.132, 270 n.105
Bernold of Constance: 18, 26 n.8, 257 n.30 – *De excommunicatis vitandis*: 18
Bertoldus elect of Bremen: see Bertram of Metz
Bertram of Metz (Bertrandus, Bertoldus): 188, 184–87 R (p. 314)
Bertrandus (glossator): 155 n.359
Bertrandus Papiensis miles: 119 n.142
Bertrand du Poujet: 155 n.364 R (p. 308)
blā.: 187 n.135, 230
Boethius: 198 n.210
Bologna, university: 13, 20, 22, 87, 89–91, 93–162, 102–09 R (p. 300), 108 R (p. 302), 165, 168–70, 170 R (p. 311), 201–02, 215, 219, 225–26, 258, 264
Boniface VIII, pope: 23, 280, 290 – *Regulae iuris* (Liber Sextus): 271
Boso, bp. of Châlons: 178 n.79 R (p. 313)
Brachylogus: 220
Bracton: 171–73 R (p. 312)
Brava, Diomede (pseudonym of G. Grandi): 52–56, 60, 69 n.120 (p. 69), IV R (p. 292), 67 R (p. 294), 73, 75
Breviarium Alaricianum (Lex Romana Visigothorum): 54, 60
Bridlington priory: 192–94 R (p. 316)
Brocarda, Brocardica, Generalia: 251–71 – definitions and etymology: 251–52, IX R (p. 321), 253 n.7 R (p. 322) – and *regulae iuris*: 268–71 & R (p. 324f.) – and *solutiones*: 253, 260 R (p. 323)

Brocarda
– *Argumentandum ex superficie litere*: 268–71 R (p. 324)
– *Argumentum a minori (Notabilia Fuldensia)*: 260 n.47, 260 n.47 R (p. 323), 263 n.60
– *Argumentum quod voluntas*: 268–71 R (p. 325)
– *Argumentum testes non esse cogendos*: 268–71 R (p. 325)
– *Dolum per subsequens purgari*: 259 R (p. 323)
– *Florianensia* (St. Florian): 261 n.50
– *In quibus casibus*: 268–71 R (p. 325)
– *Initium esse spectandum*: 268–71 R (p. 325)
– *Leges vel decretales epistole*: 226–30 R (p. 320), 268–71 R (p. 325)
– *Quem non posse facere iure suo*: 268–71 R (p. 325)
– *(Summula) de presumptionibus*: see *Perpendiculum*
– *de vitiis et virtutibus*: 268–71 R (p. 325)

Bulgarus: 22, 128, 135 n.244, 142 n.281, 171, 177, 204, 287 n.75 – *Apparatus*: 269 n. 97 – *Materia Codicis*: 256 n.27 – *Ordo iudiciorum*: 68 n.116 – on *regulae iuris*: 268–71 – *Summula de iuris et facti ignorantia*: 67
Burchard of Worms: 16, 26, 116 n.13, 180, 252 & R (p. 322)

Cacciavillanus: 135 n.244 and n. 243 R (p. 305)
Caesarius of Heisterbach: 185
Canterbury: see St. Augustine's, Canterbury, Christ Church 170 n.32
Cardinalis: 97 & R (p. 299), 167, 204, 241–42
Cassiodorus: 143 n. 286
Cathari: 278, 283
Cato: 210
Celestinus III, pope: 139 n.269, 192, 279 n.30 R (p. 326)
Christian, abp. of Mainz: 266 f.
Cicero: 143 n.286, 204 n.264 – *De re publica*: 66
Clement IV, pope: 280–81
Clement V, pope: 290

GENERAL INDEX

Codex Iustinianus, use by Gratian: 50
Codex Theodosianus: 54, 60, 70
Collatio legum Mosaicarum et Romanarum: 65
Collectio (canonum) Mutinensis: 130 n.218 & R (p. 304)
Collection in Three Books: 65 f. R (p. 293)
Collectiones decretalium: 101–02, 102 n.40 R (p. 300), 164–68, 166 R (p. 310), 168 R (p. 310 f.), 168 n.23 R (p. 311); see also Glosses
Collectio Abrincensis prima: 168 n.23, 201 n.229, 214, 227–29
– *Alcobacensis prima*: 171
– *Appendix Concilii Lateranensis*: 168, 168 R (p. 310), 181 n.101, 196, 206 n.287 (p. 318), 221, 227–30, 233
– *Bambergensis*: 101 n.39, 168, 168 n.23, 168 n.23 R (p. 311), 240 (Bamb. [O] = *Orielensis prima*), 181 n. 98, 227–28
– *Brugensis*: 178 n.79 R (p. 313 f.), 229
– *Cantuariensis prima*: 166 n.15
– *Cantuariensis secunda*: 166 n.15
– *Cassellana*: 98, 102 n.40
– *Cottoniana*: 188 n.145
– *Dertusensis III* (= *2 Dert.*): 130 n.216
– *Dunelmensis secunda*: 226 n.421
– *Estensis*: 130–31
– *Francofurtana*: 102 n.39, 168 n.23
– *Lipsiensis*: 227–30
– *Orielensis prima*: see *Bambergensis*
– *Orielensis (Oriel II)*: 181 n.98
– *Palatina II*: 139 n.269
– *Parisiensis secunda*: 113 & R 112–13 (p. 303)
– *Petrihusensis*: 167 n.19
– *Regalis* (Royal): 167 n.15
– *Romana* (Calendar of Rubrics): 152 n.336 & R (p. 308); see also Bernardus Compostellanus antiquus
– *Rotomagensis prima*: 168 n.23 & R (p. 311)
– *Salisburgensis*: 153–54 & R 153 (p. 308)
– *Sangermanensis*: 168, 196 n.199, 226–30
– *Seguntina*: 279 n.30 R (p. 326)
– *Sorbonica*: 130–31
– *Tanner*: 168 & R (p. 311), 206–07, 211 n.315, 226–30 & R (p. 320), 237–41
– *Trinitatis*: 166 R (p. 310)

– *Wigorniensis (Wig. I)*: 166 R (p. 310), 167
– *Wigorniensis altera (Wig . II)*: 166 R (p. 310), 167 n.15, 177 n.72
– see also *Compilatio,* Alanus, Gilbertus, Raynerius
Cologne, school: 183–85 & R (p. 314)
Commentaries, anon.: *Ad iuste iudicandum* (Comp. I): 132 n.226 – on the *De regulis iuris*: 184 n.120 – on the *Digestum vetus*: 171–73 R (p. 312) – *Ego dico tibi* (tract. de poen.): 144 n.293 & R (p. 306) – on the Institutes: 171, 171 n. 40 R (p. 312) – *Johannis quinto in principio*: see Petrus de Salinis – *Materia auctoris in hoc opere* (Comp. I): 132 n.226, 144 n.293, 223 n.403
Compilatio prima: 101, 104, 129, 153 n.349, 168, 196, 201, 213–14, 218 n.364, 223, 227–30, 242, 247; see also Bernard of Pavia – *secunda*: 130–31, 151, 196 n.200, 216, 230 – *tertia*: 94, 130, 148, 150, 153 & R (p. 308), 191 n.161, 193 n.184, 197 n.203; see also Petrus Beneventanus – *quarta*: 108 n.85, 152–53, 153 n.345 R (p. 308) – *quinta*: 274–75, 277 n.21, 279 n.30 R (p. 326)
Compilatio Romana: see Bernardus Compostellanus antiquus
Compilationes antiquae, French recensions: 89 f. R (p. 296)
consiliarii: 274 R (p. 326), 282 n.44, 282 R (p. 327)
Councils
– Bourges (1031): 67
– Carthage VII (418): 286 n.71 R (p. 327)
– Clermont (1130): 279 n.30 R (p. 326)
– II Lateran (1139): 279 n.30 & R (p. 326)
– III Lateran (1179): 279 n.30
– IV Lateran (1215): 274 n.6
– Lyons, I (1245): 7
– Lyons, II (1274): 7
– Paris (1212): 279 n.30 & R (p. 326)
– Reims (1131): 279 n.30
– Tours (1163); 273, 279 n.30
Coutume, droit coutumier: 276, 285, 287–89
Cresconius, *Concordia canonum*: 74 n.8, 184–87 R (p. 314), 186, 230–31

Cumba (England), church of: 172 n.42
Cyprian, saint: 286 n.71 R (p. 327)

d.: 98, 170
Damasus, Glosses on the Decretum: 156 – *Brocarda*: 261 n.50 R (p. 324) – *Quaestiones*: 142 n.282, 143 n.291, 154, 199 n.214, 201
Daniel of Morley: 208
David of London: 98 n.24 and R (p. 299), 170–71 and 170 R (p. 311)
Definitions of civil law: 171–73 R (p. 312)
Deusdedit: 16
Digesta, use by Gratian: 50
Dinus, *Apparatus* on *regulae iuris (Liber Sextus)*: 270 n.99, 271 n.109
Diplovatatius: see Thomas Diplovatatius
Dissuasio Valerii: 214 n.342 R (p.319)
Distinctio Breviter quid contrarietatis: 99 n.29, 268 n.88 – *Cantabrigenses*: 178 n.78 – *Consuetudo*: 85, 170 R (p.311) – *Delicto coram iudice manifestato*: 257 R (p. 323); see *Notabilia – Monacenses*: 85, 184, 184–87 R (p.314), 189 R (p. 315)
Doctor meus Vg.: 112 n.111, 112–13 R (p. 303)
Dominic, saint: 274 R (p. 325)
Dour: see Odo of Dover
Dunstable: 225
Duranti (Durantis): see Willielmus Duranti

E. Castellanus?: 159 n. 398
Eadsige, abp. of Canterbury: 195 R (p. 316)
Edmund, abp. of Canterbury: 216, n. 354
Egidius, *Lucubratiunculae*: 186 & R (p. 315), 200 n. 221, 230–31
Elmer (Ailmerus), prior of Canterbury (=Magister A.): 27 ff. R (p. 291)
Emo of Friesland (abbot of Bloomkamp): 210–11
Epistolae Cantuarienses: 147 n.304
Epitome Juliani: 50, 61–65 R (p. 293)
Epitome alphabetica Basiliensis: 263 n.62
Ernulphus: see Arnulphus
Etienne: see Stephen/Stephanus
Eugenius III, pope: 167, 167 R (p. 310)
Evrard of Ypres: 265 – *Summula decretalium quaestionum*: 82, 200 & R (p. 316)
Exceptiones Petri legum Romanorum: 80

Exemplum on King David: 144 n.293
Exeter, school: 207

f.: 98 n.25
Felix II (pseudo-): 69
Felix, prior of Dover: 206 n.283
Fidantia (Fidantius, Fidentius), canon of Città Castellana (Civitatensis): 98 n.25 & R (p. 299)
France, *Francia,* Roman law in: 286 n.73 & R (p. 327 f.), 287, 288 n.81 R (p. 328), 289 f.
Frederick Barbarossa: 183
French schools: 79–91, 105 n.59, 137 n.258 & R (p. 305), 142 n.281, 153 R (p. 308), 159 & R (p. 309), 173–75, 178 & R (p. 313), 190, 201, 264 n.66, 265 n.69 R (p. 324); and see Orléans, Paris, Reims, Tours
Fuero juzgo: 286 n.73 R (p. 328)
Fulgentius of Carthage, *Breviatio canonum*: 231
Fulk, dean of Reims: 174

g., G., Ge., Ger.: 102, 182, 187 n.136, 188 n.147, 189 and n. 154, 195 n.196, 201, 222
Gaius, *Institutes*: 46 n.6, 75 n.11
Gaius, pope: 75 n.11
Galfridus de Croppere: 165 n.10
Galt.: 220 n.381 R (p. 320)
Gandulph: 97, 112, 127 n.189, 195, 204
Gar.: see Warin
Garinus: see Warin
Garnerius: see Irnerius
Generalia: see *Brocarda*
Geoffrey, Geoffroy: see Godefridus
Ger.: see *g.*
Gerald of Wales (Giraldus Cambrensis): 79, 88–90, 166 n.11, 173, 180, 186 n.131, 200, 210 & 210 nn. 305, 306 R (p. 318), 210 R (p. 318) – *Quaestiones* 'Proposueram prius audire': 200 n.223 – *Speculum ecclesiae*: 210 n.305 & R (p. 318)
Gerard (Girardus, Gherardus) Pucelle: 83, 88, 170, 173, 182–89, 182 R (p. 314), 183 R (p. 314), 189 R (p. 315), 195 n.196, 230–31, 264 n.66, 266 n.84
– medieval references to his writings: 186 & 189 R (p. 315)
Gervase of Canterbury: 147 n.304

Gervase of Durham: 182
Gervase of Prémontré, abbot: 174 n.57
Gilbert Foliot, bp. of London: 98 n.24, 170, 178 n.82
Gilbert de Glanville, bp. of Rochester: 174
Gilbert de la Porrée: 204
school of: 19
Gilbertus (Anglicus): 169, 215 n.349, 216 – *Collectio decretalium*: 129 n.211, 133, 138–39, 148 R (p. 307), 151–54 – *Notabilia*: 144 n.293
Giraldus de Casamari, abbot: 225
Giraldus: see Gerald
Girardus, archd. of Paris: 222
Giseburne, monastery: 170 R (p. 311)
Glossa Ordinaria on the Decretum: 242 R (p. 321), 274 n.3, 279 n.32, 280 – Additions to Johannes Teutonicus, *Glossa Ordinaria*: 99 n.28, 106 n.69, 122–25, 122 R (p. 304), 155–62; and see Bartholomew of Brescia, Bernardus Compostellanus antiquus, Bernard of Parma, Johannes Teutonicus and Willielmus Vasco
Glossa Palatina: 52, 56 n.58, 64 n.97, 76 n.21, 98 n.25, 106–08 R (p. 301), 107–27, 135–36, 154–56, 154 n.356, 160–62, 286 n.73
Glosses
 – on *Appendix Concilii Lateranensis*: 206 n.287 & R (p. 318), 241
 – on the *Arbor consanguinitatis*: 159 n.403
 – on Bulgarus, *De regulis iuris*: 171–73 R (p. 312), 171, 269 n.97
 – on early decretal collections: 101 n.39, 102 n.40 & R (p. 300)
 – on *Coll. Alani*: 226 n.423
 – on *Coll. Cassellana*: 98 n.25 & R (p. 299)
 – on *Coll. Estensis*: 130–31
 – on *Comp.* I: 98 n.25, 129–40, 132 nn. 223 and 225, 215 n.351
 – on *Compilationes II-IV*: 98 n.25, 156 R (p. 309)
 – on *Compilatio Romana*: 150
 – on the Decretum: 95–101, 96 n.14 R (p. 297), 102–05, 105 n.59 R (p. 301), 106 n.65, 107, 109, 112, 118, 122–25, 155–62
 – on the Decretum: various MSS: 177,
179, 181, 200 n.221, 206 n.287, 209 n.301, 214
 – on Egidius, Lucubratiunculae: 187 n.136
 – on Johannes Faventinus: 110 n.96
 – on Ordo *Olim edebatur*: 171–73 R (p. 312), 171 n.39
 – *reportatio* from school of John of Tynemouth (Gonv. & Caius MS 676): 171–73 R (p. 312), 202–05 & R (p. 316 f.), 204 R (p. 317), 207, 211, 226, 227–29, 226–30 R (p. 320), 235–42
 – on Rufinus, *Summa*: 179
 – on Stephen of Tournai, *Summa*: 169 n.29, 189 R (p. 315), 239
 – on Summa *De iure canonico tractaturus*: 181
 – on Summa *Elegantius in iure divino*: 184–85 n.128
 – on Vacarius, *Liber pauperum*: 171–73 R (p. 311 f.), 192, 203 n.247, 229
Godefridus: see Goffredus, Godfrey, Geoffrey, Geoffroy
Godfrey de Luci: 165, 187 & R (p. 315)
Godfrey of St. Victor: 185, 185 n.129 R (p. 315)
Godfrey (Gottfried of Cologne): 185, 197, 265 n.69
Geoffrey Plantagenet, bp. elect of Lincoln, abp. of York: 191–95, 206 n.283
Geoffroy de Breteuil: 185 n.129
Geoffroy of Poitiers: 137 n.258
Goffredus of Trani: 277 n.21, 282 n.50
Grado, Patriarch: 273 n.1
Grandi, Guido: see Brava, Luccaberti
Gratian, archd. of Paris: 222 n.397
Gratian, card.: 167 R (p. 310)
Gratian, magister: passim
Gre.: 206, 214
Gregory I (saint), pope: 38, 56, 65, 223 n.405 & R (p. 320)
Gregory IX, pope (Hugolinus of Segni): 23, 129, 137, 154, 164, 165 n.9, 274–75, 280, 280 n.37 & R (p. 327), 288–89
Gregory VIII, pope: 99, 206, 222; see Albertus de Morra
Gregory, magister (? Gregory of London): 202–05 R (p. 316 f.), 206 & R (p. 317), 214
Gregory of S. Crisogono, card.: 16
Gualterus: see Walter

338

Guermundus, archd. of Paris: 222 n.397
    Guido Faba: 159 n.398
Guido de Baysio, *Rosarium*: 98 n.25 R
    (p. 229), 106 n.65, 108, 108 n.86 R
    (p. 302), 128, 282 n.47, 286 n.73
Guillielmus (Guillaume); see William
Gwill.: 215 n.349

h'.: 231 R (p. 320)
Henricus de Bayla: 67 n.112
Henry II, king of England: 173, 182, 186
Henry III, king of England: 276 R (p. 326)
Herbert of Bosham: 169 n.29, 169 R
    (p. 311)
Hermannus, card.: 97 R (p. 299)
Hervag, Caspar: 253 n.7 R (p. 322)
Hincmar of Reims: 70
Honorius III, pope: 137 n.258, 273 ff., 273
    n.1, 276 R (p. 326), 279–81 – const.
    'Super speculam': 159
Honorius, archdeacon of Richmond,
    magister: 189–202, 189 R (p. 315),
    191 R (p. 315), 192–94 R (p. 315 f.),
    194 R (p. 316), 206–07, 209, 210,
    212, 223 – *Summa de iure canonico
    tractaturus*: 100 n.33 R (p. 300), 181 R
    (p. 314), 190, 195 R (p. 316) – *Summa
    decretalium questionum*: 86 R (p. 295),
    141–42 n.279, 144 n.293, 181, 190,
    195–200, 195 R (p. 316), 202 n.237,
    231–35, 231 R (p. 320), 247–49
Horace: 204 n.264
Hostiensis: 274 n.3, 277, 279 nn.28 and
    31, 281 n.42, 282 nn.45 and 50, 285
    n.66, 286 n.72, 287 n.76, 288 n.81 and
    82 – *Lectura*: 137 n.258 R (p. 306)
Hubert Walter, abp. of Canterbury: 147,
    170, 170 R (p. 311), 194, 202, 206–13,
    210 n.306 and R (p. 318), 225 n.415 and
    R (p. 320)
Hugh, bp. of Lincoln: 207, 209 n. 300,
    212
Hugh of Mortagne: 34 n.49 and R (p. 291)
Hugh of Paris: 34 n.49
Hugh, abp. of Reims: 184–87 R (p. 314)
Hugh of St. Victor: 34–44, 74 n.9 & R
    (p. 294), 112–13 R (p. 303); see *Summa
    sententiarum*
Hugo Primas, poet: 184–87 R (p. 314)
Hugo du Puiset, bp. of Durham: 171 n.42
    R (p. 313)
Hugolinus of Segni: see Gregory IX

Hugolinus, glossator: 142 n.281, 144
    n.291, 157 n.389, 162, 171, 199 n.214
Huguccio: 44 n.64, 48 n.11, 62 n.85, 76
    n.21, 82, 90, 97, 96–101 R (p. 298),
    102–09 R (p. 301), 112 n.111, 181,
    196 & R (p. 316), 200 n.221, 204,
    206, 213, 218, 231 R (p. 320), 239,
    242, 242 R (p. 321), 252 R (p. 321),
    284 n.58, 286 nn.69, 73 and 74, 288
    n.80 – *Agiographia, Expositio de
    Symbolo, Derivationes*: 99 n.30 & R
    (p. 299 f.) – Glosses: 98 – *Summa* and its
    continuators: 100 n.32 & R (p. 300)

imperium, imperial authority: 285 ff.
Innocent II, pope: 167 & R (p. 310), 279
    n.30 R (p. 326)
Innocent III, pope: 23, 93 f., 97, 105, 137
    n.258 R (p. 305), 191, 193, 206, 212–13,
    278, 284 n.59, 287, 288 n.81
Innocent IV, pope: 23, 277, 278 n.27, 280
    n.33, 281 n.40, 282 n.47, 282 R
    (p. 327)
Innocent V, pope: see Peter of Tarantaise
Institutiones, use by Gratian: 50, 66
Irnerius (Garnerius): 13, 17, 20, 47, 50,
    56–58, 63 n.90, 67 n.112, 209 n.301
Isidore of Seville, *Etymologies*: 51
Ivo of Chartres, bp.: 16–18, 26 nn.7 and 8,
    33–34 n.51, 34 n.51 R (p. 291), 35, 40,
    61–65 R (p. 293), 66, 75, 79, 180, 257
    n.30 – Prologue: 18
Ivo of Chartres, magister: 173 n.49
Ivo of Cornwall, magister: 187 R
    (p. 315) Jacobus: 177 – *Summula de
    praescriptionibus*: 52

Jacobus de Albenga: 107, 156, 277 n.21
Jacobus Columbi, *Summa feudorum*: 144
    n.293 R (p. 307), 145 n.293
Jacobus Petrella, bp. of Faenza: 157
    n.381
Jacques de Révigny: 288 n.81 R (p. 328)
Jean: see Johannes
Jerome, saint: 38, 74 n.9
Johannes (Giovanni, Jean, John, Juan)
John VIII, pope: 286 n.73 R (p. 328)
John, king of England: 120, 147 n.305
Johannes Andreae: 94, 129, 148–54 R
    (p. 307), 155 n.364 R (p. 308), 201, 260
    n.48, 271 n.107, 280 n.37, 282 n.48 & R
    (p. 327), 286 n.73 R (p. 328)

GENERAL INDEX

Johannes Bassianus: 128, 135 n.244, 142 n.281, 187 n.135, 201, 204, 259 n.41, 263, 271 n.110, 282 n.49; see also *Materia ad Pandectam*
John Chrysostom, saint: 37
Johannes Colonna, card.: 284
John of Cornwall: 188, 191, 203, 207, 209, 212
Johannes Cremonensis: see Johannes Bassianus
Johannes de Deo: 166 n.15, 201, 274 n.9, 282 n.49 – *Liber quaestionum*: 143 n.284
Johannes Faventinus (John of Faenza): 52, 90, 96–101 R (p. 298), 97 n.20 & R (p. 299), 110 n.96, 112, 116 n.121, 179, 189 R (p. 315), 195, 204, 233, 237, 242, 259; see Glosses
Johannes Galensis (John of Wales): 169, 288 n.81 – Comp. II and Glosses: 130 – Glosses on Comp. III: 93 n.1, 99 n.26, 127 n.192 Johannes de Grey: 194 n.190
Johannes Hispanus (?): 112 n.111
Johannes Hispanus de Petesella: 94 n.6, 137–38 R (p. 305) Johannes of Idanha (Eginatensis): 282 n.49
John of Kent: 202–05 R (p. 317), 206 & R (p. 317)
Johannes Teutonicus: 27 n.10, 52 n.35, 98 n.25 R (p. 299), 107, 274 – *Apparatus arborum*: 108 n.85, 144 n.291 – *Apparatus* on Comp. III: 108 n.85, 108–09 R (p. 302) – *Apparatus* on IV Lateran Council: 108 n.85, 108–09 R (p. 302) – author of Comp. IV: 108 n.85 – *Glossa Ordinaria* on Decretum: 48 n.11, 52, 56 n.58, 62, 63 n.90, 64 n.97, 66 n.104, 67 n.108, 76 nn.16 and 17, 106 n.65, 107 n.77, 108–09, 108 n.83, 108 n.86 R (p. 302), 114–15, 122–25, 155–58 – Glosses on 'Super speculam': 159 n.402 – *Quaestiones*: 124 n.117, 144 n.291, 145
John of Salisbury: 79, 167 R (p. 310), 169 n.27, 169 R (p. 311), 174, 178, 182–83, 183 R (p. 314)
John of Tynemouth (de Tinemue, de Tinemuda): 101–02 nn.39 and 40 (p. 300), 202- 07, 202–05 R (p. 316 f.), 206 n.287 R (p. 318), 210–13, 211 R (p. 318), 226, 237–42
Juan: see Johannes

Julianus (iureconsultus): 138 n.260
Julianus, bp. elect of Faenza: 157 n.381
Juvenal: 204 n.264

Labbé, Charles: 150 R (p. 307)
Laborans, card.: 89
Lanfrancus: 157 n.389
Laon, school of: see Anselm of Laon
Laurentius Hispanus: 27 n.10, 224 n.409, 261 n.51, 285 n.63, 286 n.73, 288 n.81 – *Apparatus* on the Decretum, relation to Glossa Palatina: 103–04, 106–07, 106–08 R (p. 301), 109–10, 156, 160–62 – Glosses on Comp. I: 95 n.6, 104 n.55 – Glosses (*Apparatus?*) on Comp. III: 104 n.55, 115 n.120 – Glosses on *tract. de poen.*: 107 – *Quaestiones* (?): 146 n.299 & R (p. 307) – confused with Lanfrancus: 157 n.390 – see also *Apparatus Servus appellatur*
Lazarus: 38–39
Lefèvre, Nicolas: 150 R (p. 307)
Leo IX, pope: 48 n.15, 168 R(p. 310), 195 R (p. 316)
Leodegarius Piparde: 225 n.415
Lex Romana Visigothorum: see *Breviarium*
Lex Visigothorum: 286 n.73 R (p. 328)
Li Livres de Justice et de Plet: 289 R (p. 328)
Libri feudorum, Obertine recension: 145 n.293
Lincoln, school: 207–08
Literary forms and methods: 8–9, 21–23, 25–26, 81–88, 95–109, 175–76, 196–202, 251–63, 268–71; see also *Apparatus, Brocarda, Quaestiones, Summae quaestionum*
Lombard of Piacenza: 169
Lotharius, legist: 165 n.9
Louis VII, king of France: 183, 188
Lucas Bánffy, abp. of Esztergom: 182
Luccaberti, Bartolo (pseudonym of G. Grandi): 53 n.43
Lucius III, pope: 191, 222, 266–67, 284–85, 285 n.61 R (p. 327)

M.: 98 n. 25 R (p. 299), 119 n.140
Malger, bp. of Worcester: 212
Martialis: 157 n. 382
Martinus, magister: 209

Martinus Gosia, legist: 128, 204, 287 n.75 — school of: 76 R (p. 294)
Martin of Zamora (Roderici?): 95 n.6, 107, 157
Materia ad Pandectam: 252 n.3, 253 n.7 R (p. 322), 263
Mathieu: see Matthew
Matthew, archd. of Oxford: 212 n.326
Matthew of Angers: 88, 119 n.140, 173
Mauger: see Malger
Maximus, saint, bp. of Turin: 36–38
Melendus (Merandus): 119–21, 148 – Glosses on Comp. I: 119 f. R (p. 304), 133 – Glosses on the Decretum: 99, 107, 120–21 – *Quaestiones*: 146–47 & R (p. 307)
Merandus: see Melendus
Metellus, canonist: 177
Moses the Jew: 225 n.415

N. (= Huguccio): 103 n.45
Nicholas I, pope: 62
Nicholas de Aquila (de l'Aigle): 202–05 R (p. 317), 203 & R (p. 317), 205, 211, 213, 225 R (p. 320)
Nicholas de Guildford (= N. de Aquila?): 203 R (p. 317)
Nicholas of Hungary: 210
Nicolaus Fabri: see Lefèvre
Northampton, school: 208–09 & R (p. 318)
Notabilia: 254, 261 n.50; see also *Argumenta, Brocarda – Notabilia*
Argumentum quof religiosi (Pembroke MS 101): 258, 260, 268 – *Clericus apud civilem*: 179 – *Coll. Gilberti*: 144 n.293 – *Decretorum*: 144 n. 293 – *(Distinctio) Delicto coram iudice*: 257 n.31 & R (p. 323) – *Qui multum emungit*: 223 & R (p. 320) – on excommunication: 177 n.72, 180 n.96
Notulae super libello de significatione verborum: 184

Odo, magister: 178 n.82
Odo, abbot of Battle: 178 n.82
Odo, bp. of Paris: 106 n.66
Odo of Dover (de Doura, Odon de Dour), *Decreta minora*: 81 & R (p. 295), 88, 178, 220
Odo of Lucca: 34 n.49 & R (p. 291) Odo of Ourscamp: 265
Omnebene (Omnibonus, Ognibene),

Abbreviatio Decretorum: 74 & R (p. 294), 76 R (p. 294), 169 R (p. 311), 179 n.83
Ordericus clericus: 172 n.42
Ordines iudiciarii, French school: 86 f., and R at p. 295
Ordines iudiciarii
Ordo Ad summariam notitiam: 137 n.254 & R (p. 305)
– *Baltimorensis*: 168 n.24, 176 n.67 & R (p. 313), 208 n.295, 214, 230
– *Bambergensis*: see *Ordo quia iudiciorum*
– *Iudicandi formam in utroque*: 176 n.68, 220 n.380 R (p. 319)
– *Iudicium est trinus actus*: 176 n.68
– *Nota quod quicumque agit*: 202
– *Olim edebatur*: 175–76, 220
– *Quia iudiciorum (Bambergensis)*: 87, 175 & R (p. 313), 181
– *Quoniam* (var. *Quia*) *utilissimum fore putavi*: 137 n.254 & R (p. 305)
– *Scientiam*: 159 & R (p. 309)
– *Tractaturi de iudiciis*: 87, 257 n.27
– *Ulpianus de edendo*: 175 & R (p. 313)
– and see Glosses, *Summula Hactenus*
Orléans, school: 288–89
Osmund, archd. of Paris: 268 n.91
Otto of Pavia (Papiensis): 175 – *Brocarda*: 252 n.3 & R (p. 322), 253, 259 & R (p. 323)
Oxford, school: 171–73 R (p. 311 f.), 176 & R (p. 313), 207–13

p.: 133 R (p. 304), 137–38 R (p. 305)
p. b': 135 n.243 & R (p. 304 f.), 137–38 R (p. 305)
P. Hispanus (Yspanus): 137–38 R (p. 305); see Petrus
P. de Northampton, magister: 174
paleae: 47, 76, 76 n.21 R (p. 295)
Paris, anon. sermon: 281 n.43
Paris, cathedral chapter: 274 R (p. 325)
Paris, university and schools: 79–91, VI R (p. 295), 89 f. R (p. 296), 173–74, 182–83, 200, 222, 225, 264–66, 273, 274 R (p. 325), 282 R (p. 327), 283–85, 289
Paucapalea: 34 n.51, 97, 97 n.18 R (p. 299), 177, 179 n.86, 184 n.123
Paulus, *Sententiae*: 60
Pedro: see Petrus/Peter

Pelagius, pope: 65
Pelagius (Pelayo Gaitán), card.: 133 & R (p. 304), 135 n.243, 137–38 R (p. 305)
Perpendiculum (Summula de presumptionibus): 254–57, 254 R (p. 322), 256 f. R (p. 323), 267–68
persona, personatus: 279 and n.28
Peter (Pedro, Petrus, Pierre, Pietro)
Peter, card. S. Crysogono: 173 n.53, 188
Petrus Apulus: 137
Petrus de Bellapertica (Pierre de Belleperche): 253
Petrus Beneventanus (Collivaccinus): 94, 100 n.33 R (p. 300), 119–20 n.142, 150, 153
Peter of Blois (Blesensis), the archdeacon: 85 R (p. 295), 169 n. 30 and R (p. 311), 173 n.53
Peter of Blois (Blesensis), canonist: 173 n.52 and R (p. 313), 254–55 n.19, 266, 267 – *Distinctiones (Speculum iuris canonici)*: 80, 85 & R (p. 295), 88, 91, 176 n.68, 197 – *Ordo*: 86, 88
'Pierre de Blois le jeune': 85 R (p. 295)
Petrus Brito (le Breton): 89 f. R (p. 296), 107, 137 n.258 & R (p. 305 f.), 261 n.49
Peter of Capua, card.: 274 R (p. 325), 282 R (p. 327)
Petrus de Cardo <na>, card.: 137 & R (p. 306)
Peter the Chanter (Petrus Cantor, Precentor): 90, 173 n.49, 174, 174 n.55, 213, 236 & R (p. 321)
Petrus Collivaccinus: see Petrus Beneventanus
Petrus Comestor (le Mangeur): 200 n.221, 264–65 n.68 – *Historia scholastica*: 16
Petrus Hispanus (Yspanus, senior): 97, 132 n.226, 133 R (p. 304), 135 and n.243 R (p. 304), 137
Petrus Hispanus Portugalensis (Pedro Salvadores?): 137, 137–38 R (p. 305), 159 n.398
Peter Lombard: 16, 21, 37–38, 180, 185 n.124, 198 n.207, 236 R (p. 320 f.)
Peter of Louveciennes, *Prologus* to Decretum: 82, 88
Peter of Paxton, magister: 165 & R (p. 310)
Petrus Peverell (Penerclii, Penerchio, Penerell, Peneressi, Prevelli): 159 n.398 & R (p. 309)

Peter of Poitiers: 198 n.207, 203 & R (p. 317)
Petrus Prepositi (of Le Mans): 137 n.258 & R (p. 306)
Petrus de Salinis, *Lectura*: 100 n.31 R (p. 300)
Pedro Salvadores, bp. of Porto: see Petrus Hispanus Portugalensis
Pierre Sampson: 280 n.33
Peter of Tarantaise (Innocent V): 145 n.297a
Ph. (Φ): 98 n.25 & R (p. 299)
Philip Augustus, king of France: 276 & R (p. 326), 299
Philip the Fair, king of France: 289–90, 289 R (p. 328)
Philippus de Aquileia: 98 n.25 & R (p. 299)
Philip Berruyer, bp. of Orléans: 289 n.83
Philip de Calne: 174
Philip, bp. of Durham: 194 n.189
Philip of Heinsberg, abp. of Cologne: 185
Philippus Sarrazenus: 98 n.25
Philippe Séguier: see Séguier
Pierre: see Petrus / Peter
Pillius: 128, 142 n.281, 147, 165 n.9, 199 n.214 – *Libellus disputatorius*: 252–55, 258–60, 268 – *Quaestiones*: 252
Placentinus: 128, 186 R (p. 315), 201 n.228 R (p. 316), 203, 264, 270 – *Summa Codicis*: 76 R (p. 294)
plebanus: 279, 280
Polycarpus: 25 n.1
Pontigny: 169
Porretani: see Gilbert de la Porrée
Prepositinus: 183 n.111
Principium decretalium: 274 n.9
Prologus Missurus in mundum: 214 & R (p. 319) – *Omnia poma vetera et n ova*: 74 n.9 R (p. 294), 200 n.221, 266 n.76 – *Videndum que materia*: 189 R (p. 315)

Quaestiones decretales: 141, 144 n.292, 198–202, 199 R (p. 316), 200 R (p. 316), 201 n.228 (p. 316); and see Honorius, *Summa quaestionum* – *disputatae*: 140–48 & R (p. 306), 259 – *dominicales*: 124 n.170 – *legitimae*: 141, 269 n.96
Quaestionum collectiones: 124 n.150
Questiones Andegavenses (Angers MS 312; Robert Courson): 200 n.226

– *Andegavenses* (Paris lat. 11724): 86 & R (p. 295), 282 n.48 R (p. 327); see Robert Courson
– Arras 271 (*Quaest. decr.*): 201 n.228 R (p. 316)
– Avranches 149 (*Quaest. disput.*): 201 n.229
– Avranches 149 (*Summa quaest.*): 201, 214
– *Bambergenses I*: 86, 141 n.279
– Bamberg Can. 17 (*Quaest. decr.*): 201 n.228 & R (p. 316)
– Barcelona, S. Cugat 55 (*Quaest. decr.*): 200 R (p. 316)
– *Borghesianae*: 142 n.281, 274 n.5, 282 n.46
– Douai 649 (*Summulae quaest., Quaest. disput.*): 201
– *Fuldenses*: 145 n.297
– *Laudunenses*: 86 & R (p. 295); see Honorius
– *Lipsienses I*: 142 n.281
– *Londinenses* (B. L. Royal 9. E. VII): 86, VI R (p. 295), 168 n.24, 205–07 & R (p. 317), 211, 214, 225 R (p. 320), 228–29
– Montecassino 396: 197 n.203
– Munich 16083 (*Summa quaest.*): 201 & R (p. 316)
– *Orielenses*: 171–73 R (p. 312), 181 n.98, 208 n.297
– Oxford, Bodl. Selden supr. 87: 201 n.228 R (p. 316)
– *Palatinae I, II, III, VI*: 142 n.281, 143 n.283
– Paris 3934 A (*Summa quaest.*): 201
– *Patavinae*: 142 n.281
– Prague, Univ. XIV. E. 31: 142 n.281
– *Stuttgardienses*: 142 n.282, 177 n.75
– Vienna 2163 (*Summa quaest.*): 201

R. Castellanus: 159 n.398
R. de Lacy: 216 & R (p. 319)
R. de Senis: see Richard of Siena
de parvipassu: 106 R (p. 301); see Rodo(r)icus
R., Glosses on the *Arbor consanguinitatis*: 159 n.403
Rainaldus Anglicus: 217 n.358
Rainald of Dassel, abp. of Cologne: 185
Rainer (Rainier): see Raynerius
Ralph (Radulphus, Rodulphus)

Radulphus (Rodulphus) Anglicus: 148 n.307, 217 n.358
Ralph of Beauvais: 210 n.306 R (p. 318)
Ralph Niger: 173 n.49 R (p. 313), 182
Radulphus of Reims, magister: 137 n.258 R (p. 305)
Ralph de Sully: 174 n.56
Ratherius of Verona: 254 R (p. 322)
Raymond des Arènes, card. (=Cardinalis): 97 R (p. 299)
Raymond of Peñafort: 154, 274 n.5, 274, 286 n.73 R (p. 327)
Raynerius (Rainer, Rainier) of Pomposa: 149 n.314 & R (p. 308)
Regulae iuris: 268–71
Reims, school: 86, 174 Remgerus: see Renerus
Renerus, canon of St. Andrew's, Cologne (= Remgerus?), magister: 184 n.120, 185 n.127
Rex imperator in regno suo: 287
Rhetorica ecclesiastica: 86, 184–87 R (p. 314), 220 n.380
Richard I, king of England: 192, 205, 210, 210 n.306 R (p. 318)
Richard, relative of John of Salisbury: 182
Ricardus Anglicus (Richard de Mores [not de Lacy]), canonist: 100–01 n.34 & R (p. 300), 169, 181, 215–25, 216 R (p. 319), 219, 225–26, 225 R (p. 320), 286 n.69 – *Apparatus* on Comp. I: 132, 132 n.223 R (p. 304), 132 n.224 R (p. 304), 153 n.349, 215 n.351, 219, 243, 244 R (p. 321), 247, 251 n.1 & R (p. 321), 261–63 – *Brocarda seu Generalia*: 117 & R (p. 303), 144 n.293, 223, 224 n. 409, 253, 260–63, 261 n.50 R (p. 324), 270 n.100–271 n.110. – *Casus* on Comp. I: 224 – *Distinctiones*: 100, 96–101 R (p. 298), 103, 144 n.293, 156, 217 n.363 R (p. 319), 218–20, 260, 263 n.59 – *Notabilia* (?): 223 & R (p. 320) – *Ordo iudiciarius*: 76 n.17, 144 n.292, 176, 219, 223 – *Summa brevis*: 217–19, 217 R (p. 319), 223–24 n.410, 242–45, 244 R (p. 321) – *Summa quaestionum*: 141 f. n.279, 144 n.293, 196 n.199, 200, 220–25, 245–49
Ricardus Anglicus, theologian: 225 n.416
Richard (of Dover), abp. of Canterbury: 170, 187

Richard Grant, abp. of Canterbury: 215 n.253
Richard de Marisco, archd. of Richmond: 192–94 R (p. 315 f.), 195
Richard of Middleton: 215
Richard de Mores: see Ricardus Anglicus
Richard Poore: 215 & R (p. 319), 216 n.354
Richard of St. Victor: 209
Richard of Siena (R. de Senis), card.: 155, 155 f. nn.366–69 (p. 308)
Richard of Wethershed: see Richard Grant
Richard de Wych (saint), bp. of Chichester: 215 and R (p. 319), 216 n.354, 225 n.413
Richmond, archd. of: 192–94; and see Honorius, Richard de Marisco, Robert of St. Edmunds
Ro.: 98, 98 (–99) n.26 R (p. 299), 145 n.298, 148 n.307
Robertus de Anglia: 148 n.307, 212 n.328, 217 n.358 Robert Blund: 209 & R (p. 318)
Robert of Clipstone: 212
Robert of Courson: 99 n.26, 200 n.226 – *Summa*: 86 R (p. 295)
Robert of Flamborough: 180 n.96, 216
Robert de Lacy: 216 R (p. 319)
Robert of Melun: 191, 198, 209, 212
Robert Pullen: 204, 236 & R (p. 320)
Rodoicus (Rodoricus? Rotbertus?) Modicipassus: 98–99 n.26 & R (p. 299), 106 R (p. 301), 175–76, 220
Rodulphus: see Ralph, Radulphus
Roffredus Beneventanus: 142 n.281, 282 & R (p. 327) – *Libelli*: 202
Rogerius, glossator: 128 n.193, 199 n.213, 269 n.96
Roger, abbot of St. Augustine's, Canterbury: 170
Roger Bacon: 281 n.43
Roger of Hoveden: 141 n.279
Roger the Norman: 89, 173 & R (p. 313)
Roger of Pont l'Évèque, abp. of York: 171
Roger of St. Edmunds: 192–95
Roger, bp. of Worcester: 166 R (p. 310), 167 & R (p. 310), 170
Rolandus, magister: 27 n.10 & R (p. 291), 33 n.46, 98 (–99) n.26 R (p. 299), 177 & R (p. 313), 240–41 – and Alexander III: 204 & R (p. 317) – *Stroma*: 27 n.10 & R (p. 291), 48 n.13
Rolandus Bandinelli: see Alexander III; Rolandus, magister Roman law, study of: 273–90 – authority in canon law: 284–85, 284 n.58 R (p. 327) – in Gratian: 45–78, IV and V R (p. 292–94) – outside the Empire: 285–87 & R (p. 327) – in England: 171–73 & R (p. 311 f.)
Rouen, abp. of: 171 n.42
Rufinus: 82, 97, 96–101 R (p. 298), 97 n.19 R (p. 299), 112 n.112, 172, 177, 179 n.86, 180 n.93, 199 n.215, 204, 215 n.351, 233, 241 – *Summa decretorum*: 16, 48 nn.13–15, 61 n.77, 67 n.108

St. Albans, school: 208
St. Augustine's, Canterbury: 170 St. Pancras, monastery: 170
Salicta, Salictum: 253 n.12 R (p. 322)
San Salvatore, Bologna: 170 R (p. 311)
Séguier, Philippe: 150 R (p. 308)
Senatus, prior of Worcester: 210 & R (p. 318)
Seneca: 204 n.264
Sententiae divinae paginae: 32, 41 *Magistri A*: 27–32; see Elmer
Si.: 206
Sicardus (Sicard of Cremona): 82, 90, 99 n.29, 256–57, 256 f. R (p. 323), 264–67, 266 R (p. 324) – *Summa*: 187 n.137 & R (p. 315), 189 R (p. 315), 197, 199, 218 n.368 – *Sicardus abbreviatus*: 265 n.76
Silvester (Silvestre Godinho): 112 n.106, 129 & R (p. 304), 144 n.293 R (p. 307)
Silvester of Worcester, magister: 166 R (p. 310)
Simon de Apulia: 191–93, 191 R (p. 315), 224 n.405 – *Summa* (?): 191
Simon of Bisignano: 97, 112 n.106 and n.108, 187 n.135, 192 n.170, 196, 199 n.215, 221, 230, 246, 249, 260 & R (p. 323), 270 n.106, 284 n.58, 287 n.74
Simon of Derby (Derebi): 202–05 R (p. 317), 205–07 R (p. 317), 205
Simon of Sywell (Southwell, Siwelle etc.): 171, 202–07, 202–05 R (p. 317), 203 (p. 317), 210–13, 212 R (p. 318), 225 n.415
Sinibaldus, card.: see Innocent IV
Spain, Roman law in: 286 n.73 & R (p. 327 f.)
specula: 275 R (p. 326)
Stephanus Hugoneti: 155 n.364 R (p. 308)

Stephen Langton, abp. of Canterbury: 120, 202, 206 n.283, 216 – *Quaestiones*: 174
Stephen of Perche: 173 n.53
Stephen of Prague: 99 n.28, 106 n.65
Stephanus Provincialis (Etienne Bonnier): 155 n.365 & R (p. 308)
Stephen of Tournai (Stephanus Tornacensis, Etienne de Tournai): 22, 27 n.10, 48 n.13, 68 n.117, 76 R (p. 294), 81–82, 90, 97 n.18, 96–101 R (p. 298), 99, 99 n.29 R (p. 299), 112 n.106, 119 n.140, 167, 174–78, 178 R (p. 313), 182, 184 n.123, 186 R (p. 315), 187 n.135, 189 R (p. 315), 199 n.215, 265 n.69 & R (p. 324), 265 n.76, 284 n.58 R (p. 327)

Summae
– *Animal est substantia*: see *Apparatus*
– *Antiquitate et tempore*: 48 n.11, 82–83, 184–87 & R (p. 314), 265
– *Bellinensis*: 175
– *Cantabrigensis* (fragm.): 177
– *de dilatoriis*: 171–73 R (p. 312)
– *De iure canonico tractaturus*: 168 n.22, 181 & R (p. 314), 195–96, 195 R (p. 316), 221; and see Honorius
– *De iure naturali*: 178 R (p. 313)
– *De multiplici iuris divisione*: 178–80, 178 R (p. 313)
– *Dubitatur a quibusdam*: 200 n.221, 230–31, 265–66 n.76
– *Elegantius in iure divino (Coloniensis)*: 74 n.9 R (p. 294), 81, VI R (p. 295), 184–86 & R (p. 314), 189 R (p. 315), 197, 220 n.318, 285 n.61 R (p. 327)
– *Elnonensis*: 189 n.154 & R (p. 315)
– *Et est sciendum*: 83–84, 181 n.99, 197 n.203
– *Imperatorie maiestati (Monacensis)*: 81–83, 81 R (p. 295), 264
– *In eadem civitate*: 99 n.29 & R (p. 299), 265
– *In nomine*: 168 n.22, 181, 231
– *Ius aliud divinum*: 95 n.10
– *Lambethana*: see *De multiplici*
– *Magister Gratianus in hoc opere (Parisiensis)*: 47 n.11, 59 n.65, 60 n.73, 62 n.83, 67 n.108, 68 n.117, 76 n.20, 77, 80, 82, 186 & R (p. 315), 264
– *Omnis qui iuste (Lipsiensis)*: 52 n.35, 83–84, 88 VI R (p. 295), 112 n.111, 175–82, 189 n.152, 190, 195–96, 195 R (p. 316), 202, 203, 220, 246, 284 n.58
– *Permissio quedam*: 83, 170 n.37
– *Poznaniensis*: see Willielmus Vasco
– *Prima primi uxor*: 84, 214 & R (p. 319), 214 n.342 R (p. 319)
– *Quamvis leges seculares*: 84, 206, 214 & R (p. 319), 214 n.342 R (p. 319)
– *Queritur cuius sint hec verba* (fragm.), 266 n.76
– *Questio si iure naturali* (fragm.): 200 n.221
– *Quid sit symonia*: 189 n.154
– *Quoniam omissis*: 184, 184–87 R (p. 314), 220 n.380
– *Quoniam status*: 178, 178 n.79 R (p. 313)
– *Reginensis*: 100 n.33 & R (p. 300), 286 n.74 R (p. 328)
– *Reverentia sacrorum canonum*: 83
– *Sicut vetus testamentum*: 74 n.9 & R (p. 294), 95 n.10, 97 n.18 R (p. 299)
– *Tractaturus magister*: 83
– *Wigorniensis* (fragm.): 177
Summae quaestionum: 141, 144 n.292 & R (p. 306), 195–202; and see *Quaestiones decretales*
Summa sententiarum (Ps. – Hugh of St. Victor): 34, 34 n.49 R (p. 291), 37–38
Summula Hactenus on procedure: 184
Summula de dispensatione: 144 n.292
– *de praescriptionibus*: 178 n.18 – *de presumptionibus*: 254 R (p. 322), 256 f. R (p. 323); see *Perpendiculum*
Summulae et Distinctiones Casinenses: 100 n.33
Summulae and *tractatus* (in Gratian): *de accusatione*: 62–63 – *de consecratione*: 48 R (p. 292 f.), 49 – *de infamia*: 76 R (p. 294) – *de poenitentia*: 49, 48 R (p. 292 f.), 51, 77 f. n. 24 – *de praescriptione*: 52, 64–65, 64 f. R (p. 293) – *de recusatione iudicis*: 69 – *de testibus*: 69

Tancred: 129, 140, 191 R (p. 315), 202, 220, 224 n.409, 274 – *Apparatus* on Comp. I: 127–28, 131 n.219, 140 n.275, 156 n.379 – *Apparatus* on Comp. II: 127–28, 131 n.219, 154 n.354 – *Apparatus* on Comp. III: 94,

127, 140 n.275, 150 & R (p. 308), 153 n.344 – *Ordo iudiciarius*: 144 n.291 – *Quaestiones*: 145 n.297 – *Summula de criminibus*: 202 n.234 R (p. 316)
Theobald, abp. of Canterbury: 171–74
Thomas Aquinas, saint: 2–3, 141 n.279
Thomas Diplovatatius: 158 n.395
Thomas Becket (saint), abp. of Canterbury: 169–74, 169 R (p. 311), 179, 183, 187, 204, 222, 235–36, 268, 268 n.89
Thomas of Marlborough: 119–20, 169, 190, 202–03, 207, 210, 213, 216
Thomas of Tynemouth: 216 n.356
Tours, school: 174
Tv., Tu., Ty.: 206 n.287

Ulpianus de edendo: see *Ordines iudiciarii*
Urban II, pope: 18 Urban III, pope: 167

Vacarius: 168–73, 171–73 R (p. 311 f.), 171 n.42 R (p. 313), 173 n.49 R (p. 313), 185, 203, 208 R (p. 318), 209, 220, 225 – *Liber pauperum*: 171 n.38, 172, 171–73 R (p. 311 f.), 209–11, 220 n.379, 229 – Wenck's MS of *Liber*: 171–73 R (p. 312) – *Summa de matrimonio*: 172 – *Tractatus contra multiplices et varios errores*: 171 n.41, 172, 208 – *Tractatus de assumpto homine*: 171 n.41 & R (p. 312) – Commentary on the Institutes from his school: 171, 171 n.40 R (p. 312); see also Glosses on Vacarius
ūg. (= Huguccio): 103 n.45
Vaudey (de Valle Dei), abbot of: 172 n.42
Vicenza, school: 147–48
Vincentius Hispanus: 146, 146 n.302 R (p. 307), 148–54 R (p. 307), 286 n.73 R (p. 328) – *Apparatus* on Comp. I: 262 n.55 – Glosses on *Compilationes antiquae*: 137, 140 n.275, 150 R (p. 308) – Glosses on the Decretum: 107, 157 – Glosses on IV Lateran Council: 154 n.354, 155 n.359
Visigothic law: 286 n.73 R (p. 327 f.)
Vocabularius iuris utriusque: 253 n.7; see also *Epitome alphab.*
Vuolphus, Philippus: 215 R (p. 319)

Walter (Gualterus)
Walter, *Ordo scientiam*: 159

Walter Cornut (Cornuti), magister: 398 n.59 R (p. 309)
Walter of Coutances, bp. of Lincoln, abp. of Rouen: 207
Walter of London, magister, archdeacon of York: 173–74
Walter Map: 182, 214, 214 n.342 R (p. 319)
Walter of Mortagne: 34 n.49 R (p. 291)
Warin (*Gar.*, Garinus) of St. Albans: 174 n.58, 208–09, 209 n.300 (p. 318)
William (Guillaume, Guillielmus, Willielmus)
William of Auxerre, proctor of Univ. Paris: 282 R (p. 327)
William de Chemillé: 193 n.181, 203 n.246
William of Drogheda: 176, 202
Willielmus Duranti (Durantis, Guillaume Durand): 148 -54 R (p. 307), 157 n.381, 281 n.42
Willielmus Guascus: see Willielmus Vasco
William of London: 206 n.283
William of Longchamp: 86–88, 205 – *Practica legum et decretorum*: 175 & R (p. 313)
William de Monte (Montibus): 219 & R (p. 319)
Willielmus Naso: 103 n.45, 158 n.395
Willielmus Normannus: 158 n.396
Willielmus Provincialis: 120 n.142
Willielmus Vasco (Guascus): 107, 195 n.196, 214 R (p. 319), 274, 277 n.21, 287 n.78 – Additions to *Glossa ordinaria*: 122 & R (p. 304), 158–62 – *Apparatus* on Decretum: 108 R (p. 302) – *Prologus Missurus in mundum*: 108 R (p. 302), 214 & R (p. 319)
Wiz. (= Huguccio): 103 n.45

Ȳ., Ȳg. (=Huguccio): 103 n.45
York, abp. of: 171 n.42
Ysagoge in theologiam: 178 n.82

Zasius (Zäsy), Udalricus: 253 n.7 R (p. 322)
Zoën Tencararius: 277 n.21, 286 n.73 R (p. 328)

INDEX 2: PAPAL LETTERS

JK † 143: 69
JK † 157: 75 n.11
JK † 230: 69
JK † 243: 61
JK † 867: 226 n.420
JK 1033: 65
JE 1724: 65
JE 1829: 227
JE 1912: 56
JE 2796: 62
JE 3180: 286 n.73 R (p. 328)
JL 4269: 48 n.15
JL 5775: 48 n.15
JL 11872: 228
JL 11908: 171–72 n.42
JL 12117: 284 n.58 R (p. 327)
JL 12180: 113 n.113, 234
JL 12254: 113 n.113
JL 12293: 113 n.113, 228
JL 12636: 248
JL 13023: 188 n.143
JL 13032: 188 n.143 and n.145, 266 n.84
JL 13039–40: 170 n.32
JL 13162: 113 n.113, 227
JL 13735: 229
JL 13764: 248
JL 13773: 227
JL 13799: 229
JL 13854: 98 n.25 & R (p. 299)
JL 13893: 233, 248
JL 13898: 229
JL 13902: 227
JL 13912: 168 R (p. 310), 195 R (p. 316), 196 n.199, 247
JL 13917: 196 n.199
JL 13932: 230
JL 13937: 172 n.42
JL 13946: 221 n.390

JL 13948: 221 n.390
JL 13949: 221 n.390
JL 13950: 221 n.390
JL 13960: 233
JL 13967: 230
JL 13970: 113 n.113, 112–13 R (p. 303)
JL 14005: 227, 238
JL 14047: 229
JL 14055: 113 n.113
JL 14061: 170 n.35
JL 14070: 223 n.400
JL 14091: 223 n.400
JL 14156: 248
JL 14216: 228
JL 14219: 223 n.400, 229
JL 14224: 172 n.42
JL 14909: 267 n.86
JL 14965: 222 n.391
JL 14966: 222 n.391
JL 15165: see Requisivit
JL 15178: 216
JL 15189: 284 n.59, 285 n.61 & R (p. 327)
JL 15740: 172 n.42
JL 15741: 172 n.42
JL 16633: 151 n.332
JL 16829: 192 n.170
JL 17108: 192 n.170
JL 17121: 192 n.170
JL 17300: 192 n. 170
JL 17301: 192 n.170
JL 17302: 192 n.170
JL 17646: 173 R (p. 313)
JL 17648: 148 n.310
JL 17658 [17677]: see Item si quis
Po. 108: 203 n.246
Po. 275: 223 n.401
Po. 347: 172 n.42
Po. 384: see <Cum> dilectus

Po. 395: 213 n.333, 212 R (p. 318)
Po. 454: 203 n.246
Po. 457: 203 n.246
Po. 575: 203 n.246
Po. 630: 203 n.246
Po. 678: 192–94 R (p. 316)
Po. 919: 148 R (p. 307)
Po. 1190: 191 n.161, 193 n.179
Po. 1191: 191 n.161, 193 n.179
Po. 1260: 191 n.161, 193 n.181 and 182
Po. 1261: 191 n.161, 193 n.179 and 182
Po. 1262: 191 n.161, 193 n.182
Po. 1285: 191 n.161, 193 n.181 and 184
Po. 1311: 191 n.161, 193 n.182
Po. 1327: 151 n.332
Po. 1338: 191 n.161 and 162, 193 n.183
Po. 1402: 191 n.161
Po. 1560: 100 n.32 R (p. 300)
Po. 1692: 191 n.165 and 168, 193 n.181, 194 n.185
Po. 1693: 191 n.161, 194 n.185
Po. 1694: 191 n.161, 194 n.185
Po. 1695: 194 n.186
Po. 1794: 287 n.79
Po. 1858: 152
Po. 2350 (Pastoralis): 129 & R (p. 304), 137 n.258 R (p. 305), 140, 144 n.292, 144 n.293 R (p. 307)
Po. 2732: 194 n.190
Po. 2812: 125 n.174
Po. 2813: 125 n.174
Po. 3364: 148 n.310
Po. 4618–20: 137 n.258 R (p. 305)
Po. 4700: 215 R (p. 319)
Po. 5035: 191 n.161, 194 n.185
Po. 5834 (= Pressutti 1586): 284 n.60
Po. 6165 (Super speculam): see Pressutti 2267
Po. 7780 (= Pressutti 5505): 279 n.30 R (p. 326)
Po. + XIV after no. 25097: 290 n.93

Cheney & Cheney, *Letters of Innocent III concerning England and Wales* (only numbers not registered in Po. are indexed):
Cheney 249: 192–94 R (p. 316)
Cheney 250: 192–94 R (p. 316)
Cheney 270: 192–94 R (p. 316)
Cheney 271: 192–94 R (p. 316)
Cheney 284: 192–94 R (p. 316)
Cheney 417: 192–94 R (p. 316)
Cheney 420: 192–94 R (p. 316)
Cheney 1101: 192–94 R (p. 316)

Pressutti 1132: 137 n.258 R (p. 306)
Pressutti 1270: 137 n.258 & R (p. 306)
Pressutti 1303: 282 R (p. 327)
Pressutti 1586 (= Po. 5834): 284 n.60
Pressutti 2267 (= Po. 6165; Super speculam): 159, 273–290, 273 n.1 & R (p. 325)
Pressutti 5505 (= Po. 7780): 279 n.30 R (p. 326)

Auvray 318: 129 n.212
Auvray 2399: 280 n.34, 289 n.83
Auvray 2491: 282 R (p. 327)
Auvray 2792: 137 n.256
Auvray 2812: 137 n.256

Berger 5638: 280 n.36

Conquestus est nobis Ordericus: 172 n.42
Consuluit (JL 14005): 227, 238
<Cum> dilectus (Po. 384): 139 n.265
Divine sapiencie inscrutabilis altitudo: 167
Dolentes (= Po. 15570, *spuria*): 277
Gravem nec silentio (Innocent III, forsan *spuria*): 306–08 R (p. 316), (=Cheney no. 1101)
Habito (communi) cum fratribus: 280 n.37 & R (p. 327)
Item si quis (JL 17658 [17677]): 116 n.124
Miramur non modicum (Ps.-Innocent III): 155 n.358
Mortuorum: see JL 5775
Pastoralis: see Po. 2350
Recte agis: 139
Relatum est: see JL 4269
Requisivit (JL 15165): 116
Rex gloriae: 290 n.92
Sabbato proximo: 280 n.37
Super consultatione (Ps.-Innocent III): 138 n.263
Super speculam: see Pressutti 2267
Vox clamantis: 290 n.92

INDEX 3: INITIA OPERUM

Ad iuste iudicandum (Commentary on Comp. I): 132 n.226
Ad movendum (Ad monendum *male*) varie iudicem (*Distinctio* on pleading, rubr.): 257 R (p. 323)
Ad solitum suspiro metrum (Ricardus Anglicus, *Casus*, final verses): 224 n.407
Ad summariam notitiam consueti cursus causarum (? Petrus Hisp. Portugalensis, Treatise on procedure): 137 n.254 & R (p. 305)
Affinitas est propinquitas proveniens in nobis (Johannes Teutonicus, *Apparatus arborum*): 144 n.291
Agitata est causa coram episcopo (*Quaestiones Vindobonenses, Zwettlenses*): 144 n.292 and n.293
Argumentandum ex superficie litere (*Brocarda anonyma*): 268–71 R (p. 324)
Argumentum (al. Argumenta) a minori ex. De parrochiis nullus episcopus (*Brocarda anonyma*): 268–71 R (p. 325)
Argumentum a minori per negationem (*Brocarda Fuldensia*): 260 n.47
Argumentum quod nullus suo iure privetur (Bernardus Papiensis, *Argumenta [Notabilia]*; Ric. Anglicus, *Brocarda* [variant]): 117 n.127; 262 n.55 & R (p. 324)
Argumentum quod nullus privetur iure suo (*Brocarda Florianensia*): 261 n.50
Argumentum quod nullus suo privetur beneficio (Ricardus Anglicus, *Brocarda*): 262 n.55
Argumentum quod religiosi (*Notabilia Cantabrigensia*): 258
Argumentum quod voluntas pro facto reputatur (*Brocarda anonyma*): 268–71 R (p. 325)
Argumentum testes non esse cogendos (*Brocarda anonyma*): 268–71 R (p. 325)

Breviter quid contrarietatis (*Distinctiones et Generalia*): 99 n.29, 268 n.88

Canones dispensabiles propositi sunt (*Summula de dispensatione*): 144 n.292
Casus: ostenditur hic duobus (*Continuatio* of Huguccio, C. 23): 100 n.32
Circa ius naturale varie solent fieri questiones (*var.* questiones solent fieri) (Ricardus Anglicus, *Summa quaestionum*): 144 n.293, 221
Clericus apud civilem iudicem convictus *(Notabilia Decretorum)*: 179
Constitutio ergo sciatur. Ut enim Boetius ait (Gloss on Comp. I in Modena MS): 132 n.225
Cuidam coniugato dampnato ad mortem donatur vita (Honorius, *Summa quaestionum*, appendix): 197 n.203

De accusationibus quesitum est (*Lectura* or *quaestio* on 3 Comp. 4.13.2): 144 n.292
De constitutionibus: Videndum est quid sit constitutio et quot sint species (*Summa quaestionum Vindobonensis*): 144 n.292, 201
De multiplici iuris divisione (*Summa De multiplici iuris divisione*): 178 & R (p. 313)
De questionibus decretalibus tractaturi (Honorius, *Summa quaestionum*): 144 n.293

Delicto coram iudice manifestato
(*Distinctio [Notabilia]* on pleading):
257 R (p. 323)
Diligite iustitiam qui iudicatis terram
(*Summa In eadem civitate, prologus
alter* [ex Sicardo]): 265 n.76
Dolum per subsequens purgari (Otto
Papiensis, *Brocarda* rec. prior): 259 R
(p. 323)
Dominus papa contulit cuidam monasterio
tale privilegium (*Quaestiones
disputatae*): 201 n.229

Ego dico tibi: Tu es Petrus (Commentary
on *tract. de poen.*): 144 n.293 & R
(p. 306)
Ex ore sedentis in throno (? Laurentius
Hispanus, prologue of *Glossa Palatina*):
106–08 R (p. 301)
Expleto de matrimonio tractatu (? Alanus
or ? 'R. de parvi passu', *Apparatus* on
pt. III of the Decretum): 106 R (p. 301)

Gregorius: Qui multum emungit
sanguinem elicit (*Notabilia
Decretorum*): 144 n.293, 223

Hactenus Magister Gratianus egit
de personis (*Summula de ordine
iudiciario*): 184
Hec est materia processus regis David
(*Exemplum* on King David): 144 n.292
Hec sunt que suadent ne spoliatus
restituatur (*Distinctiones anonymae*):
257 R (p. 323)
Hec sunt verba magistri qui dicit
edictionem (*Apparatus* on Ricardus
Anglicus, *Ordo iudiciarius*): 144 n.292
Hic locus in iudiciis frequens
est (*Brocarda [summula] de
presumptionibus [Perpendiculum]*): 267
n.87
Humanum genus (*Abbreviatio
decretorum*): 144 n.192

Imperatorie maiestati cedit ad gloriam
(*Summa Monacensis*): 264 n.68
In eadem civitate (*Summa decretorum*):
99 n.29
In iure veteris testamenti (Bernardus
Compostellanus, Gloss on C. 16, q. 1):
122 & 121 R (p. 304)

In lege sic describuntur sponsalia
(*Quaestiones decretales de matrimonio*):
201
In quibus casibus ordo servetur (*Brocarda
anonyma*): 268–71 R (p. 325)
In quibusdam libris (*Apparatus* on Comp.
I): 137 n.258
Initium est spectandum (*Brocarda
anonyma*): 268–71 R (p. 325)
Interrogatus quis an super decimarum
(*Quaestiones*): 201 n.228 R (p. 316)
Introductis publica auctoritate renuntiare
non licet (*Brocarda de presumptionibus,
pars altera*): 258 R (p. 323)
Johannis quinto in principio dicitur (Petrus
de Salinis, *Lectura* on *de poen.*): 100
n.31 & R (p. 300)
Iudicandi formam in utroque iure (*Ordo
iudiciarius*): 176 n.68
Iudicium est trinus personarum trium actus
(*Ordo iudiciarius*): 176 n.68
Iuris scientia res quidem sanctissima
est (William of Longchamp, *Practica
legum et decretorum*): 175 R (p. 313)
Ius aliud divinum (*Summa decretorum*):
95 n.10
Ius naturale tres habet acceptationes
(Alanus, prologue of *Apparatus*): 106 R
(p. 301)

Laboris assiduitas (Huguccio,
Agiographia): 100 n.30
Leges vel decretales epistole, licet ad
certas personas directe (*Brocarda
anonyma*): 226–30 R (p. 320), 268–71
R (p. 325)

Materia auctoris in hoc opere
(Commentary on Comp. I): 132 n.226,
144 n.293, 223 n.403
Missurus in mundum (Willielmus Vasco,
prologue of *Apparatus*): 108 R (p. 302)
Moralis sapientia [est que] in libris
utriusque iuris ... (Gloss on *Summa
Coloniensis*): 184 n.121

Nam dubius in fide hereticus est (Martin
of Zamora, Glosses on Comp. IV): 157
n.383
Non valet rescriptum contra aliquos
(*Notabilia* on Gilbert's Collection): 144
n.293

INITIA OPERUM

Nota argumentum quod aliter possumus confiteri (Martin of Zamora, *Notabilia* on Comp. IV): 157 n.383

Nota in causis ecclesiasticis principaliter canones allegari (*Apparatus* on const. 'Super speculam'): 159 n.402

Nota quod quicumque agit (Tancred, *Sumulae* on procedure): 202

Notandum est quid sit prescriptio, que species prescriptionis, que inducunt (*Summula* de presciptione): 178 n.78 (?)

Nullus iure suo privandus est (*Brocarda Florianensia*, coll. altera): 261 n.50

Omnia poma vetera et nova (Prologue to Gratian): 200 n.221

Papa scribit episcopo parisiensi (*Quaestiones* in Douai MS): 145 n.297a, 201 n.230

Plus quam posse meum possit me posse iubetis (Ricardus Anglicus, *Summa brevis*): 217

Pone casum: constitutum est ut nulli detur (Second gloss on Comp. I in Modena MS): 132 n.225

Prima primi uxor Ade post primam hominis creationem (*Summa decretorum*): 214

Principium spectandum (*Brocarda de presumptionibus*, pars tertia): 258 R (p. 323)

Proposueram prius audire (Giraldus Cambrensis, *Inceptio quaestionum*): 200 n.223

Quedam rogavit quendam (*Quaestiones Zwettlenses*): 144 n.293

Quem non posse facere iure suo (*Brocarda anonyma*): 268–71 R (p. 325)

Queritur quare votum sollempne (*Quaestiones decretales*): 200 R (p. 316)

Queritur si Lazarus resurgeret (Honorius, *Summa quaestionum*, appendix): 197 n.203

Queritur utrum clericus possit compromittere (*Quaestiones* in Vienna MS): 144 n.292

Queritur utrum divisi ponantur hec tria (*Quaestiones decretales de matrimonio*): 201

Queritur utrum quicquid est contra ius naturale (*Summa quaestionum*): 201

Qui multum emungit: see Gregorius

Qui occasionem damni dat (*Brocarda de presumpt.*, pars altera [var.]): 254 R (p. 322)

Quia brevitas amica est audientie (*Apparatus* on Comp. I): 137 n.258 R (p. 305)

Quia iudiciorum quedam (*Ordo Bambergensis*): 175 R (p. 313)

Quia utilissimum fore: see Quoniam utilissimum fore

Quid sit symonia (*Summa anonyma*): 189 n.154

Quod nullus suo privetur beneficio (*var.* privetur iure suo) (Ricardus Anglicus, *Brocarda*, rubr.): 262 n.55

Quoniam ea que in civilibus (*Ulpianus de edendo*): 175 R (p. 313)

Quoniam in hac questione de prescriptionibus multa dicuntur (*Summula de prescriptione*): 178 n.78

Quoniam omissis centum distinctionibus (*Summa Decretorum*): 184

Quoniam sententia contra solitum ordinem iudiciorum prolata (*Apparatus* on Ricardus Anglicus, *Ordo iudic.*): 144 n.292

Quoniam (*var.* Quia) utilissimum fore putavi (? Petrus Hisp. Portugalensis, Treatise on procedure): 137 n.254 & R (p. 305)

Recentes auditorum animi (Egidius, *Lucubratiunculae*): 187 n.135, 230–31

Sacrosancte ac saluberrime evangelice discipline (Commentary on the Institutes): 171 n.40 R (p. 312)

Sapientiam affectant omnes (? Petrus Peverel, *Ordo iudiciarius*): 159 and n.298 R (p. 309)

Scientiam omnes naturaliter appetunt (? Walter Cornut, *Ordo iudiciarius*): 159 & R (p. 309)

Si lira delirat veniam deposco liture (Ricardus Anglicus, *Summa brevis*, final verses): 217

Sic pone casum: dividitur in quinque partes (Willielmus Vasco, Glosses on Comp. I): 160 n.404

Sicut vetus testamentum (*Summa decretorum*): 95 n.10, 97 n.18 R (p. 299)

Tractaturus igitur Gratianus de iure canonico orditur ab altiori (Ricardus Anglicus, *Summa brevis*): 217, 242–45

Utrum liceat iuramentis paganorum (*Quaestiones*): 201 n.228 R (p. 316)
Veniens quidam: see Vocatus quidam

Videndum est quid sit constitutio: see De constitutionibus

Videndum que materia que intentio (Prologue to Gratian): 189 R (p. 315)
Vocatus (*male* Veniens) quidam ad regimen civitatis (*Quaestiones* in Bamberg and Klosterneuburg MSS): 143 n.290 & R (p. 306), 143–44 n.291

INDEX 4: MANUSCRIPTS

Aachen: see Malibu

Admont
Stiftsbibliothek
7: 100 n.32
22: 98 n.25, 156 n.379, 159 n.401
48: 96 n.14
55: 132 n.223, 132 n.226, 137 n.253

Alba Julia
Biblioteca Battyanyana
292: 117 n.128 R (p. 303)

Alençon
Bibliothèque Municipale
134: 97 n.18 R (p. 299)

Amiens
Bibliothèque de la Ville
377: 112–13 R (p. 303)

Angers
Bibliothèque municipale
312: 200 n.226
370: 110 n.96

Ann Arbor, Mich.
University of Michigan Libary
52: 269 n.97

Antwerp
Museé Plantin-Moretus
M 13: 181

Arras
Bibliothèque Muncipale
271: 200 n.221, 201 n.228 & R (p. 316), 230 f.
500: 109, 118 n.137, 160

Aschaffenburg
Hof- und Stiftsbibliothek
Perg. 26: 254 R and 254 n.19 R (p. 322)

Avranches
Bibliothèque Municipale
148: 108 n.86
149: 117 n.128, 132 n.223, 144 n.292, 201, 202 n.234, 223 n.402

Baltimore
Walters Art Gallery
W 15: 176, 230
W 777 (*ol.* London, Chester Beatty Collection 46): 112 n.112 & R (p. 303), 179 & R (p. 314)

Bamberg
Staatsbibliothek
Can. 13 (P. I. 16): 102 n.42, 103 n.44 and n.48, 106 R (p. 301), 106–08 R (p. 301)
Can. 14 (P. I. 17): 107 n.72
Can. 17: 170 R (p. 311), 201 n.228 R (p. 316)
Can. 19: 274 n.6 and n.7, 81
Can. 20 (P. II. 7): 155 n.359
Can. 36: 186 n. 132
Can. 45 (P. II. 4): 117 n.128, 143, 143 n.290 R (p. 306), 145 n.295, 196 n.201, 232, 261 n.50 & R (p. 324)

Barcelona

Archivo general de la Corona de Aragón
S. Cugat 55: 140–48 R (p. 306), 200 R (p. 316), 201 n.228 R (p. 316)
S. Maria de Ripoll 34: 96–101 R (p. 298)
S. Maria de Ripoll 78: 61 R (p. 293)
– Biblioteca Universitaria 504: 96–101 R (p. 298)

Beaune

Bibliothèque Municipale 5: 108 R (p. 302), 160
Bibliothèque Municipale 19: 274 R (p. 325), 274 n.6 R (p. 326)

Berkeley, Calif.

University of California School of Law
Robbins 7 (*ol.* Vollbehr 6; Phillipps 6331): 116 n.126 R (p. 303)

Berlin

Staatsbibliothek, Stiftung preussischer Kulturbesitz:
lat. qu. 193: 169 n.29, 189 R (p. 315), 239
Phillipps 1742: 112 n.108

Biberach an der Riss

Spitalarchiv
B 3515: 96 n.14 R (p. 297)

Bonn

Universitätsbibliothek
S. 1451: 25 n.1

Bordeaux

Bibliothèque publique de la Ville
37: 96–101 R (p. 298)

Boulogne-sur-Mer

Bibliothèque Municipale
119: 99 n.29 & R (p. 299), 265 n.76, 268 n.88

Bratislava (Pressburg, Pozsonyi)

Chapter Library (administered by the Central State Archive)
13 (Jur. 210): 280 n.37
14: 61 R (p. 293)

Bremen

Universitätsbibliothek
a. 142: 96 n.14 R (p. 297)

Brugge (Bruges)

Bibliothèque de la Ville:
366: 261 n.50 R (p. 324)
– Grand Séminaire
45–144: 223 R (p. 320)

Bruxelles (Brussels)

Bibliothèque Royale
131–34 (2558): 252 n.3

Burgos

Cabildo de la Catedral
4 (?): 96 n.14 R (p. 297)

Cambrai

Bibliothèque Municipale
612 (567): 100 n.31
646: 102 n.42, 104 n.53

Cambridge

Gonville and Caius College
327: 259 R (p. 323)
676: 168 n.24, 171–73 R (p. 312), 173 n.49 R (p. 313), 202–05 & R (p. 316), 204 R (p. 317), 206, 211, 213, 226, 226–29 & R (p. 320), 235–42
– Pembroke College
101: 256 n.22, 260 n.45, 268
162: 181
– Peterhouse
114: 167 n.19
180: 167 n.19
193: 167 n.19
203: 167 n.19
– Sidney Sussex College
101: 112 n.112, 179

– Trinity College
B. I. 29: 171–73 R (p. 312), 175 R (p. 313)
B. XIV. 33: 178 n.82
O. 5. 17: 215
O. 7. 40: 178 n.78
R. 14. 9: 166 R (p. 310)
– University Library
Addit. 3321: 177
L I. II. 15: 206 n.283

Canterburry

Christ Church
D. 11 (Y. 8): 166 n.15
– Dean and Chapter Muniments
Reg. A: 206 n.283

Cesena

Biblioteca Malatestiana
II. sin. 3: 282 n.48 R (p. 327)

Charleville

Bibliothèque Municipale
269: 106 n.65, 107–10, 118, 157 n.382, 160

Chartres

Bibliothèque Municipale
173 (200): 96–101 R (p. 298)
296 (354): 98 n.25

Cividale

Museum
96: 102 n.42

Clairvaux: see Paris, B.N. lat. 18223

Colmar

Bibliothèque de la Ville
509: 223 R (p. 320)

Cologne: see Köln

Córdoba

Cabildo de la Catedral
10: 156 R (p. 309), 159 n.401 R (p. 309), 273 n.1 R (p. 325), 274 R (p. 325), 274 n.6 R (p. 326)

Cracow: see Kraków

Cues

Hospital
223: 96 n.14, 98 n.25, 102 n.42, 112 n.108
226: 201 R (p. 316), 266–67 n.85
269: 96–101 R (p. 298)

Douai

Bibliothèque Municipale
585: 77
586: 103 n.45
590: 102 n.42, 106–08 R (p. 301)
592: 105 n.59, 105 n.59 R (p. 301), 209 n.301
598: 150 R (p. 307)
640 (584): 141 n.279, 189 n.156, 197 nn. 202 and 203, 232, 234
644: 144 n.292, 223 n.402
649 (582): 100 n.34, 145 n.297a, 201, 219 n.370

Dublin

Trinity College
H. 2. 15a: 96–101 R (p. 298)
275: 101 n.34, 216–19, 242–45, 247

Durham

Cathedral Chapter
C. I. 7: 102 n.42
C. II. 1: 181
C. III. 1: 181, 189 n.153
C. III. 3: 226 n.421, 259 R (p. 323)
C. IV. 1: 179
Cosin V. III. 3: 178 R (p. 313)
– Dean and Chapter Muniments
Endpapers and Bindings No. 30: 226–30 R (p. 320), 268–71 R (p. 325)

Dyson Perrins Collections: see Malibu

Edinburgh

National Library
3.1.12: 103 n.45
6122: 268–71 R (p. 325)

Einsiedeln

Stiftsbibliothek
193 (66): 96 n.14, 96 n.14 R (p. 297)

Erlangen

Universitätsbibliothek
349: 95 n.6, 104 n.55, 129 R (p. 304)

El Escorial

Biblioteca real de San Lorenzo
c. I. 5: 106 R (p. 301)

Evreux

Bibliothèque Municipale
106: 105 n.59, 214

Exeter

Record Office
fragment (4 fols.): 267 n.88

Firenze (Florence)

Biblioteca Medicea Laurenziana
Acquisiti 93: 96 n.14
Aedil. Flor. Eccl. 96: 96 n.14, 102 n.42
Gadd. reliq. 2 (Magliab. XXXI. 46): 96 n.14, 105 n.59
Medic. Fesul. 126: 100 n.32
S. Croce I sin. 1: 96 n.14
S. Croce I sin. 4: 100 n.32
S. Croce III sin. 6: 102 n.39, 131 n.219
S. Croce IV sin. 1: 102 n.42
S. Croce IV sin. 2: 131 n.219, 132 n.223 R (p. 304)
S. Croce V sin. 4: 159 n.402, 159 n.403, 274 n.6, 274 R (p. 325), 275
S. Croce V sin. 7: 28, 30–32

– Biblioteca Nazionale Centrale
Conv. Soppr. A. II. 376: 96 n.14
Conv. Soppr. A. II. 403: 96 n.14
Conv. Soppr. G. IV. 1736: 74 n.9, 95 n.10

Frankfurt am Main

Stadt- und Universitätsbibliothek
Barth. 7 (1): 108 n.86 R (p. 302), 109 n.86

Freiburg im Breisgau

Universitätsbibliothek
361a: 129 R (p. 304), 132 n.224 R (p. 304)

Fulda

Landesbibliothek
D. 5: 131 n.221
D. 10: 145 n.297, 256 n.22, 260 n.47
D. 14: 108 R (p. 302)

Gent

Biblioteek der Rijksuniversität
1429: 184–87 R (p. 314)

Gniezno (Gnesen)

Biblioteka Kapitulna
28: 109–29 R (p. 302), 121 R (p. 304), 135 and n.243 R (p. 305), 136 n.251 R (p. 305)

Grande-Chartreuse

Monastery Library (formerly)
Jus. can. XXXVII: 106 n.61

Graz

Universitätsbibliothek
52 (40/18): 96 n.14
69 (40/4): 96 n.14
71 (40/26): 96 n.14, 102 n. 42, 108 n.86
80 (40/5): 96 n.14, 102 n.42, 108 n.86
106 (41/9): 98 n.25, 159 n.401, 160 n.404

Grenoble

Bibliothèque de la Ville
62: 108 R (p. 302)
72: 108 n.86 R (p. 302)
626 (391.1): 255 n.19, 256 n.22, 257 R (p. 323)

Halle

Universitätsbibliothek
Ye 52: 152 n.336 and R (p. 308), 262 n.55
Ye 80: 152 n.336

Hamburg

Staats- und Universitätsbibliothek
Cod. jur. 2231: 96 n.14 R (p. 297)

Heiligenkreuz

Stiftsbibliothek
43: 96 n.14
44: 96 n.14, 179 n.86

Hereford

Cathedral Chapter
O. 6. XIV: 179
P. II. 3: 96–101 R (p. 298)
P. VII. 3: 102 n.42, 112 n.108

Heverlee (Louvain)

Abbaye de Parc
fly-leaves: 96–101 R (p. 298)

Ivrea

Archivio Capitolare
67 (VIII): 112–13 R (p. 303)
72 (C): 108 n.86 R (p. 302)

Jena

Universitätsbibliothek
El. fol. 56: 102 n.42

Karlsruhe

Landesbibliothek
Aug. XXX: 216, 216 R (p. 319)

Kassel

Landesbibliothek
Jur. 11: 104 n.55

Klosterneuburg

Stiftsbibliothek
87: 108 n.86
89: 100 n.31
101: 106 n.60 and 63, 109 n.86
295: 100 n.31
656: 143–45 and nn.291, 295
1045: 132 n.326, 135 n.226 R (p. 304)
1048: 145 n.297

Köln (Cologne)

Domkapitel
128: 96 n.14 R (p. 297)
129: 96 n.14

Kraków (Cracow)

Biblioteka Jagiellónska
357: 96 n.14, 108 n.86

– Cathedral Chapter
88: 97 n.20

Laon

Bibliothèque Municipale
371 *bis*: 86 n.35, 141 n.279, 181,
195 n.198, 202 n.237, 231–34

Leipzig

Universitätsbibliothek
983: 262 n.55
984: 197 n.203
986: 195 n.198
1242: 206 n.287
Haen. 12: 184 n.120
Haen. 17: 48 R (p. 292), 77–78
and n.24
Haen. 18: 102 n.42
Rep. I. 4°. 47 (*ol.* Stadtbibl. cat.
Naumann 78): 96–101 R
(p. 298)
Rep. II. 4°. 117 (*ol.* Stadtbibl. cat.
Naumann 247): 255 n.19, 256 n.23,
257 n.31 and R (p. 323)

Leningrad (St. Petersburg)

Public Library
lat. F. II. vel 23: 96 n.14 R (p. 297),
96–101 R (p. 298)

– University Library
lat. 4: 171–73 R (p. 312)

Liège (Luik)

Grand Séminaire
6. N. 15: 189 n.154

Lilienfeld

Stiftsbibliothek
222: 96 n.14, 102, 102 n.43, 103 n.45
223: 96 n.14, 112 n.107

Lincoln

Cathedral Chapter
121: 241–42, 259 R (p. 323), 788–92 R
(p. 326)

Lindau

Stadtarchiv
P. I. 49: 96–101 R (p. 298)

Lisboa (Lisbon)

Biblioteca Nacional
Alcob. 12 (*ol.* 263): 273 n.1, 274 R (p. 325)
Alcob. 173 (*ol.* 304): 132 n.223
Alcob. 381 (*ol.* 305): 131 n.219, 159 n.402, 274 n.6

London

British Library (British Museum)
Cotton Claud. D. XII: 206 n.283
Cotton Nero C. IX: 189 n.150
Cotton Vesp. F. XV: 206 n.283
Cotton Vitell. A. III: 178
Cotton Vitell. E XIII: 188 n.145
Cotton App. XXI: 206 n.283
Harl. 391: 206 n.283
Harl. 3650: 205 n.280
Harl. 3834: 139 n.269, 150–55
Harl. 3842: 179 n.83
Harl. 3845: 150 R (p. 308)
Harl. 3868: 205 n.280
Harl. 4967: 171–73 R (p. 312), 178 R (p. 313)
Royal 2. D. IX: 168 n.23 & R (p. 311), 175 n.63 and n.66
Royal 9. B. XI: 150–55
Royal 9. C. VI: VIII (after title) R (p. 309), 268–71 R (p. 325)
Royal 9. E. VII: 140–48 R (p. 306), 205–07 (p. 317), 206 R (p. 317), 211 n.316, 225 R (p. 320), 228–29
Royal 10. A. II: 167 n.15
Royal 10. B. IV: 166 n.15, 171, 176 n.68, 178 n.78
Royal 10. C. III: 219 n.370
Royal 11. B. II: 167 n.15, 177 n.72
Royal 11. B. XV: 171–73 R (p. 312)
Royal 11. C. VII: 159 n.399
Royal 11. D. II: 214
Royal 15. B. IV: 167 n.15
Stowe 378: 112 n.107
Addit. 18325: 144 n.293, 223 n.405
Addit. 24658: 102 n.42
Addit. 24659: 171–73 R (p. 312)
Addit. 34391: 220 n.381 R (p. 320)

– Chester Beatty Collection: see **Baltimore**, Walters Art Gallery W 777

– Lambeth Palace
105: 132 n.226, 137 n.253, 139 n.269, 151–52, 214 n.345, 261 n. 49, 263 n.57
139: 178 R (p. 313), 179 n.83, 259 R (p. 323)
142: 203 & R (p. 317)
241: 206 n.283
449: 179 n.83

Louvain; see Heverlee

Lublin

Catholic University
1: 108 n.86 R (p. 302)

Lucca

Arcivescovado
20(6): 96 n.14

– Archivio di Stato
2698: 100 n.34

Luik: see Liège

Luxembourg

Bibliothèque
139: 268–71 R (p. 325)
144: 181

Luzern (Lucerne)

Zentralbibliothek
P. MS. 21: 96–101 R (p. 298)

Madrid

Biblioteca Nacional
87: 61 R (p. 293), 74 n.9 & R (p. 294)
399 (*ol.* C. 12, C. 48): 96–101 R (p. 298)
421 (*ol.* C. 41): 96–101 R (p. 298), 268–71 R (p. 325)
1136 (*ol.* S. 242): 116 n.126 R (p. 303)
11962: 96–101 R (p. 298)
12790: 108 n.86 R (p. 302), 109 n.86

– Facultad de Ciencias Politicas
1137: 96 n.14 R (p. 297)

– Fundacion Lázaro Galdiano
440: 96–101 R (p. 298)
490: 96 n.14 R (p. 297)

Malibu Calif.

J.P. Getty Museum
s. n. (*ol.* Aachen, Dr. P. Ludwig; formerly Dyson Perrins Collection MS 2): 169 R (p. 311)

Marburg

Universitätsbibliothek
33 (*ol.* C. 1): 96 n.14 R (p. 297)

Melk

Stiftsbibliothek
190 (*ol.* 333; F. 33): 117 n.127, 262 n.55 & R (p. 324)
333 (F. 33, Cat. 190): 117, n.127
518 (J. 37; Cat. 289): 134 n.355

Milano

Bibliotheca Ambrosiana
A. 238 inf.: 100 n.31 & R (p. 300)
H. 94 sup.: 95 n.10
M. 64 sup. 189 R (p. 315), 266 n.85, 266 R (p. 324)
R. 73 sup.: 99 n.29

– S. Ambrogio, Archivio Capitolare
A. 57 (*ol.* s. n.): 96 n.14

Modena

Biblioteca Estense
a. O. 6.9 (lat. 164; V. C. 11): 130 n.218
a. R. 4. 16 (lat. 968; XII. L. 8): 118 n.134, 121 n.158, 129–40, 133 R (p. 304), 150–53 n.347, 150 R (p. 308), 157 n.390, 159 n.401, 262

Montecassino

Biblioteca Abbaziale
46: 116 n.126, 132 n.223
66: 102 n.42
68: 109 n.86
136: 159 n. 399, 202 n.234 R (p. 316)
396: 100 n.32 and n.33, 110 n.97, 113 n.113, 142 n.279, 196 n.199, 197 n.203, 220–23, 245–49

Monza

Archivio Capitolare
i. 18/156 (T. VIII. Inv. CCXVII): 97 n.19
i. 19/161 (T. XII; Inv. CCXXIV): 97 n.19, 99 n.29

München (Munich)

Bayerische Staatsbibliothek
lat. 329: 156 n.369
lat. 3802: 132 n.34 R (p. 304)
lat. 3873: 96–101 R (p. 298)
lat. 3879: 191 R (p. 315)
lat. 7622: 257 n.31 R (p. 323)
lat. 8013: 254 n.19
lat. 8032: 261 n.50 R (p. 324)
lat. 10244: 98 n.25, 102 n.42 and n.44, 103 n.45 and n. 48
lat. 14024: 108 n.86 R (p. 302)
lat. 16083: 201 & R (p. 316), 224 n.407
lat. 16084: 264 n.68
lat. 28174: 106–08 R (p. 301)
lat. 28175: 109–29 R (p. 303)

Münster

Universitätsbibliothek
603 (130; *deperd.*): 96–101 R (p. 298), 189 R (p. 315)

Napoli (Naples)

Biblioteca Nazionale
XII. a. 5: 102 n.42
XII. a. 9: 102 n.42, 103 n.45

New York

Pierpont Morgan Library
M. 446: 96 n.14, 97 n.19, 102 n.42, 160 n.408

Novara

Biblioteca Capitolare
XCVI (76): 117 n.129

Nürnberg

Stadtbibliothek
Cent. II. 41: 96 n.14 R (p. 297)
Cent. IV. 94: 97 n.20
Cent. V. 95: 261 n.50

Olomouc (Olmütz)

State Archives (MSS formerly at Cathedral Chapter)
C. O. 48: 96–101 R (p. 298)
C. O. 209: 217 R (p. 319), 244 R (p. 321)
C. O. 266: 96 n.14, 181 n.99
C. O. 401: 108 f. n.86
C. O. 589: 157 n.383

Oporto (Porto)

Biblioteca Municipal
48: 280 n.37 R (p. 327)

Oslo

National Archives
Coll. fragm. 159: 97 n.18, 99 n.29

Oxford

Bodleian Library
Bodl. 423: 188 n.148
Douce 218: 179
Lat. misc. 60: 117 n. 128 R (p. 303)
Laud. lat. 17: 212 n.327
Laud. misc. 112: 96–101 R (p. 298)
Selden supr. 87: 201 n.228 R (p. 316), 217 n.363 R (p. 319), 219 n.370
Tanner 8: 74 n.8, 168 & R (p. 311), 172 n.42 & R (p. 313), 207, 226–30

– Magdalen College
258: 171–73 R (p. 312)

– New College
210: 102 n.42, 112 n.108

– Oriel College
53: 171–73 R (p. 312), 181, 208 n. 297, 208 R (p. 318)

– Queen's College
317: 178 n.78

– St. John's College
235: 96–101 R (p. 298)

– University College
17: 268–71 R (p. 324)
117: 254 n.19 R (p. 324)

Padova (Padna)

Biblioteca Antoniana
II. 35: 131 n.219

– Duomo
A. 23: 155 n.365

Paris

Bibliothèque Nationale
lat. 1566: 113 n.1566
lat. 3454: 112–13 R (p. 303), 175 R (p. 313)
lat. 3881: 28
lat. 3884: 78
lat. 3885: 103 n.45
lat. 3886: 74 n.8, 76 R (p. 294)
lat. 3886 A: 103 n.45, 200 n.221
lat. 3888: 62 n.84, 64 n.92, 65 n.98, 112 n.107
lat. 3893: 77
lat. 3895: 96 n.14 R (p. 297)
lat. 3903: 107 n.72
lat. 3905 B: 206 n.287
lat. 3922 A: 149 n.314 & R (p. 308), 168 n.23 & R (p. 311), 171–73 R (p. 312)
lat. 3922 B: 101 n.34
lat. 3932: 159 n.401
lat. 3934 A: 201, 201 n.228 R (p. 316)
lat. 3967: 286 n.73 R (p. 328)
lat. 4276: 96–101 R (p. 298)
lat. 4288: 223 R (p. 320)
lat. 4378: 268–71 R (p. 325)
lat. 4720 A: 254 n.19 R (p. 316)
lat. 11724: 282 n.48 R (p. 327)
lat. 14317: 107 n.72
lat. 14321: 274 n.6
lat. 14591: 189 n.156, 231
lat. 14606: 254 n.19 R (p. 316)
lat. 14859: 218 n.368
lat. 14877: 100 n.30
lat. 14947: 268–71 R (p. 325)
lat. 14997: 184 n.121, 185
lat. 15393: 106 n.65–109 n.92, 106 R (p. 301)
lat. 15398: 130 n.216, 131 n.219, 137 n.258, 214 n.345
lat. 15996: 131 n.219
lat. 16538: 178 n.79 & R (p. 313)
lat. 16540: 178
lat. 16898: 78
lat. 16899: 78
lat. 18223 (ol. Clairvaux M 88): 150
Baluze 77: 101 n.39
nouv. acq. lat. 1761: 74–75
nouv. acq. lat. 2127: 131 n.219

– Bibliothèque de l'Arsénal
677: 102 n.42
769: 153 .348

– Bibliothèque Mazarine
1287: 78, 106 n.65, 106–07

– Bibliothèque Sainte-Geneviève
342: 77, 102 n.42, 103, 214
1651: 188 n.144

Płock

Diocesan Seminary
64: 96 n.14, 105 n.65
67: 104 n.55
78: 154 n.353 & R (p. 308)
80: 101 n.35, 96–101 R (p. 298)

Pommersfelden

Bibliothek des Grafen Schönborn
142: 112 R (p. 304)

Porto: see Oporto Poznan

Cathedral Chapter
28: 108 R (p. 302)

Pozsonyi: see Bratislava

Praha (Prague)

Metropolitan Chapter
J. XIX: 102 n.42, 103 n.47

– National Museum
XVII. A. 5 (*ol.* I. B. IV): 280 n.37
XVII. A. 12 (*ol.* I. B. I): 99 n.28, 106 n.65, 108 n.86 R (p. 302), 118 R (p. 303)

– University Library
XIV. E. 31 (Cat. 2565): 142 n.281

Pressburg: see Bratislava

Reims

Bibliothèque Municipale
676: 102 n.42, 103 n.45, 104 n.53
684: 110 n.96
699: 280 n.37

Rein (Reun)

Stiftsbibliothek
86: 217, 217 n.363

Roma

Biblioteca Angelica
1270: 102 n.42

– Biblioteca Casanatense
1910: 202 n.234 & R (p. 316)

– Biblioteca Nazionale (formerly Vittorio Emmanuele)
1369 (Sess. 43): 186 n.135, 187 nn.136 and 137 & R (p. 315), 230

Rouen

Bibliothèque Municipale
706: 274 n.6
710: 260 n.44, 265 n.70, 284 n.58
743: 195 R (p. 316), 202 n.237, 222 n.393

St. Florian

Stiftsbibliothek
III. 5: 96 n.14, 99 n.22
XI. 346: 153 R (p. 308), 261 n.50
XI. 605: 287 n.76
XI. 720: 261 n.50

Saint-Mihiel

Bibliothèque Municipale
5: 108 n.86 R (p. 302)

Saint-Omer

Bibliothèque Municipale
192: 107 n.72
433: 78
476: 109, 118 n.137

St. Paul im Lavanttal

Stiftsbibliothek
XXV. 2. 6 (*ol.* XXV. a/25): 96 n.14

St. Petersburg: see Leningrad

Salamanca

Biblioteca de la Universidad
2077 (*ol.* Madrid, Palacio II. 735): 96–101 R (p. 298)
2399 (*ol.* Madrid, Palacio II. 163): 96–101 R (p. 298)

Salzburg

Stift St. Peter
a. IX. 18: 106 n.61, 130 n.213, 132 n.224, 153 n.349
a. XII. 9: 98 n.26, 102 n.42, 107 n.73

Seo de Urgel

Cabildo de la Catedral
2030 (124): 116 n.126 R (p. 303)
2882 (8): 106 R (p. 301)

Stockholm

Royal Library (Kungliga Biblioteket)
B. 683: 259 R (p. 323)

Stuttgart

Landesbibliothek
HB VI. 95: 106 R (p. 301)

Tarazona

Cabildo de la Catedral
41 (G. 17): 96–101 R (p. 298)
77 (G. 12): 96–101 R (p. 298)
93: 108 n.96 R (p. 302)

Toledo

Cabildo de la Catedral
24–9: 96–101 R (p. 298)

Torino (Turin)

Biblioteca Nazionale
D. IV. 40 (514; Pas. 909): 99 n.29
D. V. 2 (516; Pas. 880): 113 n.113

Tortosa

Cabildo de la Catedral
160: 130 n.216

Tours

Bibliothèque Municipale
559: 104 n.53
565: 286 n.73 R (p. 328)

Trier

Bischöfliches Seminar
8: 96 n.14, 98 n.24, 102 n.42, 112 n.108

– Stadtbibliothek
864: 131 n.219
876: 131 n.219
906: 102 n.42, 112 n.108
907: 96 n.14, 109 n.86

Troyes

Bibliothèque Municipale
961: 102 n.39
1317: 28, 31, 31 n.40

Turin: see Torino

Uppsala

University Library
C. 60: 180 R (p. 314)

Urgel: see Seo de Urgel

Utrecht

University Library
3. B. 2: 223 R (p. 320)

Valenciennes

Bibliothèque Municipale
193: 189 R (p. 315)

Vaticano, Città del

Archivio Segreto Vaticano
Regr. Vat. 14: 129 n.212

– Biblioteca Apostolica Vaticana
Vat. lat. 1367: 104 n.53, 107 n.72 and n.76, 109, 110 n.93, 114 n.119, 118, 122–25, 127 n.189, 136 R (p. 305), 155–62
Vat. lat. 1377: 136 R (p. 305)
Vat. lat. 2494: 102 n.42, 103 n.45, 112 n.108
Vat. lat. 2691: 218 n.367, 223 n.402, 242, 247, 260 n.48
Vat. lat. 4361: 28
Vat. lat. 4954: 96–101 R (p. 298)
Vat. lat. 6024: 98 n.24
Vat. lat. 10754: 260 R (p. 323)
Arch. S. Pietro A. 27: 102 n.42 Barb. lat. 1413: 96–101 R (p. 298)
Barb. 45: 274 n.9
Borgh. 250: 282 R (p. 327)
Borgh. 261: 201 n.232, 282 n.46

Borgh. 287: 27 n.10, 256, 257 n.31 R (p. 323)
Chis. lat. E. VII. 218: 261 n.50, 262 n.53
Pal. lat. 624: 27 n.10, 108 n.83, 125 n.177, 127 n.189
Pal. lat. 625: 102 n.42, 108 n.83, 125 n.177, 127 n.189
Pal. lat. 652: 132 n.224 R (p. 304)
Pal. lat. 653: 256 n.22
Pal. lat. 658: 27 n.10, 98 n.25, 108 n.83, 110 n.93, 110–19, 286 n.73
Reg. lat. 179: 188 n.142
Reg. lat. 377: 156 n.369
Reg. lat. 977: 110 n.93, 110–22, 126–27, 161–62
Reg. lat. 1039: 74 n.8 & R (p. 294), 76 R (p. 294)
Reg. lat. 1061: 100 n.33
Ross lat. 595: 102, 102 n.42 and n.43, 104 n.54, 106 n.60, 108 n.81

Vendôme

Bibiothèque Municipale
225: 117 n.129

Venezia (Venice)

Biblioteca Nazionale Marciana (S. Marco)
lat. IV. 25 (Valent. VIII. 22; progr. n.2321): 154 n.352
lat. IV. 117 (Valent. VIII. 16; progr. n. 2485): 96 n.14, 109 n.86

Vercelli

Biblioteca Capitolare
XXIII: 131 n.219
XXV: 96 n.14, 98 n.24, 102 n.42, 112 n.108
LXXXIX: 106 n.61, 130 n.213, 133 n.230, 226 n.423

Verdun

Bibliothèque Municipale
35: 184

Verona

Biblioteca Capitolare
CLXXXIV (164): 96 n.14, 102 nn.39 and 42, 112 n.108
CXCIV (169): 100 n.32

Vicenza

Biblioteca Bertoliana
17 (15.2.2; 627): 96 n.14

Vienna: see Wien

Warszawa (Warsaw)

National Library
BOZ 63: 96–101 R (p. 298)

Washington D.C.

Law Library of Congress
D 401 (*ol.* s. n.; G. 71): 63 n.87 & R (p. 293), 96 n.14 & R (p. 297 f.),
D 402 (*ol.* G. 7. Phillipps MS14953): 63 n.88 & R (p. 293) *ol.* Collection Voltbehr 6: see Berkeley

Wien (Vienna)

Österreichische Nationalbibliothek
1064: 110 n.97
2061: 96 n.14, 100 n.31
2077: 252 n.3 R (p. 322)
2082: 109 n.86
2102: 96 n.14, 107 n.73
2121: 97 n.21
2125: 184 n.121, 197 n.204, 189 R (p. 315)
2142: 101 n.35
2163: 143–48 n.307, 144 n.292 R (p. 306), 145 R (p. 307), 148 n.307 R (p. 307), 201
2172: 101 n.39
2183: 274 n.6
2436: 171–73 R (p. 312)

Wolfenbüttel

Herzog-August-Bibliothek
Helmst. 33: 102 n.42

Worcester

Cathedral Chapter
F. 14: 252 n.3, 259 R (p. 323)
F. 122: 132 n.226, 214 n.345
Q 70: 177
Q 144: 178 n.78

Würzburg

Universitätsbibliothek
Mp. th. fol. 122: 112–13 R (p. 303), 133 R (p. 304)

Zürich

Zentralbibliothek
Rh. 42 (409): 96–101 R (p. 298)

Zwettl

Stiftsbibliothek
30: 154 n.355

31: 96 n.14, 97 n.21
34: 132 n.224
162: 101 n.34, 113 n.113, 117 n.128, 129 R (p. 304), 132 n.226, 141 n.279, 144 n.293, 145 R (p. 307), 148 n.307 R (p. 307), 190, 200 n.222, 217 n.363, 220–24 n.409, 223 R (p. 320), 232, 245, 261 n.50
297: 101 n.35, 117 n.129